The War Puzzle Revisited

John A. Vasquez's *The War Puzzle* provided one of the most important scientific analyses of the causes of war of the last two decades. *The War Puzzle Revisited* updates and extends his groundbreaking work, reviewing recent research on the onset and expansion of war and the conditions of peace. Vasquez describes systematically those factors associated with wars to see if there is a pattern that suggests why war occurs, and how it might be avoided, delineating the typical path by which relatively equal states have become embroiled in wars in the modern global system. The book uses the large number of empirical findings generated in the last twenty-five years as the basis of its theorizing, and integrates these research findings so as to advance the scientific knowledge of war and peace.

John A. Vasquez is Thomas B. Mackie Scholar in International Relations at the University of Illinois at Urbana-Champaign.

Cambridge Studies in International Relations is a joint initiative of Cambridge University Press and the British International Studies Association (BISA). The series will include a wide range of material, from undergraduate textbooks and surveys to research-based monographs and collaborative volumes. The aim of the series is to publish the best new scholarship in International Studies from Europe, North America and the rest of the world.

CAMBRIDGE STUDIES IN INTERNATIONAL RELATIONS

Series list continued after index

THE WAR PUZZLE
REVISITED

JOHN A. VASQUEZ

Thomas B. Mackie Scholar in International Relations
University of Illinois at Urbana-Champaign

CAMBRIDGE
UNIVERSITY PRESS

CAMBRIDGE UNIVERSITY PRESS

Cambridge, New York, Melbourne, Madrid, Cape Town, Singapore, São Paulo, Delhi

Cambridge University Press
The Edinburgh Building, Cambridge CB2 8RU, UK

Published in the United States of America by Cambridge University Press, New York

www.cambridge.org
Information on this title: www.cambridge.org/9780521708234

10 0586770 8

First published 2009

Printed in the United Kingdom at the University Press, Cambridge

A catalogue record for this publication is available from the British Library

Library of Congress Cataloguing in Publication data
Vasquez, John A., 1945–
The war puzzle revisited / John A. Vasquez.
p.   cm.
Includes bibliographical references and index.
ISBN 978-0-521-88179-1 (hardback) – ISBN 978-0-521-70823-4 (pbk.)
1. War–Causes. I. Title.
U21.2.V378 2009
355.02′7–dc22
2009016994

ISBN 978-0-521-88179-1 hardback
ISBN 978-0-521-70823-4 paperback

To Elyse
peace of my heart

CONTENTS

ix

FIGURES

TABLES

xiii

PREFACE

Over the years I have been asked by colleagues and students if I was going to do a second edition of *The War Puzzle* or an update. I was hesitant to do so, because at a certain point the text of a book takes on a life of its own. This was particularly the case with this book, because its larger purpose was to construct an explanation of why war occurs on the basis of an inductive review of existing findings. Once that inductive explanation was constructed, the more important task was to test that explanation deductively rather than tinker with it by looking at new findings. In the last fifteen years, I have spent most of my time conducting such deductively oriented empirical tests, including several co-authored studies, particularly with the late Paul D. Senese.

It was always my intention, once that research reached a critical mass, to revisit the war puzzle to see what the new findings would tell us about the explanation set forth in the original book. The book before you is the fulfillment of that long-term goal. It is not so much a second edition as it is a book that keeps the original text intact, but supplements it with two new chapters whose purpose is not to augment the original explanation of war but appraise its scientific adequacy in light of the quantitative research conducted since 1993 that is relevant to the steps to war.

The main reason for doing this book is scientific. It is to see how the propositions in *The War Puzzle* have been tested and how the two explanations embodied in the book – the territorial explanation of war (Chapter 4) and the steps-to-war explanation (Chapter 5) have fared. Chapter 10 reviews the research on territory and Chapter 11 reviews the research on power politics. This research has been very encouraging both in terms of failing to falsify the original theory and in breaking new ground. At the same time, as one would expect, not everything has worked out. The natural domain of the theory is the classic 1816–1945 era. It fits the Cold War only partially, but the post-Cold War period seems to be returning to the patterns found in the classic era, making the theory still relevant for the immediate past and the future.

From the reader's perspective, the major difference between *The War Puzzle* and this book is that the former provided an explanation of why war occurs and this book complements the former by presenting a substantial amount of evidence that gives us an idea of where that explanation is correct and where it is not. Nonetheless, I have added to the text some brief "retrospective" commentaries after Part I and Part II. These look back on each chapter, indicating what I think now, after fifteen years have passed.

Several people have been kind enough to read the new portions of this book. Marie Henehan provided several critical readings and important advice. Sara McLaughlin Mitchell provided a close reading of Chapter 10 and Doug Gibler did the same for both Chapters 10 and 11 on short notice. My thanks also to Brandon Valeriano for suggestions on these two chapters and his work on types of war. More importantly, I thank each of them and all of the other authors cited in these chapters for the research they have conducted on interstate war and conflict. I am particularly appreciative for the research and insights of Michael Colaresi, Karen Rasler, and William Thompson on the steps to war. My thanks especially to Jack Levy, who encouraged me (more than once) to undertake this project. I am also grateful to the several anonymous referees who provided reports to Cambridge University Press, with valuable suggestions. I have not always taken everyone's advice, so I remain responsible for any errors and flaws.

My new colleagues at the University of Illinois at Urbana-Champaign, especially Paul Diehl and Colin Flint, have provided an intellectually stimulating environment in which to think and write about peace and war. As always, it has been a great pleasure working with John Haslam and Cambridge University Press. My thanks also go to various doctoral students who have worked on the steps to war in other studies: Choong-Nam Kang, Chris Leskiw, Andy Owsiak, Karen Petersen, Toby Rider, and Susan Sample. In preparing the manuscript, I am grateful to the Thomas B. Mackie research fund at the University of Illinois for support, to Delinda Swanson for preparing the references and the index, and to Audrey Cotterell for copy-editing.

The War Puzzle was completed when my daughter was eight. I dedicated the book to her because I was working on it for most of her life and because she provided me with a sense of peace conducive to working on this sort of subject. She is now twenty-three, having just finished her Master's. I re-dedicate this work to her. Raising children always has more uncertainty about it than parents want; she has provided us with more joy than we anticipated and more satisfaction than we deserve.

August 11, 2008
Block Island, Rhode Island

PREFACE TO THE ORIGINAL TEXT

This book treats war as a social phenomenon that recurs in human experience. Instead of focusing on any particular war, I am interested in systematically describing those factors which are common to wars and to the peace that follows to see if there is a pattern that suggests why war recurs and how it might be avoided or mitigated. The end result will be an explanation of the onset and expansion of war and the conditions of a stable peace. This involves explaining why and how wars occur, why some wars expand, why some historical periods and interstate relationships are more peaceful than others, why some peaces last longer than others, and how they work to avoid war.

The task set forth in this book would be almost impossible for a single individual to tackle were it not for an international community of peace researchers who have been dedicated to investigating manageable portions of the problem in a rigorous way. Their efforts have made mine possible. They have contributed a new body of evidence and insight on war and peace distinct from those provided by history, traditional discourse, and political philosophy. In this book, I seek to integrate and explain their findings in a way that will move the culmination of scientific knowledge on war and peace forward.

My greatest debt is to those peace researchers who have painstakingly worked to document generalizations about war and peace. My debt to them is acknowledged in the text every time I discuss their work and cite their studies. This is particularly the case when I am critical of an explanation or give an alternate interpretation to a finding. Just because I have disagreed with something does not mean I have not found it valuable.

I have benefited not only from the body of knowledge generated by peace researchers, but in many instances from the willingness of individual scholars to read and comment on parts of the manuscript or papers presented from it. Since this book has taken a long time to write and since I have not kept a record of every instance, I know I will forget to mention some who have provided a contribution. With apologies in advance, let me acknowledge the following who were generous with their help, time, and insights, and provided important feedback to me: Claudio Cioffi-Revilla, Paul Diehl, Brian Ferguson, Gary Goertz, Charles Gochman, Patrick James, James Turner Johnson, Charles Kegley, Jr., Sheldon Levy, Richard Lore, Manus Midlarsky, T. Clifton Morgan, Karen Rasler, James Lee Ray, Gregory Raymond, A. Bikash Roy, Alan Sabrosky, Randolph Siverson, William R. Thompson, Peter Wallensteen, and Frank Wayman.

In addition to these people, five individuals have played a special role in the evolution of this work. At the very beginning, Harold Guetzkow and J. David Singer provided models of inspiration and discipline. Harold Guetzkow's description of how to construct theory in his "Long Range Research in International Relations" provided a guiding light in uncharted academic ground. This, along with his personal encouragement and early advice on how to spend one's time, were of immense help. David Singer has probably been the key critical influence on this work. Without him, there would have been no Correlates of War project, and without that project this book would not have been possible. David Singer has been generous in giving me his time and has been supportive of my endeavors. He read early versions of the key chapters (chapters 4 through 7) and provided valuable criticisms. Steve Smith, managing editor of the Cambridge series, is one of three people who read the entire manuscript. He provided suggestions that improved the overall structure of the book and its theoretical argument. I am grateful for his long-term commitment to the project and his faith in it. Jack Levy, my new colleague at Rutgers, also read the entire manuscript – and parts of it more than once. His comments have always been stimulating, provocative, and educational. The manuscript has benefited from his readings. Marie Henehan, my partner and colleague, has read the manuscript more times than anyone with the exception of myself. Her substantive and editorial criticisms have saved me from more than several errors. More importantly, without her presence I do not think I would have been able to complete this study. I deeply appreciate her steadfast support. Even though at times I became discouraged about the project, she never did.

All of the above persons greatly improved the book, but they are in no way responsible for the omissions, errors, and misinterpretations that remain. Nor, since they do not all agree with each other, should they be seen as necessarily agreeing with the interpretations I present here. Nevertheless, I hope each will find this work as making a contribution to our common endeavor.

A book of this length requires a great deal of time and space. Block Island, a small community of people, gulls and beaches, provided the space where my ideas and thoughts could come together and eventually be expressed in the written word. Several agencies provided time. Rutgers University, in the form of the Faculty Academic Study Program and research support from the Dean of the Faculty of Arts and Sciences, permitted me to get started. A Fulbright research grant to spend a year in Beograd, Yugoslavia allowed me to maintain the momentum I had gathered on my sabbatical. My stay provided enough time and distance from the US to gain perspective and commit key parts of the manuscript to paper. My thanks to my sponsor, Radoslav Stojanovic, and to Sima Avramovic for making my stay productive and informative. Without the sabbatical and subsequent Fulbright, this book could not have been written. Several groups funded a course reduction in my teaching load from time to time which permitted me to work on the book. I thank the President's Coordinating Council (of Rutgers University) and the New Jersey Division of Higher Education for this invaluable support. My special thanks to Manus Midlarsky, Director of the Center for Conflict Resolution and Peace Studies, who not only provided funds for my work but has also provided an intellectual stimulus for serious work on conflict and peace at Rutgers. While I have felt the need to have a reduction in my teaching load in order to complete this study, I have also benefited greatly from teaching the ideas and research in this book to my undergraduate and graduate students. They have provided a constant sounding board, convincing me, as it has others, that good scholarship and good teaching feed off each other. Finally, let me express my appreciation to Michael Holdsworth who waited patiently for this manuscript and to Sheila McEnery and the staff of Cambridge University Press for the care they take in preparing manuscripts for publication.

I started research on this book the year before my daughter, Elyse, was born. She is now eight. Those have been important years. She has provided a peace for me and has helped me find my home. To her I dedicate this work of mid-life.

Block Island, Rhode Island

I

Preliminaries

~

Introduction

Much has been written on the causes of war; little has been learned about the subject. There are two reasons for this. The first is that the theoretical assumptions used to study the phenomenon are flawed and often erroneous. The second is that individual scholars have tried to do too much too soon. Typically, a single scholar working alone has tried to review a number of wars, reflect on their commonalities, and reach a conclusion. The end result has been some insightful suggestions, but little real evidence or documented generalizations. In the last twenty-five years, this has begun to change. Building on the pioneering efforts of Lewis Richardson and Quincy Wright, a community of peace researchers has emerged, with scholars testing very specific hypotheses and trying to document in a rigorous fashion the patterns of behavior associated with war.

What distinguishes this book on war from previous ones is that it will employ the large number of empirical findings generated in the last twenty-five years as the basis of its theorizing. Although this research has added important pieces of evidence that have moved the field beyond the imprecise and often contradictory explanations of the past, no clear theoretical explanation seems to be emerging from this process, although there is research that suggests such explanations. Because of inconsistencies and anomalies in the findings as well as differences in measurement and research design, the meaning and significance of these findings are hardly self-evident. Rather, they exist as a set of clues or pieces of a puzzle that need to be put together.

A scientific explanation will not just emerge from the research process, but must be constructed carefully from the evidence. While the empirical work on delineating various factors associated with war and specifying models of the war process can continue by testing various hunches, it has failed to date to provide a coherent explanation of war. One of the reasons for this may be that the dominant realist perspective that should be providing such an explanation has simply not been up to the task. It has not been able to explain inconsistencies in a satisfactory manner, and an entirely new theoretical approach may be needed, one that will put both existing findings and unresolved questions into a perspective that makes sense of both (see Vasquez, 1983a; Banks, 1985; Mansbach and Vasquez, 1981).

What needs to be done is to stand back from the findings and see what they are trying to tell us. Rather than treat the scientific process in a conservative deductive manner as suggested by philosophers of science as varied as Hempel (1966), Popper (1959), and Lakatos (1970), we might be better served by being more radically inductive, for at least the moment, and treating existing evidence as a good detective would treat clues. We would then try to piece the clues together as we would a puzzle, hoping that as we did so we would come across a clue that would suggest new hypotheses. These new hypotheses would then tell us where to find the missing pieces of the puzzle and in doing so would provide a way of deductively testing the theoretical explanation we had constructed so far. Since a number of research efforts using existing data on alliances, polarization, capability, arms races, bargaining, decision makers' perception, status, and crisis escalation (among others) have been completed or are approaching completion, this is an ideal time to implement this strategy and try to synthesize a theoretical explanation that can guide the next stage in data collection and hypothesis testing.

The scientific research on war and peace in the last twenty-five years has demonstrated that induction can bear important fruit. That research now constitutes a sufficiently critical mass of evidence to provide a real turning point in the long human effort to discover the causes of war. If the turning point comes, it will support J. David Singer's inductive notion that in attempting to understand war, emphasis must be placed on systematic data collection and description so as to produce a body of empirical generalizations. Once the patterns or correlates associated with war are known, then it will be possible to explain them. What is significant about the scientific study of war from the perspective of the philosophy of inquiry is that progress and cumulation have not come from deriving a hypothesis, testing it, and reformulating it in light of the evidence. If one takes that positivist approach, then the findings seem much more inconsistent, ambiguous, and farther away from cumulation than they in fact are. If, however, one treats the findings as an aid to discover inductively what patterns precede war, then there is greater reason for optimism.

The debate on induction versus deduction has often been confused because there has been a failure to distinguish the logic of discovery from the logic of confirmation (Nagel, 1961; Scheffler, 1967), as well as a tendency to ignore that in practice inductive and deductive procedures do not oppose each other but go hand in hand. Many of the logical arguments against induction hold only on the question of how to validly test theories (the logic of confirmation). This book is concerned primarily with the logic of discovery. I review existing findings not to see if they confirm a particular explanation, but to see if in the absence of any *confirmed* explanation a new explanation consistent with the evidence can be *discovered*.[1] This new explanation must then be tested before it can be accepted.

Methodologically, this book does not follow the typical positivist approach that specifies a proposition, operationalizes its concepts, collects data and constructs a research design that adequately tests the proposition. Instead, what this book does is employ a synoptic review of all relevant evidence to see what has and what can be learned about the onset of war – what in some disciplines is called a meta-analysis (see Hunter, *et al.*, 1982). Such efforts always raise two questions: First, is it possible to compare studies that have different statistical analyses or measures, or are designed at different levels of analysis? Second, is there not a danger that such an effort will treat findings as more definitive than they are? Both of these are important questions, but in practice they turn out not to pose insurmountable obstacles. In terms of comparing studies, this is more of a statistical dilemma than a philosophy of science problem. On the statistical level, a Pearson's r of 0.15 and a Yule's Q of a 0.15 are not equivalent and tell us different things about a relationship. Philosophically, however, they are comparable in that they both tell us that the proposition has produced a "weak" association (see Vasquez, 1983a: 179–80). Statistical findings can be compared to make philosophical assessments about the empirical adequacy of various explanations. If this could not be done, then what would be the point of doing research in the first place? More importantly, in terms of the logic of discovery, differences in research design and measurement, even flaws and measurement errors turn out to be very useful because they provide clues about what might really be going on across a series of studies, particularly those that get different results using basically the same data set.[2]

This brings us to the second question, the danger of treating findings as more definitive than they are. This, of course, can be a problem with simplistic analyses that categorically assert what "science" has found,

---

[1] Of course, explanations are not discovered as if they had a pre-existing status, but are constructed by human minds.

[2] For an example of this, see Mueller (1971) who compares different surveys using different phrasing of questions with good effect.

but it is not a problem if one is careful in assessing the evidence and explicit about one's judgments. In this analysis, I have taken pains to present the reader with all the various pieces of evidence I have examined to reach the conclusions I have drawn. Often I repeat in the text or footnotes the actual findings. If a study has been criticized or followed by studies that have inconsistent findings, I give these equal attention. In this process, I have tried to act like a judge rather than a prosecuting attorney or defense counsel.

It is important to take this perspective if one wants to get at the truth or at least learn something from research. Unfortunately, some analysts wish to pursue skepticism's agenda and seek to use scientific studies to show that nothing can be known. Ironically, it is often the anti-quantitative and anti-scientific who take this tack. They then become "super positivists" using positivist criteria to show that a research design is flawed, a measure invalid, or a finding trivial. Having satisfied themselves that scientific research cannot produce knowledge, they then proceed to ignore it and study international politics in a considerably less rigorous and even speculative manner. I hope this book will show readers who have been seduced by this attitude what they have been missing.

I have approached the literature neither in a naive nor overly skeptical way, but as a detective looking for clues. In the end, of course, I have had to make judgments about measurement validity, research designs, and how much weight to place on a particular finding. Evaluation of empirical research requires that such judgments be made. To think otherwise is to misunderstand the nature of scientific inquiry. Nevertheless, this does not mean that judgments need be arbitrary. Whenever an important question is at stake, I trace for the reader the thinking process I went through in making a particular interpretation. Although it would be tiresome to do this for each judgment, I have done it enough so that the reader can make a judgment about how much confidence to place on my evaluation of a particular body of research.

These questions are important because, in this book, I try to uncover the dynamics of war and peace in the modern global system by examining the patterns of behavior delineated by existing research. These patterns, rather than a set of axioms, will be the foundation of my explanation. Instead of assuming that people either as individuals or as collectivities act in certain ways (as rational actors or utility maximizers, for example), I will try to base my explanation on what we empirically know about how people actually behave in certain situations. In other words, I will tend to explain how one action leads to another by saying that in those kinds of circumstances, what we know about people tells us that they will act in that way for these reasons or because of these factors, rather than explaining the action by a model based on an untested axiom. What this means is that my propositions will often be linked not by mathematical or logical deduction, but by historical contingency.

War is a very complex subject, in part because war does not result from a single set of causes. There are many paths to war, and in this analysis I try to delineate the modal (typical) path by which relatively equal states have become embroiled in wars with one another in the modern state system. I had initially hoped that a single explanation of war over all of history could be constructed. Instead I have come to the conclusion that there are different types of war and that each type can be preceded by different causal sequences. To explain war requires identifying the various paths that lead to war. What makes this even more complicated is that these paths may vary over long periods of history. In this book, I believe I have identified one path, for one type of war, in one historical era, the modern global system (1495 to the present).

In trying to identify the causal sequences that precede wars, I distinguish between underlying and proximate causes. Underlying causes are fundamental causes that set off a train of events (the proximate causes) that end in war. Of all the various issues over which wars can arise, I have found territorial disputes between neighbors to be the main source of conflict that can give rise to a sequence of actions that ends in war. Since all neighbors usually must, at some point in their history, contend with this issue, and because this issue is an issue over which most neighbors are apt to fight if they are involved in a war with one another, I see territorial disputes as an underlying cause of war. Whether or not it will give rise to war, however, will depend on how the issue is treated (the proximate causes). Since how states treat each other varies according to a number of characteristics, the proximate causes of war are much more varied than the underlying causes. Thus, while territorial disputes can be the origin for all types of wars, each of the different types of wars has its own proximate causes.

In this analysis, I have tried to identify these proximate causes by looking at the foreign policy practices that lead to war. Among equals, I have found that, within the modern global system, war is likely if the practices of power politics are used to try to resolve territorial disputes. Power politics behavior, rather than preventing war, actually increases the probability that it will break out. This is because the main practices of power politics – alliances, military buildups, and the use of *realpolitik* tactics – increase insecurity and hostility motivating each side to take harder lines. Coercion fails to produce compliance or compromise because the nature of the issue at stake is such that giving in (especially to an equal) is unthinkable. Under such conditions, the use of power politics produces a set of interactions and domestic political environments that make war increasingly likely. Between equals, war is brought about by each side taking a series of steps that increase hostility and make the issue at hand more intractable. This involves the disputants in a series of crises, one of which escalates to war. Evidence on which steps increase the probability of war and which characteristics of crises make them prone to escalation has been provided by empirical research.

The use of the foreign policy practices of power politics to handle certain territorial disputes will increase the probability of war, but whether power politics will be used depends, in part, on the nature of the global political system in operation. The global institutional context, in particular whether it provides norms and "rules of the game" for resolving issues, has a major impact on whether states will resort to power politics. Preventing war and creating peace involves learning how to build structures that provide mechanisms for resolving issues through diplomacy rather than armed force.

To summarize: In the modern state system one of the main sets of factors that bring about war among equals is the rise of territorial disputes, particularly between neighbors, that in the absence or failure of a global institutional network to resolve the issue politically makes actors resort to the unilateral solutions provided by power politics. Through elaborating this skeletal outline, I will explain why and how wars occur, why some wars expand, and why some historical periods and interstate relationships are more peaceful than others.

In trying to construct these explanations from the various pieces of research, I have found it useful to think in terms of causes and consequences. Many scholars, including the leading peace researcher in the field, J. David Singer, eschew causal language. Many share Hume's reservation that the notion of "cause" inheres within the human brain and not in nature.[3] In addition, there are a host of problems in making causal inferences. Despite these concerns, it is very difficult to construct an

---

[3] Like Hume, I agree that a cause is not something that is observed empirically but is imposed by the human mind. Unlike Hume, however, I do not see this as very unusual or problematic, since we now know from linguistics and cognitive psychology that this is true of many concepts and aspects of human language. If we reject the concept of cause because of Hume's empiricist objections, we would have to reject most scientific concepts, the grammar

explanation of *why* wars occur or expand (especially if one is proceeding inductively) without thinking in causal terms at critical points in the analysis (see Dessler, 1991). Thus, I have found it important to distinguish whether some factor is really a correlate or a "cause." I have tried to see if a factor is really something that brings about war or is a consequence of war. I have thought it important in interpreting a study to see if its explanations and findings identify sufficient or necessary conditions of war. I have found it useful in determining the relative potency of variables to speak in terms of underlying and proximate causes. Without prejudicing the deeper philosophical issues, I have retained causal *language* and *thinking* at critical points in the analysis. When I have done this, I have tried to make it clear exactly what I mean by the language and to what empirical referents I am alluding.

Having said that, let me note some areas where I have found causal language misleading and have found the need to correct some of its mechanistic connotations. I have found it misleading to think of war as being brought about because a certain set of conditions or variables are in place. Such Newtonian conceptions and research based on them have not been very fruitful. Rather than seeing war as caused in this mechanical sense, I have seen war as an outcome, i.e. as something that flows out of a set of actions. Rather than seeing war as being *produced* by a set of conditions, I have found it more enlightening to speak of the probability of war increasing as certain actions are taken. To correct these misleading connotations, I have done the following. To emphasize that war comes out of a set of actions, I have spoken in terms of causal sequences and paths to war. To emphasize the probabilistic nature of war, I have spoken in terms of factors that promote or increase the probability of the onset and expansion of war, rather than of sufficient conditions – although I will use the latter phrase from time to time to distinguish these factors from necessary conditions.

My concern that war and peace have been conceptualized in an overly mechanistic manner in the scientific and traditional realist literature reflects a deeper concern that various criticisms that have been made of positivism need to be taken more seriously by those pursuing scientific inquiry. This book was written during much of the debate over positivism (see Ashley, 1987; Shapiro, 1981; Kratochwil, 1989; Lapid, 1989; Hollis and Smith, 1991; Der Derian and Shapiro, 1989), and the analysis herein

underlying language, and a host of other aspects of cognition that seem to be associated with the structure of the brain rather than the empirical environment.

has not been unaffected by that debate. In this book, the importance of history, cultural variation and the role of beliefs and social constructions of reality are emphasized over the role of single factors, like power, or rationalistic explanations. My views are considerably less positivist than even traditional scholars like Gilpin and Morgenthau who see themselves as uncovering timeless laws of politics. More fundamentally, the debate over positivism has affected how I conceive of international relations theory and has provided an opening for reflection, which I have found more congenial to serious theory construction than the strict positivism of the recent past.

These various philosophical issues are pursued in Part I of the book in which I explore the conceptual questions that need to be resolved before constructing an explanation of war and peace. In Chapter 1, I address the question of how the phenomenon of war *should* be conceptualized in order to understand and explain it. Here, I outline the theoretical assumptions about war that I have found useful to make and which are employed in the subsequent analysis. I learned early on that not all wars were alike and that different explanations would be required for different types of war. In Chapter 2, I present and justify a typology of war and argue that each type has its own causes. I then limit myself to explaining wars of rivalry, wars that are fought between relative equals. The concept of rivalry is defined and its dynamics outlined. In Chapter 3, I assess realist contributions to our understanding of war and its failure to provide an adequate understanding of the dynamics of peace and war. I argue that power politics theory, rather than providing an explanation of war and peace, actually reflects an image of the world that decision makers sometimes hold and a set of foreign policy practices that once implemented increase the probability of war. I discuss how the institution of war evolves and the role learning plays in the onset of war by creating and institutionalizing a culture of war at the global level. In a more general sense, this chapter is concerned with how and why violence is used by some collectivities in some periods, and not by all collectivities in all periods.

Part II is the heart of the book. It is devoted to constructing a scientific explanation of the onset and expansion of war and the nature of peace. In each of these chapters, the main scientific findings are put together as pieces of a puzzle to come up with an explanation of war and peace. I begin, in Chapter 4, by examining one of the main underlying causes of interstate wars – territorial disputes. I argue that territorial contiguity is the source of conflict that most frequently leads to wars, and I provide evidence to show that this is the case. The reason why human collectivities will fight over territorial issues more readily than other issues is not known, but I speculate that it may have something to do with an inherited tendency toward territoriality. A focus on territoriality can explain a number of patterns that other perspectives have not explained. Nevertheless, territoriality should not be conceived of as a drive or instinct that makes war inevitable. Territoriality makes humans very sensitive to threats to their territory, but how they deal with these issues is the main factor determining whether they will go to war. Chapter 5 specifies some of the proximate causes of war by outlining how war comes about between relative equals when they treat highly salient issues in a power politics fashion. In this chapter, I provide a detailed analysis of the empirical literature to outline the typical steps to war that rivals follow. Delineating the steps to war provides a way of explaining why some rivalries end in war while others do not. In Chapter 5, the focus is on why interactions between rivals encourage them to take certain steps that lead to war. However, domestic political factors are also important in explaining the steps to war, and these are delineated in Chapter 6, which focuses on the linkage between global and domestic factors. Chapters 5 and 6 identify the main causal sequence that leads relative equals to war. Chapter 7 identifies the causal sequence that leads some wars to expand. In that chapter, I examine the research findings on the scope, severity, and duration of war in order to explain how some wars expand to become world wars.

These three chapters specify proximate causes, but it is important to remember that structural factors have a major impact on whether the interactions that produce the steps to war are likely to be taken. Why rivals initiate the steps to war in the first place cannot be fully understood without reference to the global institutional context. This is done in Chapter 8, which examines peace structures and the role of peace in the onset of war. A full explanation of war must explain how and why a peace breaks down, encouraging states to resort to the practices of power politics. This chapter delineates the main factors associated with interstate relationships and historical periods that are comparatively peaceful. This demonstrates that world politics need not always be a struggle for power, that war is not inevitable, and that peace is possible.

The analysis presented in Part II explains war by: (1) looking at how certain issues become prone to violence if they are handled in a certain way; (2) identifying the ways in which issues are treated that are most likely to result in war between equals; and (3) examining how the global institutional structure permits or discourages political actors from handling issues in a way that will result in war. In Chapter 9, I integrate the various analyses of each of the previous chapters to construct an overall theoretical explanation of the onset and expansion of wars of rivalry. In this chapter, I also discuss the implications of the analysis for the cumulation of scientific knowledge on war and on peace. The Appendix, which the reader should not ignore, provides a more detailed specification of the theoretical argument in a propositional format. These propositions, which are keyed to each chapter, provide the best summary of the book. They also constitute a research agenda for the future.

Before turning to the body of the work, let me make some final points about the way in which this book is written and about the terminology I employ. Although it is common to review literature and summarize various approaches in theoretical works, I have avoided that in this book. I am not so interested in writing a book about what various scholars have said about war as I am about writing a book that tells us something about war. For this reason, I draw upon the literature and use it to synthesize empirical findings, rather than spend a great deal of time summarizing it. Likewise, while on occasion I will criticize other explanations, as in Chapter 3, my purpose in this book is not so much to demonstrate that one "theory" is better than another, as it is to create a new explanation. Whether it is attractive is up to the reader to decide. Whether it is true will be a matter for future research to decide.

The general reader, therefore, should be cautioned that the aspects of the analysis that are based on research can be accepted with more confidence than those aspects that break new ground, even though the latter may sometimes prove more interesting. Technically, from a scientific point of view, the explanations provided herein must be tested systematically before any of them can be accepted.

Throughout this book, I have tried to write in a style that will make it accessible to the non-specialist. Nevertheless, I do periodically use technical terms employed in the research that I have found most useful, because progress in part depends on the use of a common language. However, since much of this research has been guided by the realist paradigm, scholars often use concepts that I find to be fundamentally flawed. These include such basic concepts as power, the balance of power, hegemony, influence, deterrence, and labels such as major *power*, minor *power*, or employing shorthands, like "France," to personify societies. My main concern with each of these is whether the things these words refer to have actually existed in the way the concept or label implies they do. What, for example, are the theoretical preconceptions involved in referring to a state or some other political actor as a "power"? Have states really been deterred, or do we just assume that? What does it mean to say that France took a particular action? In this context to what does the term "France" really refer, and can we avoid the theoretical dangers inherent in using such an anthropomorphizing label?

Generally, I have avoided using theoretical terms I view as hopelessly flawed. The one area in which this proved awkward was with the terms *major power, minor power,* and *great power.* Since I do not think that countries can be treated as billiard balls that are simply a bundle of capabilities, and because I believe the realist paradigm to be an inadequate guide to scientific inquiry (see Vasquez, 1983a), I have abandoned the conceptually distorted habit of referring to countries as "powers." The capability of countries may not always be their most important characteristic; indeed the fact that countries are "states" is probably more important. For these reasons, I refer to them as "states" rather than "powers." I also avoid the term "great" because it is normatively biased in favor of the elites who ran those states.

Unfortunately, most conceptual problems are not so easily solved. Let me begin the analysis by turning to a concept that has received surprisingly little scrutiny – the idea of war. Its meaning and scientific definition are a proper subject for the first chapter.

1

Conceptualizing War

In defining a word, one may be doing a lot more than one suspects.

Definition

It seems only fitting that a scholarly work should begin with a definition of the subject at hand. Yet defining the subject of an inquiry is no light task. Although lilliputian scholars often get so bogged down in definition that they never get to the inquiry itself, poor definitions not only lead to confusion but often end up telling you more about the person who stipulated the definition than about the subject. Because the subject of definition and meaning is more complicated than appears, it needs to be analyzed before even attempting a definition of war. For this reason, I begin this chapter with a discussion of the nature of definition – how definitions are employed in and affect inquiry, the relationship between definitions and conceptualizations, and how adequate definitions and concepts can be distinguished from "flawed" ones. With this philosophical framework in mind, I argue that at the beginning of a scientific inquiry, it is best to begin with a simple working definition and to delineate the more interesting insights of complicated definitions and concepts of war as a set of theoretical assumptions separate from the definition itself.

In the second section, I select a working definition for the inquiry and elucidate some of its latent assumptions. Next, I identify the operational definition used by empirical researchers as the working definition of war in quantitative world politics discourse and analyze its latent assumptions.[1] In the third section I turn to a review and assessment of various conceptions of war by analyzing some of the more important theoretical definitions that can be found in the history of international relations

---

[1] An operational definition is one that identifies the empirical referent of a concept by stipulating what observations (or operations in the laboratory) will count as an instance (or indicator) of a concept.

thinking and in other disciplines' study of war. From these I draw out a set of insights that form an inchoate conceptualization of war. In the final section, I derive from this conceptualization the main theoretical assumptions about war I have found most useful in my own attempt to understand war and which will serve as a foundation and a perspective for this analysis.

Surprisingly, not much attention has been focused on how war *should* be defined or even on the broader question of its conceptualization. Most scholars seem content to work with modified everyday or ordinary definitions, since "we all know what a war is," a sure sign that we may not know anything theoretically significant about war.[2] Nevertheless, ordinary definitions provide, with slight modifications and stipulations, three useful functions. First, they can delimit the empirical domain of an inquiry by providing the "defining criteria" (Frohock, 1974: 56–60) that determine what phenomena will be included or excluded. Second, they try to provide at least some consistency of usage so that the word refers to the same thing. Of course, since everyday language is robust and living, most words have more than one meaning, and this can lead to ambiguity and a lack of conceptual rigor if an analyst fails to stipulate in what sense a concept is being used. Third, ordinary definitions help us get started; they allow us to talk to each other about the subject, to investigate and research it, to see it.

It is the latter function that makes words and concepts so important and, hence, scholarly decisions about how a word *should* be defined are much more complicated than was first understood. As a number of analytical philosophers have pointed out, if we do not have a word for something, it is difficult for us to even see the phenomenon and thus be aware of its importance and its connection to other phenomena. Indeed, without a word, we have trouble understanding whether the thing at hand is a single phenomenon or several (Hanson, 1965: ch. 1). One of the major contributions an intellectual or a scientist can make is the invention of a new word that permits us to see things we never saw before. Darwin's notion of evolution and natural selection, Freud's conception of the unconscious and of repression, Marx's idea of exploitation were all words that these seminal thinkers invented to communicate and see what no one else had really seen before. Once these words were uttered and applied we began to

---

[2] One can distinguish ordinary definitions which reflect the standard dictionary definition from more technical or stipulative definitions associated with the advance sciences; see Shapiro (1981: 61).

understand what before we only darkly perceived. Once having done so, our world (the phenomena we recognize) changed.

In this way, concepts have a dramatic impact on the world we perceive. The hope of science is that it can formulate concepts that illuminate what is causally significant and obfuscate the unimportant, rather than the other way around. The history of science is the history of rejected conceptions that distorted relationships more than they clarified them. Nevertheless, even when concepts appear to work scientifically, one can assume that there are aspects of a concept that are more illuminating than others.

Since science and knowledge advance, in part, by conceptual changes, the greatest task of definition is to produce a conceptualization that will result in a major breakthrough. However, because everyday definitions are derived from cultural experience rather than scientific analysis, it is highly unlikely that they will be up to this task. This makes for a predicament, because, in order to formulate a really useful scientific concept, something must be known about the subject, but in order to know something significant about the subject there must be an adequate conceptualization of it. The practices of scientific inquiry deal with this predicament by changing concepts as inquiry unfolds. The most adequate scientific concepts are the products of a fully developed theory and research program, which usually are not the concepts with which the inquiry began.

The history of science demonstrates that, while conceptualization should be taken seriously, any particular concept or definition should not be taken too seriously too early. Since the most important aspect of concept formation is to develop a conceptualization that will illuminate what is theoretically and causally significant, and since that will only be known if the concept produces hypotheses that pass scientific tests, the most important criterion for accepting an initial definition of war is that it permit research to begin. For the point of any empirical study of war, as Fukui and Turton (1979: 3, quoted in Ferguson, 1984: 4) point out, is to focus on "inspecting the phenomena and not defining the word." Once we have adopted a working definition it should lead research in a direction that will produce suggestive findings. If such findings are not produced, this may be an indication that the definition is flawed, since it is not fulfilling the purpose for which it was chosen. When a research program is producing null findings, then there is a good chance that the fault lies in poor conceptualization. Very poor concepts can produce failure and frustration.

This discussion assumes that there are no *real* definitions, definitions like those Plato sought for Justice, definitions that are absolute and reflect metaphysical verities. Instead, we remain in Plato's cave and can only develop *stipulative* definitions, working definitions that arbitrarily delimit what we are trying to study. Since science is primarily a process, it does not expect that any one stipulative definition will become a real definition that fully captures for all time the truth of a subject. Nevertheless, it should be clear that while "modern" science does not expect its definitions to reflect metaphysical verities, it strives to make its most useful concepts reflect "causal verities."

Scientists can never know if their concepts are doing this, and some question whether there are any "causal verities" in nature other than those we impose through our conceptualization. Despite this caveat, science and knowledge seem to progress by assuming that concepts that produce significant findings are capturing something about phenomena (if not nature) and not simply reflecting mental processes. The only ultimate test that science has had that it is, in fact, understanding the world is that its practices, which in a certain period of history won control over a large area of inquiry, have succeeded in providing answers that have permitted people to control and manipulate their physical worlds. Clearly, part of the promise of the scientific study of war has been the prospect of this kind of manipulation and control.

How does one get a conceptualization that will produce fruitful research that will be policy relevant? There is no easy answer to this question, but it is clear that even inductively oriented researchers do not test every possible claim. Rather, they mentally sift through ideas to see which make sense and to reformulate and make more rigorous those concepts that seem promising. Since all definitions focus on only some factors, one way of determining whether a concept is likely to produce interesting research is to uncover the latent theoretical assumptions it makes and examine the extent to which these assumptions seem plausible.

The problem with this portrayal, as critics of "positivist" interpretations of science maintain, is that it makes the process of selecting definitions appear much less complicated and fraught with pitfalls than it is. The portrayal ignores the fact that definitions and language play a variety of roles within a culture and not just the pursuit of scientific truth. In particular, it must be recognized that definitions do not simply provide a way of discussing phenomena, but help produce phenomena (see Shapiro, 1981: 5, 20–21). It is important to understand how the constituting function of language affects social inquiry and how intellectual discourse affects language.

Definitions that provide a constituting function are usually associated with an institution and its practices and for this reason can be called *institutional definitions*. Such definitions create a social institution (a set of practices) by delimiting what practices constitute the institution and what do not. In this way, they help make a certain activity come into existence and attempt to control it once in existence. Rules of games (chess, baseball) or definitions of ethical behavior and customs (like promising) are institutional definitions in that, by defining what it means to play chess or to make a promise, they provide a kind of constitutional structure for the activity.[3] This defining structure also serves to keep the institution "pure" by keeping its practices distinct from those of other activities or institutions. The "constituting" function of language is often performed by intellectual analyses, which can be scholarly, religious, political, magical, legal, and/or scientific depending on the dominant intellectual modes of a culture.

The presence of influential *institutional definitions* of a phenomenon under inquiry may not only hamper "objective" analysis, but "frame" and push inquiry in directions of which the investigator is not fully aware. For example, Grotius defined war as a legal condition between juridical equals that is declared and which regulates the way those contending by armed force may behave (see Wright, 1965: 9–10). The declaration of war is important because it sets aside normal international law and announces that a special set of laws on warfare will now govern relations. Grotius did not simply define war as it appeared historically in his day, but defined the institution of war; he defined war as an institutional fact within the existing system (and global culture) of early-seventeenth-century international law.

His definition demonstrates that definitions do not just uncover phenomena but create them. However, it should also be clear that Grotius does not start *de novo*; he inherits an ongoing activity and tries to shape and push this raw material to fit an ideal. The ideal type, if sufficiently influential (as was Grotius's analysis), can take on a life of its own. The ideal type of the activity, while rarely achieved in practice, acts as a demiurge constantly trying to shape the events of history to conform to a definitional recipe. Since this is the case, there is always the danger or the prospect (depending on one's point of view) that a new definition or concept of war can change the practice of war; that it can shape the institution

---

[3] What I have described as institutional definitions are usually discussed as institutional facts as opposed to brute facts; see Frohock (1974: 26–27) and Searle (1969).

of war the way in which both the just war tradition and Machiavelli, in different ways, attempted to do. The fact that this can occur is most obvious with legalistic definitions like Grotius's, because the institution of international law that he employed has become outdated. It has been replaced by less obvious and more informal institutions that nevertheless satisfy the definitional function, as can be seen by the fact that war is easily distinguished from riots, revolution, and ubiquitous violence.

From the perspective of the constituting function of language, what is considered war is a product of history – a product of the beliefs, formal and informal laws, and customs of a particular period. This emphasizes the notion that war is a social invention, a fact created by an institution that takes certain actions and makes them a thing. The definition of war reflects the process by which the verbs to fight and to kill become nouns, the process by which the actions become an institutional fact. In the process, that action is changed and controlled. The raw action is controlled by the dominant ideas and thoughts about the action (themselves a product of learning from engagement). These ideas try to add to and delete characteristics from the raw action, giving the action, in this case war, a goal and purpose, a strategy and a set of rituals (like declaration, surrender, treatment of prisoners, diplomatic negotiating etiquettes). However, these institutional ideas must constantly confront the raw action itself and any ideas of individual participants that may not reflect the ideals.

For the phenomenon of war, the main source of deviation from ideals is likely to come from attempts to win a war. "Innovations" of this sort are often seen as immoral and illegal. They involve things like unrestricted submarine warfare and civilian bombing. If they are successful, then they become selected out and the institution accommodates itself to them. At times, some forms of warfare are so different from prevailing customs that the term *war* is not applied to them. These forms of fighting are beyond the conceptual pale of the definition of war. When this occurs, we have a good illustration of the fact that definitions not only reflect "reality," but help create it and give it a degree of legitimacy. This is most evident today in the concept of terrorism, which is seen as something separate from war, although the case for its separation is primarily political and appears motivated by questions of legitimacy and conformity to recent historical practices, rather than a scientific delimitation of the empirical domain.

From this analysis it should be clear that the definitions of most terms do not emerge from a scientific pursuit of the truth. The history of a definition is a history of a culture's or discourse's view of the world it has created given the raw material at hand. Because we make our own world and how we have made it affects our behavior, it is always difficult to have a concept capture the world as it is. Concepts do not just reflect or capture reality, but help make reality. In the process, they distort or illuminate different aspects of the world they are shaping. In this way, a definition's history can provide the traces of those aspects of the raw action that any given age or culture saw as most important, but cultural importance is not necessarily the key to scientific understanding.

How a phenomenon should be conceptualized can become a matter of contention between science and other discourses. Why a particular concept or definition may come to dominate an age or inquiry poses a jurisdictional problem for scientific inquiry. Principles of contemporary scientific concept formation (see Hempel, 1952) try to evaluate the utility of definition and conceptualization solely on their basis for explaining empirical phenomena. Concepts and definitions, however, have purposes and consequences other than their ability to explain. Concepts may have a religious, metaphysical, ethical, or cultural utility. Statements may be believed not because they are "scientifically true," but because they help one get along in the world; live the proper way; capture the metaphysical essence of why we are here; or satisfy a group's or a "society's" political and economic interests.

One of the problems of discussing politics is that not everyone's primary purpose may be the search for "scientific truth," which is another way of saying that what is meant by the Truth is a question of debate and contention. Science wants to argue that whether we really know something is true must depend, at least in part, on the criteria people use to believe things. If some people believe things because it is in their personal or political interests or because they desire it, this does not make them "true" (nor necessarily false). However, even while those who are opposed to scientific thinking might agree with this view, this framing of the question ignores the more fundamental question, which is why should scientific (empirical) truth be the only or primary basis for accepting statements or beliefs? Once this question is asked, it becomes clearer that science itself must be seen as an institutional discourse that competes with other institutions and their discourses for the control of language and belief in certain domains.

This is the major insight suggested by Foucault's (1972; 1980: 112–14, 131–33) analysis of modern science. "Post-modern" critics, like Foucault (1980) and Shapiro (1981), have gone a long way in refuting naive positivist explanations of science as "objective." However, just because scientific discourse can be seen as competing with other discourses for control of beliefs does not mean that there are not good reasons (both epistemological and practical) for choosing scientific criteria of truth over others in questions of empirical observation (i.e. concept formation) and explanation.

Whether a scientific concept should be permitted to exercise a constituting function, thereby affecting the practice of war as an institution, is a question that must be held in abeyance for now. Suffice it to say that until the empirical study of war and peace is able to provide an adequate scientific concept, the question is moot. In the meantime, the realization that different concepts of war may affect the practice of war suggests that an analysis of different conceptions of war may provide insights about the nature of war and how it changes.

Although this discussion of the nature of definition has not answered all questions posed by the act of defining, it has made it clear that there are non-theoretical assumptions and consequences involved in accepting definitions which can make the task of defining an important social phenomenon, like war, subject to a number of pitfalls. In particular, the use of previously accepted definitions that appear highly theoretical may carry with it the unconscious acceptance of historical institutional legacies that may lead a research program in directions that would not be warranted from a purely scientific perspective. This problem can be avoided by not incorporating too many untested assumptions in a definition at an early stage of inquiry because it could produce a too narrow or distorted empirical domain for fruitful research. Rather, many useful assumptions can be taken as auxiliary hypotheticals to form a broader conceptualization of the phenomenon that both guides research and theory construction and is changed by it. In this way, the initial working definition remains fairly stable in its identification of the empirical domain and does not have to carry the weight of the entire theoretical enterprise. I will begin by selecting a working definition of war that can accommodate a number of conceptualizations and at the same time satisfy two of the main functions of ordinary definitions – demarcation of the empirical domain and consistency of use.

Definition of War

Probably the best way to move from an everyday definition of war to a working scholarly definition is to try to think of what phenomena it would be most useful to study to learn about war and what phenomena would make the effort too diffuse and divert it from its main focus. One immediately thinks of the two world wars, extended and major fights that shaped history, and a host of other more limited interstate wars, like the Franco-Prussian War. Certainly, any study should include these kinds of wars, and it is what Webster's Dictionary means by war when it defines it as "a state of usually open and declared armed hostile conflict between states or nations."

What about armed clashes between "primitive" tribes or border conflicts? Are these wars? They are organized and fought under the authority of a leader, characteristics associated with state warfare, but for some investigators these clashes are too small (in terms of the number of casualties) or too short in duration to study. Others might not want to study such clashes because they might see them as a fundamentally different human phenomenon that would tell us little about (interstate) war.

What about acts of violence like revolutions and civil wars, which take place within the same society rather than between societies? Is the distinction between what is *within* a society or a state and what is *without* the critical distinction that should be made to determine the proper domain of what is war? If so, then some of the longest and bloodiest violent political acts of history will be excluded. What is the theoretical justification for doing this and what are the implications for research?

What of interpersonal violence? Is war fundamentally different from these acts or just a special case of human violence? What about organized acts of human violence like dueling and vendetta, are these wars? And what of violence itself? Is human violence similar to animal aggression? Are the wars fought by ants for territory and the food associated with it that different from human wars? Does war have to result in death or can it still be war if no one is killed? How important are attitudes in war? Was the Cold War a war because of the extreme hostility? Are two states with a protracted border conflict that have only periodic clashes with few fatalities, at war with each other?

Such questions can be irritating, especially when they are raised by the sophist. Answering such questions, however, is much simpler than such an extended list would imply. Two things must be kept in mind. First and most important, what is or is not a war or special class of war can be determined by whether one thinks this phenomenon is caused by the same set of factors. I once met a historian who argued, perhaps facetiously, that there were as many causes of war as there were wars. For him, war simply did not exist as a general social phenomenon. Gang fights, wars among ants, and World War II can be treated as wars if we believe that they are all caused by the same factors. Since we usually do not, or at least think it not very useful to begin an inquiry with that assumption, they are not usually included as part of the class of events that we choose to call war. This is not the case, however, with civil wars, border clashes or "primitive wars" which may, in fact, have the same causes as interstate wars. Conversely, revolutions are seen as a distinct phenomenon because theories of revolution, especially those that emphasize relative deprivation (Gurr, 1970), are seen as inapplicable to interstate war. This underlines the point that what is or is not part of a phenomenon in science is determined by whether a separate theory is needed to account for it.

Second, even though we may not treat something as war, this does not mean that studying it may not give us valuable insights about the causes of war. Studying interpersonal violence, animal aggression, or even labor strikes may tell us something about the respective psychological, biological, and political dynamics associated with war. Studying phenomena that seem related to war may elucidate different aspects of war. For example, studying animal aggression may help us understand territoriality and other ecological factors associated with war. Studying family violence may add insights about the role hostility and frustration play in the onset of war. Studying gang wars and labor strikes may tell us something about war as an instrument of force. Studying interpersonal violence may elucidate psychological factors and the role of motivation and emotion in war. Studying "primitive" warfare helps us understand factors associated with war that precede modern complex societies and that may be basic to the human condition regardless of history and culture.

Eventually, science may be able to explain what makes certain acts of violence fundamentally different from each other, as well as understand how they are related and connected, if they are. It cannot be known in advance which perspective is correct. The scientific utility of these different perspectives can only be assessed in light of their ability to generate a fruitful research program that culminates in an accurate and explanatorily powerful theory. In this sense, the disciplinary division that has given rise to different approaches to war in political science, sociology, psychology, social psychology, anthropology, animal behavior, history, and geography is a useful way for social science to spread its research bets.

Given this diversity and interest from various disciplines, it is difficult to find a common working definition and nearly impossible to reach a consensus on a theoretical definition. Nevertheless, a review of the more conventional definitions shows that, while no one definition can accommodate all disciplines, there are some that can accommodate more than one. These, as would be expected, are the more straightforward and less theoretical definitions. The one that will be used for the purpose of this inquiry is that offered by Hedley Bull (1977: 184): "War is organized violence carried on by political units against each other."

The only immediate reservation that I have about this definition is the use of the term *violence*, which remains undefined. Even a narrow definition of violence as direct bodily harm through physical action (rather than broader definitions such as destruction of property, psychological domination, or harm brought about by structural conditions (see Galtung and Hoivik, 1971) seems too broad for what Hedley Bull has in mind. It would seem that war must involve organized violence that aims to kill members of another group, not simply to do them harm, otherwise war becomes too much like *force*. This reservation, however, is not so complicated that I am prompted to add to the semantics of war by giving my personal peculiar definition.

The overall advantages of Bull's definition can be readily seen by examining one of its competitors. For example, Malinowski's (1968: 247, also cited in Levy, 1983: 50) widely used anthropological definition of war as "an armed contest between two independent political units, by means of organized military force, in the pursuit of a tribal or national policy," suffers from defects not present in Bull's definition. Malinowski's emphasis on *independent* political units suggests that anti-colonial wars of liberation would not be seen as wars, neither apparently would massacres of indigenous groups like the Turkish massacres of the Armenians. Likewise, objections can be raised to confining the goals of war to tribal or national policy, or even to the notion that war is pursued for policy reasons rather than some other (including unconscious) reason.

I present these objections as illustrative of the kinds of problems confronted by working definitions. Since not much can be gained by systematically examining various working definitions and indicating why I prefer Bull's to some other, I will not dwell on my reasons for selecting his. I find Bull's definition useful for three reasons. It does not confine war to interstate war, so it is sufficiently broad to accommodate the work in political science, history, anthropology, sociology, and aspects of social psychology and geography. Second, it lacks terms that are contentious or would impose too great a theoretical perspective. Third, the main theoretical term it does include, "organized," I find particularly useful.

Since it is analytically impossible for a definition not to impose any perspective on a subject matter, it is important to make Bull's assumptions explicit. The most obvious assumption made by his definition is that war involves collective violence; it is not simply *conflict*. Bull's focus on violence is important, because it makes it clear that war and conflict are not synonymous. Conflict is a very broad and somewhat ambiguous term. One could easily argue, as E. H. Carr (1939 [1964 ed.: 42–44]) does, that conflict is pervasive and inevitable, since it cannot be assumed that there will ever be a permanent harmony of interests among political actors. Despite the reality of such conflict of interests, it is clear from the historical record that not all conflict ends in war. Indeed, war remains a relatively infrequent event in the history of most nation-states; Small and Singer (1982: 78) report that there were only 118 international wars from 1816 to 1980. Since this is the case, there must be something that distinguishes the vast majority of conflicts that do not end in war from the very few that do, which suggest that the causes of conflict are not the same as the causes of war.

Another important assumption made by the definition is that war is *organized* violence. This has three implications. First, it means that war is an ordered activity with rules and customs. This encourages an examination of how conceptions of war affect the practices of war. Second, it means that war is not random violence, but focused and directed. It reflects, no matter how irrational its overall impact or the chaos of immediate battle, some rational purpose for which it was initiated. Third, it is organized in the sense that it is collective and social, not individual. This is not interpersonal violence between individuals who have a personal dispute. Indeed, one of the theoretically interesting things about war is that it is fought by people who usually do not know each other and have no personal dispute or animus toward one another other than that which has been defined by those controlling the war.

The next critical assumption made by Hedley Bull's definition is that war is fought by political units. Again this emphasizes the collective aspect of war, but it is not violence between just any collective actors, but primarily between political organizations. Economic organizations do not fight wars, they compete in other ways. Even robbers and their victims do not typically engage in war, but in something else, and the point is not usually to kill. There is something about politics, what it does and the functions it serves, that seems to make it more prone to violence than other activities. Exactly what that is, is left unspecified by this definition.[4]

---

[4] Whatever it is, also seems to affect religious organizations, which like political organizations are prone to war under certain conditions. For a review of the anthropological literature that sees economic exchange as a substitute for war, see Ferguson (1984: 17–18).

Finally, unlike other major definitions, this definition does not indicate what is the aim or purpose of the violence except that it is directed toward the political units and only to the members of those units as a means to an end. Unlike Malinowski, Bull does not define war as aiming at a tribal or national policy. He does not tell us that war is a specific instrument to attain a particular goal that cannot be otherwise attained. Whether war, in fact, does that becomes a matter of empirical investigation and not definition.

While it is useful to delineate the assumptions of the working definition of this inquiry, it is even more important to be aware of the working definition of war that has guided research within the field of international relations. For most of the research discussed in this book, the working definitions of war have been the operational definitions of those who have collected scientific data on war. The Correlates of War project has provided the most thorough and influential quantitative data set on war, and its operational definition is: "An international war is a military conflict waged between (or among) national entities, at least one of which is a *state*, which results in at least 1000 battle deaths of military personnel" (Bremer *et al.*, 1975: 23 [1992 ed.: 387]; see also Singer and Small, 1972: 37, 39).

The use of an operational definition to guide a research program without ever explicitly developing a conceptual definition has led some to raise questions about procedure, since from a philosophy of science perspective one first has a theory and then collects the data. This did not happen with the Correlates of War project, and the fact that it did not reflects, in part, the difference between scientific ideals and practice, as well as the early stage of the scientific study of war. Singer and Small (1972) did not employ a specific concept of war because they wanted to create a data set that could be employed by the entire field to test hypotheses from a variety of theoretical perspectives. In addition, although they did not have an explicit conceptual definition, their operational definition and their actual collection of data were informed by the conceptual definitions of their two main predecessors – Quincy Wright and Lewis F. Richardson.

The problem Singer and Small faced with the work of Wright and Richardson was that these scholars' respective definitions stemmed from very different theoretical perspectives and were at times contradictory and had, as a result, produced different sets of phenomena for investigation. Like Singer and Small, Quincy Wright (1965: 636) was concerned with determining the empirical domain of the concept and eventually settled on two defining criteria: "all hostilities involving members of the family of nations, whether international, civil, colonial, or imperial, which were recognized as states of war in the legal sense or involved 50,000 troops" (Wright, 1965: 636, also quoted in Small and Singer, 1982: 37).[5] Since Wright was conducting his study during the realist–idealist debate of the inter-war period, it should not be surprising that he should combine the idealist legal emphasis with the realist emphasis on power and impact (see Vasquez, 1983a: 134–36).

Richardson (1960b), being outside the field, took a different perspective. He began by throwing out the very concept of war and replacing it with the much broader notion of "deadly quarrel." Influenced by psychology and having little respect for the scholarly study of politics (which he regarded, with reason, as unscientific), Richardson saw all killing, whether it be an individual act of crime or a war, as stemming from aggression. Therefore, for him the only thing that distinguished wars from other deadly quarrels was their magnitude, and Richardson (1960b: 6) ordered his data on the basis of the number of deaths grouped by various cut off points of the logarithm to the base ten.

Singer and Small decided to collect data on wars from 1816 on by combining lists of wars and deadly quarrels of Wright and of Richardson, since for them every instance of military combat is a potential datum (see Small and Singer, 1982: 37; their data were first published in Singer and Small, 1972). However, since Richardson included incidents that did not involve *military* combat and Wright included incidents of military combat that Singer and Small found problematic, they went through the combined list and eliminated the cases they regarded as "non-wars." For them, an incident is a non-war either because of "the inadequate political status of their participants," or because there are fewer than 1,000 battle deaths (Small and Singer, 1982: 38, 54).

Although these criteria appear innocuous enough, closer inspection reveals how difficult it is to free research from dominant perspectives, both those of the present and of the past. The first criterion, on political status, leads Singer and Small to focus primarily on the use of violence by nation-states, either against other states or against entities that the system of nation-states did not recognize as nation-states. This criterion leads them to distinguish between interstate wars and extra-systemic (imperial and colonial) wars. For interstate wars, their data set is the most definitive

---

[5] Wright (1965: 636) then makes this definition less reliable operationally by indicating that he will include some other incidents which meet neither criterion, if they "led to important legal results such as the creation or extinction of states, territorial transfers, or changes in government" (also quoted in Singer and Small, 1982: 38).

to date. For the extra-systemic wars, the data are the most accurate to date, but woefully incomplete for non-national entities, which are usually the victims in this historical period.

The discrepancy in the quality of these two data sets may be seen as part of the historical legacy of Western imperialism and racism that simply did not regard non-Western groups as civilized or as human beings equal to whites. It is not unfair to assume that such attitudes played some role in accounting for the fact that Western nations did not bother to record in any systematic way the fatalities sustained by non-national groupings in imperial wars of conquest or pacification.

This historical legacy forced Small and Singer (1982: 56) to make certain "practical" data-collection decisions which resulted in the discrepancy in the two data sets. First, Singer and Small decided to count the battle deaths only of recognized nation-states to determine what is or is not a war for their data set. This establishes a double standard in that, for an interstate war, the minimum fatality threshold for inclusion is a combined total of 1,000 battle deaths from all the sides that fought in the war; whereas for extra-systemic wars (since non-national participants' deaths are not counted) the nation-state must sustain that level by itself in order for the incident to be recorded as a war. This eliminates from consideration an entire range of unequal contests, even if they amounted to massacres.

Second, Singer and Small require that 1,000 battle deaths must be sustained by nation-states participating in an extra-systemic war *each year* in order for the war to be considered as ongoing; whereas for interstate wars once the 1,000 battle death threshold is crossed it is a war and the length of the war is determined by other factors. The reason for this research decision is that many "pacification" efforts drag on, and Singer and Small do not want these years to count as wars because it would inflate the frequency of war in the system in any given year or decade (see their discussion in Small and Singer, 1982: 56–57). Nevertheless, these decisions have the effect of making some people's deaths and wars not count, which is just the way the West viewed these conflicts in comparison to their own "real" wars.

This "coincidence" has led some (like Duvall, 1976) to charge that Singer and Small's operational definition is ideologically biased. In one sense, this is true, but, in another, this accusation is misleading since the reason the definition is biased has much more to do with previous history and governmental records than it does with Singer and Small. They are faced with the fact that others, less objective than they, have managed to shape and control the past so that part of the record is not easily reconstructed. The only alternative would have been to make crude estimates, and they were unwilling to do this because it would have greatly reduced the scientific reliability of their data.

What are the theoretical implications of this historical bias that has been handed down to researchers from the past? The clearest is that the data set on interstate wars is more complete and more valid than the data set on extra-systemic wars. This means that we can have more confidence about inferences based on the interstate data than on the extra-systemic. Since this is the case, analysis of the two data sets should be kept separate, which usually has been done. It must also be recognized that generalizations about interstate war may not apply to extra-systemic wars or to all war. The causes of interstate war may be fundamentally different from the causes of extra-systemic war; certainly the motivations (or reasons given) for these wars are different. Nor must researchers assume that the absence of interstate war means that there is no ongoing war and the system is at peace, a common mistake in data (as well as historical) analysis. If the absence of interstate war is taken as an indicator of peace when, in fact, there is ongoing extra-systemic war, then a correlation between a set of independent variables and "war/peace" may really be a correlation between independent variables and different types of war. Finally, it must also be noted that the elimination of military confrontations with fewer than 1,000 battle deaths, which means, in effect, the elimination of many border clashes, may be eliminating from observation an important set of wars and underestimating the effect of territorial considerations.

This discussion should make it clear that even the most scientific, systematic, honest and fair-minded attempts to define war with a minimum of theoretical "distortion" not only produce a number of theoretical implications, but are easily subjected to prevailing ideological assumptions about what is *really* war and what is peace.[6] Nonetheless, the solution to such problems is not less science, but more science. Better data, painstakingly reconstructed if necessary, and rated for their reliability, could be collected for extra-systemic wars. Data on wars with fewer than 1,000 battle deaths have been collected by Kende (1978) and by Gantzel

---

[6] This is because data collection is a paradigm-directed activity (see Vasquez, 1983a: ch. 5). In international relations inquiry the dominant realist paradigm carried with it much of the conservative anti-democratic ideological baggage of the aristocratic Euro-centric diplomatic elite of the post-Napoleonic era, and this is reflected, periodically, in some of the assumptions that guided the data collection.

(1981). In addition, one should not conclude in the face of problems that nothing can be learned from Correlates of War data or any data because they will always be biased and their results suspect (a conclusion Duvall [1976] comes close to making). Instead, one must be aware of the domain to which the data and the findings are applicable, a point which reminds us that we must be detectives if we are to solve the war puzzle and not expect an incontrovertible answer to emerge miraculously from the logical rigor and objectivity of research designs.

The Concept of War

Because even working and operational definitions make theoretical assumptions that may distort the world, I have avoided beginning this inquiry with an explicit theoretical definition. This keeps the empirical domain and research as open as possible. Nevertheless, since the ultimate point is to discover what is the best way of viewing the world so that we can understand the causes of war, a review of theoretical definitions provides an understanding of the various concepts of war that have existed and some insights about what may be the most useful theoretical assumptions to make in trying to explain war. Such a review also tells us something about what the various periods of history saw as the most important elements in war (or at least the wars of their time).

Quincy Wright's review of classical Western conceptions of war remains one of the most useful and will serve as a basis for beginning this review. According to Wright, one of the earliest important definitions of war comes from Cicero, who defined war as "contending by force" (quoted in Wright, 1965: 10). This suggests that war involves contention *over* something and that while war differs from other contentions in that it employs a special means, namely force, we should not lose sight of the fact that war is a form of contention. In politics, contention consists of disputes over objects of value (i.e. stakes). "Contention" is the general term applied to the various means that political actors use to resolve a dispute. From this perspective, war may be considered a violent way of getting objects of value.

As Wright (1965: 10) notes, Grotius takes exception to Cicero's definition by maintaining that war is not simply a contest, but a condition, by which he means "a legal condition." Although this may have been true in Grotius's time (and as was shown earlier, the impact of his work helped make it true), it is not necessarily true for all time. Put another way, it is possible to think of Grotius's exception as stating that war under conditions of accepted international law can become a kind of legal contest that regulates how and for what purposes armed forces may be employed.

Certainly, this is Wright's (1965: 8) view, who formally defines war as "the *legal condition* which *equally* permits two or more *hostile groups* to carry on a *conflict* by *armed* force" (italics in the original). Wright sees war as a condition or period of time in which special rules come into place which permit and regulate violence between governments. The purpose of this violence is to settle disputes. Wright also has behavioral concerns that make him wonder about the other characteristics of "the condition which prevails while groups are contending by arms" (Wright, 1938 cited in Wright, 1965: 8 n. 1). Law and custom, according to Wright (1965: 698), recognize that "when war exists, particular types of behavior or attitudes are appropriate." From this perspective, any given culture (including a global culture) consists of a number of different conditions (situations), each with its own appropriate behavior pattern. War can be seen as simply one of those conditions with custom informing neophytes how to behave when faced with such a situation, and law institutionalizing and sometimes shaping existing custom. What this appropriate behavior pattern is, what brings it about, and how regular it is throughout history and different cultures provides a latent social science conception of war within Wright's more explicit legal focus.

Today this legal focus appears less relevant, and many see this Grotian idea of international law as unrealistic. Much of this thinking is part of the legacy of the two world wars. Yet despite that dual trauma, Hedley Bull (1977: 184–89) reminds contemporary analysts that war has an order to it. It has a purpose; it is fought on a certain basis and often according to norms and rules. A world order involves an understanding of when and for what reasons war may be initiated and of who can initiate it (in the modern system only sovereign states). International society does not permit states to go to war for just any reason; it identifies either through law or intellectual argumentation the *casus belli* and legitimate reasons for war (Bull, 1977: 188). The presence of war does not mean that there is no order in the world, that all is a Hobbesian anarchy; rather, the strength of order in a global society is reflected in how it makes war. A true anarchy is not characterized by war, as Bull (1977: 185) notes, but by a "more ubiquitous violence." This, according to Bull, has been the historical alternative to war.

To understand how war differs from ubiquitous violence, we might return to Cicero's notion that war involves a contest. If, in the early seventeenth century, war had become, in part, a legal contest, then one wonders what kind of a contest it was before and what kind it has become since. Such a question makes it clearer that the word *contest* is a metaphor that implies that the "deep structure" of a contest (the elements that make a contest a contest) may also be the "deep structure" of war. In order to have a contest, in any period of time, according to the way we use the word, it is necessary for the parties to be aware of the formal and informal rules of the contest. There must be a prize, the parties must be aware that they are contending, that there are winners and losers, and that contenders have some sense of what it means to win and lose – although each may underestimate or not anticipate the most important consequences of their actions. A contest is an "institutional fact" whose meaning is only fully apprehended to the extent one understands how the practice of contests is created, sustained, and implemented. Because a contest is a human institution, it will vary with time and place, although the deep structure that is reflected in the word will provide a way of illuminating the similarities of different contests.

This analysis suggests that *legal* contests are only one kind of contest, which is another way of saying that how and why parties fight is determined by the tradition, customs, and thought of the time, which set up the rules of the contest so that the contending parties have a shared understanding of what they are doing.[7] This view comes close to an anthropological conception of war which sees war as an institution that is invented by humans and persists because it satisfies certain functions.

Margaret Mead (1940: 402) argues that war is an invention, like writing, cooking, marriage, or trial by jury. It forms part of the knowledge which is derived from the cultural inheritance of a group. For Mead (1940: 403) war is a *social invention* that gives people the idea that war is the way certain situations are to be handled. From this conception, it is clear that war is learned behavior. Since Mead defines war as fighting and killing between groups as groups, the learning is collective

---

[7] Wars that lack a shared understanding may form a special kind of war and might have a different dynamic, if not a different set of causes. This means that wars between groups that have never met before (e.g. Cortez and the Aztecs) and therefore do not have a shared conception of war are not really using violence in the same way that is typical of wars that occur among members of the same system. Wright (1965: 699) goes so far as to argue that such fights are not really wars because one side treats its opponent more "as an environmental obstacle" than an adversary in a contest. Nevertheless, his categories of "wars for the defense of civilization" and "imperial wars" are ways of including wars between those that may not have a shared understanding about how to conduct a fight (see Wright, 1965: 640). The absence of shared expectations may mitigate any moral or cultural restraints on the fighting, thus making these wars more prone to massacres.

learning. A society or tribe learns from its wisdom and folklore that when confronted with certain situations (with characteristics X, Y, Z), war is the appropriate response. As these inherited lessons are put into practice, the invention is elaborated and changed depending on the consequences. If such a conception is accurate, it would go a long way in identifying and predicting when war will occur, although not necessarily the causes of war.[8]

Mead's conception of war as a social invention provides a theoretical advance over the conception of war as a violent contest in that it suggests an explanation about the origin of war as a human phenomenon; whereas the conception of war as a contest does not tell us why violent contests appear in the first place. Mead's analysis implies that war first came about because some people learned to handle certain situations in this way. Why they learned to handle the situation in a violent manner rather than some other way is not known. Mead does point out, however, that not all societies are aware of the invention, so she concludes it is not inherent in human nature. More importantly, to eliminate war, she maintains, it will be necessary to develop a different way of handling the situations that a society handles by going to war. While such functionalist explanations are fraught with logical problems (see Brown, 1963: ch. 9), particularly the tendency to treat consequences as causes, the search for functional equivalents to war is theoretically useful in that it encourages analysts to think about what role war is playing within global society, what its manifest and latent purposes are, and how these purposes could be attained in non-violent ways.

Mead does not discuss why war became such a popular invention that it has persistently been utilized. Biologists, to the extent that they concern themselves with war, tend to explain its persistence in evolutionary terms. Biologists do not look at war, *per se*, but at animal aggression. Although only a few species exhibit behavior similar to war, a number are territorial and defend that territory by being aggressive. A biological definition of *territory* is "an area occupied more or less exclusively by an animal or group of animals by means of repulsion through overt defense or advertisement" (Wilson, 1975: 256). Animals that hold territory will fight a stranger of their own species that enters their territory. They will also fight over food, and males will fight over females, both of which can be associated with territory.

---

[8] In order to understand the causes of war it would be necessary to know why such situations arise in the first place.

Wilson (1975: 247–48) argues that territoriality evolved because a limited food supply made the territory worth defending, and the risks associated with that defense were limited. Employing conventional biological assumptions, he states that animal behavior is guided by what is advantageous over time and evolves when it has a selective advantage for certain individuals; this, in turn, increases the probability that the entire species will evolve toward that behavior. It may be that the human institution of war evolved out of this inherited tendency of vertebrates to be territorial.

For most biologists, it is inconceivable that any widespread animal characteristic, including human aggression, could not be advantageous for survival and reproduction (Wilson, 1975: 254). This has led some to argue that war persists because the clans and groups that employed war succeeded over those who did not and thereby passed on their more "aggressive tendencies." If this were correct, it may explain why people learned to handle certain situations by going to war. Such lessons might be passed on not only intellectually, but biologically, for as Wilson (1975: 255) states, "the capacity to learn certain behaviors is itself a genetically controlled and therefore evolved trait."[9] Because any evolutionary perspective is subject to teleological tendencies and overgeneralization, these arguments must be treated cautiously (see Shaw and Wong, 1987a, 1987b; Goldstein, 1987; Kitcher, 1987). Nevertheless, a biological perspective is important, because it reminds us that we have a genetic inheritance, and that may make us fight over certain things, like territory, but not others, as well as make us more predisposed to learn certain behaviors.

Clearly, humans more than any other animal have learned to use war, but for what purpose? The conception of war that places the goal and purpose of war at the center of its emphasis is that of Clausewitz. Clausewitz provided two famous definitions of war: "War is a mere continuation of policy by other means" and "War therefore is an act of violence intended to compel our opponent to fulfil our will" (Clausewitz, 1832, Book I, ch. 1, sections 2, 24, J. J. Graham translation). The first delineates the purpose of war and the second elucidates the logic of its means. For Clausewitz, war is a *political* act of *force*. The political aspect for him is the most important, and much of his treatise lectures about the need to keep the political aim of war in the forefront and not permit the dynamics and emotional

---

[9] Richard Alexander (1987) goes so far as to speculate that modern homo sapiens' main advantage may have been the capacity to learn to cooperate to form groups that could compete more successfully with neighboring groups. This, he ventures, may have allowed humans to surpass and perhaps push into extinction, close biological relatives.

aspects of force from obscuring that political aim. This focus on the instrumentality of war makes Clausewitz emphasize the rationality of war.

Clausewitz sees war as an instrument that is required by a certain activity, namely politics, and by certain situations. Clausewitz puts forth the idea that war occurs when normal politics and diplomacy fail. When the existing diplomatic practices (whether they be the simple exchange of ambassadors, or elaborate mechanisms of conflict resolution and international law) are unable to satisfactorily produce an agreement among disputants, then war becomes a means by which one side can compel its opponent to fulfil its will. War occurs when one side is not willing to lose or give up a political aim in light of the costs of fighting a war. This implies that wars are fought only over certain types of issues and that these issues may change depending on the particular historical needs, culture, or law of an era (see Luard, 1987: ch. 3; Howard, 1976).

It also suggests that, if a society has other ways of resolving disagreements in a binding or mutually satisfactory fashion, war will not be used. From this perspective, peace may be achieved by keeping certain issues off the agenda and/or providing binding alternative ways of making political decisions. Whether these are two crucial characteristics that distinguish peaceful systems from those that are war-prone is a question that has received insufficient attention. However, from the perspective of understanding the causes of war, two questions are raised by emphasizing the instrumentality of war: what is it about politics that causes certain issues to emerge and be defined in such a way that they are irresolvable, and what is it about violence that makes it such an attractive instrument?

Because politics has from earliest times involved the realm of rule and the ruled, power and authority, privilege and obligation, politics has entailed control – control of people and resources, activities and territory. Control raises at least three problems. First, who controls? Second, who benefits or is hurt by the particular set of controls? Third, how is control imposed, since control is naturally resisted and will be resisted even more by those who are hurt by it? To define the world in such terms is to create a set of issues that can in the right circumstances be viewed as life and death issues. By definition, for such issues a group is willing to fight and individuals willing to risk their lives either to assure that they do not lose, or that they will gain important privileges.

Clearly, war exists because there are fundamental conflicts of interest in the world, which cannot be harmonized away, as the utopians had hoped (Carr, 1939 [1964 ed.: 49, 51–53, 87–88]). There are some issues that call for so much change and so harm prevailing interests that they cannot be peacefully resolved. In Bismarck's words, "Not by speechifying and counting majorities are the great questions of the time to be solved ... but by iron and blood" (1862). It should come as no surprise that those issues often involve territory.

Given the fact that a certain aspect of politics consists of getting groups (not just isolated individuals; see Claude, 1962: ch. 7) to do things they do not want to do, then force, which Clausewitz would define as an act to compel our opponent to fulfil our will, is one means to achieve that end. Why? Because force is the *ultima ratio* among sovereigns (Schuman 1933 [1958: 274]) and war is the ultimate form of force. Clausewitz (1832: Book I, ch. I: sect. 4) maintains that when all else fails to convince opponents, you can change their position by making them suffer or killing their people ("place him in a situation which is more oppressive to him than the sacrifice which we demand ..."). Alternatively, in those cases where you do not need your opponents, you can gain your goal simply by removing them from the face of the earth, as Rome did to Carthage.

Historically, it can only be surmised that humans learned that force, and particularly violent force, would help establish political control and be a successful means to gain certain ends. Although the exact origins of war as a social invention are unknown, some argue that this particular use of war coincides with early agricultural civilizations, a time when human groups became more tied to particular pieces of land, and does not coincide with the more primitive hunting and gathering societies (Wright, 1965: 76; Mansfield, 1982). In addition, agricultural societies have a "higher" level of organization, and a certain level of organization is needed to marshal armies and get them to fight battles. Nevertheless, it is clear that some preneolithic societies did use violence to gain and/or defend access to water and food resources (Zur, 1987: 127). Although egalitarian societies generally have a low level of fighting, they can be expected to use violence to take over better land along a river, if faced with absolute scarcity, or some other form of circumscription that affects their material well-being (Ferguson, 1987: 9). Whatever its exact origin humans learned that collective armed violence was an important instrument in gaining one's end.

In more modern terms, violence becomes an attractive instrument because it provides a way of escaping interdependent decision making. The resolution of political issues usually requires getting others to agree with one, if not to actually take certain actions. This entails an interdependence in the sense that one cannot reach and implement a decision without others. When those who are involved in such inter-dependent decision making become stalemated, violence, provides an escape by ending one's dependence either though physical domination or elimination of the other. Force, unlike other ways of making deci-sions, is able to provide such an escape because it is a *unilateral* means (see Mansbach and Vasquez, 1981: 283–84) that depends on one's own capability and not the goodwill of others. If, in addition to these "intrin-sic" qualities, force and war have a history of success and are legitimated by custom and not overly restricted by law, then, given the right issues, it can be expected to be a widely utilized instrument for dealing with stale-mated situations. War becomes a useful invention because it provides a means of making unilateral, but binding, political decisions.

Clausewitz's emphasis on war as a form of force raises the question of whether the concept of *force* might not be a better scientific conceptual-ization of the phenomenon at hand. From this perspective, there is no need to make the causes of war a great mystery by looking for psychoana-lytical factors or the roots of human aggression. War can be explained by explaining why force rather than some other means is employed to gain a certain stake or resolve a dispute. Explain the conditions under which force is the only means, the preferred means, or the most efficient means and you have explained war – for war is but a special use of force. Other inducements, like frustration, can be seen as simply additional reasons for using force.

While a persuasive case can be made for studying force rather than war *per se*, the main objection to this view is that there may be a great deal more to the phenomenon of war than its utility as a political instru-ment. Violence may have deeper, even primordial, aspects that are diffi-cult to contain once unleashed. The use of violence may not stem from its instrumentality, but from these deeper aspects of which we are not fully conscious and which we poorly understand. Clausewitz's own need to lecture about keeping the goal of war in the forefront suggests that war is something that is inherently not easy to control, that violence toward and domination of an opponent can become ends in themselves, making war irrational.

Psychological conceptions of war emphasize the violence of war and see the need or drive of humans to kill as the main cause of war. The Clausewitzian view of war as a rational instrument has had difficulty sur-viving Freud's seminal critique of rationality. For Freud, the reasons and conscious motivations for war, whether they be derived from the cool cost-benefit calculations of military strategists or the casuistry of moral theologians, are mere rationalizations for deeper drives. Although his views of violence and of war were never fully developed, Freud (1930) saw war as an explosive reaction of the id against the increasing repression of modern civilization. The more repressive a civilization, the more severe the explosion. War is a collective and violent slip of the tongue that permits an indiscriminate satisfaction of the desires of the id. At the same time, and more ominously, Freud sees war as a product of the death instinct trying to destroy what has been created and built up by Eros (the life instinct).[10]

While it is difficult to test Freud's view scientifically, it provides a perspective for questioning political, sociological, and anthropological conceptions of war. Psychoanalysis, along with broader psychological approaches, affirms that war stems from an aspect of human nature and involves, fundamentally, not a cultural invention of a political instrument, but a *mental* state. "The state of mind" that is most associated with war is extreme hostility. This hostility often appears bizarre when it is exhibited by individuals who have not had any direct contact with people whom they consider their enemy. Nevertheless, this kind of hostility is considered part of the behavior that is typical (appropriate) to those in a condition of war. This view of war is so widespread that a number of definitions of war, including Wright's, make hostility a defining characteristic of war, and one of the dictionary definitions of war is "to be in a state of hostility." This emphasis on the mental state of war can be so great that societies are sometimes said to be "at war" even if there is no fighting (Wright, 1965: 11–12) as in "the Cold War."

To see wars where there is no killing is something most analysts, even psychologists, are not prepared to do, because for them it is the violence and not the hostility of war that they are seeking to explain. Nevertheless, conceptions of war that emphasize hostility are saying that such emotional extremes can provide reasons in and of themselves for violent actions and make it difficult to use violence in the limited coercive manner that Clausewitz advocates. This raises the question of whether some wars are fought not for political aims, but in order to satisfy aggressive feelings stemming from hostility, frustration, crowding or some other psychological condition. Whether such psychological factors are the effects or causes of conflicts of interests that help produce wars, and whether they are spontaneous or artificially inspired by leaders, it is often the case that

[10] See Freud's (1933) letter to Einstein ("Why War?") for a more optimistic view.

extreme hostility (frustration, etc.) appears to play an important part in decisions about war.

Not all conceptions of war as a mental state place emphasis on hostility. Hobbes, who lived before the era of modern psychology, declares:

> For Warre, consisteth not in Battell onely, or the act of fighting; but in a tract of time, wherein the Will to contend by Battell is sufficiently known ... War consisteth not in actual fighting, but in the known disposition thereto, during all the time there is no assurance to the contrary. All other time is PEACE.
>
> (Hobbes, 1651: pt. 1, ch. 13)

For Hobbes, individuals are at war if they are predisposed to fight and there is no assurance that they will not fight. Hobbes (1651: 205) views war as a mental state that generates what today would be called extreme insecurity, but interestingly he has little to say about hostility. He does not see hostility as a cause of war nor central to it; rather, war is a condition with "continual feare and danger of violent death." This image gets very close to capturing the immediate experience of battle, and Hobbes may have generalized from it to develop a conception of war. This apparently is where at least the English term, war, gets its meaning, since its etymology can be traced to *werra*, which means confusion, strife.

Although those who look at war in terms of mental states emphasize different experiences (hostility, insecurity, frustration), these conceptualizations generally share an assumption that violence and fighting are the most important aspect of war. It is not surprising that all of these approaches try to explain war by explaining violence, in some cases interpersonal violence, thereby making the concept of *violence* an alternative to the concept of war. Whether such an attempt is ultimately successful will depend, as stated earlier, on the extent to which violence between groups is not fundamentally different from violence between individuals.

Regardless of one's position on this question, the notion of violence as a key aspect of war is a conception that needs to be more fully explored in the literature. An emphasis on the fighting and killing in war makes it clear that war is an activity, not an object with its own ontological existence. The tendency of English (a tendency which is even worse in German) to describe activities by nouns rather than verbs fundamentally distorts the world we are trying to understand. Instead of seeing war as something mechanically caused by certain factors, it might be more illuminating to see war as an action to which states resort when faced with certain situations. In this sense, the older concept of "warfare," which Margaret

Mead employs, has a more authentic ring to it, as does Hobbes's notion of warre. The human tendency "to warre" is what we are trying to explain, and how one goes about explaining it will depend very much on whether it is conceived as a noun, whose existence must be accounted for, or a verb, whose action comes forth.

With such diverse conceptions of war, each with its own crucial assumptions, it is not wise to choose among them. Nonetheless, no serious inquiry on war and peace can proceed without addressing and making judgments on at least some of the issues that have been raised by these conceptions. From the above analysis, some basic insights about the nature of war can be gleaned to help identify what may be the most important characteristics of war, theoretically speaking. From Hedley Bull's definition, which is being used as the working definition of this analysis, from Margaret Mead's notion of warfare, and from several other definitions, it can be stipulated that war is a *group* activity, fought between and directed at collectivities. In this manner, it is fundamentally different from individual interpersonal violence in at least two ways. First, the behavior of collectivities poses conceptual problems not present in the analysis of individuals. There is reason to expect that collectivities behave differently from individuals and cannot be regarded simply as individuals writ large. This is especially true of the state and of bureaucracy, which must be treated as special collectivities. Second, war seems to require a certain level of social organization and tends not to be fought in its absence. Thus, the practice of war emerges in history as societies become more organized.

From the analysis of Cicero's definition, it can be stipulated that war involves *contention* over objects of value. As Grotius, Wright, and Hedley Bull make clear, this contention is organized in that it follows certain rules and norms that give the contention an underlying *order* from which each side derives certain expectations about its own and its competitor's behavior. The degree to which the contention (and warfare) is ordered may vary, depending on whether it is based on tacit understanding, custom, or international law. This means that war is a special kind of *contest* with winners, losers, rules, and prizes.

The metaphor of a contest implies that war is an informal institution. Margaret Mead compares warfare to other human institutions like writing, marriage, trial by jury. From her work, it can be stipulated that war is a *social invention* that is *learned* in history and shapes history.

The work of Clausewitz suggests that the purpose of this invention is to conduct politics through the use of force when other means of conducting it fail. From this it can be stipulated that war is a *political instrument of force*. It is political in that it is more frequently (except for certain "primitive" wars) associated with political activity than any other human activity. It is an instrument in that those who wage war attempt, at some point, to use it as a calculated "rational" means to an end. It is force in that it is a means that attempts to compel opponents to do something they will not do freely.

While war is political, it is also clear from the work in anthropology and biology that war has a peculiar and unknown relation to territoriality. Wars are often fought to defend or expand territory, or to enhance the wealth and status of a territorial people. Even when such objectives are not readily found, wars are territorially based contests in that they are fought over and on territory with the victor controlling the people and land of the defeated. From this it can be stipulated that wars are *territorial* in spirit, regardless of their stated aims.

Above all, war consists of fighting and killing. It is one of the most salient features of war that killing, which is generally frowned upon, if not prohibited, within a group, is encouraged and honored in war. War involves violence, and acts of violence are usually associated with certain mental states, such as extreme *hostility* or frustration. In addition, the presence or anticipation of widespread violence produces *insecurity*. These emotions, perhaps acting in conjunction with deeper unconscious motives, make war a difficult thing to control and therefore reduce its rationality. This often leads "society" (in terms of its political leaders, military officers, intellectuals, and priests) to try to carefully control war in terms of when, how, and why it is fought. From this it can be stipulated that war is an institutionalization of *violence* and is associated with clearly identifiable mental states before, during, and after wars.

War may be seen as an institutionalization of violence in the sense that the act of violence, which is a natural individual tendency, is an act which can no longer be taken by an individual without the permission of the larger group. The larger group generally prohibits the act within the group, as best it can. At the same time, it attempts to marshal the psychic and physical energy needed to carry out such acts in a concentrated form and for its own purposes and control. Thus, war requires a certain level of social organization able to bend families, clans, and individuals to a more general will. Since war makes strangers (who do not by definition feel hostile or frustrated toward each other) kill each other, the institutionalization of violence requires the artificial insemination of the collective with the mental states associated with individual acts of violence. Religion and ideology (including foreign policy ideologies, like realism) become a way for the state to institutionalize violence and bend the will of individuals and clans to its own. The psychological effects of attempting to control and channel violent tendencies, to simultaneously legitimate and prohibit violent acts, are not known, but may play a role in the unexpected "post-war moods" that follow major conflagrations and the "war hysterias" that precede them. The notion of institutionalization suggests that war is more adequately conceived as process and action that comes forth (as a *verb*), rather than a thing or object (as a noun).

Theoretical Assumptions About War

From this inchoate conceptualization of war, I make six theoretical assumptions: (1) war is learned; (2) war comes out of a long-term process; (3) war is a product of interaction and not simply systemic conditions; (4) war is a way of making decisions; (5) war is multicausal; and (6) there are different types of war. These assumptions should not be taken as untested axioms from which I will logically or mathematically deduce propositions (cf. Waltz, 1979; Zinnes, 1976). What I have done instead is to derive insights from the above conceptual work and induce some empirical generalizations and propositions from existing research to develop a set of assumptions through which to view war. These assumptions guide my inquiry and thinking about war and allow me to view war from different angles, with each angle focusing on a different aspect of war. I then use these perspectives and assumptions to interpret and help explain existing evidence, thereby constructing an explanation of war and peace. This in turn will suggest new research and avenues of inquiry, which, when completed, will undoubtedly lead to a modification of some of the assumptions. I take this inductive approach to theory construction because I believe it is the most viable way of integrating the various pieces of evidence that have emerged in the last twenty-five years (cf. Guetzkow, 1950).

War is learned

War can be conceived as learned behavior in two senses. Groups learn to make war as a general practice that is available to them, and subsequently they learn in their dealings with others that war is an appropriate response to a particular situation. Taking Mead's perspective, the first thing we want to know is how and under what circumstances war was invented. What are the origins of war and how did clans, tribes, and societies learn to fight? What is it in a people's experience that makes them accept war as an institution and adopt beliefs that provide a rationalization for and legitimation of the use of force and violence? Anthropology and studies of animal behavior provide some suggestions for answers to these questions.

In general, it is fair to assume that people have probably learned to fight by fighting. From major wars they have developed a set of lessons that helps them identify situations that are best dealt with by going to war. On the bases of previous experience, lessons are derived that recommend certain practices as a successful (good, or proper) way for dealing with war-threatening situations. These lessons become embodied in the folklore and rituals of a society and become part of its customs. In this way, war is invented and reinvented; it becomes learned as part of a culture of behavior.

Once this invention has become part of a culture, it is still necessary to explain how and why a group comes to the conclusion that a war is the best way to handle the situation facing it. Again, learning can be seen as playing a crucial role. Here a collectivity learns not how to invent a practice, but instead learns that, of the variety of existing and possible practices upon which it can draw, war is the most appropriate. If war is conceived as one of several foreign policy practices, then explaining war can, in part, be reduced to explaining why in general one foreign policy practice is chosen over another, and what in particular makes force and violence selected options.

It is assumed that any given political system, including a global political system, will have at least informal rules that influence, if not govern, what practices are appropriate to which problems. Historically, war, because of its costs and because of normative prohibitions, has never been the means of first choice, but has been resorted to only after other acceptable practices have failed. This suggests that war grows out of a sequence of interactions. Collectivities learn to go to war from the failure of "normal politics and diplomacy" to produce acceptable results.

It would be a mistake, as will be shown below, to think of this process as always culminating in a single calculated decision to go to war. Rather, what is more common is that different interactions evoke certain responses, and these responses become steps that lead one or both sides to an increasingly probable "decision" to go to war.

War results from a long-term process

While some wars, particularly between the very unequal, may emerge suddenly and from a single decision, more typically it appears that wars grow out of a long-term political relationship that has become increasingly intractable, conflictive, and hostile. These three effects lead one side, and often both, to behave in certain ways and it is these behaviors (rather than a deliberative policy *per se*) that evoke a set of interrelated actions that result in war (cf. Singer, 1984: 6). From this it follows that the outbreak of war is usually not a sudden process, but evolves out of a series of steps.

This means that a Newtonian model of mechanics (in which one or more causes appear and then there is an effect) is not an appropriate model for explaining war. I assume that we will be misled if we confine our search solely to the "causes" of war and the "conditions" of peace. We must instead try to uncover the process by which war comes about; the process by which two or more states learn that the situation they are facing is best handled by going to war. Theodore Abel (1941: 853) affirmed something like this some time ago when he maintained that war should be studied the way crime is, not by searching for the causes of crime, but by studying the process by which individuals become criminals. This is not to say (as apparently Abel would have said) that there are no correlates of crime, but only that such correlates may not be as revealing as the actual process by which individuals become criminals. To understand war, we may want to see if there is a "*pattern* according to which a war situation develops" and evolves (Abel, 1941: 853, italics in original). I assume that for many wars, especially wars between relative equals, a war situation grows out of a relationship between two political collectivities. This relationship has a history, present, and future that affects the nature of their interaction and the likelihood of war.

War is a product of interactions, not simply a result of systemic conditions

For this reason, I assume that a study of interactions (dyadic, triadic, and so forth) is going to be a more fruitful avenue of inquiry than the systemic analyses that have guided most inquiry in the past twenty-five years. What few dyadic-level studies we have support this claim (see Rummel, 1972b; Vasquez and Mansbach, 1984: 415; Bueno de Mesquita and Lalman, 1988). I want to argue in favor of a position that sees war as the outcome of the foreign policy practices of states. Some of these practices set up a dynamic of interstate interactions that produces an external and domestic political situation in which decision makers and their policy influencers are so constrained that it becomes increasingly difficult for them *not* to decide in favor of war.

The external situation has to do with the political relationship that is generated by a particular sequence of interactions. The taking of some actions decreases the probability of certain kinds of actions while increasing the probability of others. War becomes likely when the sequence of diplomatic actions fails to resolve highly salient issues, resulting in an increase in the level of conflictive actions, which in turn increases psychological hostility. This produces the kind of relationship between two (or more) countries that is prone to a conflict spiral in which the intractability leads to the taking of more conflictive actions, which produces more hostility, which makes for an atmosphere that nourishes even greater intractability and conflict. In order to explain war, it is necessary to uncover the causal dynamics that make such a relationship emerge and to understand how such a relationship acts as a set of constraints that encourage the taking of foreign policy acts that are likely to result in war.

The domestic internal situation, i.e. the domestic political context in which leaders and policy influencers operate, is shaped not only by internal political battles and competition for power, but by the effects of external interaction, which make certain policies and actions more likely than others. The impact of interstate interactions on the domestic political context has been a greatly neglected area of research. In order to explain war, it is necessary to discover whether, and then delineate how, the actions of one's opponents create in one's own society a domestic environment that encourages the adoption of bellicose policies.

War may be seen as resulting, in part, from a series of interactions which produce a dual structure (a domestic political context and an ongoing political relationship which act as a set of constraints) that encourages leaders to take steps that lead to war. It is this short-term dual structure, which foreign policy interaction produces, that has been left out of so many behavioral analyses of war. The reason for this is that these sets of constraints must operate within the broader and more long-term system structure.

Of the various systemic constraints that have been seen as playing a role in the onset of war, I see the *global institutional context*, which can be defined as those sets of formal and informal institutions that allow the members of the system to make binding political decisions, as the most important. Other system characteristics are probably less important for explaining the onset of war than they are for explaining other characteristics of war. For example, the economic structure of the system (see Wallensteen, 1981: 80–83), I see as important primarily for affecting the goals of a war (slaves, markets), and hence coloring the issues over which war might be fought. The power structure or distribution of capability, I see as important primarily for determining who will fight, when they will fight, and the type of war that will be fought.

I believe the global institutional context to be the most significant systemic characteristic not only because I believe that this is consistent with existing evidence, but because I assume that war is fundamentally a political institution that serves crucial political functions. If those functions can be satisfied by other institutions, then there is a good chance that the frequency of war can be reduced, if not eliminated altogether, without changing the economic or power structure of the system. This means that war is neither the product of any given economic system, although economic concerns and greed can motivate wars, nor the result of a particular distribution of power, although relative capabilities might determine how certain types of wars come about. Such claims are not easily tested, but it is important to make such assumptions explicit because whether one places emphasis on the political, economic, or power structure of a system will push research in very different directions. While these issues will be dealt with in a later chapter, here I will only give my reasons for emphasizing the political.

War is a way of making political decisions

What is most impressive about Clausewitz's analysis is the idea that war is a political phenomenon. Although war may grow out of psychological frustration and hostility, at the level of collectivities, these mental states themselves are the product of political stalemate – of the inability to resolve outstanding political questions. Thus, to understand war, one must first have some understanding of politics. To the extent that one focuses on or emphasizes the wrong things in one's conception of politics, then it can be expected that one will misunderstand war – why it has dominated the past and whether it will continue in the future.

I accept David Easton's (1965: 50) definition of politics as the "authoritative allocation of valued things." This conception is different from the dominant realist conceptions of world politics that define politics as "a struggle for power" (Morgenthau, 1960: 27) in that it sees politics as a process that is guided by an end and not as a process whereby the means (power) has become the only end. For Easton, or anyone who wants to seriously analyze politics within a stable relatively non-violent political system, the struggle for power is only half of the story. The other and in many ways the more important half of the story is what is done with that power once it is attained. For Easton, politics involves policy outcomes. Power is used to put certain issues on the agenda rather than others, and then to resolve those issues in one way rather than another. The outcome of this process is to take valued things and give (allocate) them to people or groups in a way that all those involved regard, at least in the short run, as legitimate and binding (authoritative).

In an earlier analysis (Mansbach and Vasquez, 1981: 57–59, 68–69, 188–89) I adopted the Eastonian definition of politics to elaborate an alternative to the dominant realist paradigm of international politics. Instead of the almost exclusive focus on the struggle for power, world politics is seen in a broader perspective as the raising and resolving of issues. From this focus, actors become involved in politics in order to keep or obtain objects of value, which can be defined as *stakes*. Stakes are usually linked to form an issue, and it is contention over issues that constitutes the substance and purpose of politics. By definition, political actors contend over issues by developing proposals for the disposition of specific stakes. Actors can then be said to agree or disagree with these proposals by taking an explicit or implicit *issue position* on each proposal.

An *issue* consists, by definition, of a set of differing proposals for the disposition of stakes among specific actors. Actors try to resolve an issue by changing each other's issue position, which is done through an interactive process of sending positive and/or negative acts. This process, however, instead of directly affecting the issue positions of an actor, determines actors' attitudes toward one another, i.e. their affect or level of friendship and hostility. From this perspective, the shape of political contention is seen as a function of three general factors: the characteristics of issues under contention, the dynamics of interaction, and the nature of the institutional context in which allocation decisions must be made.

In stable political systems, like the United States, the institution that authoritatively allocates valued things is government (Huntington, 1968). Since the current global political system lacks a government, we might ask what institutions authoritatively allocate valued things. When we do this, we find that there are numerous institutions, including some very formal ones, like the International Civil Aviation Organization (ICAO), that allocate very important things, like air traffic rules, or some informal ones, like the G-7 that plays a major role in decisions affecting the global political economy. We also find that, for certain pairs of states and in certain historical periods, war is a way of allocating some things that appear to have extremely high value, like territory, trading rights, and the form of domestic governments. This allocation can be seen as authoritative because only in rare instances does the loser of a war not regard it as the "right" of the winner to take what it had demanded during the war, even though it may regard this as unjust and reserves its own right to take it back after it recovers. War in world politics has had a certain legitimacy by custom, and this has been, at times, formally institutionalized by international law. It is the way by which independent groups resolve highly salient issues that do not appear to be resolvable by any other means.

In this sense, war serves as a kind of *allocation mechanism*, and a better sense of the political nature of war can be attained by examining other allocation mechanisms. An allocation mechanism may be defined as a set of formal and informal rules for making and implementing political decisions (see Mansbach and Vasquez, 1981: 283). An allocation mechanism is a set of procedures, norms, and/or devices for answering such questions as: how shall we decide these issues? on the basis of what procedure or norm? Two or more actors could decide to resolve a question on the basis of flipping a coin, accepting the majority vote of a previously constituted body, binding arbitration, an auction, or arm wrestling. Each of these examples embodies specific allocation mechanisms.

There are numerous allocation mechanisms that could, in theory, be employed. This means that allocation or decision making always involves two choices: first, selection of one out of the range of allocation mechanisms as the final authoritative means of reaching a decision and, second, the actual disposition of stakes under contention. What distinguishes highly institutionalized and hierarchical political systems that have stable governments from looser ones, like the current global political system, is that in the former actors have little choice over which allocation mechanism will be selected to resolve a given issue, whereas in the latter, which allocation mechanism will be the final authoritative mechanism can itself become a matter of contention, even though there may be some rules governing which allocation mechanisms must be tried first. In loosely organized political systems, allocation mechanisms that permit the unilateral resolution of an issue tend to evolve as the ultimate mechanism, because through practice they are the only ones able to make a final, authoritative (non-challengeable in the short term) and hence binding decision. These mechanisms become customary, legitimate, and even legal in due time. In the economic realm, such unilateral mechanisms have involved the exercise of wealth. In the political realm, such unilateral mechanisms have involved the exercise of force.

Despite the wide variety of specific means that can be used to make a decision, allocation mechanisms can be reduced to one of four basic types – force, bargains, votes, and games of principle – each of which is distinguished by the criterion that is used to make a decision (Mansbach and Vasquez, 1981: 283; see also Young, 1978). *Force* resolves issues on the basis of the strength of contending actors. *Bargains* aim to dispose of stakes through some sort of exchange or trade among the contending actors. *Votes* employ a consent mechanism (that specifies who may participate, whether votes will be weighted, and how the votes will be counted) to dispose of stakes. *Games of principle* resolves issues on the basis of some norm. Such norms can involve basic principles, like equality or equity (distributive justice), or more complicated normative systems, like utilitarianism, the Bible, Marxism–Leninism, or liberal capitalism (see Mansbach and Vasquez, 1981: 283–85).

This suggests that war as an institution is a form of force that has evolved within the global political system as a unilateral allocation mechanism that can make authoritative decisions. War is not simply an act of violence, but an allocation mechanism which is resorted to in the face of stalemate and the failure of normal politics to resolve fundamental issues. Since political systems that do not have functioning governments are more prone to failure, war is often seen as *a way of making authoritative decisions in the absence of government.* A more comprehensive view is to see war as emerging from a breakdown of normal politics, whether that normal politics be government, traditional diplomacy, or a negotiated regime.[11]

War as a multicausal phenomenon

Since normal politics can break down for a variety of reasons, this makes it clear that there are a number of different paths that can lead to war. In a more fundamental sense, war may be caused by other factors than just the breakdown of normal politics. Our review of the different conceptions of war revealed that there are many aspects of war, and its use as a political instrument is only one. The different aspects of war indicate that war can

---

[11] In this sense, normal politics itself must be seen as a social invention that may have emerged as a substitute for collective violence at a given historical moment.

be fought for different reasons and stem from different motivations, and therefore is probably multicausal.

For these reasons, I assume that there are a variety of factors and causes that can bring about war. This means that the hope that there are a few necessary conditions that must always be present in order for war to occur is probably not going to be fulfilled. Instead, the variety of factors associated with war and the changing nature of war through history suggests that war can be brought about by any number of sufficient conditions.

This raises a general question about causality and how we should think about the causes of war. War can be brought about by several distinct causal paths or causal sequences (see Levy, 1989: 227, 279, 281). Relations between states that follow one of these paths and are unable to take any of the exits will end in war. I assume that at this stage in the systematic study of war and peace, one of the most useful intellectual enterprises that can advance our knowledge is the delineation and documentation of such paths to war. In this book, I hope to uncover one causal sequence to war – that associated with following the foreign policy practices of power politics. I believe the sequence I have delineated is the main process by which *major* states become involved in wars with *each other* in the modern global system. In this sense, this book looks at one causal sequence to a certain type of war that is produced in a particular historical era by following the practices of power politics. While that is a theoretically very limited set, let me hasten to add that within that set are the most important wars of the last 500 years.

At this point, our knowledge is not precise enough to distinguish clearly between correlates and causes, so I will be involved primarily in trying to document through an examination of quantitative research findings the overall pattern by which such war situations develop and intensify. Although I believe the delineated pattern will include the causal sequence, it inevitably will include a number of other correlates that future research may show to be of little causal significance or even epiphenomenal. Nevertheless, I cannot be more precise than the current research permits. I have sought to err in the direction of complexity and inclusion rather than exclusion, since I hope this analysis will spur research that will identify which factors in the path to war are the most potent.

The assumption of multicausality, or equifinality as it is technically called, means that, even if I am partially successful, one will still be able to point to wars that occur even in the absence of the identified causal sequence. All this means is that the causal sequence specified here did not produce that particular war. It does not mean that the analysis is inaccurate, because all a sufficient condition requires is that when it is present there is a high probability that war will follow; it does not require that this condition be present prior to every known war. This means that trying to delineate the causes of war by only studying wars in the hopes of finding a common pattern will not be successful. As will be seen later, alliances and arms races do not precede most wars, but this does not mean that they may not play a significant role in a particular causal sequence. The latter conclusion can only be made by identifying the role alliances and arms races play in a causal sequence and then seeing if every time that causal sequence unfolds the probability of war greatly increases. In terms of policy relevance, this means that even if some causal sequences of war are identified and eliminated, war may still be caused by other factors. This makes the task of bringing about permanent peace arduous and complicated, something which should come as no surprise.

If there appear to be many causes of a given phenomenon, then it may be the case that the phenomenon under question is not a single entity but a variety of phenomena that must be distinguished before any real progress will be made. This has certainly been the case in cancer research. Only as different diseases and conditions, like leukemia, lung cancer, breast cancer, etc. were distinguished, was any progress made in identifying their causes and developing cures. This has led me to make a sixth assumption – that there are different types of war, each with different causes. I shall be confining my analysis, including the foregoing assumptions, to only certain types of war. However, since the identification of different types of war involves the construction of a theoretical typology, this last assumption requires a chapter of its own.

2

Types of War

The first step in scientific discovery is classification, but how to classify correctly?

If war is a single phenomenon that has an identifiable set of causes, then there should not be any need for a typology of war. Wars, regardless of time or place, should be associated with the same set of variables, give or take a few qualifications to account for idiosyncratic factors. On the other hand, if war is an amorphous concept that includes seemingly related but in fact very different phenomena, then there will be no clear pattern of correlates associated with war. How can one tell whether war is better conceived as a single phenomenon or several? And, if one thinks war involves several phenomena, how can one disentangle the phenomena so that the factors associated with each are elucidated?

Questions of this sort are standard in the philosophy of science, but to answer them productively requires that we become good scientific detectives – developing hypotheses in light of incomplete evidence, and then using those hypotheses to uncover new clues that will either confirm or falsify our hunches. We should think of war as several phenomena, if extensive research that conceptualizes war as a single phenomenon seems to lead nowhere. The failure of research is often a sign that conceptualization is fundamentally flawed – illuminating the unimportant and obfuscating the significant. An even more significant piece of evidence that a concept may be combining several phenomena is provided when different pieces of research inadvertently produce contradictory results – finding that sometimes war is associated positively with one set of variables and at another time negatively. Such anomalies are important "breaks," since they provide clues about how to disentangle the phenomena so as to capture the theoretical elements that will distinguish the different types.

Although even a cursory review of the historical record suggests that wars like the Second Schleswig-Holstein War, the Crimean War, and World War I are quite different, most political scientists have held on to the belief that the underlying causes of war have not changed since the Peloponnesian War. This is a widely shared view, maintained not only by quantitatively oriented scholars, like Singer, but also by traditionalists, like Morgenthau (1960), Waltz (1979), and Gilpin (1981). Yet empirical research has produced findings, including the uncovering of one crucial anomaly, that undercut important aspects of this belief and support the more common sense notion that wars differ.

I will begin this chapter by reviewing the evidence that led me to conclude that there are different kinds of wars and that a theoretical typology of wars is necessary. Then, after a brief look at the few efforts to differentiate war, I will present a formal typology and discuss why I believe that the three theoretical dimensions I have selected for constructing the typology are the most significant aspects distinguishing wars. I will conclude the chapter by indicating which kinds of wars will be the focus of this inquiry.

Is There a Need for a Typology of War?

The most direct way to see if it makes sense to differentiate wars is to empirically examine whether different wars have different causes and effects (see the symposium in Midlarsky, 1990). There is not much evidence of this sort, because few have attempted to classify wars on the basis of some theoretical characteristic. The major exception has been Rasler and Thompson (1985a, 1985b), who separate out "global wars" from all other interstate wars. They argue, on the basis of Modelski's (1978) analysis, that not all wars are the same, that a global war – a war fought among major states for the leadership of the system – is different, because of the purpose of the war and its tremendous impact on the global political system. A global war is also likely to be quite severe in terms of casualties. For these reasons, they and Modelski (1978) argue that global war is a unique type and should be differentiated from other interstate wars (see also Thompson, 1985; 1990).

Rasler and Thompson's (1983, 1985a, 1985b, 1989) research to date provides some support for their position. They find that global wars produce a long-term increase in governmental expenditures and in the tax burden, whereas other interstate wars involving major states have less of an impact (Rasler and Thompson 1985b; 1989: ch. 5). In addition, they find that while both global and interstate wars permanently increase the level of public debt in Great Britain and the United States, interstate wars do so to a much lesser extent (Rasler and Thompson, 1983: 506–12; 1989: 104–14).

Finally, they demonstrate that global wars have an abrupt but short impact on the GNP of major states, but that other interstate wars do not have any effect on the economic growth of major states (Rasler and Thompson, 1985a; 1989: ch. 6).

This evidence lends support to their notion that global war – as a type of war – has played a major role in the growth and development of the state (Rasler and Thompson, 1985b: 491, 505; 1989: ch. 8; see also Hintze, 1902, 1906). However, since interstate wars sometimes can have the same impact (albeit of lesser magnitude) as global wars (Rasler and Thompson, 1985b: 500, 503), this suggests that differences between global wars and other interstate wars might be one of degree rather than kind. This view is further supported by the fact that the US Civil War had the same kind of impact on expenditures and taxation as global wars (Rasler and Thompson, 1985b: 505 n. 16; 1989: 226 n. 17). Also, it must be pointed out that specific global and interstate wars in specific states do not always produce consistent results (Rasler and Thompson, 1985a: 530, 533; 1989: 172, 174, 192, 198, 202; Rasler, 1986: 930–31,934). This suggests that a more theoretical classification of wars might be able to produce more consistent findings across global, interstate, and civil wars. For example, Rasler and Thompson's findings imply that classifying wars on the basis of the effort put into fighting the war and its subsequent severity may account for any war's domestic and global impact.

While Rasler and Thompson produce a body of evidence that suggests the need for a typology of wars, they provide only limited assistance in telling us on what basis to construct that typology. Neither Modelski nor Rasler and Thompson develop a full typology of wars that would tell us not only on what basis global wars are different, but also how the vast majority of wars can be categorized. In this regard, it is significant that Rasler and Thompson have provided some evidence to show that global wars have a different and greater impact than other wars, but that they have not shown that these wars have fundamentally different causes from other wars that involve major states.

Greater assistance and a more compelling reason for constructing a typology is provided by Singer, Bremer, and Stuckey's (1972) seminal study of the balance of power versus preponderance of power debate. In one of the first systematic comparative analyses of that debate, they uncover a major anomaly that can be used to support the notion that there are different types of wars. A detailed examination of this study provides important clues as to how wars might be classified.

Singer, Bremer, and Stuckey (1972) find that (among major states) in the nineteenth century, less war occurs when capability in the system is dispersed, which is consistent with a parity or balance of power notion of peace; but that, in the twentieth century, less war occurs when capability in the system is concentrated, which is consistent with a preponderance of power notion. This finding is a major anomaly not only because it is unexpected, but also because the logic of realist theory cannot account for it. There is no clear reason why a balance of power should produce peace in the nineteenth century, but war in the twentieth! A scientific explanation that captures the causes of war should be fairly generalizable and not shift so radically from one century to the next, particularly since the historical causes of World War I are often seen as originating in the late nineteenth century and not at the turn of the century.

Singer *et al.*(1972: 46–47) try to account for the irenic effect of relative equality in one century and the violent effect in the next by arguing that a fundamental change in the conduct of diplomacy occurred around the turn of the century. According to them, this change was brought about by the decline of aristocratic rules of the game and the democratization of diplomacy. The latter made domestic politics intrude more in the twentieth century and therefore made world politics more uncertain. According to Singer *et al.,* for both the preponderance and the balance models, uncertainty[1] is a factor in the onset of war. The difference between the nineteenth and twentieth centuries is that, in the nineteenth, a balance of power provides sufficient certainty for an international elite to know that war will not be profitable, but in the twentieth, only a preponderance of power will convince domestic policy influencers that a war cannot be won.

There are several problems with this *ad hoc* explanation. There is little empirical evidence that the intrusion of domestic politics in democracies makes them less effective in their conduct of foreign policy (see Waltz, 1967) or that they participate in war more (or less) frequently than other kinds of states (Small and Singer, 1976; Chan, 1984; Maoz

---

[1] By uncertainty, Singer *et al.* (1972: 23) mean the difficulty elites have in discerning stratifications and blocs within the system and predicting their behavior in light of that knowledge. Elsewhere, they speak of structural clarity and low ambiguity (Singer and Bouxsein, 1975). For them, parity or a balance of power always makes for more uncertainty than a concentration or preponderance of power. Compare their definition to that of Bueno de Mesquita (1981b: 33) who defines uncertainty as "the degree to which the probability of success of a course of action is unknown," and relates it to predicting the behavior of allies and third parties in a war situation.

and Abdolali, 1989). Even if they did, there is no reason to expect and little evidence to suggest that such an impact should be felt at the turn of the century. Certainly, there was little change in French or British democracy at the turn of the century, and the intrusion of domestic concerns in German foreign policy was not that different under Bismarck in comparison with Bethmann-Hollweg and Wilhelm II. Indeed, Mayer (1981) argues that the *ancien régime* persisted into the twentieth century, a hypothesis which, if correct, would undercut the very foundation of the *ad hoc* explanation.

More damaging is that additional empirical work has failed to sustain Singer *et al.*'s (1972) findings. Bruce Bueno de Mesquita (1981a) was able to eliminate the intercentury difference. He does this by changing the dependent variable from nation-months of war, which is what Singer *et al.* employ, to the dichotomous war/no war. He argues (following Duvall, 1976) that the latter is a better measure of the onset of war and the presence of peace. Indeed, this is the case because the dichotomous variable simply describes whether, in any given period, there is war or no war; whereas nation-months measures the *amount* of war and thereby could erroneously lead to the inference that few nation-months of war was equivalent to peace. Singer *et al.*'s (1972) data analysis really tells us more about what produces wars of different sizes than it does about what is associated with the onset of war.

When Bueno de Mesquita (1981a: 564) examines the more relevant war/no war dependent variable, he finds that there is no statistically significant relationship between differences of capability (either between nations or coalitions) and the onset of war.[2] Bueno de Mesquita also elaborates the research design by examining coalitions, as well as individual major states, and finds that aggregating individual capability scores into coalitions, as one should do to properly capture balance of power thinking, does not improve the results.

Thompson (1983a: 153–54) is also able to eliminate the intercentury difference, but in his case by making changes in the measures of the independent (capability) variable. Thompson (1983a: 153–54) reduces all correlations, particularly the impressive 0.81 (for the nineteenth century), which is reduced to –0.38. When looking at only global wars, the correlation is reduced to – 0.30. Both the Thompson and Bueno de Mesquita studies suggest that there is no difference between the nineteenth and

---

[2] The inter-century difference is also eliminated in Bueno de Mesquita's (1981b: 135, 144–45) tests of an expected utility explanation of war initiation.

twentieth centuries *with regard to* the role of capability concentration and the onset of war.

These findings should come as no surprise, since the logical contradictions between the balance of power and preponderance models make it likely that neither would prove to be correct. Balance of power thinking, like all realist approaches, sees world politics as a constant struggle for power. If one state succeeds in gaining a significant degree of power over another, then it will be in a position to successfully attack that other state in order to get what it wants. The only way the state being threatened can prevent the attack is by giving in, or by securing allies that would restore a balance of power. Although balance of power logic is clearest at the dyadic or interaction level, it has been applied to the systemic level, which is the level at which Singer *et al.* (1972) test it. At this level, it is assumed that a *system* of states where power is relatively dispersed and alliances are flexible so that a balance can be maintained would be more peaceful and should protect the independence of states.

It seems that a balance of power will prevent the temptation of gaining an easy victory through coercive threats or wars of conquest. However, there is no rational reason why a mere balance of power or relative equality should *prevent* one side from attacking another. While a balance may mean no easy victory, it also means that both sides have at least a 50–50 chance of winning. Thus, as has been pointed out many times, real security lies not in a balance of power, but in a preponderance of power (Organski, 1958: 325). Only if the other side *knows* it will lose, will it be discouraged from attacking; but what then prevents the preponderant side from attacking? Sometimes the weak can save themselves by making diplomatic concessions, but the history of imperial wars shows that this is not always the case.

The difficulty in making either a balance or preponderance of power preserve the peace can be illustrated further by discussing the role of uncertainty in the decision-making process. The traditional rationale for the balance of power proposition is that states will not initiate a war unless they are pretty sure of winning it. In social science language, it is assumed that uncertainty makes states conservative and that leaders are unwilling to take risks. If you are not sure of winning, you will not attack. Since a balance of power increases uncertainty, it should decrease war. From this perspective, uncertainty produced by a relative equality of capability is seen as producing peace. According to Singer *et al.*'s (1972: 23–24) summary of the traditional wisdom, the parity (balance of power) model assumes that certainty is at the root of war, and they note that the major inhibitor to war is the lack of clarity in the power and alliance structure so that the outcome of a war is in doubt.

Conversely, the preponderance model assumes that uncertainty is at the root of war – if there is any chance you will win, then you will consider war an option. Only when the defender has a *preponderance* of power can a state be secure, for no one would initiate a war they were sure to lose. From the preponderance model perspective, Singer *et al.* (1972: 23) argue, uncertainty and a balance are associated with war because the lack of structural clarity and the ambiguity of alliance ties make for misjudgments and poor predictions.

Singer *et al.* assumed the contradiction would be resolved empirically (i.e. either certainty *or* uncertainty would be correlated with war). An alternate explanation is that the receptivity of leaders to one of these two logics may be correlated with their willingness to accept risks and tolerate ambiguity, so that any given capability distribution at either the system or dyadic level will either prevent or encourage war depending on the characteristics of the respective leadership.

Bueno de Mesquita (1981a) uses the concept of risk to build a deductive argument against the traditional wisdom that is even more persuasive than his findings. He maintains that any given configuration of power (balance or preponderance) can produce either war or peace depending on whether leaders are risk-acceptant or risk-averse. Thus, Bueno de Mesquita (1981a: 546) concludes that any individual leader's potential for initiating war will depend on his or her particular risk-taking orientation rather than any distribution of power.

Although Bueno de Mesquita uses his analysis to move toward an expected utility model, the following criticisms of realist logic can be derived from his basic insight. It can be assumed on the basis of his argument that risk-averse leaders will be prevented from initiating war when there is a balance of power, whereas those that are risk-acceptant will only be prevented from considering war when the other side has a preponderance of power. Since it is unlikely that the leaders of major states will always have the same predisposition toward risk-taking, the success of any given configuration of power in preventing war is going to vary. Sometimes a balance of power will prevent war and sometimes it will not.

Whether it does or not will probably depend on a variety of personal characteristics, not just the disposition of leaders to take risks. Other personal traits, such as tolerance of ambiguity, cognitive complexity, rigidity, open/closed-mindedness, hard-line/soft-line tendencies, and dominance may play a role (see Guetzkow and Valadez, 1981a, 1981b; M. Hermann,

1980; Etheredge, 1978). Such (utility) calculations are further complicated by the varying domestic political contexts of the contending states.
Hard-liners and political fanatics, who are willing to assume greater
costs in a war because they expect greater benefits than accommodationists and pragmatists, will be less likely to be discouraged by a balance of
power. A domestic political environment dominated by hard-liners is apt
to produce decisions and leaders that are less constrained by a balance of
power than a domestic environment dominated by accommodationists
or isolationists. Thus, the effectiveness of a given balance of power will
change as leaders and domestic political environments change. This argument shows that there is no logical reason to expect either the balance of
power or a preponderance of power to always prevent war.

How can these conclusions be resolved with Singer *et al.*'s (1972) findings? The primary difference between their analysis and that of Bueno
de Mesquita is in the measurement of war. Since they examine nation-
months of war and not the presence or absence of war, their findings are
not as germane to the question of peace as they are to the magnitude of
war. Bueno de Mesquita's (1981a) analysis must be given greater weight on
this question, because the balance of power and preponderance models
are primarily analyses of how to maintain peace and avoid war. Although
Singer *et al.* (1972) do not tell us anything about the onset of war, they
have uncovered something significant about the role of capability and the
magnitude of war. In accounting for their findings, they even say that the
two centuries "are experiencing different types of war ..." (Singer *et al.*,
1972: 48), but they do not elaborate upon this in their *ad hoc* explanation.
This suggests that *the distribution of capability will determine what form
war will take, and not whether it will occur.* Clearly, since war is relatively
rare and most dyads have either a balance or preponderance of power,
there have to be other factors that cause war. If we look at how capability
differentials affect the form war will take, then we have an empirical basis
for constructing a typology of war, especially if it is discovered that the
wars of the nineteenth century, which Singer *et al.* find associated with
a preponderance of power, are fundamentally different from the wars of
the twentieth century, which Singer *et al.* find associated with a balance
of power.

If one "unpacks" Singer *et al.*'s (1972) correlations by looking at the cases
that make up each century, then it becomes clear that the wars among
major states in the nineteenth century are, in fact, very different from
the wars among major states in the twentieth, and that this difference
is accentuated by employing nation-months as the dependent variable

rather than a dichotomous war/no war variable. Since the Correlates of War data set does not include the Napoleonic wars, their data on the nineteenth century lacks a "great power" general war (Levy, 1983: 52, 74–75). It is the absence of a general war, such as World Wars I and II, that is the primary reason that the period from 1815 to 1914 has been called the century of peace. Because there are no all-out world wars, wars involving major states in this period were considerably less destructive than in the twentieth century. Indeed, Levy (1983: 143) shows that the nineteenth century after 1815 is the least warlike period of the last five centuries.

Nevertheless, there are a number of wars involving major states in the nineteenth century data set, and based on the reasons for fighting, these can be grouped as: (1) state building wars, particularly those associated with the formation of Germany and Italy, and with the expansion of national territory at the expense of the Ottoman Empire; (2) imperial wars by the major states against considerably weaker states or nonnational entities outside the central system; and (3) limited wars between major states such as the Franco-Prussian War or the Crimean War. What these nineteenth-century wars have in common is that most of them tend to be fought between actors who are relatively unequal in power.[3] In other words, as a sample of cases, 1816–99 tends to consist of wars one would expect to be fought when one side has a clear advantage over the other. Conversely, in the twentieth century, the two world wars are the kind of wars that would be expected only when the two sides are relatively evenly matched. Because World Wars I and II (along with the Korean War) dominate the nation-months of war in the twentieth century, Singer *et al.* get a correlation associating relative equality with high war and preponderance with low war.[4] Neither of these findings means that a preponderance actually produced peace in the twentieth century or that a balance produced peace in the nineteenth century. Rather, it seems that a complex

---

[3] This seems to be true even when there is a major state on each side as in the Seven Weeks War and the Franco-Prussian War.

[4] A reanalysis and breakdown of Singer *et al.*'s (1972: 29) Table 1 shows that most war in the nineteenth century occurs from 1845 to 1871, which coincides with the highest concentration of power in that century (a range of 0.255 to 0.280). In the twentieth century, the largest wars occur after 1913, 1938, and 1950 when concentration is comparatively low for that century (0.208, 0.217 and 0.293 respectively vs. the highest concentrations of 0.371 to 0.417). Interestingly, the most peaceful periods in the twentieth century follow these three wars (1920–25, 1946–50, 1955–65) and are also periods of very high concentrations of power (0.371, 0.417, 0.331 and 0.303 respectively), the likes of which are not found in the nineteenth century. Conversely, within the nineteenth century, the periods without any war have relatively moderate concentrations (0.242, 0.243, 0.232, 0.203).

of factors, including the distribution of capability at both the dyadic and systemic levels, encouraged certain kinds of wars from 1816 to 1913 and other kinds from 1914 to 1945.

A closer inspection of the types of wars in each period suggests not only that the two periods are experiencing different forms of warfare, but that the wars of one period may have had an impact on the kinds of wars that were fought in the second period. The imperial wars of the nineteenth century along with the state-building wars of Germany and Italy and military successes of Japan eventually produced effects that led to a major power transition in the twentieth century and a set of diplomatic tensions that status quo states were unable to resolve in a manner that would assimilate new powerful states into the existing world order (see Kennedy, 1987: 203–4, 206–10; 212–15; Doran, 1989: 393; 1991). The ("small") wars of the nineteenth century created both the (relative) capabilities and the issues that were the foundation of the large wars of the twentieth century. It is not that the nineteenth century was different from the twentieth century; it is that the nineteenth century produced the twentieth century!

This analysis, along with the evidence marshaled by Rasler and Thompson (1985a, 1985b, 1989), supports the idea that wars should be differentiated and that constructing a typology of wars would be conceptually useful in explaining findings. The interpretation of the anomaly uncovered by Singer *et al.* suggests that capability differentials may be the most important theoretical dimension upon which to construct a typology.

A Typology of War

Previous efforts

Two different approaches may be taken to the construction of typologies. One is nomothetic and behavioral and strives to explain war regardless of time and place. The other is an approach that sees the specific time and place in which war occurs (i.e. the historical conditions) as the most critical factor in explaining war. A review of both approaches provides important insights and criticisms that must be taken into account before attempting to construct any new typology of wars.

One of the earliest theoretical attempts to classify wars is that of Lewis F. Richardson (1960b: 247–48), who differentiates wars according to the number of participants on each side. Richardson showed that the typical war was a dyadic war (one actor on each side) and that multiparty wars were fairly rare. Richardson was particularly interested in constructing a model that would explain the difference between these dyadic wars and more complex wars, like the world wars. His analysis is relevant because he makes it clear that the sheer number of participants, regardless of their power, can be an important factor in distinguishing different types of war.

Most behavioral approaches tend to base their typologies on the nature of the participants, especially their political power, rather than the number of participants. Typical of this approach is that of the Correlates of War project, which distinguishes between interstate and extra-systemic wars. The former must have at least one member of the international system (i.e. a nation-state) on each side, whereas the latter need have only one nation-state as a participant, which allows for the inclusion of imperial and colonial wars. This focus on nation-states stems from the realist belief that, in the modern system, nation-states are the most powerful and thus the most important actors (see Vasquez, 1983a: 134–36, 139–40). Small and Singer (1982: 46–52) make this emphasis more explicit by further breaking down interstate wars into central system wars and major power wars, depending on the political status of the belligerents. Similarly, Levy (1983: 51–52; 1990) classifies wars according to whether a great power participated on one side (wars involving great powers), both sides (great power wars), or involved most of the great powers (general wars).[5] Midlarsky (1986a, 1988) follows in this tradition by separating out "systemic" wars (e.g. World War I and World War II) as a special focus for his inquiry in order to identify the unique conditions associated with their occurrence (Midlarsky, 1986a: 109). Siverson and Sullivan (1983: 477) point out that critical aspects of balance of power theory apply only to wars that have major states on each side and not to other wars, even if they involve major states, which implies that wars with major states on each side are special in both their causes and dynamics.

Because these classifications have been constructed more for convenience and for eliminating wars than for theoretical comparison, they are of only limited aid in constructing a typology based on the capability differentials of the belligerents. More significantly, actor-based classifications can be criticized for assuming that war can be understood by looking at

---

[5] Levy's (1983: 51–52) initial criterion for a general war was at least two-thirds of the great powers. He (Levy, 1985b: 371) modified this to a war involving the leading great power and at least half of the other great powers with an intensity of 1,000 battle deaths per 1 million European population.

the power or foreign policy of a single state, rather than by looking at interactions and relationships between political actors. Research on foreign policy behavior suggests that an interaction and dyadic approach is more productive than a single-actor (or monad) approach (see Kegley and Skinner, 1976: 308–11; see also Singer, 1982: 37–38). Therefore, classifying wars on the basis of the distribution of capability across belligerents rather than the political status of the individual participants may improve analysis. One attempt to move in this direction is that of Stoll (1980), who distinguishes between *opportunity wars*, those arising from serious disputes between unequals, and *threat wars*, those arising from serious disputes between equals (see also Siverson and Tennefoss, 1982). This is an important insight that is consistent with the interpretation given of Singer *et al.*'s (1972) anomalous findings; and it will be employed later in constructing a typology of war.

The review of nomothetic approaches suggests two dimensions on which wars might be classified. The first, based on Richardson, is to distinguish dyadic wars from those involving three or more parties. The second, based on criticism of the monad approach, is to distinguish wars according to the relative capability of the opponents.

A major criticism of nomothetic approaches is that they are ahistorical. Like most positivist efforts, they can be faulted for assuming that wars, regardless of previous history, are more or less caused by the same set of variables. Marxists or students of history like Organski (1958) and Modelski (1978) would want a typology of wars that would recognize that the type of war a political unit could initiate would vary greatly depending on its own and the system's economic and historical development (see Thompson, 1983c). From this perspective, the purpose of the initiator determines the type of war that will be fought, and a search for the causes of war would start with the factors that made the initiator have that purpose in the first place and try to attain it through force of arms in the second place. Indeed, for some (e.g. Organski and Kugler, 1980; Gilpin, 1981; Modelski, 1978), the historical perspective makes them see war as natural and periodic; unlike Richardson and other more behaviorally oriented peace scientists, who try to identify the conditions of war and of peace so that the latter may be encouraged and the former prevented. Consequently, the more historically oriented investigate the causes of war by trying to identify *when* war will occur, rather than asking *whether* it will occur.

A focus on *when* wars will occur tends to lead inevitably to explaining and differentiating wars on the basis of the reasons given for fighting them. Wars tend to be classified according to their goals, and, in the more theoretical analyses, an emphasis is placed on the historical conditions associated with these goals and the historical and economic prerequisites for the initiation of war (cf. Howard, 1976). By paying more attention to such questions, we may better understand how the policies that precede these wars produce them (see Gantzel, 1981: 44). Eventually, this may make it possible to classify wars according to the policies that led to war, e.g. imperial wars, hegemonic wars. In the absence of such knowledge, classifications that have emerged from this approach have been very substantive, sometimes focusing on policy, sometimes on goals, and sometimes on the participants. Quincy Wright (1965: 638–40, Appendix XX), for example, classifies wars according to whether they are balance of power, defensive, imperial, or civil wars. Lider (1977: 195, cited in Gantzel, 1981: 48) distinguishes among wars fought between superpowers, among imperialists, between imperialists and liberation movements, and among third world states.

Some scholars wish to concentrate only on the wars that are the most important turning points in history, which they see as a special type. Modelski (1978) and Thompson (1985) view the wars that resolve the question of who will exercise leadership over the global political system, what they call *global wars*, in this manner. Those who emphasize the traditional realist struggle for power tend to speak of these wars as *hegemonic wars* (Farrar, 1977; Gilpin, 1981: 199–203; see also Toynbee, 1954: 234–87, 322–23 and Dehio, 1962, both cited in Levy, 1985b: 346) in which dominant powers and challengers fight it out. Organski and Kugler (1980: 42–47) see many of these wars as involving power transitions (see also Organski, 1958: 325–38; Doran and Parsons, 1980). In response to this discussion, Levy argues that his own category of *general war* provides the least problematic way of identifying these sorts of wars and has offered a more precise conceptualization and operationalization of his original concept (cf. Levy, 1983: 51–52 and Levy, 1985b: 364–65). While there is disagreement among these scholars over exactly which wars are the most important and why they are important, there is an emerging consensus that, of all the wars fought, only a few are influential in determining the historical structure of the world system (cf. Thompson, 1985; Levy, 1985b: 372–73, Table 1; Thompson, 1988: 105, Table 5.4).

While a truly adequate substantive classification of wars must await the outcome of more theoretically oriented historical research, like that currently being done on the world system (e.g. Braudel, 1966; Wallerstein, 1974, 1980; Thompson, 1988), it is possible to distinguish certain wars (e.g. world wars and imperial wars) that appear to be unique and historically important in their own way, and therefore worthy of studying as a type. Because the fights that lead to world wars appear sufficiently distinct to serve as a basis of differentiation and their historical impact is sufficiently great, they will be singled out in Chapter 7 for special investigation.

Big wars among major states have been the subject of considerable attention (see Midlarsky, 1990; Levy, 1990). What these wars should be called is a matter of disagreement. Some of the labels (like hegemonic wars or global wars) involve taking a theoretical stance about the causes of these wars. While it is clear that these wars have a set of causes that differentiate them from other wars, it is not clear that the specific causes (or factors) identified, respectively, by Gilpin (1981) (see also Farrar, 1977), Modelski (1978), or Organski and Kugler (1980) are the true causes or the only factors associated with these wars. This makes a more theoretically neutral label, like that of *world war*, more appropriate. Since Levy's (1983) label *general war* is not as obvious a term as *world war*, it will not be employed; however, his operational definition of these wars can provide a way of comparing and perhaps testing the different interpretations and will be incorporated in this analysis.

A *world war* may be defined as a large-scale severe war among major states that involves the leading states at some point in the war (see Levy, 1985b: 365) and most other major states in a struggle to resolve the most fundamental issues on the global political agenda (see Mansbach and Vasquez, 1981: 110–12). This definition places emphasis on who, how, and over what the war is fought, rather than on the foreign policy that led to the war, the reasons for which different parties entered the war, or the consequences of the war. The latter focus, particularly the notion that such wars could transform the structure of the system and produce a new hegemonic leader, is *not* incorporated, even though Levy (1985b: 364) is willing to pay some deference to it in his conceptual definition (as opposed to his operationalization). Instead of making such claims defining criteria, they will be treated as possible empirical outcomes of a war. I make this choice not only because it is methodologically less cumbersome, but also because I do not believe that such wars are necessarily and primarily caused by hegemonic or leadership struggles. I believe there are other factors that cause these wars and that are responsible for their scope and severity. Even though many of the wars of this type have the impact analysts see, some scholars have a tendency to discuss the causes of these wars in terms of their consequences, a logically invalid procedure.

Identifying wars of a special type, however, is still a far cry from a typology of war. Substantive classifications have not been able to serve as a complete typology of war for two reasons. First, most substantive typologies do not even pretend to be logically exhaustive (i.e. there may be a host of wars which do not easily fit any type). Second, historical classifications have to date been insufficiently theoretical. They do not identify the characteristics that are most significant for determining why the wars have different causes; they merely state that the differing goals and policies of actors (e.g. those involved in civil, imperial, and world wars) lead them to fight different kinds of wars. To overcome these problems, one must take a more nomothetic approach, but this raises the danger of creating a general typology that is ahistorical and ignores the possible changing reasons for and causes of war. Since this work is concentrating on explaining wars in the modern global system since 1495, with special emphasis on wars since 1815, that danger should be minimized.

Types of war

To construct a nomothetic typology, it is necessary to identify the theoretical characteristics of war that will most likely differentiate wars according to their causes and thereby help analysts uncover those causes. The typology offered here is based on three separate theoretical dimensions. The first and most important is the distribution of capability between the belligerents. Since the previous analysis of Singer *et al.* (1972) suggested that the distribution of capability is probably more related to the type of war than to the onset of wars, wars between equals should be separated from wars between unequals.

Wars between equals, I call *wars of rivalry*, and wars between unequals, I call *wars of inequality*. It is assumed that wars between equals are more oriented to the logic of the balance of power and prey to its deficiencies – such as mutual fear, suspicion and insecurity; arms races; and the temptation of preventive war. Wars between unequals lack all of these characteristics. These wars are more oriented to either the logic of preponderance of power and of opportunity or to the logic of revolution, depending on who is the initiator. Unlike wars between equals, where both sides tend to employ the same logic because they perceive the situation from a similar foundation of capability, wars between unequals involve two parties who employ different logics and initiate wars for different reasons – the strong seeking dominance and the weak liberation.

I call wars between equals *wars of rivalry* because one of their most distinguishing characteristics is that they are usually preceded by long-term rivalries, whereas wars between unequals are not. The presence of a long-term rivalry makes the pre-war relationship more prone to mutual hostility, while the relative capability results in mutual frustration. This makes both sides willing to hurt and harm the other side as an end in itself, often with minimal regard to the costs. Conversely, wars of inequality are more likely to be governed by rationalistic cost-benefit considerations, especially when viewed from the perspective of the initiator. Here decisions by the stronger to initiate war are more apt to follow the kind of cool, calm, and collected calculations described by expected-utility theory (see Bueno de Mesquita, 1981b). The opportunity for victory is an important prerequisite for going to war. Emotions that do enter tend to be confined to the weak who react to domination with resentment (M. Singer, 1972) and rage (Fanon, 1968), and revolt out of an inability to continue to tolerate the situation (see Oglesby, 1967). Nevertheless, if rebellion is to become successful revolution and liberation, then the war must be initiated at an opportune moment – when the normally stronger is distracted, conquered by another party, or weaker than before (see Waterman, 1981). Since inequality is responsible for the use of rational calculation, the rage of the weak, and the way the war is fought, I call these wars, *wars of inequality.*

On the whole, wars of inequality are more susceptible to cost-benefit analysis because it is clear that differences in capability will have a major impact on the outcome of the war. Conversely, in wars of rivalry, the relative equality of capability makes it less clear that the difference in capability will make a difference, thereby making the outcome appear to turn on other factors – resolve, diplomacy, military tactics, courage and will, staying power, morale, luck, support from allies.[6] Because differences in capability affect the logics that will be employed by the participants, as well as their emotions, it can be expected that the foreign policy interactions and practices preceding the two types of war will be different and

---

[6] Since an expected-utility framework can be used to calculate decisions under conditions of uncertainty and risk, the framework can still be used to analyze wars of rivalry. However, my point is that the role of uncertainty in these wars is so high that it will have much more of an impact on decision making than will any cost-benefit capability analysis. In particular, uncertainty produced by small differences in capability and by the possible unreliability of alliance commitments and third party intervention can be expected to play a major role. Conversely, in wars of inequality, cost-benefit considerations based on capability would be more determinative and uncertainty would be less influential.

that the wars will not only be fought for varying reasons but will probably be caused by different factors.

In order to differentiate wars on the basis of the relative equality of the belligerents, it is best to measure differences in capability as a dichotomous variable that would clearly demarcate dyads according to their relative capability. *Capability* may be defined as the resource base an actor can utilize to attain certain ends. It is assumed that over the long run, capability that is employed will lead to political successes or failures that give an actor a *reputation* and *status* in a global hierarchy.[7] Resource capability for individual major states has been adequately measured in the Correlates of War project in terms of its demographic, economic, and military components. Discriminant function analysis or several clustering techniques could be employed on these data to demarcate dyads as either relatively equal or unequal. Of course, in any given pairing, the differences in capability will vary, so that in some wars of rivalry, the differences will be so small that they will be difficult to measure validly; whereas, in others, like the Seven Weeks War, one side will have a clear advantage over the other, even though both sides are relatively equal. To capture this information, ordinal measures can be used to rank dyads *within* the dichotomous categories.[8]

The second dimension by which wars can be differentiated is the well-known distinction between limited and total war. This distinction is based on both the ends and means associated with war (Morgenthau, 1960: ch. 22; Kissinger, 1957: ch. 6; Osgood, 1957) and is derived from Clausewitz's (1832: book 1, ch. 1) warnings about war becoming absolute. The distinction based on means is easier to make because it refers to the extent to which an all out effort is made in fighting the war. Total wars involve a high mobilization of society, whereas limited wars command comparatively fewer resources and personnel. The degree of mobilization reflects the salience of the issue at stake in the war and, as such, affects the way in which the war is fought on the battlefield. Because total wars take on the characteristics of a fight for survival, they tend to mobilize all resources and means to wage battle with few restraints, even though

---

[7] For an elaboration of my views on the various problems with the concept of power and the ways in which capability and status can serve as substitute concepts, see Mansbach and Vasquez (1981: 213–16).

[8] Measures on relative capability could be calculated for each pair before the war and then for each war coalition once the war is initiated and after each intervention. In this way it would be possible to trace how an unequal war, like the Serbian–Austro-Hungarian war of 1914, or an equal war, like the initial Spanish Civil War, is transformed by intervention.

there may be prohibitions on specific types of weapons (like gas warfare). Limited wars are much more restrained in the means that are employed and where and how the war is fought. They may also be explicitly coercive – using force to try to get an opponent to take a specific action, although they need not be.

In terms of goals, limited wars are wars that have specific and concrete aims and leave much of the territory and independence of the opponent intact. The goals in total wars are much more open-ended and often expand as the war progresses. Total wars often demand the complete overthrow of the leadership of the other side whether through demand of unconditional surrender, as in World War II, or complete annihilation, as in the Third Punic War. As Stedman (1990: 1–2) points out, wars become total because "one or both of the antagonists comes to believe (or believes from the start) that the cause of the conflict lies in the character of the opponent," which usually means the leadership or ruling elite of the society. As a result, a peace that concludes a total war often involves attempts to reconstruct the opponent's values and institutions by some sort of social engineering scheme (Stedman, 1990: 3) that purges the society of its flawed character and elements, which are seen as residing in the leadership, policy influencers and bureaucrats. The creation of Weimar Germany and the post-World War II reconstruction of Germany and Japan all reflect such schemes. At the domestic level, civil wars and revolutions that are totalist have similar consequences, as the reconstruction following the US Civil War and the revolutionary enactments of the French, Bolshevik, and Chinese revolutions illustrate.

What distinguishes limited from total wars is the ability of participants to confine themselves to goals that are subject to bargaining and do not raise questions of survival or the ire and hostility of one side to such an extent that they fight as if survival were at stake. Two factors influence the extent to which wars will be limited. The first is the nature of the issues and the stakes over which belligerents are fighting. Wars that are fought over marginal border questions and comparatively minor changes in the dispositions of stakes (such as economic, strategic, or colonial advantages) are not going to be fought in the same manner as wars that are fought over far-reaching territorial and ideological demands, hegemonic claims, or fundamental changes in the global order and rules of the game. Of these, challenges to territory may be the most fundamental. Kugler (1990: 202–3) notes that wars between major states that become total have the core territory of states at issue, whereas limited wars, like the Crimean War, do not. The second factor that influences the extent to which wars will be limited is whether the practice of war and its related discourse in any given period restrains, by custom, the goals and means employed in war. The practices of mercenary armies of the *condottieri* of Renaissance Italy, for example, aimed to keep the loss of military personnel to a minimum, while the practices of twentieth-century armies do not. Likewise, the stylized military tactics of the eighteenth century made war limited, whereas the tactics of Napoleon encouraged total battles.

Despite the eloquence of Clausewitz, Morgenthau, and Kissinger in making the limited/total war distinction, it is the most difficult of the three dimensions to operationalize. This is because the concept itself is multidimensional and because some participants in a war can be engaged in a total struggle while others are not. This complexity bespeaks of the theoretical richness of the concept and need not be seen as an insurmountable obstacle to its use. Although this is not the place for a complete operational definition, showing how some of these problems can be overcome will make the various aspects of the concept clearer.

The distinction between limited and total is one of degree and not kind, so that it is best measured at the ordinal level by ranking wars. Since it is a comparative concept, rather than a natural dichotomy, many of the problematic cases can be taken care of by looking at the degree to which they are totalist or limited, e.g. limited wars that have totalist tendencies or total wars that are restrained in one aspect or another. Whether the means of a war are limited or total could be measured by the extent (percent) to which the population and economy of a society is mobilized to fight the war. Such indicators as the percent of production devoted to the war effort, government control of production, sharp increases in taxes and/or changes in budget allocations, the amount of credits sought and the extent of deficit spending related to the war effort are ways in which mobilization might be validly and reliably measured. A second possibility for measuring means would be to examine the military tactics employed with attention to restraints on the use of certain weapons or the avoidance of certain targets. Such a military-oriented approach would be more judgmental and not as precise as the domestic mobilization approach. In addition, the mobilization approach has the advantage of directly measuring the extent to which wars penetrate the domestic structure of a society. Nevertheless, the military approach might be useful for early wars where economic and social data are scarce.

Measuring the goals of a war is less straightforward. This is because classifying goals is judgmental and goals can change as the war evolves. Nevertheless, an examination of government documents along with public statements and memoirs should permit analysts to classify the goals of participants in a war as either limited or totalist. Limited goals can be operationalized as those confined to marginal changes in territorial, economic, or political rights. Totalist goals can be defined as those that are more hegemonic or destructionist in character and would be indicated by goals that insist on the overthrow of the head of government or ideology of one's opponent; demand large areas of the core territory of an opponent; attempt to fundamentally change the rules of the game of the global political, economic, or social systems; or seek to produce fundamental shifts in the global pecking order. Of course, what is typical of totalist goals is that they evolve in that direction, as is best illustrated in World War I, so that the most reliable classification is going to be made *ex post facto*. Nevertheless, it would be possible to code the different stages of a particular war to see how it changed – for example, before and after Hitler's invasion of the Soviet Union.

What makes measurement additionally problematic is that because goals and means refer to two different things, it is logically possible for participants to have a goal of one type and a means of another. Figure 2.1 presents four categories in which the war effort of an individual belligerent can be classified: limited means and goals, limited goals and totalist means, totalist goals and limited means, and totalist means and goals. This ordering can be used to rank a belligerent's war effort. It assumes that goals are more apt to determine means than vice versa. To distinguish the differences in war efforts, a point system can be employed so that each category is scored as 2, 4, 6, or 8 with pure limited war efforts receiving a 2 and pure totalist war efforts an 8, as indicated in Figure 2.1.

Employing a scoring system for war efforts of each belligerent provides a way of overcoming the other major problem – how to code a war when one side sees itself fighting a limited war and the other a total war. The simplest way to classify wars would be to aggregate the war effort scores of each participant. Dyadic wars would be ranked separately from complex wars. For dyadic wars, a pure limited war would be a 4 and a pure total war a 16. For complex wars, the advantages of the scheme are impressive. For example, take the Vietnam War, which as a civil war involves a total war between the Republic of Vietnam and the Democratic Republic of Vietnam, but how does one incorporate the war between North Vietnam and the US? It is a total struggle for survival by one side, but limited on the other. The scheme in Figure 2.1 would score it as an 18 (DRV-8, ROV-8, US-2) much larger than the Russo-Japanese War, but still far away from World War I and World War II. The latter wars would score over 60,

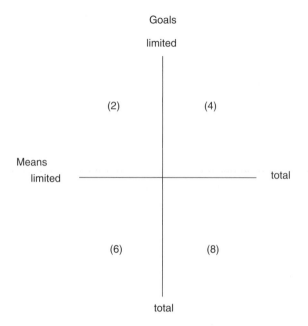

Figure 2.1 Classifying individual war efforts

with World War II scoring as more totalist because of the explicit conquest aims of Germany, Italy, and Japan and the unconditional surrender demands of the Allied states. When classifying wars, it is important
to keep in mind that the limited/total dimension is comparative across
wars within history. The point system outlined here is able to make such
comparisons admirably. More importantly, for the purposes of this analysis, the point system demonstrates that the theoretically rich concept of
limited versus total war can in principle be operationalized.

   It is assumed that wars that are fought as differently as limited and total
wars are must have different factors associated with them, if not different
causes. The dynamics of contention that precede total wars should differ
significantly from the dynamics that precede limited wars. While these
are the basic reasons for including this dimension in the typology, the
distinction between limited and total wars is also useful for distinguishing the impact of wars. Total wars are likely to have different and longer-
lasting effects than limited wars. This is true not only for internal effects,
like taxation and public debt (see Rasler and Thompson, 1985b, 1983), but
also for global effects, like the changes in global leadership that concern
Modelski (1978), Thompson (1985), and Gilpin (1981).

Combining the limited/total dimension with the previous one on differences in capability suggests some important insights. Because wars of rivalry are more prone to social psychological factors, it becomes more difficult for decision makers to follow Clausewitz's recommendations to keep war from becoming total and irrational in terms of its costs if the war drags on. In the absence of other states that can mediate a war that does not result in a quick victory, wars of rivalry are apt to become total wars.[9] Conversely, wars of inequality are less likely to become total, and if they do, they become total wars for different reasons. Rather than becoming unlimited because one side is unable to follow rational calculations, they become unlimited out of a cold calculation of what will be required to accomplish one's territorial goals. Usually this means that the stronger wants to occupy or colonize the territory of the weaker. Such wars of conquest become total when the conquered are not needed and are seen as an obstacle that must be removed, or the conquered are so culturally dissimilar that there is no desire to assimilate them. The lack of cultural similarity can serve to remove moral inhibitions about slaughtering these people and lead to genocidal acts. On the other hand, a policy of total assimilation can require that the defeated submit to the conqueror's civilization, which can mean adoption of a new religion and language, acceptance of foreign education as superior, name changes, and so forth.

The final dimension used in the typology classifies wars according to whether they are dyadic or complex (more than two participants). This distinction is derived from the work of Lewis F. Richardson (1960b: 250). In an analysis of Wright's (1942: Appendix XX) list of 200 wars (omitting civil wars) fought between 1480 and 1941 he found that 117 had only one participant on each side, 28 had two against one, 12 had three against one, etc. It is assumed that the modal dyadic wars will be easier to understand than the more complicated ones. Wars with more than three participants are called *complex*, because they may entail constructing a model of war expansion or diffusion. In addition, it can be assumed that the political dynamics of wars involving more than two participants will differ from the more straightforward dyadic wars.[10]

---

[9] It also seems that when wars of rivalry are total and involve major states on each side, these total wars are apt to spread and draw in most states in the system, i.e. total wars involving rivalries tend not to be dyadic but complex.

[10] Whether a war is complex should be determined by the number of active participants that were involved at any time from the beginning to the end of the war. Nevertheless, an analysis of complex wars might benefit from seeing if there is a difference between

Theoretically, the distinction between dyadic and complex wars is important for understanding how the onset of world wars differs from that of other wars. World wars often grow out of wars that were initiated in the expectation that they would be limited, but for some reason were unable to be confined to the initial parties (see Sabrosky, 1985: 181; see also Sabrosky, 1975). This was the case in both World War I and II where the initiator and its allies hoped that allies of the target would not fight and made efforts to keep them neutral and face them with a *fait accompli*. Nevertheless, the initiator was willing to take the risk that others might intervene. The case of the two twentieth-century wars suggests that initiators do not always employ a cost-benefit calculus in a sufficiently rational and synoptic manner, and that expected-utility theory (Bueno de Mesquita, 1981b) based primarily on capability calculations will be less successful in analyzing complex wars than dyadic wars, particularly complex total wars.

The hope of mitigating war by keeping it more limited clearly lies in understanding why major states are unwilling or unable to confine the war to initial parties. Once a war involving major states on each side becomes complex, there is an increase in the probability that it will also become total. This is because each new party that enters the war adds its entire agenda of issues to the coalition's war aims, making the issues under contention even more intractable and less susceptible to bargaining. This not only makes a negotiated end to the war more difficult (thereby lengthening the war), but the sheer number of issues encourages a total war where the winners take all. Such questions are important to explore not only by examining world wars, but by examining those cases of war expansion, like the Crimean War, that could have become a total war, but did not.

Making a distinction between dyadic and complex wars also provides a way of seeing, more generally, how and why wars expand and how alliances and contagion may affect the war process and the severity and duration of wars. Also, treating complex wars as a type will help move research beyond the finding that alliances make wars expand, to a deeper understanding of why wars become contagious. Finally, of interest is determining just how and why the causes and consequences of dyadic wars are different from the causes and consequences of complex wars.

Figure 2.2 combines the three dimensions to construct a logically exhaustive and mutually exclusive typology of war. Since difference in

wars that began as complex wars and dyadic wars that expanded. For a discussion of Richardson's (1960b) work on this topic, see Zinnes (1975: 163–74).

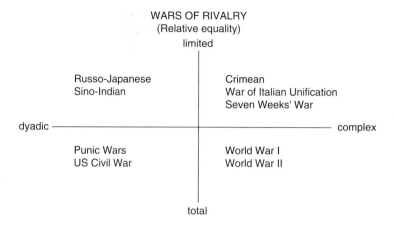

WARS OF RIVALRY
(Relative equality)
limited

Russo-Japanese Sino-Indian	Crimean War of Italian Unification Seven Weeks' War

dyadic ————————————————————————— complex

Punic Wars US Civil War	World War I World War II

total

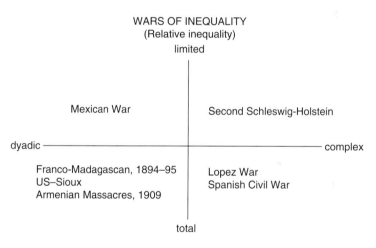

WARS OF INEQUALITY
(Relative inequality)
limited

Mexican War	Second Schleswig-Holstein

dyadic ————————————————————————— complex

Franco-Madagascan, 1894–95 US–Sioux Armenian Massacres, 1909	Lopez War Spanish Civil War

total

Figure 2.2 Typology of war

capability is seen as the most important dimension, wars of rivalry are separated from wars of inequality, and then these two basic types are broken down further in terms of the scope of the war (limited–total) and the number of participants (dyadic–complex). This results in four kinds of wars of rivalry and four kinds of wars of inequality. Among wars of rivalry, a limited dyadic war would be the Russo-Japanese War or Sino-Indian War and a limited complex war would be the Crimean War or the Seven Weeks War. Total wars of rivalry would include the Punic War as a dyadic war and World War II as a complex war. Interestingly, most civil wars of any length can be classified as total wars of rivalry that are dyadic, if there is no external intervention, while internationalized civil wars are complex.[11]

Among wars of inequality, a limited dyadic war would be the Mexican War, where a strong (and growing) state takes advantage of a weaker (and less populous) neighbor to increase its territory. A limited complex war would be the Second Schleswig-Holstein War, where two strong states, Prussia and Austria-Hungary, gang up on Denmark to gain territory. Dyadic total wars of inequality would include the many imperial wars of conquest that massacred entire sections of a population in an attempt to dominate them, and the mid-twentieth century reversal of that domination in wars of national liberation.[12] Complex total wars of inequality are rarer and usually involve the outside intervention of one or more parties in an ongoing total war that clearly tips the scale in favor of one side, as in the Lopez War or the internationalized Spanish Civil War.

The typology can be used for a variety of purposes. Significant comparative inferences can be made without employing all eight categories simultaneously. Particular wars can be compared by placing them within the categories of the typology. Wars can also be analyzed quantitatively, employing two categories at a time with two more as controls, without reducing the cases to such a small number that there would be little basis for generalization. The full typology would still be useful for "unpacking" and interpreting aggregate correlations so that they could be theoretically related to historical analyses of specific wars.

In this analysis, the typology will be used to delimit the scope of the inquiry and aid in the interpretation of evidence. If different types of wars have different causes, then any attempt to construct a scientific explanation of war must indicate what kinds of wars are being explained and *why* these wars are different from others. The typology presented in Figure 2.2 can provide satisfactory answers to both these questions. In addition, it

[11] Rasler and Thompson's (1985b: 505 n. 16) finding that the US Civil War had an impact on governmental expenditures and revenues (taxation) similar to that of the two world wars provided evidence that all three wars can be seen as total wars of rivalry.

[12] Imperial wars of inequality can only be regarded as total for both sides in the context of the territory under contention; i.e. the United States and the Sioux and the French and Madagascans were in totalist contests for control of a given piece of territory. Since the targets of imperialism were not attempting to overthrow the government of the imperial state outside the colonial area such wars can be seen as limited. Treating such dyadic wars from this more global perspective adds detail that makes this category cumbersome. Nevertheless, the typology can accommodate such distinctions by employing the scoring scheme in Figure 2.1.

allows one to sift through existing evidence and reinterpret aggregate correlations by breaking down the cases upon which they are based into the typology's theoretical categories.

As I began this inquiry, it became clear to me that a single explanation of war would not fit all cases. This confirmed my earlier suspicion that some explanations, such as rational choice cost-benefit analysis, provided an adequate model for describing decisions in some kinds of wars, but an overly simplistic and misleading account of others. As I investigated the question further, it seemed to me that some wars, like the twentieth-century world wars, were preceded by long-term rivalries with elaborate foreign policy practices, like alliance making and arms races, whereas other wars lacked these policies and appeared to start from more straight-forward instrumental calculations. The explanations with which I was working seemed to apply to the wars that were least susceptible to rational choice explanations that focus on costs and benefits and more intelligibly understood by social psychological explanations, learning models, and variables other than simply "power."

Put in another way, I suspect that wars of inequality tend to more easily conform to simple modernist ideas of rationalistic calculation of costs and benefits; whereas, wars of rivalry need to be explained by more com-plicated cognitive models of decision making.[13] The typology presented in Figure 2.2 is the result of the attempt to try to identify theoretically these wars and differentiate them from other wars. Since the explana-tions developed in this book apply only to wars of rivalry, it is important to understand the defining characteristics of these wars and how the dynamics of rivalry affect political conduct.

---

[13] I have two objections to rational choice and expected-utility analyses of war. The first is that, even though they may attempt to include risk-taking and uncertainty, they do so by making these variables modify the main variable, which they see as maximizing net benefits (see Bueno de Mesquita, 1981: 29ff). I would much prefer to include these as well as other psychological factors as separate variables in their own right. My claim is that such variables do more than just modify basic rationalistic tendencies. My second objection is that risk-taking and uncertainty are conceptualized in the very deductive and formal way they are treated in economics. I believe these concepts must be defined in light of empirical research, and I would draw upon empirical psychology to form their content. In addition, whether these two variables are the main or only variables affecting decision making I would treat as an open question, which should be actively researched. Eventually, I see such research producing an *accurate description* of how decision making takes place in a variety of situations, conditions, and cultures. It is upon such an empiri-cal base, rather than upon the more philosophical, indeed normative, base of rational choice that I think an adequate explanation of war will be built.

Conceptualizing Rivalry

It is assumed that wars between equals, particularly wars among the strongest states in the system, do not break out unless there has been a long history of conflict and hostility between the disputants. Hence, these wars have been labeled wars of rivalry. The idea of rivalry is often used in historical description. Historians speak of the rivalry between Prussia and Austria for Germany, between France and England for colonies, and of Soviet–American rivalry in the Cold War. Despite this use, the concept has not been the subject of much analysis, even though more technical definitions exist in the study of animal behavior (Wilson, 1975).

Recently, within the Correlates of War project, disputes among rivals have begun to receive attention (see Diehl, 1985a, 1985b; Diehl and Goertz, 1991; Wayman, 1983; Wayman and Jones, 1991; Gochman and Maoz, 1984: 609–11; Huth and Russett, 1991). Rivals have been identified operationally by Diehl (1985a: 334) as any two states that have had at least three militarized disputes within the last fifteen years, and by Wayman (1983: 15, 18) as any two states that have at least two disputes every ten years. Wayman and Jones (1991: 5–6) identify a "long-term" enduring rivalry as one that has at least five reciprocated militarized disputes, with the disputes spread over a twenty-five-year period.[14] While these are useful operational definitions, they do not provide a conceptualization based on a theoretical understanding of the dynamics of rivalry. There has been little reflection and no research on how and why states become rivals. The analysis in this section attempts to provide such a conceptualization.

Rivalry is, above all, a term that characterizes a competitive relationship between two actors over an issue that is of the highest salience to them. In this sense, the term can easily refer to two male deer who buck over a mate, two individuals within a company who compete to become a vice-president, or to two states, like Prussia and Austria, who struggle to achieve hegemony over a geographical region. Nevertheless, while in

---

[14] In contrast to Diehl and to Wayman, Gochman and Maoz (1984: 610) simply label the most dispute-prone dyads in a region as enduring rivalries. These range from a low of seven (Somalia–Ethiopia) to a high of twenty-four (UK–Russia/USSR). Wayman (1983: 15, 18) sees rivalries occurring when two states are involved in a chain of serious disputes. A rivalry is said to exist if two states have a second dispute within ten years of the first. The rivalry endures so long as the next dispute is within ten years of the previous one. Wayman (1983: 21) points out that the ten-year criterion produces several close calls (see his Table 1) and that a longer or shorter time period would produce a different sample. See Diehl and Goertz (1991) for a comparison of "rivalries" that the different operational definitions produce.

each of these cases a rivalry is present, the behavior that characterizes the rivalry will be extremely different. This reflects the fact that behavior is a learned response that will vary, given the prevailing customs and rules applied to a situation and the genetic tendencies of a given species, as well as the different structures of systems.

Rivalry between political collectivities is typically characterized by a sustained mutually contingent hostile interaction. Gamson and Modigliani (1971: 7–12), although they do not offer this as a definition of rivalry, characterize East–West relations in the Cold War in these terms. *Mutually contingent* can be taken to mean that each side's foreign policy actions are apprehended primarily in light of the foreign policy of the other side, and not simply as a result of internal factors or bureaucratic inertia. *Hostile interaction* is taken here to mean that a major motivation behind actions is psychological hostility, i.e. more emphasis is placed on hurting or denying something to the other side than on gaining something positive for oneself.

What distinguishes a rivalry from normal conflict is that issues are approached and ultimately defined not in terms of one's own value satisfaction, but in terms of what the gaining or loss of a stake will mean to one's competitor. An issue results from contention among actors over proposals for the disposition of stakes among them (Mansbach and Vasquez, 1981: 59). An issue, as Randle (1987: 1, 29) points out, is a disputed point or question that requires (as Coplin *et al.*, 1973: 75 argue) collective action on a proposed allocation of values.[15]

The number of disputed questions, or stakes, that are seen as part of the same issue can vary depending on how actors *link* stakes together. The underlying perceptual foundation of an issue or technically the *issue dimension* that links stakes together (see Mansbach and Vasquez, 1981: 60) can run the gamut from an extreme actor dimension, where the emphasis is on who is getting what with the focus on enemies and friends, to an extreme stake dimension, where the focus is on what is at stake and there are no permanent friends or enemies.[16]

---

[15] The action must be *collective* in that both sides are needed (if only for the sake of legitimacy) to make a decision. However, this does not mean that one side cannot unilaterally impose a settlement through brute force. It only means that contention over an issue does not usually start out that way. Contention arises out of an interdependent decision-making situation.

[16] The material in this section on issues (as opposed to rivalry) is drawn with stylistic modifications from Vasquez and Mansbach (1984) and Mansbach and Vasquez (1981: chs. 6 and 7).

Contenders that link stakes together on the basis of an *actor dimension* will have a large number of stakes in a few issues. Conversely, issues that are defined on the basis of a *stake dimension* will consist of a relatively small number of stakes that are brought together on the basis of some obvious substantive focus and/or geographical location (law of the sea, trade [or monetary] questions among OECD states). The hallmark of a rivalry is that issues are defined on the basis of an actor dimension. Indeed, as the rivalry intensifies, all issues may be collapsed and linked into a single grand issue – us versus them.

Whether an actor dimension or a stake dimension is in force has profound effects on how issue positions are determined, the types of stakes that are discussed, the kinds of proposals that are made for the disposition of these stakes, and the general pattern of cooperation and conflict that emerges in contention. The issue position an actor takes can be said to be a function of the decision-making calculus the actor employs for determining whether it is for or against a given proposal. There are three such calculi: (1) a *cost-benefit* calculus, in which actors determine whether they are in favor of or opposed to a proposal on the basis of the costs and benefits they would accrue if the proposal were adopted; (2) an *affect* calculus, in which actors determine whether they are in favor of or opposed to a proposal on the basis of whether their friends or enemies are in favor of it; and (3) an *interdependence* calculus, in which issue positions are determined on the basis of what effect the position on this issue will have on *other* issues on the agenda (see Mansbach and Vasquez, 1981: 191–97 for elaboration). Leaders in a rivalry will adopt a negative affect calculus rather than a cost-benefit or interdependence calculus. Leaders who employ a negative affect calculus favor any position that will hurt their opponents and oppose any position that will help their opponents.

A relationship between two states that is characterized by a consistent use of the negative affect calculus over time will lead each actor to link more and more stakes into a single issue, since the issue is being defined simply as what hurts one's opponent. As a result, the type of stakes under contention changes, with concrete stakes becoming infused with symbolic and transcendent importance.[17] As actors become increasingly concerned

---

[17] A concrete stake is transformed into a symbolic stake when it is seen as representing other stakes of greater value. Eventually, its value may lie primarily in the fact that it is a symbol for a host of other stakes. A stake becomes transcendent when it becomes virtually equated with the value under contention, such as democracy, survival, communism. Such stakes are discussed in highly ideological and moral terms and reflect

with relative gain and loss, stakes which may have had comparatively minor value are now seen as having great importance because they represent a commitment to bigger stakes. Thus, West Berlin in the 1960s becomes worth risking a nuclear war, because it is symbolic of America's defense of Europe. Eventually, the contention between the two actors may take on the characteristics of a titanic struggle between two ways of life or even between good and evil, particularly if leaders find it necessary to rationalize their policies with a higher purpose in order to mobilize domestic actors to make sacrifices for the coming struggle. When such highly moralistic and/or ideologically sharp language is introduced, then the contention can be seen as involving transcendent stakes.

As one moves from concrete to symbolic to transcendent stakes, issues become more intangible and hence less divisible. What little research there has been on issues shows that the more tangible an issue, the greater the likelihood of eventual resolution, while the more intangible, the more contentious and conflict-prone an issue (Vasquez, 1983b; Henehan, 1981: 13). Because some types of stakes are inherently more resolvable, the type of stakes over which actors contend will have an important effect on their interactions. Concrete stakes, because they are tangible and divisible, are more likely to permit compromise. Symbolic stakes make actors less flexible and more willing to stand firm because their symbolic nature leads to fears about losing a reputation for credibility or of establishing a bad precedent, if they entertain concessions necessary to bring about a compromise. Issues involving transcendent stakes are the most difficult to resolve, because they reflect fundamental differences over values, norms, and/or rules of the game (Vasquez and Mansbach, 1984: 426).

The issues that seem most prone to be infused with symbolic and transcendent qualities, at least in the modern global system, are territorial questions. For a variety of reasons states regard territory as the most salient stake over which contention can occur. It is not an accident then, that most rivalries originate over attempts to control the territory and space between equals. This is certainly true of the rivalry between the Valois and Hapsburgs, France and England, and Germany and France. What is ironic about this is that territory, at least on the surface, appears as a very concrete stake that could be divisible. Except for minor border changes, political actors do not perceive it this way. Instead, for reasons that perhaps stem from our evolutionary past, human collectivities treat territory

contention over fundamental rules of the political and social order (Mansbach and Vasquez, 1981: 61–62).

in symbolic and transcendent terms, infusing the concrete stake with all kinds of normative and ideological significance. Once they do that a prolonged hostile interaction is difficult to avoid. This does not mean that other issues cannot give rise to rivalry, witness the Soviet–American and Anglo-German rivalries, but that relationships between equals that contend over contiguous territory are more prone to rivalry and to rivalry that ends in war.

Rivalry is born because contention that focuses primarily on symbolic and transcendent stakes tends to be irresolvable. A relationship that is dominated by these kinds of stakes will produce conflict that tends to fester and escalate.[18] In order to resolve issues, actors indicate how they would like the stakes under contention to be distributed. Proposals for the disposition of stakes can be analyzed in terms of the way in which they propose to distribute costs and benefits between the contending parties. Initially, in any contention, each side suggests that it get most, if not all, of the benefits and the opponent bear most of the costs. Actors that contend over symbolic and transcendent stakes will not move from their initial issue positions because of the feeling that "my claims are just and yours are not." Negotiation may be further hampered when proposals of both sides take on the characteristics of a zero-sum game.

The key to whether a proposal will produce agreement and a resolution of the issue or foster disagreement and stalemate is how it assigns costs and benefits. Table 2.1 shows that there are four ways in which costs and benefits can be distributed: each side shares equally in the costs and the benefits (cell I); each side gets equal benefits, but one side bears more of the costs (cell II); or the reverse, each side shares the costs equally, but one side gets more benefits (cell III); and, finally, one side gets most of the benefits and the other bears most of the costs (cell IV). Proposals that are most apt to give rise to protracted disagreement are those in cell IV, because they call for a severely disproportional distribution of costs and benefits, with zero-sum proposals being but the most extreme of this type.

Transcendent and symbolic stakes usually give rise to type IV proposals. Successful negotiation typically entails moving initial type IV proposals to one of the other types. Some kinds of issues are more amenable to such a move than others – depending on the salience (importance) of the issue, the type of stakes that compose it, and the variety and number

[18] For evidence that transcendent and symbolic stakes are conflict prone, see Wish (1979: 544–45), who finds that ideological issues produce the most hostility of the five issues she examined, and Sullivan (1979), who shows that the use of symbolic rhetoric is associated with American escalation in the Vietnam War.

Table 2.1. *Types of proposals for disposing of stakes*

| | | Distribution of costs | |
		Equal	Unequal
Distribution of	Equal	I	II
benefits	Unequal	III	IV

Source: Vasquez and Mansbach, 1984: 427

of stakes linked in an issue. Those issues which link a large number of stakes that are infused with symbolic and transcendent significance are highly unlikely to be the subject of serious negotiation without being fundamentally redefined (i.e. defused of their emotional content and de-linked from each other). Since this is often inherently difficult and politically unfeasible, some issues simply cannot be negotiated, but must be fought out.[19]

The way in which an actor dimension affects the types of stakes under contention and the types of proposals made for disposing of those stakes clearly has an effect on the pattern of cooperation and conflict that emerges in contention. To understand why this is the case, it is necessary to have a better understanding of cooperation and conflict. *Conflict*, and its alleged opposite, *cooperation*, are two of the most ambiguous concepts within world politics. Elsewhere I have argued that to treat cooperation–conflict as a single dimension is erroneous (Mansbach and Vasquez, 1981: 234–40; Vasquez and Mansbach, 1984). The empirical research supports this conclusion in that findings consistently show that cooperation and conflict are separate and uncorrelated dimensions, and that different variables are associated with each (Rummel, 1972b: 98–99; Ward, 1982: 91, 93, 111, 118–20; see also: Salmore and Munton, 1974 and Wilkenfeld *et al.*, 1980: 183–84, 192–93, 217–29).

These findings imply that the dynamics of conflict and the dynamics of cooperation are fundamentally distinct and require different explanations. One way of moving in that direction is to analytically separate the various dimensions embodied in each of the terms. According to the way these terms are typically used in analysis, they refer to three distinct aspects of behavior: (1) agreement vs. disagreement (a similarity or difference in *opinion* on an issue); (2) positive vs. negative acts (*behavior* that

[19] Fighting either settles the issue outright or changes the emotional attachment one or both sides have toward the issue so that negotiation can proceed.

is seen as either desirable or undesirable); (3) friendship vs. hostility (*attitudes* reflecting psychological affect).

How these three dimensions interact is crucial for deciphering how a *relationship* emerges out of contention. It is assumed that differences in opinion (agreement–disagreement) shape behavior (i.e. the pattern of positive and negative acts), and behavior determines psychological affect (friendship and hostility). One of the great ironies of human interaction, pointed out by Coplin and O'Leary (1971: 9), is that conflictive (i.e. negative) acts are intended to change issue positions, but instead change affect. Typically, if an actor tries to resolve a disagreement on a salient issue by punishing another actor, this will generate hostility rather than any shift in issue position.

Spirals of conflict or cooperation occur when all three dimensions reinforce each other over time. In a conflict spiral, disagreement leads to the use of negative acts, which in turn produces hostility. The presence of hostility encourages more disagreement, which, if it persists, leads to a vicious cycle of disagreement–negative acts–hostility. One should not try to explain the pattern of negative and positive acts, but instead how "normal" interactions give rise to cooperation or conflict spirals and the effects these spirals have on determining the overall relationship between two actors. This underlines the point that *behavior* is something that comes out of and shapes a relationship. Actors do not simply behave conflictively or cooperatively; they *relate* to each other in conflictive or cooperative ways. A relationship involves all three dimensions – a pattern of agreement and disagreement, a pattern of exchanging positive and negative acts, and the residual attitude of friendship or hostility generated by the previous two patterns.

Figure 2.3 depicts how the three separate dimensions are related to each other and the various issue characteristics. What is important for understanding rivalry is that the pattern of friendship and hostility that emerges out of the pattern of agreement/disagreement and positive/negative acts has a tremendous impact on whether the issues dividing the two are defined on the basis of an actor or stake dimension. The issue dimension affects the pattern of agreement directly, as well as indirectly through its effect on the type of stakes and the nature of the stake proposal. The issue characteristics determine the pattern of cooperation and conflict, with friendship and hostility feeding back to reinforce the predominant way issues are being defined.

When an actor dimension is in effect, conflict is more likely because there is a strong tendency to reduce all contention to a single issue.

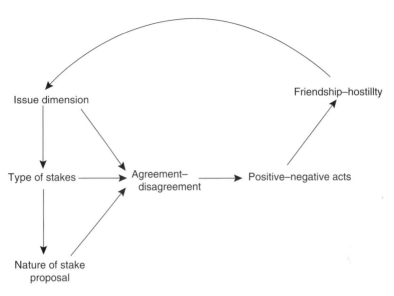

Figure 2.3 The role of issue variables and dimensions of cooperation and conflict
Source: Vasquez and Mansbach, 1984: 428

This encourages a pattern of persistent disagreement, since it reduces cross-cutting which moderates hostility (Dean and Vasquez, 1976). The presence of an actor dimension makes each side infuse concrete stakes with symbolic and eventually transcendent importance. This makes it likely that each side will offer proposals to dispose of the stakes on the basis of an unequal distribution of the costs and benefits. Such proposals promote disagreement and, if this continues, stalemates and intransigence become the order of the day, as proposals become less flexible and more zero-sum. In such a situation, conflict spirals are likely, with negative acts becoming the predominant way in which actors try to resolve differences (Vasquez and Mansbach, 1984: 428–29).

We are now in a position to delineate the most important characteristics of a rivalry with the relevant technical terms. A *rivalry* is a competitive relationship among equals that links stakes into issues on the basis of an actor dimension. The actor dimension results from a persistent disagreement and the use of negative acts which build up negative affect (psychological hostility). Hostility reinforces the actor dimension which gradually reduces all issues to a single overarching issue. Simultaneously, concrete stakes are transformed into symbolic and transcendent ones, and proposals for the disposition of stakes and the resolution of an issue distribute costs and benefits on an unequal basis. This makes for more disagreement, greater use of negative acts, and an intensification of hostility, which in turn reinforces the actor dimension. An escalating conflict spiral results, which creates an atmosphere in which crises are likely to be born.

Rivalry becomes a way of life. The relationship is difficult to change because each side is involved in a vicious circle in which hostility makes actors define issues in ways that are intractable and threatening, and actors become hostile, in part, because of the way they have defined the issues that divide them. The relative equality makes for an interdependent decision-making situation from which neither side can escape, because neither side can overcome the other.[20] Stalemate results and the issue festers. Frustration ensues, and a cost-benefit calculus of normal politics gives way to the feeling that what is of primary importance is not one's own value satisfaction, but hurting the other side.

As the issues between two equals take on these characteristics, it can be expected that the normal relationship between actors will cross a threshold in which a particular set of events sets off a conflict spiral that results in a crisis. The first crisis acts as a kind of baptism of the rivalry, crystallizing the underlying processes (Vasquez and Mansbach, 1984: 429). Rather than defining a rivalry as engaging in three or more militarized disputes within fifteen years (Diehl, 1985b: 1204) or as "enduring disputation" (Wayman, 1983: 18 n. 6), the conception offered here can predict when a pattern of crises will be likely. Because the underlying processes that have produced one crisis (the actor dimension and the resulting pattern of disagreement, negative acts, and hostility) are difficult to change, they will produce others. In a rivalry, the two sides expect their relationship to be punctuated by periodic crises.

What separates those few rivalries that have avoided war from the many that have not? Those that have avoided war have done so by breaking the pattern of crises and resolving the issues at hand. Those that have not, have adopted a set of foreign policy practices that have increased the likelihood of dangerous crises rather than reducing their occurrence. The actions they take bring them closer to war. They take these actions, in

---

[20] For this reason among others, I, unlike Wayman (1983: 18, n. 6) and Diehl and Goertz (1991: 33–35), make relative equality a defining characteristic of rivalry. Without equality there cannot be a competitive pattern where one side (for a significant period) is unable to predominate over the other, a major feature of true rivalry.

part, because the dominant global culture encourages them to do so and, in part, because some issues, namely territorial issues, are more prone to the use of coercion than other kinds of issues.

The Domain of the Analysis

In this book, I will concentrate on constructing an explanation of wars of rivalry. I am concerned with explaining the onset of these wars, delineating what factors are associated with them, and stipulating which of these factors are of causal significance. The explanations I outline will also attempt to account for the different kinds of wars of rivalry, especially total complex wars, i.e. world wars. Why are some wars between rivals limited, while others are total? Why do some wars of rivalry remain dyadic, while others involve numerous pairs? How do these complex wars draw in the various participants? Does a war between the two major protagonists in the system infect all other states, or is it the case that wars involving a minor state(s) draw in the major rivals?

Questions of this sort will be addressed by trying to delineate the factors that make wars limited or total on the one hand, and dyadic or complex, on the other. Although the answers that will be provided will apply only to wars of rivalry, it is hoped that understanding these dimensions will help in answering similar questions about wars of inequality. In this way, the typology fosters a cumulative body of knowledge of war, even though it requires separate explanations for different wars. Since the understanding of one kind of war will help us in understanding another, I will periodically allude to the types of wars I do not systematically examine when I think this analysis can shed some light on them.

Let me also note once again that the analysis presented in this book is based primarily upon studies of wars fought after 1815. While the wars after 1815 form a commonly demarcated period, there is reason to believe that all the wars fought in the modern global system (circa 1495 to the present) can be analyzed together. Because the wars from 1495 to 1815 and from 1816 to the present occur within the same historical structure, they should be caused by the same factors and therefore explicable by the same theory.

Since 1495, a number of critical events have occurred which may have had a fundamental effect on the causes, dynamics, and consequences of war that may make the wars after 1495 theoretically different from the wars that preceded them. First, two long-standing forms of political organization, the empire and the city-state, declined and were eventually replaced by a new form of organization, the nation-state (Braudel, 1966). This transformation was brought about by war, and, in turn, war seems to have been responsible for providing a competitive advantage to the nation-state as a form of organization (Tilly, 1975b, 1990; Zolberg, 1983: 280). Second, beginning in the late fifteenth and early sixteenth century, European states expanded and created a world economy (Wallerstein, 1974: 15; 1983: 305–6), which set the basis for a global political economy of what Wallerstein labels "the modern world-system." The obvious need to regulate and rule the world economy, at least in some form, gives rise to certain states taking a leadership role. Modelski (1978: 214) considers this the emergence of "the global political system." Third, prior to and throughout this time, the long transition from feudalism to capitalism and the continuing advances in science and technology produced a distinct culture of modernity, which was accentuated by industrialism and the development of bureaucracy. These four elements (the nation-state as a form of organization, capitalism, science and technology, and the culture of modernity) shaped the historical structure of the current modern global system and undoubtedly had an impact on why and how wars occurred and the consequences wars would have within the system. When attempting to explain war, I will be limiting my explanation to wars in this particular historical system, even though, on occasion, I may make allusion to earlier wars, like the Peloponnesian War and the Punic Wars, to make a specific point.

Although the reasons for limiting the scope of this analysis are justifiable, they are primarily theoretical reasons and do not reflect hard empirical or historical evidence that the causes of war in the current system are in fact (or of necessity) fundamentally different from those of earlier systems. The question of how much one can generalize about war within the current system from 1495 to the present, or between the current system and other systems, must be held open until further research is completed. I choose to limit the domain of the analysis mostly to err on the side of caution (although some will find this period much too long), and not because I am convinced that a general theory of war is impossible to construct. Since we have extensive data-based evidence on war only from 1815 to 1980 and limited data on war from 1495 to 1815, it is not realistic at this point to construct a general theory of war for all time.

I am concerned with wars of rivalry and particularly world war for several reasons. First, I focus on wars of rivalry because the empirical evidence is most plentiful on wars involving major states, with the most interesting findings dealing precisely with wars between major states that are relatively equal and with the two world wars. Second, the question of rivalry and whether and how it can be resolved without total war has been a major question in the twentieth century. Despite the ending of the Cold War, this question is still important at the regional level, where it is becoming increasingly ominous as more rivals choose to acquire nuclear weapons. The viability and feasibility of many proposals for establishing global and regional peace turn on empirical questions related to the causes of war between rivals and/or on how wars can be limited. Third, I focus on wars of rivalry and world wars, specifically, because it is these wars that realist theorists have claimed as the kinds of wars they are most able to explain, and because I believe that the realist approach to explaining war is fundamentally flawed. If international relations inquiry is ever to move beyond realism, then it will be necessary not simply to critique the realist paradigm (Vasquez, 1983a) and develop an alternative perspective (Mansbach and Vasquez, 1981), but to show that even at the heart of the paradigm (on the topics where realism claims to provide the best answers) alternative explanations can provide better answers. Thus, I have turned to these wars because of the availability of scientific evidence, their policy relevance, and their paradigmatic implications.

Because realist approaches and, more recently, neorealist explanations have so influenced theorizing about war, it is necessary to come to grips with that tradition – to indicate which of their insights are crucial to understanding war and peace, to outline where the tradition has gone wrong and what it has failed to see, and to reformulate what it can contribute to a new and broader perspective on the causes of war and the nature of peace. This is the subject of the next chapter.

3

Power Politics and War

The price of world power is death

Power politics behavior is a series of steps to war, not to peace. It is one of the great contradictions of the history of the modern global system that while the theory of power politics has been offered as the only realistic path to attain and secure peace, the practices of power politics have been associated with the outbreak of war. Power politics or *realpolitik* behavior may be defined as actions based on an image of the world as insecure and anarchic which leads to distrust, struggles for power, interest taking precedence over norms and rules, the use of Machiavellian stratagems, coercion, attempts to balance power, reliance on self-help, and the use of force and war as the *ultima ratio* (Vasquez, 1983a: 216).

Power politics behavior should be distinguished from power politics theory or realism, which is an abstract body of generalizations and prescriptions derived from and intended to shape practices in the world.[1] Much of the difficulty in creating a scientific study of world politics has stemmed from the failure to understand where power politics theory has come from, the role it has played in history, and how it both reflects and helped to create the historical conditions we have inherited. Power politics is not so much an explanation of world politics, as it is a form of behavior that must itself be explained (see Vasquez, 1983a: 215ff). Power politics theory is not simply a perspective on history, but a *datum* of history that should be subjected to scientific analysis.

When we look at power politics theory, we should not look for an explanation of war and peace that is either true or false, but we should realize that we are looking at a product of history – a set of varied reflections

---

[1] See Ashley (1981: 211, 215) for a similar distinction. The critical distinction is between theory and practice and not among *power politics, realpolitik,* or *realist,* all of which tend to refer to the same phenomenon. In this analysis, I try to reserve the term *realism* for an intellectual body of thought, whereas *power politics* and *realpolitik* (which I use synonymously) can refer to a body of practices or theory, depending on the context.

and thoughts about the practices of leaders and diplomats that have had certain consequences. My claim is that the practices of power politics have more often been associated with war rather than peace. This is not an accident, but tells us something about the kinds of foreign policy practices that lead to war and the intellectual context in which war is conceived, as well as something about the origin of, and role power politics theory has played, in creating and sustaining the modern global system.

I assume that any theory of world politics that has an impact on practice is not only a tool for understanding, but also helps construct a world. Highly influential theories, like power politics theory, must be interpreted in this larger context. The theory and practices of power politics helped in constructing the modern world of nation-states not only in terms of conceptualizing this world and thereby providing a mental construct, but more materially in global institution-building and culture-making. It helped provide both formal and informal structures that shaped behavior among the collectivities of the modern global system through the creation of customs.

For me, power politics theory provides a *description* of the kinds of behavior collectivities can be expected to engage in when war threatens, not because that behavior is natural or inherent given the structure of reality, but because realism has been accepted as a guide that tells leaders (and followers) the most appropriate way to behave in this situation, given the realities of this world. But the realities, indeed "the world" itself, have been constructed by this perspective and its practices. Power politics theory provides an accurate description of behavior to the extent that collectivities continue to adopt its perspective and/or practices. In short, it works as an intellectual guide, because its dominance has created a kind of self-fulfilling prophecy.[2] It can provide accurate predictions about how actors will respond both cognitively and behaviorally to certain war-threatening situations, but it is able to do this because power politics theory itself and the structures it has created have "taught" leaders to respond this way. The history of power politics theory provides a trace, a piece of archaeological evidence, about why some political actors adopt the foreign policies they do and take the actions they have.

---

[2] This view is consistent with Winch's (1958) notion that human behavior is rule-governed; consequently an explanation of behavior must take account of the rules which give rise to that behavior, in the first place, and guide it, in the second. Despite my agreement with Winch on this point, I do not accept his sharp distinction between social science and the physical sciences. On this question, my views are closer to Burton (1982: 23–25, 32–33) and Nicholson (1983, 1985). On realism's dominance see Smith (1987).

The foreign policies of collectivities are not made out of whole cloth; leaders do not come to power with a *tabula rasa*. They inherit both a national and global tradition about what foreign policy is all about, the range of actions that can be taken and the kinds of practices that can be engaged in. Leaders do not take actions through trial and error, but have learned from their own experience and the storehouse of traditional "wisdom" what to do in certain situations. The preeminent intellectual tradition that has guided leaders in their relations with equals in the modern global system (which has been since 1495 a Western-shaped system) has been power politics theory.

Power politics theory provides a rationale for policy and gives the actions of independent collectivities coherence by bringing together a set of related practices that define goals and means within a single tradition. For this reason, it makes sense to identify power politics as *one kind* of foreign policy. This foreign policy is formulated by decision makers drawing upon a catalog of *realpolitik* practices and its traditions to deal with current situations. In the process, they reinforce, adapt, build upon, and change those practices and traditions, and thereby draw upon lessons of the past and create new lessons (and occasionally new practices) for the future.

The theory of power politics provides a description of the kinds of behavior that lead to war, because in many ways it has served as a collective memory of the actions associated with the great traumatic wars of the past and adds on to this memory its own feeble attempts to prevent such actions from recurring. The most notable proponents of power politics – Thucydides, Machiavelli, Clausewitz, and Hans Morgenthau – all wrote in reaction to periods of severe warfare and a breakdown of their regional or global order. The same is true of Hobbes, a major source of contemporary realist images. These individuals were seared by their experiences and derived from them the fundamental lessons that became the hallmark of a power politics image of the world. Their worlds were *realpolitik* worlds and the lessons they derived from their experiences captured a historical reality, but not all history, not all worlds.

Other worlds have existed. The *Pax Romana* provided stability and order unknown in the fifth century BC of Thucydides. Italy after unification was not Machiavellian Italy. The world of the Concert of Europe was not the world of Adolf Hitler. Long-distance global trade in the nineteenth century lacked the peril of trade with the Orient in the days of Marco Polo. What is significantly different about these other worlds is that they have ways of making authoritative allocations without going to war. In addition, the issues they resolve are issues that the loser can afford to lose. In the long run, the loser expects to derive benefits from the stability of the system and future victories that will outweigh any current loss. Not only do *realpolitik* worlds have few non-violent allocative mechanisms, they raise life and death issues, which make it difficult for actors to live with each other. Clearly the practices of foreign policy in *realpolitik* worlds are going to be different, as will be the frequency of war.

If this analysis is correct, then not all periods should experience the same amount of war. The empirical evidence supports this expectation. Not all historical periods (see Levy, 1983: 138–44; Wallensteen, 1984) and not all actors (or dyads) experience the same amount of war (see Bremer, 1980; Small and Singer, 1982: ch. 10). This suggests that war is not as culturally acceptable in some times and places as in others. In fact, not only does the frequency of war differ, but the goals of war, the rules of its conduct, even the reasons justifying war vary from time to time (Johnson, 1975; 1981).

All of this underlines the fact that war is part of a global political culture and that the practices derived from the lessons of war are meant to cope with and survive war, not avoid it. In that sense, it is not surprising that a power politics image of the world and a foreign policy based on it will lead actors to take steps that will bring them progressively closer to the brink of war. The culture of war, like the culture of vendetta and dueling, is a trap. Once in the culture, one must adopt the image and practices of the culture in order to survive, but to do that one must fight. Realism may provide clues to the dynamics of processes that lead to war, but it will provide little aid in understanding how such worlds of war originate or can be superseded.

Power politics theory does not provide a complete explanation of world politics because it confuses one form of politics with all politics; it does not provide an accurate explanation of the causes of war and of peace because the consequences it predicts for its policies do not occur. The scientific inaccuracy of realism is evident in the fact that the practices it recommends for dealing with a war-threatening situation do not lead to peace but to war; indeed they often increase the prospect of war. This indicates that the underlying theory of war and peace from which these practices are derived is flawed.

An adequate theory of world politics would seek to discover when policy makers adopt a power politics image of the world, what kinds of behavior this image fosters, and when such behavior results in war. This implies that non-power-politics images and behavior have existed in history and that an adequate theory should be able to delineate the conditions that promote power politics behavior and non-power politics behavior, and how a system or issue area characterized by one mode of behavior might be transformed to the other. Such an approach would provide an authentic alternative to realism, because it would not only explain everything realism purported to explain but would also be able to discover and explain a vast area of behavior that realism ignores (see Vasquez, 1983a: 216). In terms of an explanation of war, this requires identifying other kinds of foreign policy and other practices to see whether they are associated with war, and specifying with what kinds of wars power politics is associated. Of course, while it is expected that power politics behavior will be associated with certain kinds of war, it should not be assumed that the absence of power politics behavior or realist beliefs will produce peace. The latter would only be the case if there were a single path to war.

Foreign Policy and War

In this book, I will focus on the foreign policy practices of power politics that lead to wars of rivalry. I am interested in identifying a specific set of foreign policy practices that increase the probability of war. To do this it is important to distinguish foreign policy *practices* from other aspects of foreign policy. Three interrelated aspects of foreign policy are relevant for assessing the relationship between foreign policy and war. First is the substantive *policy* (the bundle of goals and means that provide the overall guiding light for leaders *vis-à-vis* a specific issue and the actors contending on that issue).[3] Second is *foreign policy behavior* (the acts [words and deeds] collectivities take toward each other and the resulting pattern of interactions that emerges). Third are the *foreign policy practices* that collectivities follow in conducting their diplomacy, including the implementation of their policy. Foreign policy practices are special kinds of behavior, like alliance making, that have become sufficiently customary and institutionalized that they take on a recognizable "form of life" that

---

[3] Of course, a state has many policies, not one. It can have several foreign policies on a single issue that may emphasize different aspects of the issue and in the process may end up contradicting each other. It must also be kept in mind that most nation-states, most of the time, do not have a clearly coordinated policy they consciously follow on most issues. Nevertheless, on the most salient issues, and especially on those that end up in war, states usually have recognizable policies that they have followed, and these can be identified because the makers of these policies as well as contemporary observers often discuss these policies and even give them names, like containment or mercantilism.

distinguishes this behavior from the other interactions that surround it. In this sense, practices are similar to games in that they are social creations, they have their own rules, and these rules give rise to a set of expectations about why certain actions are taken and what future actions can be anticipated.[4]

Each of these aspects of foreign policy (policy, behavior, practices) can be a factor in the onset of war, but some are more important than others, and which are seen as the most crucial has important research implications. If it is assumed that certain kinds of goals (and their attendant means) lead to war, then war can be explained by asking what makes states have those goals. If it is assumed that certain kinds of behavior (Hermann and Mason, 1980) or practices (e.g. *realpolitik* bargaining styles) lead to war, then war can be explained by asking why states take those actions or adopt such practices. To understand how foreign policy is related to war, and specifically how power politics is related to war, it is necessary to distinguish more carefully substantive policy, behavior, and practices and then delineate the possible roles each may play in the onset of war. Once this is done, we will understand where realist theories were correct about war and where they were misled.

Foreign policy *behavior* is clearly different from policy in that *policy* is a mental construct shared by individuals, whereas foreign policy behavior refers to what political actors say and do to one another. *Practices* differ from *policies* in that practices are sets of behavior and not purely mental constructs. Practices are subordinated to policies and can serve a number of different policies; whereas policies (in normally functioning states) are never subordinated to practices. A practice is a set of behaviors that have become institutionalized, and for that reason can be interpreted as a special kind of behavior. Just as medicine involves certain practices, like surgery, with identifiable procedures, tools, and even rituals that permit the doctor to achieve his or her ends, so too does diplomacy. Alliance making, negotiation, and war itself are all practices within the repertoire of diplomacy. These practices are sets of behavior that evolved over time and are an historical inheritance that can be drawn upon in the appropriate situation. Practices are ways of dealing with certain situations, usually difficult and dangerous situations. While a political actor will engage

---

[4] The term "form of life" is derived from Wittgenstein who argued that actions and utterance always presuppose a form of life (see M. Shapiro, 1981: 14). Practices are distinguishable from other behavior in that actors are more conscious that a particular and temporary form of life is being engaged in. For a discussion of how the global system can be defined in terms of its common practices, see Kratochwil (1986: 33).

in a variety of behaviors to support its policy, it may also adopt certain historically recognized practices to aid its cause. At times its own behavior may be so ingenious and novel and successful that it may institute a new practice (like subversion or terrorism) that future generations adopt.

Elsewhere (Vasquez, 1986) I have created a taxonomy of the major kinds of foreign policy in the modern global system relevant to the security issue area. This was done by grouping various policies that could be found throughout history, like balance of power, coercive diplomacy, and concert of power, into "families of foreign policies." Six families were identified – power politics, hegemony, messianism, non-involvement, clientelism, and world order.[5] Some kinds of policies, simply because of their goals, are much more apt to produce war. The goals of hegemonic policies, for example, often result in war, as do most messianic policies; whereas the goals of non-involvement (isolationism) are not likely to result in war. Goals alone, however, are not determinative; means are also important. The goals of world order policies, like those of the victors at the Congress of Vienna or at Versailles, can be as grand in scope as those of hegemony, but in the absence of unilateral attempts to impose an order the question of force and war does not arise. In contrast, the policies of power politics lack the grandiose goals of world order, hegemony, or messianism, but because they place unilateral efforts and the use of force at the center of world politics, they are often associated with war.

These examples suggest two important points about the relationship between foreign policy and war. First, the policy of power politics is not exclusively associated with war; other policies, namely hegemony and messianism, are also likely to result in war. Second, as a *policy*, power politics is related to war not because of its goals, but because of the means associated with it. The first point tells us something about why realist theorists thought power politics was not associated with war. For them, war is brought about because of unlimited ambitions (see Morgenthau,

---

[5] A detailed description of each of the families of foreign policies is provided in Vasquez (1986: 214–18). Suffice it to say here that families of foreign policies are identified by grouping together specific foreign policies that share one or more common characteristic. Thus, the policies of coercive diplomacy, balance of power, deterrence, containment, and spheres of influence are policies that are grouped together as a family of policies that can be labeled power politics since each of these policies tends to emphasize interest and reject moral constraints and norms, employs and/or threatens force, is concerned primarily with the goal of managing the struggle for power, and is implemented unilaterally. The policies of hegemony differ from those of the power politics family in that their goals are concerned with establishing hegemony over territory and people and hence are much more expansionist and revisionist.

1960: ch. 3; Gilpin, 1981, 1989). They look at history and they see revisionist states with newly acquired power adopting the policies of hegemony or messianism as the main source of war. To them, war results from the adoption of certain substantive policies, and they discuss the causes of war in terms of what makes those policies possible, namely changes in power (Gilpin, 1981; Dehio, 1962). For the more pessimistic realists (like Gilpin, Dehio, and Organski and Kugler [1980: 63]), such fundamental policy challenges arise inevitably out of long-term changes in power; for others, like Morgenthau (1951) and Kennan (1951), such challenges can be avoided by states learning to refrain from pursuing hegemonic claims or moralistic tendencies and, instead, keeping their goals confined to their immediate national interests (defined in term of territorial sovereignty and political independence).

Even though realists disagree about the extent to which self-restraint is possible, they agree that what are called hegemonic and messianic policies here are the main sources of war. They also agree that the policies of power politics (balance of power, coercive diplomacy, etc.) are the best defense against the policies of messianism and hegemony. They have overestimated, however, the extent to which such defensive stances can avoid war and greatly underestimated the extent to which the behavior and practices associated with realist *policies* are themselves sources of war. Thus, while realists have identified two of the major policy sources of war, they have failed to identify the third.

A full explanation of why power politics is associated with war must look not at power politics as a policy of goals, but at power politics in terms of the behavior it generates and the practice it adopts. When I say that power politics is associated with war, I am referring principally to the practices and behavior associated with power politics, rather than the substantive goals. It is my argument that the practices that have evolved out of the history of power politics, and the behavior power politics theorists have prescribed on how to handle security-threatening situations, do not prevent war, but *reflect* the way equals, especially those who have become rivals, go to war.

One of the interesting things about rivalry is that, while relative equality does not require rivalry, once rivalry emerges, it tends to produce within the modern global system the same kind of behavior and a reliance on the same set of practices regardless of the kind of policy (hegemony, messianism, or power politics) that produces the initial threat. Because I believe this is the case, realism as a theory aids in developing a description of how equals go to war, but to explain why equals go to war, it is necessary to ask why realist practices and behavior result in war. This will be the subject of Chapter 5, which will look at power politics as a sequence of behavior (a series of steps between equals) that leads to a certain kind of war. If one can explain why that sequence results in war and why the steps that produce the sequence are taken, then one has gone a long way in identifying one of the main correlational patterns that leads to the onset of dyadic wars of rivalry. If one can add to this, as I hope to do in Chapter 7, an explanation of how wars expand, then one has provided a fairly comprehensive explanation of wars of rivalry. Before turning to those analyses, it remains to be seen why realist explanations of war as a result of changes in power do not provide an adequate understanding of the subject.

Power-Based Explanations of War

The first thing that must be kept in mind when looking at realist explanations of war is that they are not all the same, some are much more precise than others. In addition, not all suffer from the same problems. Nevertheless, from the broad sweeping claims of Toynbee on the rise and decline of empires to the *realpolitik* policy eruditions of Kissinger and other Cold Warriors about the balance of power and power vacuums, there lies an ambiguous, unverified, but oft-repeated and firmly held view of the nature of reality. What exactly can this realist view tell us about the war, and is what it tells us true? If it is not always true, are there situations in which interstate behavior conforms to that depicted by the realists?

Since I have already discussed the traditional balance of power account of war, I will not treat systematically all of the various realist emendations of this argument that have been made. Instead, I will concentrate on those contemporary accounts that still focus on power or changes of power as the most important cause of war. These include Gilpin's "neo-realist" reformulation of hegemonic theory of war, Organski's criticism of balance of power theory and his power transition explanation of the onset of war, and Modelski's long cycle theory, which sees global war as arising out of a leadership struggle brought about by long-term capability shifts in the global political economy. Not all of these explicitly link themselves to realism (see Kugler and Organski, 1989: 172–73; Thompson, 1988: 44),[6] but all

---

[6] Thompson (1988: 44) objects to others' having categorized Modelski's long cycle analysis as neo-realist. While I would not see it as neo-realist in the sense of structural realism, I do treat it as a power approach because the major emphasis on shifts in capability makes it a rival explanation to the approach being developed here. Nevertheless, the recognition that there is a global political system with a global leader that provides global

these accounts have attempted to make power-based explanations more sophisticated by adapting and changing the traditional folklore to answer critics and take account of complexities and subtleties that earlier views skimmed over. While each of these three explanations gets further away from traditional realism in order to answer deficiencies in that approach, each still clings to the notion of changes in power as critical in explaining the onset of war. Together they constitute the most sophisticated accounts of the onset of war that focus on the structure of power. Any non-realist explanation of war must show that these accounts are seriously deficient and that it can offer a more plausible explanation.

Gilpin's work is important because it provides a reformulation of realist philosophy of history in terms of an economic logic. Gilpin (1981: 197) argues that war has been "the primary means of resolving" a disequilibrium in the international system between the structure of the system (which reflects the interests of those who created the structure) and a new (re)distribution of power (see also Gilpin, 1987: 55, 351; 1989: 18–19, 25–26). Gilpin assumes that the most powerful state in the system, the hegemon, builds an international system to reflect and protect its interests. No attempt is made to change this system unless the expected benefits exceed the expected costs (Gilpin, 1981: 50). As the hegemon declines and a new "power" ascends, the latter will not only be able (capable) to change the system, but presumably will be motivated to do so because (what others have called) "the mobilization of bias" (Bachrach and Baratz, 1962) of the political system is so great that the anticipated benefits of changing the system are worth the expected costs (of war). The main evidence to support this explanation is the sweeping view of history that sees the rise and fall of empires and hegemonies as the rise and decline of power. War, in turn, is seen as the means by which empires and hegemonies are built, protected, and destroyed.

There are several problems with this as an explanation for the onset of war. The first is how the concept of power is used to explain the onset of war. The inference that, just because there is a capability for war, there will be a motivation for war is much too facile. There may not be any motivation to challenge the hegemon, and, even if there is, that may not lead to a challenge to the system. Nor can it be assumed that war would be the only means that would resolve such challenges if they did occur. In short, this

political management clearly rejects the anarchy assumption of Waltz (1979, 1988) and is compatible with the world society/issue politics paradigm that is the basis of this analysis (Burton et al., 1974; Mansbach and Vasquez, 1981).

explanation confuses possibility with causality; just because two major states are able to fight does not explain *why* they do.[7] How war emerges from a disequilibrium is not elaborated nor really discussed. Hardly any detail is given about what happens during the long time lag between the disequilibrium and the onset of war.

It is assumed that just because a state may be capable of challenging another, it will. Such explanations are psychologically persuasive in a culture long used to realist thinking, but the prediction needs to be checked empirically. When this is done the great anomaly for hegemonic theory is the surpassing of Britain by the US. From the end of the nineteenth century to 1945, the US in terms of its economic capacity replaces Britain as the hegemon of the global system and yet there is no war between them. As the US increased in power it did not challenge Britain any more frequently than it had from 1776 to 1895; indeed it threatened it even less as it became more powerful. Nor did the US show any great motivation to use its capability as a hegemon despite a great "power vacuum." Only in 1947 (when practically forced by Britain) did the US finally accept a hegemonic leadership role. These three historical events – the absence of war, the reduction in conflict, and the unwillingness to play a hegemonic role – are not what the hegemonic theory expects and must be explained away.

A second problem with hegemonic theory is the nature of the evidence marshaled on its behalf. It is grand and overarching rather than precise and falsifiable; as a result, there are few safeguards against oversimplification and overgeneralization. While wars may occur in some instances when the hegemon is overtaken by another state, they need not occur in every instance, as demonstrated by the rise of the US during the *Pax Britannica*. Since the explanation can be evaluated only on the few instances of hegemonic transition that exist, failure to account adequately for one or more cases is a serious flaw.

It also seems that the hegemonic wars that do occur do not evolve in the manner that the explanation leads one to expect. This is a critical problem for all three power explanations in one form or another. From the perspective of hegemonic theory, as well as power transition or long cycle theory one would explain the onset of World War I by saying that the war occurs

---

[7] Gilpin himself seems somewhat ambivalent about this point. In a more recent statement, Gilpin (1987: 55) says that a redistribution of power accentuates conflict between the rising and declining states, and: "If this conflict is *not resolved* [my emphasis] it can lead to ... a hegemonic war ..." This qualification, however, is abandoned later on p. 351 when he says that, "The historical record suggests that the transition to a new hegemon has always been attended by ... a hegemonic war."

because Germany is surpassing Britain in capability and challenging it for hegemonic leadership.[8] This all makes sense until one remembers that it is the US that becomes the number one power, not Germany at the close of the nineteenth century (Bremer, 1980: 64; Kugler and Organski, 1989: 181). Even if one accepts the various *ad hoc* explanations of why the US and UK did not fight or of why Germany and the US were not global rivals, it is hardly established, although often assumed, that World War I starts because of Anglo-German rivalry. World War I does not start because of German challenges to British hegemony, but with a dispute between Austria-Hungary and Serbia, which is linked to the French–German dispute over Alsace-Lorraine via alliances with Russia. Instead of seeking to fight Britain in 1914, Germany sought to keep it neutral. This does not sound like a war that is caused by a hegemonic struggle.

Likewise, the explanation for World War II, a hegemonic war if there ever was one, is wanting. By 1939, clearly it is the US that is the most powerful state in the system. Yet the US was brought into the war by Japan, a comparatively weak state that could not be seen as a rising hegemonic rival (particularly in economic terms) of the US. Japan attacked not because of the exigency of some alleged power or economic cycle, but because of a complex set of specific factors. The ways in which the two world wars of the twentieth century occurred and evolved are major anomalies for the hegemonic theory of war, as well as the power transition and long cycle explanations.

A third problem with hegemonic theory is that several of its causal inferences need to be established better. Even if changes in capability were to be shown to be associated with the rise and decline of empires or hegemons, it is not clear that these changes actually cause these events. Changes in capability may be coincidental. Since empires and hegemons come and go, states change and grow, and wars occur every twenty to thirty years, it is easy to assume an association among all three, when in fact they may be three independent, but regularly occurring phenomena. This is especially the case when no precise time frame is employed and no actual correlation calculated.

When a correlation is calculated as with Spiezio (1990), it is not very strong. Spiezio's test is limited to a study of British hegemony from 1815 to 1939. While he finds that hegemonic power (generally) is inversely related to the frequency of war, all this may mean is that after major world wars, when power is concentrated in a hegemon, the wars that occur

---

[8] See Gilpin (1989: 23, 33–34), for his discussion of the two world wars.

are small. More importantly, not all tests show a statistically significant relationship, and those that are significant account for only 33 percent of the variance, at most. For great power wars, which is the subset hegemonic theory is trying to explain; only 22 percent of the variance is accounted for (Spiezio, 1990: 176, 179, Tables 2, 4). As Spiezio (1990: 179) concludes, the magnitude of these correlations does not support "Gilpin's view that hegemonic power is the single most important factor" in explaining war. Of even more significance is that most wars that are fought by Britain while it is a rising hegemon (ten of twelve wars) are fought at the peak of its power cycle from 1845 to 1860 (Spiezio, 1990: 175, 178), something which does not strictly conform to the logic of hegemonic theory.

Finally, tests of hegemonic theory that also draw upon the work of Wallerstein (1974, 1980) raise serious questions. In one of the earliest tests of hegemonic theory, Raimo Väyrynen (1983) analyzes the economic history of the post-Napoleonic period to classify world history into four stages of a hegemonic cycle – ascending hegemony, hegemonic victory, hegemonic maturity, and hegemonic decline. He then examines the amount of war among major states in each stage. Significant major power warfare occurs in all stages except hegemonic decline (see Väyrynen, 1983: 411, Table 5). World wars occur during ascending hegemony when they are expected, but also in the period of hegemonic victory, when they are not. They occur in periods of accelerated and decelerated economic growth. Likewise, Boswell and Sweat (1991: 139–40) find no statistical association between war intensity and hegemonic ascent, victory or decline. They do, however, find mature hegemony and hegemonic power (generally) negatively associated with intensity. The latter, along with a similar finding of Spiezio, suggests that when a single country has overwhelming power, large wars are not fought. This implies that Gilpin's insights about how peace is sustained may have some merit and will be taken up again in Chapter 8, but his explanation that wars occur primarily because of declining power appears incorrect. It provides no explanation of most interstate wars, and it encounters a number of empirical and logical problems with the few cases it does seek to explain.

These problems with hegemonic theory are further aggravated by the theory's reluctance to specify clearly what evidence will falsify it. Thus, Gilpin (1989: 26) argues that the theory predicts neither the initiator of the war nor its consequences. In the end, it seems that hegemonic theory does not even outline the sufficient conditions of war. Gilpin (1989: 17) states that: "The structure of the international system at the outbreak of such a war is a necessary, but not a sufficient cause of the war." The failure to discuss sufficient conditions of war means that the major realist theory of war does not specify the main factors that produce wars. In practice, however, it actually turns out that these necessary structural conditions either produce the unspecified sufficient conditions or act like sufficient conditions since the transition to a new hegemon is always attended by war. This vacillation (which, as will be seen, is even more problematic with the power transition explanation) allows defenders of the theory to give an apparently plausible explanation of the onset of world war, while at the same time not having to explain the absence of war in the presence of every major structural power change in the system.

Many of the problems of the realist and hegemonic analysis of war stem from the imprecision and lack of detail in philosophy of history, and a number are resolved by Organski's (1958: ch. 12) power transition explanation. One of the great advances Organski makes over the traditional folklore is that he makes the theory more generalizable while making it testable. War occurs when the capability of the major challenger in the system catches up to and surpasses the capability of the dominant state. It is the transition of the number two state supplanting the number one state that leads to war. This analysis makes it clear that a relative balance of power, i.e. relative equality, should not prevent war, but reflect the condition in which war is most likely. Peace should occur when there is a preponderance of power.

The logic and structure of Organski's explanation is superior to that of hegemonic theory. If Organski is correct, then it would seem that whenever a power transition between the strongest states approaches or occurs, there should be a war. The problem with this expectation is that the logic of the analysis makes it possible to interpret the power transition as either a sufficient or a necessary condition of major war, and both interpretations have been made (cf. Organski and Kugler, 1980 and Houweling and Siccama, 1988a). While the theoretical analysis in Organski (1958: ch. 12) and Organski and Kugler (1980) does not always make it clear that they intended to confine their explanation to necessary conditions, their research design and subsequent elaborations by Kugler do (Kugler and Organski, 1989: 179). Thus, they identify the wars which they think require a power transition and then see if every war of this type is preceded by a power transition any time twenty years prior to the war. This means that if their hypothesis is correct, major wars will not be preceded by a period where the dominant state and its allies have a preponderance of power.

Organski and Kugler (1980) begin their data analysis by testing their claim that the balance of power is associated with neither peace nor war. They do this by demonstrating that there is no statistically strong relationship between the distribution of capability (as measured by GNP) and war (see Organski and Kugler, 1980: 52, Table 1.5); i.e. war can occur when there is an equal or unequal distribution of power. (This lends credence to the view developed in Chapter 2 that differences in capability *per se* do not cause or prevent war.)

Organski and Kugler then seek to demonstrate that war occurs only with equality of power and overtaking, i.e. a power transition. They show that a power transition affects the war involvement of the top two or three states (what Organski and Kugler call "contenders"), but it does not affect when other major states go to war (see Organski and Kugler, 1980: 52, Table 1.5).[9] In a study confined to 1860–1939, they find that among contenders war breaks out only when a power transition has occurred; a finding that produces a moderate 0.50 (Tau C) (in their Table 1.5). They then go on to show (Organski and Kugler, 1980: 55) that the more rapidly the transition occurs, the greater the danger of war.

These findings apply only to the very strongest states in the system. Non-contenders – weaker major states, like Italy, and major states in the periphery (i.e. outside Europe prior to 1945), like Japan, the US, and China – are unaffected by the power transition. There is no statistically significant relationship between capability (GNP) distributions and when major states in the periphery or other major states in the center fight wars (see Organski and Kugler, 1980: 52, Table 1.7). If differences in capability do not affect the other major states, what does? Apparently, they are drawn into wars when there is a tightening alliance structure in the system (Organski and Kugler, 1980: 55–56).

These results make it clear that the power transition explanation is applicable only to the strongest two or three states in the (European) Center and not to all major states. It is curious that the power transition effect would turn out to be so limited, given the great theoretical emphasis placed in realist analysis on the role of power and changes in power for

---

[9] Organski and Kugler (1980: 44–45) operationally define *contenders* as the strongest state in the central system and any other state that has at least 80 percent of the GNP of the strongest state. If no state meets the 80 percent threshold, then the three strongest states are considered contenders. It should be noted that because the strongest state in the *central* system is taken as a criterion, the United States is not considered a contender until 1945, even though Organski and Kugler admit that the US had the highest GNP in the world by the end of the nineteenth century.

shaping behavior. As a result, while Organski and Kugler's findings lend some support to their proposition, they also make it clear that the power transition is an inappropriate and inadequate explanation for most of the interstate wars that have been fought in human history. In this sense, the empirical findings can be seen as indicating a deficiency in the explanatory power of the proposition, especially since it is unclear why the logic of the power transition would apply only to the top states and not to all states, or at least to all major states (see Houweling and Siccama, 1988a: 95).

Do the findings support the conclusion that the power transition accounts for at least the wars among the strongest states? Although these findings appear impressive and are highly suggestive, some important caveats must be noted. First, the findings are primarily a function of the two world wars, which is a very limited sample. For various reasons the actual data base of Organski and Kugler's (1980) test is confined to the Franco-Prussian War, the Russo-Japanese War, and the two world wars, which they admit might mean the results are produced by chance (Kugler and Organski, 1989: 180). Clearly, the last two wars are very relevant to the theory; however, the inclusion of the first two without including a number of other (basically dyadic) wars of that type makes less sense.[10] In addition, it is not clear whether the relevant wars prior to 1815 or wars between regional rivals would fit the power transition explanation. Thompson's (1983b) analysis of global wars prior to 1815 suggests that attacks are often premature (occurring before a transition) and that some global wars occur without any transition at all (see Kugler and Organski, 1989: 182–84 for their response).

More problems are encountered if the power transition is treated as a sufficient condition for major war. Here one must identify all power transitions and then see if they lead to war. This allows for the possibility of there being power transitions among contenders without a war. Houweling and Siccama (1988a, see also 1988b: ch. 9) provide such a test using a twenty-year test period. Employing data collected by Doran and Parsons (1980) that measures capability on the basis of economic, demographic, and military indicators,[11] they find a slight relationship between

---

[10] Organski and Kugler (1980: 45–46) eliminate all interstate wars which have a major state on each side if: (a) the war did *not* have a higher level of battle deaths than any previous war and (b) the war did not result in a loss of territory and population for the defeated.

[11] This measure, probably because of its emphasis on population and the size of the standing armies, produces certain "power transitions" that Organski and Kugler and most others would not accept as valid, such as China overtaking the US in 1960 and the USSR overtaking the US in 1970 (see Houweling and Siccama, 1988a: 98 for the data).

a power transition and war for all major states and slightly more of a relationship when the sample is confined to the top three or four major states during the 1816–1975 period. The latter provides further evidence that Organski and Kugler are correct in seeing the power transition as something which affects the top three or four states, rather than all major states, and Houweling and Siccama (1988a: 101) conclude by supporting the power transition explanation.

However, a close inspection of Houweling and Siccama's (1988a: 100–1) findings, which are reprinted in Table 3.1, raises questions. It turns out that the association between different types of power distribution and war for all major states is very weak (the highest Tau C equaling 0.159), so this general hypothesis should be rejected, even though it is statistically significant and slightly higher than Organski and Kugler's (1980: 52) – 0.03. More importantly, the association for the top three to four states is only 0.306. This is quite a reduction from the 0.50 Tau C that Organski and Kugler (1980: 52) had found. If one looks at the actual numbers of cases in which a power transition occurs, then it is clear that, at the most, only about half the cases result in war (for Organski and Kugler five in ten power transition cases are associated with war, and for Houweling and Siccama eight result in war and nine do not). What this means is that the power transition effect is not very strong. It has no effect on major states in the periphery or on major states that are not among the top two or three states – and, among the very top states that experience a power transition, their chances of going to war are as great as their chances of avoiding war. Clearly, since both the set of eight cases that go to war and the set of nine that do not go to war experience a power transition, there is likely to be some other factor that is causing the onset of war. This raises the possibility, particularly in light of the findings on other major states, that the relationship between power transitions and war is random or spurious.

This suspicion is further fueled by the use of a twenty-year time lag by both Organski and Kugler and Houweling and Siccama. While some time lag is reasonable, a twenty-year lag poses a problem in that major wars tend to occur in the modern system around every twenty to thirty years (see Denton and Phillips, 1968; Small and Singer, 1982: 150–56), raising the possibility that any association between a power transition and war is coincidental.[12] This turns out to be a serious problem, because if a ten-year time span is taken to see if a war occurs either just before

---

[12] This is also a problem with Doran and Parsons (1980) who employ a twenty-year period in the test of their power cycle.

Table 3.1. *Houweling and Siccama's findings on the power transition*

Power distributions and the incidence of war (all major powers), 1816–1975							
	Unequal			Equal, on overtaking			Overtaking
	20%	10%	5%	20%	10%	5%		N
No war	58	63	70	14	9	2	14	86
War	17	20	21	4	1	0	12	33
	75	83	91	18	10	2	26	119

	Tau C	Significance
20%	0.15931	0.0167
10%	0.12796	0.0255
5%	0.14914	0.0477

Power distributions and the incidence of war (three or four strongest nations), 1816–1975							
	Unequal			Equal no overtaking			Overtaking
	20%	10%	5%	20%	10%	5%		N
No war	10	12	15	6	4	1	9	25
War	2	3	3	1	0	0	8	11
	12	15	18	7	4	1	17	36

	Tau C	Significance
20%	0.30556	0.0327
10%	0.27469	0.0459
5%	0.30247	0.0267

Source: Houweling and Siccama, 1988a: 100–01

or after a power transition, then the relationship disappears. In a much more systematic text than Organski and Kugler, Peter Wallensteen (1981: 80–81) examined all pairs of major states from 1816 to 1976 and found no relationship between war and one major state catching up with and economically surpassing another. Employing a measure based on iron and steel production, Wallensteen found a power transition occurring in eleven of fifty-three pairs of major states, but in these eleven pairs war took place within ten years only *three* times. Of these three instances, only two are really legitimate examples – Prussia surpassing Austria and the Seven Weeks War of 1866, Prussia surpassing France and the Franco-Prussian War of 1870. The third case is China surpassing France in 1960 and the previous Korean War in 1950 when China technically attacked France as part of the United Nations.

Equally important are the instances of transition that do *not* lead to war. Wallensteen points out that Russia surpassed France at the end of the 1890s and instead of war there was an alliance. Likewise, in the classic case, which Organski (1958: 323–25) himself recognizes as an exception (the major power transition of our time), the US surpassing Britain in the 1890s does not lead to war, but to a collaborative and peaceful transition.

As a sufficient condition of war, power transition does not seem to lead to war on any regular basis. Sometimes it does and sometimes it does not. Often Organski and Kugler are misread as dealing with sufficient conditions because they attempt to specify the conditions under which a power transition will result in war; namely, that one state must be dissatisfied with the status quo including the rules of the game the dominant state has set up. If this is the case, then it appears that political variables (particularly such non-realist variables as norms, rules of the game, the political structure of the global system, and the amount of political institutionalization) are more potent than the distribution of power. Even though the political structure may be created and sustained by the political power of the victors of the last major war, what determines a peaceful or violent transition is not the power shift, but whether the rising state(s) can be accommodated by the existing political order, including the rules it has for bringing about change (see Kugler, 1990: 209–11).

Here the work of Doran (1971, 1991) is important because he makes it clearer that while a power cycle increases the probability of war, whether war will actually break out is determined by the ability of the global political arrangements to handle new issues. To the extent that the power transition thesis can be reformulated to be made more adequate, the focus seems to be to de-emphasize the power variable and begin to think in broader terms. Organski's (1958) criticisms of balance of power were an important step in that direction and the more recent work of Kugler and Organski (1989: 172–73; Kugler, 1990: 209–11) has extended that tendency. Thus, the criticism that balance of power is associated with war, the notion that peace is associated with preponderance of power, and the recognition that power transitions do not lead to war except under certain conditions not directly related to power variables are all steps in the right direction. Nevertheless, the core of the power transition explanation is the logic it provides for how shifts in power will bring about war, and this seems inadequate.

Nowhere is this more evident than in trying to apply this logic to the specific details of the onset of World War I and World War II. Organski and Kugler (1980: 43–45) argue that major wars have their origin in the second ranked contending state overtaking the first. Indeed, Bremer (1980: 69) shows empirically that this is often the case. One would assume, then, that the two world wars result from the second-ranked state overtaking and attacking the first. Organski and Kugler (1980: 58) maintain that prior to World War I, Germany caught up with Britain (in GNP) by 1905 and by 1913 had surpassed Britain. It then fell behind Britain after 1919 and caught up again in the early twenties, retaining a small advantage for the rest of the decade (Organski and Kugler, 1980: 59). On this basis the two world wars produced the aggregate statistical findings.

A closer look raises some problems. First, Germany is the second-ranked state only because the US is not included in the contender sample until 1945. To eliminate the US as a contender because the US did not view itself as part of the central system or because Britain and the US did not view themselves as mutually threatening or as members of competing regimes (Organski and Kugler, 1980: 45; Kugler, 1990: 209) is too convenient. Certainly, the US viewed itself as a rival to Britain in the Western Hemisphere and as a player in the Pacific, and their relations, prior to 1895, were hostile. During this time Irish immigrants in the US also provided a domestic political incentive for "twisting the (British) Lion's tail." All these factors indicate that the US cannot be assumed automatically to be a "satisfied ally" at the period of transitions as Organski and Kugler assume (see Kugler 1990: 209).

In this regard, power transition theory is particularly deficient in explaining why Britain found Germany more of a threat than the US given America's economic and naval capability. Why as Britain began to decline, did it choose to resolve its outstanding issues with rising nations, like the US (1895) and Japan (1902), and with old rivals, like France (1904) and Russia (1907), but was unable to settle accounts with Germany? There were important acts of cooperation between Britain and Germany, some just before the outbreak of the Great War, as well as significant and long-standing royal ties that formed a foundation for a peaceful settlement. Also unlike relations between France and Germany there were no outstanding disputes involving territorial contiguity. Nor were the colonial disputes as serious as those that had been resolved between Britain and France or Britain and Russia.

It is a further anomaly for the power transition hypothesis that Germany did not seek to challenge and fight Britain, but Britain's former rivals, France and Russia. Why were the most forceful challenges made toward these states and not toward the declining hegemon, Britain, or the rising hegemon, the US? There are some obvious geopolitical and historical answers to this question, which will be explored in the next few chapters. The fault of the power transition explanation and hegemonic theory is that they ignore these answers and instead emphasize an abstract single factor that seems procrustean.

Likewise, it is not clear that actors confine their initiations of war to times when they have caught up to and surpassed a rival or that they are able to make such calculations correctly. Japan, for instance, attacked Russia in 1904 and the US in 1941 when it was weaker, hoping that surprise and military strategy would overcome overall capability. In one case, it succeeded and in the other it was humiliated. In World War I and World War II, Germany attacked when it had greater capability than its immediate opponent, but it was unable to adequately assess the strength of the coalition it would face or determine whether it could keep certain nations from entering the war. Thus, it attacked while its coalition was weaker. As even Organski and Kugler (1980: 57–60) readily admit, certain attacks are premature and the challenger loses badly. All of this emphasizes the importance of human error, unanticipated consequences, and failure play in the onset of war – factors which the power transition and other capability explanations obscure.

The power transition hypothesis has a number of empirical deficiencies that prevent it from being accepted as an accurate or dependable account of the onset of war. Organski and Kugler admit that, as a sufficient condition, the presence of a power transition does not produce war. Half of the time war should occur (because a power transition has occurred), it does not ensue. As a necessary condition, the explanation is also very limited, since it does not apply to major states in the periphery, even if they are the rising hegemon. Nor when the details of World War I and World War II are examined does the power transition provide much insight; instead it raises a host of questions. Finally, if it is taken solely as a necessary condition of war, then it has failed to provide an explanation of the sufficient conditions of war; i.e., it does not have an explanation of the onset of war.

This discussion of power transition has important implications for the hegemonic theory of war. It seems that, as the power transition explanation makes hegemonic theory more specific and precise so that it can be tested, then the evidence tends not to support it. Only when one remains vague, ambiguous, and rhetorically forceful (as Toynbee, Dehio, and to a lesser extent Gilpin do) does the theory appear psychologically per-suasive. The quantitative tests of Väyrynen (1983), Spiezio (1990), and Boswell and Sweat (1991) (while not definitive), further the impression that hegemonic theory cannot stand up to systematic testing.

Suffering from similar problems is Modelski's (1978) long cycle theory. Modelski posits a long cycle of leadership in which the state dominating the global trading system exercises political leadership over the system. For Modelski (1978) global wars are struggles over who will lead the system (see also Thompson and Rasler, 1988: 337; Thompson, 1988: 44–54). Modelski and Thompson (1989: 42, 45) see global wars providing a selection mechanism by which a new global leader is chosen. War is seen as part of a natural cycle of four stages in which *Global War* concentrates *World Power*, which then becomes *Delegitimated* and finally *De-concentrated*, only to be followed by another global war (Modelski, 1978; Thompson, 1988: 76–77; Modelski and Thompson, 1989: 24, 27). Modelski empha-sizes the natural role war plays in the global system and sees global war as continuing unless some "substitute mechanism of global decision mak-ing" evolves (Modelski and Thompson, 1989: 42). Although the system has not had an alternative to global war, Modelski (1990: 21–24) believes that such a mechanism may in fact evolve.

To the extent that Modelski and Thompson try to explain war, they do so by looking not at its causes, but at the function and consequences it has for the global system. In doing this, they explicitly eschew the delineation of the causes of war:

> In our argument global wars are likewise part of the political calendar. If there is merit in regarding global wars as a form of macrodecision, the puzzle over its causes assumes a much reduced, if not a minor, form.
>
> In reality, a reformulation of the question is needed. In a most basic sense, the "cause" of a global war is the absence of an alternative.
>
> (Modelski and Thompson, 1989: 42)

Given this view of the causes of war, it is not clear how much aid the long cycle approach can be in constructing a causal explanation. From the perspective of *why* wars occur and what brings about war, the long cycle approach is of limited use. At best, it promises to tell us when and under what conditions global wars occur, but even here its view on the causes of war does not make it clear that these conditions can be interpreted as sufficient conditions.

What we are left with are a specification of when and under what conditions global wars will occur and the claim that global wars occur because there is no alternative mechanism for selecting a global leader. These are no mean contributions, but how adequate are they as explanations of war? If they are empirically accurate, then a deconcentration of power should be followed by a global war and global wars should be wars of leadership succession. An examination of each of these claims raises serious questions.

First, Geller (1992: 277) finds that the relationship between increasing/decreasing concentration at the system level and the frequency of war (1820–1976) is statistically insignificant. He concludes that wars among major states are no more likely to occur during periods of deconcentration than in periods of rising concentration. What he does find is that a power transition at the dyadic level is more apt to result in a war when power at the systemic level is decreasing in concentration. However, this association is low, Kendall's Tau C = 0.26 (Geller, 1992: 278–79). As with Spiezio's (1990) test of Gilpin (1981), these findings imply that changes in capability, at best, play only a minor role in the onset of war.

Nevertheless, Geller's test makes a major contribution in that it shows that power transitions at the dyadic level are affected by systemic conditions.[13] While Geller focuses on systemic capability concentration, the low association suggests that other systemic characteristics (e.g. the global institutional context; see Chapter 8, below) might be more important.

Further evidence that saying that global wars occur in a deconcentration phase does not provide a very precise description of the period preceding global wars can be marshalled from Thompson's (1983b) test of Organski and Kugler's power transition thesis. Thompson measures power as seagoing power and therefore is more in tune with Modelski's view of power than with Organski's. Before reviewing that study, it must be pointed out that, as with Organski and Kugler (1980), Thompson's (1983b) test first identifies the global war and then looks at the preceding period (in his case, twenty-five years!) to see if a power transition occurs. This, of course, reduces capability shifts to a necessary condition of global war and does

---

[13] In work in progress, Rasler and Thompson (1992) following up Geller's insight show that an increase in regional concentration (e.g. unipolarity) coupled with the decline of the global leader (global deconcentration) is the most dangerous situation for the onset of global war (see also Thompson, 1993). Two caveats, however, must be noted. First, only significance tests are conducted and any correlation may be low, as in Geller's analysis. Second, World War I does not fit the model, since there was no regional concentration prior to 1914. This means that the attempt to explain the onset of global wars using the long cycle approach is still incomplete.

not show that fundamental changes in capability produce challenges to global leadership. Also, such a long time period raises the possibility that any association between global wars and capability changes will be coincidental. Despite these "biases" in favor of the proposition, some of Thompson's findings raise serious questions about the ability of the long cycle to provide a coherent explanation of global war consistent with the evidence.

Thompson (1983b; 1988: ch. 10) shows that there is no single sea-power transition pattern associated with global war. For example, Thompson (1983b: 107; cf. Thompson, 1988: 234, 235, Table 10.2, Figure 10.3) finds that in the first cycle (1517–1608), England is equal with Portugal in naval strength in 1564 and then surpasses Portugal in 1576–77; yet there is no war. In 1581 Spain catches England and England continues to decline, yet England defeats Spain. In the second cycle (1609–1713), England and the Netherlands are declining and France is rising, eventually surpassing both states in 1669–70, but in the last decade (1676–87), France levels off and is no longer a rising state prior to the global war (Thompson, 1983b: 107; see also Thompson, 1988: 236, Figure 10.4). The same thing happens very clearly in the second half (1779–91) of the third cycle when France and Britain are declining but flat (Thompson, 1983b: 109; see also Thompson, 1988: 237, Figure 10.5). This suggests that global wars can occur when there is a decline and rise, as in cycle one, or a relative stability as in cycles two and three. Such evidence shows that explaining global wars as a result of global deconcentration is much too vague and imprecise; instead the evidence supports the contrary view that global wars can occur with any kind of transition pattern or the absence of one. Indeed, prior to global war in cycles three and four (1714–1815, 1816–1945), there is no transition to speak of (Thompson, 1983b: 108; see also Thompson, 1988: 237–39, Figures 10.5, 10.6, 10.7). Thompson (1983b: 109) concludes that the image of a second-ranked challenger contesting the leading world power fits only one of the four cycles, a conclusion which undercuts not only Organski and Kugler, but Modelski as well.

Second, it is not clear that calling global wars, wars of leadership succession, explains why they occur. To the extent that global wars provide a way of resolving questions of succession, this does not mean that such a role or function can be seen as a *cause* of war (and this may be why Modelski and Thompson [1989] eschew that language). At any rate, Modelski and Thompson do not claim that leadership succession is an explicit motivation for global wars. What they find is that the succession wars are not of the variety that a rising challenger and declining hegemon fight it out with one becoming the new leader. The leaders who succeed – Netherlands, Great Britain (twice), and the United States – are usually not the challengers to the previous leader. Modelski (1978: 225) lists Spain as the challenger to Portugal with the Netherlands succeeding, France challenging the Netherlands with Britain succeeding, France challenging Britain with Britain succeeding (the only case that proceeds as one would expect), Germany challenging Britain with the US succeeding (see also Thompson, 1983b: 106; cf. Thompson, 1988: 46, 50).

Such discontinuities are more extensive than one would expect given the logic of the long cycle and suggest that perhaps global wars are not direct struggles for leadership succession and that economic factors, more than war, are critical in the rise of hegemony. What connection wars have with a leadership cycle, then, is not fully captured by Modelski. At best, global wars remove a challenger and perhaps weaken the dominant power, thereby clearing the way for a new successor, which is the conclusion that Modelski and Thompson (1989: 46–47) and Gilpin (1989: 26) accept. Why the eventual successor is not more fully involved in the beginning is an unanswered puzzle. This indicates that a less teleological and functional approach is warranted. A few wars may have the consequence of selecting out a new global (economic) leader (usually by exhausting both the old leader and a challenger), but it appears empirically incorrect (as well as logically invalid)[14] to infer from this occasional consequence the cause of global wars. Such world wars are caused by a complex of factors, with contagion playing a key role, and they are typically, as with the start of World War I, not planned or initiated as succession struggles.

The conclusion that world wars need not necessarily be succession wars or follow a long cycle is further supported by the fact that there appear to be some wars that are authentic world wars and that play an important role in the history and making of the modern world system, but do not give rise to new system leaders and/or appear to occur at the wrong times if the long cycle is operating the way it should, a point emphasized by Levy (1990). Both the Thirty Years War and the Seven Years War are especially problematic in this regard. Modelski handles this problem by not recognizing these wars as *global* wars (see Thompson, 1985: 485), but, except for the fact that they do not produce a new global leader, they appear to be global wars according to the criteria Modelski and Thompson adumbrate

[14] It is logically invalid to infer cause from consequence, since a *cause* must precede an event, not follow it. What Modelski and Thompson are really saying is that changes in capability make for leadership struggles, which then result in war, making their proposition not dissimilar from those of Gilpin and Organski.

(see Levy, 1991: 157–58; see also Levy, 1985b).[15] To eliminate the Thirty Years War is a serious omission because of the severity of the war and the significance of the Peace of Westphalia. Certainly, if any war gave rise to a new political order, it was this one. To eliminate this war simply because England did not play an active role appears much too myopic. To eliminate the Seven Years War is not as drastic, but because of the global reach of this war and its impact on the future of Western colonization and the spreading of a world political economy, it is not clear why this is not a global war.

Further questions about global wars being wars of leadership are raised by Thompson's (1983b: 109) admission that the Anglo-Dutch naval wars of the second cycle are associated with a set of capability intersections (between 1664 and 1688), but never become the global war they should have been. In other words, one has the kind of power configuration and challenge within the long cycle that should lead to a global leadership succession through war, but it does not occur. At other times, a series of small wars can produce changes in leadership, as Levy (1990: 217–18) shows; which suggests that global wars are a neither sufficient nor necessary condition for system transformation.

In addition, a number of academics have questioned Modelski's claim that Portugal rather than Spain should be treated as the world leader in the first cycle. If Modelski is correct that seagoing power is the best indicator of leadership of the global political system, then why is Spain, a non-naval power, able to take over as the leading world power in 1580 without a global war (see Thompson, 1983b: 107–8)? Does it not make more sense to think of Spain as not simply the dominant continental state, but the leading world power, even if it does not play the kind of role in trade that Portugal did?

Finally, if one looks at all the wars that take place *within* each of the long cycles, one sees that wars, including some very major ones, occur fairly frequently, once again supporting the notion that any kind of distribution of capability can be associated with the use of force, even though certain forms of capability distribution may be associated with certain types of war (see Chapters 2 and 7 herein). As with the power transition explanation, most of the wars of human history are left unexplained. A scientific explanation of the onset of war should at least, if only by implication, say

---

[15] Modelski and Thompson (1989: 43–45) list the following criteria for determining a global war: they are the most violent wars in history; they are global as opposed to regional; they decide the constitution of the global system.

something about other wars in the system. Modelski and Thompson have not shown why a general theory of war with the proper caveats cannot be constructed. Only by showing how their explanation of a few rare cases (the global wars) is consistent with what is known about the typical cases (dyadic interstate wars) can we be assured that the long cycle explanation is not generalizing from a few coincidences.

In terms of providing an adequate scientific explanation of the onset of war, the long cycle approach suffers from a number of problems. Nevertheless, there have been some important contributions. Modelski's analysis provides critical insights about the role global wars have played in politically constituting the system, ideas which are compatible with those of Gilpin (1981). From a scientific point of view, even more signifi- cant have been the documentation and elaboration of the impact of global wars on the global system and domestic political systems in the research of Rasler and Thompson (1989; see also Rasler, 1986, Thompson, 1988). Both conceptually and in terms of the research associated with it, the long cycle approach is more relevant for understanding the impact of certain wars on the nature of the global political system than for elucidating the causes of global wars.

Two significant conclusions can be made about power-based expla- nations of war. First, the explanations are confined to only a few wars; there is no explicit explanation of other wars, except to say that war is an inevitable part of the struggle for power. Second, the explanations for the large major wars are fraught with problems of inference, ambiguity, weak explanatory power, lack of fit to the historical record, and a failure to pass quantitative tests.

This is not a very good record for a theoretical approach whose main aim is to explain war and show how it can be mitigated. It would seem we could do better. The analyses in Part II of this book offer an alternative non-realist explanation of war. Chapters 4–6 present something which the power explanations have to date failed to present – a precise, testable explanation of all wars between relative equals that delineates the suffi- cient conditions of war. Rather than focusing on a handful of major wars, it seeks to explain all interstate wars of a certain type without focusing on power as the main explanatory variable and then goes on to explain the few major wars on which the power theorists have concentrated. It pro- vides answers where the realist paradigm has provided only the promise of answers.

The analysis of world war in Chapter 7 provides a non-realist alternative to hegemonic, balance of power, power transition, and long cycle theory.

It seeks to explain world war, the major set of cases with which realism is concerned, even though there are only a few cases. As an alternative explanation, it has fewer theoretical problems, makes fewer untested assumptions, is more historically precise and detailed, more consistent with the historical record, more generalizable, less teleological and less deterministic. It delineates not only the sufficient conditions of world war, but also the necessary conditions of world war. On the bases of these criteria, the alternative explanation of world war seeks to demonstrate that even at the heart of the realist paradigm, a counter-realist analysis can provide better answers to what brings about "hegemonic wars," and in particular what brought about the wars realism has been most concerned with – World War I and World War II.

Does this mean that realism and the power-based explanations offer no insights? No. The work of Gilpin, Organski and Kugler, Modelski and Thompson all show that the establishment of peace is associated with creating a structure for resolving issues without having to resort to all-out war. They are correct in seeing the creation of that structure as being the result of an exercise of a preponderance of power (albeit not necessarily a single state), and they are correct in seeing the creation of global structures as occurring as a consequence of a few major global wars that act as watersheds in the history of the modern global system. They also suggest the insight that as a peace structure is unable to resolve certain issues, the probability of resorting to war increases. These are not minor contributions and will be incorporated in the discussion of peace in Chapter 8. To deny that power should be the focus of analysis or that it is not the main variable in explaining war, does not mean it plays no role. The remainder of the chapter will outline the specific roles capability should be seen as playing.

The Role of Capability in the Onset of War

It has already been argued in Chapter 2 that capability is important in determining the form war will take. Capability is also very important in determining who will win a war (Rosen, 1972). What is being rejected here is the overly mechanistic view that fundamental changes in power cause wars. In this section, I will take a second look at the empirical evidence to see if it offers any clues as to what role capability might play in the onset of war. Since the most suggestive clues are based on limited evidence, a number of the inferences made in this section must be seen as tentative until they are tested further.

Wallensteen's (1981) examination of the power transition thesis is an important place to start. Although his data analysis shows that a power transition between major states has little effect on their going to war with each other, he finds that power transitions increase conflict by increasing the number of military confrontations between major states. Whereas only 27 percent of the eleven dyads that experienced a power transition went to war, 91 percent were involved in at least one militarized dispute with another major state. This is slightly more than would be expected statistically.[16]

This finding suggests what might be the true effect of secular or long-term changes in capability in the major state system. Actors who have an increase in capability can be expected to place demands on the political system, but these demands need not result in war if the political system can handle them (see Doran, 1991: chs. 1 and 7). For example, a significant increase in an actor's capability will lead it to place its special issues or concerns on the political agenda or give existing issues new emphasis. This places demands on those members of the system who are able to do something to resolve the issues. Depending on the nature of the issue, its salience to the involved parties, and the procedures available for resolving conflicting issue positions, these demands can lead to militarized disputes in the global system, but from 1816 to 1976 they frequently did not lead to war. A power transition, in and of itself, then, does not have to result in war (Doran, 1991: 7–8, 22, 117, 166–71, 174–80).

These changes are not that different from the role sharp changes in capability play in a domestic political system. A dramatic increase in the capability of some group or class is going to lead it to make new demands. In many domestic political systems, new capabilities are usually accommodated. However, revolutions and civil wars do occur and domestic political crises occur with even greater frequency. In both domestic and global political systems, a power transition may set off a series of events that ultimately result in war, but usually this is not the case.

Theoretically, what is it that separates the cases where power transitions end in war from the cases where it does not? The existence of accepted procedures for resolving political issues is a key factor that separates not only

---

[16] Wallensteen notes that 85 percent of all major state pairs from 1816 to 1976 have at least one military confrontation. This means that power transition pairs (as a group) are 6 percent above "what we would expect to be 'normal' in the system" (Wallensteen, 1981: 83). Other characteristics that are equally or more closely associated with militarized disputes are: differences in government (94 percent), geographical contiguity (93 percent), and changes in government (91 percent).

domestic society from global society, but effective domestic governments from unstable ones. Is there any evidence that certain systems of major states are less able to deal with a power transition than others? While a review of this evidence must wait until Chapter 8, suffice it to say here that both Väyrynen (1983) and Wallensteen (1984) provide evidence to show that periods that are considerably more peaceful than others are those characterized by certain agreed upon rules of the game that manage relations between actors, while those which only allow issues to be resolved through the unilateral action of states are more war prone.

These findings are consistent with Gilpin's (1981) notion that after a hegemonic war, the leading state establishes rules of the game that provide a political order. Likewise, these findings are supportive of Modelski and Thompson's belief that the global system is not completely anarchic, but has a political structure with a leading state. Väyrynen's and Wallensteen's findings also support Organski and Kugler's idea that war is associated with a challenger being dissatisfied with the rules by which the system is run (Kugler and Organski, 1989: 173).

To understand whether and why a power transition ends in war, it is necessary to examine how other actors, particularly those that had used their capability to maintain the status quo, treat a newly empowered challenger. If the nature of the issues is such that they are not highly salient to those supporting the status quo, then there is no need to plunge the system into war. Clearly, the nature of the issue (how it is defined and the type of stakes involved) will be important.

There is considerable evidence that questions of territory are usually associated with escalation to war (Wallensteen, 1981: 84; Gochman and Leng, 1983; Diehl, 1985b). Consequently, contiguous states that have outstanding grievances with each other will be more affected by a power transition than those that are widely separated. Territorial contiguity, rather than Organski's (1958) notion of satisfied versus dissatisfied states, better explains why Germany was less concerned with the declining and rising hegemons – Britain and the United States – and more concerned with France and Russia. The absence of contiguity between Germany and Britain may explain why Germany felt compelled to plan a war with France and Russia in the early 1900s, while with England it sought to avoid war and to keep it neutral. A focus on issues and the role of territorial contiguity makes much more sense of the actual foreign policy objectives and behavior of states than reliance on such abstract laws as: all nations struggle for power, or, global wars are caused by struggles for leadership of the global system.

This means that whether capability changes between two actors are important will depend on whether they have outstanding grievances, particularly those involving territorial questions, and whether their prior interaction has been hostile or friendly. War between major states is not produced by one major state simply overtaking another. Japan overtaking Italy and then Austria-Hungary in the early 1900s (Houweling and Siccama, 1988a: 99) is not going to result in a war, but Japan will initiate wars with major states that in statistical terms it is not about to overtake (Russia in 1904 and the US in 1941). Japan is not prevented from initiating war because there is no power transition (as it should be if a power transition is a necessary condition of war). Instead it initiates war in 1904 and 1941 because: (a) it was unable to resolve outstanding differences with these states on a set of territorially related issues; (b) it needed to make a space for itself in an area which had been open to Western interference and it felt it had to establish a new status for itself in a world where non-whites were regarded as inferior; (c) its domestic political context placed a high regard on militarism and the use of force as a foreign policy tool, and so forth. Likewise, the United States did not enter World War I because it had earlier overtaken Britain and was economically superior to Germany and France, nor did it enter the war because it had any interest in the territorial issues that gave rise to the war. Rather, in this case, it was because America's economic relation with belligerents was becoming a critical variable in the outcome of the war.

The presence of war-prone issues, however, is not sufficient to explain the onset of war. Equally important are the allocation mechanisms (see Mansbach and Vasquez, 1981: 283–85) available for dealing with contentious issues. One of the problems of a system guided by realist principles is that the set of practices available to states does not contain many techniques for resolving highly salient issues, i.e. for solving the problems that give rise to the disagreements and conflict at hand.

Political actors in realist systems typically seek to resolve issues by the unilateral threat or use of force. Their primary non-violent technique is to encourage negotiation and disposition of stakes on the basis of existing capability, but to get one side to bargain may require the threat or use of force (i.e. the initiation of a crisis). Once bargaining begins, threat or force can be used as either a way of measuring the salience of the issue to a party and its commitment to its position or as a way of settling disagreements over existing capability. It should come as no surprise that Wallensteen (1981: 84) finds that power transitions increase militarized disputes.

Crisis bargaining is not a very efficient technique for resolving disagreements. When the participants are relatively equal and the issues are very salient to both, stalemates are likely. The failure to resolve issues can lead to a series of repeated confrontations between the disputants, which Wallensteen (1981: 84) shows increases the probability of war. Thus, the absence of non-violent allocation mechanisms means that the increased militarized disputes brought about by a power transition can lead to a pattern of repeated crises. In a system that is guided by principles of power politics, when actors are plagued with intractable demands and faced with threatening crises, they will try to increase their capability as best they can.

The history of realist practice, especially in Europe, has provided a set of practices, namely military buildups and alliance making, that actors can engage in when faced with this kind of situation. As will be argued in Chapter 5, these practices make war more likely rather than less likely. Realist practices make war more likely, because they produce unanticipated consequences that increase threat and insecurity, rather than ameliorating them.[17]

Power transitions, then, can be said to produce war, only to the extent that they generate or resurrect issues that make political actors rely on those foreign policy practices that are primarily responsible for bringing about a war-triggering situation. These issues are frequently territorial issues involving major states and their allies. In this way, realist practices are more a preparation for war (albeit sometimes unwittingly) than a way of avoiding war. Put another way, some power transitions result in war because they encourage actors to take the first of a series of steps that will lead to war. On the whole, however, most wars, global as well as interstate, begin because of the presence of intractable, usually territorial, issues whose presence is unrelated to power transitions or long cycles.

---

[17] It is by examining whether such realist practices as alliance making, military buildups, and the use of *realpolitik* tactics increase the probability of war that the association between power politics and war presented in this chapter can be most efficiently tested. Such a test is easier than trying to measure whether the presence or absence of realist beliefs and norms in a particular period increases the probability of war. The latter test is an appropriate way of assessing the analysis in this chapter, but it must be kept in mind that the realist construction of reality tends to be a constant in a particular period and only produces war when specific practices are enacted to resolve certain kinds of issues.

Examining the effects of specific realist practices also makes it clear that realist policies are not defined as simply any policy that results in war, thereby making the analysis tautological. Instead, the realist practices that have been identified as associated with war (e.g. alliances and increasing military strength) are typically seen in realist thought as ways of preventing war.

All of the above suggests that when power politics is a way of life, war is more likely to occur. Realists would complain that it is impossible for life in international politics to be anything but power politics. Is there any evidence that they are wrong? Empirically, it must be recalled that Organski and Kugler (1980: 52) found that the power transition affected only the top two or three states in the center and not major states in the periphery, even if the state in the periphery was the ascending hegemon. Interestingly, Charles Gochman (1980) has also found a difference between the way major states in the center and in the periphery behave. He found that, in Europe, major states become involved in militarized disputes according to an opportunity model, while, in the periphery, states (US, China, and Japan) get involved in militarized disputes because of a status inconsistency model.

The opportunity model reflects the realist assumption that states need no special motivation to threaten or use force; rather, they are always predisposed to do so, unless restrained by certain contextual variables (Gochman, 1980: 87). The traditional European major states, namely Britain, France, Germany, Austria-Hungary, Italy, and Russia, tended to become involved in militarized disputes unless restrained by unfavorable circumstances (Gochman 1980: 118). In the periphery, a clear motivation must be present for the major states to become involved in militarized disputes, and that motivation is status inconsistency, i.e. they are not receiving the recognition due them given their capability; which means they probably feel they are ranked lower in the pecking order than they should be and/or that they are receiving less consideration and fewer rewards than those to which they are entitled.[18] Gochman's (1980)

---

[18] In the twentieth century, the opportunity model accounts for an average of 54 percent of the variance of European major state behavior and a status inconsistency model accounts for an average of 56 percent of the variance of major states' behavior in the periphery (Gochman 1980: 115). The models do less well in the nineteenth century, but this may be in part because the three periphery states (United States, China, and Japan) are not major states in the nineteenth century.

It is interesting to point out that in the nineteenth century the opportunity model applies to Britain and Russia and the status inconsistency model to the two new states Germany and Italy and to the declining major state, Austria-Hungary. France's behavior in the nineteenth century also fits a status inconsistency model, but it accounts for only 2 percent of the variance (Gochman, 1980: 110). Although the findings are weaker, they are not that inconsistent with the twentieth century in that newly arrived states follow a status inconsistency model and more traditional states that have been part of the system do not.

It is also noteworthy that a straight capability model, which predicts that states will threaten or use force the more powerful they are, does not do as well as the opportunity or findings confirm (unintentionally) Organski's and Kugler's finding that the periphery is different. Together, the two studies provide evidence that not all major states and not all systems follow the laws of behavior laid down by the principles of power politics.

What can be made of these findings? Let me suggest, in a speculative manner, that these findings imply that a power transition is going to have more of an effect in a system whose rules for allocating values place great emphasis on power and unilateral action. In other words, a system that is socially constructed on general principles of power politics in which political actors are ranked according to their power, and political influence and reward are distributed according to that ranking, is going to be more seriously affected by a power transition than some other system. Because changes in capability imply eventual changes in rank and reward, mere statistical changes in GNP, military troops, or naval strength are not sufficient to bring about a change in status. Before they can move in rank, such actors must demonstrate their potential through success in a test of arms; at least this seems to have been the case in late nineteenth-century and early twentieth-century Europe.

The reason power transition wars occur primarily among the top dogs of Europe may be that the European system was a social construction of reality that placed great emphasis on power and pecking order, but had no peaceful mechanism to permit succession to new ranks. As a result, power transitions placed the system under stress and resulted in war in about half the cases. Once you move to the periphery where nations are not socialized to realist reality, then states do not behave this way. In the United States, the rules of power politics were consciously rejected. In Japan, the rules would have been acceptable if they had been permitted to play, instead they saw themselves as being excluded for racial reasons. In the Soviet Union, the rules were rejected for ideological reasons.[19] Such

status inconsistency models. This provides further evidence that major states can become involved in wars and crises either when they are increasing or declining in strength. Prussia in 1866 and 1870 is the classic case of a state that engages in wars when its capability is overtaking a neighbor that is "overrecognized," but Prussia also engages in disputes when its capability is declining, albeit usually with weaker opponents (Gochman 1980: 112). The United States, on the other hand, is more prone to become involved in disputes when its capabilities are declining relative to others (Gochman, 1980: 118).

[19] The Soviet Union, as opposed to Tsarist Russia, is an interesting case, because it is not only on the geographical periphery, but socially distant and (like the United States) committed in the two world wars to overthrowing the power politics of Europe. Gochman may not find any difference between the Soviet Union and other European states because he looks at participation in militarized disputes rather than initiation (Gochman, 1980: 93),

states would be less affected by power transitions *per se* and would become involved in wars for other reasons. Hence Organski and Kugler's model does not fit their behavior. Yet as Gochman's (1980) findings suggest, when these states face the center, they must come to grips with a power politics reality and assert their place in a pecking order. Therefore, their behavior becomes explicable in terms of a status inconsistency model, rather than a basic power politics opportunity model.[20]

The implication of this reasoning is that the role capability plays in the onset of war will vary depending on the social construction of reality that underlies a system. For many periods in European history, the diplomatic system was a *realpolitik*-based system. Upsets in the balance of power, of which power transitions are but a dramatic instance, sometimes were associated with wars because the rules of the system placed so much emphasis on power for determining rewards, and changes in rank were only recognized through a test of arms. While war was not produced because of a self-fulfilling prophecy, such rules made war an inherent part of the system. Realism then became in imperfect intellectualization of a social construction of reality that encouraged and institutionalized certain forms of behavior, collective warfare being one of them. It had certain predictions about what events were threatening. When these events, like an increase in power, occurred, they were interpreted by the rules at hand, i.e. they were seen as threatening. However, the reason they were threatening was that changes in power were one of the ways the rules permitted a redistribution of stakes.

War is a way that a culture has of handling certain situations; realist culture saw power transitions (or even the possibility of power transitions) as giving rise to situations that might have to be handled by war. Since all social constructions are imperfect, it is not surprising that wars did not always occur when they were expected. As it was, European states had a hard time responding to power transitions in a consistent and "rational" fashion. Sometimes they would attack long before they had reached a transition. More frequently, they would attack after overtaking, but then were often unable to judge the effect of opposing alliances on undercutting

and because he does not separate Tsarist Russia from the Soviet Union. I note here only that Houweling and Siccama (1988a: 98) show the Soviet Union passing Germany in 1930 without the Soviet Union initiating a war, making Hitler's attack in 1941 another instance in which a major war occurs without the proper power transition.

[20] Whether the "peripheral states" will become more like the center states as they are socialized, as Gochman (1980: 116) argues, or whether they will change the basic construction of the system as they become the center remains an open question.

their new capability, thereby making their attack premature. Realism as a reflection of the social construction of a power politics reality did not fully comprehend the system that was in operation. In part, this was due to the frailty of human understanding and to human inconsistency.

Nevertheless, like all social constructions of reality, this one too is arbitrary (Ashley, 1987: 408–9). It need not be the only construction possible, i.e. it was a reality imposed by people not by nature, God, or History. With the rise of major states in the periphery, the arbitrariness of the system, in principle, became clearer because these states were not behaving according to the model, leading the model to mispredict or fail to predict critical events. Even within European history, other social constructions, like the Concert of Europe, had emerged, tenuously trying to coexist with it. Because of cognitive failures – like selective inattention, denial, *ad hoc* explanations, *post hoc* reasoning, and an unwillingness to use rigorous procedures to collect evidence and make inferences from it – and a commitment to the modernist narrative, the arbitrariness of the power politics social construction is still not recognized. For realism, this is reality.

Although philosophically arbitrary, this does not mean that power politics is a form of behavior that could arise in any historical condition. It may well turn out that power politics and its reliance on war is peculiarly associated with a system that has many autonomous, relatively equal, contiguous states that have been unable to resolve, in any permanent fashion, territorial disputes.[21] Systems having few contiguous states, like North America, may be more insulated from these effects.

How much of a role changes in capability play in the onset of war will depend on the social construction of reality that holds sway over a particular system. A social construction of reality that is based on principles of power politics is going to place more of an emphasis on capability, because of the greater role given to warfare as a means of resolving intractable issues. Here Doran's (1991: ch. 4 and Doran and Parsons, 1980) analysis moves in the right direction by emphasizing not so much the actual shifts in capability, but the effect such shifts have on the insecurities and perceptions of decision makers. By introducing these intervening variables he provides an explanation of how shifts in capability can lead to war, whereas the other theorists discussed in this chapter do not. However, I see the perceptual effects Doran postulates as arising only in a power

---

[21] In this sense, it would not be surprising that such socially distant and separate systems as the Italian city-state system and the Chinese warlord system would give rise to balance of power thinking (cf. Franke [1968] and Chi [1968]).

politics culture that places great importance on such shifts. Such shifts are not always discernible and not really worth noticing, but if they are thought to be of significance, then they will become important.

To measure capability in terms of relative shares of demographic, economic, and military resources, as Doran (1991: chs. 2 and 3), Kennedy (1987: 198–203, 210–12, 226–29), and realists do, constructs a zero-sum world that by definition is a struggle for power. Yet to believe what is of value in this world is distributed on a zero-sum basis flies in the face of modern historical experience, which shows that the pool of value can increase. This is certainly true of wealth and technological ability. It is also probably true of security. A focus on relative shares distorts this experience and creates a perceptual orientation that need not occur and can appear quite bizarre. For example, are the people, and even the leaders, of England worse off today than they were when England was the hegemon?

Having said that a power politics culture encourages such a perspective, it must be pointed out that it is still debatable whether, even within the center of such a system (Europe), shifts in relative capability actually produced the fears Doran suggests. Rather it seems that various states (leaders and policy influencers) had concerns about their status based on imprecise measures and inferences. Nevertheless, Doran (1991) recognizes that these concerns appear associated with war when most of the states in the European system are undergoing shifts in relative capability, which implies that uncertainty and other cognitive variables associated with the breakdown of the system, rather than power *per se*, are the main factors related to the onset of world war.

It can be concluded that within power politics reality, capability plays two distinct roles in explaining the onset of war depending on whether it is long-term secular changes of capability or short-term changes that are being discussed. Long-term changes can sometimes play a role in initiating a series of events that end in war. Drastic changes in capability can lead political actors to place demands on the system and/or find a place in the pecking order. This often leads to crises and the adoption of a series of foreign policy practices that may ultimately end in war. Such an outcome is not inevitable. Indeed, within recent European history, power transitions resulted in war only half the time. Other regional systems, as well as stable domestic political systems, seem to be immune from this effect. The behavior of mid-ranked states, and hence most of the wars in history, are not explained by power transitions. One can think of this role of capability as a possible source of conflict to which an observer might be able to trace back the origins of a war. However, this is not necessarily the ultimate cause, since one could probably go further back to look at the role of previous wars and the long-term relationship between the involved parties. Since such secular changes in capability are so far removed from the actual outbreak of a war, it is difficult to tell what effect, if any, they really have. Because they do not always result in war and they are only one of several possible sources of conflict, they can not be expected, in a properly specified research design, to account for much of the variance.

The same is not true for short-term changes in capability or decision makers' concerns about capability. Perceptions of threat are reinforced by changes in capability, and this can lead to attempts to increase one's own capability, which in turn can have negative effects. Increases in military expenditures and calculations about capability immediately prior to the outbreak of a war should be seen more as an attempt to prepare for a coming war and to time it to one's advantage, rather than as a "true cause" of war. If, however, it is revealed that the opponent has engaged in such measures or if a calculation of relative strength should reveal that this is the only opportune moment for some time to initiate a war, then such *information* may play an important role in a domestic political debate between those who want to go to war and those who do not.

When all is said and done, capability, the most observable aspect of power, plays a very narrow role in explaining the onset of war. Not much more should have been expected, since *power* is a concept taken from immediate experience to explain that experience, rather than a scientific concept derived from careful and rigorous observation. If one wants to understand war, one has to conceptualize more precisely the sequence of events that precede wars and follow them. This will lead to an understanding of the proximate causes of war. To get at some of the underlying causes, i.e. the factors that give rise to the sequence of events that precede certain types of wars is more difficult. It involves looking at the world from a perspective different from that of the realist paradigm and asking some new questions. These are among the tasks of the second part of the book.

~

Retrospective Commentary on Part I

In this retrospective, I would like to talk briefly about the book's connection to my previous books and elucidate some of the sources for the approach I take in Chapters 1–3. *The War Puzzle* was my third major book. The first stemmed from my dissertation, *The Power of Paradigms* (1974), which was a Kuhnian intellectual history of the field (see Kuhn, 1970) and a critique of the realist paradigm. It was a quantitative analysis of all statistical findings published in journals since 1956, showing that most of this research was guided by the realist paradigm, but that there were very few strong findings, indicating that the paradigm itself was probably fundamentally flawed.

When I arrived at Rutgers in 1975, the natural second book to write would be an alternative to the realist paradigm. My graduate mentors, William D. Coplin and Michael K. O'Leary, had already begun work in this direction with their PRINCE computer simulation (Coplin, Mills, and O'Leary, 1973) and World Policy Process paradigm (see Dean and Vasquez, 1976). To actually come up with a full-blown alternative paradigm was a highly ambitious project, but Dick Mansbach had similar ideas and had critiqued the dominant state-centric paradigm in the field for ignoring non-state actors (Mansbach, Ferguson, and Lambert, 1976). A four-year collaboration with him resulted in my second book – *In Search of Theory: A New Paradigm for Global Politics* (Mansbach and Vasquez, 1981). Although this book was written second, it came out before the revised dissertation, *The Power of Power Politics: A Critique* (1983).[1]

With one book at press, a second under contract, and six refereed peer-reviewed articles, I got tenure in 1980. There was enough in the pipeline to keep me busy for the next couple of years, but essentially I took a deep breath (after five years of teaching six preps a year – Rutgers College still

---

[1] I had of course published articles from the dissertation and related work on an issues politics paradigm. I had received a contract for this book in 1979 and submitted the final typescript in 1980, but because of problems in the press, it did not come out until 1983.

had its liberal arts teaching load, although that would soon go by the boards) and asked myself what I wanted to do next. I had entered the field because of an abiding concern with peace, intensified by the Vietnam War. Even though I knew it would be highly ambitious, I decided that my next project would be a study of the "causes of war" in the hope, similar to that of Lewis Richardson (1960b), that elucidating the causes would make it more possible to achieve peace. The new project would be connected with my previous work in two ways. First, I would seek to provide a non-realist explanation of war, thereby showing that a new paradigm could explain not only "low politics," but the most important aspects of "high politics" as well. Second, I would begin the task by reviewing all the relevant statistical findings on war to see what they could tell us, a procedure I had adopted in my dissertation, although now I would be more interpretative.

Nevertheless, this would be a daunting task, since I did not know the literature in this area, and I did not have many contacts with those working in the area, especially within the Correlates of War project – most of my contacts were in the area of comparative foreign policy. I decided to begin by teaching an undergraduate course on the subject. This gave me time to read and think about the literature, and test out ideas with students, long before committing them to print. In 1983–84, after nine years of teaching, I took my first sabbatical. It was the first time since graduate school that I could work on my research full time. This was very energizing and ideas began to flow one upon the other, which I duly recorded in my "war journal." After a semester return, I got a research Fulbright for a year in Beograd, Yugoslavia that allowed me to capitalize on the sabbatical and complete the first two articles for what would become *The War Puzzle*.

As stated in the Introduction, my strategy for coming up with an explanation was to be inductive. I did this for three reasons. First, there were numerous findings and one had to put them together to make sense of them. Second, it was the strategy J. David Singer was following – first elucidate patterns then explain them. Third, and most important, I thought the theoretical perspective by which much of this research was being guided and interpreted, i.e. the realist paradigm, was fundamentally flawed. In my view, to emphasize the theory, especially in interpreting findings, was actually to be misled. A good theory can hide the truth more effectively than a good lie. I wanted to stand back as much as possible and try to figure out what the research was trying to tell us; hence, the notion that the book was trying to piece together a puzzle.

Given this stance, Part I spent more time on fundamentals – philosophy of science and definition – than is typical for such a book. This emphasis was accentuated by the fact that this was also the time when post-modernism (Ashley, 1987) and post-positivism (Lapid, 1989) were raising their critiques. Chapter 1 was very much influenced by the post-modernist work, especially that which built on the work in philosophy and sociology that saw concepts as institutional facts that could construct a social reality (Berger and Luckmann, 1966). To me this is what realism had done, beginning with the Peace of Westphalia, and now I wanted to investigate how the concept of war (and changes in the concept) had affected the institution of war (and our theoretical understanding of it). This led some, in retrospect, to see Chapter 1 as a constructivist analysis. The analysis really pre-dated constructivism, and I saw it more as an analysis informed by post-modernist thinking, which of course shaped much of constructivism.[2] The notion that the concept of war would shape the practice of war and that war itself could change over time was a far cry from a strict positivist notion that the concept of war is merely a label that refers to a constant unchanging phenomenon. At the same time, however, I was still empirically oriented and thought that tracing the history of the concept could tell us something about the world itself and how war was socially learned. I was not fully post-modern, in that I believed that ideas and practice are a two-way street. Just as the concept of war could affect its practice, so too could the material practice of war (and its success and failure) influence what concepts and definitions of war prevailed in any given era.

This same kind of ideational orientation was played out on a larger surface in Chapter 3. While most of this chapter dealt with criticizing the prevailing theories of war that placed emphasis on power, part of it looked at power politics as a construction of reality that came out of realist theorizing and was institutionalized in practice, especially with the Peace of Westphalia. I saw realism and power politics, specifically, as providing a kind of diplomatic culture (see Johnston, 1996) that guided decision makers and told them how to handle certain situations they might face. Based on this assumption, I argued that classical realism could be used to tell us how states would behave in crisis situations. Power politics, then, was seen as a set of behaviors or practices, and not so much as an "objective" theory that captured "reality." Because decision makers believed in it, they would follow its precepts, and scholars could then use it to predict their foreign

[2] In fact, constructivism in many ways is a watered down and de-radicalized version of aspects of post-modernism that is acceptable to mainstream international relations (IR) inquiry.

policy behavior. However, because it did not fully capture the underlying forces of international relations, the kinds of consequences that "realist theory" foresaw, especially things like peace through strength, would not come about. Instead, cognitive psychological explanations would lead us to suspect that many realist practices would actually make war more likely rather than increasing the prospects of peace. From this assumption came the idea that realist practices were a series of steps to war.

In an indirect way, and parts of this were stated in Chapter 2, realism provided a shared culture or *Weltanschauung* for leaders that helped bring about war. Sometimes that claim has been taken as a constructivist hypothesis that implies that I believe that the idea of power politics is a cause of war. This is not my position, which I have recently made clearer (see Senese and Vasquez, 2008: 33). What causes war is not a diplomatic culture or any particular set of ideas, but what states do to each other. *The War Puzzle* is an explanation of the issues and the foreign policy practices that give rise to war, based on the assumption that dyadic interstate interactions are the key factors bringing it about. Other levels of analysis, including the norms in the global political system (see Chapter 8) or the prevailing diplomatic culture of the time (i.e. power politics from 1648 on) also have an impact, but these are system wide and more contextual than immediate in their impact. Thus, power politics as a set of ideas is indirectly responsible for the onset of war because it provides guidance to decision makers in their selection of actions, but it is the acts themselves and the reactions to those acts that make for peace or war. In the end, the steps-to-war explanation is a more psychological and behavioral theory than a constructivist one.

The other major point made in Part II, both at the end of Chapter 1 and throughout Chapter 2, is that war is multicausal. Again, this was another abandonment of positivist hopes – namely that a single set of causes of war could be found for all of history. The post-modernist attack on the Enlightenment (Foucault, 1980) and the stress on historicity (Alker, 1996b: 386–93) led me to this realization, but of equal importance was the pattern of statistical findings themselves. The findings were simply too varied for there to be only one path to war (see also Levy, 1989: 227, 279, 281). Given this assumption, Chapter 2 is devoted primarily to constructing a typology of war that would identify the sorts of wars that will have different factors associated with their onset. The two key distinctions are between dyadic and complex wars (with the latter being the main set of wars requiring some sort of diffusion model) and between wars of equality (wars of rivalry) and wars of inequality (asymmetric wars). The steps to war are meant to apply to wars of rivalry, and it is suggested that other theories, such as imperialism, are better candidates to explain wars of inequality.

The idea of types of war is an intriguing idea, but herein its role was primarily to set the domain of the analysis. The typology and the claim that there are different paths to war are still very rudimentary in the book. In recent years, I have returned to this idea and have with Brandon Valeriano tried to more seriously classify wars according to the steps-to-war explanation – examining the issue that gives rise to a war and the use of one or more of the practices of power politics (alliances, rivalry, arms races). We attempt to classify each of the seventy-nine interstate wars from 1816 to 1997 using these variables (Vasquez and Valeriano, 2008). We also look at the special factors that make multiparty wars complex and how one might go about classifying them (see Valeriano and Vasquez, 2010). The conceptual scheme underlying this classification exercise can also be used to identify the various paths to war that have been traversed since 1815.

Chapter 1 defined the concept of war and outlines my theoretical assumption about war. Chapter 2 developed a typology of war and sets the domains of the analysis. Chapter 3 gave an overview of the role of power politics in shaping foreign policy while at the same time arguing that explanations of war based on power were inadequate. Aspects of each of the chapters were also unconventional at the time. Chapter 1 had what later would be seen as a "constructivist ring" about it. Chapter 2 rejected the idea that a single explanation of war will explain all wars in all times. Chapter 3 found fault with the major existing explanations of war. Together the three chapters set the foundation for the book. With these in hand it was possible to actually review the statistical findings and integrate them into a coherent explanation. Part II presents that explanation.

I I

The onset and expansion of wars of rivalry

4

Territorial Contiguity as a Source of Conflict Leading to War

Territoriality is the cloth from which humanity's shroud is woven.

Why does warfare occur? Why do some wars expand to encompass the entire system? Can more peaceful structures be built? These have been some of the burning questions of the twentieth century. Practical politics has provided answers to these questions. Scientific analysis has found those answers wanting.

The next five chapters will carefully sift through the last twenty-five years of scientific research to piece together new answers to these questions. These answers will be suggestive, not definitive. How much confidence we can have in them depends on the success of the research that has been conducted to date. I seek to present all the relevant scientific findings as pieces of evidence that must then be examined and synthesized, before they can be used to provide answers. The analysis of war presented in this part of the book, therefore, must be seen as an exercise in theory construction. I am seeking to explain war by explaining existing findings, but since these findings are sometimes inconsistent and incomplete, a full explanation of war, particularly its onset, requires not only that I interpret the evidence, but that, at times, I go beyond the evidence and hypothesize on the basis of historical example or inductive reasoning. When I do this, and I will do it at certain critical junctures in the argument, it should be clear from the context and the absence of references to data. For this reason, as well as standard criteria of scientific rigor, the explanations offered in this part of the book must be seen as tentative until they are tested deductively.

Of all the issues over which collectivities can contend, some are more prone to violence than others. This chapter will examine the source of conflict most likely to give rise to war in the modern global system. For some reason, collectivities have been more discriminating about what they will fight over than have individuals. From the time humans have enclosed land, the territory where two states or communities meet has been a source of potential conflict and contention. In the modern global system, and long before then, it has been territorial issues, particularly issues involving territorial contiguity, that are the source of conflict most likely to end in war.

The theoretical significance of territory has been neglected because the realist paradigm has not viewed the substance of world politics, the issues under contention, as important or central to understanding. Once the focus shifts from treating world politics as a struggle for power to treating it as the raising and resolving of issues, it is easy to see and appreciate the connection between territory and war. A paradigm shift toward issue politics leads to such inquiries as: over what issues are wars fought? are some issues more war-prone than others? if so, what is it about the issues that makes them war-prone?

All wars begin with issues, but not all issues are resolved by war. It is argued here that concerns over territory, not power, have been the underlying and fundamental source of conflict that ends in war. Few wars are fought primarily to gain power and/or hegemony (Holsti, 1991: 308), and only about half of the time do power transitions or other shifts in capability end in war (Chapter 3, above). Conversely, most of the interstate wars that are fought are between neighbors. This suggests that issues of territorial contiguity, i.e. issues involving disputes over land adjacent to states, have often led to war. In this sense, it is *territoriality*, the tendency for humans to occupy and, if necessary, defend territory, rather than the struggle for power, that is the key to understanding interstate war.

Territorial disputes, particularly those involving contiguity, are so much more war-prone than others that they are viewed in this analysis as one underlying cause of war. They can be regarded as an underlying cause in two senses. First, they are *underlying* in the sense that instead of leading immediately or inevitably to war, they usually produce a sequence of events that results in war. Because they are intractable, they tend to give rise in the modern global system to the foreign policy practices of power politics, which can lead to a series of steps that end in war. Power politics is not the only way to settle territorial issues, and, if this sequence of events is avoided, war may be prevented. Second, they are *causes* in the sense that if claims over contiguous territory are settled amicably at one point in the history of two states, it is highly unlikely that a dyadic war will break out between the two neighbors regardless of other issues that may arise in the future. This means that a dispute over territorial contiguity is of *causal* significance in that its presence makes war possible and its absence makes war highly unlikely.

Other issues may give rise to war by encouraging the use of power politics, so this analysis does not claim to identify all of the sources of conflict that result in war. However, since wars between neighbors are so prevalent and other wars infrequent, disputes over territorial contiguity may be the typical starting point for interstate wars.

The chapter begins by presenting evidence that of all the possible issues that could end in war, issues involving territorial contiguity are indeed the most war prone. The second section presents findings that show that most wars and rivalries are between neighbors. The third section places the evidence within a broader theoretical context and uses it to construct an explanation of the underlying causes of interstate wars with emphasis on wars of rivalry. The final section looks at the role power politics plays in making wars recur and how other methods of resolving territorial issues can lead to peaceful relations.

Sources of Conflict Leading to War

If one wants to understand the sequence of events that precedes wars of rivalry, the place to begin is by examining what started the sequence in the first place. This logically leads to an examination of what the actors are fighting over. Conflict, i.e. disagreement, is pervasive, but only a few disagreements are settled by war. What are the issues and stakes that are sources of conflict that lead to war?

There has been little data-based research on this question, but what research exists can be supplemented by some recent historically informed theoretical analyses. The thrust of the evidence shows that only certain kinds of issues are commonly associated with war, despite the fact that war is an act of force that, logically, could be used to resolve any issue. A substantial body of data-based evidence has been found linking territorial contiguity as an important factor associated with confrontations and war. Wallensteen (1981) identifies contiguity as an important factor associated with confrontations and war. Ninety-three percent of contiguous major state pairs have military confrontations and 64 percent of these pairs have wars; whereas, on the average 85 percent of pairs have militarized confrontations and 55 percent have wars. This is impressive evidence that contiguity is a source of conflict that produces both military confrontations and war, particularly since Wallensteen analysis may underestimate the relationship by not controlling for pairs that had settled border issues prior to 1816.

Wallensteen's analysis suggests two conclusions. First, geopolitical conflict, specifically territorial contiguity, is a major source of disagreement leading to the use of military force and war. Second, since Wallensteen (1981: 83–85) also finds differences in type of government associated with conflict that leads to war, it can be inferred that while disputes stemming from contiguity are probably difficult for all states, regardless of their form of government, to resolve non-violently, differences in ideology exacerbate territorial conflicts. One of the problems, however, with trying to draw these conclusions is that all Wallensteen shows is that contiguous states engage in confrontations; he has not shown that the confrontations are over territorial issues. The extent to which his findings and others are produced by territorial disputes or simply emerge from frequent interactions is a question that will be addressed throughout this chapter. Suffice to say here that, at minimum, Wallensteen has identified contiguity as an area prone to conflict.

Additional and somewhat clearer evidence that this site of confrontation is prone to war is provided by Diehl (1985b). He finds that among enduring rivalries between major states, a militarized dispute occurring in a site within or contiguous to one of the rivals is much more likely to escalate than those involving other stakes. About one-fourth of these disputes, twelve of fifty, escalate to war, whereas only one of fifty-four non-contiguous disputes (2 percent) escalate (Diehl, 1985b: 1207).[1] In addition, of the thirteen wars in Diehl's (1985b: 1206) sample, twelve started with a dispute contiguous to one or both of the parties, indicating that issues involving contiguous territory are an important condition for war among rivals. It is not known how many disputes in Diehl's sample actually involve territorial issues; nevertheless, his evidence makes it pretty clear that *if* states have militarized disputes over contiguous territory, they are more likely to become involved in wars than states that have disputes in another area.

Is it possible to go one step further, and posit the site of a dispute as a sufficient condition for war? One objection to this conclusion is that Diehl (1985b) finds that only one-fourth of the disputes involving contiguity escalate to war. This indicates that disputes involving contiguity need not always result in war. While this is a correct inference, it underestimates the extent to which territorial contiguity may produce persistent disputes that prove irresolvable even in the face of intense bargaining. The proper question is not whether there is a strong direct relationship between

---

[1] The first figure is based on my recalculation of Diehl's (1985b) Table 1. Interestingly, the only non-contiguous dispute to escalate is the one that began in 1940 between the United States and Japan.

disputes involving contiguity and the outbreak of war, but whether issues of territorial contiguity produce effects that eventually result in war – i.e. a series of crises that intensify bargaining, hostility, and intractability so that they eventually produce a crisis that escalates to war (see Chapter 5).

In this regard, it is also important to take note of an equally facile, but often persuasive, objection regarding the role of territorial contiguity in the onset of war, namely, that contiguity is not a sufficient condition for war, because contiguity is constant but war infrequent (for instance, Allan, 1983: 7). This objection involves something of a sleight of hand in that it is not contiguity, *per se*, that is a sufficient condition for war, but *disputes* involving territorial contiguity. Furthermore, such disputes are not directly responsible for war, but rather set off a train of events which, if unchecked, result in war.

More definitive evidence that territorial contiguity is the key characteristic associated with disputes that escalate to war is provided in a recent study by Bremer (1992). Bremer finds that of seven theoretically significant characteristics that are suggested in the literature as promoting war between two states, contiguity is by far the most potent. The probability of war breaking out between contiguous states is thirty-five times higher than for non-contiguous states (0.00455 vs. 0.00013). Although the actual probability of war breaking out in any given year between contiguous states is not, as one would expect, very high, it is still considerably higher than the other characteristics and twice as high as the next ranked characteristic.[2] More significantly, when Bremer controls for contiguity, he finds that contiguity is more important than any of the other characteristics. Other factors – like whether the state is a major state or a minor state, is non-democratic, has great economic capability, or has an alliance – only have a major effect on war if the states are contiguous. While contiguity is the most potent variable, combining contiguity with these other characteristics does increase the probability of war. Thus, the most dangerous dyads are: those that are contiguous with both highly militarized (probability of war in a given year = 0.00686), those that are contiguous and have a major state on one side (0.00662 if major–minor; 0.00654 if major–major), those that are contiguous

---

[2] After contiguous dyads, the probability of war breaking out is highest if both states in a dyad are major states (0.00221). As Bremer (1992) points out, the probability of war breaking out in one dyad in any given year is small because there are not that many wars initiated in a given year. Nevertheless, as the number of trials increases, the probability of at least one war breaking out goes up considerably and war is likely to break out in the dyad that has the most war-prone characteristics.

with both undemocratic (0.00644), those that are contiguous and have a medium difference in power (0.00559), those that are contiguous and neither has great economic capability (0.00503) (Bremer, 1990: 21). From these findings, it is clear that contiguity is almost a prerequisite for war to break out in a dyad.

War, however, does not always break out between neighbors, because contiguity does not always give rise to disputes. Contiguity does not constantly give rise to conflict. Instead, what is being said here is that territorial contiguity is a very sensitive area that can give rise to conflict and disputes and that if it does, these disputes are much more apt to lead to war than other disputes. The research reviewed so far has shown that disputes involving contiguous states are much more apt to escalate than other disputes, and it has shown that wars are much more frequent between contiguous states than noncontiguous states. These are important clues that territory and territorial contiguity may be of great theoretical significance. What has not been shown, and what needs to be shown if a territorial explanation of war is to be accepted, is that contiguous states actually fight over territory.

There is little data-based evidence on this question, since most dispute data are not coded for the issues at stake. An exception is the study by Gochman and Leng (1983). They analyze a random sample of thirty disputes to see which escalate to war and which do not. Gochman and Leng (1983) find that disputes that involve a physical threat to vital issues, which they define as involving questions of political independence or control of one's own or contiguous territory, are more likely to escalate to war than disputes over other issues. This holds for 82 percent (nine of eleven) of militarized disputes (rt = 0.50), where both factors (physical threat and vital issue) are present; when only one factor is present, the association drops (Gochman and Leng, 1983: 101).

The evidence from this small sample is consistent with historical evidence presented in two sweeping (and less operationally precise) surveys of wars in the modern global system. The historical evidence provided in each of these theoretical analyses of war shows that territorial issues are the most frequent issues at stake in most wars. K. J. Holsti (1991: 19), in his review of major wars from 1648 to 1989, attempts to delineate, albeit on the basis of historical judgment, the various issues over which decision makers claimed wars were fought. He divides his temporal domain into five standard historical periods: 1648–1714, 1715–1814, 1815–1914, 1918–41, and 1945–89. Territorial issues are the only ones that have been among the dominant issues in each of the periods. In four of the five periods, more wars have involved territorial issues (including boundary questions) than any other kind of issue,[3] exceeded only in 1815–1914 by the "maintain integrity of state/empire" issue, which is an issue obviously related to territorial concerns. In 1648–1714, territorial and boundary issues were at stake in 55 percent of the wars; in 1715–1814, 68 percent; in 1815–1914, 42 percent in 1918–41, 47 percent; and in 1945–89, 31 percent (Holsti, 1991: 307–9). This means that for most of the modern global system, contests over territory (including boundaries) generated more wars than any other issue.

Wars, of course, often have more than one issue at stake, and Holsti accordingly lists multiple issues (often narrowly defined) for each war. Many of these other issues also involve territorial questions, although they involve characteristics that permit Holsti to distinguish them from direct contests over specific pieces of territory. Thus, Holsti (1991: 51–52) classifies strategic territory and questions of irredenta as separate issues from "territory," although they obviously involve territory. If these three issues are combined, then the percentages of wars involving territory, strategic territory or irredenta in each of the periods would be considerably higher.

One of the problems with attempting to combine issues is that a war fought over boundaries and a war fought over some other territorial issue, like strategic territory, are counted separately by Holsti, so that a simple combining of his percentages will inflate the number of wars having territorial questions at issue. For example, combining Holsti's (1991: 308)

---

[3] There seems to be no conceptual reason not to combine boundary issues and territorial issues. Holsti (1990: 307–8) himself does this. In addition, boundary issues as defined by Holsti appear only in two periods and account for a low percentage of wars (1 percent 1815–1914 and 7 percent 1945–89), compared to the territorial issues (42 percent and 24 percent in these two periods). If the two are not combined, then territorial issues rank first in three periods, second in 1814–1914, and second in 1945–89 with 24 percent of the wars (but following three issues [maintain integrity of state/empire, national liberation/state creation, government composition] each tied for first place with 28 percent of the wars) (see Holsti: 1990: 282).

The ranking in the most recent period reflects the large number of anti-colonial wars, which Holsti classifies as *national liberation* from the perspective of the colony and *maintain empire* from the perspective of the imperial state. Part of the reason these and government composition issues exceed territorial issues (without including boundary wars) may be due to the kinds of cases Holsti includes. The 1945–89 period has the most wars (fifty-eight vs. twenty-two to thirty-six for the other periods) and a number involve insurgencies (e.g. Jewish settlers vs. Britain 1946–47), secessions (e.g. Katanga, 1961), or superpower interventions that would not be classified as wars in Correlates of War data (e.g. United States intervention in Lebanon in 1983). Given these considerations, combining territorial issues and boundary wars does not seem too distorting.

percentages of wars involving territory (67 percent), strategic territory (17 percent), and boundaries (1 percent) from 1715 to 1814 would indicate that only 15 percent of the wars did not have some territorial issue. In fact, 28 percent of the wars did not have any territorial questions at issue. Since wars that have territory as an issue may also have strategic territory as an issue, Holsti's percentages cannot be combined. In order to determine in how many wars territory appears as an issue in any form and in how many wars it is completely absent, Holsti's judgments on each war, which are published in his book, were examined and grouped. Table 4.1 lists the number of wars that had one of the three main territorial issues present, the number of wars that had some other aspect of territoriality present, and the number of wars that had neither present (and were presumably not affected in any significant way by territorial questions). Keeping in mind that Holsti's identification of issues and lists of wars are historical judgments and not operationally precise data, Table 4.1 suggests that territorial issues (even when narrowly defined) have persistently dominated warfare for almost 350 years. The percentage of wars fought having territory, boundaries, strategic territory, or irredenta as an issue was 77 percent, 72 percent, 58 percent, 73 percent, and 47 percent for each period, respectively.

In addition, a number of the other issues appearing frequently as a source of war have a *territoriality* dimension to them. These include such issues as: the creation (or unification) of a national state, maintaining the integrity of a state or empire, empire creation, state/regime survival, and dynastic rights/succession (a basic principle for transferring territory). Some of these issues are fairly frequent. The combination of national liberation and national unification/consolidation are issues present in 55 percent of the wars from 1815–1914 and 52 percent of the wars after 1945 (including wars of succession), even though they appear in less than 14 percent of the wars in the other three periods (Holsti, 1991: 308). When these wars are combined in Table 4.1 with those focusing on narrower territorial questions, then concerns about territoriality are present in 86 percent, 83 percent, 84 percent, 93 percent, and 79 percent of the wars of each period. This means that only 14 percent, 17 percent, 16 percent, 7 percent, and 21 percent of the wars in each of the five periods have had no connection with territoriality.

Issues that clearly are not related to territoriality include: commerce/ navigation, protecting nationals/commercial interests, protecting religious confrères, protecting ethnic confrères, defending an ally, ideological liberation, government composition, enforcing treaty terms, and

Table 4.1. *Frequency of wars involving a particular issue[a]*

Type of issue	Historical periods				
	I (1648–1714)	II (1715–1814)	III (1815–1914)	IV (1918–41)	V (1945–)
Territory[b]	17 (77%)	26 (72%)	18 (58%)	22 (73%)	27 (47%)
Territoriality related issues[c]	2	4	8	6	19
Subtotal					
Cumulative %	(86%)	(83%)	(84%)	(93%)	(79%)
None of the above	3 (14%)	6 (17%)	5 (16%)	2 (7%)	12 (21%)
Total wars	22	36	31	30	58

[a] Frequency based on classification of historical judgments listed in Holsti (1991: 48–49, 85–87, 140–42, 214–16, 274–78).
[b] Includes Holsti's (1991: 308) "territory," "boundary," "strategic territory," and "irredenta" issues.
[c] Includes Holsti's (1991: 308) national liberation/state creation, secession/state creation, national unification/consolidation; maintain integrity of state/empire, dynastic/succession.

balance of power, among others. These issues are less frequent than those involving just the three narrow territorial issues. Holsti (1991: 308), for instance, finds the widely touted balance-of-power issue present in only 9 percent, 1 percent, 3 percent, 3 percent, and 0 percent of the wars of each period. More prevalent are ideological issues (the combination of ideological liberation and government composition) which are present in 0 percent, 15 percent, 23 percent, 27 percent, and 42 percent of the wars of each period (Holsti: 1991: 308, 311–13). The presence of these non-territoriality issues is important because they show that territoriality is not being so broadly defined as to include every possible issue that might lead to war. The presence of these non-territoriality issues as a motivation for war demonstrates that the territoriality finding is not a function of a tautological argument.

These figures, although exploratory, suggest that while war is an act of force that can be used to resolve a number of different issues, it has been frequently and commonly tied to questions of territoriality. Issues related to this phenomenon crop up again and again, and they are inevitably the issues that are the sources of conflict that lead to war. Further historical evidence to support these conclusions can be derived from Luard's (1986) theoretical analysis of wars from 1400 to 1983.

Luard's analysis is similar to Holsti's (1991) in its methodological approach, but he takes a different theoretical perspective, which permits one book to be used as something of a check on the other. One of the main differences between the two books is the periodization. Luard also has five periods, but this is for 583 years (as opposed to 341 years) and the dates do not usually overlap. Luard (1985: 24–64) divides his time span into the age of dynasties (1400–1559), the age of religions (1559–1648), the age of sovereignty (1648–1789) (Holsti's first and second periods up to the French Revolution), the age of nationalism (1789–1917) (end of Holsti's second and all of his third period), and the age of ideology (1917–) (Holsti's fourth and fifth periods).

Despite the differences in the books, Luard also finds territorial and border issues (in terms of specific claims to land) to be the focus of a number of wars in each of his periods (see the descriptions in Luard, 1986: 90, 96, 99, 101, 107, 117–18, 121, 125–26). Luard's (1986: 127–31, 182) more general point, however, is that the issues and motives that dominate wars in each period vary fairly radically. The age of dynasties was concerned with issues of succession, the age of religion with religious beliefs, the age of sovereignty with territorial questions, the age of nationalism with the creation of national states, and the age of ideology with imposing certain forms of government or socioeconomic organization. This issue variation leads Luard (1986: 313, 128) to conclude that there is no consistency in the issues that have given rise to war and that there is no "single overriding passion – whether nationalism, economic interest, the competition for power, or political concern – which continually causes nations or peoples to engage in war against each other."

From a purely substantive perspective this is correct, but Luard overlooks the extent to which the various issues he sees dominating each age are connected to territoriality. The fact that territorial acquisition, particularly in Europe, is a dominant issue primarily in the age of sovereignty does not mean that concerns about territory are absent from the issues dominating the other periods. Succession and dynastic disputes were usually about who would inherit a crown and the territory that went with it. Attempts to create nation-states after the French Revolution as well as after 1945 were attempts by peoples or their leaders to give a nationality or group a territory that it could control for itself. The fact that these issues are substantively different, but that the human animal defines them in terms of territoriality and, once having done so, fights wars over these issues, cannot be without significance.

The closest Luard (1986: 129) comes to recognizing this is when he states that in almost every age wars arise in situations where there is an ambiguity over who has sovereignty. Although Luard (1986: 182) does not discuss territoriality, he describes the motives underlying the major issues of each age in a way that implicitly points out the role of territory (italics added):

> The aim that most often brought rulers into war with each other in the age of dynasties, [was] the acquisition of a throne *elsewhere* ...
> The desire to protect a religious faith or to impose it on another *land* ... often led to war in the second of the ages ...
> The aim of promoting state power by the acquisition of *territories* seen as being strategically, commercially or otherwise valuable, [was] a major source of war in the age of sovereignty ...
> The demand for national *independence* or national *integration,* [was] common as a source of war in Europe in the last century ...
> Finally, the desire to see governments of a particular political persuasion in power in *neighboring* countries ... has become the most frequent single incentive for warlike action in the age in which we now live.

Even though Luard's main point in this paragraph is to show that the particular substantive definitions of issues that dominate the global agenda may shift from one period to the next, i.e. from dynastic claims to religion, to state sovereignty, to nationalism, to imperialism, to ideological rivalry and national liberation, the italicized words show that these larger purposes have a way of being linked to territorial proclivities. When they are so linked, they become war-prone.

On the basis of the evidence reviewed in this section, it can be concluded that states that are contiguous and/or involved in disputes over territorial contiguity tend to go to war with each other more frequently than other states, and that they probably are fighting over territorial issues of one sort or another. This means that the findings uncovered by Wallensteen (1981), Diehl (1985b), and Bremer (1990, 1992) are produced not simply because of the site of the dispute, but because the dispute is over the control of the territory located on that site. This suggests that territorial issues broadly defined are not like other issues, but are unusual in their proneness to violence. This does not mean that other issues, like ideological questions, can not give rise to conflict that leads to war. All that is being said is that territorial issues are for some reason or other apt to give rise to disagreements and that those disagreements have more often than other kinds of disagreements ended up being resolved by war. Since these issues do not always lead to war and often are resolved permanently, territorial issues are at most an underlying cause of war and not by themselves a sufficient condition for war.

Interstate War and Neighbors: An Overlooked Relationship

Although the evidence suggests that territorial contiguity and disputes over it are more potent predictors than any other single variable of the onset of war, it is equally clear that most disputes involving contiguity do not escalate to war and that most contiguous dyads are not constantly at war or even in serious conflict with one another (Diehl, 1985b; Bremer, 1992). It is rather surprising therefore that a careful examination of the population of interstate wars reveals wars fought between neighbors to be so high. This is an important clue whose significance for explaining the onset of war has been generally overlooked, although the new interest in geographical explanations may rapidly change that situation (see Starr, 1991; Diehl, 1991; Ward, 1992). This section will take a new look at the relationship between war and neighbors and the implications of that relationship for developing a unified explanation of violence and war.

The obvious way to begin the analysis is to ask: what are the implications of territorial contiguity being an underlying cause of war, in light of the evidence in the previous section? To say that territorial contiguity is an underlying cause of war implies that human proclivities toward territoriality are *a*, if not *the*, fundamental factor that leads collectivities to take actions that eventually result in war. Territoriality is the natural tendency of the human animal to occupy and, if necessary, defend territory. This factor is fundamental in that, without its presence, the use of collective violence would be greatly reduced. Just how fundamental a factor it is should be evident in the traces it leaves in the history of war and confrontation. Since neighbors are more apt to have concerns about each other's territorial ambitions than about those of other countries, it would be expected that if territoriality is a fundamental factor in the onset of collective violence then wars, rivalries, protracted conflict, and militarized disputes would be unusually clustered between neighbors.

Of the interstate wars listed in Correlates of War data, most are between neighbors. There are sixty-seven interstate wars from 1816 to 1980 (Small and Singer, 1982: 82–95); all but eight are between neighbors or begin that way (see Table 4.2a).[4] If imperial wars (like the Franco-Mexican War, the Spanish–American War, or the Boxer Rebellion) are removed, then all of the wars are between neighbors. Since all imperial wars involve a major state, then all wars in the sample are either between neighbors or involve a major state. This means that all interstate wars are either between neighbors or involve a major state in overseas expansion.

A review of Holsti's (1991: 48–49, 85–87) lists of wars, 1648–1815, produces a similar observation (see Table 4.2b). All but a handful (fifty-three of fifty-eight wars) are between neighbors, with the major exception being wars between Spain and Britain, and these often involve colonial competition.[5] Except for the phenomenon of imperialism, in which a clearly stronger and expanding state attacks a weaker country, most interstate wars are confined to neighbors. These patterns can hardly be an accident and must occur for some deeper reason.

One possible deeper reason is territoriality, i.e. that human proclivities to territoriality lead neighboring states to use violence and aggressive displays to demark their territory, especially the areas contiguous to another state. If territoriality is acting in this manner, then it should also play a role in cases of persistent confrontation. Specifically, it would be expected that neighbors should be disproportionately represented in interstate rivalries and protracted conflict between unequals. An examination of the twenty-eight rivalries between equals and protracted conflicts between unequals[6] identified by Wayman and Jones (1991: 6) (on the basis of states that have at least five militarized disputes within a certain time frame) supports this expectation (see Table 4.2c). Twenty-four of the twenty-eight cases (86 percent) are between neighbors. Of the four exceptions, two involve imperial legacies (UK–US pre-1816–61 and

---

[4] Using unpublished data, Singer (1990: 9) reports that fifty-seven of seventy wars are between neighbors. Although Singer goes on to dismiss this finding as somewhat trivial, his report of the finding led me to pursue this line of inquiry here.

[5] Even though there are no precise operational measures of contiguity for this period, it appears that the only wars not involving any neighbors in Holsti's (1991: 48, 85) list are one war in the first period (Great Britain–Spain, 1655–59) and four wars in the second period, two between Spain and Britain, 1727–29, 1739–40, and two between the American colonies (United States) and Britain, 1776–83, 1812–14.

[6] Wayman and Jones treat major–minor disputes that persist as indicating the presence of an enduring rivalry. For reasons outlined in Chapter 2, I define rivalry as a process characteristic of relative equals. So as not to use the term rivalry in contradictory ways, when reporting Wayman and Jones's findings on major-minor dyads, I refer to major–minor cases having five or more confrontations as a relationship of protracted conflict between unequals.

8 body.

Table 4.2a. *Interstate wars 1816–1980*

Interstate wars involving neighbors[a]	Other interstate wars[b]	Total
59 (88%)	8 (12%)	67

[a] Neighbors were defined as contiguous states or those separated by water by 150 miles or less.

[b] Wars between non-neighbors include: Anglo-Persian, 1856–57; Franco-Mexican, 1862–67; Spanish–Chilean, 1865–66; Sino-French, 1884–85; Spanish–American, 1898; Boxer Rebellion, 1900; Italo-Ethiopian, 1936; Franco-Thai, 1940–41 *(Small and Singer data, 1982)*

Table 4.2b. *Major wars 1648–1814*

	Wars involving neighbors	Other wars[b]	Total
1648–1713	21	1	22
1714–1814	32	4	36
Total	53 (91%)	5 (9%)	58

[a] Contiguity data were derived from Palmer (1961).

[b] These include the following wars: Great Britain–Spain, 1655–59; 1727–29; 1739–40; American colonies (US)–Great Britain, 1776–83; 1812–14 *(Holsti's (1991: 48–49, 85–87) list)[a]*

Table 4.2c. *Rivalries 1816–1986*

Rivalries between neighbors	Other rivalries	Total
24 (86%)	4 (14%)	28

(Wayman and Jones sample, 1991)

US–Spain, 1850–98) and two ideological rivalries (US–USSR,[7] 1946–86 and US–China, 1949–74).[8] These exceptions illustrate some of the other

[7] After 1959 when Alaska is granted statehood, Correlates of War data treat US–USSR as contiguous by water. I do not consider them neighbors because they are continental nations that are proximate only in areas that are very far from population centers.

[8] Of the rivalries involving equals, only one of the fifteen rivalries between two minor states is between non-neighbors, and this case, Spain–US 1850–98, really involves a former major state and a rising major state, as well as colonial territory contiguous to the

sources of conflict that might give rise to violence and are consistent with Wallensteen's (1981) findings, but the thrust of the evidence shows that territoriality is related to not only war but persistent confrontations. This is an important relationship, because as Wallensteen (1981: 84) shows, repeated confrontations are a source of war.

It follows from this logic that territorial contiguity might also be associated with the general use of force. Gochman (1990) groups militarized disputes from 1816 to 1976 according to the amount of force employed: threat of force (verbal), display of force, actual use of limited force (short of war), and war. In each instance, he finds that neighbors are responsible for most instances of force. Neighbors account for about two-thirds of the militarized disputes (Gochman, 1990: 8, Table 2) with the overwhelming number of disputes being between states that are contiguous by land. Furthermore, the frequency of neighbors being involved increases as the intensity (and cost) of threat increases. The percentage of disputes involving neighbors goes from 63.8 percent for verbal threats to 64.1 percent for displays of force to 66.3 percent for limited force to 78 percent for war (Gochman, 1990: Table 2). Gochman's (1990) findings demonstrate that contiguity is important in all phases of the use of violent force.

These various pieces of evidence show that territoriality is operating as an underlying cause of war. It makes the territory contiguous to states a very sensitive area that can generate confrontations, long-term rivalry, and/or war until it is settled. Other issues do not have these effects, even if they may occasionally be a source of war.

Although this is new evidence, the hypothesis on contiguity and war has been in the literature in various forms for some time. One of the reasons it has been discounted is the belief that wars are fought between contiguous pairs more frequently than other pairs not for any causally significant reason, but simply because it is difficult to fight wars if the two sides cannot reach each other. Thus, it is highly unlikely that Paraguay and Mali would ever fight a war.

United States. This suggests two inferences – first, that minor states get involved in rivalries (between equals) only with neighbors and, second, that major states that are able to project their capability to new territories beyond their homeland are the primary states likely to become involved in confrontations and wars with non-neighbors.

In the modern global period, major states seem to extend themselves for two reasons – imperialism and ideological competition. While both of these reasons increase confrontation, they seem to lead to war among non-neighbors only when an issue of territorial contiguity is involved (usually through an ally, as in the Korean War, or through a colonial area, as in Cuba in 1898).

From this perspective, it is the proximity, which is a relatively trivial characteristic, that is accounting for the relationship and not the territoriality. It is argued that as states get further apart, a loss-of-strength gradient makes it less likely that they will get involved in wars, because they are less capable of fighting such wars and winning them once they start. The idea of a loss-of-strength gradient, initially suggested by Boulding (1962), makes a great deal of sense, but it does not necessarily follow that because states experience a loss-of-strength gradient, that territoriality is not causally significant. Are there tests that would be able to discern between the two explanations of why territorial contiguity and war are related? One explanation emphasizes the contiguity and says that it is the proximity aspect that is driving the relationship and that territorial factors are theoretically insignificant. The second explanation emphasizes the territorial aspect and says that territoriality is of causal importance in the use of violence.

One possible test, which has been suggested by those who take the proximity explanation seriously, is that technological innovations in transportation, communication, and weaponry should reduce the loss-of-strength gradient, thereby making proximity less relevant in the twentieth century than earlier. Gochman (1990) has conducted such a test. He predicts, on the basis of the strength-of-gradient proposition, that as technological advances shorten distances, contiguity should be less of a factor in militarized confrontations. Somewhat to his surprise, he finds the opposite: contiguity is associated with more confrontations after 1870 than before.[9] Such a finding is not consistent with the proximity proposition and must be explained away.[10] The finding is, however, consistent with the territorial explanation, which would

---

[9] Specifically, Gochman (1990: Table 3) finds that in 1816–48 and 1849–70, 53.7 percent and 47.8 percent of the disputes involve neighbors, but after that, the rates are 59.7 percent (1871–90), 67.8 percent (1891–1918), 71.1 percent (1919–45), and 72.0 percent (1946–76). Controlling for type of disputes generally produces the same results (see Gochman, 1990: Table 5).

[10] Gochman tries to explain away the finding by saying that the increase in contiguous disputes may be due to an increase in disputes among less industrialized states. This is partially true, but this explanation is more appropriate after Western colonies are liberated. The ad hoc explanation does not fit the earlier five periods. Nor is Gochman, given his data, able to demonstrate that technologically advanced states are engaging in noncontiguous confrontations as frequently as they would have engaged in contiguous confrontations when they were not technologically advanced. If increased interaction makes war more probable and technology reduces the loss-of-strength gradient, then states should fight more frequently and wars should not be clustered between neighbors as time goes on. Neither of these expectations seems to result.

see technology as having a minimal impact on the proportion of wars fought between neighbors. From the territorial perspective, technological advances may increase the number of imperial wars slightly, but most wars should still be between neighbors who have not yet settled their territorial claims.

On the basis of this test alone, the proximity proposition could be eliminated. A second possible test is to look at the war involvements of states whose territory is non-contiguous. The dynastic states of early modern Europe provide several examples as do some contemporary states such as Pakistan (East and West) and Western colonial empires. If territoriality is the key and is of causal significance, then a dynasty will fight to hold any territory to which it has a legitimate claim regardless of whether it is contiguous or closer to its center of capability than some other territory. A cursory examination of noncontiguous states, like the Hapsburg Empire or even England in the Hundred Years War, seems to support the territoriality explanation. As Luard (1986: 96) notes, in the age of dynasties (1400–1559), wars to maintain distant non-contiguous territory were not uncommon. The Spanish Hapsburgs were not less concerned with the Spanish Netherlands than the areas adjacent to Spain; nor were the Austrian Hapsburgs less willing to fight wars to hold their distant territory than to fight over conflicts stemming from areas nearer the center. This is further illustrated by the costly Hundred Years War, where the Kings of England fought in France to claim feudal and dynastic rights and to hold territory in southwestern France despite its great distance, by land and sea, from England. The Hundred Years War illustrates that it is the violation of norms for holding and transferring territory and not proximity that makes for war.

Similar propensities are at work in Pakistan's defense of East Pakistan and Palestinian efforts to defend Gaza as well as the West Bank. In these contemporary cases, the norm for holding territory has changed (it is now self-determination and nationalism), but violation of it still leads to war. If proximity were the key variable, none of the above wars and efforts should have occurred in the manner they did.

These examples are often overlooked because there is a shift in Western history, as Luard (1986: 101, 110) notes, away from dynastic succession as the key norm for holding and transferring territory to attempts by sovereign states to round out their territory by taking over contiguous areas. This is amply evinced in the evolution of Prussia, France, Italy, and Germany, as well as in the continental conquests of Russia and the United States. This historical shift, however, does not mean that contiguity is more important than the territorial aspect, since territoriality can easily explain and predict such a shift. What makes for war is not that states are contiguous and unable to fight far away (this is true enough); what makes for war is that territory once seen as legitimately owned will be defended by the use of violence where other issues are less likely to be.

Another reason the hypothesis between contiguity and war has been discounted is the argument that to see wars as related to territory is tautological because every war must logically take place in a certain time and space; hence wars will always be fought on some piece of territory. Just because war must be fought *on* some piece of territory does not mean, of course, that it is fought *over* territory. What this argument ignores is that the territoriality explanation does not say that wars are fought territorially, but that they are fought over territorial issues and motivated by a sense of territoriality. Such an explanation gives rise, as shall be noted below, to a variety of tests that can falsify it and does not simply predict that wars take place on territory.

While it is a truism that wars are fought in a particular time and place, that does not mean that findings which show that wars are clustered in particular times (historical periods) and places should be ignored. It is important to look at why such clustering occurs. If war is absent from some periods, this provides an opportunity to see what these peaceful periods have in common (Wallensteen, 1984; Chapter 8, below). Likewise, the clustering of wars in contiguous states suggests that there is a theoretically significant factor making contiguous places prone to conflict and war. Territoriality is such a factor and, if it is significant, it should operate not only in contiguous areas, but also evince itself in other spheres of behavior.

If the relationship between contiguity and war is taken as real and non-trivial, then the question arises as to how to explain it. The only main competitor to the territoriality explanation, and the one non-trivial explanation that has received attention in the international relations literature, is the interaction explanation (see Bremer, 1992; Gochman, 1990: 1). It sees wars as arising out of contiguity because contiguity encourages interactions, which makes for disagreements and conflicts of interest, a certain number of which may give rise to the use of force and violence. This explanation does not see territory, let alone territoriality, as crucial, but is based on the general proposition that the more interactions the more conflict, and the more conflict the greater the probability of war, at some point. Two tests can be used to discriminate between the interaction and territory explanation. First, if the interaction explanation is true, then all issues have an equal probability of going to war, and this is patently not the case! Whereas, if the territorial explanation is true, disputes involving territorial questions should be more likely to result in war, which seems to be the case.

The difference between the interaction explanation and one based on territoriality is that the latter sees territory as a special issue prone to violence. If the interaction explanation were correct, then the number of issues over which wars are fought should not be so clustered around territorial questions and disputes. There should be more crises involving non-territorial issues between contiguous parties and these should be just as likely to escalate to war as those involving territorial disputes. Although more systematic research on this question remains to be done, this does not seem to be the case.

A second test can be based on the fact that the interaction explanation, like the proximity explanation, assumes that advances in technology should make war more likely between non-contiguous pairs. As communication and contact between some non-contiguous pairs approaches the level of interaction typical of contiguous pairs then the probability of war between these non-contiguous states should be equal to that of contiguous states. That, as Gochman's (1990) tests show, has not happened. All the clues point in one direction and suggest that a greater emphasis in international relations should be placed on elaborating a territorial explanation of war.

A Territorial Explanation of Interstate War

The work on animal behavior provides some insight on why contiguity might be so problematic.[11] Even though most other animals do not fight wars, humans are not alone in using aggressive displays to keep and gain territory. Virtually all vertebrate animals are territorial (see Valzelli, 1981: 81 for documentation). This tendency is deeply ingrained and is part of humanity's collective genetic inheritance. In other words, humans may fight over territory because *classes* of animals have been territorial.

---

[11] Clearly, animal studies cannot be used to make logically valid inferences about human behavior, but discussions of human behavior should be aware of the biological basis of behavior and relevant studies in ethology. On the need for social scientists to examine the life sciences and for a justification for using ethological and zoological research see Masters (1989) and Shaw and Wong (1989: 6–10). For some cautionary notes on extrapolating to humans see Huntingford (1989: 29–33).

Humans are not "hard-wired" the way determinists maintained, but may be, as Somit (1990: 569) expresses it, "'soft-wired' to favor certain behaviors and cultural options." This probably includes a proclivity to react with violence over the issue of territory (see Huntingford, 1989: 33; Valzelli, 1981: 64–65, 81).

This position is very different from the position that war is a result of innate aggression or a drive for territoriality (McDougal, 1915; Lorenz, 1966; Ardrey, 1966; all discussed in Ferguson, 1984: 8–13). One of the problems with these innatist positions is that they leave no room for learning or for differentiation in behavior. Human warfare is not the result of a drive or an instinct like hunger, thirst, and sex are. The latter involve internal chemical and hormonal states that motivate humans and other animals to engage in certain kinds of behavior that either relieve or control the internal state. Typically a *drive* is distinguished from an *instinct* in that a drive is triggered by an internal state whereas an instinct needs an external stimulus to be induced (McGuinness, 1987: x) and then gives rise to a characteristic pattern of behavior associated with the species. Human warfare, and indeed killing, are too rare to be the product of a drive that needs to be satisfied. There is no drive or instinct that builds up, gives rise to aggression, is satiated upon release, and then builds up again until the next cycle (see Huntingford, 1989: 26–27; Bateson, 1989: 41; see also Valzelli, 1981: 67). Likewise, if it were the product of an instinct then warfare and killing should not vary as widely as it does or be as susceptible to other influences as it seems to be. Furthermore, humans also have a genetic inheritance shared with fellow primates for peacemaking (de Waal, 1989), and that propensity must also be factored into the equation.

Instead, it seems that humans learn both how to go to war and how to make peace. There is no instinct or drive determining behavior. Nevertheless, humans as a species are predisposed by their genetic inheritance and culture to learn some things more readily than others. Through most of history humans have learned that territorial issues can give rise to situations that are "best" handled by the use of force and violence.

These insights provide a broader theoretical context for understanding why territorial contiguity is an underlying cause of war and can serve as the basis for a broader territorial explanation of war. Let us assume that human collectivities (because of their genetic inheritance) behave in regard to territory according to a certain pattern, i.e. they use aggressive displays and acts to establish and maintain a territory and its boundaries. All other things being equal, it can be posited that two states bordering on each other will use aggressive displays to establish a border in areas where they meet. If this territoriality axiom were operating within the modern global political system, what kinds of behavior would be expected? First, it would be expected that states would divide up the Earth into territorial units and that territory would usually be claimed and often held through the use of force. Second, states would pay a great deal of attention to their boundaries, would be highly sensitive to any threats to their territory, and would be prepared to meet these threats with force. Indeed, it would be expected that the rationalization for military forces would in some way or another be related to the need to defend (or gain) territory. Third, with certain exceptions, any two contiguous states that were relatively equal in capability could be expected to establish boundaries through a struggle involving the use of force. This would mean that war or the threat of war should characterize the history of contiguous areas at some point in time. Such war, however, need not be constant since one of the effects of war might be to clearly establish one state's claims over another. Fourth, any new state that emerges could be expected to pose a threat to existing territorial divisions, and if fears arise that it cannot be accommodated, then violence or the threat of violence is likely.

Clearly, the first two expectations, that human groups would divide up the Earth into territorial units and pay a great deal of attention to boundaries, conform to some of the most obvious forms of behavior that have existed in world politics. These tendencies toward territoriality explain why most wars and enduring rivalries are between neighbors and why even acts of force short of war are clustered among neighbors. They also explain why other issues, when not linked to territory, do not give rise to many wars, even though armed force appears to be fairly fungible.

The third expectation, that contiguous states struggle to establish boundaries, is not so obvious in everyday life. If true, it means that every border, all other factors being equal, is going to be contested at some point in the history of two neighbors, although the contesting need not necessarily be violent. Likewise, any major change that might portend a change in the acceptance of existing divisions will give rise to threats.

Change that gives rise to threats can come from a variety of sources. Geography, demographic shifts, economic change, and shifts in the domestic political coalition in neighboring states can produce clear threats and challenges to existing territorial divisions. A river can move, leaving the land of one country in another. Movements of people, particularly if they are of different ethnolinguistic background, into border areas can establish the foundation for new claims. Changing economic modes can create new values and needs, making old territory more attractive or less desirable. The raising of sheep as opposed to cattle, the discovery that oil had practical uses, the opening of new trade routes all put great pressure on existing territorial distributions. Changes in the attitudes of the political coalition ruling neighbors can portend the raising of new claims or the resurrecting of old territorial disputes.

If such challenges are coupled with shifts in capabilities (demographic, economic, and military) or power transitions that enable one side to enforce its demands, then the probability of confrontation increases, if more normal diplomatic means have failed. Territorial issues, however, do not have their origin in such changes of capability, rather the capability permits existing concerns to move up on the political agenda.

The logic of this analysis implies that states with more borders should experience more wars. This proposition was tested some time ago by Richardson (1960b: 176–77, 297), and he found a 0.77 correlation between the number of frontiers a state had (including colonial frontiers) and the number of external wars in which it became involved. Subsequent research has confirmed this relationship (see Rummel, 1972a; Starr and Most, 1976, 1978).

Not all borders are contested, however. Sometimes natural geographical characteristics, like mountain ranges, deserts, and the sea separate human communities. It is only when communities come in direct contact that border contests are a possibility. Still, it is known from human history that this need not always be the case. In certain situations and periods of history, borders were not fixed nor were they always associated with aggressive displays. Nomadic societies are an obvious example. Also, Quincy Wright (1965: 39, 829–30) thought some time ago that war may have had its origin with the enclosing of land and the development of animal husbandry and agriculture (see also Fried, 1967: 115–16). Contemporary anthropologists (see Ferguson, 1987: 6–7, 9) find that inter-riverine Amazonian societies engage in territorial battles only when there is an intensive resource use pattern coupled with a scarcity of food and an inability to move on (i.e. some form of circumscription is involved).

Because territory is the primary means by which vertebrates gain their food, territoriality is not unrelated to economics. Some may argue that it is not territory *per se*, but the food and resources on the territory or the lack of them that may be the ultimate factor that makes territory so prone to violence (see Alcock, 1989: 518–20). Nevertheless, it seems fair to say that somewhere in evolution or in human history concerns with territory took on a life of their own, at least for large societies organized as states. Few interstate wars are fought for commercial gain unless they are connected with territory (see Holsti, 1991: 308, 316–17), and wars have been fought over territory that for all practical purposes is devoid of value (see Goertz and Diehl, 1992).

The fourth expectation, that wars are associated with new states, is supported by some recent research findings of Zeev Maoz (1989). Maoz is not looking directly at the question of territory, but at whether attempts by new states (or regimes) to join the club of nations give rise to militarized disputes. Nevertheless, Maoz's findings are relevant to the proposition on territory being presented here. If it is the case that territoriality makes states prone to use violence to establish their boundaries, then as the number of states in the system increases, the number of militarized disputes should also increase, since the establishment of new borders will entail more disputes. Consistent with this expectation, Maoz (1989: 202) finds a strong correlation (0.795) between the number of states in the system and the number of disputes in the system (see also Gochman and Maoz, 1984: 592–93, 600–1; Goertz and Diehl, 1988). Similarly, Small and Singer (1982: 130, 141) find that as the number of states goes up, so does the number of wars. Thus, the territoriality axiom can take a well-established association between system size and conflict and gives it a theoretically significant explanation.

Maoz (1989) points out, however, that how a state enters the system will have an effect on the amount of conflict it generates. States that enter the system through a violent revolutionary struggle are going to be regarded as more of a threat than those whose independence and state formation is characterized by a non-violent evolutionary process. According to Maoz (1989: 204), evolutionary states are not very disruptive of existing understandings. They have maintained close ties to a colonial power who has served to reassure other states and the new leaders that existing practices and relations will continue more or less as they have. More importantly, their route to independence has gradually adapted them to existing structures so that they are accepted, and their leaders have no reason to expect anything but acceptance. Revolutionary states, by contrast, are more likely to be less accepting of the status quo and their revolution usually portends a radical change in foreign policy goals and alignments.

In terms of the analysis being presented here, evolutionary states can be expected to pose less of a threat to existing understandings about boundaries; whereas revolutionary states may not accept old boundaries and any threat to existing boundaries will pose a source of conflict prone to war. Unless they have patrons who will do it for them, new states must make a place for themselves in the system. On the most literal level, this means that they must secure a physical location. Because of the sense of territoriality guiding human collectivities, such efforts are fraught with danger.

Maoz (1989: 207–8) also points out that changes in regimes can also generate militarized disputes. Here too, the new regime (as opposed to state) must make a place for itself. It must create the social and political space to allow its values, rules, and lifestyle (see Foucault, 1980: 68–70, 77) to exist, and it must do this on a territorial base, since the institutionalization of ideas often requires a location in which they can be put into practice and nurtured. Here a violent revolutionary change is an indicator that a new regime is disrupting a social space and thereby posing a threat. This is particularly the case if the new regime is going to challenge existing boundaries. What is equally likely, of course, is that the process of change will provide an opportunity for enemies to settle old scores. Since territorial questions often fester while they are dormant, changes in regime may produce a perceived shift in the balance of forces that permits the issue to be rectified.

On the basis of these various rationales, it can be predicted that revolutionary regimes entering the system should produce more conflict than evolutionary regimes, even when the system size does not change (as it would not when a state changes regimes) (see Maoz, 1989: 205–8, 214–26). Maoz (1989: 216–17) shows that this is, in fact, the case; for about the first twenty years after they enter the system, revolutionary states are much more likely to be involved in militarized disputes than evolutionary states. In addition, the greater the level of revolutionary change in the system, the more likely disputes will become contagious. Maoz (1989: 225) finds that the mean number of disputes begun when the level of revolutionary change is low is 3.41, but when there is a medium or high level of revolutionary change this increases to 8.86 and 11.50, respectively.

Maoz's findings suggest that Most and Starr (1980: 935) are correct in seeing borders as creating "structures of risks and opportunities that constrain the range of possible inter-nation interactions and make certain types of conflictive behavior more or less likely." Any fundamental change in the regime will create opportunities to raise territorial concerns that had been previously resolved and thereby put the new regime at risk. At the same time, the closest states provide the most immediate opportunities for the new revolutionary regime to spread its view of the world and/or to raise irredentist claims of its own, and thereby put the neighbor at risk. In these ways regime changes can have a contagious effect, breaking down an order and its stability of expectations (see Rummel, 1979: 160, 246, 255).

The ability of the territorial axiom to give rise to and explain the four expectations is testimony to its theoretical significance. Territoriality can explain very common and pervasive phenomena like the division of the world into units, as well as less obvious patterns like the connection between contiguity and rivalry, and between war and changes in regimes.

From the perspective of territoriality, interstate wars arise from attempts by human collectivities to demark territorial units, which form the basis for economic survival and well being. Economic pressures may give rise to new demands for territory; conversely, abundance may reduce the salience of territorial concerns. Territory that is not inhabited or of very little value may be left vacant. On the whole, however, states tend to struggle over contiguous territory. Aggressive displays and force, sometimes leading to violence and war, are used to establish boundaries in areas where two different societies are in direct contact. As a result, most wars are between neighbors: the more states in the system, the more wars that can be expected; the more borders a state has the greater its war involvements.

Territoriality is such a powerful concern that it shapes not only involvement in wars but involvement in crises and enduring rivalries. Most enduring rivalries and protracted conflicts are between neighbors, and neighbors are responsible for about two-thirds of the interstate militarized confrontations that occur. These patterns suggest that territoriality is an underlying force shaping world politics. Few other issues between states produce armed conflict unless they are linked with territorial issues. The exact reason why human collectivities fight over territory rather than other issues remains a focus for future research, but it seems to be connected with genetic proclivities associated with territoriality, which in turn may be related to the connection between territory and biological sustenance.

Although concerns over territoriality underlie all interstate wars, how different parties go to war and the events associated with the onset of war vary according to the capability of the two sides. The logic of interaction between relative equals is different from the logic of interaction between unequals. Wars between equals have different correlates and different proximate causes than wars between unequals. To explain interactions that lead to war, it is necessary to go beyond territoriality and examine how states learn to deal with their proclivities and needs. Politics is the key intervening variable, not only for explaining the type of war, but for predicting whether war will occur at all.

Territory, Politics, and Violence

Territory, and territorial contiguity in particular, is an underlying source of conflict that leads to war, but if that conflict is resolved, it need not constantly give rise to war. Territoriality is a basic tendency in state behavior, but once a territory is established, territoriality need not provoke confrontation and violence. If territoriality is so important, why does not contiguity constantly produce disputes? The answer is that while contiguity does give rise to conflict that is frequently settled by force or the threat of force, territorial and border conflict need not continue for the entire relationship of two states. This explains in part why the probability levels in Bremer's (1992) study are so low. Often a major war or series of wars stabilize the situation, and the two states are able to work out their relative status so as to avoid continual warfare. The United States' relations with Mexico and Canada illustrate two different ways in which this can occur. With Mexico, the United States fought a war and so defeated Mexico that it was able to strip it of large areas. The absence of ethno-linguistic links between Texas and Mexico prevented an irredentist issue from emerging (see Roy, 1991). With Canada, a series of crises, mostly with Britain, eventually produced a mutually acceptable solution without a major war. The establishment of this border, nevertheless, was shaped by experiences in the French and Indian war, the Revolutionary war, and the War of 1812. Other states have been less successful in resolving border claims and have been involved in a series of wars. These include Russia and Turkey, Germany and its neighbors, and Israel and its neighbors. While not a substitute for systematic research, these illustrations do indicate that contiguity can be a serious problem at one point in time without its being a persistent issue.

If the territorial divisions among neighbors are not challenged but accepted as legitimate, peaceful relations can govern. Most borders once satisfactorily settled remain so for long periods of time. A tremendous increase in England's capability *vis à vis* France is not going to lead the English to reclaim Guienne and Gascony. Nor is Sweden likely to seek the return of Estonia and Livonia. Nor will Mexico enter an alliance with Germany to try to get back the Southwest of the United States. Changes in capability become dangerous only when there are existing territorial disputes, old scores to settle, or new issues raised because of economic or demographic shifts. While these three factors often make capability shifts threatening, in regions where borders are fixed and considered legitimate, they do not. For much of European history after the fall of the Roman Empire, borders were a subject of contention. Since 1945, the borders of Western Europe have not been prone to violent change. Those issues are now considered settled or subject to non-violent change based on norms of self-determination and diplomatic recognition by the European community.

How territorial issues are settled will have a profound effect on relations between neighbors, determining the extent to which they will be basically hostile or friendly. Attempts to impose borders or acquire new territory through the use of force produce hostility. Imposed borders, especially between relative equals, are much more likely to lead to enduring rivalry (or protracted conflict between unequals) than borders established through mutual accommodation and diplomatic agreement. The use of force only leads to settlement when one side attains an overwhelming victory and is able to maintain a preponderance of power over the other side (see Weede, 1976 and Garnham, 1976 for evidence consistent with this claim). Anything short of that will make territorial issues fester and produce long-term hostile relationships. In this context, shifts in capability can be expected to lead to a renewal of claims. Thus, there is a curvilinear relationship between the use of war to establish a border and the recurrence of disputes, with settlement by the two extremes of overwhelming victory and diplomatic accommodation both associated with peace, but the use of force short of overwhelming victory associated with recurring disputes.

Much of European history has been plagued by recurring wars and disputes because force was used between relative equals. The same pieces of territory – because of dynastic claims, strategic location, or ethnolinguistic composition – were the focus of confrontation over and over again. When territorial disputes are not settled, relations with neighbors become a struggle for power. Much of power politics thinking probably derives from such experiences. So long as there is a struggle over contiguous territory, then world politics is a struggle for power, but once boundaries are settled, world politics has other characteristics. Conflict and disagreement are still present, but violence is less likely and power transitions no longer war producing.

This suggests that the very idea of power politics and its practices are derived from an inability to settle territorial questions. Power politics is not the key fact of existence, as the realist paradigm would have us believe, but may simply be an epiphenomenon of territoriality. Realism and the practices of power politics come out of a particular set of struggles and construct a world appropriate to those struggles. Once those struggles end, however, the ideas are less relevant and even counter-productive. The great mistake of realism has been to assume that a struggle for power is a constant verité of history, when in fact it is most characteristic only of (contention on) one kind of issue – territory. A cursory review of the periods of history most associated with the intellectual origins of realist thought and power politics behavior lends credence to this idea. Renaissance Italy, early modern Europe, Ancient China in the Warring States period, and the India of Kautilya were all periods of intense struggle over contiguous territory. More systematic research would provide an important test of these claims.

While persistent rivalry and confrontation over contiguous territory is associated with power politics beliefs and practices, this does not mean that territorial disputes *always* give rise to this sort of contention. Much depends on the nature of the interactions and diplomacy of a period. Territorial conflict can be reduced considerably if norms have evolved for dealing with territorial claims and transfers. All norms generally reduce confrontation, but some may be more successful than others. For example, in Western history during the age of nationalism, the principle of national self-determination evolved for justifying territorial claims. Such a principle once applied makes territory that is ethnolinguistically homogeneous less open to periodic challenge, because it is unlikely that the ethnic composition of an area will change very rapidly. Conversely, in the age of dynasties, every death of a monarch had the potential of raising a claim if the succession was ambiguous.

These examples show that norms can play an important role in making territorial issues less prone to violence. This assumes, of course, that there can be an agreement on norms. If there are conflicting norms in a period or a shift from one norm to a radically different one, then there may be attempts to redraw the entire map of a region or the known world. The territoriality axiom suggests that if this were to happen, there would be widespread violence. In European history, the shift from the age of dynasties to the age of sovereignty and then to the age of nationalism produced something like this (see Luard, 1986: 110). Territory which was held exclusively on the principle of dynastic right gave way to a situation in which the modern nation-state sought to acquire contiguous areas with "natural" frontiers. After 1789, the idea of nation required that people of similar ethnolinguistic heritage take control of their own destiny by living within a single state. Because of these shifts in norms, the map of Europe was redrawn at least twice, and in some areas, several times. Understanding that there is a link between territoriality and violence should make people better aware of the possible consequences of changing territorial divisions or changing the norms underlying those divisions.

Nevertheless, the fact that norms are often able to determine the legitimacy of territorial claims shows that territorial disputes can be settled politically without the use of violent force. Disputes tend to arise only when norms are ambiguous or non-existent. Succession to other thrones in the age of dynasties (1400–1559) led to confrontation and war primarily in situations where there was no consensus on the rules to succession. In these circumstances, more than one claimant could appear, and existing norms were unable to resolve the dispute. Luard (1986: 87) lists some of the questions that the norms of the time were unable to answer definitively: "Could succession pass through the female line …? … Could a brother inherit before a son …? … Could a mother inherit from a son …" A number of wars were fought over these questions, because there was sharp division over the correct answers. Presumably, if a consensus or set of rules for resolving these questions could have been developed, fewer challengers could have garnered support and many of these wars would have been avoided. Perhaps if diplomats had understood better the connection between territory and war, they would have been more motivated to make norms more comprehensive and improve the procedures for transferring territory or dealing with disputants' claims.

If politics truly is an intervening variable and territoriality is not a drive or instinct, but simply an underlying cause, then settling territorial disputes non-violently should lead to a long-term peaceful relationship. One of the most effective ways, in modern times, to resolve territorial disputes has been through the creation of buffer zones. This is an ingenious discovery that works. Wallensteen (1984: 247) shows that when efforts are made to separate major states by the creation of buffer zones, wars no longer occur and militarized confrontations go way down.[12] Conversely, when major states treat the areas between them as political vacuums that

---

[12] It is significant that studies of animal behavior show that once territory is used to space animals and keep them at a certain distance from each other aggression goes down (see Valzelli, 1981: 64, 70–71; Huntingford, 1989: 32–33). For an analysis of buffer states and their role in establishing peace see the studies in Chay and Ross (1986).

must be filled, wars result. This indicates that disputes over territorial contiguity can be peacefully resolved.

The creation of buffer zones in history also forms a kind of natural experiment in which the causal significance of territory can be assessed. If the creation of buffer zones ends wars and contiguity promotes wars, this is dramatic evidence that territory is a cause of war, since "manipulating" the cause in one direction produces peace and "manipulating" it in the other direction produces war. Such an effect could not result if the relationship between territorial contiguity and war were tautological or trivial. Since buffer states are contiguous to each state, the interaction or loss-of-strength gradient explanations can not explain why buffer zones work. Because buffer states are contiguous states they should, according to these two explanations, not produce any more peace than the typical contiguous dyad, since they still would be the subject of frequent interactions, and not very distant. Of course, differences in capability play a role, but such differences do not always prevent weaker states (like Serbia) from pursuing territorial claims.

The way to peace, then, lies with handling territorial issues better. One way to do this is to pay more attention to norms governing territory and its transfer. Another is to avoid linking non-territorial issues with questions of territory. Taking either tack can reduce war and confrontation as demonstrated by the issue of international navigation and commerce. In mercantilist times, states claimed large areas of the ocean as their territory, and there were few rules governing navigation and commerce (Holsti, 1991: 315). In addition, trade was considered the exclusive right of the state that held a colonial territory. As trade was opened up, as the oceans were no longer subject to the sovereignty of any state, and as rules and procedures were developed for regulating commerce and navigation, disputes and wars related to these economic issues declined rapidly (Holsti, 1991: 315). All of these changes became possible because the mercantilist belief that wealth and trade were zero-sum games was abandoned. Since they were now treated as non-zero-sum, and in some quarters as positive-sum games, there was no point to attaching economic issues to exclusive territorial claims.

The example of trade and navigation suggests a new way of achieving peace, namely to "de-territorialize" an issue by stripping it away from its territorial base. Trade was de-territorialized when who owned a territory became irrelevant to whether one could trade with the inhabitants. The oceans (and navigation) were de-territorialized when state sovereignty was limited to a 3-mile territorial sea. To de-territorialize an issue is to see that the needs and values giving rise to the issue can be satisfied without it being necessary to have exclusive control over a given piece of territory. In the contemporary period, nationalist aspirations (in terms of identity issues) and ideological preferences are treated as zero-sum and territorialized. Nationalism preaches that each people is a nation and to protect its cultural identity and autonomy it must have its own territory with its own state. It is not clear, however, that identity is zero-sum or that its only protection is to divide the world into national territorial units. What is clear is that such efforts increase the probability of war and attempts to de-territorialize identity issues would make them easier to resolve.

Territoriality and the territorial concerns to which it gives rise make war neither inevitable nor constant. Rather, they form a structure of predispositions within which collectivities must learn to interact to meet their mutual needs. How neighboring states deal with their concerns shapes the relationship they will have and helps construct the world in which they live. How states throughout the known world deal with territorial concerns sets examples and precedents and creates a structure of expectations in which all states operate (see Kratochwil, 1986, 1989). Territorial issues are so fundamental that the behavior associated with their settlement literally constructs a world order (including a world of anarchy). The institution of war and the behavior correlated with it that was outlined in Chapter 1 and the foreign policy practices of power politics delineated in Chapter 3 must be seen as originating in the ways states learn to deal with their territorial concerns. In these various ways, territoriality is an underlying force shaping world politics. Learning how to deal with that force can have a profound effect on the nature of the world in which we live – and die.

Conclusion

Territory, given the nature of the animal we are, will probably always be the subject of disagreement, but that disagreement need not always be resolved by war. The way to peace is not to try to eliminate all sources of conflict, but to understand what kinds of issues are prone to violence and how they might be dealt with differently. The analysis in this chapter has shown that wars, rivalries, and confrontations are unusually clustered between neighbors. This relationship is probably not an accident but reflects an underlying cause. Of all the issues over which wars could logically be fought, territorial issues seem to be the ones most often associated with wars. Few interstate wars are fought without any territorial issue being involved in one way or another.

This has led to the conclusion that territory is a peculiarly sensitive area for human collectivities. They will fight over it more readily than over any other question, and any issue linked with territory becomes subject to violence and the use of force. The reason for this is not known, but it may very well lie in an inherited tendency toward territoriality. A focus on territoriality can explain a number of patterns not explained by other perspectives. It also suggests solutions to war, like the creation of buffer states and de-territorializing issues, that seem to work and produce peaceful relations.

Territoriality is treated here as a proclivity that humans have and not as a drive or instinct that makes war inevitable. Human collectivities are prone to use violence and force to resolve territorial issues, but these are instruments that we have been predisposed to learn to use and that have been selected out, in part, by their perceived success. These are not the only instruments human collectivities have used to settle territorial disputes, however, and non-violent means have produced better relationships between neighbors. In addition, territoriality and violence are not so intimately bound that territorial concerns are constant and always giving rise to violent solutions. Indeed, for most neighbors, once territorial issues are resolved, peaceful relations eventually ensue. They learn to live with each other. This is true especially if they cannot destroy each other, but it is also true that they learn that they need not destroy each other.

The history of most neighbors is characterized by a period of confrontation and war, followed by a period of peace. War is a period in the history of neighbors, not a constant. Since most interstate wars are between neighbors, this implies that once all neighbors resolve territorial questions, the world will be at peace. This can happen if states learn how to resolve these issues and avoid practices that increase the probability of war. War comes about not simply because humans are territorial, but because they deal with territorial issues in certain ways. The ways they select to resolve territorial issues determine whether there will be war or peace. For this reason, the foreign policy practices of states can be seen as the proximate causes of war. Among equals, the surest way to war is to use the practices of power politics to resolve territorial disputes. This is the topic of the next chapter.

5

The Realist Road to War

The road to war is well marked, even though the destination may turn out to be a surprise to many.

It is often the case that when questions have failed to be answered for a long time, as is the case with many of the questions on war, it is because the questions themselves have been posed in an unelucidating way. Much of the analysis in the previous chapters has been devoted to trying to pose questions about war in a manner that will make satisfactory answers more likely.

How should we ask questions about the causes of war? First, not all wars are alike, so this analysis seeks to explain one category of wars – wars of rivalry. Within that category, the focus is on wars of rivalry among the *strongest* states in the system, since more research exists on these states and their wars than on others. Second, not all wars are equal in their social or theoretical significance, so this analysis will place special emphasis on explaining the onset of world war. To do so means explaining why wars become total and complex; i.e., how and why most, if not all, of the major states are drawn into a war and why it is a war fought to the finish. Third, not all wars have the same causes, so while this analysis seeks to identify some of the sufficient conditions of wars of rivalry, it will not identify every causal sequence leading to war. And of the possible sufficient conditions, this analysis will focus primarily on identifying the foreign policy practices in the modern global system that appear to be associated with the onset of wars of rivalry. Systemic, domestic, and individual factors (e.g. aspects of human nature) will not be systematically discussed; to do so would make the analysis overly diffuse. Nevertheless, the aspects of these factors that are seen as most critical in explaining war will be drawn into the analysis by showing how they give rise to or flow out of the foreign policy practices that are associated with wars of rivalry.

In this analysis, wars of rivalry in the modern global system, including twentieth-century world wars, will be explained by asking what factors led to the foreign policy practices that made war highly probable. If we think of war as a foreign policy practice, then we can explain the onset of war by looking at the pattern of interstate interactions, the domestic political factors, and the global institutional context that give rise to a situation that makes leaders adopt this foreign policy practice. When conceived in this way, the behavior that leads to war can be seen as setting up three different structures which, under the right conditions, establish a set of reinforcing constraints that make at least one side (and frequently both sides in a war of rivalry) feel that they have no choice but to go to war. What is significant is that interstate interactions have a way of moving each of the structures to a position where all three push the actors toward selecting out war as the most appropriate response.

While this may appear as if war is a rational or inevitable response to an unbearable situation this is the case only so long as one internalizes the logic of realist folklore. As one steps out of that perspective or examines the actual consequences of each action that is taken, one finds it anything but rational. Misperception, miscalculation, self-fulfilling prophecies, and error often produce disasters that might have been avoided if actors had behaved differently. War also cannot be regarded as a rational outcome because political actors are not fully conscious of the process that gets them involved in war. This is because the factors within the three structures that produce war often emerge as unanticipated consequences of previous actions. This is particularly the case with world war, which is rarely anticipated.

In this chapter, the sequence of behavior that has usually preceded wars and how and why this sequence results in war will be examined.[1] The emphasis will be on delineating how a rivalry is converted into a war relationship. In Chapter 6, attention will be given to how foreign policy interactions produce a domestic political context that favors war. In Chapter 7, how foreign policy interactions can convert dyadic wars of rivalry into world wars will be analyzed. In Chapter 8, attention will turn to the global institutional context – discussing how foreign policy interactions can lead a peace to decay and examining the role war plays in establishing a peace.

The analysis in this chapter will synthesize from existing scientific findings an overall picture of the factors that lead to wars of rivalry. An

---

[1] Because it is stylistically cumbersome to always state "wars of rivalry among the strongest states in the system," the reader should note that all explanatory statements about war in this part of the book are confined to wars of rivalry among the strongest states, unless otherwise noted.

explanation of war will be constructed by looking at: (1) how security issues arise; (2) how alliances are a response to the rise of security issues and how they affect the onset of war; (3) how military buildups and arms races are a response to security issues; and (4) why some crises escalate to war and others do not.

Explaining War as a Series of Steps

If we piece together some of the findings and theoretical suggestions made in the literature on the scientific study of war, we get the following picture of the process that leads two or more actors to a war of rivalry, a process best characterized as steps to war. As a situation develops that might portend the use of force, leaders and various policy influencers become concerned primarily with security goals and/or the use of force to gain stakes that they have been unable to attain up to this point (Singer, 1982: 40). In order to test their rival and to demonstrate resolve, leaders rely on threats and coercive tactics, which involves them in crises (or militarized disputes) (Rummel, 1979: 186; Maoz, 1983). Leaders respond to a crisis and to security issues that are perceived as posing a long-term threat by attempting to increase their military power through alliances and/or a military buildup (Wallace, 1972; Most and Siverson, 1987). In a tense environment, military buildups lead to arms races, and alliance making may result in a polarization (of blocs), both of which increase insecurity. In militarized disputes between equals, actors employ *realpolitik* tactics (Leng, 1983). Eventually, a dispute arises that escalates to war. Disputes or crises are most likely to escalate if there is an ongoing arms race (Wallace, 1979), and if (1) they are triggered by physical threats to vital issues (Gochman and Leng, 1983); (2) they are the second or third crisis with the same rival (with *realpolitik* tactics becoming more coercive and hostile in each succeeding crisis) (Leng, 1983); (3) a hostile interaction spiral emerges during the crisis (Holsti, North, and Brody, 1968); and (4) hard-liners dominate the leadership of at least one side.

This process is based on the assumption that wars of rivalry result from a series of steps taken by each side. Each step produces, in succession, a situation that encourages the adoption of foreign policy practices that set the stage for the involved parties' taking another step that is closer to war. It should not be concluded that each of these steps is a cause of war, like a variable in a path analysis. The steps must be seen as the adoption of a social practice that the dominant folklore recommends to decision makers in light of the situation they are facing. The realist tradition has suggested that, in the face of threatening security issues, one must build up power. To increase power, the tradition tells leaders to make alliances and/or enlarge their military. These practices are not the only ones possible, nor do they always work. They are, however, the practices that have been selected out by the realist tradition, and that tradition has guided the modern global system. As with war, these practices are social inventions that have been created as a way of handling a particular situation.

The recommendations of the realist folklore often involve hedging one's bets. The recommendation to build alliances and one's military is seen as a strategy that will prevent an adversary from attacking, but if this fails, these practices also increase the probability of victory. What the realists overlook, of course, is that such behavior among equals tends not to prevent war, but to encourage it. This is because situations arise in which each side becomes involved more with preparing for war and eventually winning it, rather than taking those actions that would help prevent a war (see Wayman [1990: 20] who refers to this as "the Phillips curve of international security"). For this reason, these social practices and steps can be expected to be associated with wars of rivalry, but how many are truly causes and which are epiphenomena will have to be the subject of future research.

An analysis of the steps to war becomes a way of uncovering the dynamics by which leaders and their followers learn to adopt social practices that their culture makes available to them. The claim of this chapter is that, among equals, war is resorted to only after these other practices have failed to resolve the issue at hand. During this period, leaders and their followers become convinced (i.e. they learn) that war is the best (and probably only) way of handling the situation facing them.

In other words, if war is thought of as a foreign policy practice, then it can be asked what global institutional factors, what pattern of interstate interactions, and what domestic political contexts in the contending parties make leaders select war as the most appropriate foreign policy practice for handling the situation at hand. Foreign policy actions and practices can be seen as operating within these three general types of constraints or structures. The most basic is the political structure of the system, i.e. the global institutional mechanisms (including accepted rules of the game) that exist for authoritatively resolving global issues. When such structures work, they are often called peace systems or regimes (see Doran, 1971; Randle, 1987), and when they do not, the structure is said to be anarchic (see Waltz, 1959, 1979). Suffice it to say here that a global institutional structure that makes war possible by institutionalizing it or reduces its likelihood by providing other practices to deal with its functions is a systemic structure that has been socially constructed and institutionally built by the previous acts of states or other collectivities. In any given historical period, the extent to which the global institutional context favors or hinders the use of war as a foreign policy practice will vary.

The second structure in which political actors must operate emerges out of the pattern of interactions with their rivals. The history of prior interactions, particularly since the last major war, establishes a set of expectations and a reservoir of psychological hostility or friendship (see Mansbach and Vasquez, 1981: 203–7) that act as a set of constraints on existing interactions. Nevertheless, existing interactions can determine the present and future relationship, if they are sufficiently intense and frequent. What happens prior to wars of rivalry is that the relationship becomes increasingly hostile in terms of psychological affect, thereby encouraging the selection of war as a foreign policy practice.

The third structure in which foreign policy practices are selected is the domestic political context. Regardless of the type of political regime within a state, a coalition needs to come together that favors war. The formation of that coalition must minimally involve the leadership, but more often than not it must usually involve the entire government (including its bureaucracy), the state's elite, and the mass public. How threatening or how accommodative a leadership can be toward a rival will depend on the influence and predispositions of the domestic political context in which that leadership must operate. The domestic political context itself, however, is shaped by the foreign policy actions taken against the opponent and the opponent's reactions.

Not all foreign policy practices and actions are equally favored; the three structures can differ in the degree to which they push forward one practice or another. War is selected as a practice when all three structures constrain a leader so that no other option seems possible, or comparatively desirable, given one's goals. What realism's dominance of the modern global system has accomplished is that it provides an overall cognitive structure which, under the right conditions, tends to push each of these three structures in the same direction. Namely, it pushes the system toward anarchy and unilateral behavior, the interactions toward hostility, and the domestic political context toward hardline preferences.

This chapter will focus on how interactions lead to steps that bring states closer to war, while the next chapter will examine how the internal effects of these interactions privilege hard-line actions. A discussion of the effects of the global institutional structure will be delayed until Chapter 8.

The Rise of Security Issues

The beginnings of wars can be traced to those situations in which some leaders believe that their state's security is threatened and start to take measures to protect themselves. Contrary to realist assertions, however, not all actors, particularly states, are always engaged in a struggle for power. It seems more accurate to assume that security issues and the power-politics behavior associated with them only occur at certain stages in interstate relationships and predominate only in certain periods of history.[2]

If realists have been generally too alarmist in their assumptions about the pervasiveness of war and threats to security, they have been more accurate in describing the kinds of behavior associated with the rise of security issues between equals. Such issues are usually raised by one actor testing another's willingness to use its capability (diplomatic, economic, or military) to maintain a given distribution of political stakes. In such a situation, actors believe that victory is most likely to be associated with some demonstration of resolve; that is, making it credible that they are more willing than the other side to use force and risk escalation and war, either to defend or to advance their position (see Maoz, 1983; Leng, 1980).

It is logical to assume that only after such threats appear, especially if they are perceived as long-term threats, will actors seek allies or build up their military. The research on this question and on the factors that precede alliance making and military buildups has been neither extensive nor conclusive, however.[3] Most research has centered, instead, on the effects of alliances, capabilities, and arms races.

---

[2] War is a relatively rare event. Only sixty-seven interstate and fifty-one other wars (involving at least one nation-state) were fought between 1815 and 1980 (Small and Singer, 1982: 59–60). According to these data, war is an even rarer event in the history of specific interstate relations. Likewise, some periods of history are more peaceful than others. Peter Wallensteen (1984: 245–46) shows that 1816–48, 1871–95, 1919–32, and 1963–76 are devoid of major power wars and have fewer military confrontations between major states than other periods.

[3] For some of the empirical work that examines the factors that lead actors to become involved in disputes see Maoz (1982), especially chapters 4 and 5, Gochman (1980), and Wallace (1972). For some initial thoughts on what causes rivalry and hence the rise of

Responding to Security Issues: Alliances

Alliances and the culture of war

Realist thinkers see alliances as a response to anarchy and the insecurity it produces. Some writers, particularly Waltz (1979: 118), see alliances as a product of structural anarchy, whereas others, for example Morgenthau (1960: 181–82), see alliances as resulting from a foreign policy decision. This analysis, taking a foreign policy perspective, sees alliances as a way political actors in the modern global system attempt to cope with threatening security issues that arise. Since there are other ways of dealing with security issues, alliances do not always form when security issues are present (Most and Starr, 1984; Most and Siverson, 1987: 149–51; Choucri and North, 1975: 203).

Unlike traditional realism, this analysis assumes that alliance formation is not an inevitable behavior that arises in certain conditions, but is something which is historically contingent. Alliances are a learned social practice made available by realist culture, but whose popularity changes. Furthermore, this analysis does not assume that the conditions realism typically sees as producing alliances, namely anarchy and insecurity, are as prevalent as realism posits. Nor does it assume that anarchy always produces insecurity or that anarchy is the predominant structure of every global system.

For realists, making an alliance can be a way of avoiding war and promoting peace through strength. The empirical research does not bear out this assumption, however. Alliances do not prevent war or promote peace; instead, they are associated with war. Although this may be because specific alliances are unable to increase strength sufficiently or because they provoke counter-alliances, it is important to establish the fact that alliance making typically does not result in peace and often is followed by war, although alliances are probably not a cause of war.

The first data-based study of the relationship between alliances and war was that of Singer and Small (1966). They examine the alliances and war behavior of states from 1815 to 1945 and find that states that rank high on alliance activity also rank high on the amount of war they experience, whereas states that rank low on alliance making rank low on war involvement.[4] States that rank high on alliance activity, rank

---

security issues, see Mansbach and Vasquez (1981: ch. 6). For some thoughts on why states seek alliances see Walt (1987).

[4] A subsequent study by Levy (1981: Tables 3–6) may appear to contradict this finding in that it shows a small negative relationship between number of alliances in the system and

high not only on the number of wars in which they become engaged, but also on the total number of battle deaths they have suffered and the number of years of war they have experienced. This implies that alliances not only encourage states to become involved in wars, but that when they do, these wars are longer and more severe than wars fought in the absence of alliances. These relationships hold mostly for defense pacts (not ententes) and are stronger for central system members (those major and minor states most important for the Eurocentric system that has dominated the modern global system) than for all members of the system.[5]

One of the problems with this kind of research design, which Singer and Small point out, is that the findings may simply reflect the fact that some states are more active than others – participating more in all of the practices of the system. Singer and Small (1966: 134) want to make sure that the high alliance activity is preceding wars, so they rank states only by pre-war alliances that were made at least three months before the outbreak of war. When they do this, the values of the Spearman's rho go up. This means that the most war-prone states are making alliances prior to their wars, especially when the wars are in the central system or with other major states.

An examination of specific cases makes it clear that the chances of an allied major state staying out of a war are not very good (Singer and Small, 1966: 134–35). Indeed, the evidence indicates that major states within the central system herald their wars by alliances. For example, all of Austria-Hungary's, Prussia/Germany's, and Russia's wars (seven, seven, and eight wars, respectively) are preceded by alliances. All but one of Britain's four wars in the central system are preceded by alliances (Singer and Small, 1966: 126, Table 5).[6] Further inspection of Singer and

war in the system. Levy's systemic measure of alliances may really be tapping the amount of polarization in the system. Singer and Small (1966) do not look at the number of alliances in the system (for that see Singer and Small, 1968), but at whether states that make alliances then experience wars. When Levy (1981: Tables 7–9) examines the latter question he gets similar results; see below.

[5] For the central system the Spearman's rho values between number of defense pacts and: number of wars, number of wars vs. majors, battle deaths, and years of war are, respectively, 0.51, 0.52, 0.51, 0.47. With the total system they are lower (0.36, 0.44, 0.31, 0.25), and with ententes they are generally negative, but below 0.20 (see Singer and Small, 1966: 135–36, Tables 8 and 9).

[6] The accuracy of these figures, which have been derived from Table 5, has been confirmed by Melvin Small in a personal communication to me. Note that if Britain's wars outside the central system are counted, only three of Britain's five wars are preceded by an alliance.

Small's (1966: 124, Table 4) data shows that six of France's nine wars, eight of Italy's eleven wars, and five of Japan's seven wars are preceded by alliances.

Singer and Small (1966: 136–38) also find that the longer a state is a member of a system, the more wars and the more alliances it will have.[7] This raises the possibility that the relationship between alliances and war might be spurious, especially given that some of the tests that control for a state's membership duration weaken many of the associations. However, not too much emphasis should be placed on this reduction in the associations, since further tests (Singer and Small, 1966: 137–38, Table 14) show little change in association between the number of pre-war alliances of a state and war involvement modified for duration of membership. More significantly, the control test can be interpreted to show in what ways alliances lead to war.

For instance, Singer and Small's findings make it clear that the central system has proportionally more alliance activity and more wars than the total system. Since the central system is clearly more guided by a realist culture, it makes sense that the longer a state was in the system, the more it would conform to the norms of the system. The argument presented in Chapter 3, that war and power politics are social inventions shaped by realist discourse, would suggest that the longer a state was a member of the system, the more wars *and* the more alliances it would have. The fact that most of the reduction in the association between alliance and war is brought about by newer states (Singer and Small, 1966: 138), which may not yet have been fully socialized, is consistent with this interpretation.

Indeed, an inspection of Singer and Small's (1966) Table 4 shows that newer states in the periphery that resist the norms of the system, e.g. the United States, or weaker states that are unable to practice the norms of the central system are the ones involved in wars without having been previously involved in an alliance. Thus, only one of the United States' five wars is preceded by an alliance. Similarly, only two of China's five wars and none of Turkey's nine wars are preceded by alliances (figures compiled from Singer and Small, 1966: 124–25, Table 4).

These criticisms do not impugn the relationship between alliances and war, but limit it to the central system and major states. For these states, the

---

[7] The number of years a state has in the central system has a strong association with number of wars (0.66) and a moderate association with alliances (number of defense pacts = 0.34; pacts with majors = 0.42). The associations for the total system are similar, but slightly lower; see Singer and Small (1966: 136, Table 11).

relationship between alliance and war is very real, and for major states in certain periods of history, alliance involvement is almost a prerequisite for war. Since weaker and newer states, as well as those outside the central system, do not conform to this behavior, this suggests that alliances are probably not a cause of war, but an aspect of a larger package of behavior associated with war. *Alliances can be seen as part of a political culture of war* that has been constituted by realist discourse and shaped by the practices of power politics. Making an alliance becomes a way of handling security issues and of preparing oneself in case war might occur. Not all states can make an alliance and not all states, particularly newer states and those on the periphery, accept this norm, so the relationship is far from perfect.

Further evidence that war might result not so much from a single cause, but from a syndrome of behavior, is provided by Gochman (1980) and by Bremer (1980). Gochman provides more detailed evidence that newer and peripheral major states behave differently from the more central older major states. As noted earlier (in Chapter 3: 122–23, especially note 18), he finds that, in the twentieth century, older European states, with the exception of Britain, follow an opportunity model in their participation in serious disputes; whereas the latecomers from outside Europe follow an inequity or status-inconsistency model (Gochman, 1980: 107, 115–16). An opportunity model implies that major states will engage in power politics behavior unless restrained.

This is precisely the kind of behavior profile one would expect states to have in a culture where realist norms prevailed. Just as it should come as no surprise that male individuals who live in a culture of dueling or a culture of vendetta should have a behavior profile consistent with those cultures, so too it should be unsurprising that alliance making, involvement in serious disputes, and participation in war should be the hallmark of major states in the central system. The fact that newcomers to the system behave differently and require a stronger motivation before resorting to force underscores the importance of learning and cultural norms for shaping conflict and violent behavior. Gochman (1980: 116) even speculates that as the newcomers actually become acculturated they will follow a traditional opportunity model. Such a conclusion may underestimate the extent to which new major states may be able to transform the system and/or the extent to which realist norms and practices are a historical product of the peculiar geographical configuration and resource base of Europe, but it does support the point that alliance and war behavior are something learned from the norms of the system.

Bremer (1980) provides additional evidence that major states behave differently and are more likely to be involved in war than other states. He shows that power does not prevent war, but is associated with it. Specifically, he finds that stronger states are involved in more wars, initiate more wars and have more deaths per war.[8] Examining only the top sixteen states, Bremer (1980: 74) found that the higher a state is in its capability ranking, the greater the number of wars in which it becomes involved ($R^2 = 0.65$). Subsequent studies extending Bremer's study have found that the more powerful states are, the more involved they become in militarized disputes (Eberwein, 1982; Gochman and Maoz, 1984: 606–9). Bremer's analysis suggests that the most powerful states in the system are caught in a culture of war and that the more powerful they are, the more they are unable to avoid war. Power (and probably attempts to increase power) does not prevent war, but makes it more likely. As Bremer (1980: 79) concludes:

> Over the past 150 years there is no evidence to support the contention that the possession of military capability in large quantities ensures peace. On the contrary, the evidence suggests that, regardless of whether nations arm to prevent war or to wage war, in the long run there is a positive association between the possession of military capability and its ultimate use.

The findings of Gochman, Bremer, and Singer and Small show that power, alliances, war, and length of time in the central system are all bound together. The norms and practices of this system often encourage war, even if states may seek to avoid it. Nevertheless, these are general tendencies and they do not have to hold for all periods. This is particularly true for alliances. For instance, Singer and Small (1966: 139) show that 1871–1900 was a period of high alliance levels but infrequent war, which implies that under the proper conditions (e.g. in the way alliances are used, or the global institutional context in which they are made) alliances can be stripped of their bellicose effects. Also, eliminating alliances will not eliminate war, since Singer and Small (1966: 138–39) find that even in a period of low alliance levels, such as 1815–70, there still can be frequent war. Alliances then can be seen as a path, and not necessarily a direct one, nor the only one, through which states become involved in war.

---

[8] For the entire period these correlations are respectively 0.60 (rate of war involvement), 0.64 (rate of war initiation) and 0.64 (battle deaths, i.e. *absolute* deaths as opposed to *percent* population loss) (Bremer, 1980: 73, Table 3.5).

Alliances and war in the last 500 years

Singer and Small (1966) look at only 1815–1945. More extensive evidence that alliances do not prevent war, but are associated with it, is presented in an article by Jack Levy, who supplements Correlates of War data on the nineteenth and twentieth centuries with his own data on alliances and war involving major states from the sixteenth through eighteenth centuries. Levy (1981: 597–98, Table 7) finds that, except for the nineteenth century, the majority of alliances (56 to 100 percent, depending on type) have been followed, within five years of their formation, by war involving at least one of the allies. Moreover, all "great-power" alliances in the sixteenth, seventeenth, and twentieth centuries have been followed, within five years, by a war involving a major state (Levy, 1981: 597–98, Table 7).[9] Additional tests show that none of these findings are due to the effects of chance (see Levy, 1981: 600–2). Levy's analysis goes a long way in dispelling the notion that alliances promote peace.

Furthermore, Levy's finding that "great power" alliances are more frequently followed by war than other alliances indicates that alliances involving major states are more war-prone than other alliances. Although Levy does not examine the question, two different processes and effects are probably at work in producing this relationship. The first and most obvious way in which a "great power" alliance results in war is when an alliance is formed during on ongoing rivalry and gives rise to counter-alliances, eventually producing a situation that ends in war. Levy's evidence, as well as Singer and Small's, is consistent with the notion that alliances formed during a rivalry are much more likely to result in war than alliances formed in other situations. Thus, the strongest relationship Levy finds between alliances and war is when he looks at "great power" alliances followed by "great power" war (wars involving "great powers" on each side), while controlling for random effects. Here, he finds that alliances were followed by war in the seventeenth century 72 percent more frequently than expected by chance, 82 percent more frequently in the eighteenth century, and 85 percent more frequently in the twentieth than expected by chance (Levy, 1981: 601, Table 9).

The second and less obvious way in which alliances between major states give rise to war is discussed by Schroeder (1976) and demonstrated by Moul (1988b). Moul (1988b: 34–35) shows that there is a tendency for disputes between unequals to escalate to war more frequently when a

---

[9] In the eighteenth century, 71 percent of the "great power" alliances are followed by war.

predatory major state has a non-aggression pact or entente with another major state than when such alliances are absent. This finding appears to indicate that alliances between major states, particularly those that are competitors, can serve as a way of legitimizing and/or permitting the use of force against weaker parties, while simultaneously limiting the impact of the war. Schroeder's (1976) historical analysis supports this conclusion. When alliances are used in this way, they are a form of management, a pact of restraint (*pacto de contrahendo*) that helps control unilateral behavior (Schroeder, 1976: 230–31). It is significant that even while such alliances may help keep the peace, they prevent one kind of war by permitting another. Nevertheless, alliances as a tool of management require an understanding among major states about what the rules of the game are. It is not surprising, therefore, that Moul (1988b: 36–37) finds the relationship to be stronger in the nineteenth century than the twentieth, and for disputes that occur in the central system (where permission would be more apt to be needed) rather than in the periphery.

The findings by Levy that have been discussed so far are based on an analysis of the number of alliances and wars in the *system*. When the behavior of specific states is examined to see how many of their alliances are followed by war, the findings are sustained. In the sixteenth to eighteenth centuries, alliances of individual major states were often followed by war. This was true over two-thirds of the time for two-thirds of the major states (geographically isolated Sweden being the major exception) (Levy, 1981: 602–3). This, of course, is a reflection of the fact that prior to 1815, alliances were formed for offensive purposes whereas later the motives leading states to form alliances were more diverse (Osgood and Tucker, 1967: 71–75 cited in Levy, 1981: 604). For the twentieth century, the findings are more complicated, but for most major states, entering an alliance is followed by a war. For example, in "great power" alliances in the twentieth century, six of the seven major states find themselves at war with each other after entering such an alliance; for three states this happens one-third to two-thirds of the time, and for three others, this occurs over two-thirds of the time (Levy, 1981: 603, Table 10). This set of findings provides clear evidence that, as a foreign policy practice, alliances are generally bellicose in their effects. Nevertheless, how much of a factor they play in causing war is difficult to discern, since alliances are not always followed by war (and even when they are, some alliances may form because actors anticipate war).

The fact that some alliances form because states fear or anticipate war, however, should not be seen as a reason for trivializing the association between alliance formation and war. First, many realists think that forming alliances in response to a threat will help prevent a war. Levy provides evidence that this is generally not the case. Second, there can be a long time lag between alliance formation and war. If alliance formation were just an *indicator* that war is about to happen, then there should be no time lag. Rather, as will be demonstrated in the next section, alliances do not simply grow out of a war-threatening situation, but aggravate that situation so as to increase the probability of war. This is the typical effect that alliances have, but, as Levy shows, alliances need not always result in war.

It was in the nineteenth century that alliances were least likely to be followed by war. Indeed, the nineteenth century is the only time in the last 500 years that the bellicose effects of alliances have been moderated. Only 44 percent of all alliances were followed by war (compared with 100 percent, 89 percent, 73 percent, and 81 percent in the sixteenth, seventeenth, eighteenth, and twentieth centuries), and none of the "great power" alliances were followed by a "great power" war within five years of their initiation (Levy, 1981: 598, Table 7). These data show that wars do not always have to result from alliances, and even when they do, war can be limited (as Schroeder [1976] and Moul [1988b] show). The changing strength of the relationship over the centuries indicates that there are different types of alliances, some more dangerous than others.

Levy's longer perspective shows that the so-called one hundred years of peace between 1815 and 1914 did leave a statistical impact on the amount of war between major states. This was due, in part, to the Concert of Europe system established at the Congress of Vienna. It can be inferred that under certain conditions, most likely a functioning global institutional context, alliances can become part of a broader functioning peace system, if they are used as a means of restraining unilateral behavior and encouraging states to follow rules of the game, rather than as a means of increasing power.

Levy's analysis is also important for demonstrating that alliances are not a necessary condition for war. Most wars occur without an alliance preceding them. From the sixteenth to the twentieth century, only 26 percent of the wars, on average, were preceded by an alliance involving one of the war participants (Levy, 1981: 599, Table 8). Alliances, however, are still an indicator of some systemic disturbance that is associated with war. For example, from the sixteenth to twentieth century, 43 percent of the wars involving a major state are preceded by an alliance involving a major state, although the major state that was a member of the alliance may not have been involved in the subsequent war. Furthermore, wars between major states (e.g. a war of rivalry) are more likely to require a preceding alliance than wars between a major and a minor state (e.g. a war of inequality). This is particularly true in the seventeenth, eighteenth, and twentieth centuries.[10] Nevertheless, since roughly half of the wars involving a major state occur without a preceding alliance, other factors besides alliances must give rise to war. Hence, eliminating alliances will not necessarily produce peace, although it may prevent specific wars or *types* of war.

Further evidence that alliances are associated with war is provided by Ostrom and Hoole (1978). In a reformulation of some of the propositions on alliance aggregation and war examined by Singer and Small (1968), they compare the number of dyads experiencing interstate war with the number of dyads having defense alliances. They find that within the first three years of alliance formation, as the number of alliance dyads increases, so does the number of war dyads. After three years, this positive correlation is reversed, and the more alliance commitments, the fewer war dyads. After twelve years, there is no relationship. This suggests that soon after alliances are made, there is a danger of war, but four to twelve years later there is not. After twelve years, it is probably a new game in which old alliances are irrelevant in questions of war and peace.[11]

[10] Thus, for wars between great powers, a great power alliance precedes the war 29 percent of the time in the seventeenth century, 50 percent in the eighteenth and 60 percent in the twentieth, compared to 24 percent (in the seventeenth century), 41 percent (eighteenth century), and 47 percent (twentieth century) for wars involving only one great power (Levy, 1983: 599, Table 8). One would suspect for wars not involving a major state the necessity of an alliance preceding a war would be weaker still.

It should be noted that since Levy's analysis does not include non-aggression pacts and ententes, it may underestimate the extent to which alliances between major states precede wars between unequals (see Moul, 1988b: 36 n. 12).

[11] Wayman (1990) finds that war peaks one to five years and eight to nine years after alliances are formed. This, in principle, is not that different from Ostrom and Hoole's findings. Ostrom and Hoole's periodization is probably more precise for our purposes since they look at dyads.

Wayman (1990) it should be noted rejects the idea that alliances are associated with war, because he argues that in order to infer that alliances have an impact the amount of war following alliance making must be statistically greater than the amount of war preceding alliance making. This is a much too stringent test. Nevertheless, since he finds wars peaking ten to nine years *before* alliances and one to five years and eight to nine years *after*, he argues alliances have no impact on the onset of war. In my view the logic of this test blinds us to the fact that war is following alliance formation. The reason why war (at the system level) also precedes alliance activity ten to nine years before is a separate problem that should be treated independently.

The role of alliances in the onset and prevention of war

Since Ostrom and Hoole show that there is often an interval between an alliance and the outbreak of war, it is a legitimate inference that alliances do not directly cause war, but help to aggravate a situation that makes war more likely. How might alliances do this? Let us focus on the possible role the formation of an alliance might play in an ongoing rivalry. Rivalry, by definition, already embodies a considerable amount of negative interaction and hostility stemming from persistent disagreement over a fundamental issue. The formation of an alliance in such a situation cannot be regarded as anything but threatening, and the most obvious (and appropriate) way to respond to this threat is with a counter-alliance. A counter-alliance can offset most, if not all, of the capability advantages created by the initial alliance. This eliminates the possibility of alliances acting as a kind of preventative (or "deterrent") of war through the marshaling of overwhelming power. Instead, it increases insecurity, because even if the alliances keep the relative balance the same, the absolute threat, in terms of the destructive power facing each side, has gone up. This can lead to a scramble for more allies which promotes an atmosphere that polarizes the system. Rivalry among major states and polarization often go together. The result is to institutionalize hostility and reduce the moderating effects of cross-cutting (Dean and Vasquez, 1976; Wallace, 1973). If the scramble for allies takes on the focus of lining up countries that are strategically located (see Morgenthau, 1970: 98 cited in Kegley and Raymond, 1991), then alliance behavior has subtlly shifted from a focus on war prevention to preparation-for-war-if-it-comes. A host of other factors, such as coordinating military plans, working out the terms of *casus foederis*, produce the same kind of shift. With such shifts, no matter why they might be brought about, one already has a psychological condition of war.

Since the making of alliances in an ongoing rivalry often does not produce the results that were desired, it is unlikely that those who enter alliances can accurately anticipate their consequences. It has already been seen how the attempt to use the device of an alliance to increase relative military power usually fails because of the formation of a counter-alliance. The result is greater, rather than less, insecurity. Counter-alliances also produce greater uncertainty, because of the possibility that one or more allies will not honor their commitments. Such uncertainty complicates last-minute calculations about who might win a war, and therefore whether it is "rational" to initiate a war. In many ways, Germany in World War I miscalculated by hoping that England would not enter the war (Choucri and North, 1975: 225).

If realists are incorrect about the ability of alliances to prevent war, they are correct that alliances better prepare a side for war, if it comes. Although no one has examined the question directly, there are a number of statistical findings which can be used to show that alliances make wars deadlier and longer. Singer and Small (1966: 123, 136, Table 9 [central system]), for example, consistently report that a high ranking on defense pacts is significantly associated with a high ranking on battle deaths (Spearman's *rho* = 0.51 [0.55 with defense pacts with a major state]) and duration (number of years vs. major at war (0.47 [0.52 with defense pacts with a major state]). Likewise, the greater the number of years a state has been allied, the more battle deaths it suffers (0.48) and the more years of war it experiences (0.39). For pre-war alliances, these associations are even stronger. The higher the ranking a state has on the number of times it has belonged to an alliance, the more battle deaths it has had (0.72) and the more years of war it has fought (0.64) (Singer and Small, 1966: 136, Table 10).

Table 5.1 shows that among major states those who have had the most alliances have tended to have the most battle deaths and experienced the most years of war (with a major state). If one compares column 1 with column 3 (battle deaths) and one eliminates the two peripheral states (China and Japan), who have few alliances, a close relationship is produced, particularly if it is kept in mind that Britain's low ranking on battle deaths is a result of the fact that it is a naval power.

One of the ways alliances make wars longer and more severe, in addition to better preparing each side, is to expand the war. Alliances tend to bring states into a war, and, as a war spreads, it is likely to become longer and more severe to the extent that intervention makes each side equal to the other. To do this, alliances must be pervasive, i.e. they must polarize the system. In this way, alliances are probably more responsible for the severity, magnitude, and duration of war than for its onset. Thus, an unanticipated effect of alliances helping states prepare for war is that they do such a good job that wars become more devastating. Several studies provide evidence that alliances expand wars, a topic that will be treated in Chapter 7. Suffice it to say for now, that one of the effects of alliance making prior to a war of rivalry is that it can polarize the system and, if a war should occur under these circumstances, it is likely to become a complex war.

In the light of the above analysis, what can be concluded about alliances? Most important, in terms of realist foreign policy prescriptions, is that

Table 5.1. *Ranking of major states by alliance and severity and amount of war*

No. allies w/major	No. allies	Battle deaths	Years war vs. major (duration)
(1) Russia	(1) Russia	(1) Russia	(1) Britain
(2) Germany	(2) Germany	(2) Germany	(2) Russia
(3) Britain	(3) Austria-Hungary	(3) China	(3) Germany
(4) France	(4.5) Britain	(4) France	(4) Italy
(5.5) Austria-Hungary	(4.5) France	(5) Japan	(5) China
(5.5) Italy	(6) Italy	(6) Austria-Hungary	(6.5) Japan
		(7) Britain	(6.5) Turkey
		(8) Italy	(8) France
			(9) Austria-Hungary

Source: Compiled from Singer and Small (1966: 130–31, Table 6) data.

alliances do not prevent war. Instead, they appear to be associated with war, particularly when an alliance is made with a major state. Alliances, however, are probably not a direct cause of war, since there is a considerable interval between an alliance forming and the outbreak of war. Instead of calling alliances a cause of war, it is probably more accurate to see alliances formed within an ongoing rivalry as a step toward war that aggravates an already tense relationship. This may account for why alliances among major states are more frequently followed by war than other types of alliances. Such a consequence is not inevitable, and under some conditions, for example between 1815 and 1900, alliances among major states can be stripped of their bellicose effects. Whether this is due to the type of alliance that is formed or, more likely, to a particular global institutional context needs to be researched further. Nevertheless, except for the nineteenth century, alliances can be seen as a way of preparing for war. Among major states, such preparation strengthens both sides, but often leaves the blocs relatively balanced. The result, if war does break out, is to make the war expand, thereby making it longer and more severe. Finally, many wars occur in the absence of alliances, so avoiding alliances is not a guarantee of peace. Despite this, alliances do seem to be an essential condition for certain types of war, namely complex wars of rivalry among major states.

In terms of outlining the realist road to war, it can be seen that alliances have important and unanticipated effects. In particular, as a response by major states to insecurity and threat, they fail and usually increase insecurity and uncertainty. Because of this failure, actors place greater emphasis on the other major solution realism offers for meeting security problems – building up their own military. Even if this step had been taken previously, it now receives new impetus in the minds of leaders and policy influencers. It may, however, take a crisis before domestic constituents can be convinced of the need to make the sacrifices necessary to provide increased military expenditures, if the rival's making of an alliance has not already sufficiently mobilized the public to recognize the external threat. The building up of the military involves actors taking yet another step toward war. Military buildups during a rivalry can easily lead to an arms race, particularly if initiated after alliances have polarized the system.

Differences Between the Nineteenth and the Twentieth Century: Alliances and Arms Races

Before examining the role of arms races, it is important to explore why alliances in the nineteenth century deviate from the general pattern of the last 500 years. One possibility is that alliances are one step to war, but not the final step, so that under the right circumstances it might be possible to avoid taking the next step. If this were the case in the nineteenth century, it would be expected that alliances in the nineteenth century would not give rise to arms races, whereas those in the twentieth would. One reason arms races might have been avoided is that, given the more ordered and less anarchic global institutional context of the Concert of Europe/Bismarckian system, the kinds of alliances that formed in this period may have been sufficiently different so as to avoid the unilateral power politics behavior typically associated with alliances. Instead of being unilateral attempts at power politics meant to intimidate opponents, the important alliances of this period might have functioned as a way of bringing opponents together to resolve issues and dispose of stakes on the basis of some principle all parties regarded as legitimate. If this were the case, then the alliances of this period might be looked at as an inchoate means of governance within a larger peace system. If such a system were able to partially satisfy the major states, it might sufficiently raise the provocation threshold for war to make it an undesirable means for gaining one's ends. This in turn would make any additional steps toward war unnecessary, since existing security questions were being handled adequately.

Such an explanation has not been tested, nor could it be easily tested with existing data. Nevertheless, there are findings (such as Moul, 1988b, see above) that are consistent with it and add to its plausibility. An even more interesting piece of evidence comes from some ongoing research of Michael Wallace (cited in Wallace, 1985: 110–11). In trying to account for his previous research (Wallace, 1973), which found a strong relationship between polarization and the magnitude and severity of war in the twentieth century but only a weak relationship in the nineteenth, he notes that after 1903, major power alliances that were aimed at another major power always produced a sharp increase in the rate of growth of the target's military expenditures. Prior to 1903, this effect did not occur; Wallace speculates that, in the twentieth century, alliances were formed to build winning coalitions, whereas in the nineteenth century they were equilibrium mechanisms in the classic balance-of-power fashion.

In my view, it is not the balance-of-power aspect that is the significant difference: in the nineteenth century, alliances more frequently aimed to prevent war between major states by coming to an understanding about how to deal with major issues (including the use of force); failing that, they aimed to keep any war that did occur limited. This claim seems to hold for the two most peaceful periods within the nineteenth century – the Concert of Europe era from 1816 to 1848 and the Bismarckian era from 1871 to 1895. The Concert of Europe and the alliance of major states growing out of the Congress of Vienna acted in a way that attempted to govern relations and establish rules of the game that would curb unilateral behavior. They did not pose any threat to the existing major states, since they reflected a consensus and a set of understandings among status quo states about how to deal with non-governmental actors (revolutionaries) or minor states. In this way, these alliances did not give rise to arms races because they posed no direct threat to major states.

Bismarck's system was more power politics oriented, based on deception, and committed to certain changes, but he did attempt through an intricate network of alliances to restrain unilateral behavior. Bismarck used alliances as part of a broader policy to fight limited wars that would change the status quo but prevent the war from expanding by keeping the target isolated. The purpose of alliances here was to keep other parties neutral while trying to buy them off, and show them that Prussia posed no threat because it had only limited aims. Since prior to both the Seven Weeks and Franco-Prussian wars it also appeared that Prussia had limited means, this was believed. When Kaiser Wilhelm II abandoned this approach in favor of a more direct, less duplicitous, but boisterous approach, the threat was clearer and gave rise to counter-alliances and arms races. This suggests that revisionist states are apt to be more successful if they use alliances to divide status quo states, rather than alert and alarm them by forming a war-fighting coalition.

Clearly, the kinds of alliances that are formed will make a big difference in whether wars will be limited or become general. For research to progress, there is a need to create more theoretical typologies of alliances. Despite the variety of purposes served by alliances in different historical contexts, the critical distinction in terms of a comparative analysis of the causes of war seems to be whether an alliance is perceived as preparing for war through the creation of a winning coalition.

The immediate effect of alliances that seek to form a winning coalition is to intensify military expenditures and to embroil actors in arms races. It is through the creation of these arms races that alliances are linked to the onset of war. Some evidence to support this argument comes from an early path analysis of Wallace's (1972: 64) in which he finds that alliance aggregation in the system leads to arms expenditures, but not the reverse: arms expenditures do not lead to alliances. This analysis, however, is based on systemic measures of the aggregate amount of alliances and arms expenditures and such an inference leaves open the possibility of an ecological fallacy, since specific states and their interactions have not been examined to see if arms races always follow alliances and none precedes them. Indeed, as will be shown later, increases in military expenditures (although they may not be arms races) can precede alliance making, suggesting that the Wallace (1972) finding may be an effect of alliance polarization in the system rather than an effect produced by the making of any specific alliance. Nevertheless, in his more recent research, he maintains that major power alliances after 1903 *always* led those who were targeted by the alliance to increase the rate of growth of their armed forces; in turn this *always* produced a counter-response which led to an arms race (Wallace, 1985: 110–11).

This implies that alliances that do not produce arms races will not lead to war, explaining why Levy (1981) finds that while many alliances are associated with war, not *all* are, and especially not those in the nineteenth century (see also Wayman, 1985: 133–35). Some evidence that alliances not followed by military buildups do not lead to war is provided by Bremer (1992). He shows that contiguous dyads who are allied with each other have a lower probability of going to war than contiguous dyads who are not allied with each other. Here the alliance is probably an indicator that the two states have resolved their outstanding issues (especially territorial questions). However, if the two contiguous states have an alliance and are both building up their military, then Bremer finds that the probability of their going to war increases. Bremer's (1992) findings provide evidence that alliances coupled with military buildups are much more war-prone than alliances not followed by military buildups. Along with Wallace's research this suggests that part of what might be going on during the typical three-year (or so) time lag between the formation of alliances and the onset of war is the building up of the military of each side so that an arms race results.

The different ways in which alliances can lead to arms races can be illustrated by looking at the rivalries preceding World War I and the Korean War. World War I is the more extensively studied case. It is possible to argue that as the major European states expanded, their interests intersected at geographical meeting points outside of Europe. These often produced crises that the political system attempted to resolve, sometimes successfully. As disputes continued to arise, alliances formed which began to polarize the system. These alliances were followed by large increases in military expenditures and arms races (Choucri and North, 1975: 106–11, 117).

A detailed examination of the period preceding World War I, however, will reveal that military expenditures both precede and follow alliance formation. Choucri and North (1975) find that although the military expenditures of major states are correlated primarily with the previous military expenditures of the state, they are also correlated with the military expenditures of non-allies and the intensity of interactions in colonial areas. In addition, they find that the number of alliances a state has is correlated with the military expenditures of non-allies and the intensity of interactions.

Although the exact pattern and variables depend on the specific state in question, Choucri and North uncover a dynamic pattern in which what one state does affects the other. The increases in military expenditures that precede and follow alliance making can be seen as reflecting threats and responses to threats. The pattern may not be as neat as Wallace suspects, but that is not critical, since Choucri and North (1975: 203–5) point out that a state that feels threatened in one dimension, e.g. alliance, may respond not in a reciprocal pattern but by taking action on another dimension, e.g. increasing expenditures. The British felt sufficiently threatened by Germany to resolve a number of issues with rivals France, Russia, Japan and the US after the turn of the century. Germany's leaders viewed this as encirclement and saw it as one of the reasons it was necessary to build up its army and navy (Choucri and North, 1975: 207, 226–27). Germany could not gain any more allies, since they were all taken up. The increase in military expenditure made the entente countries view Germany as more threatening, therefore making the entente more of an alliance, while the absence of potential allies made Germany more willing to support Austria-Hungary (Choucri and North, 1975: 225). The attempt to build up a German navy increased military expenditures all around and led to a full-blown arms race with Britain (Choucri and North, 1975: 205, 207), a phenomenon found to hold in several wars (see Wayman, Singer, and Goertz, 1983).

World War I can be regarded as a classic model of how alliances and military buildups lead to war. What is significant about the model is that each step taken to increase security is viewed (rightly so) as an increased threat to the other rival. Tension builds, and each side moves from trying to prevent attack to preparing for war. Alliances demark the sides that will fight and consolidate them, while military expenditures prepare the armies and navies. When the war comes, no one is really surprised, although it may turn out to be a war no one anticipated.

The Korean War illustrates a different kind of model of how alliances might produce war. Here there is no direct war between the major rivals, and the effect of alliances is more systemic and indirect. Nevertheless, war comes, and when it does, it is more of a surprise and unwanted. Within the quantitative literature, the Korean War is a case supporting the generalization that alliances are followed by war. In 1949 NATO is formed, in Levy's terms a "great power" alliance, and it is followed within three years by a war involving at least one of the "great powers." If China is considered a "major power," as Small and Singer (1982: 50), consider it, then the Korean War is a war between major powers. Likewise, Wayman (1985: 129) found that alliance polarization increased just prior to the Korean War. Yet, clearly NATO did not cause the Korean War, and how NATO gave rise to the Korean War is different from how the Triple Entente and Dual Alliance gave rise to World War I.

The case of NATO clarifies how alliances can be an important step toward war without being a cause of war and provides some insights about the impact of alliances on a rivalry. The formation of NATO not only posed a threat to the Soviet Union, but also crystallized the hostile and threatening image of the Soviet Union that American decision makers and elites had been deriving from events in Europe since the defeat of Hitler. The need to break American isolationism and convert its domestic supporters required framing the Soviet threat in transcendent terms. This was, after all, what Acheson did in his famous meeting with Congressional leaders in March 1947 and what Senator Vandenberg recommended Truman do when he addressed Congress in what became the speech announcing the Truman Doctrine (Jones, 1955: 142). Many scholars now see this as an exaggeration of the threat in order to secure domestic support (Lowi, 1967: 320–23). Because the formation of NATO required breaking an American tradition on avoiding entangling alliances and a fundamental shift away from isolationism (requiring the intellectual and political defeat of its supporters), it involved a radical change in beliefs. Consequently, once the image of the Soviet/communist threat and the social construction of a Cold War reality was in place, it could not be changed easily.

The formation of NATO biased the American foreign policy establishment toward a hard line by defining the situation the United States was facing as one requiring a policy of containment and vigilance. So strong was this conceptual framing of reality among American leaders, that almost anything that happened would be interpreted as confirming this view of the world. When the North Koreans attacked in June 1950, Truman and his advisors were surprised; they had expected a move in Europe not in the periphery. Indeed, Truman hesitated in his commitment of troops because he thought this might be a diversionary attack with the main onslaught to come elsewhere (May, 1984: 218; Truman, 1956, Vol. II: 341, 343, 345–46). The Cold War framework was applied to interpret what was going on and how the US should respond. Stalin's hand was seen as guiding the North Koreans, and the attack as a probe that compelled a strong response. The very success of NATO in containing the Soviet Union to Eastern Europe, although it was hardly over a year old, was seen as making Stalin shift to the softer Asian front (see Spanier, 1973: 70 for an example of this mindset). The equally plausible interpretation that the attack might reflect local initiatives and interests did not receive serious consideration until recently (see Small, 1980: ch. 6; Cumings, 1981, 1990).

The North Atlantic Treaty, by institutionalizing a social construction of reality, made the United States enter a war it had never dreamed it would fight. From this, it might be generalized that the making of an alliance within an ongoing rivalry not only increases tensions between the two sides, but helps instill images and a definition of the situation where events are seen as more threatening than intended. In these circumstances, any use of force in a crisis can lead to an armed response in order to avoid creating a precedent. Once the United States intervenes and approaches the Yalu, the same processes probably occurred in China, triggering its intervention. If this is the case, it would show that a severe crisis can have an effect similar to the formation of a hostile alliance.

What is significant about the Korean War is that many of the effects attributed to alliances prior to the First World War – e.g. the formation of a counter-alliance, increases in military expenditure, and mobilization of domestic elites – are produced not by NATO, but by the Korean War. NATO does not give rise to a counter-alliance (the Warsaw Pact) until 1955, well after the Korean War. Indeed, as Jervis (1980: 569, 580) argues, the North Atlantic Treaty does not really become an organization with a central headquarters and an army until after the North Korean attack. More importantly, it is the Korean War and not NATO or the ideology of the Cold War that produces a permanent and dramatic increase in US military expenditures (Russett, 1970; Diehl and Goertz, 1985), makes Congress compliant (see Henehan, 1989: 261–63), encourages an atmosphere where dissent is silenced and viewed as un-American, and further institutionalizes the Cold War construction of reality and its major policies (Jervis, 1980; May, 1984: 211). For the American public and many policy influencers, including the Congress, the Cold War does not really begin until the Korean War. That war itself was unwanted and a function of a definition of the situation crystallized by the formation of an alliance.

The Korean case shows that alliances must not be viewed mechanically as a condition that will inevitably produce the same effects. Instead, they must be seen as part of a dynamic in which crises, alliance making, and military buildups interact and reinforce each other. This dynamic shapes a hostile relationship, constructing images and definitions of a situation and then institutionalizing and extending them. The Cold War rivalry results from a set of crises (from the 1947 crisis in Greece and Turkey to the 1948 crises in Czechoslovakia and Berlin) which in turn help spur the formation of an alliance. Fears of Soviet military strength, especially in light of the 1949 Soviet A-bomb test, increase the perception of threat and make American leaders want to increase military expenditures (NSC-68; Jervis, 1980: 576–78). All of these factors intensify the sense of rivalry and make decision makers sensitive to any use of force within the system. Such uses, as in Korea, can trigger war. Since the war is not a total war, it functions as a crisis, leading to mobilization of domestic elites and the public and an increase in military expenditures. It also eventually results in a counter-alliance by the other side, increases in their military expenditures, and an intensification of hostility and rivalry, resulting in a nuclear arms race.

Although this analysis of World War I and Korea portrays the different ways in which alliances can result in war, it leaves unanswered the question of why some alliances, like many in the nineteenth century, do not lead to arms races. The answer may lie with the level of hostility between rivals preceding and following the formation of an alliance. Alliances that attempt to build a winning coalition are born in a hostile environment and pose a new threat that increases the level of hostility and sense of insecurity. Alliances that do not seek a winning coalition pose less of a threat, and thus do not add to existing hostility. Alliances and arms races may thus be critical intervening variables that increase the level of hostility until it is sufficient to generate the kinds of disputes that escalate to war. The level of hostility, in turn, it can be argued, is a function of the failure of the parties to resolve existing issues, which is very much a function of the kinds of issues they have raised (see Mansbach and Vasquez, 1981: ch. 7).

Other than the studies of the 1914 crisis by Holsti, North and Brody (1968) and by Zinnes (1968) that found that perceived hostility correlated with violent behavior, little research on hostility has been conducted, primarily because of the difficulty of measuring hostility. In this regard, Wayman (1984b) provides an important contribution in an analysis that measures changes in hostility in the Middle East. He develops a measure of friendship–hostility by asking the US State Department, Pentagon, and academic Middle East specialists to rank various Middle East dyads from 0 (highest hostility) to 100 (highest friendship). He then is able to correlate his measures with various scales of World Events Interaction Survey (WEIS) cooperation–conflict event data and to a lesser extent Correlates of War data on serious disputes. He finds that hostility–friendship judgments are most closely associated with the pattern of conflict in the crisis years of 1970 and 1973 and with whether a dyad has ever had a serious dispute. These findings, Wayman rightly argues, indicate that hostility results from learning during dramatic events, which have a major and lasting impact on images, much like Jervis (1976: ch. 6) describes.

Wayman then combines the 1970–74 friendship–hostility judgments and the WEIS conflict and cooperation events to "predict" the WEIS events of 1976–78. He finds that an interactive model, initially developed by Mansbach and Vasquez (1981: ch. 7) and which he operationalizes by multiplying prior cooperation–conflict times the friendship–hostility judgments, accounts for 88 percent of the variance. This means that the impact of conflict is reduced if countries are friendly, and that the impact of cooperation is reduced if countries are hostile. In other words, hostility makes countries discount any cooperative acts, which makes it difficult for them to break out of a hostile pattern of interaction. On the basis of this analysis, it can be hypothesized that hostility is produced by dramatic changes in relations between actors and that the presence of hostility produces a step-level effect in subsequent behavior, making actors more sensitive to negative acts and leading them to discount positive ones.

If this hypothesis were confirmed by further research, it would identify the operating force that gets actors from one step to war to the next: it shows that the taking of one step, instead of reducing threat, leads to a permanent increase in hostility, which leads to the taking of more threatening steps by the other side, which in turn are matched by the first. Such a hypothesis helps to explain how some alliances lead to arms races, while others do not. It also underlines the fact that alliances, like most practices associated with war, are important as part of a dynamic reciprocal process (Vasquez, 1987: 134–35).

Responding to Security Issues: Arms Races

Most of the threads of an explanation of why arms races begin have long been part of the literature (see Richardson, 1960a; Singer, 1958, 1970b). There is a consensus that arms races presuppose rivalry, at least at some level, and intensify that rivalry once they are under way. In terms of the steps outlined here, the key motivation for arms races is the insecurity resulting from perceived threat and hostility. This general insecurity, which is awakened whenever a situation occurs that might portend force, becomes a specific fear whenever a rival state is perceived as having a larger military capacity, as building arms, or as increasing its capability by making an alliance (see Singer, 1958 [1979: 33–34]).

Even though such factors may lead decision makers to seek a military buildup, decision makers are unlikely to get domestic support without some concrete manifestation of the threat posed by the rival. This usually comes in the form of an international crisis, although the formation of an alliance itself can so alarm leaders that it may be seen (by them and the public) as a crisis. Since crises make threats clear, the greater the number of crises between two rivals, the harder it will be to avoid an arms race.

In order to generate the necessary domestic mobilization for arms races – such as increased taxes, a shift in resources and spending, and the adoption of some form of conscription – leaders often exaggerate the external threat (see Singer, 1970b [1979: 73], 1958 [36–37]; Lowi, 1967: 320–23; Wayman *et al.* 1983: 498). In turn, this increases the fear in the other side, extends the influence of hard-liners in both camps, and helps to produce an arms race spiral (see Singer, 1970a [1979: 77–78], 1970b [1979: 151–52]).

In such an atmosphere, war is likely but not inevitable. The trigger that is needed to explode the various elements that have been put in place is an international crisis, and the mere presence of an ongoing arms race makes it more probable that such a crisis will be the *kind* that will escalate to war. The first systematic evidence that arms races are, in themselves, a major factor in the onset of war was published by Michael Wallace (1979: 14–15). He examines ninety-nine serious disputes between 1816 and 1965, which he divides into those that escalated to war and those that did not. He then asks whether the presence of an ongoing arms race is what distinguishes the relatively few serious disputes that escalate from the many that do not. Of the twenty-eight serious disputes that occurred in the presence of an ongoing arms race, twenty-three escalated to war; of the seventy-one serious disputes that occurred where there was no arms race, only three escalated to war. This is impressive evidence that arms races are a crucial factor in determining whether serious disputes will escalate to war; it produces strong measures of association (Yule's $Q = 0.96$ and phi coefficient $= 0.75$).

Erich Weede (1980) has criticized Wallace for treating each arms race and serious dispute as a dyadic case rather than counting all disputes and wars involving the same set of participants as a single case, regardless of the number of dyads. This is particularly important for World War I and World War II, both of which Wallace treats as several discrete cases. Wallace (1982: 46) reanalyzed the data and eliminated all cases in which two or more allies simultaneously entered the war against a common foe, thereby reducing the twenty-eight cases of serious disputes having arms races to fifteen. Nevertheless, the relationship still holds: eleven of the fifteen serious disputes escalate to war while only four do not. Conversely, only two of the sixty-five serious disputes escalate when there is no ongoing arms race (phi coefficient $= 0.67$).

Paul Diehl's (1983) challenge to Wallace's findings is more serious, since he eliminates most of the relationship Wallace establishes by using new measures of what he calls military buildups and by changing the sample. Diehl (1983: note 3) removes seventeen cases associated with ongoing war. He argues that seven or eight large wars are treated by Wallace as twenty-six dyadic cases. For Diehl, if one dispute (such as the 1914 crisis) escalates to war and then other dyads having arms races become involved in the war, this is only one case supporting the proposition, not several. Wallace, as in his response to Weede, is prepared to eliminate some but not all of these cases. By removing these cases Diehl reduces the number of cases supporting the proposition. In addition to dropping certain cases, Diehl also adds cases since 1965, as well as others which Wallace's preliminary data may have missed. Among the recent cases, many that do not escalate to war in the presence of ongoing military buildups involve states having nuclear weapons. Normally, such changes in the sample would be too extensive to support a conclusion that arms races are unrelated to the escalation of serious disputes. However, Diehl has argued that Wallace's index of arms races cannot be replicated (see Siverson and Diehl, 1989: 218 n. 4), and he replaces it with a new measure of arms races that is simpler and more straightforward.

Wallace's (1990) response to this criticism is to apply Diehl's index to a revised set of his own cases that reduces some of the double counting, but still leaves in multiple cases within a world war that historians regard as separate wars (e.g. Japan and US in World War II). When he does this, he finds that, of the fifty-nine disputes that occur without an ongoing arms race, only three escalate; however, of the forty-three disputes with ongoing arms races, twenty-four escalate and nineteen do not. This is still a statistically significant relationship (p < 0.001), but the strength of association drops (phi = 0.30).

The controversy between Diehl and Wallace and their related findings support two conclusions. First, militarized disputes that occur in the absence of an arms race (or military buildup) rarely escalate to war. Second, many disputes can arise during an ongoing mutual military buildup (as measured by Diehl) *without* escalating to war.

Diehl's measure of arms races identifies arms races within ongoing disputes that do not have a tendency to escalate (see also Altfeld, 1983). Methodologically, this means that Wallace's measure, which is difficult to calculate, is sensitive to changes in operational definition, a point substantiated by Houweling and Siccama's (1981: 176–78) comparison of Smith's (1980) and Wallace's lists of arms races (see also Houweling and Siccama, 1988b: 156–57). Theoretically, this raises the possibility that some military buildups or arms races may not be pernicious (see Richardson, 1960a; Singer, 1970b; Smith, 1980). Whether this is because of some inherent characteristic of the arms race process (whether the race is mathematically stable or unstable [Smith 1980], or whether it is bureaucratically or enemy driven [Singer, 1970b; 1979: 152]) or some other set of factors must be investigated further. Nevertheless, different scholars, working independently of each other, have had some success in distinguishing the kinds of arms races that lead directly to war from those that do not (Smith, 1980; Morrow, 1989).

Although Wallace's (1982) conclusions cannot be accepted until his arms race index is replicated, his analysis and later defense do raise the possibility that some measure of military expenditures will be able to discriminate between arms races (or buildups) that lead to dispute escalation and those that do not. Evidence that military buildups, if not arms races *per se*, may be associated with the escalation of militarized disputes between rivals that are major states is provided even by Diehl (1985a) himself. In a refined analysis of three distinct measures of military allocations (level of defense burden, unilateral or asymmetrical arms races, and mutual buildups or arms races) he uncovers circumstances in which each of these measures is associated with escalation to war. Interestingly, he finds a statistically significant relationship between the defense burden of a state and the onset of war through escalation.[12] The likelihood of a dispute escalating to war goes from 8 percent when the defense burden is low to 50 percent when the defense burden is high (Diehl, 1985a: 339). This means that relatively few states engage in war who have not previously prepared for it; such preparation may very well reduce caution within a crisis. Adequate defense preparations in the twentieth century appear to be a prerequisite for escalation; low defense preparation can prevent escalation to war even when other necessary conditions are in place (Diehl, 1985a: 342). Of course, this makes sense, since in a rivalry, an unprepared state would rather take a loss in a militarized dispute (as Russia did in 1908), and then prepare for war, rather than enter a war unprepared.

This implies, as Diehl finds, that military preparation need not take the technical form of an arms race to result in war. Sometimes unilateral buildups (which are not seen as arms races by Diehl [1983] and Smith [1980]) can result in war. In the nineteenth century, Diehl (1985a: 340) finds the asymmetric buildup between Austria and France and the unilateral German buildup against France eventually producing a situation that resulted in war. In the twentieth century, he sees the unilateral buildup of Germany against France prior to the two world wars playing the same role. In these cases the military buildup resulted in relative equality

---

[12] Phi = 0.30, p. 339. Diehl's concept of defense burden is meant to tap the ratio of military personnel to population and the ratio of military expenditures to economic productivity (for the precise measures see Diehl, 1985a: 337, especially note 8).

among the rivals. At other times, a mutual buildup or an arms race can prevent a revisionist state from gaining its ends through increased capability and frustrate a state in its attempt to gain relative equality so that the end result is war. This, according to Diehl (1985a: 341), appears to have been the result of the Japanese buildup in the 1930s. Clearly this was also the result of the German naval buildup prior to World War I.

Diehl's (1985a: 342–43) analysis of rivalries suggests that military buildups, whether they are unilateral or take the form of arms races, are at least critical indirect factors in the escalation of disputes. They seem to be important in bringing about short-term shifts in overall capability that have the effect of increasing tensions and hostility or preventing certain shifts that frustrate an opponent and thereby increase hostility. In particular, military buildups that are perceived by one side as creating immediate disadvantages for it may make it prone to war at a later date when the timing is more opportune; while buildups that are perceived as creating long-term disadvantages may make a side more prone to strike while the iron it hot, if it is pressed. In either case, a crisis involving a salient stake and that has followed a series of crises may provide the trigger.[13]

In light of the Wallace, Weede, and Diehl controversy, what can be concluded and what avenues of inquiry seem worth pursuing? First, it would be fruitful to see if the disputes that occur in the presence of military buildups but do not escalate have identifiable characteristics. An examination of Diehl's and Wallace's findings suggests that non-escalating disputes may be the first or second of a series of crises, that they may occur between dyads that are not contiguous, and that they may involve disputes between nuclear states. Diehl's (1985a: 335) sample of disputes between

---

[13] Diehl (1985a: 342–43) sees prior militarized disputes, a dispute whose site is contiguous to one of the rivals, and an escalatory distribution of power as three necessary conditions of escalation. He sees military buildups as important because they shift rivals toward or away from an escalatory distribution of power. I have not incorporated the last variable in my analysis and have tried to reinterpret it in terms of perceptions of threat. The reason for this, in addition to possible tautological problems with the concept of "escalatory" distribution of power, is that Diehl finds parity among rivals as escalatory in the nineteenth and preponderance as escalatory in the twentieth. This, it should be noted, is just the opposite distribution of capability *at the system level* of the one that Singer, Bremer, and Stuckey (1972) found associated with war (they found war associated with system preponderance in the nineteenth century and with system parity in the twentieth). Diehl (1985a: 344) himself is hard-pressed to explain the inter-century difference, and I take this as further evidence that any distribution of capability can be associated with war. The key factor, as I tried to make clear in my interpretation, is not the distribution of capability, but how power is used and what effect attempts to increase capability have on perceptions of threat and hostility.

rivals is heavily weighed in favor of post-1945 disputes that did not result in war (see Diehl, 1985a: 335). Defining rivalry as two states engaging in at least three militarized disputes within fifteen years (Diehl, 1985a: 334), he finds that war usually occurs relatively late in a rivalry. This raises the possibility that a number of Diehl's disputes in the earlier analysis that had an ongoing arms race and did not escalate to war may eventually have escalated. As is known from Leng's (1983) study, frequently a series of crises must occur before war breaks out. Thus, a number of disputes that do not escalate in the presence of an arms race may simply be the first of a series of crises that eventually do escalate. In addition, the rivalries that do not go to war in Diehl's sample (e.g. US–USSR, UK–USSR, UK–China, France-USSR) are not contiguous and have nuclear weapons, both of which may dampen the escalatory effect of arms races. Diehl's (1985a: 342–43) analysis, then, while it does not show a strong direct association between arms races (technically defined) and escalation of disputes, does suggest the circumstances under which such a relationship holds; namely, contiguous rivals having a series of disputes. In addition, even though he eschews the idea of arms races, he provides support for the explanation that efforts to increase capability through military buildups are a step to war within an ongoing rivalry.

A second avenue of inquiry is that arms races are associated with only certain types of wars. Diehl's (1983) manipulation of the sample shows that much of Wallace's finding depends on the presence of ongoing wars and on World War I and World War II (on the latter see Houweling and Siccama, 1981: 160–61 n. 13). This implies that, while arms races may escalate disputes between rivals (relative equals), they may not be a factor in other types of wars. This hypothesis would also help to account for Diehl's (1983: 209) finding that 77 percent of the "major power wars" that occur are not preceded by an arms race, since many of these wars may be wars between relative unequals. Finally, the connection among arms races, escalation of disputes, and ongoing wars may provide a clue about how wars spread to become world wars. The presence of a series of disputes that might escalate to war may encourage others to arm because of the threatening environment, and thereby encourage war, when it comes, to enlarge. Several ongoing arms races are also likely to make the war bloodier once it comes.

A third avenue of inquiry is that certain types of military buildups or arms races may prevent wars (by a process of creating peace through strength). The claim that some military buildups might prevent war has attracted some impressive deductive analysis (e.g. Intrilligator and Brito, 1984), but has generated little empirical support. The peace-through-strength hypothesis goes back at least to the Roman general Vegetius. Wallace (1982) recognizes that a serious theoretical challenge to his findings comes from the peace-through-strength counter-hypothesis and attempts to compare that hypothesis with the armament–tension spiral hypothesis. Wallace (1982) argues that the peace-through-strength hypothesis maintains that it is not the presence of an arms race, but who is winning it, that is the key factor. If this logic were coupled with Organski's distinction between satisfied and dissatisfied states (or revisionist and status quo actors), then it could be expected that serious disputes would be likely to escalate to war only if revisionist states were winning the arms race. Wallace examines this claim by comparing the relative adequacy of this peace-through-strength approach with his own and Singer's armament–tension spiral approach.

In a number of tests, Wallace finds no statistically significant relationship (and hardly any association) between whether arms races favor (or are won by) revisionist actors and whether serious disputes escalate. It can be concluded that spending more on arms than one's rival is not related to the escalation of serious disputes – which means that strength of arms neither prevents war nor leads to war. Wallace goes on to demonstrate that the peace-through-strength hypothesis has nowhere near the accuracy of the armament–tension spiral hypothesis by showing that, whether a revisionist state is "superior" or "weaker," arms races still lead to escalation. Of the ten serious disputes that occur when there is an ongoing arms race while the revisionist state is "superior," eight escalate and two do not. Conversely, of the eighteen disputes that occur when there is no arms race and the revisionist state is "superior," only one dispute escalates, and seventeen do not. The cases involving "weaker" revisionist states exhibit the same pattern. In the eighteen disputes that occur when there is an ongoing arms race while the revisionist state is "weaker," fifteen escalate to war and only three do not. Conversely, of the fifty-three disputes that occur when there is no arms race and the revisionist state is "weaker," only two escalate, and fifty-one do not. In light of such consistent findings (even though they are based on Wallace's index and not Diehl's), it must be concluded that the peace-through-strength hypothesis has little support and does not compare well with the armament–tension spiral hypothesis. It should be noted that Diehl (1985a: 343, 346), in his analysis of rivalries, also finds the *para bellum* hypothesis deficient.

On the basis of these various tests, it does appear that military build-ups do in fact, by their mere presence, make it more likely that a serious dispute will escalate to war, but as Diehl and Houweling and Siccama have argued, this will occur only *in certain circumstances.* One of those circumstances is relative equality, and hence rivalry, between major states.[14] The circumstances under which disputes may not escalate are when the disputants are not contiguous or it is the first crisis between them.[15] In terms of the explanation being built here, this means that the findings support the conclusion that military buildups that occur within a rivalry, where the states are contiguous, are an important step toward war, and clearly not a step toward peace, as some hard-liners argue.

However, it is also clear from Wallace's research design and from Houweling and Siccama's (1981: 170–75) analysis that arms races alone do not produce war, as some accommodationists argue. Arms races and military buildups are dangerous in the context of an ongoing militarized dispute or crisis. This implies that, in the absence of persistent crises, war can still be avoided during an arms race. Although this inference is plausible, there has been no test of whether this factor distinguishes arms races that lead to war from those that do not. Further, it is unclear whether crises can be avoided in a relationship marked by an arms race.

Crisis Escalation

The mere presence of an arms race or military buildup may not be what leads disputes to escalate; it may just be that a military buildup introduces greater insecurity and hostility in political relationships and therefore makes it likely that actors will become involved in the kinds of crises that are likely to escalate. Although the evidence makes it difficult to discern whether arms races encourage actors to become involved in the kinds of serious disputes that are apt to escalate, current research has made it clear that rivals usually go to war after a series of crises, the last of which escalates.

---

[14] This follows from the fact that Wallace's analyses are confined to major states, and he is not sure that the relationship would hold for disputes between minor states (Wallace, 1990). It should also be noted that because the evidence is so tied to the two twentieth-century world wars, it is not clear whether a rivalry must involve three or more major states before it produces an unstable arms race.

[15] I have dropped nuclear weapons as a condition preventing escalation, because (1) in Diehl's sample it is always coterminous with the absence of contiguity and (2) although nuclear weapons may raise the provocation threshold, I do not think they will prevent war if other factors promoting war are in place (see Vasquez, 1991).

Once there is a pattern of repeated military confrontations, it becomes increasingly difficult to avoid war.[16] Peter Wallensteen (1981: 74–75, 84), in his study of major states from 1816 to 1976, found that 75 percent (twelve of sixteen) of the pairs of states that had repeated confrontations also experienced war. Russell Leng (1983) found that, among relative equals who are involved in successive disputes, war is increasingly likely by the third dispute. Diehl (1985a: 340, 342), in his study of rivalries, found that over 90 percent (nineteen of twenty-two) of the rivalries "go through at least two militarized disputes" before escalation to war is likely.

Houweling and Siccama, (1981: 170–72; see also Houweling and Siccama, 1988b: ch. 8) find a statistically significant and fairly strong link between the presence of serious disputes and the outbreak of war (Yule's Q = 0.96 and phi = 0.42). Their data analysis indicates that the presence of serious disputes is more directly related to the outbreak of war than is the presence of arms races (which are not as strongly associated with war, Yule's Q = 0.60 and phi = 0.10). Finally, and of critical importance, they find a strong association between arms races and serious disputes (Yule's Q = 0.72 and phi = 0.22), which they argue means that arms races promote serious disputes (Houweling and Siccama, 1981: 170). Since crises both precede and follow arms races, it is probably more precise to say that military buildups so intensify the hostility within a rivalry that they increase the probability that a crisis will escalate to war.

An alternative interpretation is that military buildups may produce new kinds of disputes, the *kind* of crises that are most apt to escalate. It may not be the mere presence of arms races that leads disputes to escalate, but the fact that persistent confrontation makes rivals feel that force is the only way to resolve the issue at hand, and that existing (or projected) military preparations make this a viable option for at least one side. As a result of this conviction and new capability, at least one side engages in behavior in the confrontation that makes it likely that the crisis will escalate. The research on crisis escalation has identified a number of behavioral characteristics that distinguish serious disputes that escalate to war from

---

[16] The terms *military confrontation, serious disputes*, and *militarized dispute* are variations on terminology that researchers have used to refer to what in effect is an evolving data set (cf. Gochman, 1980; Wallace, 1979; Maoz, 1982; Gochman and Maoz, 1984; Leng and Singer, 1988 for technical differences). Since most of the disputes that escalate to war can be taken as crises (using Snyder and Diesing's (1977: 6) definition of that concept), I take research using the data set as a way of telling us something about crisis escalation. Leng (1983; 1993; see also Leng and Singer, 1988) has developed criteria for distinguishing crises from lower-level serious disputes in Correlates of War data.

those that do not and thereby provides some insight into how and why certain crises escalate to war.

Since there have been a large number of militarized disputes, but only a few crises that have escalated to war (see Gochman and Maoz, 1984: 600, 602; Cusack and Eberwein, 1982: 19), identifying any patterns associated with the latter will greatly elucidate how and why war occurs. Most researchers have focused on characteristics related to crisis escalation that are in one way or another internal to the crisis itself. One set of factors that has received a great deal of attention consists of the bargaining tactics and strategy employed by the participants, especially the initiators, and the effects these have on hostility. Another set of factors that is often considered is the characteristics of the issues that make them intractable, leading crises to repeat. This section will examine the research on both of these factors and its implications for explaining the onset of war.

The effect of bargaining

In a series of studies that usually employ a small random or representative sample, Russell Leng has uncovered a number of suggestive findings about the role of bargaining in crisis escalation. At the most basic level, Leng and Wheeler (1979) found that a bullying strategy is usually associated with disputes escalating to war, and that a reciprocating strategy provides the best overall outcome while avoiding war. More significantly, in a later study on tactics, Leng (1980: 143–56) finds that threats – especially negative inducements that are highly credible – are apt to produce extreme responses: either outright compliance or defiance (in terms of counter-threats or punishments). Defiant responses, however, are most likely to occur when the disputants are relatively equal in capability. There is also some indirect evidence that defiant responses are associated with war. These results suggest that, while decision makers may behave in crises in ways that conform to the descriptions provided by realists like Morgenthau and conflict strategists like Schelling, this behavior often leads (among equals) to war, rather than diplomatic success.

Apparently, the key to understanding how *realpolitik* tactics lead to escalation of disputes lies in the way in which leaders change their behavior toward a rival from one dispute to the next. In a review of six pairs of evenly matched states that were involved in three successive disputes, Leng (1983) uncovers a definite learning pattern. He finds that the loser of the previous dispute attributes the loss to a failure to demonstrate sufficient resolve (i.e., commitment to force), and is likely to initiate the second dispute. Among equals, the threat of force is usually met with defiance, and equals tend to meet force with force (Leng, 1986: 54). As a result, both participants tend to escalate the level of coercion in each successive crisis (a finding that holds true for seventeen of twenty-four cases), with war becoming increasingly likely by the third dispute, if it has not occurred earlier.[17] This suggests that, as the underlying issue fails to be resolved, bargaining techniques in successive disputes will become more coercive and more likely to escalate.

Leng shows that this pattern of behavior occurs in direct contradiction to realists' prescriptions about prudence and what realists would expect about the effect of power on bargaining. Leng (1983: 410) maintains that Morgenthau would expect that a state which experiences a decrease in capability from one crisis to the next would tend to be more accommodative or at least less coercive. However, in four of the five instances where an unambiguous shift has taken place, the weaker state moves to more coercive bargaining (Leng, 1983: 412). The only exception is Soviet behavior in the Cuban missile crisis. This indicates that while leaders may follow certain aspects of realist folklore, they appear unable to follow those aspects that caution prudence (Leng, 1986: 53–55).

One of the reasons why leaders may not be able to be as prudent as realists would like is that coercion produces hostility, which makes leaders committed to respond in kind, regardless of their immediate prospects of success. As Leng (1986: 55) notes, attempts at coercion are likely to challenge a leader's pride and the status of a state. This means that targets of coercion, instead of reacting like rational calculators, as a realist rational actor model would maintain, are reacting like human beings who refuse to be coerced, despite the power balance, since their honor and sense of dignity are now at stake. Because such human reactions are very common, particularly when the domestic political context is hostile to a challenger, realist dictates of prudence are a bit of wishful thinking rather than something which will be heeded.

Leng's (1983, 1986) analyses tell us something important about the characteristics and effects of coercion. Among relative equals, coercion tends to give rise to coercion. In successive disputes, political actors learn

---

[17] An examination of Leng (1983: Table 2) shows that only major states require a series of crises before war breaks out. Among minor states that are relatively equal (e.g. Israel and the Arabs; India and Pakistan) war breaks out in the first crisis. These cases show that major states are more cautious than minor states, a conclusion consistent with other empirical findings (see Brecher and Wilkenfeld, 1989: ch. 10).

to behave more coercively, rather than resolve their dispute. The use of coercion, then, tends to be contagious, with one party imitating the behavior of the other. As Leng (1983: 412) points out, a similar pattern occurs within a crisis with coercion begetting more coercion (see Leng and Wheeler, 1979). There is considerable evidence in international relations that behavior, particularly conflict behavior, follows an action–reaction model (see Ward, 1982: 97–98, 105–7, 122–23; Wilkenfeld *et al.*, 1980: 170–72, 192; Milstein, 1972; Wilkenfeld *et al.*, 1989), in a tense situation where leaders have each other's attention (Phillips and Crain, 1974; W. Phillips, 1973; Synder and Diesing, 1977).

These studies of Leng's make it clear that how one bargains within a crisis makes a difference as to whether war breaks out. How one bargains within a crisis may, in turn, be a function of how a militarized dispute starts and over what is at issue. Gochman and Leng (1983: 101), for example, find that disputes between equals that pose a physical threat to vital territorial issues are more apt to escalate than disputes triggered by other events. Among equals, these tactics meet with defiant responses and lead to successive crises.

More extensive evidence that how a crisis begins will shape the subsequent level of violence is presented by James and Wilkenfeld (1984), who examine ninety-two crises from 1945 to 1975. They argue that how a crisis is triggered sets the tone for how actors will pursue their goals and restricts the choices available for response (James and Wilkenfeld, 1984: 37, 38; see also Gochman and Leng, 1983: 100). Although they do not look explicitly at the question of which crises escalate to war, they do find that crises initiated by a violent trigger are much more likely to be characterized by a bargaining pattern where violence is preeminent. Of the crises that begin violently, 44 percent will continue to have violence as their preeminent characteristic, compared to 24 percent of the crises that begin non-violently. In addition, crises that have violent triggers are likely to give rise to a recurrence of crisis among the same parties within the subsequent five-year period. Fifty-six per cent of the crises initiated by violent triggers will be followed by additional crises, whereas only 27 percent of the crises that started with a non-violent action will be followed by a crisis in the next five-year period (both sets of findings are statistically significant; see James and Wilkenfeld, 1984: 42–43, 49). This study confirms, with a large sample, the hypothesis that the use of violence begets violence in both the short and long run. This probably occurs because the likely effects of the use of violence are to escalate tensions and increase hostility.

In follow-up studies Brecher and Wilkenfeld (1989: chs. 9–10) and Brecher and James (1988) show that crises that repeat (and hence are more apt to end in war) tend to be triggered by violent acts, have basic values (such as "threats to existence") at stake, and use violence as a central conflict management technique. These "protracted conflicts" tend to have more ambiguous outcomes and more unilateral acts than conflicts that do not suffer from repeated crises. Each of the identified factors suggests why these crises fester and repeat, and the findings are consistent with Leng's (1983) study, but based on a much larger sample. In addition, Brecher and James (1988) provide evidence to show that it is the characteristics of crises and not the region in which they occur that is responsible for the behavioral syndrome they exhibit.[18]

Leng's studies, along with the supporting evidence of James and Wilkenfeld and of Brecher and Wilkenfeld, go a long way in demonstrating that the use of *realpolitik* tactics, particularly in their hard-line mode, makes crises escalate to war. This is yet another piece of evidence to indicate that realist practices are more associated with the outbreak of war than with peace. As stated earlier, this is because realism frequently offers prescriptions that, while trying to avoid war, also try to assure victory in case war breaks out. The bargaining practices associated with *realpolitik* are especially susceptible to this logic, often assuming that tough acts will aid victory and reduce the likelihood of war. Obviously, they do not reduce the likelihood of war. What is their effect on victory?

Here the realist folklore tends to be correct. Indeed, as Maoz (1983) shows, resolve is more important than capability in determining the outcome of a dispute. Employing a random sample of disputes, Maoz (1983: 215) finds that actors (usually initiators) who show more resolve (i.e. they engage in more hostile or violent acts and they maintain a higher degree of control over the escalatory sequence) than their opponents tend to win. These variables better predict who will win a dispute than do differences in capability.[19]

---

[18] In his study of dispute escalation involving major states, Zeev Maoz (1984: 396) attempts to go beyond the previously discussed studies by trying to distinguish which specific acts of military confrontation during a crisis are associated with escalation to war and which are not. He finds that acts such as alerts, full scale mobilization, occupation of territory, and threats to use force are consistently related to war; whereas threats to blockade, general uses of force, clashes, and seizure of material and personnel are not. Although highly inductive and tentative, Maoz's study does provide a more precise understanding of the kinds of acts and tactics within a crisis that are apt to lead to war.

[19] While these variables tend to be more important then differences in capability, in disputes between major states, military expenditure ratios and mobilization rates are also related to the outcome (Maoz, 1983: 215).

Maoz (1983: 223–24) also finds, however, that when both sides display "high levels of recklessness, a high degree of control over the interaction sequence," and the willingness to risk war rather than give in, then the dispute is apt to escalate to war. Interestingly, disputes that escalate are also related to the military expenditure ratios of the actors (Maoz, 1983: 215), as Wallace (1982) and Diehl (1985a) found, and Singer (1982: 40) suggested. *Realpolitik* tactics may produce victory, but under certain conditions they may also produce war.

It can be surmised that war is likely when both sides feel so strongly about an issue that neither is willing to give in. They both show a willingness to risk war and they both have prepared for war. This probably indicates that they have been unable to come to some sort of agreement about an issue that is of high mutual salience to them. Only issues of this type can command such risks. Issues dealing with territory, especially territorial contiguity, are the kinds of issues that are of high mutual salience and prove to be intractable.

It might be hypothesized that because territorial issues are difficult to resolve, actors employ increasingly coercive tactics to get the other side to give in. By the third crisis, if not before, all of the characteristics Leng found associated with escalation (initiation by physical threat, vital issues, previous learning, increasingly coercive tactics, adequate military preparation) are in place, and war breaks out. It is in this manner that the nature of the issue and its irresolvability acts as a force that drives actors to take steps that increase hostility and bring them closer and closer to war. From this perspective, it is not a mindless struggle for power that produces war, but certain kinds of issues that generate an inherent conflict of interest which, when the parties attempt to resolve it according to realist practices, frequently results in increasing hostility and insecurity.

Other factors making issues intractable

While territorial concerns may be the fundamental factor that gives rise to a set of interactions that lead to war, it must be remembered that whether war occurs will depend very much on how disputants perceive their issue and how they contend over it. Barringer's (1972) cluster analysis of 300 characteristics of 18 conflicts helps establish this point.[20] His

---

[20] These range from violent incidents like the Bay of Pigs and the 1962 India–China conflict to protracted conflicts and wars like the Cyprus war of independence, Kashmir conflict, Greek insurgency, and Spanish Civil War (see Barringer, 1972: 49).

early inductive findings take on greater significance because they are compatible with the more recent findings on crisis escalation discussed above. Barringer (1972: 102–15) finds that one of the main distinctions between the non-military and military *phases* of a conflict is the way the issues at stake are perceived. At least one side no longer feels that the issue can be negotiated and both sides feel that they have made a public commitment that is now vitally at stake in the dispute (Barringer, 1972: 104–5). Barringer (1972: 107–8, 110) also finds that domestic mobilization is associated with the militarization of disputes. Attitudes among the public on each side are more supportive of hostilities, and ideological differences that had been previously mild are now extreme. He finds that both sides tend to equalize their military forces just prior to the war, whereas they had earlier been unequal.[21] Often, any shift in the military balance is seized upon to gain an immediate advantage (Barringer, 1972: 111–12). Finally, Barringer (1972: 105) finds that military hostilities tend to erupt after a crisis and a change in the leadership of one side.

Once a militarized dispute or war is under way, Barringer (1972: 115) finds that escalation in military tactics has two common factors: pessimism about what will happen if victory is not achieved, which can be seen as an indicator of the salience of the issue, and a recent shift in the military balance. Clearly the two factors are related, with the first providing the motivation and the second the means. Thus, while the outbreak of hostilities is associated with relative equality in military capability, escalation in tactics is brought about by a shift in favor of the party that was previously disadvantaged (Barringer, 1972: 114). The intervention or continued support of a major state is important for the latter, since it will tend to increase its involvement in order to avert an unfavorable military balance. This encourages escalation by discouraging a losing side from negotiating, since it does not have to face the limits of its own ability (Barringer, 1972: 114–15). In this regard, it is important to note that deescalation within a war is associated with a shift in the military balance against one of the parties, particularly if it is against the party that is suffering greater losses (Barringer, 1972: 114). Such shifts often bring about deescalation when they are associated with the prospect that the advantaged party will receive even more third-party support than the disadvantaged in the near future.

---

[21] Singer (1982: 40) hypothesizes that the more equal the protagonists are militarily, the more likely escalation; see also the findings of Diehl (1985a) and Moul (1988a).

As with other analyses, Barringer finds that the underlying issues are an important factor in producing a war-prone situation. It is only when the issues appear to be unresolvable through political accommodation and reasonable alternatives have been foreclosed that military solutions become implemented (Barringer, 1972: 105). It has already been seen how one of the other factors that make issues intractable is their association with territorial contiguity. Barringer's analysis also provides evidence to show that one of the factors that makes issues intractable is the number of parties involved in the dispute. He finds that third-party intervention by a "great power" tends to increase the likelihood that a "conflict" will move into its militarized phase and that escalation will occur. For his sample of cases, which includes mostly "conflicts" in the periphery rather than direct confrontations between major states, he finds "great power" involvement and support to be the single most influential factor in the outbreak and escalation of militarized hostilities (Barringer, 1972: 112, 114). This suggests that crises involving more than two parties are more difficult to manage.

More systematic evidence to support this conclusion is provided by Cusack and Eberwein (1982), who find that issues that involve several parties are explosive. In their review of 634 twentieth-century militarized disputes, they find that, while about three-fourths of these disputes were dyadic, they are among the least likely to escalate (Cusack and Eberwein, 1982: 11, 24–26). Conversely, disputes involving three or more parties are prone to escalation, with disputes involving major states (either directly confronting each other or in alliance with minor states) most likely to escalate. The major exception to the size principle is disputes between coalitions (at least two states on each side) consisting exclusively of minor states; none of these escalate to war. Cusack and Eberwein (1982: 27) conclude that intervention in an ongoing dispute increases the probability of war.

Since intervention by a major state has an impact on escalation, it is not only the size of the dispute, but who enlarges the dispute that is important. While on average only one of every nine disputes culminates in war, disputes between exclusively major states escalate a little over one in five times. Mixed disputes, involving major and minor states, escalate slightly less frequently, but disputes between minor states culminate in war roughly only one out of twenty times (Cusack and Eberwein, 1982: 26–27). These findings indicate that the expansion of disputes, and hence anything that produces that expansion (like alliances), makes war more likely. In this regard, Cusack and Eberwein provide indirect evidence that alliance making, to the extent that it encourages subsequent intervention, is a step toward war.

These findings have been reconfirmed by Gochman and Maoz (1984: 601–2) on a more complete data set (960 militarized disputes from 1816 to 1976). They find that 22 percent of the multiparty disputes escalated to war compared to 5 percent of the dyadic disputes. In addition, while they find that minor states have been more prone than major states to become involved in militarized disputes, these have not frequently escalated to war, whereas those involving major states have. Gochman and Maoz (1984: 602) argue that multiparty disputes are more apt to escalate to war because they "are likely to provide a larger aggregate of capabilities to sustain large-scale hostilities," particularly since they are apt to involve more than one major state. More importantly, multiparty disputes, they argue, probably make it difficult to keep interactions from getting out of control in an escalatory spiral. Finally, the inclusion of more than one major state in a dispute leaves few others to play the role of neutral mediators. They suggest that one of the reasons that disputes involving only minor states may not escalate to war is that major states acting as mediators may be able to prevent such wars. Gochman and Leng (1983: 115), for example, find that disputes in which major states are mediators are less likely to escalate to war (see also Raymond and Kegley, 1985).

Additional evidence that the size of a dispute has an effect on its dynamics is provided by James and Wilkenfeld (1984). In their study of post-World War II crises, they find that crises that involve three or more participants tend to be longer and produce less satisfactory outcomes. The latter finding is important because, even though they show that crises having three or more disputants are more apt to result in some form of agreement than dyadic crises, that agreement is considerably less satisfactory and hence less likely to last.[22] James and Wilkenfeld (1984: 39–40, 46) explain these findings by noting that coalitional dynamics make crisis bargaining more complicated and hence more protracted. Differences between the parties are also less likely to lead to complete satisfaction. These same characteristics can, under some circumstances, also make an issue under contention more intractable.

The size of a dispute is probably related to the intangibility of the issue under contention. Elsewhere, I have argued that the more intangible an

---

[22] James and Wilkenfeld (1984: 45) find that while 54 percent of the dyadic crises produce an agreement compared to 74 percent of the multilateral crises, only 9 percent of the latter showed complete satisfaction with the agreement compared with 33 percent of the dyadic crises.

issue, the more likely it will attract a larger number of contenders, and the more likely it will engender conflict, especially if the contention persists and it links several issues (Vasquez, 1983a). Evidence based on event data that consist primarily of verbal conflict, but include conflictive deeds, lends support to these claims (see Vasquez, 1983a: 183–89). Issues that involve intangible ends and means include moral and/or ideological issues which tend to produce more interactions and more persistent contention than issues with tangible ends and means (Vasquez, 1983b: 180–81; Rosenau, 1966 [1971: 145–47]; Henehan, 1981). The reason for this is that tangible issues, with the exception of territory, can be divided and resolved through compromise (Lowi, 1964).[23] Issues with intangible goals, however, cannot be divided, and they often result in a stalemate where both sides prefer a winner-take-all solution. The inability to compromise means that routine, as well as crisis, interactions usually fail to resolve the issue in a satisfactory manner. Consequently, contention persists and festers, making conflict more intense and eventually producing a hostile relationship.

Under the right circumstances, and among equals, such issues can produce a rivalry. As indicated in Chapter 2, what is most significant about rivalry is that it reduces all stakes and issues under contention to a single grand overarching issue whose goals and means are intangible. In a rivalry, such an issue produces persistent conflict and even crises, but it does not seem to produce war. Rivalry establishes an important context for the rise of security issues and subsequent steps to war, but it often appears that before the intractability of contention and the irresolvability of the issue will actually trigger war, a crisis must emerge in which territorial contiguity is directly under contention.[24] Since rivals are not always contiguous or can sometimes avoid conflicts along a direct border, they are often brought to war by intervening in a crisis that emerges in an area contiguous to one of the rivals. This intervention usually occurs because of an alliance bond with a minor state.

---

[23] Territory, of course, can be divided, and many fights that are stalemated end this way, but, unlike other tangible issues, humans seem to prefer to fight a contest over territory where the winner takes all, rather than divide the territory in dispute. This makes territorial issues very different from other tangible issues, e.g. most economic questions which are usually very susceptible to bargaining. Hence, the most salient issues in any society are territorial issues and intangible issues that have been linked and infused with transcendent qualities.

[24] Territorial issues are needed for an increased probability of war not because they are necessary conditions, but because the probability of disputes over territory escalating to war is much higher than disputes over intangible issues escalating to war.

Barringer (1972: 112) elucidates how rivalry, with its scramble for spheres of influence, not only aggravates conflict among minor states, but brings major states into a dispute that involves territorial contiguity:

> It is an irony that while it is perhaps only through the progressive expansion of local conflict that the great powers are likely to come to confront each other directly, it is they who must be held largely responsible for the course of development of those conflicts. In the pursuit of spheres of influence and in the name of righteous principles, the great powers have generally supplied the public support and the military hardware that are the very fuel of local conflict, even while withholding or failing to furnish the agencies of impartial accommodation.

Because rivalry often involves a search for allies, who then bring with them their particular issues, rivalry has a tendency to put territorial issues on the agenda.

If this analysis is correct, then what separates rivalries that end in war from those that do not is the ability to avoid crises involving contiguous territorial disputes. In both World War I and World War II, alliance commitments were able to plunge Germany and France into war by introducing territorial disputes into their rivalry, even though there was no direct border crisis prior to the war. Austria-Hungary's dispute with contiguous Serbia brought about World War I, and Hitler's persistent aggrandizement of contiguous areas led to World War II. Conversely, despite the rivalry, arms race, and several crises between the United States and the Soviet Union, direct war was avoided in the Cold War probably because of the absence of a salient territorial dispute involving a contiguous area (see Vasquez, 1991).

On the basis of the above analysis, it can be concluded that crises will tend to escalate when: they are triggered by a violent action on a territorial issue, the bargaining becomes intractable and positions harden, the dispute involves more than two parties, and a major state intervenes. Intangible issues tend to increase the number of parties in a dispute and the possibility of a major state intervening, but they do not lead to war unless they are linked to a territorial dispute. Rivalries that do not end in war are those that for one reason or another have avoided disputing over territory contiguous to one of the rivals. The avoidance of territorial issues is difficult, however, because the intangible quality of the issues separating rivals leads them to search for allies and link as many issues on the global agenda as possible into one overarching issue. This process normally brings in an issue involving contiguous territory, particularly since notions of a balance of power encourage rivals to ally with minor states bordering on their opponent.

The evidence on issues suggests that it is not bargaining alone that accounts for the escalation of crises to war. Certain issues – territorial issues, particularly those involving major states and more than two parties – make conflict persist, so that even if the bargaining in one crisis does not result in war, the issue will give rise to other crises, which will be even harder to manage. To get a full sense of why bargaining becomes so difficult to manage by the third crisis (rather than becoming easier with experience), it is necessary go beyond the bargaining factors that arise within a crisis and examine the nature of the leadership (and the domestic political context within which it operates). Although this topic will be treated in the next chapter, it is important to point out here that the domestic political environment is not immune from the effects of previous crises and in turn plays an important role in shaping the crisis that eventually escalates to war.

Singer (1970a [1979: 72–78], 1982: 40) recognized long ago that there is an interaction between the international and domestic political contexts that encourages leaders to take escalatory actions and makes it difficult to initiate conciliatory moves within a dispute. Domestically, in the attempt to mobilize the public and gain support for military expenditures, leaders paint a picture of a hostile enemy and create a climate that is responsive to hard-line and jingoistic appeals. This tendency is reinforced by traditional realist advice that one must show firmness (and resolve) in the struggle for power. Domestic and global factors interact to produce self-aggravating propensities that increase hostility and make compromise impossible.

Such factors affect decision makers' perception, encouraging both sides to develop not only mirror-images (Bronfenbrenner, 1961; White, 1970), but a shared intellectual context that sees power politics as a legitimate and useful means for dealing with the adversary. In this climate, it is not surprising that perceived hostility is correlated with violent behavior and that crisis interactions generate a hostile interaction spiral in which each side overreacts to the other while thinking its own policy is less hostile than that of the other (Holsti *et al.*, 1968: 146, 148, 152–57). The development of this kind of hostile spiral is the final step to war. If the spiraling effect can be avoided through diplomatic skill and bold leadership, the crisis can be successfully managed and war averted (see McClelland, 1972).[25] This is difficult, however, because of the weight of all the previous

---

[25] For an attempt to model different hostile spirals so as to distinguish those that will escalate to war from those that will not see Zinnes and Muncaster (1984).

decisions (steps) that have been taken and have brought the parties to where they now stand.

This means that, while the decisions taken in crises are crucial, they are not the fundamental causes of war. Psychological stress, selective inattention, and poor decision making may make it hard to avoid war at the last minute, but, even if a particular crisis is successfully managed, another will inevitably come along (and will be more intense and more difficult to manage) if there is no fundamental change in policy (goals and means). It is not the dynamics of decision making that produce war, but a set of foreign policy goals and a sequence of practices which create a political relationship and an atmosphere that is apt to result in war given the right set of triggers.

Conclusion

What separates the rivalries that have avoided war from those that have not is that the former are able to break the pattern of behavior associated with the steps to war, whereas the latter are unable to do so. One of the main factors that make it less probable that war will be avoided is the intrusion of territorial disputes involving both rivals. Linking such violence-prone issues with the highly salient intangible issues fueling the rivalry makes it less likely that any of the issues separating the parties can be resolved in a mutually acceptable manner. This pushes actors toward the unilateral policies of power politics, setting them off on the realist road to war.

For rivals, the road to war is a long one in which each side learns from its interactions with the other that force and ultimately war are the only way of resolving certain mutually salient issues. How states react to the policies and actions of their rival is not determined simply by what the other side does at any given moment, but by the entire history of their relationship, as interpreted by general lessons of history, which have become embedded in the folklore of the system. Political actors are predisposed to learn certain things over others. In the modern global system, realist folklore has provided a guide and cultural inheritance for Western states that has shaped and patterned the behavior of major states in certain situations. From its lessons of history, realism has given rise to a set of power politics practices and recommendations which states that are faced with security issues can draw upon. These prescriptions include increasing power through alliance making and/or military buildups, being willing to use coercion and force to gain one's ends, and showing resolve when faced with threats.

The fact that political actors in the modern global political system adopt common realist practices like alliance making, military buildups, balancing of power, and *realpolitik* tactics should come as no surprise. Since realism is part of the system's folklore that has shaped behavior, it does provide observers with a rough description of the kinds of behavior that one would expect to be associated with the onset of war. What is crucial to understand is that against equals, these practices do not produce peace and security, as realists maintain, but increased insecurity, coercion, and entanglement in a process and series of steps that may lead to war. Each step leads decision makers further and further into a trap (both globally and domestically) where they have little choice but to fight.

The empirical research reviewed in this chapter shows that not every step has to be taken in a particular order. Military buildups both precede and follow alliances. Crises punctuate the history of a rivalry. The key factor is that each step taken produces discernible effects that intensify hostility and make further steps more likely and harder to resist. Also, each step better prepares the rivals for war, and this has an effect on the magnitude, severity, and duration of the war that will be fought.

The empirical research also shows that no single factor makes war inevitable. As David Singer is fond of saying, there are many exits along the road to war. Even if security issues arise, war, and especially certain kinds of war, can be avoided, if alliances are eschewed. Even if an alliance is signed, war probably can be prevented if threatening military buildups are avoided. If arms races occur, rivals may still escape war, if they can elude a series of crises. Even if they cannot do that, a crisis may not escalate to war, if the bargaining tactics can be properly managed and hostile spirals bypassed.

Although the steps-to-war analysis must be seen as a working outline that needs to be further tested, refined, and fitted to specific historical cases, its propositions provide the kind of precision and non-obvious findings that are the true hallmarks of an adequate scientific explanation. Unlike the realist description that has been derived from a vast contradictory and ambiguous folklore, the explanation given here provides a broad understanding of both how and why war occurs and how it might be avoided. Realism does neither. Realism cannot be seen as an adequate explanation of war and peace, since not only do many of its practices help bring about war, but many of the things it believes causes war or will produce peace do not do so. Realism and power politics are not so much explanations of war and peace as they are part of the behavior comprising the road to war that must be explained. The analysis presented in this chapter, in large part, has accomplished that task.

The analysis also suggests why war has been with us for so long. War is an institution within the modern global political system that serves an important political function – the resolution of intractable issues. Until there is a functional equivalent to this institution, war will remain a way of handling certain situations. War and the steps and practices that lead to it must be seen as part of a culture of violence that has given birth to these practices. In light of subsequent experiences, war and the practices of power politics have been changed, shaped and ordered to fit a given period and relationship. Peace, when it comes, involves not only establishing alternative ways of dealing with certain issues (or avoiding them entirely), but establishing a different culture. Cultures of violence – whether they be of dueling, vendetta, or war – can only be superseded by creating new worlds based on a different culture and social construction of reality.

Some of these themes and the systemic factors associated with the creation of peace will be treated in Chapter 8. Before taking up the question of peace, however, an important question about the onset of war remains: What role do domestic factors play in the onset of war? These factors seem to be the main reason why it is so difficult for leaders to avoid taking the next step to war, once they have taken the initial step. Interactions between rivals teach not only leaders, but also their publics and policy influencers, that war is the answer. Chapter 6 looks at how domestic political actors are mobilized and shows how this is a prerequisite to a war of rivalry.

6

The Domestic Prerequisites of Wars of Rivalry

> Wars of rivalry are not decided upon by a unitary rational calculator, but by
> the inexorable movement of an entire society.

The actions states take toward one another are of primary importance
in determining whether a rivalry will result in war. From their interactions, states learn that force and war are the only way of resolving
the issue at hand. In this sense, interstate interactions can be viewed
as one set of constraints in which the leadership of a state operates.
The dynamics of the relationship close off certain possibilities, while
encouraging other actions that will increase tensions. These interactions, however, do not take place in isolation; they interact with a second
set of constraints, the domestic political context in which the leadership
of each side must operate. This chapter will examine how external interactions produce those domestic consequences which encourage more
hostile (and escalatory) steps to be taken within a rivalry and within a
crisis.

Although various aspects of the causes of war have been researched by
those taking a scientific approach to international relations, the domestic
prerequisites have received little attention. Not much consideration has
been given to how leaders try to mobilize a society for the decision to go
to war or how the domestic political environment encourages a government to make, or restrains it from making, a foreign policy that is apt to
lead to war. For those who black-box the domestic political environment
or concentrate exclusively on a systemic perspective, it is as if the decision
to go to war were not a foreign policy problem at all, and as if the factors
that affect foreign policy decision making had no impact on the outbreak
of war. In this chapter, I hope to show the importance of domestic politics
in making decisions about war, but since this area has been researched so
little, most of my effort will be confined to outlining the role domestic factors probably play and suggesting new hypotheses, rather than presenting
and interpreting evidence.

There are two ways in which the domestic political environment affects the onset of war. First, the steps to war nation-states take not only intensify hostility between the two sides, but produce reactions that increase the probability of war. Hostile domestic images of the rival encourage the leadership to continue to move along the road to war, taking steps closer and closer to war, rather than reversing direction or exiting. The domestic reaction to international interactions is part of the dynamic that moves states from one step to the other. Domestic hostility toward a rival can reach a feverish pitch, which can become critical in shaping how a crisis is managed. It is likely that in a crisis that escalates to war, hard-liners will dominate the leadership of at least one side and frequently both, since the previous interactions have driven out those who have sought accommodation. The presence of hard-liners is an important prerequisite for a war of rivalry, for, without their influence, it is unlikely that the bargaining tactics most associated with crisis escalation would be taken.

Second, the domestic political environment affects the timing of a war of rivalry. Before a war can occur, at least one side must be mobilized. If there is no domestic mobilization (raising an army, taxes, etc.), leaders will not be able to fight and win a war, and therefore they will be hesitant to initiate or enter one. In addition, the public must be mobilized not only to accept the decision, but to fight and sacrifice enthusiastically in order to give the state the highest chances of success. Because wars between equals are likely to be severe and their outcome uncertain, leaders are not wont to risk war unless their society is psychically prepared. For this reason, even if the decision makers wants to go to war, he (or she) may not initiate it because of domestic constraints. This was certainly the case with Franklin Delano Roosevelt prior to the attack on Pearl Harbor, and it was also the case with Bethmann-Hollweg, who in 1914 wanted the war to come in a way that would make it clear to the Social Democrats that Germany was not at fault.

Clearly, the two ways in which the domestic political environment affects the onset of war interact. The previous steps that have been taken toward war help to create a constituency for hard-liners, who in turn help mobilize the public and encourage leaders to take those actions, such as a military buildup, that make it prepared for war. Without such preparations, a leader would be more cautious in a crisis. What is important to keep in mind is the interacting dynamic that makes various aspects of the entire society (from the leadership to domestic critics) come to the decision to go to war. The decision to go to war is rarely made by a single leader as if he (or she) alone had this thought and informed the country of it. Instead, what happens is that a growing number of people begin to feel that war may be necessary and this shift in attitude convinces the leadership that certain actions can be taken. These actions, in turn, produce consequences which in turn convince more people and groups that war is justified.

The steps to war, then, must be viewed as foreign policy *decisions* that are interrelated and cumulative. They are not statistically independent, but reflect a process of increasing hostility between rivals and a mobilization of domestic resources and public attitudes in preparation for war. Such domestic consequences stiffen an elite's determination and ability not to give in to the opponent. When specific actions fail to produce the desired outcomes, costlier and riskier actions consistent with the overall policy are tried. A more complete explanation of the steps to war requires discovering how leaders and their society learn to go to war. In order to address this question, we need some classification system for differentiating leaders, elites, and policy influencers according to their willingness to adopt the practices and tactics associated with war. Since it is known that power politics behavior and the use of *realpolitik* tactics in crises are associated with war, what is needed is a classification of domestic political actors that separates those who advocate power politics from those who do not. Once this is constructed, it will be possible to analyze what aspects of the domestic political environment increase the influence of those advocating policies that increase the probability of war.

Classifying Domestic Political Actors

Historians have recognized the need to classify the various domestic elements that either favored or opposed going to war. Often they indicate that among European monarchies the court was frequently divided over whether a policy of war or peace should be pursued. Typically, these factions are referred to as the war party and peace party (see Braudel, 1966 [1973: 940]). This nomenclature appears tautological for our purposes in that it does not precisely identify the characteristics of each faction that lead them to advocate their respective policies. The work of Frederick Hoffmann (1970) provides some insight on this question. In an analysis of legislative arms debates, he finds that conservative and radical arguments are always presented and seem unaffected by external factors. This leads him to conclude that a person's security views are not derived from "objective" factors, but are a function of individual beliefs and predispositions. This is a valuable piece of evidence and it suggests that power politics practices may be advocated, in part, because of personal predispositions, but his labels of conservative and radical seem much too broad, especially to describe arguments over military expenditures.

Crude as they are, such attempts offer two insights. First, as a rivalry develops and there is a possibility of war, domestic advisors tend to be reduced to two groups, those willing to go to war and those seeking to avoid it. Second, membership in these groups may not depend solely on the objective situation, but on certain prior beliefs and predispositions. In light of the analysis of the previous chapters, it would be expected that debate over foreign policy would be among those who wanted to follow power politics to its fullest (e.g. demonstrating resolve, engaging in strong action) and those who outright opposed such action or who, operating within the realist tradition, counseled prudence. This suggests that personal predispositions may be associated not only with different beliefs, but with different emphases within the same intellectual tradition.

A classification that captures this insight and that is more precise than Hoffmann's (1970) conservative/radical scheme is the hard-line/soft-line distinction (see Snyder and Diesing, 1977: 297–310). It is much clearer that hard-liners, as opposed to soft-liners, are prone to adopting power politics practices, whereas either conservatives or radicals can be hard-liners. One of the problems with the hard-liner/soft-liner distinction is that it is unclear whether it refers to differences in personality or to beliefs and strategies. The problem with treating the distinction as a personality trait is that individual behavior varies and can change over time. For example, Snyder and Diesing (1977: 309–10) find some individuals to be hard-liners on one issue but soft-liners on another. This means that the distinction is not a personality trait and is better kept as a classification of beliefs and strategies. In addition, scholars should be wary of efforts to connect personality characteristics with beliefs, since such efforts often can be ideologically biased (e.g. those with whom one disagrees are measured as psychologically deviant).

In this connection, one of the problems with the terms hard-liner and soft-liner is that they can both be regarded as somewhat pejorative from at least some point of view. An alternative would be to use the more neutral "hawk–dove" distinction but this is too time-bound to the Vietnam War debate in the United States for an analysis meant to explain 500 years of war. The term soft-liner can be replaced by "accommodationist," following the lead of Wittkopf and Maggiotto (1983), who compare hard-liners and accommodationists within the public and the elite. This seems appropriate, since policy influencers never say they are advocating a "soft line," but often do express the need to take a "hard line." In addition, the term hard-liner, although sometimes used pejoratively, seems less pejorative than other terms such as militarist, the latter label being widely used in the period following World War I. Finally, the hard-liner/accommodationist distinction is compatible with Singer's (1970a) analysis of how hardliners within a society aggravate tendencies toward escalation and his later (Singer, 1982: 43) proposal to delineate the conditions that generate "hawkish and doveish moves."

If in fact hard-liners and accommodationists are domestic rivals who will continually debate with one another because of personal predispositions, it will always be difficult to avoid negative connotations, since each faction will always impugn the motives and policies of the other. The responsibility of the analyst is to define recognizable labels in a manner that is fairly neutral and precise enough so that one faction can be empirically distinguished from the other. Here, Margaret Hermann's (1980) argument that there are four types of personal characteristics that can affect foreign policy decisions – beliefs, motives, decision style, and interpersonal style – can be of help. For now all that is necessary is to focus on beliefs and leave open the question of why those beliefs are held. Beliefs are easier to identify and a focus on them does not impugn anyone's motives or style.

For the purpose of this analysis, *accommodationists* can be defined as individuals who have a personal predisposition (due to the beliefs they hold) that finds the use of force, especially war, repugnant, and advocates a foreign policy that will avoid war through compromise, negotiation, and the creation of rules and norms for non-violent conflict resolution. Conversely, *hard-liners* can be defined as individuals who have a personal predisposition (due to their beliefs) to adopt a foreign policy that is adamant in not compromising its goals and who argue in favor of the efficacy and legitimacy of threats and force.

The hard-liner/accommodationist distinction is also useful because it makes it clear that not all realists will advocate or favor war. Although hard-liners have a general predisposition to power politics practices, hard-liners and realists are not identical. The twentieth-century realism of E. H. Carr, Morgenthau, Niebuhr, and Waltz (as opposed to the realist folklore that has been around for several centuries) is a detailed intellectual position that is more subtle and sophisticated than the general stance connoted by the term hard-line. This means that hard-liners will tend to emphasize the coercive aspects of power politics and neglect advice on prudence (see Leng, 1983: 410–12, 416) and messianism. This suggests, of course, that there can be both hard-line (i.e., militant) idealists and accommodative realists.[1]

On the whole, it does seem that the hard-liner/accommodationist distinction can be useful for tracing changes within the domestic political environment. Snyder and Diesing (1977) find it conceptually useful in discussing crisis bargaining. More significantly, Wittkopf and Maggiotto (1983) (see also Wittkopf, 1987) employ the concept to identify two (of four) groupings of elite and mass opinion on foreign policy (hard-liners, accommodationists, isolationists, and internationalists). Their analysis shows that operational indicators can be provided for each of the categories, and that they have an empirical referent.

Their study is also important for pointing out that the main opponents of hard-liners may not be accommodationists, but isolationists. This means that the domestic critics of hard-liners will vary depending on the nation and its history. Thus, in the 1930s, the main critics in the United States were isolationists. Similarly, in Bolshevik Russia after Lenin's death, those who opposed Trotsky's permanent revolution and advocated with Stalin, socialism in one country, can be regarded as isolationists. In the Cold War, critics of hard-liners in the United States, Soviet Union, and China were not isolationists (as was sometimes charged in the United States), but accommodationists (see Vasquez, 1985: 666). Critics of hard-liners, then, tend to be either accommodationists or isolationists.[2]

Even though hard-liners will, by definition, always be in the forefront of advocating violence, their political complexion will vary by nation-state, since the sentiments of hard-liners can be linked to other national issues. Thus in post-1945 France, hard-liners are associated with the Empire, conservatism, and the Catholic Church. In Nazi Germany, they are associated with nationalism and racism. In Trotsky's Russia, they are associated with internationalism and the spreading of the revolution. In the United States during the two world wars, they are associated with democratic liberalism. In any case, since what is of concern here is to trace the rise and influence of hard-liners, I have not tried

---

[1] Wilson and Kissinger would be examples of each of these types. For some empirical evidence about the characteristics of militant idealists which makes clear their similarity to those of hard-liners, see Shapiro (1966, cited in Guetzkow and Valadez, 1981a: 204–6).

[2] Internationalists tend to be more sympathetic to the hard-line position, as the external threat intensifies. As war approaches, I believe it becomes increasingly difficult to differentiate internationalists from hard-liners the way I define them and describe their behavior in this chapter, although in normal times they are a clearly identifiable opinion group. A clear example that supports this point is Franklin D. Roosevelt.

to construct or utilize a complete typology along the lines of Wittkopf and Maggiotto (1983). All that is essential is that a distinction can be made in the foreign policy elite and the public between hard-liners, on the one hand, and all other non-hard-liners, on the other (whether they be accommodationists or isolationists). While I will employ the term accommodationists in the analysis, the reader should keep in mind that in any specific country, the main non-hard-liners may very well be isolationists. Nevertheless, the behavior I attribute to accommodationists and the dynamic between hard-liners and accommodationists should apply equally well to isolationists and all other domestic critics of the hard-liners.

Although the hard-line/accommodationist distinction is useful at this stage of inquiry, it should be clear that the concept suffers from an imprecision that raises concerns about tautological tendencies. I have tried to avoid this in the definitions I have given above and by making a distinction between hard-liners and realists. Thus, it is not inevitable that all realists will always seek to use force; they may counsel prudence or negotiation. In the Western democracies, hard-liners have drawn upon and emphasized the most virulent aspect of the global realist culture. In a Marxist or Christian political culture, hard-liners could be expected to do the same thing, and, instead of having hard-line realists, one would have hard-line Marxists or Christians. Nevertheless, as research progresses, it will be useful to identify specific personal traits as well as personality tendencies that might be associated with the use of force and violence. At this point, the term *hard-liner* is an initial attempt to capture some of those traits without knowing exactly what they are.

What are the traits that make hard-liners prone to the most dangerous and least prudent aspects of the realist folklore? One likely candidate is risk-taking. Clearly, hard-liners will be much more willing to take risks, but this in part may be a function of the fact that what is at issue is of greater salience to them than to accommodationists or others. Michael Haas (1974: 110–25), in his study of thirty-two major decisions, found the propensity to take risks related to the use of violence. Crow and Noel (1977: 400; cited in Guetzkow and Valadez, 1981a: 206) found that players in a simulation who were risk-takers tended to use higher levels of military force in responding to a crisis than those who were more risk-averse, but that these tendencies were moderated when players worked within a group. Although we can assume that within a crisis hard-liners would be more willing to take risks, research shows that the tendency to take risks will be affected by the context in which the decision takes place

(Guetzkow and Valadez, 1981b: 275–76) and whether a decision maker is facing the prospect of losses or gains (Kahneman and Tversky, 1979).

Another major factor affecting the use of force is the cognitive complexity of an individual, i.e. the extent to which a person's thinking and concepts tend to be abstract and elaborate, as opposed to concrete (Guetzkow and Valadez, 1981a: 203–4). Driver (1977: 342; cited in Guetzkow and Valadez, 1981b: 261) found that players with simple (as opposed to complex) cognitive structures tend to involve their simulated nations in more aggressive behavior. Margaret Hermann (1974: 220–23; see also M. Hermann, 1980) uncovered a similar finding in her content analysis of national leaders' speeches; she found those with low cognitive complexity engaging in more conflict. Suedfeld and Tetlock (1977) in a content analysis of documents find that complexity of information processing and communication is lower in crises that ended in war (1914 and Korea) than in those that were peacefully settled (1911 Moroccan crisis, Berlin Blockade, and Cuban Missile crisis). Similarly, they also find complexity declining in UN speeches dealing with the Middle East situation just prior to the outbreak of war (Suedfeld, Tetlock, and Ramirez, 1977). A refined measure of integrative complexity of archival sources, which examines the ability of leaders to differentiate a number of dimensions in information and integrate these into combinations, was found to decline during American–Soviet crises (Wallace and Suedfeld, 1988). These findings, however, may be measuring the effects of decision makers' stress; when Levi and Tetlock (1980) examine the cognitive complexity of Japanese decision makers' planning to attack Pearl Harbor, they found that complexity was high not low, indicating that when war is premeditated and initiated, cognitive complexity is not low.[3]

It makes sense that hard-liners would look at the use of force as a simple way of resolving problems, and the fact that Leng (1983) found that leaders did not follow realist advice about prudence seems to support this conclusion. Nevertheless, the fact remains that force is usually a last resort. It may be that by this time the situation appears cognitively simple because

[3] We can speculate that complexity indicators go down in crises that uncontrollably escalate to war, because the call for a hard-line response appears as relatively concrete and direct, whereas crises that end without going to war require much more elaborate and abstract schemes in order to work out some sort of accommodation. Therefore, it is not surprising that measures of integrative complexity might be positively associated both with accommodation and deliberate war initiation (both of which require elaborate planning), but inversely correlated with involvement in crises that escalate to war by getting out of control. If this were the case, we would expect integrative complexity to be low prior to unwanted wars and high, in at least one side, prior to planned wars.

no other options are perceived as possible. In this regard, it is interesting that Margaret Hermann (1974: 220–23) finds conflict associated with leaders not having a great belief in their ability to control events, a finding similar to Holsti's (1972: 151) evidence showing that in the 1914 crisis leaders perceived their adversaries as having more options than they had themselves. As Wallace and Suedfeld (1988: 442, 449–50) argue, integrative complexity may be a behavioral variable that is affected by external events, and, therefore, as crises intensify and war looms it will go down.

Other studies of the Inter-Nation Simulation have found that players who are nationalistic and who hold a militaristic world view are more apt to escalate conflict than are others (Crow and Noel, 1965: 8, 20; Guetzkow and Valadez, 1981a: 206–7). M. Hermann (1974) also found nationalistic leaders to be more conflictive. Similarly, Etheredge (1978), in a study of US State Department personnel, found that those who have an idealized view of American diplomatic history are more prone to advocate force than those who have a more revisionist view of American diplomatic history. That hard-liners would be more nationalistic makes sense. We would expect hard-liners to emphasize the importance of force and to be nationalistic, particularly as a rivalry progressed and war seemed more likely. This also emphasizes the point that hard-line predispositions are not invariant, but grow as the prospect of war grows, so that in the end more and more of the elite and domestic populace become hard-liners. Thus, it is significant that studies have found distrust and hostility to be associated with the advocacy of violence (Etheredge, 1978: 127; M. Haas, 1974: 110–25; Driver, 1977; Brody, 1963; see also Holsti et al. 1968). Furthermore, Driver (1977: 350 cited in Guetzkow and Valadez, 1981a: 204, 210) found that a simple cognitive structure is associated with violence when the individual is distrustful.

One of the few studies dealing with foreign policy that find a clear personality trait associated with violence is Etheredge's (1978) content analysis of US presidents and their advisors. He finds that when there is disagreement among high-level foreign policy makers, interpersonal style becomes an important factor (see also M. Hermann 1978 for other situations when personal characteristics are seen as being able to have an impact). Etheredge (1978: 79, 85) finds that those whom he scored high on personal dominance are more apt to advocate the use of force and oppose conciliatory moves. This was true in thirty-eight of the forty-nine cases he (77.5 percent) studied. Graham Shepard (1988) replicated Etheredge's study for the 1969–84 period and found that in the presence of disagreement, decision makers with a high dominance interpersonal style tend to advocate the use of force, while those with a low dominance style do not. Shepard (1988: 120) found this to be the case in 76.9 percent of the 108 cases he studied.

Although these studies must be regarded as highly tentative, they do offer a more detailed portrait of the beliefs and attitudes that make the hard-liner more predisposed to engage in power politics and escalatory actions. The hard-liners' cognitive map of the world tends to be simple rather than complex. Hard-liners tend to be nationalistic and hold a militaristic view of the world. The hard-liner as a type is hostile toward and distrustful of the other nation, and feels unable to control events. In a crisis they are risk-takers. In personal relations they are prone to dominance.

Except for the last, which is a personality characteristic, it is clear that the characteristics hard-liners share are something they have learned from their experience or imbibed from the culture around them. The remainder of this chapter will attempt to delineate how the steps to war create a domestic political environment in which hard-liners flourish and more and more people learn to become hard-liners, whether they like it or not.

Determining the Initial Balance Between Hard-Liners and Accommodationists

This analysis has presupposed that once hard-liners are in power, or are highly influential in the domestic environment, power politics practices will be favored over other practices. So, to uncover the domestic political roots of war we must explain the rise of hard-liners. It can be assumed that there are always hard-liners and accommodationists within a population, and what Karl Mannheim (1952: 304–7, 315–18) calls the "spirit of the times" will determine which will prevail. It is this nebulous spirit of the times that must be more precisely analyzed if we are to discover under what domestic and global conditions hard-liners are likely to be influential within the elite and in the public. It is not inconceivable that these domestic and global conditions are so powerful that hard-liners will push accommodationists out of the body politic. We will begin by looking at an initial domestic political context and then see how that is changed by external factors.

To determine whether a domestic political context is initially more favorable to the influence of hard-liners or accommodationists, all one has to do is to look at the "lessons of the past" that prevail in the national political culture. This is not a difficult task since these lessons are reflected in the popular media and the publications of the intelligentsia. The crucial question is: where do these lessons come from? It seems that in all societies these lessons are derived from the most traumatic experiences that the society as a whole goes through. For most, this is the last major war. Subsequent events, particularly more limited wars, will affect those lessons, but for the generation that lived through the traumatic experience, only another major war will lead to an opportunity for rethinking the lessons. Using a general learning model (Vasquez, 1976), one can assume that these lessons will be passed on to the next generation through socialization and will be accepted, although with less emotional attachment.

Lessons of history (May, 1973; Jervis, 1976: 266–69) seem to be debated just before, during, and/or just after a major war, and then once again as a new war looms. Whether hard-liners or accommodationists are favored in the post-war environment depends on whether hard-line policies are judged to have succeeded or failed during the last war. The main effect of the failure of a policy is the rethinking of its underlying assumptions and the beliefs associated with it. Severe failures, especially at war, can lead to very drastic policy changes as indicated by Germany in 1918 and Japan in 1945. Even more limited failures, like the United States in Vietnam, can lead to a significant restructuring of belief systems (see Russett, 1975: 5–6; Holsti and Rosenau, 1984: 102–6, 214; Wittkopf and Maggiotto 1983: 222). It is important to remember that policy failures actually lead to changes in people's attitudes and to a sense of learning and development across generations, even though they will have their greatest impact on the generation for which foreign policy is having a direct and sustained impact on personal experience for the first time (Mannheim, 1952: 276–82, 297–301; Jervis, 1976: 239–43). Domestic realignments on foreign policy involve conversions of beliefs and are not produced simply by the addition of new people or a cohort to the population (see Bobrow and Cutler, 1967).[4]

The key variables in assessing the failure or success of a hard-line policy are whether the war was won or lost and whether the effort was regarded

---

[4] Although there is little research on how people learn from international events and how their life experiences affect that learning, there is some evidence that traumatic events shape beliefs for long periods. Bobrow and Cutler (1967: 51) find that cohort is more important than external situation or life-stage for the salience attributed to foreign policy or defense problems, the expectation of war, negative economic expectations, and negative images of certain states. In addition, they find different cohorts will be sensitive to the failure of particular policies; for example, the Great Depression cohort is more pessimistic about collective security (Bobrow and Cutler, 1967: 47).

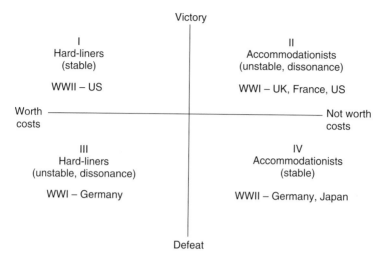

Figure 6.1 Classification of domestic political environment

as being worth the costs in terms of what was gained. This produces four possible outcomes, as illustrated in Figure 6.1. The more determinative variable is costs, with casualties being the major factor (Mueller, 1971). Extreme hard-liners will always see the war as worth the costs, in part because of their attitude toward force and in part because they attach a higher value to what is at stake in a war. Extreme accommodationists will always find the costs too high because they generally regard war as repugnant, if not an immoral practice that produces few benefits. Which position will prevail will be determined by how most people, between these two ends of the continuum, adduce the costs. Wars that are adduced as not having been worth the costs lead to a post-war domestic political context in which accommodationists tend to prevail. Conversely, wars that are adduced to have been worth the costs lead to a domestic political context in which hard-liners prevail.

The second variable, victory or defeat, determines the stability of the domestic political context and the extent to which the derived lessons are susceptible to internal debate and external influence. A victory that is seen as not worth the costs and a defeat in a war that is seen as worth the effort are highly volatile domestic situations filled with cognitive dissonance. Such situations tend to divide the population more than the cognitively consistent situations and lead to recriminating questions, such as why an unnecessary war was fought, why an important war was lost. World War I produced such a situation. Each of the major victors felt the victory was not worth the costs (so their inter-war leaderships and domestic political environments were dominated by accommodationists). In contrast, Germany had important segments of its society feeling that the war was worth the costs and had been lost because of a stab in the back.

Of course, the outcomes and assessments of some wars are clearer than others, so that each variable is treated as a continuum with a stalemate demarked at the origin of the y-axis. The less drastic the victory or defeat, the less stable the subsequent domestic political context. In this sense, it is interesting to compare World War II with World War I. Figure 6.1 portrays the post-war domestic environment of the winners and losers. World War II was not only a more drastic defeat for Germany, but a clearer victory for the allies. In Germany, as well as Japan, the hard-liners were purged by the victors so that there was no one left to make the case that the war was worth the costs, although the tremendous costs would have made it difficult for the hard-liners to regain power after the disgrace of such a defeat. In the allies, accommodationists were soundly defeated because they and their policies were seen as bringing about the war in the first place, which hard-liners believed (probably incorrectly) could have been avoided by a hard-line policy. Such a situation is less likely to lead to a repeat of war between the same two parties than the situation produced after World War I.

Figure 6.1 provides a framework for determining and predicting the initial domestic political context prior to the rise of a new critical issue and external threat. It is hypothesized that after an appropriate time lag, in which hard-liners and accommodationists battle over the lessons of the last war, the domestic political context will be determined by whether the war was won or lost and whether it was adduced as worth the costs.[5] The analysis assumes that a kind of law of political inertia will operate, allowing hard-line or accommodationist tendencies to prevail and be played out in a state's foreign policy until disturbed by some external factor or by

---

[5] This analysis assumes that there may be a time lag before the predicted group prevails, but that by the time a new issue and threat arises (around fifteen years after the war) the domestic context should be clear. Thus, after 1918, Lloyd George and the French took a hard line, while the Germans were accommodative during the Weimar Republic. This was to change in each side, thereby sustaining the description given in Figure 6.1. In the United States, the change in sentiment was heralded by the defeat of the Versailles Treaty and Wilson's League of Nations, but even more significant were the Neutrality Acts of 1935–39.

a non-foreign-policy domestic issue.[6] Having outlined the initial general tendencies of the domestic political context, it is now possible to delineate the effect of interstate interactions on this domestic balance.

Before doing so in detail, it can be seen from Figure 6.1 that the lessons derived from the last war already set up a structural relationship between two societies that push them toward or away from war. Thus, war is most likely to occur when the previous war results in hard-liners dominating both sides, (i.e. when two rivals' domestic political contexts fall within quadrant I, III, or across I–III). The wars between Israel and the Arabs have frequently produced domestic political situations of this sort. War is also likely to occur in a situation in which hard-liners prevailed in the losers and the accommodationists in the winners (i.e. when two rivals are across quadrants III–II). This was the situation at the end of World War I that eventually led to World War II. The remaining situations (except I–IV) should be associated with peace, but if they produce a war, it would occur only by changing the domestic political environment into one where hardliners dominated at least one side.

The tendencies portrayed in the four quadrants should not be interpreted in an overly deterministic manner. They simply delineate some of the structural constraints under which the two rivals and their domestic political actors interact with each other. Whether they will meet or be able to resist the destiny that the burden of their history has laid out for them will depend on the choices and decisions they make.

Domestic Reactions to the Steps to War

Once a major war has resolved the fundamental issues in a rivalry – wars like World War II, the Thirty Years War, and the Napoleonic Wars – the domestic political context will begin to change only when a new critical issue (embodying a new rivalry or the resurrection of the old one) emerges on the global political agenda (see Mansbach and Vasquez, 1981: ch. 4; Vasquez, 1985). The new critical issue and the rise of an external threat are usually heralded by a crisis or an incident that takes on the characteristics of a crisis. The effect of the crisis is to make domestic constituencies more aware of the importance their leaders are attributing to the new critical issue.

---

[6] While the domestic political environment may favor either a hard-line or an accommodationist tendency, the leadership of a state may not hold the prevalent position if it was brought to power on a non-foreign policy issue. Such leadership, however, will still be constrained by the domestic context.

The involvement of the state in major incidents and crises that increase the possibility of war and the hostile interactions generated between the contending states has a major impact on the basic images individuals (both those active in foreign policy and the general populace) develop of their foreign opponents and friends. Deutsch and Merritt (1965: 135–37, 183), for example, provide evidence to show that changes in images are most likely to occur when spectacular events are followed by reinforcing cumulative events and leadership stances. As leaders react hostilely toward another state, the public tends to develop images and attitudes consistent with the behavior of its own state (Abravanel and Hughes, 1975).

The number of incidents and crises needed to bring about a change in images is a matter that needs further research. It is clear, however, that each major surprise and crisis builds upon and reinforces others. The greater the surprise and the more intense the crisis (i.e. the higher the perceived threat and the greater the danger of war), the more rapidly these events will change the psychological affect that existed between the actors prior to the rise of the new issue. In the absence of research, all we can say is that the external situation must not be only sufficiently threatening to produce a cohort effect on those entering adulthood, but also profound enough to weaken the resistance to conversion by older cohorts and those in life-stages not prone to derive the obvious lessons everyone else is deriving.[7]

At the beginning of the Cold War, for example, three major events played a critical role in transforming American–Soviet disagreements into a shift from ally to enemy: The Greek–Turkish crisis culminating in the March 1947 Truman Doctrine, the Czech coup of February 1948, and the 1948 Berlin blockade and airlift. The 1947 crisis was important in converting the Truman administration and critical elements in Congress; the other two were crucial in convincing doubters in the elite and attentive public. More recently, the seizure of American hostages in Iran during the

---

[7] Bobrow and Cutler (1967) show that, at least for support for military expenditures, the external situation can have this kind of an impact, and it is more important than cohort or life-stage. The relative impact of external situation, cohort, and life-stage on foreign policy beliefs is an area where little is known. Bobrow and Cutler (1967) (see also Cutler, 1970) find that each can have an effect depending on the circumstances. Earlier (note 4) it was shown that the views of a cohort or an entire generation can be shaped by a traumatic event. Also, as persons go through different life-stages, they are more receptive to certain lessons than others. Bobrow and Cutler (1967), for instance, find that life-stage (operationalized as ages: 21–25, 31–35, 51–55, 71–75) is more important than external situation or cohort for advocating war.

Carter administration illustrates how a crisis-like incident can drastically change the image that the public has of a state.

For leaders, the initial crisis provides a way of employing external events to capitalize on a rally-round-the-flag effect in order to defeat opponents and get members of the legislature (or the party), various policy influencers, the media, mobilizables, and opinion leaders to adopt their policy line. Often, to gain the commitment of domestic groups, leaders exaggerate the nature of the threat, thereby infusing the critical issue with further symbolic and transcendent qualities (Lowi, 1967: 320–23; Mansbach and Vasquez, 1981: 57–67). All too many domestic actors who are aligned with the leader accept the need for this benevolent deception of other actors and the general public.[8]

The effects of exaggerating the threat are to make images among the less knowledgeable more rigid and to create constituencies more susceptible to hard-line stances. This in turn makes it difficult for decision makers to reduce the salience of the issue or to alter their positions radically (see Singer, 1970a [1979: 72–73]). Thus, Truman in 1947 took Vandenberg's advice to couch his request to Congress for aid to Greece and Turkey in highly ideological terms, but this virulent anti-communism came back to haunt Truman and Acheson in 1949 when they were accused of "losing China," a metaphor that subsequent administrations also feared might be used against them if they "lost" a country to the communists (May, 1973: 99–100).

All other factors being equal, hard-liners will prefer power politics practices over all other options, but will adopt the least costly first. Once power politics tactics are adopted by one side, it is difficult for the target not to eventually respond in kind. This is because, if the target is accommodative, that will only encourage the initiator to repeat its previously successful strategy. If the strategy is repeated, then the accommodationists in the target will lose influence to the hard-liners. Conversely, if the power politics tactics are resisted, this leads to an escalation in means (see Vasquez and Mansbach, 1984: 428–29; Leng, 1983).

The introduction of power politics drives out accommodative influences and leaders on both sides and increases the influence and power of hard-liners in each rival. As Singer (1970a [1979: 75]) notes:

> In the process of mobilizing public and subelite support for these [military] preparedness activities, however, two new conditions are

---

[8] For one example of a scholar recommending, unabashedly, the deception of the public, see Thomas A. Bailey's *The Man in the Street* (1948), cited in Dahl (1950: 271).

generally created. First, the adversary is not likely to sit idly by, watching its superiority disappear; its regime therefore embarks on a similar set of programs. Second, both publics must become more persuaded of the need to resist the menace to their nation's security, and as a consequence, offer a more fertile ground for any militant domestic opposition.

The end result is that leaders paint themselves and their rivals into a corner (Singer, 1970a [1979: 74]). This is reinforced by the tendency of the leadership and media in both sides to whip up patriotic fervor. Hard-liners also gain influence because their predictions that the other side poses a threat seem to be confirmed by the actions the other side takes. The success of these predictions, however, rests in part on a self-fulfilling prophecy.

A domestic context dominated by hard-liners will constantly push the leadership to take actions that are riskier and more hard-line than they would normally take. From the point of view of a decision maker facing a crisis, it is certain that strong actions will be supported domestically, while anything less will be criticized as being soft. Thus, after the second Moroccan crisis, the Pan-German press attacked the Kaiser as weak, and conservative leaders in the Reichstag claimed that the state had failed to give a "strong answer" and called for increased naval expenditures (Fischer, 1967: 25–26). Lebow (1981: 138–39, 176, 184) sees the fear of such criticisms leading decision makers in Germany in 1914, in the United States in 1950, and in India in 1962 to take hard-line actions. Existing realist norms about demonstrating resolve and avoiding a precedent also encourage this sort of response (Singer, 1970a [1979: 72–73]).

In order to keep domestic support, leaders try to placate hard-liners, but, in the absence of success, this is difficult, since there are always some policy influencers who will advocate riskier actions than leaders take. Consequently, policy disagreements arising out of ambiguous evidence about the intentions of the other side tend to be resolved in favor of the hard-line (Singer, 1970a [1979: 77]) and compromise becomes difficult to pursue. This may be one reason why McClelland (1972: 100) finds that when leaders reduce their conflictive deeds in a crisis so as to abate a hostile spiral, they do so under a cover of verbal abuse.[9]

If a crisis drags on or there is a series of crises, the leadership will try to get out of a situation that portends to drain domestic support by adopting

---

[9] McClelland (1972: 98–99) finds that, while conflict deeds in the abatement phase of a crisis go down to 10.9 percent in the Berlin crises (in comparison to what they were during the non-crisis period), verbal combat (confrontation) increases 18.2 percent (compared to the non-crisis period). The same trend was found in the Taiwan crises – conflict deeds declined by 26.7 percent, while verbal confrontation increased 17.0 percent.

any policy or strategy that may result in victory, despite the risks.[10] While this is generally true as rivals move from one crisis to the next, it is probably especially true of states that have been successful in previous wars. The leaders of such states, as Singer (1982: 46) notes, are more willing to take risks; whereas, leaders of states that have been unsuccessful in war are probably risk-averse.[11] Psychologically, it can be expected that a leader will be less likely to oppose a bold action that holds out the promise of victory, because it provides a way of escaping the external and internal trap that is enclosing him (or her). Kahneman and Tversky (1979), for example, provide evidence to show that people are more willing to take risks if they see them as a way of avoiding a certain loss. These psychological and domestic factors reinforce the tendency produced by crisis interactions to escalate moves that fail either within a crisis or from one crisis to the next.

If leaders resist these domestic pressures and do not produce a success, then they are apt to be replaced. In this way, hard-liners literally replace leaders if they have not been able to convert them. They can do this because the steps to war produce such powerful domestic reactions. The classic example is Churchill replacing Chamberlain, but such developments are not confined to democracies. Bethmann-Hollweg was driven from office in the midst of World War I, in part, for opposing unrestricted submarine warfare, a policy which hard-liners knew would risk American intervention, but which they thought would bring victory before American participation could make a difference (Fischer, 1967: 288–93).

Similar factors are at work at the bureaucratic level. Each bureaucracy, as well as each bureaucratic decision maker, wants to avoid failure. In a crisis or war, the military will push for the use of the greatest firepower because they regard this action as most likely to produce victory (which makes it for them the least risky policy). They are aided by hard-liners in the public and legislature (or party) who demand all possible means

---

[10] These same factors play a role in the escalation of tactics during a war and appear to apply to both open and closed polities.

[11] Although this hypothesis has not been extensively tested, Singer and Small (1974 [1979: 313–14]) find that victory is related to future involvement in war. When examining individual nations, rather than systemic trends, they find that of seventy-three states that initiated a war, only thirteen initiated another war within a decade, but of these all but one had won the first war. Similarly, of the ninety-eight states that were attacked, only eleven subsequently initiated a war within ten years, but ten of the eleven had won their previous war. I would argue that one of the factors bringing about this tendency is that successful war experiences set the domestic political balance in favor of hard-liners.

be used. In addition, in the military and the foreign policy-making establishment, some individuals see the crisis (or war) as an opportunity for rapid career advancement if they can develop a successful solution to the foreign policy (or military) problem. These individuals, who are probably risk-acceptant, advocate the bold action. Thus, the prevalence of hard-liners in the domestic political environment not only increases the probability that the leadership will be hard-line, but sets up partisan and bureaucratic incentives for taking harder and riskier policies.

These act as a set of domestic "stabilizers" for a hard-line policy. Kjell Goldmann (1982) uses the concept of stabilizers as a way of describing how a policy becomes established and persists within a state. A policy can be considered stabilized when there exists within the bureaucracy: a set of standard operating procedures, a set of contingency plans, and beliefs among bureaucrats sufficiently consistent that leaders are able to select delegates who, regardless of individual differences, will produce the same decisions by applying the general policy to the given situation (Goldmann, 1982: 245–46, 248–50). Outside the bureaucracy, a policy will be stable to the extent to which there is a domestic consensus, the policy has been enmeshed in a set of global agreements and expectations (e.g. alliances), the policy is linked to other policies (i.e. it is seen as facilitating the success of another policy), and a level of global interdependence has grown up around the policy that would be threatened if the policy were changed drastically (Goldmann, 1982: 253–55, 261–62).

The stabilization of a hard-line policy can be seen as a process by which the psychological preparation for war brought about by crises and leadership stances is now converted into a military doctrine and set of war plans that can be used when needed. The presence of a set of war plans and the commitments it entails (military buildups and coordination with allies) increase the likelihood of war, as Snyder (1984) and Van Evera (1984) point out, by biasing the leadership in favor of actions that increase the risk of war, engender misperception, and increase the sense of threat and insecurity within one's opponent. Standard operating procedures, like that responsible for the Russian mobilization in 1914, and contingency plans, like Germany's Schlieffen plan, are well-known examples of how the military unconsciously restricts the actions decision makers take to those that make war more probable.

The reason for this is that the institutional bias of the military is to produce a military doctrine that assures victory, not a doctrine that reduces the likelihood of war. As a result, there can be a tendency to adopt offensive rather than defensive strategies, as was done prior to World War I

(Snyder, 1984). The trade-off in realism between peace and victory, the so-called Phillips curve of international security (Wayman, 1990: 20), is now at the extreme end. In addition, patriotic fervor interacts with military virtues and nationalistic views of history to aid mythmaking and socialization supportive of war (Van Evera, 1984). In these ways, the attitudes of the military and of the nationalistic sentiments of the population feed off each other to create a domestic political situation in which hard-liners flourish.

Stabilization is also aided by those who benefit economically or politically from the hard-line policy. Within the government, the military and intelligence agencies have their budgets increased because of the external threat and command the attention of the national leadership (and thereby have greater influence). If the threat were to subside, these political benefits would decrease. Outside the government, defense industries and workers, sections of the country that house those industries or military bases, and partisan leaders who "represent"[12] these areas receive direct economic benefits from the maintenance of a strong defense and high military budgets. Academic consultants also benefit in this way, as the government calls upon their expertise, and universities generally benefit from an external threat as the government provides sums for basic research and training in everything from area study programs to advanced mathematics in order to prepare its people to meet any challenge. With economic benefits thus spread around, a cobweb of vested interests is created that lend support to the policy among those who are not necessarily predisposed to support a hard line. Vested interests, even when they are not crassly pursued, cannot help having an effect on the way in which organizations, if not individuals, perceive events and define situations, as well as moderating any criticism they make.

While there has been little empirical work done on these questions, some evidence to support these claims is provided by Nancy Edelman Phillips (1973), who in a survey of 381 men in New London, Connecticut, finds that workers in US defense industries tend to be more supportive of belligerent policies than non-defense workers. Even less research has been done on other states, but Alex Mintz (1985: 636) finds that in Israel

---

[12] "Represent" should be interpreted in the broad sense of expressing the interest of a region or group, even if one is not elected to do so. In this way, party leaders in closed societies are covered by this analysis. Generally, I see little fundamental difference in the forces that shape the domestic behavior of open and closed societies as they approach war, especially a war of rivalry.

the heads of the military and government-owned defense industries act as a powerful interest group that enjoys considerable autonomy.

Stabilization of a hard-line policy brings in an entire new set of forces that push the domestic political environment along the road to war. Stabilization, however, is a gradual process that becomes ingrained after various practices, like alliance making and military buildups, have taken place. The domestic reactions, along with the external interactions, create a self-amplifying feedback that makes *not* taking the next step difficult. Thus, crises lead to alliances, and alliances to military buildups, which can aggravate the kinds of crisis produced. Meanwhile, crises increase the influence of the military, who often encourage hard-line tactics (Alker and Bock, 1972: proposition 2.29a).

A movement toward war is forecast by the increasing salience of the issue. Leaders, again anticipating the need for commitment, escalate the degree to which the issue is infused with transcendent qualities.[13] Those who are not swept along by the patriotic fervor are silenced by the explosive "war fever" now gripping the land. The few who would oppose the war or seem potentially "disloyal" (often for ethnic or racial reasons) are purged from influence and/or incarcerated.[14] Now, nearly all in the collective are hard-liners of one sort or another.

War Initiation

As nations get ready for war, each side (leadership and populace) tends to develop mirror images. Ralph White (1966: 4–5; 1970) sees each side developing a diabolical image of the enemy, a virile self-image, and a moral self-image just before the onset of war with decision makers prone to selective inattention, an absence of empathy, and military overconfidence. Although derived from a review of only the two world wars and the Vietnam War, White's analysis forms a basis for more systematic research that should look at who in the elite has these images and trace how more and more develop these images as war is approached. One would hypothesize that crises which occurred in the presence of these six tendencies would be more apt to escalate to war.

---

[13] For example, in June 1913 while the army bill was being voted by the Reichstag, the German Chancellor Bethmann-Hollweg alluded to the coming war as a "struggle between Teutons and Slavs," and the press immediately seized upon the slogan (Geiss, 1976: 148, 150).

[14] These actions occur even in societies, like the US, in World War II or the McCarthy era, that pride themselves on standing for democratic civil liberties.

Such tendencies are probably correlated with the presence of a hostile spiral like that which led to World War I. Detailed analyses of this case suggest the following generalizations: In the presence of hostility, one expresses hostility (Zinnes, Zinnes and McClure, 1972). Perceptions of hostility lead to violence (Holsti, North, and Brody, 1968). Both sides tend to exaggerate threats, and both sides think the other side is being more hostile than it is, while misperceiving their own actions as less hostile than they actually are (Holsti *et al.*, 1968). Both sides see the other as having more options than themselves (Holsti, 1972: 150–68). The implication of these analyses is that certain wars are associated with a hostile escalating spiral involving perceived hostility in the face of one's own accommodation.

While certain wars are triggered by this phenomenon, there is an equal chance that not all wars are. Clearly, wars between unequals that are planned by the stronger, preventive wars, or wars that begin with a preemptive strike (like Pearl Harbor or the 1904 Russo-Japanese War) would be less prone to starting because of an uncontrolled hostile spiral within a crisis. One would expect hostile spirals to occur when neither side was really sure it wanted a war, although both were prepared to fight it. Such wars would be more apt to be complex wars of rivalry, like World War I. However, even some wars of rivalry might be precipitated by enacting a well thought out grand strategy (for example, the Japanese attack on Pearl Harbor and Hitler's attack on the USSR) and hence lack some of the psychological misperceptions and stress associated with unpremeditated wars.

Midlarsky's (1988: 131–32) distinction between structural and mobilization (world) wars is of some use here. Midlarsky (1988: 131–32, 143, 146 n. 1) sees structural wars, like World War I, as unwitting and unwanted conflagrations, while mobilization wars, like World War II, are planned by strong leaders who have an explicit "aggressive intent," and who mobilize the population for a major war to resolve the critical issue of the time. The contradictory evidence of Suedfeld and Tetlock (1977) and Levi and Tetlock (1980) that cognitive complexity went down prior to World War I, the Korean War, and the Middle East wars, but was high in the Japanese decision to attack Pearl Harbor would be explained by Midlarsky's distinction.[15] Nevertheless, although mobilization wars may not arise out of a hostile spiral with its attendant reduction in integrative

[15] This implies that Wallace and Suedfeld's (1988) measure of integrative complexity would be low for structural wars, but high (for the initiator) in mobilization wars.

complexity, these wars do conform to the general dynamic of an increased hardening of positions in the face of the resolve of the other side. The distinction between structural and mobilization war, however, does imply that the nature of the internal decision-making dynamics of states in the final step to war can vary among world wars.

We would expect that wars that are even more different – e.g. wars of rivalry and wars of inequality – would exhibit clear differences in the domestic politics that preceded them. One can mentally compare the interactions and domestic factors associated with imperial wars as opposed to structural world wars to see how this might be the case. The kinds of conflict preceding wars of rivalry are likely to be so drawn out and more emotion-laden that hostility may color leaders' calculations. This would be true of both structural and mobilization wars. Hence, even when by certain objective factors nation-states are weaker than their opponents, they may still attack first, counting on allied support or the absence of intervention to carry the day.

Interestingly, two quantitative analyses, one of World War I and one of World War II, find the axis countries attacking even when they had a lower capability. Zinnes, North, and Koch (1961) argue that both Germany and Austria-Hungary were weaker than the entente, but attacked anyway. They conclude that hostility is more important than perceptions of capability. Doran and Parsons (1980: 956–57, also cited in Midlarsky, 1988: 146–47) find Germany had less latent military capability than others in the system and a more rapid decline in relative capability than any other major state just prior to the outbreak of World War II.

War cannot be initiated, as expected utility models would have us believe, just by a simple decision of the leader. Before a decision maker would even consider such a calculation, most of the factors outlined in this chapter would have to already be in place. If they were in place and the calculation came out wrong (i.e. it showed that the other side was stronger or apt to win), then a resolution to go to war might still be made, which is what Germany did in the two world wars. Alternatively, if a side were really weak, the final decision to go to war might be postponed to a more opportune moment. In the meantime, the leader would prepare better. Thus, Russia in the 1908 Bosnian crisis was willing to be subjected to humiliation rather than enter a war unprepared, but its leaders vowed that this would not happen again (and in 1914 they did go to war). Expected utility affects not so much whether a war can occur (since in a dyad someone will usually have a positive utility to war), but the *timing* of the war, once the factors promoting war are in place. By black-boxing the domestic political environment, scholars leave many of the key factors associated with the onset of war out of the analysis.

Bueno de Mesquita and others who support rational models of this sort would argue that we can live without the detail presented in this chapter, that we can live without even knowing the actual decision rules leaders take, if we have a deductive set of rules with which the actions of leaders are consonant and which therefore accurately predict their behavior (Singer, 1984: 20). While Bueno de Mesquita (1981b) accurately predicts many of the cases he examines, he does not predict all, and the ones he has trouble in predicting turn out to be very interesting and very important. The critical ones are the two world wars, both of which he treats as dyadic cases in which he accurately predicts that the stronger Austria-Hungary will initiate war against Serbia and the stronger Germany will initiate war against Poland, but he fails to predict the outcome.[16] He omits from his data analysis decisions to expand or intervene in ongoing wars. He does not include in his data analysis, for instance, the Japanese attack on the United States and the equally flawed decision of Hitler to invade the USSR, although he states that he offers a proposition to explain the Japanese decision (Bueno de Mesquita, 1981b: 85–86). If we add to this the fact that the theory incorrectly predicts the outcome of the Vietnam War and the data analysis omits the American and Chinese interventions in the Korean War, we begin to wonder whether the theory can only explain the easy cases. More critically, can we accept a theory that provides us with no aid in avoiding the great mistakes (and miscalculations) of our recent past?

These problems alone would not warrant abandoning the approach, but coupled with its other limitations (see Nicholson, 1987) they do suggest that the claims for the model must be qualified. One begins with cost-benefit analysis, to see how much that explains. Then one looks at the deviations. In the end, probably more will be learned by explaining

---

[16] To treat these wars in this manner does not tell us very much. In particular, to use only dyads for the two world wars (even though the possibility of intervention is measured) produces an expected utility score that is too high, in that it makes the initiation of war appear as a much more rational and calculating decision than it was. My argument is that the "calculations" in complex wars involving more than two parties are so difficult for leaders to make, that explanations other than expected utility must be introduced to account for state behavior. Bueno de Mesquita (1981b: 158–59) himself recognizes that in certain circumstances (e.g. with non-aligned states), utility calculations may become so difficult that leaders are either behaving less like utility maximizers or are more prone to miscalculate. For his justification of the way he treats the two world wars, see Bueno de Mesquita (1981b: 99–100).

deviations from rational behavior than by formal models themselves (see Rapoport and Chammah, 1965: 11).

If one looks at the kind of cases where expected utility seems to be best able to make unproblematic predictions, then the domain of its applicability will be found. Dyadic wars rather than complex wars would be easier for this model to predict, and it is noteworthy that Bueno de Mesquita treats World War I and World War II as dyadic wars. Since dyadic wars involve fewer comparisons and considerably less uncertainty, they should produce fewer errors and doubts within the minds of leaders. Second, wars of inequality should be more susceptible to accurate calculation, since great disparities of capability are easier to discern than close ones. Third, wars of inequality are not likely to be preceded by long periods of conflict and hostility; therefore, calculations are less likely to be emotionally clouded.

With these caveats, expected utility calculations or more traditional calculations of capability can be factored into the steps-to-war analysis in the final stages of certain types of wars. All other factors being equal, the side that thinks it will win, in technical terms, the side with an expected utility for war, will tend to be the initiator. It makes sense that, once a war is likely, the side with the greater capability and commitment from allies will try to initiate the war, and the side with less capability and weaker commitment from allies will try to delay the start of war. *If* there is going to be a war, then you would want to make last-minute calculations about the likelihood of your winning and act accordingly. Bueno de Mesquita's (1981b) findings tell us something about who is likely to initiate wars, once other factors bring about a war situation.[17] However, the findings seem to apply only to dyadic wars and not to complex wars, like World War I and World War II. Nevertheless, these findings when put into perspective uncover an important piece of the puzzle.

Domestic Constraints on War

While the analysis in this chapter has dwelt on the influence of hard-liners within the domestic context, it should not be concluded that the

---

[17] It should be noted that Bueno de Mesquita (1981b) never claims to delineate the sufficient conditions of war, but only the necessary conditions. For this reason, he does not need to explain why in the many cases where a deductive utility for war could be found, war was not initiated. In the steps-to-war analysis, such calculations are not seen as true necessary conditions, because (1) their absence does not always prevent war and (2) their role is relatively minor compared to some of the other factors that have been delineated.

growth of hard-liners is automatic or easy. Hard-liners must battle their way into influence, and they often lose. Wars, as we know, are infrequent, and the difficulty hard-liners have in bringing together the factors that have been identified to actually produce a crisis that will escalate to war should not be underestimated. Simple models can be too alarmist in their predictions. Singer (1982: 44), for example, reports that a model that predicts escalation to war if both sides have high stakes and relatively equal capability actually predicts 25 of the 28 wars that arise out of 225 serious disputes. But it also predicts that 37 additional serious disputes should have escalated to war when they do not. It behooves us to try to identify what restrains hard-liners and aids accommodationists.

The probability that an actor will employ any *realpolitik* practices in order to gain stakes, and hence increase the prospect of war, must be discounted by whether a global institutional context exists with effective procedures for resolving issues, especially security issues (see Kegley and Raymond, 1986). Since states, including those led by hard-liners, will always adopt the strategy that seems to be the most effective, but least costly, they will use the non-violent "rules of the game" first. If the system is too rigged and the issues too fundamental, however, they will resort to the various unilateral means within the power politics arsenal (see Mansbach and Vasquez, 1981: 310–13).

This suggests, *ceteris paribus*, that hard-liners have a more difficult time than accommodationists in getting policies accepted because the rules of the game are usually followed first, and force is both costly and risky. Accommodationists maintain their influence by using both of these factors to their advantage. When accommodationists prevail after a war, their main concern is to establish a post-war order that will prevent the use of force and war. This can lead to attempts to create a new global order, including a system of rules and norms that preserves a world order but allows for the settlement of disputes (as was done at Versailles and the Congress of Vienna), and/or to attempts to prevent national participation in another war (as in the constitutional provisions in the Federal Republic of Germany and in Japan after World War II). In either case, accommodationists establish a set of rules (or laws) that correct the errors (or conditions) that led to the previous war. Just as the military prepares to fight the previous war, accommodationists try to prevent the last war (see Jervis, 1976: 267). The US Neutrality Acts provide an excellent illustration of this. Correctly assessing that the United States becomes involved in World War I because of its insistence on trading with belligerents, the acts strictly regulated, and sometimes prohibited outright, American trade with belligerents. In the Vietnam War, accommodationists passed the War Powers Act not only to prevent the President from unilaterally involving the country in a war, but also to correct the process that led the nation into a war it need not have fought.

The rules accommodationists establish, whether at the global or domestic level, have the effect of preserving their influence and reducing that of hard-liners. Domestically, their rules are obstacles to implementing previous practices or positions that led to war, and these usually include, either explicitly or indirectly, a variety of hard-line options. At the global level, the new norms and rules have a legitimacy that requires that they must be first tried before any unilateral (and hence hard-line) action can be initiated. This means that accommodative actions will always be taken first, and hard-liners will not be in a position to influence policy unless those actions fail. Learning theory suggests that failure must be persistent before there is a drastic change in policy, since the initial response to failure is incremental change (see Vasquez, 1976).

Accommodationists also establish their prevalence more directly by creating a dominance over intellectual and popular opinion about the lessons to be derived from the previous war. Often they find hard-liners responsible for the war. Revisionist accounts of diplomatic history reveal nationalistic accounts to be self-serving, and patriotic sentiments to be emotional jingoistic appeals that distort objective understanding. Militarism and military values are disparaged. Similar sentiments are directed toward defense industries, which are regarded as war profiteers and may, as in World War I, be seen as one of the causes of war. These sentiments, along with a reduction in military personnel and expenditures due to the end of the war, lead to a further reduction in the influence of the two natural institutional bases of hard-liner support – the military and defense industries.[18] These decreases in capability, in turn, make it more difficult to take hard-line actions.

The prevalence of accommodationists is also aided by the fact that the use of force and war is an almost irreversible act and, hence, requires a high degree of commitment and certainty to overcome the natural inertia and conservativeness of collectivities, a conservativeness that has been immeasurably increased by the negative lessons associated with the last war. This effect will be particularly powerful within the bureaucracy,

---

[18] Reductions in military expenditures, however, do not always return to pre-war levels. This has especially been the case in the US (see Russett, 1970; Diehl and Goertz, 1985), as compared to some European states (see Rasler and Thompson, 1985b).

whose members take their cue from the accommodationist leadership that hard-line advocacy will not advance one's career. Even within the military, there will be an unwillingness to become involved in any action unless it is clear that there will be a rapid and clear victory that will lead to a rehabilitation of the military's lost reputation in the previous war. The unwillingness of the foreign policy bureaucracy and the military to advocate risky hard lines will be reinforced by popular sentiment which, under accommodationist sway, will be seen as difficult to mobilize for war, thereby making hard-line actions more costly and uncertain (see Russett, 1975; Holsti and Rosenau, 1984).

These internal actions are not without external effects. A state with a reduced military, low military expenditures, and a public that is difficult to mobilize is not very threatening. The willingness of the leadership to take accommodative actions also makes war less likely by their reluctance to take steps that intensify hostility and increase the influence of hard-liners in the opposing side. Such steps include an unwillingness to compromise, the use of coercion and force, the making of alliances, and the decision to build up the military. Of course, if the opponent takes advantage of the accommodationists to push too far, then support for accommodationist policies declines and the sentiment for a change in policy rises. Accommodationists have a difficult time maintaining influence in the face of coercion and hostility. The human tendency to strike back in the face of persistent hostility overwhelms accommodationists' ability to control the situation and plays into the hands of hard-liners.

War, then, is most likely to be avoided when accommodationists are firmly in control in each side or when accommodationists dominate potentially revisionist states (as indicated in quadrant IV in Figure 6.1). One of the reasons why structural wars may be followed by mobilization wars, whereas mobilization wars are followed by peace (see Midlarsky, 1988: 141–42) is that structural wars probably produce a post-war domestic political context in each side that is unstable and dissonant (quadrants II–III in Figure 6.1). As can be seen in the figure, this is the kind of situation that followed World War I with accommodationists in the allies and hard-liners in Germany. Structural wars seem to have a way of producing hard-liners in revisionist states after the war, and this sets up the possibility of another war. This is because revisionist states that have lost one war will seek to use war again (but this time effectively [!], i.e. according to the dictates of hard-line philosophy), just as those who are defeated in one crisis are more apt to initiate a second crisis and employ more escalatory tactics (Leng, 1983).

Conversely, mobilization wars are probably followed by long periods of peace because they purge hard-liners from the defeated. After World War II, accommodationists were dominant in the defeated revisionist states and hard-liners dominant in the victors, who were more status-quo oriented (see Figure 6.1). As would be expected, the domestic political context is important not only for explaining why war erupts, but how peace is maintained.

Conclusion

The above analysis is meant to demonstrate that a more complete and accurate account of the outbreak of wars of rivalry can be attained by identifying the kind of domestic political context that encourages the adoption of power politics behavior. The driving out of accommodationist influences in the domestic environment of both rivals is an important step toward war and a domestic prerequisite for public mobilization. The introduction of each new power politics practice – alliance formation, military buildup, and crisis diplomacy – has domestic consequences in the other side that increase the influence of hard-liners and support for more escalatory actions. Simultaneously, these practices lead to an increase in hostility between rivals and greater insecurity. This is a process that convinces the domestic populace of each side that they are facing a situation that can only be handled by going to war.

This act is rare within the global system, because even hard-liners will only adopt it after the more available, less costly means have failed, and only after they have learned that *realpolitik* practices short of war fail to achieve their goals. Once these practices are adopted, however, they usually produce unanticipated consequences. One of the least anticipated is the expansion of the war to a world war, which is the subject of the next chapter.

7

Explaining World War: Its Scope, Severity, and Duration

World wars are the great accidents of European history.

World war has been the scourge of the twentieth century. The world wars of this century have fundamentally altered the modern global system. The idyllic aristocratic way of life that had lingered in Europe since 1815 (cf. Mayer, 1981) came to a crashing end in the summer of 1914. The legacy of the cataclysm produced an even more destructive and total war for the next generation. In that war, the search for the ultimate weapon inaugurated an ominous nuclear era with the prospect of complete annihilation. Such has been the inheritance of the twentieth century, and it accounts in large part for the persuasiveness of realist thought and its obsession with power.

Realists have explained world war as part of a hegemonic struggle for power that is endemic in history. This chapter provides an alternative explanation to show that even where the realist paradigm has focused most of its attention a more plausible and less problematic interpretation of the major events of this century can be derived from a non-realist perspective.

While the alternative explanation treats world war as special, it does not, like most realist accounts, see world war as requiring its own theory of war. The steps-to-war analysis presented in this book assumes that the causes of world wars are the same as the causes of any war of rivalry; that is, they flow out of attempts to use power politics. Yet, world wars are different. More than any other kind of war, their specific characteristics and their profound impact on both global and domestic systems are unanticipated. The reason for this is that, while following the steps to war is likely to result in war, only following them in a certain way and under certain circumstances will produce world war. Although most wars can be understood primarily in terms of the interactions that lead to them, world wars need to be understood also in terms of the context in which they are fought and the systemic conditions associated with them. For these reasons, as well as other theoretical reasons outlined below, world wars are treated as a special case requiring special explanation. Nevertheless, world war is treated as a general phenomenon that occurs throughout history and for which there might be an identifiable set of causes or correlates.

In this chapter, I attempt to construct a scientific explanation of world war by delineating the various factors that have been shown to be statistically associated with world war. One of the problems with developing an explanation of world war, *per se*, of course, is that it is logically risky to generalize from such a small number of cases. Before beginning, several important points need to be addressed concerning this issue. First, the analysis is not based simply on generalizing from two world wars; rather the inductions are made by comparing statistical findings on the entire population of sixty-seven interstate wars from 1816 to 1980 with various subsets of that population, e.g. wars with major states on each side. Inferences are made by, in effect, comparing world wars with other wars, dyadic wars with complex wars, wars among major states with wars between major and minor states. Because of such comparisons, although based on samples of statistical data, the number of cases is much larger than a handful of cases.

Second, even if this analysis only offered an explanation of World War I and World War II, that would be no mean achievement. These, after all, are the wars realists have promised to explain, and I believe the analysis given here is much more precise and able to account for a greater variety of findings than hegemonic theory, the power transition hypothesis or long cycles.

Third, because this analysis is based on evidence since 1816 but meant to apply to all world wars in the modern global system since 1495, the period prior to 1816 provides a set of general wars with which the propositions can be tested and falsified. The veracity of the explanation should be seen as an open question subject to testing and should not be simply dismissed because of a logical point regarding the number of cases, particularly since realist explanations are not based on a greater number of cases. Indeed, one of the advantages this explanation has over realist explanations is that it treats world war within the context of a larger unified explanation of wars of rivalry.

I begin the analysis by developing a clearer concept of world war. Next, I review the findings relevant to the expansion of war to see to what extent factors that promote diffusion and contagion can be viewed as sufficient conditions of world war. In the third section, I systematically delineate the necessary conditions of world war and briefly discuss why world wars are total wars. Finally, in the last section, I apply some of the general findings on the duration and length of wars to account for some of the peculiar factors affecting the duration of world war.

What are World Wars?

To explain world wars involves not only a definition of that phenomenon, but a conceptualization that makes implicit assumptions about what is the best way to treat these wars in comparison to other wars. The first assumption in even talking about world wars is that these wars can be usefully differentiated from other wars. It is not difficult to historically identify and separate out these wars, and a number of scholars have (Modelski, 1978: 226–27; Gilpin, 1981: 197–203; Midlarsky, 1988: 12–14), even though there may be disagreements about whether certain cases are really world wars (cf. Levy, 1985b and Thompson, 1985 [1988: ch. 5]).[1] Normally, the second assumption in talking about world wars is that there is a theoretical reason for differentiating them, usually that the causes of these wars are different from other wars. My reasons for separating out these wars from others, however, is not that I see them as having unique causes (I believe they are triggered in the same way as any war of rivalry), but because they require a different explanatory model from the typical causal sequence used in analyzing war.

My approach to this subject is to view world war as a type of *warfare* that emerges once there is an ongoing war. This "model" brackets what causes war in general and tries to explain world wars by explaining the characteristics that distinguish these wars from other wars. Such an approach begins by focusing on and trying to explain why some wars of rivalry expand and enlarge and others do not (Sabrosky, 1985) or by applying contagion or diffusion models (see Siverson and King, 1979; Most and Starr, 1980).

In Chapter 2, world war was defined simply as a large-scale severe war among major states that involves the leading states at some point in the war and most other major states in a struggle to resolve the

---

[1] There are eleven possible candidates: Italian wars (1494–1525), War of Dutch Independence/Spanish Armada, Thirty Years War, Dutch War of Louis XIV, War of the League of Augsburg, War of the Spanish Succession, War of Jenkins' Ear/Austrian Succession, Seven Years War, French Revolutionary and Napoleonic Wars, World War I, and World War II. Levy (1985b: 371–72) includes the last ten; Modelski and Thompson exclude: the Thirty Years War, the Dutch War of Louis XIV, the War of Jenkins' Ear, and the Seven Years War (Thompson, 1988: 105).

most fundamental issues on the global political agenda. Figure 2.1 in Chapter 2 can be used to provide a more theoretical definition of world war that elucidates in what ways it is similar to and different from other wars. Since world wars are between relative equals, they are clearly wars of rivalry. Since they involve more than two states, they are complex wars. And since their participants do not limit their goals and means and frequently view themselves as being in a fight to the finish, they are total wars. *World wars*, then, can be defined theoretically as *total* wars that are *complex* and fought between relatively *equal* major states.

Each of these three dimensions provides a clue as to what might be important in distinguishing warfare in world wars from other wars. The equality of capability of the individual states may be important in giving rise to a long-term rivalry that makes wars more likely to be total rather than limited if the territory of one of the major states is at stake. In addition, the fact that world wars are not dyadic, but complex, may reduce "rationality" (making any calculations of cost-benefit difficult and prone to error because of increased uncertainty), decrease the ability of any one state to manage and control the situation, and intensify frustration and hostility. Each of these factors aids in making wars fights to the finish rather than limited ventures. Also, since most wars are dyadic rather than complex (see Richardson, 1960b: 257, 275), this suggests that factors which normally keep wars relatively dyadic are not operating. Finally, the fact that world wars are complex may affect the nature of their duration.

World Wars can be compared to other wars in terms of their scope, severity, and duration. The *scope, severity,* and *duration* of war consist, respectively, in the number of participants (how widespread it is),[2] the number of battle deaths, and its length. If we can find wars that differ on each of these characteristics, then we can begin to get an idea of the factors that are associated with each of them. If we could subsequently identify certain foreign policy practices or global structural characteristics that bring these separate factors together in their most explosive combination, we would be well on our way to explaining world war as a social phenomenon.

Each of these three characteristics of world war has been measured in the empirical literature, and we have some evidence about the factors associated with them. No one has attempted to piece this evidence together for the explicit purpose of explaining the degree to which, and

---

[2] My thanks to Jack Levy for his suggestion that I use the term *scope* (rather than magnitude) to refer to how widespread a war is.

the reasons why, world wars differ from other wars – mostly because this literature has been concerned primarily with other questions, such as bipolarity and multipolarity. In addition, many who have used measures of magnitude and severity have used them as indicators of the amount of war in the system and to test hypotheses about the onset of war rather than the dynamics of warfare. Since this has been the case and since some of my definitions differ from the exact measures that have been employed by this research, it is necessary to discuss how existing evidence will be treated.

It must be made clear at the outset that only a few pieces of research are directly concerned with explaining the scope and severity of war; most attempt to explain the onset of war. Nevertheless, as several scholars have pointed out, interval measures like nation-months and battle deaths in the Correlates of War project do not tap the onset of war as readily as the dichotomous variable – war/no war. The fact that the latter measure frequently produces different findings (see for example Bueno de Mesquita, 1981a) than the former adds considerable weight to the claim that the interval measure is probably tapping characteristics of warfare and not the extent to which a period is prone to war or peace. If one really wants to get at the causes of war, one must measure the true absence of war and not simply compare, as some analysts have done, small amounts of war with large amounts of war. This means that individual pieces of research cannot be taken at face value.

Before turning to a detailed review of the findings, therefore, let me make some general points about how I interpret some of the principal measures that have been employed in the research on war – the Correlates of War indicators of the severity, duration, and magnitude of war. As with Small and Singer (1982: 69), I take battle deaths as a measure of severity, even though there may not be a perfect correlation between battle deaths and civilian deaths. I believe duration can be measured by the length of a war from the first month in which fighting began to the last month when fighting ended, regardless of the number of participants (see Bueno de Mesquita, 1978: 253).

Nevertheless, many studies that examine nation-months of war provide some insights about duration. Measuring war in terms of nation-months is a widely used indicator in quantitative studies of war. Small and Singer (1982: 64–69) offer this indicator as an operationalization of *magnitude*. The main problem with this is that "nation-months" taps not only how widespread the war is in terms of the number of participants (its scope), but also its duration. This is the case because wars that had three nations would have different magnitudes depending on the number of months each nation participated. While it is certainly the case that Small and Singer have other measures that can clearly distinguish the number of participants from the length of the war, the problem is that when faced with a set of correlations on nation-months, one cannot readily infer the extent to which the correlation is a function of the nations or the months or the combination of the two. I am primarily interested in magnitude for determining how *widespread* a given war is. This is important for an explanation of world war, since it is the ability of such wars to spread and involve all major states (as well as a number of minor states) that makes them so distinct. Therefore, unless otherwise stated, I use indicators of nation-months in this chapter to make inferences about the *scope* of a war, i.e. the number of participants in a war and how widespread it is. With these caveats in mind, let me turn to an analysis of the relevant evidence.

Factors Promoting the Expansion of War

One of the first things a review of the evidence and historical record indicates is that world wars are usually not initiated as world wars, but become world wars by spreading. This suggests that there is one set of factors that cause war and another set of factors that make wars spread. In the presence of these special factors (or in the absence of certain constraints), any given war could spread. This suggests that models of contagion and diffusion might be appropriate.

World wars begin in two ways. A few begin with two major states attacking each other and then dragging in other states. More typically, however, world wars begin with a major state intimidating or attacking a minor state and a rival of the major state coming to the aid of the minor state. Both World War I and World War II began this way and not with a direct military confrontation between the main rivals. There is increasing and diverse evidence indicating that two main rivals can often manage to avoid war when left alone, but are unable to do the same when others, particularly weaker states, become involved.

Alan Sabrosky (1985), employing the Correlates of War data set, has uncovered some important details on the kinds of wars that are likely to enlarge and the role alliances play in that process. He provides a useful conceptual framework for studying how wars spread by distinguishing among *localized* wars, which are confined to the original belligerents; *expanded* wars, which have a subsequent increase in the number of belligerents; and *enlarged* wars, which are wars that expand to include a major state on each side (Sabrosky, 1985: 148). He finds that of the fifty interstate wars recorded between 1816 and 1965, forty remained localized. Crucial to the point being made here is that *none* of the wars that initially involved major states on each side expanded; they remained localized. Major states that were neutral at the beginning of these wars remained so (Sabrosky, 1985: 151, 181). Of course, while this is a dramatic finding, it must be remembered that the probability of any war expanding is not high.[3] Nevertheless, it is probably not a coincidence that all of the wars that have expanded have involved minor states in their initial stages.

Even more intriguing is Sabrosky's (1985: 181) finding that *if* a war between a major and minor state expanded, it was highly likely that it would also be enlarged; that is, the war would have a major state on each side. Of the five major–minor wars that expanded, four were enlarged; whereas, of the five minor–minor wars that expanded, only one war enlarged. While this is a small number of cases, the major–minor wars that enlarged were: the Crimean War, the War of Italian Unification, World War I, and World War II, indicating that the main complex wars among major states since 1815 began through intervention to help a minor state. Interestingly, the one minor–minor war that was enlarged was the Korean War, which the United States perceived as a case of North Korea acting under the direction of the Soviet Union.

Further and more impressive evidence of the importance of the major–minor combination in the occurrence of world wars is provided by Manus Midlarsky (1984, 1986a, 1986b, 1988). Midlarsky argues that the onset of systemic or world war (a structural war, like World War I) is associated with a buildup and accumulation of disputes in the system. By contrast, no world wars occur (during 1816 to 1899) when the system is able to keep disputes (statistically) independent and the total number of disputes relatively constant (i.e. in statistical equilibrium so that for every new dispute that is begun one must end to avoid a buildup) (Midlarsky, 1984: 564). Midlarsky hypothesizes that, so long as disputes are independent and in equilibrium, a system will be stable; however, if disputes become connected, build up, and accumulate, the system will become unstable and degenerate into war.

Employing Correlates of War data on militarized disputes, Midlarsky examines whether disputes are randomly distributed in a system in a

---

[3] The probability of a war between a major and a minor state expanding is 0.208 (five of twenty-four wars expanded) and for a war between minor states, 0.227 (five of twenty-two wars expanded). These figures are based on my recalculation of Sabrosky's (1985: 151, 181) findings.

particular period and for a specific set of actors. He finds that the periods prior to the two world wars, 1893–1914 and 1919–39, are statistically unstable (i.e. disputes build up). Midlarsky has made a major contribution by developing a mathematical analysis and a statistical measure that are able to confirm the well-known historical fact that prior to the two world wars, crises came upon one another fast and furious and could not be handled by the major states. What his quantitative analysis demonstrates that was not fully understood before is that instability occurs in these years *only* when the disputes involving just major states are combined in the sample with disputes between major states that involve a "central power" (like Serbia or Romania). If the sample is restricted to disputes between solely two or more major states, then there is no instability and no prediction of war (Midlarsky, 1984: 570–74; 1986b: 92–93). These findings support the claim that world wars result not so much from the inability of major states to manage crises among themselves as from their inability to manage those crises in combination with crises involving minor states.

Midlarsky's analysis suggests that wars spread because of major states' entanglement with minor but important allies. While we will see later that alliances are indeed a critical factor in the spreading of war, Midlarsky (1986b) takes us one step further by arguing that systemic wars come about because of the inability of major states that are the heads of coalitions to tightly control allies and when necessary ignore their interests. Midlarsky (1986b) argues that when there is a great disparity of power and a large number of non-aligned small states (a hierarchical equilibrium), this permits the heads of coalitions to tightly control or ignore allies. However, when there is an insufficient disparity of power within a coalition and most states are aligned then heads of coalitions cannot ignore allies and find it more difficult to control them. While this is plausible, it must be made clear that Midlarsky does not provide a direct test of hierarchical equilibrium theory by measuring the distribution of power within a coalition or the extent to which all states are aligned. Hierarchical equilibrium theory must be seen as an interpretation of his findings.

An alternate, but not necessarily incompatible, interpretation can be derived by focusing on the role issues play in keeping militarized disputes (or crises) independent and in equilibrium. What Midlarsky has not fully explained is how and why crises build up and become connected. He does argue (1986a) that disputes that lead to war are connected by memory, by which he means that there is a statistical relationship indicating that previous interactions affect current ones. But this does not really provide an explanation. Russell Leng's (1983) research provides some help by showing that actors not only remember previous crises but *learn* from them. In an analysis of recurrent crises (including some of the very crises Midlarsky analyzes), Leng shows, as was discussed in Chapter 5, that, as actors go from one crisis to the next, they learn to escalate their bargaining by intensifying their resolve and conflictive actions.

One can explain Leng's (1983) finding on escalation by the irresolvability of the issues underlying the crises. Escalation occurs because actors are unwilling to change their issue positions. They thereupon threaten to impose a settlement. While the need to rely on threats to reach a settlement may stem from a variety of factors, one factor must be seen as coming from the very nature of the issue under contention. Certainly, the irresolvability of an issue that precedes world war must be seen as a function of the fact that rivals have combined a number of political stakes over which they are contending into a single overarching grand issue and then through coalitions have linked the individual issues of allies with this grand issue, making it difficult to resolve any part of one issue without an overall settlement.

There is some empirical research to show that linking stakes and issues increases conflict (see Vasquez, 1983b: 188). The linkage of issues explains not only how crises accumulate and build up, it also explains part of the dynamics that lead major states to become rivals and seek allies among minor states in the first place (see Vasquez and Mansbach, 1984, for elaboration). In terms of the onset of world war, this suggests that: (1) the linkage of issues reduces the resolvability of issues, thereby helping to generate rivalry between major states; (2) this rivalry leads major states to seek allies, which results in even more issues being linked and increases the probability of linking with violence-prone territorial issues; (3) this issue linkage ensures that crises will not be independent; (4) since linkage also makes issues less likely to be resolved, this makes crises recur and build up, thereby reducing equilibrium.

Combining this interpretation with Midlarsky's own interpretation of his findings suggests that the fact that world wars frequently start by a major state coming to the aid of a minor state is not simply a mistake that can be avoided, but the product of deep underlying dynamics that are not easily changed. These dynamics involve complicated relations of issue linkages, rivalry, and management, which bring to the forefront those factors that bring about the diffusion of disputes that makes war spread.

It should be clear from the above that the analysis in this chapter does not offer an explanation of why wars occur, but focuses on why violence spreads, once it breaks out. Once a war is ongoing, what factors promote or inhibit its expansion? Six factors seem to be responsible for the spread of war: the presence of alliances with one of the belligerents, territorial contiguity, the presence of a rivalry, bandwagon effects, the breakdown of a political order, and economic dependence. Each of these factors can be seen as increasing the probability of war spreading. However, since world wars also require necessary conditions (which are outlined in the next section), these six factors only produce a world war if they occur in the presence of three necessary conditions. This means that in the absence of the necessary conditions, they will not be sufficient to bring about a world war, although they may promote some expansion.

There is empirical evidence that alliances, territorial contiguity, and processes involving bandwagon effects play an important role in the occurrence of world wars. Alliances seem to expand an existing war by having previously committed states and now drawing them in, regardless of the legal nature of their commitment; whereas contiguity expands wars through escalation and considerations of military strategy (strategic location and geopolitics). Although there is little systematic research on the question, anecdotal evidence supports the notion that wars are more apt to spread if they break out in a system dominated by an unrestrained rivalry, than if they break out in a system where rivalries are absent. Likewise, although there is little quantitative evidence that bears on the question, world wars seem to differ from other wars that spread in that they create a dynamic that so breaks down established patterns of order and stability that actors, particularly small states and non-state actors, see it as a rare opportunity to achieve long-held goals that the pre-war structure has stymied. Finally, as wars become protracted, states who trade with belligerents or have economic resources they need tend to be drawn into the war. These inductive conclusions should make it clear that world war must be viewed not simply as a single war that drags in other participants, but also as a process in which more and more dyads (or triads) resort to war to settle their differences. In this way, world war can also be seen as a set of concurrent interrelated wars. How this is the case can be seen by examining each of the six factors in more detail.

Alliances

One of the main practices that can be suspected of spreading war is alliance making. There is a growing body of evidence that supports the conclusion that alliances act as a contagion device, making wars spread. Two studies by Randolph Siverson and Joel King provide direct evidence that alliances expand wars. Siverson and King (1979) hypothesize that a war begun between two states that do not participate in an alliance has a much lower probability of spreading than if two states with allies begin fighting. Using Correlates of War data on interstate wars from 1816 to 1965, they identify 188 instances in which an actor participates in war (note that 50 interstate wars generate these 188 war participations). They find that in 112 of these instances an actor fought in coalition with others, and in 76 it fought alone. What determines whether a war will involve a coalition and not just dyadic combat? Of the 112 participants who fought war in coalition, 76 had pre-war alliance bonds and 36 did not. Conversely, of the 76 participants who had fought the war alone, 52 had made no pre-war alliances and only 24 had (Yule's Q = 0.64; Siverson and King, 1979: 45). This means that when a war breaks out among states that have alliances with non-belligerents, those non-belligerents have an increased probability of being drawn into the war. In this way, alliances act as a contagion mechanism by which war spreads and expands.

On the basis of this analysis, it might be expected that where there are few alliances wars will be small; Siverson and King (1979: 48) find this to be the case. In nineteen (38 percent) of the fifty interstate wars between 1816 and 1965 where neither party had a pre-war alliance, all but three were dyadic. And those three had only three parties involved. Siverson and King (1979: 48) remind us that in 1870, France had no allies and fought alone, but in 1914, it had plenty of allies.[4]

Although alliances can make wars spread, it must be remembered that most wars do not spread even when belligerents have allies. In a follow-up study, Siverson and King (1980: 2) point out that of the 290 instances of a state being allied to a belligerent, three-fourths of the time (233 or 76.9 percent) the ally does not become involved in the war. About one-fourth of the time they do. From this it can be concluded that not all alliances are equally susceptible to contagion. Siverson and King (1980: 8–9, 13) then show that the kinds of alliances that are prone to expanding war have identifiable characteristics. They find that allies of belligerents are more apt to be drawn in as more of their allies enter the war, the allies they join are minor states, the alliance is a defense pact (as opposed to a neutrality pact or an entente), the alliance is relatively new, and they have relatively few alliance partners but belong to many alliances (i.e. a state with many

---

[4] This finding implies that a *system* with extensive alliances will tend to have wars with many participants, whereas a system with few alliances will tend to have small wars.

partners in a few large alliances is not as prone to being dragged into a war as a state with a large number of small alliances). The latter, of course, would be a state like the United States which because of its rivalry with the Soviet Union, is trying to get as many allies as possible.

A separation of the data by century, however, shows that while the overall findings are stable, the specific war-prone characteristics are not always stable and sometimes vary by century (Siverson and King, 1980: 10–11). Significantly, the twentieth century contains 214 of the 290 instances of an alliance with a belligerent; this clearly reflects the impact of the two world wars on these data. In both centuries, being involved in a new alliance with a minor state that becomes involved in a war tends to drag in the non-belligerent ally. In the nineteenth century, the contagion process itself is a potent influence, for the more allies that are involved in the war, the more difficult it is to remain neutral (this is the single most important variable in the nineteenth century).[5] Whereas, in the twentieth century, this factor is supplanted by belonging to a large number of small defense pacts.

Nevertheless, using these variables, Siverson and King (1980: 10–11) are able to successfully retrodict 89 percent (of the 76) nineteenth-century cases and 84 percent (of the 214) twentieth-century cases. They then examine the deviant cases with some interesting results. First, ten of the twelve cases that should have participated in the war, but did not, involved minor states. Minor states seem much more able to avoid being dragged into war than major states. Second, eighteen of the thirty-two cases that should not have participated in the war, but did, involved major states (Siverson and King, 1980: 12), which suggests that major states have a much harder time resisting entry into war. This seems to be especially true once a war spreads. These findings are consistent with those of Sabrosky (1985) and Midlarsky (1983, 1986b) on the expansion of war. Siverson and King show that, for the nineteenth and twentieth centuries, having an alliance with a minor state that becomes involved in a war tends to drag in the non-belligerent. Although it was not directly tested, this seems to be especially the case if the non-belligerent ally is a major state.

Further evidence that alliance making may be responsible for both entangling major and minor states and combining the disputes in the system is provided by Midlarsky's (1986a: chs. 4 and 5; 1983) analysis of alliance behavior. As in his analysis of disputes, Midlarsky argues that

---

[5] The standardized discriminant function coefficient = 0.89.

a random distribution of existing and newly formed alliances reflects a stability and equilibrium in the system. He shows that the alliance system is in equilibrium for most of the nineteenth century (Midlarsky, 1986a: ch. 4) but, after 1871, alliances follow a diffusion model in which they are no longer formed independently, and the number of new alliances (or new members of existing alliances) does not equal the number of alliances that dissolve (or members that leave an alliance) (Midlarsky, 1983). This is consistent with McGowan and Rood (1975), who find a dramatic decrease in the ability of the Poisson distribution to describe alliance changes at the end of the nineteenth century (see Midlarsky, 1986a: 76). In addition, it is likely that alliances may now be formed in a more reactive process, with one state creating or entering an alliance because of what another state has done. Thus, Midlarsky has demonstrated that the total number of alliances in the system, as well as the number of disputes, accumulates. Once this is made evident, it is not too great an inference to assume that alliances are in some way responsible for combining the disputes of minor states with those between major states, a combination which appears related to the onset of both world wars.

All of the above suggests that alliances are a key factor in wars expanding, but they are not the only factor. As Siverson and King (1979: 46–47) point out, the three largest wars that occur after 1815 in terms of participants (the two world wars and the Korean War) contain intervening participants who do not have previous alliance commitments – two in World War I, six in Korea, and eight in World War II. Very large wars, then, must involve other factors. One of these factors is contiguous territory, which played an important role in the spreading of World War I, World War II, and the Korean War.

Territorial contiguity

Since Lewis Richardson's (1960b: 176–83, chs. 11 and 12) pathbreaking work, numerous studies, as noted in Chapter 4, have demonstrated that territorial contiguity is an important factor in the onset of war (Garnham, 1976; Gochman and Leng, 1983; Diehl, 1985b; Ward, 1992). Whatever it is about territorial disputes that makes them associated with war, it is also likely that it makes territorial contiguity play a role in the spreading of war. Benjamin Most and Harvey Starr (1980), in an analysis of wars and armed conflicts in the post-World War II period (1946–65), provide some evidence to support this conclusion. They find that when a state has a warring state on its border in one period, there is an increased probability that it will become involved in a war in the next period. Although derived from a complex research design, this finding does support the notion that some wars diffuse by bringing in non-belligerents that are contiguous. As such, it provides a clue about the factors that may spread wars to non-allies and is worth a closer examination.

Most and Starr (1980) divide their sample into different time periods and examine those cases in which nation-states at peace in the first period subsequently participated in war in the second period. In order to test the effects of territorial contiguity, they further divide their sample of states that are involved in war in the second period into two subsamples – those that received an experimental "treatment" (having had a warring nation-state on their border in the first period) and those that did not. They argue that if there is a positive spatial diffusion of war brought about by territorial contiguity, then the cases with bordering warring states that go from peace to war should greatly outnumber the cases that go from peace to war without a warring state on their border (in the first period). This expectation is supported in all but two of forty-three observations (across three data sets). This means that at any given period most states at war had a warring nation-state on their border in the previous five-year period. Now, as Most and Starr (1980: 942) point out, while having a war on one's border does not make it necessary that one would be involved in a war in the subsequent five-year period, *"it does increase the odds"* (their emphasis).

Two questions are raised by these findings. First, will Most and Starr's findings on the post-1945 period hold for the 1816–1945 period, and second, what is the relative potency of contiguity and alliance in the spreading of war? Siverson and Starr (1990, 1991), who analyze all wars for both major and minor states from 1816 to 1965, provide interesting findings on both of these questions. First, they show, using the standard interstate war data for the 1816–1965 period, that sharing an alliance or a border with a belligerent increases the probability that a state will be drawn into war. The probability of being dragged into a war is greatest for contiguous areas, less for areas across water, and least (but still positive) for wars on colonial borders. For alliances, the probability of being dragged into war is greatest for defense pacts and less (but still positive) for ententes and non-aggression pacts.

Second, Siverson and Starr (1990: 57, 58, 60; 1991: 58–61) find that alliances are a much stronger variable than borders (see also Most et al., 1987). What is even more significant is that having both alliances and borders with a belligerent greatly increases the probability of entering a war,[6] with the most potent combination being defense pacts and contiguous borders (Siverson and Starr, 1990: 55–57, 60–61; 1991: 59–60). These findings mean that the individual effects of alliances and borders are separate and cumulative.

Although these relationships generally hold for both major and minor states, there are differences in the behavior of the two types of states. First, major states are much more apt to be drawn into a war. Thus, for major states 40 percent of the test cases for alliances and 17.5 percent of the test cases for borders diffuse to war as opposed to 21.5 percent and 7.3 percent, respectively, of the test cases for minor states (Siverson and Starr, 1990: 58, Table 6; 1991: 61, 63, Tables 3.6, 3.8). Second, although major states are more involved in wars, Siverson and Starr's (1990: 69, Table 7; 1991: 62, 65, Tables 3.7, 3.9) figures indicate that minor states are more affected by these variables, particularly the combination of defense pacts and contiguous borders. Thus, while this combination produces a 302 percent increase in the major-state cases diffusing to war, it produces a 1089 percent increase in the minor-state cases diffusing to war. This means that minor states are not only less able to resist the effects of alliances and contiguity, but also that major states are probably being dragged into wars for other reasons, since they have a much higher rate of war participation.[7] Nevertheless, Siverson and Starr (1990) clearly document that both alliances and contiguity play a role in spreading war, but have different effects on different states.

Exactly why and how territorial contiguity acts to spread war is not fully explained by these findings. Most and Starr (1980: 935–36) and Siverson

---

[6] Defining each alliance and each border contact as a treatment, Siverson and Starr (1990: 55–56; 1991: 54–55) find that the greater the number of treatments, the greater the probability of becoming involved in a war (eta = 0.45). For example, when there are two treatments only 4.3 percent of the cases (n = 389) diffuse, but when there are more than six treatments 50 percent of the cases (n = 30) diffuse.

[7] Although further research is necessary, major states may not be as sensitive to border problems as minor states, even though they are, as Siverson and King (1980) point out, sensitive to having a warring alliance partner. (This is probably because major states have previously resolved border problems.) In light of Midlarsky's and Sabrosky's findings on the expansion of war, it might be speculated that while minor states drag in major states because they have alliances with them, they do not drag in major states simply by being at war, even if the minor state is contiguous to the major state. In other words, war between two minor states will not drag in a bordering major state *unless* one of the minor states has an alliance with the major state. Conversely, it seems probable that minor states would be particularly likely to be dragged into a war if the warring nation on its border were a major state.

and Starr (1990: 48–50; 1991: ch. 2) do suggest that borders are an area of uncertainty and risk as well as opportunity for states. This structure of risks and opportunity is likely to change once a war is under way in a neighboring country. An ongoing war, no matter what its initial cause, is likely to change the existing political world of those contiguous to the belligerents, creating new opportunities, as well as threats. These factors would operate to expand any war, but they probably become very potent in wars among major states. Since opportunity and threats are a function of the capability of political actors, a war among major states is going to create more opportunities and threats for neighbors than a war between minor states.

Although there is very little systematic research on this question, examples drawn from World War I and World War II can illustrate the process by which wars among major states become widespread. In both twentieth-century world wars, geography and territorial contiguity provided a physical point of contact for the diffusion of war. Some data-based evidence that is consistent with this conclusion is provided by Houweling and Siccama (1988: ch. 7) who show that wars are clustered not only in time, but in space. The latter implies that battlefields are close together and that wars spread from one area to an adjacent or nearby area.

One of the reasons this occurs is because of considerations of military strategy, which affects the diffusion of war in several ways. First, the spreading of world wars must be seen in part as a function of escalation, which can be seen as a product of both the failure of existing strategy to win the war and the success of military operations in achieving important goals. The high salience that war generates for the political stakes under contention makes states escalate their actions in the face of failure (see Smoke, 1977; Leng, 1983). The fighting on the Western front in World War I illustrates the extremes to which this tendency can go. Conversely, military success can create new opportunities by placing a victor in a new geographical position, allowing it to contend for stakes that were not previously at hand, as the United States did in Korea.

Second, the successful use of violence can act in the short run as a positive reinforcement, encouraging political actors to repeat their use of violence.[8] The initial success of Hitler, and to a lesser extent of Mussolini, encouraged the seeking of broader objectives, particularly in Eastern Europe. Finally, escalation helps spread wars because the actual dynamics

---

[8] In the long run, however, there seems to be little positive reinforcement in the use of coercion: see Bremer (1982: 51–53).

of warfare may make certain areas strategic locations of vital significance. The Soviet and British occupation of Iran in World War II provides an example of this effect.

Alliances and territorial contiguity are the key factors that empirical research has identified in the diffusion of war, but it also seems that rivalry, and in particular, how a rivalry is managed, can play an important role in the spreading of war.

Rivalry

A cursory review of global history suggests that one of the factors that distinguish wars that spread from wars that remain dyadic is whether or not wars occur in the absence or presence of an ongoing regional or global rivalry. One would expect that wars erupting in the absence of a rivalry would be much less likely to spread, especially if the other contagion factors discussed in this chapter are absent. Regions or periods of global history not marked by an enduring rivalry, then, should not experience *large* wars, but dyadic or other small wars (e.g. three-party wars). The presence of rivalry, however, should not be seen as ensuring that wars will spread. Whether they do will depend very much on the extent to which rivals are able to manage relations among themselves and control their allies.

One of the main ways within Western history that rivals have been able to avoid entangling wars has been by establishing certain rules of the game for determining when, and over what, war would be permitted and how war should be conducted. Such rules are often reflected in *pacta de contrahendo* (pacts of restraint) between major states, which serve as a way of legitimizing and/or permitting the use of force against weaker parties. When alliances are used in this way, they are a form of management that helps control unilateral behavior and prevents a war between a major and a minor state from spreading by in effect asking permission from other relevant major states to go to war.

The second way in which wars may be inhibited from spreading in the presence of a rivalry is when the major states are able to control their minor allies and thereby prevent these minor states from dragging them into a war. If war is to be avoided or contained, rivals must not allow the interests of minor states to become a *casus belli* for a war between the rivals. This, as is obvious from a host of wars, including the Korean War, Vietnam War, and World War I, is not an easy task.

In the absence of tight control, another way of preventing war from spreading is through working out a set of understandings with the rival

262 THE ONSET AND EXPANSION OF WARS OF RIVALRY

over how to limit war if it should break out. Sometimes this can be done through secret diplomacy. Bismarck was a master of this practice, using alliances to keep wars limited by making sure his targets would have to fight without major support. At other times, tacit understandings evolve in a relationship that serves to reduce the likelihood of war or keep it limited, if it breaks out. During the Cold War, it became understood that, despite rhetoric and even covert support, the United States would not use military force to prevent Soviet domination of Eastern Europe. Likewise, it became clear that if one side intervened militarily to support an ally, the other would confine its intervention to aid. This occurred in Korea, Vietnam, Africa, and Afghanistan. In addition, within the modern global system, certain practices have evolved to limit intervention. These include such historical practices as spheres of influence and the realist principle of non-interference in the domestic affairs of states. The latter is a particularly significant "rule of the game" in limiting the internationalization of domestic conflicts.

The nature of rivalry, however, is to place no limits, to always seek advantage. If a war should break out in the system under these conditions, there is, obviously, pressure for the rivals to become involved. Thus, wars spread, not simply because a belligerent has an alliance with a non-belligerent as Siverson and King (1979) show, but also because rivals have a perceived interest in any conflict within the theater of their rivalry. Furthermore, since rivalries between states lead them to make alliances, there is a strong probability that if a war breaks out, one of the rivals will already have an alliance with one of the belligerents. In these ways, rivalry and alliance making go hand in hand, and the more intense the rivalry, the less likely a rival can control its minor ally and separate its ally's interests from its own.

Understanding the role rivalry plays in a system also gives us some idea of how and why crises build up and become connected. The irresolvability of an issue that precedes large wars must be seen as a function of the fact that rivals have combined a number of political stakes over which they are contending into a single overarching grand issue, and then through coalitions have linked the individual issues of allies with this grand issue. This makes it difficult to resolve any part of one issue without an overall settlement.

Up to this point we have identified three factors associated with the spread of war – alliances, territorial contiguity, and rivalry. The contagion and diffusion effects of the first two factors have been documented by research and the third factor is suggested by theoretical analysis and needs to be empirically documented. It is assumed that these are the basic factors promoting an initial intervention in an ongoing war. Once parties are brought in by one of these factors, then it appears that there is a tendency for the mere fact of intervention to increase the probability that others who are unaffected by the three basic factors will also intervene. In other words, pure contagion takes over to generate bandwagon effects.

Bandwagon effects

Some political actors, especially major states, intervene in an ongoing war even when none of the basic factors are present (see Siverson and King, 1980: 12). Some of the reasons why this might be the case are uncovered by Yamamoto and Bremer (1980: 216–17), who examine three probability models to see which best explains (fits) the decision of a major state to enter an ongoing war. The three models they examine are an independent choice model, which assumes that the decision of one actor has no effect on the decision of another; a one-way conditional choice model, which assumes that a decision to enter the war has a great impact on what others do, but that a decision to remain neutral has no effect; and a two-way conditional choice model, which assumes that whatever an actor decides encourages the other actors to make the same decision.

Of the fifty interstate wars from 1816 to 1965, only eight involve the intervention of major states, so their sample is very small. Nevertheless, they are able to show that the two-way conditional choice model fits the data better than the one-way conditional choice model and much better than the independent choice model, which does not fit at all. This means that if an actor intervenes in an ongoing war, that increases the probability of others intervening; if it remains neutral, that increases the likelihood of others being neutral. Although the two-way conditional model holds for both the nineteenth and twentieth centuries, the finding is stronger for the twentieth. Major states in the twentieth century were more likely to intervene in ongoing wars, and were more affected by what others did (Yamamoto and Bremer, 1980: 218–21). While this inference is based on a very small number of cases, it is consistent with the intercentury difference uncovered by Siverson and King (1980: 10–11) and implies that alliances in the twentieth century were more dangerous than in the nineteenth.

Yamamoto and Bremer do not investigate the role of alliances or contiguity, but simply find that major states, when faced with an ongoing war, will do what other major states do. Thus, *once* there is an intervention, the probability of other major states intervening will go up. In light of Siverson and Starr's (1990, 1991) findings, it might be inferred that the presence of alliance bonds or contiguity increases the likelihood of an initial intervention, and once this occurs other major states eventually follow suit, whether or not they have alliance bonds or share a border with a belligerent.[9] On the basis of these findings it can be hypothesized that the greater the number of major states involved in a war, the greater the tendency of the war to encompass more states.

Additional statistical evidence of contagion is found by Houweling and Siccama (1988: ch. 7). They show that wars cluster in time and space. This means that wars are not randomly distributed but connected. This suggests that one of the causes of war is war itself. War begins and its mere presence draws in others. They find that outbreaks of war are more likely to cluster when the analysis is confined to major states, but there is a clustering of war for all nations when interstate wars are combined with civil wars.

Of course, although war is probably a cause of war, it is clear from the historical record that most wars do not spread. Richardson (1960: ch. X), in his pathbreaking analysis, showed that the typical war is a dyadic war and that there are only a few very large wars. Houweling and Siccama's findings lead one to ask: under what conditions do wars spread? A pure contagion model would imply that, after a certain point, interventions are not motivated or "caused" by one of the basic factors but by the dynamics of the ongoing war process.

One of the problems with using Houweling and Siccama's (1988: ch. 7) findings to support a pure contagion explanation is that all they show is that war is clustered. They do not identify the factor producing the contagion, and although their evidence is consistent with the explanation that war leads to war, they do not show how this is the case, nor test this explanation before the fact. The problem of testability is handled by Yamamoto and Bremer (1980), so that need not be a major concern. The problem of explaining how war leads to war can be resolved by looking at how other forms of conflict and force produce contagion effects. Here the Bremer (1982) study is particularly illuminating.

The pure contagion or bandwagon model assumes that once states begin to resort to coercion, there is a tendency for other states also to resort to it. In an analysis of twentieth-century militarized disputes (i.e. disputes involving the threat or use of armed force), Bremer (1982: 42–46, 53–54)

---

[9] Note that this does not explain why and how minor states are drawn into the war.

provides evidence to support this assumption. He demonstrates that the initiation of a serious dispute increases the likelihood that another serious dispute will emerge within that region shortly thereafter (see also Maoz, 1989: 225). In other words, the use of coercion becomes infectious, with other actors now resorting to it in order to gain their ends. This can be regarded as a breakdown of prohibitions against violence and unilateral behavior. At the same time, the spread of such behavior institutionalizes a norm that legitimizes the use of violence. As Gurr (1970: 170) shows for internal violence, such norms are correlated with the outbreak of violence.

All these findings show that the use of force by one party leads others to use force. They substantiate that as the use of force spreads, there is little that can be done to stop it except, as Cicero pointed out long ago, resorting to force oneself (cited in Waltz, 1959: 159). Reinforcing this tendency is the fact that as more major states are drawn into the war, there are few major states left that can restrain the belligerents; whereas, in dyadic wars or in wars among minor states, the more powerful non-belligerents can impose restraints to keep the war from spreading.

The use of coercion and armed force is highly contagious because the dominant realist political culture holds that little can be done against it except to use violence against violence. This theoretical analysis of the empirical findings suggests that one of the factors that lead violence to spread is that actors get caught up in a bandwagon of violence. As more states intervene more, and more major states feel compelled to intervene, this can have severe effects and lead to a breakdown of the political order, which spreads war further.

Breakdown of the political order and economic dependence

When fighting spreads, particularly among major states, this can lead to a breakdown of order which can expand war in several ways. Firstly, the breakdown of order entails a breakdown in the constraints that had been placed on those who are seeking to bring about fundamental changes in the status quo. For small states, this may be the only opportunity to act because the vacuum created by the war allows them the freedom to unilaterally pursue long-held objectives. For leaders of small states, war among the major states can produce a feeling that they had better act now because they may not have another chance in their lifetime to gain the support of major states for the changes they want in their region. Serbian nationalists certainly felt this way during World War I.

Secondly, this feeling makes leaders more willing to take risks. As concern about opportunity becomes the focus of attention, it upsets calculations of expected utility based on relative capability. Consequently, states may initiate attacks now that they would not do in a strictly dyadic situation. The breakdown of order, of restraints, and of prohibitions against violence permits smaller states (as well as non-state and revolutionary actors) to fight wars of their own within the larger context of an ongoing war. These smaller dyadic wars (as well as civil wars) can be seen as examples of contagion in that they reflect an imitation of violent behavior which has become possible because the larger ongoing war has provided an opportunity for violence, which in peacetime the existing order had prevented.

Thirdly, war spreads by major states actually bargaining with middle-sized states for their intervention, as Germany and the allies did with Romania in World War I. Likewise, war in a region may provide the opportunity for domestic minorities or dissident factions to gain power through collaboration with an external state, as the Croatian fascists did in Yugoslavia during World War II. In these ways, the breakdown in order provides great and rare opportunities for fundamental change.

Lastly, as the war spreads and grows, it becomes more contagious because it appears that more of the existing pre-war political and economic order will be changed. This begins to threaten the interests of the remaining non-belligerents. Some become drawn into the war because they develop more of a stake in who will win. For weaker states or holdouts, the further extension of the war may produce a bandwagon effect in which they attempt to get in on the war before their support is no longer needed.

War also spreads because the economic needs of belligerents draw in those who can satisfy those needs either willingly or unwillingly. Although the invasion of certain areas to gain economic resources is an obvious vehicle by which war can spread, the effects of such decisions can be far-reaching. For example, the Japanese decision to get oil by invading the Dutch East Indies led them to attack Pearl Harbor, because they felt, perhaps erroneously, that since the invasion would bring American intervention, they should reap the advantage of a surprise attack. The more subtle way war is spread is through neutrals trading or financing the war effort of one side. Trade, in particular, as was the case in World War I, can lead one of the belligerents to directly attack shipping, if it believes it can increase its chances of victory by interrupting or ending the trade of its opponent. Credit, which is an important factor in winning a war

(Rasler and Thompson, 1983; Kennedy, 1987: 76–82, 263, 268), may not lead to such direct attacks, but gives the creditor nation (and powerful groups within that nation) a vested interest in the outcome of the war. This may predispose it to intervention under the right circumstances, as well as raise the ire of the side that is not being supported. Often, however, credit and trade are conflated.

Conclusion

By these paths, war becomes contagious and subject to diffusion. Although these two terms are used in the literature somewhat interchangeably, they suggest different metaphors and can be distinguished according to which metaphor seems more appropriate to a specific factor.[10] Contagion is a medical, not spatial, term. It implies that learning and example are important in spreading war. It also suggests that what "infects" one political actor to go to war may affect others. Diffusion is a physical and mechanical metaphor; it suggests that one can study how war spreads as one studies the spilling (and spreading) of a liquid. The focus is on geography and direct contact.

Using these distinctions, war can be seen as contagious in the sense that contact with a belligerent or a war increases the probability of involvement in the war. This contact differs from the contact involved in the diffusion of war. Here the contact is through choice, often a pre-war alliance or trading relationship, whereas in diffusion the contact is geographical or involves the direct effects of war on existing structures (boundaries, location, political order). War that spreads through alliances, rivalry, or economic relationships can be seen as contagious in the sense that the set of interests that make one belligerent go to war may be shared by others and might under certain conditions make them go to war. This is particularly the case if a belligerent can make it clear that a non-belligerent's interests are bound up with its own success in the war. In this way, pre-war alliances and trading relationships can be indicators of shared interests that make actors support each other when those interests are threatened, and not simply the reflection of an expedient bargain.

War spreads by diffusion usually through escalation and the adoption of new objectives brought about by conquest. The dynamics of battle can enlarge the theater of war, particularly if no strong neutral states can

---

[10] For a mathematical distinction between diffusion and contagion, see Midlarsky (1983: 78 n. 1; 1978).

constrain the expansion of war or if major states, such as England and France in the Seven Years War, have far-flung territorial bases. This geographical diffusion of war can bring with it the breakdown of a regional order and create the kinds of opportunities and risks that make the use of violence infectious (contagious).

What is noteworthy about the six factors is that they frequently work in conjunction with each other. Territorial contiguity between equals often produces a period of rivalry. Rivalry produces a search for alliances. This raises the question of how the variables might be combined, or whether they need to be combined, to have their specified effect.

There are two plausible theoretical specifications. One approach would be to specify, inductively if need be, the relative probability each factor has in making war spread by itself and then in combination with the other variables. For example, territorial contiguity is a very powerful variable and might account for much of the variance, meaning that states contiguous to an ongoing war would be much more apt to be drawn in than other states. However, this does not mean that most states who share this characteristic would be drawn in; in fact most wars are fought dyadically. By itself, territorial contiguity is not a sufficient condition; rather, it carries a certain probability of drawing states into an ongoing violent situation. The same is true with the other basic factors, such as sharing an alliance or an ongoing rivalry being present. Instead of thinking of contagion in terms of necessary and sufficient conditions, a better approach would be that taken in epidemiology or meteorology, in which certain conditions (combinations of variables or exposure to a disease) are associated with a certain probability of rain occurring or a disease being caught.

In this approach each of the three basic factors is seen as not having a very high probability of making war spread, but as having a statistically significant impact. Each variable is posited as having a separate but independent effect. The presence of more than one variable greatly increases the probability of contagion. This model specifies that one or more of the three basic factors – alliances, territorial contiguity, and rivalry – must provoke contagion before the last three factors go into effect. A model that combined the factors according to probability levels seems appropriate for explaining violent contagion if this were a fairly frequent phenomenon. War contagion in the modern global system is fairly rare, however, and expansion to world war is rarer still.

This suggests that a conjunctional relationship is a more appropriate model; that is, all six variables must co-appear in order to have contagion. Such a model has the advantage of eliminating the alarmist tendencies in the analysis; that is, since one or more of the six factors appear fairly frequently, they would successfully predict existing cases of expanded wars but at the same time they would probably predict war expansion much more frequently than it occurs. Specifying a conjunctural relationship would greatly reduce this problem and increase accuracy in prediction. Nevertheless, world wars are so rare that not only would a conjunctural relationship be required, but also it is likely that the conjunctural relationship would have to occur within a particular systemic structure. Identification of this structure would be tantamount to specifying the necessary conditions of world war.

The Necessary Conditions of World War

A careful analysis of statistical findings on interstate wars from 1816 to 1965 reveals that world wars are associated with three necessary conditions: (1) a multipolar distribution of capability in the system; (2) an alliance system that reduces this multipolarity to two hostile blocs; and (3) the creation of two blocs in which one does not have a clear preponderance of capability over the other. Under these three conditions wars that expand will expand to their widest scope and most extreme severity. Conversely, in the absence of any one condition a war of rivalry will not become a world war.

The three necessary conditions have been derived from quantitative studies of polarity. If it is assumed that the Correlates of War measure of nation-months does indicate something about how many participants there are in a war and that the measure of battle deaths is a valid indicator of severity, then the work on polarity provides clues for uncovering the correlates of the scope and severity of war. The implications of this research for the expansion of war have not been grasped because the work has been viewed primarily in terms of the polarity debate. In addition, the findings relevant to the debate have sometimes been inconsistent and the research exceedingly complicated (Singer, 1981: 8–9). The reason for this is that different definitions and measures of polarity have been employed, some based on the number of blocs (sometimes called polarization or cluster polarity), some on the distribution of power, and some, most notably that of Wallace (1985), based on a combination of the two dimensions.[11] Differences in definitions have been further aggravated by

---

[11] Wayman (1985: 128–31) shows that polarity based on the number of blocs and polarity based on the distribution of power are two uncorrelated and empirically separate

differences in the measurement of both the independent and dependent variables and differences in research design. Because it is far from obvious how these findings fit together, some important evidence about the scope and severity of wars has been overlooked.

Two recent pieces of research that look at polarity in terms of the distribution of power provide important evidence to show that wars of great scope occur when a multipolar distribution of capability provides a foundation for subsequent alliance making. Jack Levy's (1985a) analysis is important because it extends the purview of inquiry from two centuries to five with some interesting comparisons. His findings challenge the earlier findings of Michael Haas (1970) and the persuasive argument of Rosecrance (1966). His data analysis of five centuries shows that periods of bipolar distributions of power are more stable than multipolar periods. He finds that bipolar periods have more frequent wars, but these are less severe and of lower magnitude than the wars of multipolar periods. This is the opposite of what had been earlier believed to be the case.

In addition, Levy and Morgan (1984) show that if wars are frequent in any given period, they tend not to be severe, but if they are severe, they tend to be infrequent. This inverse relationship holds from 1500 to 1974. Since multipolar periods are associated with extremely severe wars (Levy 1985a: 50–52, 58), this implies that in these periods one large war is fought in which all the major actors become involved; whereas, in bipolar periods there are probably frequent dyadic wars which are confined to the initial participants.

Levy (1985a) also finds that unipolar periods are very unstable, having the wars of the highest magnitude and duration. However, by unipolar, Levy means the emergence of a single hegemonic state, which is usually involved and frequently defeated in a general or hegemonic war involving all leading states. Wallace (1985: 108–9) has challenged whether these periods should be described as unipolar. In many ways, they are similar to the multipolar periods. One of the problems of Levy's analysis is that his classification of periods as unipolar, bipolar, and multipolar is based on a historical judgment of wide spans of time, rather than precise decade or half-decade measures.[12] This is not to say that

---

dimensions (0.01 for 1816–1965). See also Wayman (1984a: 74–75) for his extended review and correlation of the various measures.

[12] For example, Wayman (1985) is able to measure shifts in polarity within the nineteenth and twentieth centuries, where Levy (1985a) codes the entire 1815–1945 period as multipolar. Compare Levy (1985a: 49, Table 3) with Wayman (1985: 127, Table 2).

the classifications are arbitrary, but only that more evidence is needed to assess his suggestive findings.

Here the research of Frank Whelon Wayman (1984a, 1985) proves to be very interesting. Wayman's analysis is the most thorough to date, employing measures of polarity based on both the distribution of power (power polarity) and the number of blocs (cluster polarity or polarization). Using a variation of Singer, Bremer, and Stuckey's (1972) capabilities index, he examines the percentage of system capabilities of the two most powerful states for each half-decade from 1816 to 1965. Employing a cutoff point of over 50 percent for bipolarity, Wayman (1985: 126–27, 131) finds, similar to Levy (1985a) and contrary to Rosecrance (1966) and Michael Haas (1970), that a bipolar distribution of capability is characterized by wars of a lower magnitude (fewer nation-months) than a multipolar distribution of capability, which is associated with the great world wars. In power multipolarity, 75 percent of the *high* magnitude wars occur, and in power bipolarity, 73 percent of the *low* magnitude wars occur (Wayman, 1985: 131–32).

Table 7.1 reproduces Wayman's measure of a bipolar–multipolar concentration of power. His "TWOCON" measure is the percentage of capability held by the two strongest states. I have marked the key multipolar periods, and it can be seen that the two world wars are preceded by a relative decline of concentration in capability in the two strongest states. After 1865, there appears to be a shift from a bipolar to a multipolar distribution of capability with a further deconcentration after 1895. After World War I, there is a brief bipolar concentration of power, but by 1925 the system is once again multipolar and remains so until the conclusion of World War II, which results in the highest bipolar concentration of power since 1815.

The long lead times (1875–1913 and 1925–38) make it clear that a multipolar distribution of capability across more than two states is not a cause of world war in the sense of a potent sufficient condition of war that results fairly soon in world war. Instead, the multipolar condition seems to establish a foundation for making a war widespread once it is brought about by other factors. What is important here is the fact that world wars are complex wars that involve three or more major states as participants, and not wars in which there are only two major states with a host of minor states, or simply dyadic wars between the two strongest states without

Nevertheless, Levy can make a plausible argument that the 1815–1945 period is relatively multipolar when compared to other periods from 1495 to 1975.

Table 7.1. *Wayman's power polarization data*

Year	CON[a]	TWOCON[b]	Year	CON	TWOCON
1815	–	–	1895	0.223	0.47
1820	0.241	0.58	1900	0.202	0.44
1825	0.233	0.58	1905	0.207	0.43
1830	0.242	0.58	1910	0.212	0.45
1835	0.243	0.57	1913	0.208	0.46 ←
1840	0.232	0.57	1920	0.371	0.61
1845	0.257	0.57	1925	0.247	0.52
1850	0.260	0.57	1930	0.241	0.48
1855	0.276	0.58	1935	0.228	0.51
1860	0.280	0.57	1938	0.217	0.48 ←
1865	0.255	0.56	1946	0.417	0.90
1870	0.233	0.51	1950	0.293	0.65
1875	0.225	0.50	1955	0.331	0.69
1880	0.226	0.49	1960	0.303	0.66
1885	0.208	0.48	1965	–	–
1890	0.203	0.48			

[a] CON is the concentration index of major power capabilities reported in Singer, Bremer, and Stuckey, (1972: 22).
[b] TWOCON is the percentage of major power capabilities held by the two largest powers.
Source: Wayman, 1985: 127.

any allies whatsoever. From this body of evidence provided by Wayman (1984a, 1985) and Levy (1985a), it can be inferred that world wars originate from a multipolar distribution of capability across three to five states; that is, a distribution of capability where the two strongest states do not have much more than 50 percent of the demographic, economic, and military capability of the system.

If the multipolar distribution of capability provides a foundation for making war widespread, what actualizes this potential? By what process are the separate poles brought together? Alliances seem to be the main factor that brings about this actualization in that their end result is to combine (cluster) the separate "poles" (major states) into two competing coalitions (blocs). Alliances not only reduce the separate poles to two sides (thereby making it likely that if war occurs it will be one of great scope), but they do so in a manner that seems to increase the severity of war – to make the war a total war. Alliances that cluster poles into two hostile blocs can be said (by definition) to have *polarized* the system.

Several pieces of research provide evidence that the wars of the greatest scope and severity are apt to occur when the system is highly polarized (maximum polarization would be two blocs) or had no polarization at all (minimum polarization would be no blocs); whereas a moderate amount of war or no war is associated with moderate polarization. Measuring the amount of war in terms of nation-months and battle deaths, Wallace (1973: 597–99) uncovered this curvilinear relationship between polarization and these indicators of (what can be considered) the scope and severity of war. This finding can be interpreted as meaning that when there are no alliances, the weak fall victim to the strong, but when most actors are bonded to two blocs, intense rivalry and preparation for war develop. One would suspect that the findings produced by very low or no polarization would be the result of many wars not directly connected, while the finding on high polarization would be the result of large complex wars, like the two world wars.

Wallace (1973: 598–99) also finds a moderate curvilinear relationship between cross-cutting (links across blocs) and the magnitude and severity of war, with moderate cross-cutting reducing the intensity of war, and very low and very high cross-cutting increasing it. This finding is of interest, because it means that systems that are very polarized and have no (or very low) cross-cutting will be subject to wars of great scope and severity. Wallace's finding on cross-cutting is also consistent with the finding of Kegley and Raymond (1982: 588–89) that shows that when alliance structures are extremely flexible or extremely rigid, the amount of war is high.

The findings on both polarization and cross-cutting are consistent with the findings of Siverson and King (1979) that alliances serve to expand wars. Since Wallace does not look at the expansion of wars, it is not clear whether a polarized alliance structure can give rise immediately to a complex war, or whether such wars tend to result from the expansion of dyadic wars. Sabrosky (1985) argues that wars will expand and enlarge when the system has a high concentration of military capabilities in major states, a high level of alliance aggregation, and an increase in both of these factors in the previous five years. While he has some success using these variables to retrodict which wars would expand and enlarge, he was unable to retrodict which wars remained localized. Nevertheless, Sabrosky's findings in light of Wallace's (1983) suggest that world wars occur through expansion and that expansion is associated with high polarization. In this sense, Wallace's curvilinear finding is somewhat misleading in that the high values of nation-months and battle deaths may be produced in one situation by a single large war and in the other by a series of non-connected wars.

More direct evidence on how alliances expand wars is provided in Organski and Kugler's (1980: 49) study of the Franco-Prussian War, Russo-Japanese War, World War I, and World War II. Employing a measure of the tightness of alliances developed by Bueno de Mesquita (1978), they find that in nine of the eleven pairs of states that go to war, alliances tightened just before the war. In only one pair did alliances loosen (Organski and Kugler, 1980: 53–54). While this adds evidence on the role of alliances, what is more significant is that the tightening of alliances is associated only with some states' participation in war and not all states. Organski and Kugler (1980: 54–56) argue that the tightening of alliances does not explain why *contenders* (the strongest two or three states in the Eurocentric system) become involved in war, but is associated with the involvement of other major states in war.[13]

This means that the reasons *contenders* fight are different from the reasons that other major states fight. It is a fair inference that within a region, the strongest rivals become involved in a war on different sides and then other major states are brought in because of their alliance bonds. This suggests that the underlying grievances of the strongest rivals are more important in bringing them to war than the fact that they belong to different alliances. It also implies that the grievances of the strong determine the shape of the polarization of the system that will then bring the other major states into a war. Nevertheless, Midlarsky's (1988) and Sabrosky's (1985) analyses make it clear that once an alliance system is polarized, world war is likely to emerge by a *contender* coming to the aid of an ally.

Bueno de Mesquita's (1978: 258–60) analysis, which Organski and Kugler build upon, takes us a step further than the previously discussed studies in that he finds that it is not so much the structure of polarity that is important, but the change in the tightness of the blocs, which can be viewed as an increase in polarization. Using a dichotomous war/no war dependent variable, Bueno de Mesquita finds a relationship between change in tightness and the onset of war, but only for the twentieth century and only for wars involving major states. Given these limitations, it is fair to assume that Bueno de Mesquita (1978) has not uncovered a general

---

[13] Alliance tightening accounts for only 6 percent of the variance of the behavior of *contenders*, but accounts for 26 percent of the variance of the behavior of major states that are non-contenders (Organski and Kugler, 1980: 55).

tendency, but a pattern associated with the two world wars of the twentieth century. Thus, it is probably theoretically significant that the probit correlations between increasing tightness (polarization) and the occurrence of war is 0.47 for wars involving major states, but only 0.29 for all interstate wars (Bueno de Mesquita, 1978: 260). In a direct test of the relationship between increasing tightness and the extent to which war is widespread, Bueno de Mesquita (1978: 259–60) finds that nearly 80 percent of the wars from 1816 to 1965 involving more than one participant on each side (i.e. complex wars) occur in periods of rising tightness, and no complex war occurs following a decline in systemic tightness.[14] The fact that a change in tightness occurs just prior to war suggests that alliances are needed to convert the multipolar distribution of capability into a tight two-bloc system before world war will occur.

Wayman (1985) provides specific evidence that this did occur just prior to the two twentieth-century world wars. He finds that prior to these two wars, alliance patterns were becoming more polarized (clustering major states into two blocs, which Wayman calls cluster bipolarity). He finds that an increase in polarization among major states in the twentieth century is associated with an increase in the subsequent magnitude of war (r = –0.48 between alliance multipolarity and nation-months of war, Wayman, 1985: 135).

A close inspection of Wayman's data on alliance polarization, which is reproduced in Table 7.2, shows how this occurs. Wayman (1985: 128) measures cluster polarity (the number of blocs in the system) by the ratio of actual poles to potential poles among major states. This gives him a scale that ranges from 1.00 – for the maximum number of poles (no blocs) or complete depolarization and the absence of alliances – to scores that would approach 0.00 when there is a cluster bipolarity or complete polarization. As can be seen from Table 7.2, beginning with 1870, which has no blocs (score of 1.00), the system gradually sees more alliances develop until it is polarized at 0.50 in 1905, where it remains until the onset of World War I. At the end of the war the system sees a rapid disintegration

---

[14] Change in polarization or tightness also seems to play a role in the onset of wars, but more for the twentieth century than the nineteenth century. Bueno de Mesquita (1978: 259) finds that 84 percent of twentieth-century wars begin after a rise in systemic tightness, making this an almost necessary condition for war. Conversely, war almost never occurs after periods of declining tightness: 89 percent of these periods in the twentieth century are followed by peace. For the nineteenth century, 63 percent of the years wars began followed rising systemic tightness, and more than three-fourths of the periods of declining tightness preceded years of peace. This is evidence that alliances are associated with the preparation for war, not the preservation of peace.

Table 7.2. *Wayman's alliance polarization data*

Year	Alliance polarization[a]	Year	Alliance polarization
1815	0.40	1895	0.56
1820	0.20	1900	0.62
	(UNIPOLAR)	1905	0.50
1825	0.80	1910	0.50
1830	0.80	1913	0.50 ←
1835	0.60	1920	0.80
1840	0.40	1925	1.00
1845	0.60	1930	1.00
1850	0.80	1935	0.86
1855	0.80	1938	0.86 ←
1860	0.83	1946	1.00
1865	0.83	1950	0.40
1870	1.00 ←	1955	0.40
1875	0.83	1960	0.40
1880	0.83	1965	0.60
1885	0.67		
1890	0.67		

[a] A value of 1.0 represents maximum alliance multipolarity. Low values represent clustering of the system into blocs, thereby tending toward alliance bipolarity.
Source: Wayman, 1985: 129

of blocs (score 0.80 for 1920, and 1.00 from 1925 to 1935), which then build up again just before World War II with a score of 0.86 in 1938, and disintegrate at the end of the war (score 1.00). Although there is a movement toward polarization just before World War I and World War II (as well as Korea), the score of 0.86 for 1938 is a bit disconcerting. Before the hypothesis that an increase in polarization produces an increase in the scope of war can be accepted, it must be asked why there is not a greater increase in polarization just prior to World War II.

The answer is that the really dramatic increase in polarization does not occur in 1938, but in 1941! Previous to that time, Hitler had succeeded in neutralizing the Soviet Union and avoiding war with the United States, thereby keeping these two major states out of the Western alliance. In addition, the German–Japanese alliance and Soviet–German non-aggression pact worked to keep the wars of Europe separate from the wars of Asia. In 1941, this fell apart when, through their folly, Hitler and Japan succeeded in polarizing the system by attacking the Soviet Union and the United States, respectively. These two expansions of the war account for much of its scope, as well as its severity and duration. When the alliance structure from 1939 to 1941 is examined, the evidence becomes more consistent with that of World War I.

Wayman's (1985) findings make it clear that while formal alliances are critical in bringing about polarization, as prior to World War I, other factors that bring about alignments that polarize the system can also bring about world war, as happened in World War II. Polarization and the underlying alignments of interest it represents is the crucial variable, whether or not it is embodied in a formal alliance. Avoiding alliances *per se*, therefore, will not necessarily avoid war, if the underlying alignment of conflict of interests is ignored.

Increasing the scope of war is not the only effect of increasing polarization. Bueno de Mesquita (1978: 263) provides a convincing argument that a main effect of increasing tightness of blocs is to encourage each side to prepare better for war. Increasing tightness reflects each side's ability to get its own house in order, by firming up commitments and pooling resources. Although Bueno de Mesquita makes this argument in the context of explaining how polarization makes wars longer (see below), it should be clear that such preparation and pooling of resources will also make war more severe, if the system is polarized to make each side relatively equal. In other words, world wars are severe because alliances take a multipolar distribution of capability and reduce it to two *relatively equal* polarized blocs in the sense that no side has a clear preponderance over the other. If this is correct, then this would mean that alliances are associated with the expansion and scope of war, while capability is associated with severity and duration.[15]

Evidence that a relatively equal distribution of capability is associated with world wars can be derived from Singer, Bremer, and Stuckey (1972). However, since they did not test this hypothesis, nor interpret their findings in this manner, this evidence must be seen as indirect. They find that, in the twentieth century, a relative equality of power in the system is associated with more war and a relative preponderance or concentration of systemic power with less war (see Chapter 2 herein). It is also clear from even a casual historical review of the two world wars that polarization of

---

[15] To the extent that polarization produces relative equality of capability between blocs, it can be seen as having an indirect association with the severity and duration of war.

blocs prior to each war occurred in a way that made the distribution of capability between the two blocs *relatively* equal. Unfortunately, because Singer *et al.* (1972) confine their analysis to nation-months of war and do not look at battle deaths, it is not known whether equality of capability is associated with scope or severity, or both.

The association with magnitude alone must be questioned, because it is not clear what theoretical rationale would explain why relative capability should be associated with the spread of war. What may be likely is that the correlation with scope is spurious and what is really occurring is that nation-months, which would be correlated with battle deaths in the twentieth century, is acting as an indicator of the severity of war. This makes more sense theoretically in that a relative equality should typically produce more battle deaths (as well as a longer war) than relative inequality.

Any association between capability and severity, however, is going to be greatly affected by the objectives of the war and the extent to which one or both sides commit their resources; i.e. whether participants see themselves as fighting a limited or total war. Clearly, total wars will always be more severe than limited wars, but within this context, it could be hypothesized that when two sides are relatively equal in capability, any given (limited or total) war will be more severe (and longer) for both sides than when the sides are not equal.

To fully explain the severity of war, it is necessary to identify the factors that are primarily responsible for making war total once war occurs. Although there is not any evidence on this question, the findings on polarization suggest that polarization involves more than simply the division of the system into two blocs. It reflects a deep underlying polarization of hostility that has led to the disintegration of a political system and the previous peace that produced it. Kugler (1990: 202–3) argues that one of the factors that distinguish total wars from limited wars is that total wars put the core territory of a major state at stake. Once such an issue is at stake, then it can be expected that the major state affected will treat the war as a fight for survival. This suggests that total wars come out of a long-term political relationship that has grown more threatening and hostile and that has so poisoned the system that its normal restrictions on what kinds of issues can be placed on the agenda have broken down. Once core territory is at issue then normal restrictions on behavior and fighting go by the board.

We are now in a position to see why the necessary conditions make wars widespread, severe, and usually total. The process by which a polarization that reflects a deep, irresolvable conflict of interests produces total wars has not been fully explained in the literature, but what seems plausible is that in a protracted conflict between equals that becomes a rivalry, the making of an alliance by one side will lead to the making of a counter-alliance and a competition for allies. This will polarize the system and produce a number of effects all of which increase perceived threat and lead to behavior that is more conflictual.

First, polarization increases perceived threat by increasing the military capability of each side and enlarging the possible theater of war. This creates a foundation for the later diffusion of war, but at the time naturally leads each side to prepare for a worst-case scenario and to increase its military expenditures. The increase in military expenditures produces arms races. Several empirical studies have suggested that, more than any other type of war, world wars are associated with a number of ongoing dyadic arms races (see the critiques of Wallace 1979 by Weede [1980: 285–87], Diehl [1983: 210], and Houweling and Siccama [1981: 161 n. 13]). These arms races are not only associated with the kinds of militarized disputes that are most apt to escalate to war (Wallace 1979, 1982), but generate an arsenal that provides the destructive capability necessary for severe wars. More importantly, because these arms races involve several countries that are geographically dispersed, they make each side less vulnerable than if only two states faced each other (in that one state can come to the aid of another). A state fighting alone might be more easily defeated than one which could rely on others. This means that complex wars will be more severe and longer than other wars, particularly since these wars are more likely to be preceded by long arms races, whereas dyadic wars usually are not preceded by arms races or, at best, short bursts of military expenditures just prior to the initiation of fighting.

Second, polarization focuses the attention of each side on the main issues that divide them and reduces the salience of cross-cutting issues. This promotes persistent disagreement; makes all minor stakes symbolic of larger ones (thereby collapsing all issues between the main rivals into one overarching issue); and greatly accentuates rivalry and hostility. The long-term rivalry has probably also territorialized a number of stakes, thereby making them more prone to violence. At the same time, polarization that involves contiguous rivals insures that any outbreak of war will make the core territory of one or more major states at issue. This means that if a war should break out it will be a total war.

Third, complete polarization removes the possibility of any major state acting as a mediator and reflects the fact that no one is committed to rules and norms (from the last peace) to resolve disputes, but measures of self-help are relied on, thereby indicating that violence is a legitimate and perhaps the only effective means for resolving the fundamental issues at hand. Further, the bringing in of allies along with their particular issues makes it more difficult to reach any compromise, prevents the war from being limited, and encourages total war. This is because the war becomes an opportunity to resolve all major differences among all parties (major and minor). The increase in military expenditures and the competition for allies is also likely to make each side relatively equal and therefore make the war, once it comes, severe, long, and widespread.

One might conclude that the making of alliances has two different sets of effects. The first is that it leads to polarization that is a step to war in that it produces behavior and territorial objectives that increase the probability of a *total* war. The second is that increasing tightness of blocs indicates that each side is making last-minute preparations for war, which usually are successful, and that produces wars of greater scope, severity, and duration. Exactly how these factors affect the duration of war must be explored more fully.

Duration

The idea that alliances affect the duration of war is based on the assumption that alliances, rather than preventing war, are ways of preparing for war. It seems that alliances associated with world wars have been very successful in preparing the future war participants so that when the war comes, it is longer than it would have been in the absence of polarization. The major evidence to support this argument comes from Bueno de Mesquita (1978: 262–63), who finds that, in the nineteenth and twentieth centuries, a change (increase) in the number of poles is associated with longer wars involving major states (but not related to longer wars in general). He infers that an increase in poles produces uncertainty and encourages nations to be prepared for war. This probably results, in my view, in arms races and attempts to secure commitments from allies, thereby also producing greater tightness and discreteness (i.e. more polarization). While Bueno de Mesquita (1978: 262–63) does not examine the effect of an increase in poles on changes in tightness and discreteness of blocs, he does find that, in the twentieth century, increases in systemic tightness and discreteness do produce longer wars (both wars involving major states and interstate wars in general). Since increasing discreteness (few bonds across blocs) means little cross-cutting, this finding is consistent with Wallace's (1973) finding that the absence of cross-cutting is associated with severe wars.

An increase in tightness produces longer wars, most likely because it reflects each side's success in integrating its resources at least at some level, which means that alliances that work result in longer wars. Since Steven Rosen (1972) has shown that the outcome (and probably the length) of war is a function of the comparative amount of revenue available and the percentage of population loss, allies that can effectively pool resources will have a larger aggregate of revenue and population to sustain longer wars than they would if they fought dyadically. Added evidence that it is the economic resources of the state that are important in determining who will win a war (and thus the length of war) is provided by Wayman, Singer, and Goetz (1983: 506–11). They show, in an analysis of militarized disputes between 1816 and 1976, that the single best capability predictor of whether an initiator will win a war is its industrial capability rather than its military capability or demographic strength.

The way in which alliances work to prolong war through the successful pooling of resources is demonstrated in Paul Kennedy's (1984) analysis of World War I. Kennedy shows that allies prolong wars by providing additional resources, particularly economic staying power, at critical junctures. It is the industrial and financial base and the goods and credits they can supply (and not military power and skill, which tends to be canceled out) that make the real differences in World War I (Kennedy, 1984: 22, 26; see also Kennedy, 1987: 262–74). Economic support from an ally makes war longer by making a state that would have collapsed, if it were fighting alone, hang on, especially when a stronger ally couples this economic support with political pressure.

Kennedy (1984: 11) argues that Austria-Hungary is prevented by Germany from getting out of the war after 1916, that Italy after Caporetto would have left, and that France after Verdun might have negotiated a peace if they had been fighting alone. The kinds of pressures and inducements one government can place on another are illustrated in the case of Russia, which after it left the war saw the allies intervening to forcibly keep its front open. For Kennedy (1984: 24–26), World War I continued despite a series of incidents where individual allies became exhausted. When the stalemate between France and Germany was broken to Germany's advantage, British economic resources and armed forces permitted France to hang on. By 1917, US intervention was critical not so much for its troops as for the infusion of its economic resources, including munitions that it could provide for the allies.

The impression one gets from Kennedy's analysis is that world war has elements of a relay race in which the less economically sound members of a coalition are sustained by various states taking over the economic burden of the war at crucial points; without that support the war might have ended. The important insight is that coalitions are successful not so much for their initial pooling of resources as for their ability to get different states to provide relief to allies just before they are exhausted and collapse. This clarifies how world wars differ from dyadic wars. The evidence on the latter shows that revenue and access to credit are important predictors of the outcome of war (Rosen, 1972; Organski and Kugler, 1980: ch. 2; Rasler and Thompson, 1983). Kennedy's analysis demonstrates how coalitions unconsciously manipulate these variables to sustain allies that would have otherwise collapsed.

On the basis of Bueno de Mesquita's and Kennedy's analysis, it can be hypothesized that the duration of war is a function of the economic resources available to each side. The more equal those resources, the longer the war. If the ability of each side to efficiently manage these economic resources is equal, and its military skill is relatively equal, then the outcome of the war will be determined by the absolute size of a state's economic resources and its ability to bring those resources to the field of battle. Complex wars are longer and more uncertain than typical dyadic wars, because they allow different states to take over the economic burden through increased commitment or through the entry of new war participants. Since economic resources are so crucial, non-belligerents trading with one side are apt to be drawn into the war, because those who are hurt by the trade attempt to end it, by force, if necessary, and those who benefit from the trade attempt to get the non-belligerents to take over more of the economic burden by providing credits, protecting vessels, etc. It is through this process that trade and the providing of credits becomes a contagion mechanism by which non-belligerents literally "catch a war" through (economic) contact.[16] In this way, the scope of the war interacts with the duration of war, but in a way in which early entrants prolong the war by making both sides relatively equal, while late entrants shorten the war by giving one side the edge.

Resources themselves, however, end a war only because they allow one state to kill off a large percentage of another state's population

---

[16] In light of Most and Starr (1980), it can be hypothesized that the catching of a war will be even more likely and faster if the trading partner shares a border with one of the belligerents.

(Rosen, 1972). The ability of a state, such as France in World War I, to sustain causalities larger than 4.0 percent of its population (the percentage that usually leads to surrender, if it has not already occurred) is probably a function of a stronger ally promising troops and aid, if only the weaker ally can hang on. Of course, they want to hang on because part of their core territory is usually at stake. In this way, the scope and duration of war is associated with its severity (see Richardson's 1960b: 257ff evidence on this), since the more economic resources available and the longer the war, the more severe it will be.

Conclusion

Although the various factors accounting for the scope, severity, and duration of war involve complicated interactions, it should be clear that a multipolar distribution of capability, polarization of blocs, and a relatively equal distribution of capability between sides all play an important role in producing the unique characteristics of world war. A multipolar distribution of capability is associated with wars of great scope (Wayman, 1984a, 1985), and if that distribution is polarized into two blocs, as was the case in World War I and World War II (Wayman, 1984a, 1985), and there is no preponderance of power between the belligerents (Singer, Bremer, and Stuckey, 1972), then war will also be severe. An increase in polarization as measured by tightness is associated with an increase in the duration of wars (Bueno de Mesquita, 1978). All other factors being equal, it can be concluded that a multipolar distribution of capability that has been polarized into two blocs makes for wars of greater scope, equal capability between blocs increases the severity of wars, and increasing polarization of blocs produces longer wars. Because alliance making can affect each of these variables, it has the peculiar consequence of bringing each of these factors together in their most disastrous and explosive combination, so that a war that occurs in this context is most likely to become a general war, eventually encompassing most major states. We know from Sabrosky (1985) that, in the twentieth century, the situation that is most likely to trigger such a general war is a war between a major state and a minor state, in which another major state intervenes to aid the minor state. Whether world wars in other centuries are facilitated by a minor state acting as a trigger is a question that needs further investigation.

World war is an unintended highly complex social phenomenon brought about by the rare coincidence of several factors. The analysis in this chapter should make it clear that world war cannot be adequately explained by a simple realist model of secular shifts in capability. The realist and power model of world war lacks the precision of the analysis presented in this chapter, which shows that world wars are not so much inexorable conflagrations brought about by fundamental shifts in capability as they are the unintended consequence of limited actions. Ironically, it seems that the practices of power politics not only lead rivals to take steps that lead to war, but to follow practices which, under certain conditions, make the wars that do occur into world wars.

Humanity, however, need not be enslaved by these practices and the scourge they produce. The promise of the scientific study of war and peace is that through rigorous observation the unintended consequences of actions can be elucidated. The identification of the drastic effects of the combination of multipolarity, polarization of blocs, and equal strength is a partial fulfillment of that promise. If further research shows that these three conditions also preceded world wars prior to 1816, then this analysis will have succeeded in uncovering the necessary conditions of world war. Avoidance of any one of them would prevent a repeat of the great slaughters of the past.

Peace involves more than just the avoidance of the conditions of war, however, and the avoidance of world war does not eliminate other wars. To bring about peace involves understanding why the practices of power politics are resorted to in the first place. To do that we must identify the periods of peace that have existed in the past, understand why they were peaceful, and uncover the factors that made the peace break down.

8

Peace

The key to understanding war lies in understanding peace.

Until now we have looked at the onset of war in terms of how interactions have constrained choice by producing a relationship of rivalry and domestic political environments that select out threatening practices and hostile behavior. These lead actors to resort to realist practices and begin a long journey down the road to war. The presence of disagreements and of hostility need not always have this result, however. Whether and how quickly actors will resort to power politics depends on the extent to which the global institutional context provides alternative mechanisms for handling issues.

Part of the reason power politics results in war, especially between equals, is that coercion short of war usually does not resolve a highly salient issue. War occurs because within realist culture it is an institution by which binding political decisions can be made. To the extent that there are other ways of making authoritative decisions, it can be expected that war will be less frequent, especially since these alternative mechanisms will probably be less costly and morally preferred.

Even realists admit that, at the domestic level, government and economic bargaining are allocation mechanisms that are employed to make critical decisions affecting the everyday life of millions of people. Only rarely in established states does war (either in the form of civil war or social revolution) become a way of resolving a political issue. Realists have spent some time trying to understand and to show why the domestic solution to violence cannot be applied globally.[1]

---

[1] See Niebuhr (1946), Morgenthau (1960: ch. 29), Claude, (1962: 255–71), and Waltz (1979: 88–101); see also Suganami (1989) for a review of the domestic analogy. Realists argue with some cogency that a world government would presuppose a world community, and since there is no world community, a world government cannot be expected to emerge. Further, any attempt to impose a government where there is no communal foundation would simply produce an ineffective government which would be plagued by civil wars and domestic strife, rather than interstate wars.

In their effort to avoid illusions, however, realists have overlooked a very obvious fact; namely, there have been thousands of important political decisions made in the modern global system, but comparatively few wars. This means that global political actors have found ways of resolving issues in the absence of government and without going to war. If the mechanisms by which these decisions were made can be identified, then some important insights can be gained about how to prevent war and maintain peace.

The first section of this chapter will review international relations theory to see what insights can be garnered about the nature of peace – what it consists of and how it works. The second section will examine the empirical research to delineate the characteristics of peaceful periods that distinguish them from war-prone periods. The final section will look at the relationship between peace and war.

The Nature of Peace

Inquiry into the nature of peace and how to build it can be framed in two ways. From the systemic perspective, it can be conceptualized as a world system where the probability of war, especially war among major states, goes way down. From an interaction perspective, it can be conceptualized as a great reduction in the probability that political actors will resort to violence to achieve their ends. International relations theory has provided analyses about both of these conditions and has assumed that political actors will not resort to violence to achieve their ends if there are more efficient, less costly, and more legitimate ways of attaining their ends. Empirical research has shown that peaceful periods are ones in which there has been a rich global institutional context in which major states have consciously attempted to establish rules for the conduct of relations and implement practices and institutions (usually informal) for resolving disputes (see Wallensteen, 1984; Väyrynen, 1983). In addition, these periods have established norms and a body of international law that circumscribe the use of force and war, thereby limiting its impact while legitimizing it and making it part of the system. Peace appears to occur when there is a working political system, even if there is no government.

One would expect that the key element in an effective political system would be providing institutions that are the functional equivalent to war. At the domestic level, government has been the main functional equivalent. Understanding that government and war provide some of the same functions elucidates what would be needed in a working political system that was based neither on government nor war. If we view war as a social invention, then we must also see government, and politics itself, as social inventions. Everyday politics (like party politics or diplomacy) is distinguishable from war in that it is an interdependent system of decision making, whereas war is an attempt to escape that interdependence. Government is useful because it not only institutionalizes interdependences, but provides ways of breaking stalemates to which very equal interdependences are prone. War is not simply an act of violence, but a way of conducting politics. Like government, it also is a way of breaking stalemates, but unlike government it provides a unilateral solution for the resolution of issues, and this has been the main reason why actors have found it so attractive, despite its costs.

War and government are functional equivalents, and in the West since Hobbes this has been generally accepted as a truth. Nevertheless, government alone does not prevent war, rather it is only *effective* government that avoids war. Even here, however, it is clear that certain issues arise that cause governments that had been previously effective to falter and collapse. Issues like slavery, which touch upon fundamental ways of organizing life, are not easily resolved by government, especially when divisions are along sectional (territorial) lines. Questions of social justice that linger for decades likewise can explode. Government cannot always avoid war, and its breakdown usually forebodes war.

It would be a mistake to assume that there are no social inventions available to conduct politics between the extremes of effective government and war. There are many institutional arrangements short of government by which politics can be conducted. Peace reflects and is the outcome of a kind of governance, i.e. the presence of peace indicates that conflicts of interest are being controlled by an invisible exercise of authority and not subject solely to the unilateral behavior of contenders. In this sense, peace is not simply the absence of war (see Rock, 1989), but involves political rule to settle disagreements. Political rule without government has been tried in the global system, providing an historical record that can be examined to determine the factors associated with its success. The successful systems have not been rationalistically drafted with pen and paper and then implemented, but are the "outcome of iterative adjustments" (Rummel, 1979: 331) that have evolved through a process of conflictive and cooperative interactions.

A successful global political system would, like government, institutionalize interdependent decision making, but should also, like war, provide a set of rules that permit political actors to break stalemates by escaping that interdependence. In addition, like both government and war, effective political systems should establish a context in which actors feel constrained to accept the outcome of the system's institutions, even if they lose. Actors accept this outcome for the same reasons they accept negative outcomes from government or from a war; namely, that the attempts to employ alternative institutions are too costly or uncertain, that generally the overall rewards of the system outweigh the specific loss, or that the actor has no choice – either because the system provides no other options and/or the actor is incapable (physically or ideologically) of pursuing the legitimate or illegitimate options that might be available.

It should be clear from this analysis that peace is not something that is caused by inanimate forces, but something that is consciously made by human beings. How well it is made determines how long it will last, for it is the success or failure of a peace in creating a global political system that will determine the frequency of war in the presence of intractable issues. Peace is an historically determined process, a social construction of a political system – complete with rules of the game, allocation mechanisms, and decision games. Each historical period (and its global culture) has its own form of war and its own form of peace, and the nature of its peace will determine whether war can be avoided for a long or short period of time.

After any war, a peace settlement resolves the outstanding issues between the parties, typically with the defeated acceding to the position of the victor. It is the *acceptance* of this practice – that the loser accede to the general position of the victor on the issue in dispute – that makes war serve as an authoritative allocation of value. After major wars, like a world war, the peace settlement typically establishes a system for resolving future disputes and conducting relations between states. Sometimes this will be done formally in a treaty and by the creation of international organizations. At minimum, the way in which the peace settlement is arranged, and the new status hierarchy it reflects, creates precedents on how the system is to be governed in the future. In a limited dyadic war, a peace settlement has similar consequences, but is confined to shaping the relationship between the two parties.

A peace reflects the interest of those who create it in that it distributes stakes and resolves issues to institutionalize a status quo that will be enforced by (as well as reflect) the dominant balance of forces (Gilpin, 1981). Its rules and procedures create a mobilization of bias (Bachrach and Baratz, 1962) in favor of those who created the system. The end of a war gives rise to a structure of expectations about how actors will behave toward one another and how issues will be resolved (Rummel, 1979: 368, 372, 375). A structure of expectations shapes behavior in that it provides a framework by which actors understand and perceive each other (Rummel, 1979: 114). This structure evolves, as interaction gives rise to patterns of behavior. The status quo established in the peace mirrors and is enforced by a balance of interests, capabilities, and wills (Rummel, 1979: 268, 317–18). The mutual willingness of all sides to accept the outcome of a war and the new status quo is a result of their common perception that the nature of this balance would make further contention unprofitable (Rummel, 1979: 318).

The peace also embodies an inchoate political system, and it is the ability of this political system to resolve *new* issues and accommodate new actors that will determine how long the peace will last. It cannot be supposed as Rummel (1979), Gilpin (1981), and to a lesser extent Modelski (1978) do, that a change in the balance of powers or the rise of a challenger to the hegemon will result in a new major war. Although these analyses provide some important insights about how peace ends a specific war and about the foundation of power upon which that peace rests, their realist emphasis on the power foundation makes them over-look the extent to which a peace and a structure of expectations do more than resolve the issues that led to a war and give rise to a new status hierarchy. The rise of new actors and changes in capabilities will, of course, place new demands on the political system, but whether those demands will result in a breakdown of the system and a new major war depends on the nature of those demands (the type of issue being raised) and the characteristics of the political system (e.g. the existence of pro-cedures and institutions able to handle highly salient issues, especially territorial issues).

Not all peace systems break down in the face of new powerful actors. Some do, of course, but others only slowly decay. Realists ignore the most important variable cluster at the systemic level, namely the global institu-tional context the peace has created. If the global institutional context is important, then some peace systems should be much more effective than others in the face of secular changes in power. In fact, certain types of peace have been fairly successful in avoiding a repeat of the war, while others have actually promoted a war's recurrence (see Doran, 1971).

Realists overlook the theoretical significance of peace, because they see anarchy and power politics as prevailing. Waltz (1959, 1979) argues that a structure of anarchy makes war possible, and since anarchy is endemic, power politics dominates. However, if the structure of the system is not always anarchic, then power politics behavior might wane and war might not be the main way of resolving fundamental issues.

Most scholars assume that the global system is fundamentally anarchic, but is this the case? If one means by anarchy the absence of hierarchical domestic-type government, then it is, but if one means the absence of all governance and order, then it is not. Despite the analogy to domestic government, most realists, including Waltz, *use* the term *anarchy* to mean not simply the absence of hierarchical government, but the presence of a Hobbesian state of nature.

In the modern global system since 1495, anarchy-as-a-state-of-nature, while present at times, has not been as pervasive as Waltz (1979) would have us believe (see Bull, 1977; Alker, 1996a). Indeed, as David Campbell (1989: 104) astutely observes, the defining characteristic of the international system since the sixteenth century has been capitalism, not anarchy. To see the modern global system as "anarchic" is to hide the historical fact that an arbitrary system of organization (i.e. nation-states and a capitalist world economy) evolved at a particular period of history and has been guided by clear principles of order which makes this system much more of a society than a state of nature. The fact that international capitalism is consonant with a multiplicity of states which relate to each other on the basis of an interstate anarchy (i.e. in the absence of legal hierarchy), rather than empire (Braudel, 1966; Wallerstein, 1974; Ashley, 1987), substantiates the claim that interstate anarchy is a constructed and contingent condition, rather than an eternal verité of world politics.

One of the reasons Waltz underestimates the amount of order in the system is that he treats the anarchy/order distinction as a dichotomy when it is better seen as a continuum. Major wars have given rise to political orders and most wars are not fought in conditions of anarchy but within a regional or global order that shapes the way in which the war is fought, as well as containing the war (i.e. the order usually confines the war to the two parties and often limits its goals and means). The kind of anarchy Waltz and Hobbes talk about only emerges with the complete breakdown of a political system, which occurs only during world wars in the global system and civil wars and social revolutions in domestic systems.

The ability of a global system to avoid war seems to be a function of the extent to which it has an ordered structure. All other factors being equal, it can be argued that the more ordered the global structure; the fewer wars, the less intense the wars that occur, and the fewer the military confrontations. A system can be considered *ordered* to the extent to which actors are constrained from unilaterally imposing their issue preference on others. In an ordered political system, actors officially recognize and feel it necessary to follow certain rules of the game, and institutions exist for the resolution of issues.

What empirical evidence exists on the nature of peace provides support for the above generalizations. If we examine the periods which are peaceful and delineate what the interactions are like and what the structure is like, it is possible to identify some of the factors associated with peace. In this way we are able to investigate the adequacy of the above proposition and begin to uncover the correlates of peace.

Characteristics of Peaceful Periods

Can war ever be avoided, or is humanity condemned to a history of war and a struggle for power? There are some interesting findings that demonstrate that the frequency of war varies in different periods and systems; there are cases where political actors do not exhibit the kind of power politics behavior involved in the steps to war. Realism is incorrect in asserting that all periods are a struggle for power.

Peter Wallensteen (1984: Table 2, 246) marshals evidence to show that when major states make concerted efforts to work out a set of rules to guide their relations (what he calls "universalist policies"), no wars among major states are fought, military confrontations are drastically reduced, and even wars and confrontations between major and minor states are somewhat attenuated. Conversely, when major states do not (or are unable to) create an order based on acceptable rules, and fall back on "particularist policies" based on unilateral actions, war breaks out among them and confrontations increase two-fold. Specifically, he finds that from 1816 to 1976, in universalist periods, there are no wars between major states, but, in particularist periods there are ten wars. In universalist periods, there are twenty-four militarized disputes between major states compared to forty-nine militarized disputes in particularist periods.

Wallensteen's definition of universalist policies implies that periods of peace are associated with informal decision games that are able to resolve disputes or with procedures – such as third party mediation or conferences among major states – that can manage crises and/or reduce tensions in relations. Rules and norms set up expectations about general standards of behaviour that not only control escalation if crises should develop, but push actors to deal with disputes by making them try certain actions before turning toward more drastic action. Universalist policies try to reduce and eliminate certain types of behavior, particularly unilateral acts, while establishing certain preferred means of interaction.

Rules and norms create ways of adjudicating disagreements. Even though such rules and norms may be part of a conscious policy by one or more of the actors, it is probably a mistake to imply, as Wallensteen does, that the rules themselves are policies *per se*. They can be nothing more than informal understandings set up after the last major war to demark the bounds of normal relations among major states. These norms can be refined into rules, tacitly, through interaction. Since it is the rules rather than the policies that shape behavior, instead of speaking about universalist periods, one might speak of periods in which rules of the game have been established.

How rules of the game shape behavior and help avoid war can be seen by looking at what Wallensteen calls *particularist policies*. When these policies dominate, unilateral actions and practices guide states. There are few or no means to adjudicate disagreements. Actors in an interdependent decision-making situation can reach agreement through making a bargain (each trading something to get what they can), if the friendship–hostility level of their relationship permits it. Otherwise, there are few norms, mechanisms, or institutions (formal or informal) in particularist periods for the resolution of persistent conflicts of interest. In such a global or regional context, a stalemate over a very salient issue leads actors to take unilateral acts to resolve the dispute in their favor. This leads to a focus on questions of power and capability, which leads in the modern global system to an adoption of realist perspectives and practices, and from these toward the steps to war.

It is the unilateral nature of actions that appears to be of significance in distinguishing periods of peace from periods that have extensive warfare. When rules govern behavior and establish a structure of expectations that political actors will not act on their own to secure their issue positions, then confrontations are reduced and wars non-existent among major states. However, in the absence of rules, political actors seem to have little choice but to take unilateral action or give up their issue position.

Typically, wars are preceded by periods of unilateral behavior, but is this of causal significance, simply descriptive of some deeper phenomenon, or perhaps even tautological? Wallensteen (1984: 246) raises the latter possibility by recognizing that since his demarcation of universalist policies is based on the assessment of historians, they might be "quicker" to identify an order when there are no major-state wars. Yet he points out that in his classification this has not been the case, noting that none of his periods of universalism end in war. His criteria identify periods of particularism and only at a much later date does war erupt, the earliest being in the sixth year of a particularist policy (Wallensteen, 1984: 246, 256, note 4). This shows that Wallensteen's criteria for particularist and universalist periods are separate from his dependent variables. Second, he finds that his universalist and particularist policies are associated with several other forms of behavior (which are more operationally visible and less susceptible to the tautological accusation). He argues that the forms of behavior in universalist periods help reduce conflict and reflect policies "that have been designed to support one another." Likewise, particularist periods also are characterized by distinguishable forms of behavior, but instead of reducing conflict they tend to reflect "a pattern of internally consistent policies... [that reinforce] the underlying conflict" (Wallensteen, 1984: 250).

Even though these forms of behavior may not always indicate conscious designs, it does seem that the peaceful periods are characterized by distinguishable acts that not only create peaceful relations, but maintain a way of interacting that reduces the probability of war, even in the presence of conflict. Conversely, in particularist periods, conflict is intensified and hostility increased because of the practices that are employed to handle it, although the underlying issues in particularist periods may be inherently less resolvable than those in peaceful periods. The key point to keep in mind for now is that in both periods behavior tends to be reinforcing, consistent, and prone to amplifying feedback, but whether it moves towards a more accommodative direction or a more confrontational direction depends on the presence or absence of rules of the game.

Wallensteen finds periods of peace distinguished by four other characteristics, but his research on this question is exploratory and needs to be investigated in more detail. First, peaceful periods are associated with conscious attempts to geographically separate major states so that they do not border on each other. This is usually done through the creation of buffer zones. In particularist periods, just the opposite occurs. Territory separating major states is seen as a "vacuum" that needs to be filled and over which rivals compete (Wallensteen, 1984: 247, 250). Since territorial issues are the most likely to end in war, Wallensteen's observation probably indicates that one of the ways in which peaceful periods are truly distinguishable from periods that are more war prone is the practices and procedures they have for dealing with territorial questions.

In light of Wallensteen's analysis and the evidence and analysis presented in Chapter 4, it appears that territorial contiguity has causal significance. Since serious disputes over territorial contiguity can lead to war, efforts which reduce those disputes, especially by eliminating the contiguity, will reduce the probability of war. Thus, one of the ways in which rules of the game probably produce peaceful relations is by establishing practices for handling the territorial disputes between major states. The diplomats of the one hundred years of peace between 1815 and 1914 were particularly adept in this regard. Not only did they employ the practice of buffer zones in the core area of Europe, but also in the periphery to manage colonial claims and rivalries.

The creation of buffer zones was only one practice used in the nineteenth century to handle territorial questions. Equally important was the practice of *compensation* (see Morgenthau, 1960: 179–80; Craig and George, 1983: 34; Lauren, 1983: 33). Compensation embodies the principle that among major states, especially rivals, advantages given to one state must be offset by advantages given to competing states. Territorial distributions and allocations of spheres of influence often followed this principle in the nineteenth century. Thus, if one major state won new territory by taking over a weaker political actor, other major states were entitled to compensation. Clearly, such rules go a long way in avoiding war between major states. Without such rules and the games they construct, other major states have to either acquiesce or take unilateral action. The practice of compensation not only made such a choice unnecessary, but kept hostility within manageable bounds so as to keep the cost-benefit aspect of decision making paramount.

The use of buffer zones and compensation illustrates how specific practices can produce peaceful relations. It must be remembered, however, that such practices typically are part of a broader system of rules and understandings. In the nineteenth century, the use of buffer zones and compensation reflected the workings of an inchoate political system created at the Congress of Vienna for the settlement of the French Revolutionary and Napoleonic wars. The Concert of Europe was a conscious attempt to govern the world and manage relations among major states. Although it broke down mid-way through the century (see Rosecrance, 1973: 36–38), it created a set of precedents and rules of the game that served the system right up to 1914.

For example, the legacy of the Concert seems to have been critical in avoiding war in the scramble for Africa in the late nineteenth century. Through a series of interactions and subsequent conferences, like that at Berlin (1884–85), the major states were able to handle important territorial questions without fighting wars with one another. In Africa, as in other areas before, this peace allowed the major states to divide the world among themselves and to fight wars of inequality without fear of interference. In this case, as in others, it should not be assumed that peace will necessarily enhance the net balance of values. In the nineteenth century, peace in one area of the world established the foundation for war, dominance, and social injustice in another.[2]

Nevertheless, it can be concluded that to the extent to which major states are able to develop practices and a system for dealing with territorial issues, then peace is more likely. Practices that succeed in handling territorial questions are likely to be associated with rules that can handle other issues as well, so that peaceful systems will tend to take on the characteristics of a political system that is governed by an elite.

A second characteristic of peaceful periods that occurs in conjunction with the establishment of rules of the game, according to Wallensteen (1984), is the absence of messianism and expansionist ideologies. In peaceful periods, there is more of a willingness to tolerate differences (cf. Craig and George, 1983: 33–35). States are basically satisfied with the status quo and change is confined to the margins. Classical realism has long recognized that moral and ideological issues dealing with how life should be lived are war-prone and has extolled rules that have sought to keep such issues off the agenda. Realist prescriptions and rules about non-interference in the internal affairs of other nation-states, conducting diplomacy prudently so as not to overextend one's power or threaten the vital interests of another, as well as the need to make foreign policy on the basis of interests rather than morality (see Kennan, 1951; Morgenthau, 1960: 3–14) can be understood in this light.

The realist emphasis on prudence is a latent recognition that not all issues affect politics in the same way. Certain issues are so fundamental and have such profound and far-reaching consequences, depending on how they might be resolved, that they become life and death issues. Whether a society shall be organized and ruled on the basis of feudalistic norms, the divine right of kings, or a social contract, or whether groups should be treated equally or on the basis of some ascribed or achieved status (e.g. race or class) are not questions that can be settled through compromise. In the realm of ideas, they often involve almost incommensurable perspectives that make it difficult to find common intellectual

---

[2] Wallensteen (1984: 247–48), for example, points out that both British and French extension into the Middle East in the 1880s and 1920s, as well as the scramble for Africa in the early 1880s occurred in universalist periods, but that decolonialization occurred in the particularist and tense period of the Cold War.

ground that does not bias the discussion in favor of one of the parties. In the realm of practice, the acceptance of one position, even aspects of the position of one side, can tear apart the social fabric of a community and initiate a series of changes in relationships. American abolitionists, Vietnamese and Algerian revolutionaries, Christian settlers in the New World, German fascists, and Puritans in seventeenth-century England are not posing questions that are easily settled. It is difficult to organize a society based on slavery and individual freedom. Slavery is more than the ownership of human beings. It is a way of life. To abolish it is to do more than free human beings, it is to destroy an entire way of living. Those who benefit from the way of living and believe in it are not likely to relinquish their dominance without a fight. Actors have no choice but to attempt to settle things unilaterally.

The history of civil wars and social revolutions shows that it is the case that certain human issues place too great a demand on even the most established political system, i.e. government. On these kinds of issues, no one believes they can afford to lose, and so if in any given procedure or game they do lose, they will turn to another game or procedure whereby they think they might win. Ultimately, one side is apt to break out of the system and engage in unilateral action to secure its issue position. If this analysis is correct, it means that one of the things that make certain periods peaceful and political systems stable is the ability to keep certain types of issues off the political agenda; namely, life and death issues that are prone to unilateral action. Ideologies and religions that seek exclusive rights to institutionalize their way of life on a territory obviously raise fundamental issues of life and death.

It is not surprising in this light that Wallensteen (1984: 252) finds that fundamental changes in the ruling political formula of a major political actor (as in the French and Bolshevik revolutions, the creation of the Third Reich, the overthrow of Metternich, Louis Philippe, or the Shah of Iran) have unsettled the dominant global or regional political order and sometimes transformed it from a universalist period to a particularist period. Revolutionary changes can bring about new and fundamental ideological concerns that the old rules of the game are probably ill-prepared to handle. The revolutionary regime may be seen as threatening because it provides an alternative way of living and organizing social life and because it is viewed as unlikely to accept the status quo (which the existing rules of the game have institutionalized). However, unless dissatisfied states are capable of challenging the older states (Bolshevik Russia was not), the system will not be placed under much stress. Likewise, war may be avoided if the satisfied states are willing to change the status quo to accommodate the needs of challengers (as Britain did during decolonization).

The extent to which a challenger is accommodated depends not only on the willingness of satisfied states, but also on the ability of the political system to establish a structure that encourages both parties to reach some sort of understanding and believe that the rules of the game, if one is patient enough, will work. When a political system fails to resolve an issue, actors must give up or take matters into their own hands. The kinds of unilateral actions they have favored can be seen by examining Wallensteen's particularist periods.

In particularist periods, states rely on alliance making and arms build-ups, precisely the kinds of practices that in Chapter 5 were seen as steps to war. Wallensteen (1984: 248) argues that since in universalist periods attention is focused on diplomacy to work out problems, there should be less emphasis on building up one's military and the role of alliances should be diminished. He finds this to be the case in three of his four universalist periods, the exception being the early detente period of 1963–76.[3] In contrast, three of the four particularist periods show a rapid arms buildup, the exception being 1849–70 (Wallensteen, 1984: 248). Likewise, Wallensteen finds alliance systems to be loose in peaceful periods and tight in particularist periods. Most universalist periods have loose alliance systems, with the only possible exception being 1963–76, but even this shows a breakdown in blocs with the defection of France from NATO and of China from the Eastern bloc. Three of the four particularist periods show tight alliance structures, with the 1849–70 period again being the exception.

Wallensteen (1984: 248) believes that there is an interaction between alliances and arms buildups. When no major allies can be had (usually because the world has been polarized) then the only way to increase capability is a military buildup. Alliance polarization would be expected to encourage military buildups, and he finds this to be the case in 1896–1918, 1933–44, and in the post-1945 era.[4]

---

[3] In the long run, however, this was not an exception, since Soviet–American arms control agreements eventually led to a relaxation of the Cold War and its ending with the rise of Gorbachev.

[4] Wallensteen (1984: 249–50) also examines whether economic relations differ in universalist and particularist periods, but no clear patterns are found, except that after 1895, universalist periods seem to have increased economic interaction, while particularist periods have not. Wallensteen (1984: 250) also notes that in particularist periods trade becomes an instrument of coercion and/or exclusion. This last finding is not that different from the role economics played in the Cold War; i.e. hostility reduces trade, which leads to

Wallensteen's examination of the characteristics of particularist periods provides significant additional evidence that the steps-to-war analysis is on the right track. Realist practices are associated with war, and peaceful systems are associated with an emphasis on other practices. Peaceful systems are exemplified by the use of practices like buffer states, compensation, and concerts of power that bring major states together to form a network of institutions that provide governance for the system. The creation of rules of the game that can handle certain kinds of issues – territorial and ideological questions – and/or keep them off the agenda seems to be a crucial variable in producing peace.

Additional evidence on the import of rules and norms is provided in a series of studies by Kegley and Raymond (1982, 1984, 1986, 1990) that are operationally more precise than Wallensteen's (1984) analysis. Kegley and Raymond provide evidence that when states accept norms, the incidence of war and military confrontation is reduced. They find that peace is associated with periods in which alliance norms are considered binding and the unilateral abrogation of commitments and treaties illegitimate. The rules imposed by the global political culture in these periods result in fewer militarized disputes and wars between major states. In addition, the wars that occur are kept at lower levels of severity, magnitude, and duration (i.e. they are limited wars).

Kegley and Raymond attempt to measure the extent to which global cultural norms restrain major states by looking at whether international law and commentary on it sees treaties and alliances as binding. They note that there have been two traditions in international law – *pacta sunt servanda*, which maintains that agreements are binding, and *clausa rebus sic stantibus*, which says that treaties are signed "as matters stand" and that any change in circumstances since the treaty was signed permits a party to withdraw unilaterally. One of the advantages the Kegley–Raymond studies have over Wallensteen (1984) is that they are able to develop reliable measures of the extent to which in any given half-decade the tradition in international law emphasizes the *rebus* or *pacta sunt servanda* tradition. This indicator is important not only because it focuses in on the question of unilateral actions, but because it can serve as an indicator of how well the peace system is working. The *pacta sunt servanda* tradition implies a more constraining political system and robust institutional context which should provide an alternative to war.

increased hostility and less need of the other side, which removes one restraint on keeping relations friendly.

Kegley and Raymond (1982: 586) find that in half-decades (from 1820 to 1914) when treaties are considered non-binding (*rebus*), wars between major states occur in every half-decade (100 percent), but when treaties are considered binding (*pacta sunt servanda*), wars between major states occur in only 50 percent of the half-decades. The Cramer's V for this relationship is 0.66. When the sample is expanded to include all states in the central system, Cramer's V is 0.44, indicating that global norms have more impact on preventing war between major states. Nevertheless, among central system states between 1820 and 1939, war occurred in 93 percent of the half-decades where the *rebus* tradition dominated and in only 60 percent of the half-decades where the *pacta sunt servanda* tradition dominated.

In a subsequent analysis of militarized disputes from 1820 to 1914, Kegley and Raymond (1984: 207–11) find that there is a negative relationship between binding norms and the frequency and scope of disputes short of war. In periods when the global culture accepts the *pacta sunt servanda* tradition as the norm, the number of military disputes goes down and the number of major states involved in a dispute decreases. Although the relationship is of moderate strength, it is not eliminated by other variables, namely alliance flexibility. As Kegley and Raymond (1984: 213) point out, this means "that in periods when the opportunistic renunciation of commitments" is condoned, militarized disputes are more likely to occur and to spread. The finding that norms can reduce the frequency and scope of disputes is significant evidence that rules can permit actors to successfully control and manage disputes so that they are not contagious and they do not escalate to war. These findings are consistent with Wallensteen's (1984) and suggest that one of the ways rules help prevent war is by reducing, limiting, and managing disputes short of war.

While alliance norms and the legal tradition governing commitments may be important, it is unlikely that, in and of themselves, they would have such an impact on the onset of war; rather the presence of such norms is an indicator of a much broader consensus (on rules of the game) that diminishes unilateral action. In a later analysis, Kegley and Raymond (1986: 217–24) use the notion of rules to explain their findings and to account in detail for actual historical practices. They conclude that a consensus among major states about rules is a precondition for the avoidance of war (Kegley and Raymond, 1986: 223). Interestingly, they note that an essential element in avoiding war is to set up rules that "permit, but place limits on, the uses of force short of war" (Kegley and Raymond, 1986: 223).

Kegley and Raymond (1986) also provide evidence to support the claim made earlier in the chapter that rules come out of peace settlements made to conclude the last major war. They find that norm formation is associated with the outbreak of violence, but that the force of these rules erodes with time. They suggest that the horrors of war make leaders establish rules so as to avoid war, but as memory fades and new generations and political actors emerge, the salience of the rules wanes, especially in the face of new issues (Kegley and Raymond, 1986: 224). Leaders then need to relearn their painful lessons about the acceptability of war as a way of handling disagreement.

The importance of rules is underlined in Väyrynen's (1983) study of the role of economic cycles and power transitions in wars among major states. He finds war less frequent among major states when the system of "political management" of interstate relations restrains unilateral actions. When alliances and institutionalized norms are restraining – as in a system managed by a concert of states or institutionalized regional or global organizations – then wars among major states are less frequent. When the system is unrestrained – as in a balance of power system in which management is based solely on calculations of distribution of power – war is more frequent. On the basis of an historical analysis, Väyrynen (1983: 402–10) classifies 1854–71, 1890–1914, and 1920–39 as unrestraining. If we place his nine wars in these periods, we see that seven of his nine major wars occur when the system is unrestraining – the Seven Weeks War (1866), Franco-Prussian War (1870–71), Russo-Japanese War (1904–5), World War I (1914–18), Russian Civil War (1917–21), Soviet–Japanese War (1939), and World War II. If we eliminate the questionable cases of the Russian Civil War and Soviet–Japanese War (1939) then five of seven wars since 1815 have occurred in unrestraining periods. Only two wars occur when the political management of the system has been restraining – the Crimean War (1853–56) and the Korean War (1951–53) – and the Korean War was unwanted by both major states (the United States and China). Although Väyrynen's (1983: 403) measurement of the political management variable is *ex post facto* and his study is concerned primarily with the role of economic cycles, his analysis implies that the ability of a political system to restrain allies and adversaries by setting up norms and rules to resolve disputes is an important factor in reducing the probability of war.

All of the above studies suggest that one of the keys to peace is to get major states to control their unilateral actions in favor of some set of rules that will allow them to contend over certain issues, while leaving other more highly salient (and less resolvable) issues off the political agenda. When major states have been unable or unwilling to institutionalize such rules, they have had to rely on their own unilateral actions, which in the modern global system means they have relied on the practices of power politics to gain their ends. War is a way of making authoritative decisions unilaterally. Since force and war are costly ways of making decisions, it can be assumed that war will decrease when alternative ways of making authoritative decisions exist. Likewise, it is plausible to assume that when there is a strong global order, rules and norms will limit war, even when it occurs, by restricting the situations under which it can be initiated and circumscribing how it may be fought. Many of these ideas about peace have been circulating for some time; what is significant about the above studies is that they provide systematic evidence to support these conclusions.

On the basis of Wallensteen's (1984), Kegley and Raymond's (1982, 1984, 1986, 1990), and Väyrynen's (1983) findings, the following inductions can be made about the characteristics associated with peace. In peaceful periods, rules of the game have been created and norms are not unilaterally abrogated. The system as a whole restrains the contention of actors by offering them practices other than power politics for the resolution of issues. In particular, practices – such as buffer states, compensation, and concerts of power – that permit states to deal with territorial issues have been implemented. Issues involving severe threats to territory, especially to the core territory of major states, and certain life and death issues are kept off the agenda through the creation of a tolerable status quo and the avoidance of messianism. In addition, it can be inferred from Doran's (1971) study that the system must permit the status quo to change in order to accommodate new actors and new issues that come to the fore after the system has been created.

Empirical evidence that peace is associated with the creation of a political system after a major system-wide war is provided, indirectly, by several studies. Early on, Singer and Wallace (1970) found that war and the number of intergovernmental organizations in the system go hand in hand, with war giving rise to new international organizations after it is concluded. Singer and Wallace were looking for a negative relationship between the number of intergovernmental organizations and war; when they failed to uncover such a relationship and instead found a positive one between international organization and war, the implications of the latter finding were not pursued. While the Singer and Wallace (1970) study shows there is no simple relationship between peace and the presence of intergovernmental organizations, it also shows that large wars do give birth to attempts to enrich the global institutional context. These attempts can in light of our understanding of the history of the modern global system be seen as efforts to create a political system (see Doran, 1971, 1991).

A later study by Wallace (1972) makes clearer the role intergovernmental organizations play in producing peace. In this analysis, Wallace uncovers distinct paths to war and to peace. He finds that large amounts of war in the system are associated with a path that begins with changes in capability producing status inconsistency. This in turn eventually gives rise to alliance polarization and then to arms buildups that are correlated with war. Obviously, this model of the path to war is a rudimentary forerunner of the steps to war outlined in the previous chapter.

What is interesting is that this path to war is complemented by a path to peace in which the number of intergovernmental organizations in the system is *inversely* related to the amount of war in the system. In this path, status inconsistency is negatively associated with the number of intergovernmental organizations in the system. This makes sense in that, as he points out (Wallace, 1972: 55), intergovernmental organizations are most likely to be created and function well when there is little dispute over the global pecking order. Thus, Wallace (1972: 66) finds that the greater the number of intergovernmental organizations (IGOs) in the system (and presumably the more effective their use), the less frequently arms buildups occur in the system, which the model finds correlated positively with war.

This means that as IGOs are created and function, there is less of a resort to arms buildups in the system, so wars are less frequent. In terms of the steps-to-war analysis, one would expect that when global institutions exist for the resolution of issues, power politics behavior should decrease. There should be little making of alliances, no polarization, few arms races, and crises that do occur should not escalate to war, but be mediated by international organizations or major states. War would result from the breakdown of such a system, and in this light it is theoretically significant that Kjell Skjelsbaek (1971) finds that shared membership in intergovernmental organizations decreases prior to the outbreak of war.

Evidence that Wallace's (1972) IGO indicator is probably tapping the richness and effectiveness of the global institutional context is provided by Faber and Weaver (1984). Their analysis provides data to show that what is important in establishing peace is not the mere existence of IGOs, but that there is a set of institutions and practices that present an alternative way of handling political decisions. Confining their study to the

European system (including Turkey, Russia, and the United States) from 1816 to 1915, Faber and Weaver (1984: 525) look at the extent to which, in any given period, states participated in international conferences and signed treaties to settle issues. They then analyze the short-term effects such participation has on war, in terms of the number of participants in war and nation-months of war. Faber and Weaver (1984: 523) argue that, especially in 1816–70, it was through conferences and bilateral diplomatic consultations rather than IGOs that most conflict resolution took place. Additionally, they control for whether the issues discussed were military (alliance formation, non-aggression pacts, and peace settlements), peaceful settlement of territorial issues, economic issues, or some other issue. They then compare "military issues" with "peace-related issues" (a combination of the last three). Although this is not the most refined nomenclature, they uncover some interesting relationships.

Faber and Weaver (1984: 531) reconfirm Singer and Wallace's (1970) analysis, finding that one to three years after warfare, states tend to intensify their participation in international conferences and treaties. However, when they control for the type of issue, they uncover two different patterns. Conferences and treaties devoted to issues of alliances and peace settlements are related positively to warfare, while conferences and treaties devoted to the non-violent resolution of territorial questions (especially borders), economic questions, and other issues are negatively related to war (Faber and Weaver, 1984: 532–33). These findings imply that international conferences and treaties can serve as a functional equivalent to war; it is significant that attempts to resolve territorial questions are negatively related to war.[5] It appears that if certain issues, namely territorial questions, can be resolved by the system, the prospects for peace are good. Conversely, issues that are dealt with by alliances are likely to give rise to war.

Wallace's (1972) analysis along with Faber and Weaver's (1984) elaborations are theoretically important because they provide evidence linking the presence of a rich global institutional context with the absence of power politics and war. Such a link is highly congruent with the findings of Wallensteen (1984) and Kegley and Raymond (1982, 1984, 1986, 1990). Since war and force are ways of making political decisions under

[5] It would be interesting to know how much of the relationship is accounted for by territorial issues and how much by the other two types of issues, but Faber and Weaver do not present their data on this. The findings also reconfirm the association between the practice of alliance making and warfare, which indicates that Wallace (1972) is correct in seeing this as a path to war.

anarchy, the creation of a global set of institutions and rules of the game by which to make political decisions reduces the need of major states for war. It does this by providing allocation mechanisms other than force for resolving issues. Actors accept the outcomes of using those mechanisms, even if it means they will lose a particular contest. This acceptance, in turn, is probably a function of their ability to avoid raising fundamental issues of life and death.

If it is assumed that war avoidance at the domestic, regional, or global level involves the creation of a political system or regime capable of making decisions, then how long a peace that ends a major war will last depends upon its success in creating an order that institutionalizes procedures for the resolution of political demands. In this way the global institutional context has a direct impact on whether and when war will occur. The global institutional context, which is created by the previous interactions of states, forms a structure that either encourages or discourages steps to war.

The Relationship of Peace to War

According to Waltz the condition of anarchy provides a structure that makes war permissible (Waltz, 1959: ch. 6; 1979: 111; 1988: 41–44). Because anarchy provides few ways of making authoritative decisions, it follows that when certain issues are present, war is more likely than in a structure where there are a variety of ways of making authoritative decisions. In other words, a rich global institutional context should provide a structure that will make war less probable. A system's structure can be seen as ranging from one of little order (e.g. anarchy) to one which is highly ordered (e.g. government in stable societies). Force and war tend to be more frequent in a condition of anarchy (defined as the absence of order) simply because when no practices permitting interdependent decision making are available, unilateral practices dominate by default. War is less frequent in an ordered system that provides more efficient means of resolving issues, particularly when norms proscribe and deprecate the use of war.

It must be remembered, however, that war is a social invention, and the ways in which it is fought and the situations that are handled through war will vary according to cultural traditions. The structure of any system, whether it be global or domestic, must be seen not as something that is given by nature, but something that has been socially constructed by the combination of practices that have been employed by political actors. Structure is historically contingent and reflects the informal institutionalization of previous practices.

In this sense, anarchy or "the" state of nature should not be viewed as a primeval condition, but as an outcome of a set of social constructions (Campbell, 1989: 114, 122–25; Ashley, 1987, 1988). Global anarchy is a constructed condition that institutionalizes how actors *should* treat each other in their relationships. The "billiard ball model" must be seen as a normative model of exemplary behavior that is prone to a self-fulfilling prophecy, rather than an "objective" description of "natural" behavior. The model is a description of aspects of actors' behavior that conform to an earlier set of prescriptions, but since those prescriptions are not always followed and fail to guide behavior in certain realms, the model often falls short as a description and predictor of actual practice.

Structures, including anarchy, usually evolve from tacit behavior, from practices that have been legitimated, and from more explicit attempts to shape relationships. As actors deal with an interdependent decision-making situation, it becomes necessary for them to settle upon rules for interacting with each other. Such rules initially are little more than expectations derived from previous behavior. Nevertheless, they set up mutually understood procedures by which actors will contend for and dispose of stakes. Such expectations establish criteria for determining what is legitimate behavior and how a stake can be won or lost. Only when such expectations exist – whether they emerge from tacit bargaining or formal rules – is it possible to engage in decision making. The remainder of this chapter will outline how peace is related to war by showing how structures of order emerge to create peaceful periods and how these structures break down to give rise to unilateral policies and war.

Patterns that are repeated and associated with certain rules may be called decision games.[6] A decision game is any set of recognizable procedures used to dispose of a stake. The key element in a decision game is its *allocation mechanism*. As discussed in Chapter 1, allocation mechanisms can be grouped into four types: force, bargains, votes, and principle, depending on whether a stake is disposed of on the basis of coercion, a trade, voting, or some set of agreed upon standards (e.g. equality or status). Decision games emerge and are characterized by actors favoring

---

[6] The conceptual framework dealing with decision games, allocation mechanisms, systemic rules, and their characteristics that is employed below was initially developed in Mansbach and Vasquez (1981: 282–313).

a certain mix of allocation mechanisms based on the following of specific procedures and use of certain techniques in a predictable sequence. As a result, interaction takes on a gamelike quality with actors able to anticipate each other's moves (Mansbach and Vasquez, 1981: 287). Decision games usually evolve through *ad hoc* interaction, with the parties seeking to find new rules by probing and testing one another in a trial and error fashion. In this way, they learn what each is willing to accept and how they can make decisions. Dyadic relationships, however, must be understood in terms of the larger systemic norms that have been developed.

System-wide rules and norms usually reflect custom. Every peace within the system helps establish a set of norms, rules, and conventions about how states should relate to each other and when war can serve as a way of resolving issues. Thus, the history of neighbors usually is a history that involves establishing boundaries, a status hierarchy, and a political relationship that sets precedents about the manner in which each side will deal with the other. At certain critical moments in history, however, major states attempt to develop in a more formal manner a set of rules and decision games. This typically occurs after a major global war, when the victors sit down (sometimes with the new representatives of the vanquished) to establish a new world order. Formal attempts at rule making usually derive from a mutual realization that prior interaction games, especially total war, should be avoided and replaced by less costly ways of conducting politics. Some of these formal rule-making efforts, like the Peace of Westphalia and the Congress of Vienna, have been highly successful in resolving the issues that led to war and mitigating the use of violence. Others, such as the Versailles system, have been disastrous, bringing about the very war they tried to prevent. Since systems that follow major wars are acts of creation that are historically contingent, their precise nature will vary.

Unlike stable domestic societies, global society does not have a dominant decision game, like government. This means that actors contend not only over stakes, but over which interaction game should be employed to reach a decision. All other factors being equal, an actor will select that interaction game which will give it the highest probability of winning with the least costs. This means that an actor will favor the interaction games for which it has ample resources. Wealthy states would be expected to prefer that the market allocate, rather than distributing stakes by voting. Militarily strong states will insist that allocation and political influence reflect capability. The weak will favor games of principle, especially those based on equality and equity (Mansbach and Vasquez, 1981: 294–95).

Although global society does not have a clear hierarchy among decision games, it often does have rules about which games must be tried first. Since a variety of games would give rise to numerous conflicts over which game should be used, rules develop about which decision games should be used for what purposes and at what times. These overarching or "systemic rules" help order the system and make it less "anarchic" by restraining the autonomy of individual actors. Indeed, one of the main functions of a peace system is to develop a set of systemic rules along with decision games.

The systemic rules as well as individual decision games are characterized by three dimensions: institutionalization, hierarchy, and legitimacy (see Mansbach and Vasquez, 1981: 290–91). Institutionalization refers to the extent to which the systemic rules and decision games are ingrained in the system. With high institutionalization, rules are understood and norms followed. There is little uncertainty and expectations are fulfilled. Hierarchy refers to the extent decision games are ordered; that is, whether certain channels must be followed before others can be tried. Legitimacy refers to whether the rules and decision games are regarded as the correct and proper way of conducting politics. Legitimacy captures the degree to which rules and norms are widely accepted.

The idea of systemic rules and the extent to which they are institutionalized, hierarchical, and legitimate help elucidate: how decision games are selected when there is more than one game available; how political actors switch from one game to another; and how new games are created. Systemic rules (and precedents and expectations when rules are not fully constructed) determine initial game selection. This means that, at least in the first game, the system and not the actors determine the locus of contention. If there were no systemic order, it would be expected that individual actors would strive to get their issue "heard" in the "forum" and resolved by the "practice" or allocation mechanism which would make it most likely to win at the minimal cost. However, this cost-benefit desire, as well as any other motivating factor, is overridden by the rules and norms of the system which have evolved. Individual preference accedes to systemic demand. Thus, strong actors, like the United States, often listen to the claims of weaker actors in fora that favor the weak (e.g. those governed by one vote one state) even though they prefer not discussing the issue at all or dealing with it bilaterally or among an elite.

Political actors follow the rules, especially on initial game selection, because the rules promise to provide greater value satisfaction for actors as a group over the long term than the benefits derived from breaking the rules in a particular instance (Mansbach and Vasquez, 1981: 298). This is especially the case since defection is not without cost. Actors have an interest in carrying the burden of the collective good because they realize that numerous defections could undermine the system and be very costly in terms of engendering disagreement over game selection, stymieing collective problem solving, and increasing uncertainty and decision costs (i.e. the minimal time and energy necessary to make a decision). Since rules are created through trial and error attempts to avoid the errors of the past, the experience by which actors have created the rules reflects an investment that is not easily risked. In addition, following systemic rules may be important to gain the support of domestic political groups.

As the systemic rules (and the peace system that embodies them) appear to work, the beneficial aspects of following the rules is recognized, and the rules gain in legitimacy. Actors become accustomed to discussing certain issues in a particular manner. Inertia sets in and norms give rise to custom. Historical learning tends to be conservative; collective actors are unwilling to challenge a situation that provides overall value satisfaction even when the particular instance may produce a loss. Furthermore, it is probably not certain that challenging the rules of the system may produce a net benefit. This is particularly the case if a "hegemon" or a concert of major states is willing to enforce the rules of the system (Mansbach and Vasquez, 1981: 298; Keohane, 1984). Finally, actors accept the rules on game selection because, even if the preferred game leads to a loss, the rules usually provide a way to shift to a more favorable game; even highly structural political systems permit a right to appeal or a channel to mobilize new support (see Vasquez, 1976: 305–8).

One of the most important ways by which systemic rules maintain a peace and reduce the likelihood of war is by regulating how one actor may make an unwilling actor shift contention on an issue to a new site and decision game. Through precedents, custom, and socialization, the systemic rules produce a cognitive map of the system that governs the sequence by which actors can shift from one game to another and informs actors which channels can be used and for what purpose. In global society, as in any anarchical society, more options are provided than in hierarchical domestic societies. In a hierarchical society, an actor may have only one channel open at a time, while in an anarchical society, the system may not privilege one channel but allow several to be utilized. Nevertheless, the systemic rules will probably restrict the choice to a *set* of channels and not allow some games or channels to be selected out of order. Even when such rules are not formal, the costs associated with certain channels order the sequence in which they will be played.

Two classic psychological principles, the "law of effect" and the "principle of least effort," help explain how actors learn to shift between games.[7] The law of effect states that rewards strengthen a bond between a stimulus and response while punishments weaken the bond (Thorndike, 1898). This implies that behavior that is rewarded will be repeated and behavior that has been punished will be avoided, all other factors being equal. Learning, for Thorndike (1898), consists of a trial and error search for behavior that produces rewards. The principle of least effort was developed by Tolman (1932) who argued that insight as well as trial and error governed the search for rewards. Tolman maintained that animals, as well as people, develop a cognitive map of their environment that tells them which paths or channels will lead to a desired goal. The principle of least effort maintains that the shortest path or least costly one will be selected.

These two principles help make evident how systemic rules might emerge from tacit behavior and how they regulate the shift between games and practices. In any given system, political actors learn through their successes and failures that certain channels will produce value satisfaction at an acceptable price and that others will not, and some may be exceedingly costly and dangerous. These lessons are derived from immediate experience, as well as the folklore handed down interpreting previous experience. Insight confirmed by trial and error gives rise to cognitive maps about the best way to proceed. Cognitive maps provide a guide to the reality that is being practiced and thereby determine what set of practices (games or channels) will be selected in what order.[8]

Equipped with cognitive maps, actors have clear ideas of what is expected of them and what they think will work. Actors are more likely to adhere to rules, especially in the beginning, if defeat in one instance allows them an opportunity to try other channels (Vasquez, 1976: 304).

---

[7] The use of these principles initially developed to explain the action of collective actors in Vasquez (1976).

[8] Cognitive maps vary by issue area and by historical period. What is considered legitimate in one issue area or period may not be considered legitimate and appropriate in another. Actors will permit infringements on their autonomy for some issues, but not on others. This emphasizes that rules and "laws of politics" are social constructions and not reflections of an independent reality. To a certain extent, what works depends on what the system wants to work, i.e. the system's mobilization of bias privileges certain practices and actors. Although this is true, it is equally the case that much of what humans hope to attain in creating systems often fails to come to fruition, so that many conscious social constructions are utopian.

In global society such opportunities abound, but with the understanding that force and war should only be used after other channels have been tried (although it is clearly not the case that, in practice, war is the last resort). Shifts occur because actors will not accept a loss in one game if they think they can win in another (Mansbach and Vasquez, 1981: 300). The systemic rules (i.e. the understandings, expectations, and precedents of previous practice) permit this, so there is little the actor who would have won can do. The rules, however, do *not* permit a shift to *any* game. They will, in conformity to the principle of least effort, select games or channels which keep the costs of contention relatively low, but higher than the previous game or set of games. In this way, a peace system insures that only the most salient issues will produce a "crisis" for the system. If it seems like there may be a war, then a system may have a host of conflict-resolution practices that come into effect in order to avoid that eventuality – mediation, concerts, intervention. A system may also have a set of games that permit limited or controlled use of violence to resolve a dispute as a way of regulating the impact of war on the system.

By providing multiple channels for contention with each channel incrementally increasing the costs to actors who fail to resolve their dispute, a political system can delay, perhaps even avert, war. Each channel can provide an authoritative decision, but this is held in abeyance or provides an interim disposition, if the losing actor seeks to expend more resources. Ultimately, a series of decisions, if somewhat consistent, takes on a final quality.

Clearly, some peace systems will be more successful in avoiding future war than others. Some will succeed because they manage to avoid war-threatening issues, and they probably are able to do that because they have consciously established a set of practices to keep those issues from arising. It has already been seen how the nineteenth-century practices of buffer states, compensation, and the use of concerts of power did this. Other systems will succeed because their system is better equipped to deal with political relations in a manner that controls hostility and avoids actions that are apt to escalate tensions.

Regardless of the structure of a system, war, especially war between equals, does not break out at the initial stages of contending over an issue. The onset of war must be seen as occurring only after actors have failed to resolve their issue by following the non-violent practices and games which the systemic rules have presented as the most legitimate. War emerges from a process by which actors shift from one game to the next. Depending on the specific historical context, games utilizing principles or votes as their allocation mechanism give way to bargains (Mansbach and Vasquez, 1981: 311). Games embodying these nonviolent allocation mechanisms can be regarded as ways of jointly dealing with an interdependent decision-making situation. As these games fail to resolve the issue, actors entertain unilateral solutions. In the modern global system, these solutions have been the practices of power politics. As these fail to resolve the issue, actors shift from one to another, learning that war is the only escape.

In wars between equals, this process is intertwined with an intensification of rivalry. In a robust global institution environment, the presence of many games makes the rivalry more competitive than hostile. So long as the rivals are willing to accept some authoritative resolutions, and the losses they imply, then the rivalry can be successfully managed. As issues take on a more symbolic quality and transcendent issues define the relationship, actors are wont to reject any interim disposition and shift from game to game, increasing hostility and frustration. The fear and threat associated with salient security issues drives them toward the legitimate unilateral actions made available by realist practices. Zero-sum perceptions are bred, and the entire concatenation of global and domestic factors associated with war, as outlined in Chapters 5 and 6, come into play.

Legitimate realist practices may be supplemented by new tactics that violate existing norms, which aggravates distrust and hostility. In general, however, the process of war involves not so much the abandonment of all the rules as the breakdown of the non-violent political system and a complete switch to and reliance upon a unilateral system of coercion and force which has its own rules of the game. In modern global politics there has been a dual system in operation, one governing normal politics and one governing war that has been institutionalized and regulated by international law. As Grotius (1625) argued, a shift to the war game sets normal international law into abeyance and brings into force a special international law of war. For traditional international law, this shift required an open declaration of war that would formally and unilaterally bring the special set of international law into operation. By the mid-twentieth century, the declaration statute had fallen into disuse, so that war and related acts, like the covert toppling of governments, could be conducted without an open announcement.[9]

---

[9] Although this is done for strategic advantage, the domestic political advantages of circumventing an open declaration and keeping the action secret are of enormous benefit to democracies. As a result, in recent times, it has been clearer that the shift to war has been the culmination of a number of acts that have produced a war-prone relationship.

The analysis presented in this section suggests war comes with the progressive failure of non-violent games to resolve issues and the feeling that only a reliance on unilateral practices will get one what one wants. With such a change in expectations, the system (or dyad) moves from Wallace's (1972) path to peace to the path of war.

The extent to which systemic rules are institutionalized, hierarchical, and legitimate can serve as a measure of how likely a given peace system will succeed. A successful peace system will have several accepted channels for resolving issues and rules that tell actors which channel to use at what stage of contention. Wallace's (1972) delineation of a path to peace that is negatively correlated to the path to war suggests that as long as a set of intergovernmental organizations is working, the unilateral practices of power politics will be minimized, making the chances for system-wide war low. In the absence of a rich institutional context, war is more likely because there are few channels available to resolve highly salient issues. Conversely, when there is a system of global institutions, war is less likely, but how much less likely and whether it can be avoided will depend on the specific nature of the channels available.

Only in knowing whether peace has produced a political system able to resolve issues is it possible to assess the probability of war. The outbreak of war does not follow cycles (see Singer and Cusack, 1981; Small and Singer, 1982: 150–56; Levy, 1983: 137) because *when* a war will occur depends not so much on inexorable shifts of capability (Gilpin, 1981; Organski and Kugler, 1980; Modelski, 1978; Thompson, 1988) but on how well the peace system created after the last major war is able to manage existing issues and new issues that arise.

This provides some hope for humanity, for it seems that people can learn to conduct politics on a more peaceful basis. The creation of new games comes about after existing practices have failed to resolve issues or have resolved them at great human cost. The capacity for insight and learning provides a way of restructuring the cognitive map to provide better channels and new paths, although clearly such changes are difficult to bring about and occur rarely. Prolonged stalemates like that of the Cold War or great conflagrations like World War I break the bond between following existing rules and the expectation of value satisfaction. Failure that results in great human suffering promotes a search for new ways of doing things, not only because leaders and intellectuals begin to learn to think differently, but because domestic political forces push aside those who are committed to the old ways of doing things. It is not an accident that the creation of new global systems and practices is associated with the conclusion of the major world wars of the past and the creation of new domestic political systems is associated with revolution and civil war. Peace is learned through pain and the domestic reaction to that pain.[10]

The search for new games occurs through the examination of precedents (Vasquez, 1976: 304–5; Mansbach and Vasquez, 1981: 302). Actors search for analogous situations and attempt to apply what has worked in the past. This always creates the possibility of overgeneralizing (Jervis, 1976: 281–82). The negative example of the immediate past is instrumental in developing new practices that attempt to avoid the disastrous consequences of the former way of conducting politics. Such rationalistic schemes can become utopian as in Wilsonianism. More lasting norms are apt to come out of a process of mutual probing that tacitly works out how major states will treat each other. This in turn may produce an atmosphere where more creative practices can be born. The exact manner in which effective new social inventions come about is an area that needs considerable investigation.

What can be concluded about the relationship of peace to the causes and avoidance of war? The global institutional context, like any structural variable, must be seen as a fundamental permissive cause that either allows or (generally) prevents a certain kind of behavior from occurring. A system that lacks rules and is unordered is going to have few ways of resolving issues, forcing actors to rely on unilateral actions. During certain periods and in certain regions, the lack of order in the system along with a realist culture has permitted war to occur. However, since this structure has been constant for all actors within certain periods, it cannot explain why most dyads have not been engaged in constant warfare. A structure may encourage war, but specific wars are brought about by the long-term interstate interactions and domestic effects outlined in Chapters 5 and 6. These interactions are characterized by unilateral actions, but even their use is not a sufficient condition of war. Rather, they must be seen as putting actors on a course, where in the presence of the right kinds of issues, states take steps that produce the domestic political environments and increased hostility that are congenial to the kinds of crises that trigger war.

No global institutional context in and of itself can cause war, but certain global institutional contexts can eliminate the conditions in which disputes and practices related to war become ingrained and highly

[10] States and regions that suffer highly costly wars may develop a negative attitude against war in general, which can raise their provocation threshold (see Mueller, 1989).

functional. The importance of the kind of structure a peace system establishes for maintaining peace cannot be overestimated. The structure of the system determines how long war can be delayed and the type of war that will predominate. Some peace settlements structure the system so as to reduce the probability of future war. A structure that has one kind of disposition of stakes, rules and practices, and distribution of capability is likely to have a different war profile from a peace settlement that structures these factors in a different manner. In working political systems, war is avoided for a long time or highly restrained and ritualized. Learning why some post-war systems fail can help us uncover the flaws within a political structure that might be avoided in constructing a new peace system.

Peace is not simply a negative phenomenon, but the active creation of relationships that permit actors to contend over issues whose resolution will enhance or harm their value satisfaction. Nations not only learn how to go to war; nations also learn how to construct a peace. Just as there is a culture of war that shapes behavior, so too is there a culture of peace that guides relations. If peace is to be maintained among equals, then institutions for resolving issues must be created and non-violent ways of contending for stakes must be learned. With the decline of Soviet–American rivalry and the emergence of a post-Cold War era, it is now politically possible to utilize some of these insights to construct a theoretically sound peace for the twenty-first century.

9

Conclusion: Solving the Puzzle of War

> Before something is understood, it appears both more complex and simpler than it actually is.

It is now time to put the pieces of the puzzle together. Each of the previous chapters has sifted through the evidence trying to distinguish real clues from false leads. With major parts of the puzzle completed and all the pieces laid out on the table, it remains to be seen if the various parts can be fitted together to make a whole. This is the way in which scientific theory can be inductively constructed.

Induction involves generalization from a few cases to a population. True induction, however, is not confined simply to stating that the findings from some cases apply to many, it involves deriving general principles from a few instances. It is these general principles that are used to integrate findings and resolve puzzles so that a coherent explanation of the phenomenon is provided. This chapter attempts to provide such an explanation by weaving together the various threads of analysis in the previous chapters into a concise statement of the factors that bring about the onset and explanation of wars of rivalry in the modern global system.

The analysis is guided by two assumptions, one methodological and the other theoretical. Methodologically, it is assumed that there are several causal paths to war. This book has attempted to delineate one of them, i.e. the path to war resulting from disputes over territory and the adoption of the foreign policy practices of power politics between relative equals. It is argued further that this path is the typical path by which a certain type of war, wars of rivalry (i.e. wars between relative equals), is brought about in the modern global system.

Theoretically, it is assumed that war is a social invention (Mead, 1940: 402–3). It is a human institution that evolves and changes in history for the purpose of using collective violence. War is not ubiquitous or random violence (Bull, 1977: 185), but has an underlying order to it. War is a contest of violence with winners, losers, rules, and prizes.

The rules of the contest tell political actors the reasons for which they can go to war, and how it should be conducted. The rules are derived from the practice of war and the discourse associated with it. War is one of several practices available to states and as such must be understood within the context of the larger social construction of reality within which it is embedded. To understand why war is brought about, it is necessary to understand why, of the numerous practices available to states, war is selected.

The Onset of War

War is an act of force that parties learn to use in certain circumstances. So, to explain war, one must identify the circumstances under which parties feel compelled to resort to violent force. Such circumstances will vary with the cultural traditions of an historical period. Nevertheless, within these social constructions, some patterns emerge depending on the type of war.[1]

In the modern global system, war among equals has followed the failure of power politics to settle certain highly salient issues, and the resort to power politics has followed the failure of the global political system to provide mechanisms that could decide issues authoritatively without the threat or use of force. To understand why war occurs, it is necessary to understand what kinds of issues are most prone to the use of force and violence (the underlying causes) and how these issues might be handled differently (the proximate causes) depending on the structure of the global political system.

Underlying causes

Of all the possible issues states can fight over, the evidence overwhelmingly indicates that issues involving territory, especially territorial contiguity, are the main ones prone to collective violence. It is remarkable how many interstate wars (regardless of type) from 1816 to 1980 involve states that are neighbors (i.e. contiguous or indirectly contiguous because of water). These findings provide more than a strong hint that war is intimately connected with struggles over contiguous territory.

---

[1] Since the purpose of this chapter is to outline the overall theoretical argument of the book, citations of evidence and specific historical examples, which have been provided in each chapter, will not be repeated here. A detailed formal summary of the argument with citations to each chapter is provided in the propositional inventory in the Appendix.

In this analysis, territory is seen as a general underlying cause of war. Geographical proximity provides an opportunity for war only because humans, as other animals, have a tendency to demark and protect their territory, if necessary. This means that it is probable that disputes over where one's territory ends and another's begins will arise at some point in the history of two states and, depending on how the issue is treated, war can result. Unlike most other questions that arise between states, territorial contiguity is a highly sensitive issue, which under the right conditions can lead to the use of violence. There must be a reason why human collectivities are more prepared to fight and kill over territory, especially contiguous territory, than over any other issue.

The predisposition to kill over territory cannot be explained fully without taking cognizance of the similarity of this behavior to the behavior of other territorial animals. This does not mean that war is inevitable or automatic. What it does mean is that when it comes to territorial contiguity, humans are predisposed to *learn* to deal with this situation by using aggression and, if need be, violence. It is highly likely that not only have ideas about war and violence been selected out by the history of warfare, but so has a genetic inheritance that predisposes people toward violence primarily when facing only certain kinds of situations. Violent behavior, like all "human behavior[,] is the product of an active interplay between genetically programmed proclivities, on one hand, and environmental situations and stimuli, on the other" (Somit, 1990: 569).

How and whether humans kill is learned; a proclivity is not the same as a "drive" or instinct. All that is being said here is that of the various sources of conflict giving rise to the threat or use of force, territorial disputes are the most likely to result in war if other means are unable to resolve the issue. Whether war will result or whether other means are available depends on other variables, including the dominant social constructions of a period.

Nevertheless, because there is a tendency to fight rather than give in over questions of territorial contiguity, it is likely that the use of power politics as a coercive instrument will fail, since if one side attempts to gain territory through the use of force, that attempt will be resisted. The failure of power politics between equals usually results in war. In this manner, disputes over territory, especially territorial contiguity, can be seen as the underlying cause of war. They are the intractable issues that drive political actors from one step to war to the next.

Assuming some tendency toward territoriality in human collectivities, it can be posited (all other factors being equal) that any two states

318   THE ONSET AND EXPANSION OF WARS OF RIVALRY

next to each other will use aggressive displays to establish a border in an area where they both have frequent contact. If all other things were equal, one would expect aggression in some form to occur between all contiguous states. Since all things are not equal, sometimes border areas have characteristics that do not provoke aggression. These instances of peace would be likely to occur where natural frontiers, like high mountain ranges, bodies of water, or desert form a border. In addition, areas that are not inhabited or are seen as having little value, and therefore act as a kind of buffer zone, would not be subject to aggressive displays. All other contiguous areas would be seen as a potential source of some conflict.

The tendency to see territory as something important is not unrelated to the fact that territory for most animals is the basis of securing a livelihood. Where territory is not perceived to have this relationship, either because the social and economic organization does not depend on fixed territory (as with nomads) or there is an abundance of game as in certain hunter-gathering societies, territorial concerns will not be as salient. In the modern global system this has usually not been the case, so territory has been a major focus of contention.

How violent that contention will be and whether it will produce wars depends very much on the nature of the interactions that take place. If political actors use force and violence to gain territory and establish borders, as was typically the case in Europe and the Mediterranean, then wars will be frequent, because any change in power (either a decline in one side or a rise in the other) will be used to redress the status quo. A power transition will be even more likely to intensify conflict. Indeed, much of the power politics thinking and the perception that the world is a struggle for power probably stemmed from this historical experience. The error in realist thinking is to assume from this experience that there is a constant struggle for power operating, when in fact there may be only a struggle over contiguous territory. Once the struggle over contiguous territory is resolved, the probability of armed conflict may go way down.

Most struggles over contiguous territory do eventually get resolved, and how they are resolved is very predictive of future wars. If leaders of relatively equal states attempt to deal with territorial disputes by engaging in power politics, then they will likely find themselves at war. This is because between relative equals, coercion on highly salient issues does not normally result in victory, but in stalemate and escalation. If it does result in a victory, then the outcome is likely to produce an irredentist mentality in which the losing state will take advantage of any change in capability to rectify the situation. In either case, the use of power politics, including war, tends to lead to recurrent disputes.

The major exception to this is when the victory in a war is so overwhelming that the other side is unable to recover sufficiently to pose a future armed challenge. The extreme instance of this is Rome's destruction of Carthage. Victories of this sort are rare, however, and only when a defeated state goes into decline and the victor continues to rise in capability so that they are no longer relative equals does peace emerge (albeit one based on dominance). The Great Northern War between Russia and Sweden provides an example of this process as do the wars between Russia and the Ottoman Empire. Nevertheless, even in these instances, some tensions remain, as evinced by Stalin's attempts to get some consideration for Russian influence over the straits at the end of World War II and attempts in 1991 by the Baltic states to establish links with Sweden while still within the USSR.

Victory in war is more apt to lead to peace if it is coupled with an attempt to reach an accommodative solution with the defeated party or to acquire territory that is not so salient to the defeated. Territory that has few or no ethnolinguistic links with the defeated is less likely to provoke future wars than territory that contains people of the same ethnic heritage. In part, this was why the United States was able to absorb Texas in the Mexican War. Likewise, if the defeated party has no historical rights to a territory, it is less likely to lead to recurrent disputes.

Reaching an accommodation with one's neighbor is the basic way in which recurrent wars are prevented and the way in which, in some cases, war is avoided altogether. Although some rivalries that stem from territorial contiguity can go on for several hundred years, as that between France and England, most neighbors settle the issue one way or another. Concerns about territorial contiguity need not dominate the relationship of two states for their entire history. It is for this reason that contiguous states are not constantly at war. Contiguity may be the most important factor in the history of a state, but it is not the only factor that shapes the relationship between neighbors.

Nevertheless, how the border is established will have a long-lasting effect. The best way to peace, as Burton (1984) points out, is through some negotiated settlement that tries to accommodate the mutual needs of both parties. Of course, reaching such a settlement is much easier when scarcity is not a factor and the area in question does not have characteristics that make it prone to the use of violence (such as overlapping ethnolinguistic links and the absence of natural frontiers). Between equals, negotiated settlements can often be reached through the creation of buffer zones.

Of course, negotiation need not be bilateral. Frequently the most effective settlements involve third party intervention or the imposition of borders by a concert of the most powerful states in the system. When the latter occurs, it is an example of how a peace system, whether it be regional or global, can provide a structure that is able to control war or prevent it by providing alternative mechanisms or a set of rules of the game for settling disputes and resolving conflicts. Examples of such instances are the conference at Berlin in 1884–85 avoiding possible war in Africa between colonizing states by adopting the principle of effective occupation to establish a claim on the coast, and in the contemporary era the insistence of the Organization of African Unity (OAU) that colonial boundaries not be changed, which has been seen as avoiding a host of disputes.

Territorial contiguity need not lead to war, but it can and often does set off processes that result in war. These processes can be regarded as proximate causes of war. Between equals, the process most often leading to war has been the one in which the practices of power politics fail to achieve a coercive victory and as a result escalate to war.[2] Thus, while the analysis has revealed that territorial contiguity is a sensitive area stemming from both a biological inheritance and economic needs, it is not so deterministic that changes in structure (which close off a process) or behavior (which change a process) are unable to make for peace.

Proximate causes

Whether and when war will occur depends on the nature of the global political system that is in operation. If the global system provides no mechanisms or rules for deciding issues, if it is totally devoid of all practices or customs for resolving disagreements, then political actors must rely on their own unilateral acts. Reliance on unilateral acts often means a reliance on force, with war being the ultimate use of force. Such a structure has ominous implications for dealing with disputes over territorial contiguity.

Ironically, the repeated use of unilateral acts sets up a structure of expectations, gives rises to practices, and sets up an order, even under

---

[2] Between unequals, the process is more direct – it is not necessary to go through alliance making, arms races, and several crises. This is especially the case for imperial wars.

conditions of anarchy. Within the modern global system, the realist tradition has embodied a set of lessons about how to act in a condition of anarchy. A rich and long discourse about these lessons, usually derived from experiencing war or traumatic crises, has evolved and has helped select out of the diplomacy of states a set of practices that leaders resort to in the conduct of their foreign policy. These foreign policy practices are not, as realists believe, the only or the best practices available. Rather they must be seen as social constructions that create and institutionalize a "reality."

The reality constructed by the practices of power politics provides a host of channels for the conduct of interstate politics. Some of these are intended to be guides to the successful use of force capable of breaking stalemates. Others are practices that allow political actors to defend themselves from the threat of extinction. Actors have learned from experience the various uses to which collective violence and the threat of violence can be put. From this experience, the institution of war was created. The institution is defined by rules which tell political actors what practices constitute and do not constitute war. The rules also embody an understanding of what constitutes a legitimate *casus belli*, so that actors know what situations are best handled by going to war. However, since the institution of war is based on practice, its rules are never fixed, but constantly subject to emendation.

At some point in the history of humanity, war became a way of attaining goals. Since the goal was often getting the other side to agree to one's decision on an issue, war became a way of making decisions. Because it was an effective way of making decisions, war became selected as a practice of the system. However, it was never the only way of making decisions, and if it was costly, as it often was, it was not the preferred way.

So when a war will break out between relative equals depends on the rules extant in the system. If the system provides a set of viable channels, i.e. decision games and allocation mechanisms, for the raising and resolving of issues, then war will break out later rather than sooner. Global political systems are typically created at the end of a major cataclysmic war as part of the peace that ended the war. The probability of another major war breaking out and how long this peace system can be expected to last will depend on the extent to which the peace is able to resolve outstanding issues and create a set of "rules of the game" for resolving future issues. The nature and characteristics of the peace system are intimately related to the onset of war. When the rules of the game are no longer able to make decisions that satisfy the major states, then the peace system is

322   THE ONSET AND EXPANSION OF WARS OF RIVALRY

beginning (by definition) to decay. As the peace system decays, because of the rise of new powerful actors, the recovery of defeated ones, or the inability to keep certain types of issues off the global political agenda, then the probability of war increases.

War becomes more probable because states rely on unilateral acts rather than utilizing whatever existing channels the political system has for interdependent decision making. In the modern global system, the most effective unilateral acts have been perceived as those associated with power politics. While many of these practices have been overtly coercive, many have also been intended to prevent war by increasing capability. Empirical research has shown, however, that between equals, practicing power politics has not been associated with peace, but with an increased likelihood that war will break out.

While no one act or practice of power politics is a sufficient condition for war, the taking of one act usually increases insecurity and hostility, leading to counter-measures, which then lead to the taking of other steps that bring the parties even closer to war. Typically, the realist road to war begins with a situation that portends the use of force and makes leaders concerned primarily with security goals. In the face of such a threat, the realist tradition suggests increasing one's power through alliances and/or a military buildup. Both of these practices, alliances and military build-ups, instead of reducing insecurity, increase it because among equals they tend to result in counter-alliances and arms races or mutual military buildups. These intensify hostility and increase the probability of a crisis breaking out. Eventually, a crisis comes along that escalates to war. Some kinds of crises are much more apt to escalate than others. Those that are apt to escalate have known characteristics and their emergence is no accident, but the product of a long train of events that the decision makers and their followers are unable to avert. Ultimately, one side reaches a point where the logic of the situation makes war the best alternative.

Leaders on both sides are unable to avert these events because they learn from the realist tradition, as confirmed by the logic of the "reality" under which they are living, that when faced with a situation of such and such characteristics, they are to enact certain kinds of policies, e.g. make an alliance, build up the military, hang tough. The realist tradition teaches them how to respond to an opponent when faced with certain interactions. Each major set of interactions is teaching each side that the other is hostile and threatening. The very actions each side takes increase the hostility and threats, producing an upward spiral. This tendency is reinforced by leaders exaggerating threats to mobilize the population and maintain support. This leads to an increase in hard-liners which makes it more likely that the leadership will take hard-line action. War breaks out when a situation emerges which the global political culture (as interpreted by the realist tradition) sees as best handled by going to war. This situation, however, has emerged because of the previous actions of each side.

In the modern global system, the situations that will give rise to war and the actions that are apt to put one in such a situation are pretty much understood. Because history is open-ended and because many of these actions have gamelike qualities, actors never know whether war will really occur, but they do know that war is a real risk.

The causal paths and steps to war are embedded in the social construction of a global society. Put another way, the language and grammar of war is already in the system. This implies that if one were able to uncover the political language of global society, one could uncover the paths actors follow that get them into war. Realist folklore provides a guide to the language of war that is embedded in the political culture of the modern global system. Following its cues will let the observer know when the probability of war goes up. While realist discourse provides some cues about war, and the practices of power politics are often associated with war, neither the discourse nor the practices provide much of a guide to peace. In part, this is because they are more concerned about survival and winning than avoiding war. More significantly, it is because as folklore realist discourse overgeneralizes the experience of war and the struggle for power, underestimating the possibility for peace, order, and cooperation. It is a language born of trauma, and generalization based on trauma is more concerned with avoiding certain threats than with understanding.

Like the language of dueling and of vendetta, the language of power politics will not provide a way to end the war system. The very practices it suggests as a way of gaining peace – making alliances, building up the military, employing *realpolitik* tactics in crises – have been shown to be more associated with war than with peace. There is a realist road to war, and the further one goes down it, the greater the probability of fighting.

To avoid war, one must avoid going from one step to war to another. If alliances are made, avoid military buildups. If buildups occur, avoid crises over issues involving territorial contiguity. If crises occur, avoid certain types of bargaining and try to manage the crisis. Above all, avoid successive crises with the same party. Try to resolve the underlying issue on the basis of a mutual accommodation. The influence of hard-liners in the domestic politics of each side, which is a function of all the previous interactions, will make this difficult, however. If crises repeat and none of the other factors have changed, then war is highly likely.

Wars of rivalry, unlike wars between unequals, are usually the outcome of a process. This process makes the relationship increasingly hostile, and any set of factors that gets the process started in the first place is apt to produce war. It is in this sense that the process, i.e. the foreign policy practices of power politics, is a proximate cause of war – a road equals take before fighting. Although anything that starts actors down the road can ultimately produce war, it appears that disputes over territorial contiguity are most associated with the initiation of the process.

Now that a causal sequence to war has been identified on the basis of an inductive analysis, the next step is to formulate propositions that can be tested deductively to see if they will hold up. To that end, major propositions on the onset of war derived from each chapter are listed in the Appendix. The next section identifies the causal sequence responsible for the expansion of war.

The Expansion of War

The typical interstate war in the modern global system has been a *dyadic* war. Why and how do some wars spread? This analysis assumes that wars involving more than three parties, i.e. *complex* wars, have the same underlying and proximate causes as dyadic wars. What makes complex wars different from dyadic wars is not their initial causes, but that they are fought in a context and under systemic conditions that make them expand and enlarge. To explain complex wars, including world wars, it is necessary to identify the factors that bring about contagion and diffusion once there is an ongoing war.

The two main factors known to be responsible for the spreading of war are alliances and territorial contiguity. Indeed, the main effect of alliances is not to directly cause war, but to make it expand once it breaks out. A considerable amount of evidence shows that a dyadic war fought within the context of a network of alliances is much more apt to spread than a dyadic war fought in the absence of alliances. This means that non-belligerents that are allies of one of the belligerents are more likely to be drawn into the war than non-belligerents that do not have an alliance tie to one of the dueling parties. It must be kept in mind that since most wars do not spread, the probability of being dragged into an ongoing war, even if one has an alliance with a belligerent, is not very high. Nevertheless, it is much more probable than for states that have no alliances.

The probability goes up further depending on the kind of alliance it is and the behavior of others in the alliance. Alliances between major and minor states seem the most explosive. Alliances between these two types of actors have the effect of combining issues and disputes in a way that makes it much more likely that war will spread if it breaks out. Although the precise characteristics of war-expanding alliances may vary by century, it appears that the allies of belligerents are more apt to be drawn into a war if the alliance is a defense pact, if the allies they join are minor states, if the alliance is fairly new, if they are major states, and if they have a tendency to join a large number of small alliances.[3]

At the interaction level, then, alliances act as a contagion mechanism; the same thing occurs at the systemic level. A system that is polarized into two blocs tends to have large wars, while those that are not polarized (meaning they have fewer alliances) have smaller wars.

Polarization affects not only the scope of the war, but also its severity. One of the effects of alliances and polarization is that they can make each side better prepared for a war, if it comes. The result is more battle deaths. Thus, it is probably not a coincidence that just before the two world wars of the twentieth century, alliances tightened, and those wars were quite severe. In this regard, polarization and alliance making probably also help explain why military buildups are associated more strongly with world wars than with dyadic wars. The presence of these military buildups increases the destructive capability of each side, thereby increasing the severity of the war. If, in addition, the buildups make each side relatively equal in the sense that one side is not preponderant over the other, then they probably also increase the duration of the war.

After alliances, territorial contiguity is the most important factor in spreading war. A state that has a belligerent on its border in one period is more likely to experience a war in a subsequent period than some other state. This means that war can spread by dragging the neighbor into the ongoing war or by creating some regional disturbance that makes for a second war. The first is an example of spatial diffusion and the second of infectious contagion.

Existing research has shown that while territorial contiguity is not as potent a variable in spreading war as alliances, it does have an

[3] These characteristics often hold for two powerful competing rivals, which indicates that alliances driven by rivalry are more war prone than other alliances.

independent and cumulative effect (Siverson and Starr, 1990, 1991). This means that bordering non-belligerents do not need to have an alliance in order to be dragged into a war. However, if they do have an alliance, then the probability of their becoming involved in the war is higher than it is for states that have only an alliance or only share a border with a belligerent.

In addition to alliances and territorial contiguity, rivalry itself is a factor in the spread of war. Although there is little scientific evidence on the question, it does seem plausible that wars fought in the context of some ongoing regional or global rivalry are more likely to be the target of intervention than wars fought in the absence of rivalry. Concerns about rivalry explain why major states intervene in a war even when they do not have an alliance with one of the belligerents and are not contiguous to one of them. Rivalry also indirectly promotes the expansion of war because it is a motivating force behind much of the alliance making and polarization of the system that is going on.

Once these basic factors (alliances, territorial contiguity, rivalry) provoke an initial intervention, then the mere intervention of major states makes it more likely that other major states will intervene; i.e. a bandwagon effect is produced. As more and more states intervene, it becomes harder and harder for other states, particularly those trading with belligerents, not to become dragged in, whether or not they share an alliance or a border with one of the belligerents. This can result in a breakdown of the political order, which provokes even further expansion.

Each of these factors increases the probability of war spreading, but none of them individually can be seen as a sufficient condition. Instead of thinking in terms of sufficient conditions, it is better to think of the presence (or combination) of factors as associated with a certain probability that war will spread (as in the probability that rain will occur a certain percent of the time under x conditions). The highest probability of war's spreading would be when all three basic factors are present.

For rare complex wars, like world wars, certain necessary conditions are required before they will be fought. Even a conjunctural relationship with all factors present (the three basic factors plus the intervention of other major states, the breakdown of order, and economic dependence) would not be sufficient, because world wars seem to emerge only within a particular systemic structure. There appear to be three necessary conditions for world war. First, the distribution of capability in the system is multipolar. Second, this multipolar distribution of power is reduced to two hostile blocs and this polarization tightens just before the outbreak of war. Third, the polarization of blocs occurs in a way that gives neither side a clear preponderance of power over the other. If any one of these conditions is absent, world war will not occur. Because alliance making plays a role in bringing about each of these conditions in their most explosive combination, alliances must be seen as the single most dangerous practice within world politics.

World war can be explained as a complex war among major states that occurs in a fairly unusual systemic situation. These systemic conditions are the primary factors that distinguish world wars from less widespread wars. World wars tend to become total wars, because as they spread they inevitably involve contiguous rivals who make the core territory of a major state part of the issue under contention. Once this is done, the major state makes the war a fight to the finish.

It should be clear, however, that these systemic conditions and the consequences they produce are mainly a product of the foreign policy practices of the major states, particularly the practice of alliance making, and not the result of more long-term secular processes. This means that the conditions necessary for world war can be prevented from arising by changing the actions of states without having to alter the more basic economic and power structure.

Peace Research and Cumulation of Scientific Knowledge

Humanity has faced a number of puzzles in its history. Answers have not been wanting, but answers based on a rigorous method capable of correcting errors and prevailing prejudices have not been so easy to find. Because war has such a profound impact on politics and society, explanations of it have been wrapped in folklore, rationalizations, and justifications for previous decisions. Solving the puzzle of war has meant clearing away much of this and developing a theoretical perspective that will illuminate more than it obfuscates. The scientific study of war and peace has spent much of its energy and limited resources testing erroneous ideas. It is not that scientific analysis is unable to explain world politics, but that scientific analysis has been testing an inaccurate understanding of the world (see Vasquez, 1983a).

The scientific study of war, because it utilizes a method for testing, falsifying, and rejecting empirical statements, has provided a body of evidence that raises serious questions about the adequacy and accuracy of realist explanations of war. At the same time, it has uncovered relationships that suggest a broader explanation for the onset and expansion of war. This analysis has sought to construct an explanation of the patterns uncovered by existing research by providing a new theoretical perspective and synthesis. It has sought to literally place *in perspective* the role of power and the practices of power politics in the conduct of world politics.

The scientific findings, sometimes no more than clues, have been the foundation for the explanations given here. Treating these findings as pieces of a puzzle that need to be put together has shown that scientific research has been more cumulative and less contradictory than is widely believed. The analysis has shown that induction can play an important role in the construction of theory, but that induction alone does not give rise to explanation. This book began with the assumption that further progress in the understanding of war and peace required the construction of an explanation of war that was able to integrate existing findings and explain anomalies. The theoretical analysis provided in this book, by explaining one type of war and its expansion, has taken a major step in achieving that goal.

Two major tasks remain. The first is to explain other types of war. The second is to assess the adequacy of the theoretical approach outlined here. In terms of other types of war, some insights have been provided, and the identification of the processes leading to wars of rivalry provides a basis for comparison that may help analysts make inferences about wars of inequality. First, it appears that control of territory has been an underlying source of conflict leading to all kinds of interstate wars. A major difference between wars of inequality and wars of rivalry has been that wars of inequality include a number of wars where the stronger state has been able to project its capability to non-contiguous areas, so that concerns about territory and the economic motivation underlying that concern become more of a focus than contiguity *per se.* To explain this set of wars within the general category (of wars of inequality), it will be necessary to explain why some states expand beyond their neighboring areas. Here, explanations of imperialism and lateral pressure are relevant (Choucri and North, 1975; Choucri *et al.*, 1992). Second, this means that the main difference between wars of inequality and wars of rivalry lies not so much in the underlying cause, but in the proximate causes. Dyadic wars of inequality follow few if any of the steps to war characteristic of wars between equals, especially major states. Identifying what patterns they do follow will be a major area for future research. Third, this analysis has suggested that complex wars of inequality, if they involve at least one major state on each side, expand for the same reasons that wars of rivalry expand. Lastly, how non-interstate wars and wars before the modern global system differ from the wars treated in this book is an area wide open to research. Nevertheless, it is hoped that the conceptualization of war provided by this analysis will at least offer a starting point .

The second task involves evaluating the theoretical analysis constructed for wars of rivalry. As soon as any set of explanations is constructed, this question comes immediately to mind. Clearly, a systematic assessment is beyond the scope of this book, but any answer should begin by outlining the criteria of adequacy that any scientific theory should meet. Within the philosophy of science, there are rules and norms for what constitutes scientific explanation and certain standard criteria of adequacy for evaluating those explanations.

In terms of achieving the goal of constructing a scientific explanation of war, the analyses offered in this book do satisfy the formal criteria for what constitutes *scientific explanation*. First, they answer the question *why?* They tell us what causes certain types of war, and they distinguish the correlates from the causes of war. They tell us what brings about world wars and why these are so rare. Second, they offer testable propositions that clearly specify in advance the evidence that will falsify them. Third, the explanations are generalizable, albeit much more qualified than positivist, or traditional realist, theorists would like. Instead of offering one explanation of all war from ancient times to the present, the analyses posit several types of wars, each with its own causal dynamic that is likely to vary given the historical and cultural traditions of a period. Each type of war is seen as resulting from any of several causal paths. The explanation of the onset of war given here has identified only one such path for one type of war in one historical period, but it is an important step forward because the path identified is the typical path by which wars between major states come about.

In terms of satisfying the criteria of adequacy, it is important to specify exactly what these criteria are. The most important criteria maintain that theories should be *accurate*, be *consistent* with other areas of knowledge, have *explanatory power*, give rise to a *fruitful* and *productive* research program, and provide some *guide to practice* or manipulation of the world (see Vasquez, 1992). The criterion of accuracy is the most fundamental. By attempting to construct explanations, this analysis has been working at the *level of discovery*. Now that the explanations have been systematized, it is possible to move to the *level of confirmation*. If the explanations and their propositions pass empirical tests and are further supported by comparative case studies, then the cumulation of knowledge will advance. Only then will the accuracy of the explanations given here be able to be rigorously assessed.

As they stand, the explanations and propositions are consistent with existing evidence on war. Of no less importance is that by building upon work in the other social sciences and on ethology, the explanations are consistent with what is known about violence outside the field of international relations. Despite the limits on the generalizability of some of the propositions, this multidisciplinary perspective makes it possible to integrate this analysis of interstate war within a unified theory of conflict and violence.

The analysis also seems able to exhibit a significant amount of explanatory power. It can explain anomalies and puzzles that could not be explained before. If applied to specific cases, it should demonstrate great explanatory power. It should be able to predict (before the fact) the process that will lead to certain types of war and explain *ex post facto* the process that resulted in a war. It should be able to deal with counter-factuals telling us how a war of rivalry could have been prevented, or a situation that did not result in war could have ended in war. Whether the analysis is able to fulfill these promises will be an important test of its contribution to our understanding of war.

The more fundamental test is whether the explanations can guide scientific research in a productive direction. The explanations offer a theoretical structure and research program that promises to be progressive rather than degenerative (Lakatos, 1970). To this end the Appendix provides a list of propositions and queries that can serve as a research agenda on the onset and expansion of war. It is hoped that following this research agenda will provide a firmer and more sympathetic foundation to the scientific study of war and peace than realism has been able to offer. Its promise and the test of its superiority over realism will be in its ability to produce a fruitful and productive research program in which findings cumulate and become increasingly policy relevant.

Lastly, the analysis seems to have the potential for providing a better-informed and hence more effective guide to practice, at least in terms of war avoidance, than that provided by realist folklore. One of the main differences between this analysis and traditional realist folklore is its view of what are the most important theoretically significant facts in terms of the causes of war and the establishment of peaceful relations. For realism, the focus is on power. For this analysis, the focus is on how to resolve certain types of issues, particularly disputes over territorial contiguity. To avoid war, one must look at the source of conflict most likely to result in war, and that is a territorial contiguity with one's neighbor. The issue of boundaries, not the issue of relative power, is what will determine the probability of war for most states. Even a very simple solution, like the creation of a buffer zone, can go a long way in transforming a war-prone relationship into a peaceful one.

In the post-Cold War era, the insight that disputes over territorial contiguity might be the most war-prone issues is not without important policy implications. It suggests that pressures for devolution and a resurgence of nationalism must be treated cautiously. It also underlines the wisdom of the early decision of countries freed of colonialism not to readjust borders along ethnic lines.

Territorial contiguity also plays a role in expanding war. Most rivals that do not border on each other but still go to war with each other do so by being dragged into a war through alliance commitments with a belligerent involved in a war that began as a war between neighbors. The advice to advocates of peace is clear: if you want to avoid war, learn how to settle territorial disputes non-violently.

It has long been a hope of peace research that once some of the causes of war were understood, the lessons for peace would be fairly apparent and some might even involve simply being aware of the real consequences of certain practices. This initial specification of the explanation of the onset and expansion of war provides some substantiation for these hopes. A major conclusion of this analysis for the conduct of international relations is that the practices of power politics may help a state to win and survive a war, but will not prevent war. Indeed, their use is highly prone to self-fulfilling prophecy. Alliances are dangerous because they can lead to military buildups and make war spread if it breaks out. Arms races increase the severity of war and make it more probable that a crisis will emerge that escalates to war. Among equals, the use of coercion leads to more coercion, escalation, stalemate, and hostility. There is a realist road to war and it is marked by the practices of power politics. To get off that road one must stop taking the steps that power politics preaches.

Instead, one must construct a different road – one in which rules of the game restrict the use of unilateral acts, one that creates new practices and channels for the resolution of issues and the making of authoritative decisions. Once the paths by which wars of rivalry occur and expand to become world wars are identified, the implications for peace are obvious: to avoid war, block the paths to war and create functional equivalents to war. Unlike realist thought, this analysis makes it clear that peace systems have existed and their characteristics can be delineated. One of the most hopeful lessons of the inquiry is that peace is possible. Peace can be learned. Humanity need not be condemned to living in a world constructed around war.

~

Retrospective Commentary on Part II

Of all the chapters in *The War Puzzle*, Chapter 4 on territory attracted the most attention, and with good reason – it was the most original in terms of its explanation of war. Although others, like Ardrey (1966), had talked about the importance of territory, he had done so in a very deterministic manner. Even those studies within the field of international relations, as recent as Shaw and Wong (1989), were unable to bring territorial perspectives on war into mainstream IR. There was a distinct intellectual bias against biological perspectives on war within the field, especially if they discussed territory and biology. In part, this was a legacy of the Nazis' geopolitical justifications for their claims to *Lebensraum*. Indeed, I worried that including territory, even in the very non-deterministic manner that I did, might lead to the book being consigned to the dustbin.

Nonetheless, I felt territory was a missing piece that I had overlooked. I had basically completed the book and was reflecting on its argument, which was centered on a critique of power politics, and realized that I had written an entire book on war without talking much about the issues that lead to war. This was ironic, given that I had written a book about a decade earlier arguing that issues are the key to politics (Mansbach and Vasquez, 1981). What role did issues play in the onset of war? Were there certain issues that were more war-prone than others? These were questions that I had ignored.[1] I thought again of Rosenau's (1966) pre-theory and his discussion of territory. I held the book back for over a year and worked on these questions; out of that thinking came Chapter 4.

Although I grounded my theorizing on human territoriality and stressed the importance of the life sciences for political science and IR, this deeper theoretical rationale did not catch on. Others working in the area, like Huth (1996b), Hensel (1996a), and Senese (1996), did not pick up on the underlying biological foundation. Instead, the influence of the

---

[1] It is interesting to note that territory is not discussed in the original steps-to-war article (Vasquez, 1987b).

chapter and its companion piece (Vasquez, 1995) can be attributed to two other factors. The first is that it presented new evidence, although very sketchy, that territorial issues were over-represented in wars and in rivalries, and that neighbors fight the most wars and have the most rivalries (see Tables 4.1 and 4.2, herein). On the basis of a territoriality explanation, I argued that the reason most neighbors fight is that they have territorial disagreements.

The findings on territorial issues were new, and the findings on neighbors were interpreted in a radically new way (from the prevailing contiguity and interaction explanation of why neighbors fight). I believe it was this evidence that first attracted attention and accounted for the influence of the chapter. Even today, when scholars want to document that territorial disputes are highly war-prone, they frequently cite Chapter 4, even though that evidence was very limited and preliminary. Its chief merit is that it was among the first pieces of quantitative evidence in IR that territory was important.

The second and most important reason for its influence was the release of the Militarized Interstate Dispute (MID 2.1) data with their inclusion of a variable coding territorial (and policy and regime) disputes. I still believe that if it were not for the availability of these data on territorial disputes, not much would have come of Chapter 4, and what I have called the territorial explanation of war. The coding of militarized interstate disputes in terms of the type of revision in the status quo an actor was trying to bring about by the threat or use of force became a gold mine for testing the propositions in Chapter 4. At the time *The War Puzzle* was released, only a few people knew about the revision type variable, and I was not one of them. Indeed, data for it seem to have been collected as an afterthought simply to make the data logically complete.[2]

Within a few years, data analyses using this variable began to show that territory was more conflict- and war-prone than other types of disputes (Hensel, 1996a; Senese, 1996; Vasquez, 1996b). The data also proved useful in addressing certain criticisms, such as the one claiming that this explanation was tautological and non-falsifiable (see Vasquez, 2000).[3] At the same time, Huth (1996b) collected a data set on territorial disagreements between all states from 1950 to 1990, which provided more data and attention to the role of territory in international politics. Together

---

[2] For example, at the time event data typically coded for the issue at stake.
[3] Having data that showed that other types of issues could give rise to war demonstrated that territorial disputes were not defined in a tautological manner that would prevent the territorial explanation of war from being falsified.

with the MID data, this led to a steady flow of research on territory and conflict. The end result of this research, as will be detailed in Chapter 10, is that the propositions in Chapter 4 have been rigorously tested and supported much more strongly than even I thought would occur when I first set out the territorial explanation of war.

In retrospect, if there is a weakness in Chapter 4, it is that I underestimated the importance of territory. Concern about the bias against the life sciences led me to be overly cautious about following out the logic of territoriality. Even today I wish I had the time to read widely (and even be trained) in ethology and neuroscience so that I could formalize the underlying logic of the territorial explanation of war and understand better the biological basis of violence and conflict. I opted instead to do what I had to do, treat these factors as exogenous. The constraints of my academic career proved too rigid to do otherwise. The challenge of bringing in the life sciences is an immense task that others, following the lead of Masters (1989), will need to take up. The start-up costs are huge, but so too will be the benefits. For example, new breakthroughs in neuroscience (see Rosen, 2005) could uncover the ways in which territorial issues resonate within the human brain. Evolutionary theory can map how we inherit territoriality.

The other chapter that has received a great deal of attention is Chapter 5, which is an extensive elaboration of the original steps-to-war explanation (Vasquez, 1987b). The work on alliances and arms racing had always received a great deal of attention within the Correlates of War project. Now there was an explicit non-realist framework for guiding such work. I was also fortunate to have two extraordinary doctoral students who were willing to work on each of these variables – Douglas Gibler on alliances (going back to 1495) and Susan Sample on the debate over arms races. These dissertations and their later work provided important tests of the propositions in Chapter 5, using new data, which each collected.

Advances in research require not only exceptional students but sometimes also exceptional collaborators and often external funding. I wanted to work with someone who had state-of-the-art methodological skills, so I entered into a collaboration with Paul Senese, who had been trained by Glenn Palmer and Stuart Bremer at Binghamton and had worked on the MID 2.1 data. In 1999, we received a major National Science Foundation grant to test the steps-to-war explanation, including the propositions on territory. After two years of data work, we were able to complete a series of studies that culminated in Senese and Vasquez (2008). The grant permitted me to do what I had planned in the beginning (as early as 1987) – deductively test an inductively constructed explanation of war.

At the same time, a number of other scholars were publishing relevant studies on the steps to war to make, in effect, a research program. Some of this research was explicitly guided by the steps-to-war explanation; some, like that on rivalry (Diehl and Goertz, 2000), was not, but was highly relevant. All of this research will be reviewed in Chapter 12. While this research is not as consistently supportive as the research on territory, it is consonant with the steps-to-war explanation, especially for the classic 1816–1945 international politics era. The nuclear Cold War era provides some anomalies, especially for alliances, but this seems to be due to nuclear weapons. Nonetheless, since the end of the Cold War, alliances again seem to be operating according to the way they are depicted in Chapter 5.

The other chapters in Part II have received less attention. Chapter 6 attempted something rarely done at the time, which was to develop an explanation of war that incorporated domestic politics within an explanation that detailed the role of interstate interactions and the global system in bringing about war. In *The War Puzzle*, I was committed to constructing an explanation that would look at how all the major levels of analysis worked together to bring about war. In terms of quantitative international politics, hardly anything was known about the impact of domestic politics in terms of how it affected interstate interactions that produced war, although there was a body of work in comparative foreign policy related to conflict in general. There had, of course, been important historical work debating the relative influence of *Innenpolitik* versus *Aussenpolitik* (see Kehr, 1977). The German debate over foreign policy, however, often looked at whether internal or external politics was more critical, while what I wanted to do was to provide an integrated explanation that would look at the impact of external interaction on domestic politics and vice versa. The model I was interested in was more like Gourevitch's (1978) second image reversed, although I was looking at interstate interactions and not just the system. To do this, I needed to come up with a general conceptual framework by which to compare very different types of states over time. I settled on the hard-line/accommodationist distinction, because the hard-line/soft-line distinction was in the literature and some historians had talked about war parties and peace parties.

The earliest version of Chapter 6 was written in 1985 while I was on a Fulbright in Yugoslavia and published in Vasquez (1987a). This was before Putnam's (1988) two-level games idea. In many ways, the scheme presented in Chapter 6 presents a more elaborate framework than two-level games – nth-level games would be an appropriate appellation. If I had used the game theoretic language, which is about all Putnam (1988) took from game theory proper, it would have attracted more attention. By the time the book was complete in 1992, I saw no need to re-write the chapter in light of Putnam's framework. In retrospect, it would have been interesting to explore two-level game theory in a more serious vein to see what that could tell us about the domestic–international–domestic linkage. At the time my interest was oriented more toward the role of foreign policy critical issues (see Vasquez, 1985; see also Henehan, 2000). Nevertheless, when all is said and done, Chapter 6 does what it sets out to do – it provides a theoretical rationale for explaining the domestic politics of how external hostile interactions from one side produce hostile reactions from the other side. I wanted to provide an explanation of the "O" in the "S-O-R" model of crisis escalation (see Holsti, North, and Brody, 1968) and the chapter does that. If we ever get reliable data on hard-liners (see Hagan, 2003), then perhaps the propositions in this chapter will get tested.

Of all the chapters in Part II, I thought Chapter 7 on world war would spark more attention than it has. When I first presented it at the International Studies Association in 1987, David Singer thought it was even better than the original steps-to-war article in *World Politics* (Vasquez, 1987b). He liked the synthesis of the Correlates of War findings with regard to large wars. I should have published it then, but instead I held it back so that there would be something new in the book. By the time I finished the book, I had re-designed and completely re-written the piece, so an important opportunity was missed. Nonetheless, the chapter was instrumental in guiding my subsequent case studies on World War II (Vasquez, 1996c; Vasquez and Gibler, 2001). I still think it is a very interesting chapter, and in many ways, more original than Chapter 5. As diffusion models get more attention, I think it will guide more research in the field. My current interdisciplinary work on ConflictSpace (see Flint *et al.*, 2008) that utilizes spatial and network analysis to look at the spread of World War I builds on Chapter 5.

Chapter 8 in many ways is a purely theoretical chapter, although it does review the few pieces of research available on the characteristics of peace. It makes important points about governance and norms and how these make peace possible. One of its key points is that peace must be constructed; it is not simply the absence of war. It also makes the point that peace requires ways of making binding decisions other than power politics. This means that peace should be associated with the absence of power politics. Conducting politics without resorting to violence usually also means that certain issues (namely salient territorial issues) are kept off the agenda. In making these points, Chapter 8 sets the stage for a peace science that would truly study peace and not just the absence of war. We are still a long way from such a peace science today, although we are closer now than in 1993.

One of the reasons we are closer is the research program on the democratic peace, which was just beginning to take off when *The War Puzzle* was published (see Maoz and Russett, 1993; Russett, 1993; but also see Rummel, 1983; Doyle, 1986; Maoz and Abdolali, 1989). The biggest lacuna in Chapter 8 is my failure to take account of the democratic peace (as my colleague James Lee Ray has pointed out on several occasions) and its implications for the territorial explanation of war and the steps to war. Since then that has been corrected (see Chapters 10 and 11). It turns out that the absence of territorial disputes and infrequent use of power politics between democratic states are important factors for understanding why they are at peace.

As will be seen in the last part of the book, much research on the steps to war has been completed, but the process has been slow. As a field, we have made the progress we have because we have moved beyond the model of relying on a single scholar discovering the causes of war to a community of scholars collecting and using scientific data to crack the problem. This effort is still inhibited by the current university structure that prevents us from working collectively full time on the causes of war and the conditions of peace. Shortly after World War II, Harold Guetzkow (1950) made a proposal for an institute that would engage in long-range research to prevent the kind of war that had just been fought. The proposal was not funded, but that is precisely the kind of institute(s) that we need now to make more headway. Full-time researchers, properly funded, interacting with each other (and graduate students), will make our progress not only more rapid but more likely to generate conceptual and empirical breakthroughs. The Correlates of War project under David Singer was the closest we as a field have ever gotten to such an institute. As the data collection phase of that project becomes more institutionalized, we need to think more about how to build an institutional structure to create the time and space our community of scholars needs to uncover the "causes" of war. If there had been such an institute, it would not have taken fifteen years to conduct the research reported in the last two chapters of this book.

III

Findings on the Steps to War, 1994–2008

10

Research Findings on Territory, War, Peace

Facts then theory then back to facts again, and so on and so forth, until you get at the truth.

The War Puzzle (Vasquez, 1993) was born in an intellectual milieu that was still dominated by the realist paradigm, which had held sway since the end of World War II. It seemed like it would continue to hold sway no matter what sorts of criticisms were leveled at it. At the same time, there had emerged a body of research findings spearheaded by the Correlates of War project about the factors associated with the onset of war. These findings, while often, but not always, growing out of realist hunches about the causes of war, were far from consistent, rather incomplete, and in need of a coherent theoretical explanation, whether it be realist or not. *The War Puzzle* was a conscious attempt to explain these findings from a non-realist perspective, that while built on realist insights, rejected the core assumptions of the realist paradigm, in particular the importance of power for explaining politics and war. When the dominant theory of a field is fundamentally flawed, then facts take on new meaning. They suddenly become puzzles that need to be put together and explained. This was the intellectual climate when *The War Puzzle* was written.

The explanation of war constructed in this book was based on an inductive strategy that synthesized the existing findings of the time, although as stated in the Introduction, no construction of theory is ever purely inductive. Once this was completed, the focus turned to a deductive testing of the hypotheses derived from the theory. The fifteen years or so since the publication of this book have been quite fruitful in terms of testing some of the central propositions it laid out. This chapter and the next will review that research and provide an assessment of what these "new facts" tell us about the adequacy of the steps-to-war explanation. The first two sections of this chapter will review the work on territory and war and then territory and peace. The next chapter will review the findings on power politics and war. The last section of each chapter will provide a review of the patterns delineated and an overall assessment of the explanation in light of the research to date.

One of the key problems in testing an explanation that has been inductively constructed is that, in order to be properly tested, it must employ a body of data and evidence separate from the data that produced the theory. It was fortuitous, therefore, that shortly after the book was published, the Correlates of War project released the long-awaited militarized interstate dispute (MID) data set (Jones, Bremer, and Singer, 1996). Whereas most of the findings in this book, with a couple of exceptions, were derived from the war data (which went from 1816 to 1965) of the Correlates of War project, the new data contained a much larger body of evidence. These data purport to include every instance of the threat or use of force between legally recognized nation-states from 1816 through 1992 (now updated to 2001, Ghosn, Palmer, and Bremer, 2004). These data permitted the peace science and international relations fields to study war in a new way; namely, to compare the few MIDs that escalate to war with the many that do not (see Bremer, 1992, 1995). These data are very different from the war data; they provide an independent data base on which to test the numerous propositions listed in Appendix I.

The research that will be reviewed can be classified into two categories. First, there is general research on MIDs and war that is very relevant to the propositions herein and that typically was conducted independently of those working within the steps-to-war research program and frequently testing hypotheses separate from those presented in *The War Puzzle*. Second, there is the research specifically designed to test the propositions initially presented in the original text. That research was greatly aided by a National Science Foundation grant (SES 9818557) to Paul D. Senese and myself in 1999. Our work and that of several collaborators and the dissertations and subsequent work of several students, especially Douglas Gibler and Susan Sample, permitted the accumulation of a fairly large body of work on territory, alliances, rivalry, and arms races as they relate to the steps to war.

Philosophically, the quality of the resulting evidence from the above research is of two sorts. The evidence from the work that deductively tests the explanation is of a higher quality because it reflects the ability of the explanation's hypotheses to fail to be falsified. Sometimes even work not directly testing the steps-to-war explanation may be of this sort, if the hypotheses it tests are similar to those of the explanation. Other research, however, may simply provide evidence consistent with the explanation, but which is not a product of an attempt to falsify. This evidence is of a lesser quality, philosophically, because, as Popper (1963: 45–48) emphasizes, it is always easier to find instances (and marshal evidence) in favor of a theory than to specify in advance what (in the data) would lead one to reject a theory and then see if such falsifying evidence exists.

The research will be reviewed topically, with an emphasis on what empirical patterns have actually been documented and how these patterns compare to the theoretical expectations originally delineated in 1993. The review will be organized in terms of a kind of natural history of how and why war comes about, with technical details about measurement and research design introduced as appropriate. The main findings will be summarized and listed in Appendix II as a supplement to the propositional inventory in Appendix I, so that the reader can see which propositions have been tested, which have not, and which have passed empirical testing. Within this appendix the main studies that produced the finding will also be cited.

Territory and War

There are three major sources of data on territory and war that have produced most of the findings, and understanding the nature of these data sets will make the findings clearer. The basic data source is the MID data of the Correlates of War project. Within the data, actors are categorized as either revisionist or non-revisionist. If an actor is revisionist, then the revision of the status quo the actor is trying to bring about is coded into one of four categories: territory (one side is disputing the territorial claims of another); policy (one side disagrees with the foreign policy of another on a particular point); regime (one side is trying to topple the government or leadership of a state from power or is challenging its legitimacy); or a miscellaneous "other" category (Jones, Bremer, and Singer, 1996: 178). These demands for revision must be made by officials of the state and must be made prior to the threat or use of force. Only demands coupled with the threat or use of militarized force are recorded.

This last requirement is what separates the MID data from the other two main data sets – Huth's (1996b) and Huth and Allee's (2002) data on territorial claims and the ICOW (Issue Correlates of War) issue data (see Hensel, 2001; Hensel et al., 2008). Both the Huth and ICOW data record territorial claims made by one state on another regardless of whether they are coupled with the threat or use of force. The Huth (1996b) data were originally collected from 1950 to 1990 and now go back to 1919 (see Huth and Allee, 2002). Huth is primarily interested in the different types of territorial disagreements between states and codes them as either strategic, economic, or involving ethnic questions (including national unification). His data are useful primarily for looking at the conflict propensity of different types of territorial issues, rather than comparing the war-proneness of territorial issues with that of non-territorial issues.[1]

The ICOW data are similar to the Huth data in that they include disagreements that do not resort to the threat or use of force; however, they are broader both in the types of issues and their temporal domain. In principle, the ICOW data set could include all issue disagreements between nation-states; however, such an effort would take an enormous amount of resources and time. Hensel (2001: 90–94) has instead started with all territorial disagreements, subsuming Huth's data, but going back to 1816 so as to be compatible with the rest of the Correlates of War data (see also www.paulhensel.org/icow.html).

The data set also includes two other types of issues: maritime issues and river claims. As of this writing, the territorial issue data are completed only for the Western Hemisphere and Western Europe (including the Nordic countries), with the Middle East almost complete. The maritime issues and river claims data cover the same regions, but only for 1900–2001 (Hensel *et al.*, 2008: 127–28).

What does the research on these three data sets tell us about territory and conflict? In general, this research has shown that territory is a key to understanding war and perhaps peace. The resort to war is often the culmination of conflict that has gone on for some time, and territorial disagreements are an important source of conflict that ends in war. The mere presence of territorial issues between states increases the likelihood that they will resort to the threat or use of force in the form of a militarized interstate dispute. The presence of a territorial issue increases the likelihood of any MID and not just a territorial MID. This provides evidence that territorial issues are special. Humans are more likely to resort to a use of force to try to settle them.

The research supporting these conclusions is based on an analysis of the 1919–95 period, using Huth's territorial claim data for the entire

---

[1] Huth calls his data territorial disputes; however, in order to distinguish them from the Militarized Interstate Dispute data and to emphasize that his data include variables prior to the rise of MIDs, I and others often refer to Huth's data as territorial claims or issue data.

world. Data for the entire world prior to 1919 are not yet available. Once the ICOW data for territorial issues are completed, these will make a replication test possible to further test the proposition that the presence of territorial claims increases the likelihood of MIDs. A major test was conducted by Senese and Vasquez (2003; 2008: ch. 3); they find that in any given year, a dyad (i.e. a pair of states) in the absence of any territorial claim has a .0011 probability of having a MID, but this increases to .0085 if they have a territorial disagreement in that year.[2] Although these numbers are small, as one would expect for the probability of any two states having a MID in any given year, this does reflect an almost eight times increase in the probability of having a MID. The relationship between a territorial claim and having a MID is statistically significant and the difference between the .0085 and .0011 is statistically significant (see Senese and Vasquez, 2008: Tables 3.2 and 3.3, 92, 97).

The finding implies that once a pair of states has a territorial disagreement, this contention is apt to so sour relations that they are prone to have a MID on any issue. Chances are, however, that they will eventually resort to the threat or use of force on the territorial issue over which they are contending. Indeed, Colaresi, Rasler, and Thompson (2007: 253) find that 92.6 percent of Huth and Allee's (2002) cases of territorial disagreements have a MID. We also know that territorial MIDs are more apt to be reciprocated (Hensel and Diehl, 1994; Hensel, 1996a). Once dyads have a territorial MID, they have taken a major step toward war, since we know that territorial disputes (MIDs) tend to recur (Hensel, 1994, 1996a, 1998). Hensel (1998: 197–98), looking at all dyads and their MIDs from 1816 to 1992, finds that the odds of territorial disputes recurring are twice as high (1.9 odds ratio) as for a non-territorial dispute.

This is important because the steps-to-war explanation posits that any issue that festers is apt to evince an increase in escalation as crises repeat (see Chapter 5 and proposition 36 [see Appendix I, herein] and the finding by Leng, 1983). What we now know that was not fully documented in the early 1990s is that disputes that recur are highly likely to escalate to war (see the findings on rivalry below). Because territorial disputes have a propensity to recur and presumably to fester, they are more likely to eventually escalate to war.

---

[2] This finding is produced by conducting a two-stage probit analysis using dyad-year data. The 2008 study uses updated MID (3.02) data to extend the earlier study from 1992 through 1995. The reported predicted probabilities can be found in Senese and Vasquez (2008: Table 3.3, 97).

States that have recurring MIDs are classified, by definition, as enduring rivals (Diehl and Goertz, 2000; see also Wayman and Jones, 1991). If territorial MIDs are apt to recur, as Hensel (1994, 1998) finds, then states contending over territorial disputes are more apt to become rivals than states contending over other types of questions. If territory is a source of interstate rivalry, a proposition initially posited in Chapter 4 and proposition 11, herein, that would underline the importance of territory for understanding international politics. Some indirect evidence that territorial disputes are responsible for rivalry was presented in Chapter 4: Table 4.2c. Since there were no data on territorial disputes *c.* 1992, the analysis in Chapter 4 assumes that most confrontations between neighbors will be over territorial issues. Assuming that neighbors are disagreeing about their borders, it was predicted that this will lead to repeated confrontations, which means that the list of interstate rivals compiled by Wayman and Jones (1991) should be dominated by neighbors. This was found to be the case.

This evidence was presented in Chapter 4 as suggestive and preliminary, merely to show that the idea that territoriality could be at the heart of international politics might be plausible. Since 1993, the proposition that states that contend over territory through the threat or use of force are more apt to become enduring rivals compared to states that resort to MIDs over other questions has been more rigorously tested. Using a standard measure of enduring rivalry as the presence of six or more MIDs within a twenty-year span (Goertz and Diehl, 1992), Vasquez and Leskiw (2001) show that dyads that have at least 25 percent of their MIDs over territory have a statistically significant greater likelihood of becoming enduring rivals than those that have fewer than 25 percent of their MIDs over territory.[3] Using a different research design, Tir and Diehl (2002: 274) get a similar result showing that enduring rivals tend to be those that have territorial MIDs.[4] Both these studies provide evidence to show that the origin of interstate rivalry lies in territorial disputes. Interestingly, Huth (1996a) finds that territorial issues involving ethnic questions are more likely to give rise to rivalries. Rasler and Thompson (2000) and Colaresi, Rasler, and Thompson (2007: 79–80, 188) also recognize the prevalence

---

[3] Using a 50 percent threshold does not change the result; in other words, dyads that have under 50 percent of their MIDs on territorial questions are less likely to become enduring rivals than dyads that have at least 50 percent of their MIDs over territory.

[4] They find that 81 percent of the enduring rivals have one or more territorial MIDs and 27 percent have 50 percent or more of their MIDs over territory (Tir and Diehl, 2001: Tables 1 and 2, 274–75).

and importance of spatial rivalries (i.e. territorial rivals) – which dominate minor–minor states – for international politics.[5]

In addition to recurring, territorial MIDs are also apt to result in fatalities. In other words, such disputes are so important to states that they are willing to use deadly force in contending over them, perhaps even willing to go to the brink of war. Two studies find that territorial MIDs are prone to fatalities – Senese (1996) and Hensel (2000). Dividing MIDs into those that produce fatalities and those that do not, Senese (1996) finds territorial disputes are more apt to result in deaths than non-territorial disputes. Separating MIDs according to whether they have fatalities is one measure of the seriousness with which decision makers are willing to contend to get their preferred issue position adopted.

Similarly, Hensel (2000: Table 4.4, 73) finds that dyadic territorial disputes always result in fatalities more frequently than non-territorial disputes. Controlling for contiguity, he finds that roughly 24 percent to 26 percent of the non-territorial MIDs from 1816 to 1992 result in fatalities (percentages refer to non-contiguous vs. contiguous dyads) compared to 52 percent to 42 percent (non-contiguous vs. contiguous dyads) of the territorial MIDs. This is a statistically significant difference. Hensel (2000: Table 4.5, 74) goes on to compare dyads that have MIDs in terms of whether they also have had a prior territorial claim as measured by Huth's (1996b) data for 1950 to 1990. This permits him to separate MIDs where the parties have had territorial issues on the agenda from where they do not. He finds that when territorial claims have not been at stake, only about 25 percent of the disputes result in fatalities compared to about 42 percent of the MIDs when territorial claims have been at stake. This is an odds ratio of about 2 to 1, which is statistically significant.

---

[5] Vasquez and Leskiw's (2001) finding that territorial disputes are a source of rivalry is driven by equal dyads (minor–minor and major–major) and is most pronounced among minor–minor dyads. It does not hold for unequal dyads (major–minor). In fact, over 60 percent (twenty of thirty-one) of the minor–minor rivals and 55 percent (5 of 9) of the major–major rivals have at least 25 percent of their MIDs over territory. If the threshold is raised to 50 percent territorial MIDs, the finding for minor–minor states is still robust (50 percent), but for major–major dyads, seven of nine are dominated by policy disputes. Rasler and Thompson (2000) argue that while most minor–minor dyads are spatial (i.e. territorial) rivals, major–major states are more apt to have positional issues (i.e. involve a struggle over power and global leadership). Their scheme is not mutually exclusive, so rivalries can have both spatial and positional elements. In this regard, Colaresi, Rasler, and Thompson (2007: 80) find that all major–major rivals have some positional issues at stake. All of the above findings show that the role and importance of territorial disputes for major–major rivals needs further investigation.

Both these studies show that territorial disputes are more likely to spark a resort to deadly force than non-territorial issues. This pattern suggests that decision makers are more willing to sacrifice lives for questions of territory than for non-territorial disputes. So too apparently are publics, although there is no systemic evidence on this question.[6]

Simmons (1999) provides some indirect evidence on the saliency of territory for publics by showing that leaders (in Latin America) will submit territorial disputes to arbitration in order to avoid domestic costs. She also finds that if the external settlement goes against the country, then the leader submitting the claim may be toppled and/or the country will not comply. Likewise, Allee and Huth (2006a), using a broader data set on territorial disagreement, find that states will use legal procedures over negotiations when leaders want to provide political cover for possible concessions because of potentially high domestic costs.[7] Thus, they find that states will opt for legal settlement when leaders need to deal with territorial issues that are very salient to domestic audiences and/or when leaders are democratically accountable.[8]

Roy (1997), looking at two sets of cases (Russia–Turkey in the nineteenth century and Pakistan–India in the twentieth), finds that domestic politics are important in making states intervene against neighbors even when decision makers do not think their actions will be effective in settling the underlying ethnic issues. He finds nationalism, especially in conjunction with non-state actors stirring up communal strife, and domestic pressures to pursue hard-line policies are critical variables in making these states intervene. These case-study findings are consistent with the steps-to-war explanation that domestic pressures by hard liners play an important role in the escalation of territorial disputes, indicating that publics are sensitive to such issues.

These findings on fatalities and the public are consistent with the underlying idea of the territorial explanation of war that territorial issues

---

[6] Of course there is plenty of non-systematic anecdotal evidence: for example, Milosevic riding the nationalist (Kosovo) card to power. Also, it is interesting to point out that once the Japanese attacked US territory, the heretofore powerful isolationist movement within the US public and the Congress dissipated overnight.

[7] Interestingly, and consistent with other findings discussed in this section, territorial issues involving ethnic questions or a rival are more likely to produce an attempt to avoid domestic costs and seek political cover by resorting to legal settlement procedures (Allee and Huth, 2006a: 231).

[8] This would also account for their earlier finding that democratic leaders are more apt to negotiate and offer concessions right after elections and when they have a large majority in the legislature (Huth and Allee, 2002: 205–10, 293).

are different from other types of issues, and because of that people are willing to die and fight for these issues more readily than for other issues.[9] They are, according to the explanation, seen as intrinsically more salient.

If territorial issues are intrinsically more salient, we would expect that decision makers would resort to all sorts of means to try to resolve them, including non-violent means. In other words, territorial issues (more so than non-territorial issues) should also spark other serious attempts to settle. Hensel (2001) finds some evidence consistent with this claim. Measuring the salience solely of territorial issues (for Western Hemisphere dyads from 1816 to 1992), he finds that highly salient territorial issues (measured on a six-point index) are more likely to engage in bilateral nego-tiations, non-binding arbitration, *and* militarized disputes (Hensel, 2001: Tables 3–5, 100–02). An update of the data to include Western Europe produces a similar finding (Hensel *et al.*, 2008; see also Ben-Yehuda, 2004). The more salient a territorial issue, the more likely that decision makers feel pressured "to do something" about the issue. To the extent that ter-ritorial issues are generally more salient than non-territorial issues, we would expect them to receive more attention than non-territorial issues, but the latter proposition has not been fully tested.[10]

One would expect that decision makers, even if not fully rational utility maximizers, would generally try to settle issues in the least costly man-ner, so that non-violent means would be tried first, all other factors being equal. Hensel's (2001) findings are consistent with this assumption. He also explicitly states that attempts at negotiation and arbitration and ini-tiation of MIDs should be seen as substitutable (Hensel, 2001: 83). The fact that territorial disputes can often be peacefully settled does not necessarily contradict the finding that territorial disputes are also more likely to result in war than expected by chance or than other types of disputes. Hensel (2001: 86–89) outlines a more sophisticated model that tries to delineate

---

[9] Senese (1996) and Hensel (1996a) do not further divide fatal MIDs into those that escalate to wars (i.e. have at least 1,000 battle deaths) from those with fewer than 1,000 deaths. This raises the question of whether the relationship between territorial disputes and fatalities is merely a function of the fact that territorial MIDs are more apt to go to war.

[10] Hensel *et al.* (2008: 132) compare salient territorial claims with salient maritime issues and river claims to see if the former are generally more prone to MIDs, but the measures of salience are not fully comparable even though they have made important progress in measuring salience. For example, we cannot be sure that territory that has a permanent population is as salient as a river used for navigation. Likewise, Hensel *et al.* (2008: 131) explicitly state that "a river claim with a salience score of six … is not necessarily more salient overall than a territorial claim with a salience score of six." Also there are no data yet on regime or policy claims.

and explain the conditions under which states with territorial issues will resort to a particular settlement procedure. The model explicitly recognizes that the failure of peaceful attempts to settle the issue can give rise to a resort to force (MIDs) (see also proposition 40, herein) and the failure of war to settle the issue is likely to lead to a return to the use of peaceful settlement attempts. This last finding implies that the relationship between non-violent and violent settlement procedures is better characterized as a pattern of "sequencing" rather than "substitutability"[11] in that the selection of settlement techniques is governed by their success.[12]

At the same time it is important to note that Hensel (2001) finds that salient territorial claims are less likely to be submitted to arbitration than they are to be negotaited bilaterally or subject to the use of force (i.e. a MID). This underlines that salient territorial claims are different. Mitchell and Hensel (2007) add a bit more evidence in this regard. In a general analysis of territorial, maritime, and river claims within the Western Hemisphere, they find that the active involvement of an international institution increases the likelihood of compliance with an agreement, especially if the parties have agreed to binding arbitration. Likewise, just having shared membership in inter-government organizations (IGOs) increases compliance, although not as much as the active involvement of an international organization (IO). Nonetheless, they also find that this relationship and the likelihood of reaching an agreement in the first place are negatively related to the salience of the issue (territorial claims are often salient). A specification of the non-compliance cases shows that some very famous territorial claims are associated with failing to live up to an agreement once it is made; these cases include Chaco, Patagonia, Beagle Channel, Falklands, even the El Chamizal dispute between the USA and Mexico. Indeed, seven of the eight non-compliance cases of binding agreement made by third party (non-IOs) are territerial (Mitchell and Hensel, 2007: 733). These findings are consistent with those of Simmons (1999) that even when agreements are made over territorial claims they may be broken if the issue is very salient to domestic publics.

[11] This point in general terms is taken from Todd Allee, comments made at a talk at the University of Illinois at Urbana-Champaign, April 17, 2008.

[12] A sequencing conception allows the observer to predict the order in which different settlement procedures will be chosen; whereas a substitutability conception simply posits that a variety of policies can satisfy the same function or fill a need without specifying whether and how one policy leads to another. Of course, it may be that conflict management strategies are neither sequenced nor following a "substitutability" pattern, but that "states use multiple strategies sometimes simultaneously" (personal communication from Sara McLaughlin Mitchell, November 23, 2008).

Further evidence that states contending over territorial disputes tend to be involved in more severe conflict is provided by Tir and Diehl (2002: 275–76). They find that enduring rivals that are dominated by territorial issues (i.e. having 50 percent of their MIDs over territory) are apt to have more MIDs per year than enduring rivalries not dominated by territorial MIDs. This is probably a function of the fact that territorial MIDs tend to recur, as shown earlier. More significantly, they find that predominantly territorial enduring rivalries have significantly more severe MIDs (as measured on a 200-point scale) than those in other rivalries. In a similar vein, Petersen (2008), using a hazard model, finds that dyads with a history of territorial MIDs go to war much more quickly than dyads without a history of territorial disputes. This implies that a dyad that experiences a territorial dispute will more quickly have its relationship turn hostile and give rise to a war than a dyad that does not experience a territorial dispute.

The above findings delineate three important patterns regarding interstate conflict. First, territorial issues, in and of themselves, increase the likelihood of militarized interstate disputes and of crises (i.e. MIDs). Second, once a territorial MID occurs between two states, it tends to recur. Third, territorial disputes are among the most serious of MIDs and are more likely to be severe and to result in fatalities than non-territorial disputes. All three findings are consistent with proposition 5 (herein) that territorial disputes are likely to go to war and are a source of conflict more likely to result in war than other issues.

The relationship between war and territorial disputes was the earliest of the propositions derived from the territorial explanation of war and has been the most extensively tested. The basic proposition is that territorial disputes are more likely to go to war than expected by chance and more war-prone than other types of issues. The most systematic test of this claim is conducted by Vasquez and Henehan (2001). In a set of explicit tests of the territorial explanation of war, they look at three MID data samples – a dispute sample (whose unit of analysis is the MID regardless of the number of participants); a dyadic-dispute sample (which breaks down each multiparty dispute into its dyadic components, thereby increasing the number of cases, which gives large wars like the two world wars more weight); and a dyad sample (which treats each dyad from 1816 on as one unit of observation and examines what issue dominates its overall relations).

They find for the first two samples that territorial disputes have a significantly higher (conditional) probability of escalating to war than the overall (base) probability of war. They also find, using their third sample, that pairs of states whose relations are dominated by territorial MIDs (i.e. 50 percent of their MIDs are over territory or their modal MID is over territory) have a significantly higher (conditional) probability of having a war than the overall (base) probability of a dyad having a war. In addition, they find that the conditional probability of territorial disputes going to war is always higher than policy disputes (the modal category of MIDs) and generally higher than regime disputes. A logit analysis confirms that this finding is statistically significant (Vasquez and Henehan, 2001: Tables I and II, 128–31).

This study is the first to break down non-territorial disputes into their component categories. On the whole, it is found that regime disputes are more likely to go to war than policy disputes, which tend to have a lower probability of going to war than expected by chance. A further analysis shows that territorial disputes are more likely to go to war than expected by chance in the 1816 to 1945 and post-1945 periods and more likely to go to war regardless of whether the dyad consists of major–major, major–minor, or minor–minor states. In all but two of the tests, territorial disputes have the highest probability of going to war. However, regime disputes in the post-World War II period (for the dispute sample only) and for minor–minor dyads (for the dispute sample only) have a higher probability of going to war than territorial MIDs. This finding does not hold, however, for the dyadic dispute and dyad samples.

Vasquez and Henehan (2001) confirm and extend the earlier analyses of Hensel (1996a) and Senese (1996) that show that territorial MIDs are more likely to escalate than non-territorial MIDs (see also Vasquez, 1996c). Additional studies have in various ways reconfirmed the relationship between territorial disputes and the probability of war (see in particular Hensel, 1996b, as well as Hensel, 1996a). In terms of having confidence in the finding, one would want to know if the relationship would hold if a different data set were used. The most obvious alternate data set to use to investigate this question is the international crisis behavior (ICB) data of Brecher and Wilkenfeld (1997). These data differ from the MID data in that they focus primarily on crises, a narrower category than MIDs, and they include a number of decision-making and bargaining variables absent from the MID data.[13] These data, however, only go back to 1918 (with most analyses covering through 1994, but with very recent analyses, like Ben-Yehuda [2004], using data updated through 2001).

---

[13] See Hewitt (2003) for a systematic comparison of the two data sets; see Brecher *et al.* (2000) for a comparison of ICB and Correlates of War findings.

The two major sets of tests relevant to the proposition that territorial disputes are more apt to escalate to war are those of Ben-Yehuda (1997, 2004). She finds that when crises involve threats to territory, existence, or general conflict over territory, they are more apt to escalate to war than other crises and to utilize violent techniques, although different types of territorial issues and their location will have different impacts. These findings hold primarily for escalation to war and do not always hold for lower levels of violence (Ben-Yehuda, 2004: 97) where differences between different types of territorial crises and non-territorial crises are less stark. These tests using different data sets show that the finding on the war-proneness of territorial disputes is fairly robust.

Another test of the territorial explanation is to look at the number of wars that arise out of territorial MIDs. If territorial conflict is a major source of interstate war, then this should have an impact on the distribution of wars. Vasquez and Valeriano (2008) provide a test of this claim. They classify the seventy-nine interstate wars that occur from 1816 to 1997 in terms of the MIDs that give rise to them as territorial, policy, or regime wars. They find that the majority of wars arise out of territorial MIDs – forty-three of seventy-nine (54.4 percent) compared to nineteen of seventy-nine (24.1 percent) for policy wars and nine of seventy-nine (11.4 percent) for regime wars (see also Vasquez and Henehan, 2001: 131).[14] If a slightly broader criterion of territorial wars is employed,[15] forty-seven of seventy-nine wars (59.5 percent) are territorial. These findings show that territorial wars are the largest class of interstate wars fought from 1816 to 2001, constituting more than a majority of wars. This pattern shows that territorial disputes are not only more prone to war, they produce the most wars that have been fought.

Can we go further and say that one of the most common types of war is a war between neighbors over contiguous territory, as Vasquez avers (1993: 140–41, 145, 310 [proposition 7])? Vasquez and Valeriano (2008) show that, among the seventy-nine interstate wars, dyadic wars and wars arising between neighbors are the most common. The former constitute

[14] Vasquez and Henehan (2001) have similar percentages, but they are based on ninety-seven disputes that go to war. This is larger than the seventy-nine interstate wars because more than one dispute can give rise to the same war.

[15] This broader criterion includes wars as territorial if (1) the two parties' relations have been dominated by territorial disputes even though the specific MID that escalates to war is not classified as territorial (an example is the Bangladesh War), or (2) if the MID escalating to war is classified as "other" but an examination of the case indicates a strong territorial element (an example is the Football War) (see Vasquez and Valeriano, 2008).

fifty-one of the seventy-nine (64.6 percent) and the latter sixty-six of the seventy-nine (83.5 percent) wars. Of these interstate wars, thirty-nine are dyadic wars between neighbors. These constitute 77 percent of the dyadic wars (thirty-nine of fifty-one) and 49 percent (thirty-nine of seventy-nine) of all interstate wars. If one looks solely at dyadic wars between neighbors, their modal war is over territory. Of the thirty-nine dyadic wars between neighbors, eighteen are over territory (46.2 percent) and thirteen are over policy (33 percent). If the broader definition of territorial war is employed, then twenty-three are over territory (59 percent). All these findings support the contention that wars between neighbors over territory are a very common type of war in history, although not the only type.

Although the above findings show that territorial disputes increase the probability of war, are some territorial issues more likely to go to war than others? Huth (1996b), looking at territorial issues from 1950 to 1990, finds that different types of territorial issues have different propensities to escalation to a MID. He finds that territorial issues associated with ethnicity are most apt to produce what we would call a MID; issues related to the economic value of the territory are the least likely to escalate. Strategic territory falls in between these two types in its conflict-proneness (see also Huth and Allee, 2002: ch. 9). Huth shows that the substantive nature of the territorial issue is important for determining the level of conflict it is apt to produce.

Hensel et al. (2008) use a salience measure of territorial issues (claims) and show, like Huth, that certain types of issues are more apt to result in the threat or use of force (i.e. a MID). Looking only at the Western Hemisphere and Western Europe from 1816 to 2001, they find that territorial issues that they classify as more salient are more apt to result in a MID. Territory (1) that involves homeland versus colonial territory; (2) that has a permanent population; (3) that has been subject to the sovereignty of the state within the previous two centuries; (4) that has valuable resources; (5) is of strategic value; and (6) that entails an explicit ethnic, religious or other identity claim, is more likely to result in a MID than those that do not have these characteristics. The more salient characteristics that an issue has, the more likely a MID.[16] This study complements and extends the findings of Huth (1996b) and of Huth and Allee (2002). Using the same salience measure, Hensel and Mitchell (2005) provide evidence to show that ethnic issues, which they see as more intangible, are

---

[16] This study does not break down the individual characteristics.

also more war-prone. This is important evidence that ethnic territorial claims are not only more apt to give rise to a MID, but to go to war.

Ethnic issues related to territory are also seen as crucial in civil wars. Toft (2003) finds for the former Soviet Union that when ethnic grievances are made by groups that are concentrated geographically, they are more apt to result in violence than those where the ethnic groups are widely dispersed. In a study of numerous civil wars in the post-World War II era, Walter (2002: 80–82, 87) finds that groups that have territorial goals are much more unwilling to sign settlement agreements, making these types of civil wars more intractable. Likewise, Sambanis (2000) finds a relationship between ethnicity and civil war risk.[17]

Are there other characteristics of territorial issues that distinguish those that are prone to war from those that are at less risk to end in war? The general conflict resolution literature, as well as the steps-to-war explanation (see above, p. 81; and Vasquez, 1983b; Rubin and Brown, 1975; Bercovitch and Langley, 1993), maintain that any issue that is intangible tends to be indivisible and prone to zero-sum perceptions that make it difficult to reach a bargain. The inability to reach a bargain makes the issue susceptible to the use of force and violence. This appears strange for territorial issues because they are often (but mistakenly) taken as a concrete and tangible stake that can be divided (see Walter, 2002: 82). While territory appears as tangible and divisible, it is often infused with symbolic and transcendent qualities that make it both intangible and indivisible.

Mansbach and Vasquez (1981: 242) provide an analysis of how this happens. According to them, what occurs is that persistent disagreement over an issue, to which territorial issues are prone, leads to an over-reliance on conflict behavior to resolve the issue, which instead of changing issue position leads to psychological hostility. Over time, this leads to a sense of rivalry among the actors and to their infusing the stake in contention with symbolic qualities whereby any given stake is treated not only in terms of its intrinsic merits but also in terms of the precedents it might create for related stakes for which it might stand. Thus, during the Cold War, West Berlin, which was only half a city (and during 1948 in the first Berlin crisis not a very valuable piece of property), was symbolic of all of the western part of Germany, and later of all Western Europe.

Walter (2003) frames this process in terms of reputation effects and sees territorial issues in civil wars as intractable despite their potential

---

[17] Fearon and Laitin (2003) do not, however; but their study seems to be an exception.

divisibility because of these effects. While reputation is an important component, as the concept of symbolic stake makes clear, the process is more complex than that because many territorial issues and certainly the most salient are not only infused with symbolic value, but also with what might be called transcendent value, which involves a further transformation, making a given stake embody certain fundamental (typically moral) values like freedom, honor, identity. West Berlin at some point early in the Cold War stands not only for other pieces of territory in the West, but for the Free World and the democratic way of life. For Yugoslavia, Kosovo Polje stands not for a parcel of land or the memory of a battle fought long ago in 1389, but for the very soul of the Serbian nation, for the heart of their identity – an intangible stake that must be kept at all costs. In extreme cases, as at the height of the Cold War, transcendent stakes are seen as embodying a struggle between good and evil. Such framing makes actors see their disagreement as a zero-sum game and thus makes them oriented to resort to force rather than try to reach a mutually acceptable bargain. From this theoretical perspective, what makes ethnic territorial issues prone to conflict is that they are typically infused with symbolic and transcendent qualities that make the issue intangible and thereby intractable (see also Newman, 2006).[18]

What limited research has been done on the tangibility of territorial issues shows that intangible territorial issues are, in fact, more prone to conflict than tangible territorial issues. The main research demonstrating this is Hensel and Mitchell (2005). Intangible territorial issues (claims) are more apt to give rise to a MID, a fatal MID, and a war than tangible territorial issues. However, in something of an aberration of bargaining theory, Hensel and Mitchell (2005) do not find that intangible territorial issues are less likely to be settled peacefully compared to tangible territorial issues.[19] Actually, the opposite is the case; intangible territorial claims are more likely to result in peaceful settlements than tangible territorial issues. This finding is very similar to Hensel's (2001) finding on salient territorial claims in general (i.e. that salient territorial issues,

---

[18] It is important to note that it is not so much that *conflicts* are intractable but that the underlying *issues* are intractable. Inquiry will be more fruitful if we think in terms of intractable issues rather than intractable conflicts. Certain issues are more difficult to resolve because the issues under contention have certain characteristics, like being intangible or centered on territory involving ethnic claims.

[19] This is something of an aberration because it is expected that tangible stakes are more apt to produce bargains. The tangibility of stakes should make it clearer how a stake could be divided, thereby making the zone of agreement and each side's reservation point clearer.

without controlling for their tangibility, are apt to be more prone to both militarized conflict *and* peaceful settlement. While this finding may raise some questions about conventional bargaining theory and the divisibility of issues (as Hensel and Mitchell [2005] point out), it underlines the point that violent and non-violent means can be seen as sequential (or substitutable) and that the salience of the issue pushes decision makers to get some resolution. Nevertheless, this research makes it clear that one characteristic that separates territorial issues that go to war from those that do not is their intangibility.

The above findings on ethnicity and intangibility mean that not all territorial disputes are equally likely to go to war. From the beginning, the territorial explanation of war stated that territorial issues do not have to inevitably end in war. This is confirmed in the analysis of Senese and Vasquez (2008: ch. 6), who show that most dyadic territorial MIDs from 1816 through 2001 do not escalate to war; in their data, only 174 of 1,012 (17.2 percent) territorial disputes escalate to war.[20] In addition, Hensel *et al.* (2008: 133; Hensel, 2001: 99) show that most territorial claims give rise to more peaceful settlement attempts than to MIDs.

Are there characteristics other than the nature of the substantive issue that distinguish those territorial issues that go to war from those that do not? The most obvious answer would be the processes by which disputes are handled (propositions 36a, 37 herein). In other words, what separates territorial issues and disputes that go to war from those that do not is not only certain substantive characteristics intrinsic to the issue, but also the process by which they are handled. How they are handled in turn depends on the underlying relationship between the two contending states. The *relationship*, in terms of the overall level of friendship–hostility (see Mansbach and Vasquez, 1981: ch. 6; herein, pp. 84–86) between two actors, is the key to understanding why certain disputes go to war and others do not.

The general steps-to-war explanation (Chapter 5 herein) maintains that the use of power politics increases the likelihood that any dispute will escalate to war. Since territorial disputes are seen as more war-prone, it would be expected that they would have a higher likelihood of going to war than other types of disputes when power politics are used. Vasquez (2004) looks at the use of three different power politics practices by states – the

---

[20] This figure is calculated from the MID 3.02 territorial data used in Senese and Vasquez (2008: Table 6.1, 192). If one looks at the number of MIDs that escalate to war within five years, the percentage increases to 28.5 percent (288 of 1,012).

making of alliances, repeated confrontations (that lead to an enduring rivalry), and engaging in arms races. Each of these practices is seen as a step to war, and as they combine, there should also be a step-level increase in the probability of war. Vasquez (2004: Table 2) finds this to be the case. The overall predicted probability of a pair of states (whose relations are dominated by territorial disputes when neither side has an outside ally) going to war at least once in their history (1816 to 1992) is .499.[21] If both sides have outside alliances, the probability increases to .589. If both parties are also engaged in an enduring rivalry (six or more MIDs within twenty years) the probability increases further to .856. If all of these conditions are present and they are also engaged in an arms race, the probability of having at least one war is extremely high: .951.

These tests provide ample opportunity for the steps-to-war explanation to be falsified; instead the findings are highly consistent with its theoretical expectations (see p. 169 and proposition 22). They show that one of the main factors that separate territorial disputes that go to war from those that do not is handling them through certain power politics processes. They also show that combining power politics processes produces a higher probability of war, with the presence of all three practices making war almost inevitable.

Senese and Vasquez (2005, 2008) reconfirm these findings by looking at individual dyadic territorial disputes. Senese and Vasquez (2008: Table 6.3, 197) find the overall predicted probability of a territorial MID escalating to war within five years (during the 1816 to 1945 period) when neither side has an outside ally is .165. If both sides have outside alliances, the probability increases to .486. If both parties have engaged in a series of MIDs (at least fifteen [the modal number of MIDs for dyads]), then the probability increases further to .692, and if all these conditions are present and they are also engaged in an arms race, the probability of war within five years is an extremely high: .921. They also find that when non-territorial disputes (policy and regime disputes) are handled in a power politics fashion, there is a similar increase in the prospects for war, although, as anticipated, the probabilities of war are always lower than for territorial disputes. This means that power politics is a separate and independent set of factors from territory that bring about war (as stated in Chapter 5, herein), a claim that will be more fully discussed in Chapter 11.

---

[21] This study uses dyad-history data with one observation for each dyad over its history, discussed above in the review of Vasquez and Henehan (2001). For a more refined analysis of this data sample for the 1816–1945, 1946–89, and 1990–2001 eras, see Senese and Vasquez (2008: ch. 5).

If Senese and Vasquez (2008: Table 6.5, 204) provide more precise evidence on the relationship between the use of power politics and escalation of disputes to war, they also show that this pattern of behavior does not fully hold during the Cold War nuclear era (1946 to 1989). Here the probability of war is generally much lower, and having both sides with outside alliances actually decreases the probability of war. Territorial disputes, however, still have a higher probability of going to war in this period than policy or regime disputes, but the probabilities are much lower than pre-1946. When dyads contend over territorial disputes, the probability of war is .045 for both sides with allies, but it increases to .121 if they are also rivals. Adding an arms race increases the probability of war further to .139, but while this is in the correct direction it is not a statistically significant increase.

This means that the steps-to-war explanation best fits the 1816 to 1945 era, and that the likelihood of territorial disputes escalating, though still more war-prone than other issues, can go down in certain periods, presumably because of certain processes operating during that historical era. During the Cold War, Senese and Vasquez (2008: chs. 5–7) show that the East–West alliance structure greatly reduces the probability of war. Whether that was unique to the nuclear Cold War is an open question, but their analysis of the few years in the post-Cold War era (1990 to 2001) suggests that alliances are no longer playing this irenic role. The most recent period seems to be more like the earlier 1816–1945 period.

Additional evidence that process is important comes from the work of Hassner (2006/07). He notes that the longer territorial disputes are contested the more difficult it is to reach a settlement. Hassner and Hironaka (2002; cited in Hassner, 2006/07: 109) confirm through statistical analysis that while 50 percent of the disputes in their data are settled within twenty years, only 6 percent are settled in the next twenty years, and another 5 percent in seventy-five years from their origin. Hassner argues that such territorial disputes become entrenched over time because of specific actions that states take that make it more difficult to offer compromises. Using a case study method (with an emphasis on the Golan Heights, but also looking at other cases), he maintains that over time states build a number of material links (e.g. roads) and symbolic links (temples, churches) to the disputed territory. This makes the new border more clearly defined and the disputed territory more integrated into the occupying state. States build cultural structures that symbolically emphasize the religious and ethnic links to the homeland state, while simultaneously eliminating such structures of the competing actor. These material, functional, and symbolic entrenchments, as Hassner (2006/07: 114–18) calls them, can be seen as a set of sunk costs and emotional attachments (which most likely create domestic hard-line constituencies in the new territory and the homeland) that make the dispute intractable. Territorial disputes that have not been physically changed in this manner are more amenable to negotiation, which makes the point that process is important. His recommendation is to settle territorial disputes early before entrenchment processes take over. Likewise, Goddard (2006), looking at the Northern Ireland issue, sees the indivisibility of an issue as a product of the process by which actors, especially during negotiations, legitimate their claims.

From these findings and the earlier findings on intangibility and ethnicity, we know that the processes by which territorial disputes are handled as well as their substance are key variables separating the relatively few MIDs that go to war from the many that do not. Territorial issues involving intangible qualities are more prone to have severe militarized confrontations, including war, than tangible territorial issues. Even though the evidence is limited, territorial issues that involve ethnic claims are also more likely to go to war than territorial issues involving other sorts of stakes. In addition, it seems reasonable to expect that territorial issues with such attributes are apt to recur and become more intractable over time. The substantive nature of issues and disputes (i.e. whether they are territorial or intangible) may very well be related to the processes by which they are handled, although there has been limited research on this question. What we do know is that territorial issues handled in a power politics fashion have a pronounced likelihood of going to war. This body of quantitative research – with the couple of exceptions on alliances and arms races in the Cold War – is very supportive of the territorial explanation of war and the steps-to-war explanation. Given the variety of opportunities for key parts of the territorial explanation to be falsified, it can be concluded that territorial disputes are more war-prone than other types of disputes.

Is it a better explanation than the competing contiguity explanation of why neighbors fight that is laid out in Chapter 4?[22] We now know, based on three separate empirical tests, that the territorial explanation is superior to the contiguity explanation. Vasquez (2001) offers a crucial

---

[22] The best evidence for the latter comes from Bremer (1992) and Bennett and Stam (2004); see also Gleditsch and Singer (1975) and Halvard and Gleditsch (2006: 209–12), but none of these studies directly compares the contiguity and territorial explanations.

experiment to decide between the two explanations. He maintains that if the contiguity explanation is superior, then contiguous states should be more likely to have a war whether they have territorial disputes or not, and if the territorial explanation of war is superior, then states that have territorial disputes should be more likely to have a war whether or not they are contiguous. He finds that non-contiguous dyads that have 25 percent or more of their MIDs over territory have a .730 probability of having a war, and contiguous dyads that have 25 percent or more of their disputes over territory have a .422 probability of having a war. Conversely, dyads with few territorial MIDs have lower probabilities of going to war (.230 and .222 – for contiguous and non-contiguous dyads, respectively) (Vasquez, 2001: 161).[23]

Hensel (2000: 73) has similar findings when he looks at specific dyadic disputes and whether they are prone to fatalities. A larger percentage of territorial MIDs have fatalities whether or not they are contiguous (52 percent and 42 percent – non-contiguous and contiguous) and a lower percentage of non-territorial disputes have fatalities whether or not they are contiguous (24 percent and 26 percent – non-contiguous and contiguous). He concludes that the territorial explanation is stronger than the contiguity explanation (Hensel, 2000: 77).

As Hensel points out, these findings do not mean that contiguity plays no role in conflict. The definitive study in this area is that of Senese (2005). Using a two-stage analysis, he finds that contiguity increases the probability of a dyad having a MID (of any sort), but that the presence of a territorial MID is a much better predictor of war than contiguity, as the early studies of Vasquez (2001) and Hensel (2000) show. Contiguity, then, plays an important role in bringing about militarized conflict (any MID) in the first place, but even when controlling for this, it is the type of MID, namely territorial MIDs, that bring about war and not whether states are contiguous.

This last point raises one final criticism that has been made of some of the research findings on territory and war that utilize the MID data set. At the time, in the late 1990s, it was argued that merely showing that territorial MIDs are more likely to go to war than non-territorial MIDs does not necessarily mean that the territorial explanation of war is correct, because it may be that the factor (which remained unspecified by critics) that gives rise to MIDs in the first place is what really accounts

---

[23] These are conditional probabilities, each of which is significantly different from the base probability of war (.328) in this sample of MIDs from 1816 to 1992.

for the onset of war. Put in more technical language, these critics argue that there may be a selection effect operating in the data that limits inferences. Senese (2005) explicitly tests for this possibility and finds no general selection effect operating nor one that affects the posited relationship between territorial MIDs and war when controlling for the effect of contiguity on increasing the likelihood of a MID.

Another study of selection effects by Senese and Vasquez (2003) that looks at the role of territorial claims as a possible factor making for both MIDs and war also finds no selection effect operating. Again it is found that it is not merely the presence of territorial issues that makes for war, but the resort to force and the rise of a territorial MID out of them that is critical. In other words, it is not territorial issues that make for war, but how those issues are handled. The lack of a selection effect that changes the relationship between war and territorial disputes is also confirmed by Rasler and Thompson (2006).[24]

These additional findings provide robust support for the territorial explanation of war, not only in terms of the sheer amount of evidence, but also in terms of providing a crucial test that supports it over the competing contiguity explanation of war. The evidence from a number of tests has shown that territorial disputes are a major factor associated with interstate war. If territorial disputes are a key to understanding war, are they also a key to understanding peace?

Territory and Peace

One of the main testable differences between the territorial explanation of war and realism is that the former maintains that once neighbors settle their borders, violently or non-violently, they can have peaceful relations even if other salient issues arise (herein: pp. 160–61). In contrast, realism maintains that issues are unimportant because all issues can be reduced to the issue of power (Morgenthau, 1960: 27); for realism, war is a natural consequence of the struggle for power (Vasquez, 2002) and not a function of certain issues.

The research on the relationship between the settlement of territorial disputes and peace is considerably less extensive than the research on the war-proneness of territorial disputes. Nevertheless, certain patterns

---

[24] See also Braithwaite and Palmer (2003), who present an extensive set of tests on selection bias in the MID data and find none regarding the impact of territorial MIDs on several dependent variables, including war.

can be gleaned, although it must be remembered that the narrow evidentiary base of this research makes this pattern more suggestive than confirmed.

The most important pattern is that neighbors who have accepted their boundaries as legitimate have a much lower probability of having a war than states that do not mutually recognize the legitimacy of their borders. The earliest evidence on this is provided by Kocs (1995). He examines the legal status of a state's boundaries from 1945 to 1987, and he finds that when neighboring states have formally and legally accepted their boundaries, as opposed to claiming the same territory between them, then the probability of war is almost 40 times less. Kocs (1995) also finds that once a boundary is legally settled, this has a durable rather than temporary impact on peace. He concludes that interstate war is "largely a function of the legal status of boundaries" (Kocs, 1995: 173).

Using entirely different data, Huth (1996b: 72, 86, 90–91, 182) produces similar findings. He finds that challengers tend not to contest territory (i.e. raise a claim) if it means overturning a prior signed agreement on the boundary. This holds even if ethnic groups are separated and there are changes in the situation, like an increase in capability, that might encourage raising the issue (Huth, 1996b: 79–80, 90–91). Although his data look at prior agreements before 1950, a focus just on signed agreements after 1950 and their impact on territorial claims re-emerging shows that there are 45 border agreements, of which only one gives rise to territorial conflict in light of a signed agreement (Huth, 1996b: 92).

Kocs (1995) also theoretically fits in with more recent work on neighborhood effects. Mitchell (2002) finds that as more dyads in the world become democratic, then even non-democratic dyads begin to adopt the dominant norms of democratic states for settling disputes, at least within the Americas. This implies a kind of tipping point in certain regions and a neighborhood effect.[25] Maoz (1996) sees certain PRIEs (politically relevant international environments) as prone to war because of the characteristics of their neighborhoods, and has recently explored looking at some of the PRIE characteristics as a way of predicting peaceful dyads and states (Maoz, 2004). Likewise, Senese and

[25] Mitchell (2002) thinks of the finding on the number of democratic states in the system as a general finding holding across regions even though she has tested it only on the Americas but I am suggesting that the finding may be generalized to only certain kinds of regions (e.g. post-1945 Western Europe, but not the Middle East).

Vasquez (2008: ch. 8) see certain neighborhoods as peaceful because of their characteristics. The neighborhood, then, can have an impact on dyadic relations that either enhances or reduces the violence potential of territorial disagreements – compare Europe in the 1930s with Europe after 1945. In light of this theoretical perspective, Kocs's (1995) findings may also be a function of the extent to which a neighborhood, as a whole, has legally accepted its boundaries. Gibler (2007) makes a similar point about stable borders (see below, as well as Gibler and Wolford, 2006). For all these reasons, neighborhood effects should be a focus for understanding how peace spreads (see also Gleditsch, 2002).

Gibler (1996, 1997b) also finds some evidence that settling territorial disagreements leads to peaceful relations. He finds that when states that have had territorial disagreements settle them with an alliance, they tend not to go to war. There are twenty-seven such alliances from 1816 to 1980, and only one is followed by war within five years, whereas in general Gibler (1996) finds that other types of alliances are significantly more likely to be followed by war. He also finds, in another study, that when states that are rivals settle their territorial disputes through an alliance, that dampens the rivalry and results in a significant reduction in the number of MIDs (Gibler, 1997a).

Compelling evidence that settling territorial issues also reduces the likelihood of future militarized conflict is provided by Hensel's (2006) preliminary research of ICOW data for the Western Hemisphere and Western Europe. He examines a broader set of behaviors than MIDs by looking at all territorial claims. He finds that if the claim is settled – either peacefully or through war – the likelihood of having any MID goes down. This suggests, consistent with the territorial explanation of war, that reducing territorial conflict has an impact on the general underlying relationship between states and can serve as a foundation for overall peaceful relations. States that settle their territorial issues are not only likely to avoid war, but have fewer MIDs of any kind in comparison to those that have outstanding territorial claims.

What is theoretically significant about Hensel's (2006) findings and Kocs's (1995) earlier finding is the impact of settling territorial issues on future militarized conflict and war. While other conflict, and paths to war, can occur, these analyses show that settling territorial conflict can have a positive irenic impact across the board, presumably by changing the underlying relationship between the two states. These findings are consistent with the territorial explanation's claims that peace is possible and that the settling of territorial issues between neighbors is a potent path to peace. This is a far cry from the picture painted by classical realism, as well as structural realism and offensive realism, of the constancy of the struggle for power and of war (cf. Morgenthau, 1960, Waltz, 1979, Mearsheimer, 2001, respectively).

It follows from all of the above that peaceful historical eras, regions, and dyads should have few territorial disputes (see Vasquez, 2001: 164). The territorial explanation of war would expect this, but realism would not since war and the struggle for power are endemic to anarchy (Waltz, 1979) and major power relations (Morgenthau, 1960). Henehan and Vasquez (2006) explicitly test the non-realist claim for different historical eras. They find that periods in which there are no wars between major states[26] have few territorial MIDs (see also Vasquez, 2001: 164–66).[27] More systematically, their evidence shows that in the 101 "relatively peaceful years," there are only .16 territorial MIDs per year, whereas in the 73 "relatively war-prone years," there are .84 territorial MIDs per year. This statistical evidence implies that the peaceful historical eras from 1816 to 1991 are associated with keeping territorial MIDs off the agenda.

The Henehan and Vasquez (2006) analysis is an explicit test of the irenic proposition within the territorial explanation of war and as such provides an opportunity to falsify the explanation. From a philosophy of science perspective (Popper, 1959, 1963), it is an important *test* and not simply an attempt to marshal instances of confirmation. More in the area of marshalling evidence would be to ask if peaceful regions or peaceful dyads are those that do not have many territorial issues or disputes.

Vasquez (1998: 211) and Vasquez and Valeriano (2008: 200–01) argue that the West European peace that emerges after 1945 is an anomaly for realism because a region that has been continuously torn by war is now at peace. This peace can be explained by the mutual acceptance, after World War II, of all major boundaries between states and the concomitant integration of West European economies to increase trade and wealth. While the acceptance of borders was not the main strategy

---

[26] These periods are based on Wallensteen's (1984) operational definition of periods of "universalist" policies in which major states attempt to develop rules to guide their behavior, and his finding that in these periods there are no wars between major states. The peaceful periods are: 1816–48, 1871–95, 1919–32, and 1963–91.

[27] There are fewer than five in the first three periods – 1816–48, 1871–95, 1919–32 – and eleven in the more dispute-prone Cold War period, but these are considerably fewer than in the pre-détente era.

pursued by Schuman and the subsequent leaders of the EEC, it was an essential side effect that separates this period of economic integration from that preceding World War I (Vasquez and Valeriano, 2008: 200). The formation of the EU institutionalized and spread this side effect by making the peaceful settlement of territorial issues a requirement for the admission of new members. As a result, since 1945 there have been comparatively few territorial MIDs within the European community (EEC, EFTA, and EU). In terms of the territorial explanation of war, one of the most theoretically significant (and overlooked) events for the future of peace in Europe was the acceptance of the German–Polish border by the newly unified Germany in 1990. Without that, despite all the economic integration and the end of the Cold War nuclear threat, Europe would have been back where it was in the late 1930s. The West European peace is a case highly consistent with the territorial explanation of war.[28]

Miller (2007) explores a similar but more general issue – what is it that separates peaceful regions, like South America and Western Europe after 1945, from war-torn ones, like the Middle East and the Balkans? Building on Van Evera's (1994) work, he argues that the state-to-nation balance in a region is key. Where states and nations (self-identifying collections of people) in a region are in balance, liberal theories are more applicable and (warm) peace prevalent, but when there is an imbalance between states and nations, the region is more war-torn (Miller, 2007: 12–13). His in-depth comparative case studies of South America, Western Europe, the Middle East, and the Balkans in the post-World War II period support his analysis.

The case studies are also highly consistent with the claims of the territorial explanation of war, which would see the war-prone regions as those with many territorial MIDs and the peaceful regions as those with few territorial MIDs. The reason the state-to-nation imbalance is associated with war in Miller's cases is that the nations without states are seeking to become states by gaining their own self-governing territory. Without the territorial claim, there would be no conflict. Thus, when the nations and states are "balanced" there is peace, which in Miller's scheme means basically that all the nations have their own states. The state-to-nation balance

---

[28] Mearsheimer (1990) argues that the peace is a product of the external Soviet threat and thus consistent with realism. With the end of that threat, he maintains that West European states would turn against each other, and we would soon grow to miss the Cold War. Although a provocative argument, time has proved it to be false, since the Western European peace has expanded eastward and shows no sign, almost twenty years later, of crumbling.

RESEARCH FINDINGS ON TERRITORY, WAR, PEACE

is merely a proxy for territorial issues and typically territorial MIDs. Thus, the evidence is consistent with both theoretical arguments.[29]

While Miller's (2007) evidence is consistent with the territorial explanation of war, is the latter a more explanatorily powerful theory? The main limitation in Miller's analysis, and that of Van Evera (1994), is that they both use nationalism and ethnicity as the main causal variables and not territory *per se* (see Miller, 2007: 34, 57). This is a problem because nationalism and the ideational construction of national identity are fairly recent phenomena (nineteenth century), and war is very ancient. Any nationalist explanation of war cannot explain pre-nationalist wars, such as the many dynastic wars of the modern global system beginning in 1495. The territorial explanation can, because it is territory and the desire to get and hold it, and not nationalism, that makes humans fight and die. Nationalism is merely the most recent idealization of human territoriality; prior to that it was dynastic legitimacy (see Luard, 1986; Vasquez, herein: 162–63).

What makes territory so important? Miller (2007: 6) argues that those who see territory as important "do not provide a theoretical explanation of *why* [his emphasis] such wars occur so frequently, and under what conditions territorial conflicts are more likely to escalate to large-scale regional violence." Neither of these criticisms is justified. The territorial explanation of war maintains that the underlying cause of war has a biological basis – human territoriality. This genetic inheritance makes humans more willing to defend territory with the use of violence. This tendency is mediated by the particular learned cultural practices of the time (see Chapter 1: 18–19, 32–33, 41–43, 49, herein) of which the institution of war is one. Animals in general are soft programmed to learn some things more easily than others, and using aggressive displays and violence as a way (one way) to deal with territorial competition is easily learned by humans. The proclivity to use collective violence for other types of issues, while not absent, is less likely to be utilized because it lacks this biological grounding. Precisely how this works is left exogenous in the explanation because the topic lies in the purview of biology, ethology, psychology, and the other life sciences. Nonetheless, the reason *why* territory *causes* war is outlined.

---

[29] What Miller (2007) adds that is new is to couple this territorial analysis with an explanation of the role of outside great powers in aggravating or improving relations within regions. Nevertheless, he maintains that war or true peace (what he calls warm peace) is a function primarily of the regional actors themselves and thus the state-to-nation balance.

What political science can provide is documentation of whether territory is a source of conflict that is apt to lead to war and an explanation of how this comes about politically (Senese and Vasquez, 2008: 11). In doing so, it specifies the conditions under which territorial concerns result in war, contrary to what Miller (2007: 32) says. The territorial explanation of war coupled with the steps-to-war explanation maintains clearly that not all territorial issues end in war and that what determines whether they do is how they are handled (herein: 159–60, 162–65). If states utilize the practices of power politics (alliance making, recurring crises, arms racing), they become involved in a security dilemma, which increases threat perception and the risk of war every time one of these practices is adopted. Each use of a different power politics practice is seen as a step to war. These factors are the proximate causes of war in contradiction to Miller's (2007: 20) realist proximate causes (balance of power, offense/defense balance).

The last fifteen years of research have tested a variety of hypotheses related to these steps-to-war hypotheses and found considerable support for them. Territorial disputes handled by making outside alliances, the use of repeated crises to gain one's way, and arms racing are more likely to escalate to war as each of these practices is employed and less likely as each is absent (see the discussion in Chapter 11 on power politics along with its caveats). The territorial explanation of war has not only posited the conditions under which territorial disagreements might result in war, but its research program has confirmed that those conditions are in actuality the key conditions for increasing the likelihood of war for most of the post-Napoleonic era.

The territorial explanation can distinguish the peaceful regions from the more war-torn ones. It can also, albeit after the fact, distinguish the peaceful dyads from the more war-prone ones. In the past fifteen to twenty years, the research program of the democratic peace has documented that of all pairs of states, those where both sides are democracies are the most peaceful and the least likely to go to war (see Maoz and Russett, 1993; Russett and Oneal, 2001; Ray, 1995; Chernoff, 2004). Even when they have major disagreements and militarized disputes, these are often settled through non-violent procedures (Dixon, 1993, 1994; Raymond, 1994).

The territorial explanation would predict that such dyads would be relatively free of territorial disputes. Is that the case? Mitchell and Prins (1999) have conducted an analysis relevant to this question: in looking at pairs of joint democratic states they find that they have mainly maritime disputes and few territorial MIDs. In fact democratic dyads where both sides score a "10" on the Polity scale have no territorial MIDs. Additionally, Huth and Allee (2002: 267) show that one of the ways in which mature democratic dyads keep their territorial claims from becoming territorial disputes (MIDs) is by using negotiations instead. Likewise, Allee and Huth (2006b: 15) find that democratic dyads are about three times more likely than non-democratic dyads to use legal procedures to settle territorial issues (see also Allee and Huth, 2006a: 230). They (Huth and Allee, 2002: 267) conclude that one of the main reasons democratic dyads do not go to war over territorial issues is that they rarely threaten to use force over these issues in the first place.[30] These findings support the claim that keeping territorial disputes off the agenda is a key to peace and implies that one of the reasons democratic dyads do not go to war is that they do not contend over life-and-death issues.

Although only three studies, Mitchell and Prins (1999), Allee and Huth (2006b), and Huth and Allee (2002), show that the systemic pattern found in Henehan and Vasquez (2006) is also present at the dyadic level. A more systematic and deductive test of the irenic proposition would be to see if non-joint democratic dyads that are at peace also have few territorial disputes. Maoz (2004) has produced a list of states and dyads that have never had a war since 1815. He has also measured the rate at which states and dyads have MIDs. Both of these could serve as dependent variables. While Maoz (2004) tests several factors to see if they are associated with these "pacifist" cases, as he calls them, he does not include the absence of territorial disputes. So this would be an excellent sample on which to deductively test the irenic proposition, albeit looking only at necessary conditions.

The most far-reaching set of findings on territory and the democratic peace, however, comes out of the research of Gibler (2007). He finds, looking at dyad years from 1946 to 1999, that stable borders increase the likelihood that a dyad will be a joint democracy and that it will have few MIDs of any kind.[31] His most important finding is that when controlling for his proxy indicators of stable borders,[32] the relationship between joint

---

[30] This is consistent with Reed's (2000) analysis that the democratic peace occurs primarily because democratic dyads have few MIDs to begin with.

[31] In a related study, Gibler and Wolford (2006) take having a defense pact with all contiguous states as a proxy for stabilized borders and find that these allied states (typically in large regional alliances like NATO and the OAS) tend not to have territorial MIDs with each other.

[32] These consist of two sets of variables – geographic focal points that can facilitate the identification of a border (border salient variables) and predictors of border strength (i.e. factors that might affect the continued acceptance of a previously drawn border).

democracy and MID onset becomes statistically insignificant (Gibler, 2007: 527–29; see also James, Park, and Choi, 2006). This is one of the few studies that successfully wipe out the statistical significance between joint democracy and peace (see also Reed, 2000; Mousseau, 2000).[33]

Gibler (2007: 529) goes on to offer a territorial logic for the democratic peace. He states that stable borders decrease the likelihood of war, which over time diminishes the need for highly centralized states to meet security needs (Tilly, 1975b; Rasler and Thompson, 1989). Stable borders and the absence of territorial disputes provide a propitious environment for the emergence of democratic dyads.[34] For Gibler, as well as the territorial explanation of war (see Vasquez, 1998: 383), one of the reasons democratic states do not fight each other is that they cluster in space and have previously settled their border conflicts with each other (see also herein: 160–61). Gibler (2007: 528) even goes so far as to say that zones of peace are a "contagion effect of stabilized borders."

Gibler's findings are supportive of the claim that once neighbors settle their territorial disputes and accept their borders they can have long periods of peace. It is also important to point out that this claim and his findings apply to all states and not just democratic dyads. All neighbors are apt to be at peace if they accept their borders. What Gibler adds that is new is that the spread of stable borders creates an environment where democracy can flourish.[35] Gibler (2007: 529) argues that non-territorial issues are less likely to be associated with alliances, militarization, mutual military build-ups, and aggressive bargaining (i.e. power politics).[36]

There are three border salient variables that indicate that a border is unstable: similar terrain (% mountainous – with many mountains indicating instability, because of the difficulty of drawing a line); ethnic groups straddling a border; and similar colonial heritage. There are four border strength variables: state power or capability (with preponderance indicating stability); length of peace across the border; age of the dyad; and outbreak of civil war within one member of the dyad (Gibler, 2007: 519–21).

[33] Henderson (2002) also overturns the relationship, but there is less consensus on this; see Ray (2003a: 15–16).

[34] Tir and Gibler (forthcoming) find consistent with this claim that settling territorial diputes by peaceful transfers leads to stable borders and democratic transitions.

[35] Stable borders, then, become a key neighborhood effect.

[36] This analysis suggests two hypotheses that have not been extensively tested: (1) that the absence of territorial claims (or MIDs) is associated with less of a reliance on power politics (alliance making, recurrent MIDs [especially escalatory ones] and arms racing); and (2) joint democratic dyads are less likely to resort to power politics when dealing with one another. On the latter, see Gibler and Wolford (2006), who find that states in (typically regional) alliances with all their neighbors (which tend to be democracies) rarely target each other with territorial MIDs (see also Huth and Allee, 2002: 267).

If there is a weakness in Gibler's (2007) data analysis, it is that his measures of stable borders are proxies, although they have the merit of being conceptually distinct from Kocs's (1995) indicators and "harder" data while producing a similar pattern. Nevertheless, while it is plausible that borders will be stable in the absence of a civil war, when a border does not divide an ethnic group, or where one side is preponderant, these indicators do not directly measure the mutual acceptance of a border. It is therefore of theoretical interest that Hutchison and Gibler (2007) are able to test the relationship between territory and democracy using a more direct measure of territorial threat.

Hutchison and Gibler (2007) replicate an important study (Peffley and Rohrschneider, 2003) of internal political tolerance (i.e. of a key democratic value). They find that the level of political tolerance is determined not only by conventional political variables (like democratic ideals, free speech, political interests) and individual variables (like age, education, gender), but also by the presence of external territorial threat (measured by targeted territorial MIDs). The significance of an external international relations variable is not eliminated by these internal variables which have successfully predicted democratic values in the past; in fact its inclusion actually reduces the amount of unexplained variance (Hutchison and Gibler, 2007: 139). However, when territory is included, democratic duration is not significant as a predictor of cross-national variation in tolerance. This study provides separate evidence that the presence of territorial disputes has a negative impact on an important democratic value, which is consistent with Gibler's (2007) broader claim that the absence of territorial disputes is associated with democracy.

Each of these studies from Kocs (1995) to Gibler (2007) provides evidence for the proposition that settling territorial disputes and mutually accepting borders can produce peace. Although it is not tested as extensively as the relationship between territorial disputes and war, all of the evidence conforms with the irenic proposition embodied in Chapter 4 (herein). This is especially noteworthy since the claims about peace being a function of settling territorial issues is one of the major testable differences between realism and the territorial explanation of war.

Conclusion

Research in the last fifteen years has tested some of the most important propositions of the territorial explanation of war outlined in this book. All of these tests have failed to falsify the propositions derived from the territorial explanation. In addition, the overall logic of the explanation has suggested new insights about world politics and history that have broadened its explanatory power as evinced by Gibler's (2007) territorial explanation of the democratic peace.

What has the research told us that we did not know before? The presence of a territorial disagreement (claim) between two states is apt to result in a militarized dispute (MID) (Senese and Vasquez, 2003). Militarized disputes are also a function of being neighbors (Senese, 2005). Neither the presence of a territorial issue (claim) nor contiguity, however, is the "real cause" of war. What produces war is the use of force to settle a territorial claim. It is not territorial issues *per se* that cause war, but how they are handled. Only when territorial issues give rise to territorial MIDs is there a significant increase in the probability of war. Part of the reason for this is that unlike other types of disputes – specifically policy and regime disputes – territorial MIDs tend to recur (Hensel, 1994, 1998).

Recurrence of disputes between the same pairs of states produces a sense of rivalry, and rivalry, even if not fueled by territorial disputes, increases the likelihood of war (Diehl and Goertz, 2000). Nevertheless, because territorial MIDs tend to recur it is not surprising that most interstate rivalries arise out of territorial disputes (Vasquez and Leskiw, 2001; Tir and Diehl 2002), especially among minor–minor dyads (Colaresi, Rasler, and Thompson, 2007: ch. 3). In fact, recurring territorial disputes, even when they do not reach the technical threshold of rivalry, increase the likelihood of war and can have a separate and independent effect from rivalry.[37] In addition, territorial enduring rivals, have more severe MIDs than other rivals (Tir and Diehl, 2002: 275–76). Likewise, states that have territorial disputes are more apt to have fatal MIDs than states that contend over non-territorial disputes (Senese, 1996; Hensel, 2000). These findings are indicators that leaders and their publics are more willing to fight and die for territory than for other issues.

All these patterns help explain why territorial MIDs, once they emerge, are much more likely to escalate to war (Hensel, 1996b) than non-territorial disputes, i.e. policy or regime disputes (Vasquez and Henehan, 2001). With few exceptions, this holds for major–major, major–minor, and minor–minor dyads, as well as across three historical eras (1816–1945, 1946–89, 1990–2001) (Vasquez and Henehan, 2001; Senese and Vasquez, 2008: ch. 6). Similarly, a pair of states whose relations over its history are

---

[37] Senese and Vasquez (2008: ch. 6) find that four or more territorial disputes have a similar impact to six or more MIDs.

dominated by territorial disputes is more likely to go to war than one whose relations are dominated by policy and regime disputes (Vasquez, 2001; Senese and Vasquez, 2008: ch. 5). Indeed, pairs of states whose relations are dominated by policy or regime disputes are much more apt to avoid war altogether (Vasquez, 2004).

Not all territorial issues and disputes, however, have an equal probability of escalating to war. Certain types are more war-prone. Territorial issues that are intangible are much more likely to have MIDs and go to war than those that are tangible (Hensel and Mitchell, 2005). Additionally, territorial issues that are more salient are more susceptible to militarized confrontations. Thus, territorial issues involving homeland territory, ethnic claims, and a long history of sovereign rule, among other characteristics, are more conflict- and war-prone.

Territorial claims involving ethnicity (and presumably all identity issues) are the most conflict-prone and apt to give rise to the use of force (Huth, 1996b; Huth and Allee, 2002; see also Hensel et al., 2008). Strategic territory is also at risk of militarized conflict, although less so than ethnic territory. Disputes over territory involving economic resources are the most apt to be peacefully settled, apparently because it is divisible and provides mutual gains (Huth, 1996b; Huth and Allee, 2002). Similarly, territorial issues involving ethnicity are more apt to go to war (Hensel and Mitchell, 2005, although the evidence on this is still limited). Likewise, ethnic and territorial issues are important for civil war (Toft, 2003; Walter, 2002; Sambanis, 2000).

The substantive characteristics of territorial issues are one basis by which the many territorial MIDs that do not go to war are separated from the few that do. Process or the way contending parties handle the issue is equally important. It has already been mentioned that territorial MIDs tend to recur, and one of the major factors that distinguish territorial MIDs that do not go to war from those that do is that they are the first or second MID between the pair of states rather than the fourth, fifth, or nth MID.

Dyads that handle territorial disputes through the use of power politics generally have an increased risk of going to war. The making of alliances, the recurrence of disputes (and the rise of rivalry), and arms races individually make a territorial MID more likely to escalate to war than territorial disputes that are not handled in this manner. In addition, as each of these practices is added, there is a step-wise increase in the probability of war as predicted by the steps-to-war explanation. The probability of war can range from .16 for territorial MIDs that are not handled in a power politics fashion up to .90+ when all three power politics practices are employed (Vasquez, 2004; Senese and Vasquez, 2008: chs. 5 and 6). Power politics, then, has a separate and independent effect from territory on the probability of war, especially since it also increases the probability of non-territorial disputes going to war.[38] These findings suggest that the underlying relationship between two states is a key factor in whether they resort to power politics and how they handle territorial disputes.

The above findings hold for most of the two centuries in the MID data set – 1816–2001 and 1816–1945 – but not for the nuclear Cold War era. In the latter, territorial disputes are still more likely to escalate to war than other disputes, but certain kinds of alliance patterns, specifically having both sides with outside alliances, actually reduces the likelihood of war rather than increasing it. This implies that in certain historical eras (or systems), the probability of war can decrease depending on certain characteristics associated with that era. In the Cold War, the East–West polarized alliance system (and presumably nuclear weapons) has this irenic effect. This impact, however, is unique to the Cold War, since already in the short post-Cold War period (1990–2001), alliances seem to be returning to their traditional bellicose impact (Senese and Vasquez, 2008: chs. 5 and 6). This means that the steps-to-war explanation is not just of historical interest, but relevant to the present as well. These findings provide ample support for the territorial explanation of war and the steps-to-war logic. Comparing them with the competing contiguity explanation (Hensel, 2000; Vasquez, 2001; Senese, 2005) also shows the territorial explanation to be superior.

What about the relationship between territory and peace? The major difference between realism and the territorial explanation of war is that the latter sees peace as possible once territorial issues are settled. It is much more optimistic than realism, even going so far as seeing power politics itself as arising primarily out of struggles over borders (herein: 161–62).

The research on territory and peace has been much more limited than that on territory and war, but what work has been done is quite consistent with the irenic proposition that once states have settled their territorial disagreements they can have long periods of peace even if other salient issues arise. Research in the last fifteen years has shown that states that mutually accept the legal status of their borders are considerably less likely to have a war (Kocs, 1995). States are very unwilling to contest territory if

---

[38] Non-territorial disputes, however, have a lower probability of war than territorial disputes (Senese and Vasquez, 2008: ch. 6).

there has been a prior agreement on the border (Huth, 1996b). Similarly, if they settle a territorial disagreement and seal that agreement with an alliance, they are highly unlikely to have a war within the next five years (Gibler, 1996). In addition, enduring rivals who settle their territorial disputes see a significant reduction in the number of MIDs they have and an increase in the number of years between their MIDs, indicating a muting of the frequency of militarized conflict (Gibler, 1997a).

Most importantly, if states settle their territorial claims, the likelihood of militarized conflict (having a MID) of any kind goes way down (Hensel, 2006). This means that settling territorial issues does seem to have a positive impact on future relations the way the territorial explanation of war predicts. War and violent conflict need not be a constant feature of international politics.

It is also theoretically significant that the peaceful eras that do exist in the post-Napoleonic era have few territorial disputes on the agenda (Henehan and Vasquez, 2006; see also Vasquez, 2001). In a similar vein, peaceful regions in the contemporary world, like Western Europe since 1945, have few territorial MIDs on the agenda, whereas war-torn regions, like the Middle East, are rife with territorial disputes. Likewise, it is significant that joint democracies, which rarely if ever fight a war, have few territorial MIDs. Instead their militarized conflict is more characterized by maritime and economic disputes (Mitchell and Prins, 1999). Thus, peaceful eras, peaceful regions, and peaceful dyads are all associated with few territorial MIDs.

It may even be the case that much of the democratic peace is a function of having stable borders. Gibler (2007) argues that when states have stable borders war is less likely and this reduces the need for the centralization of the state, thereby making democracy and democratic dyads more likely. He finds that stable borders are related to joint democracy and that controlling for stable borders eliminates the significance between joint democracy and militarized conflict (MID onset). Hutchison and Gibler (2007) add to this evidence by finding that the absence of an external territorial threat in the form of a MID is associated with more domestic political tolerance, which provides further evidence that stable borders are associated with democracy.[39] Gibler's (2007) application

---

[39] Gibler (2007: 524) deals with the question of endogeneity by arguing that geographic indicators of stable borders are constants and therefore not subject to change and that, historically, democratic dyads frequently have settled their borders before they became democratic states. The latter is best illustrated by France and England, but a systematic test of the claim has not yet been conducted.

of a territorial logic to subsume the democratic peace and to account for non-democratic peaceful dyads shows the potential explanatory power of the territorial explanation and in many ways can be seen as a progressive turn in the latter's research program (see Lakatos, 1970; cf. Ray, 2003b; Chernoff, 2004).

The findings on territory in terms of their variety, the opportunities they present to falsify the explanation, and their overall consistency with explicit propositions and the logic of the explanation are impressive. They certainly are much more extensive than one would expect for a new theory that has not undergone any revisions since it was first presented in Chapter 4. The research agenda is far from completed and the new line of inquiry opened by Gibler and the new ICOW data provided by Hensel and Mitchell augur well for a vibrant and progressive future research program. Can the same be said for the research on power politics and war? The next chapter examines this question.

11

Research Findings on Power Politics and War

Power politics is not a theory of war, but a syndrome of behavior that produces war.

Research in the last decade and a half has tested numerous aspects of the steps-to-war explanation concerning power politics and war. This chapter will review that research by looking first at the role of alliances in war, then rivalry, arms races, and lastly the impact of combining the various steps.

Chapter 5 argues that the use of power politics does not prevent war, but actually increases the risk of war. That chapter marshals evidence from the research of the time to make the case that forming alliances, engaging in repeated crises, and building up one's military all increase the probability that a crisis will emerge that escalates to war. Since 1993, each of these claims and the steps-to-war explanation proper has been extensively tested. What does this research indicate?

Alliances and War

Previous research indicated that wars tend to follow the making of alliances and certainly do not prevent war (Singer and Small, 1966; Ostrom and Hoole, 1978; Levy, 1981). The major exception to this is in the nineteenth century, when alliances are followed by peace (Levy, 1981: 598). The analysis of alliances in Chapter 5 (herein: 187) calls for the construction of a typology that would distinguish between those alliances that are followed by peace, as in the nineteenth century, and those that are followed by war.

Gibler (1997b, 2000) has been in the forefront of creating such a typology. Classical realists believe that in the face of threat, states should increase their power, and one way of doing that is by making alliances. Adopting the steps-to-war logic, Gibler (1997b) maintains that alliances that threaten another state's security will not prevent war nor result in "peace through strength" the way most realists would expect (see Morgenthau, 1960: 30, cited in Wallace, 1982: 37–38), but increased insecurity. Threat perception is a key for distinguishing alliances that will have a bellicose effect from those that do not. In a very original move, Gibler (1997b, 2000) maintains that alliances made up of a coalition where all members either have been successful in their last war, are dissatisfied with the status quo, and/or are major states will be perceived by those facing such alliances as highly threatening; whereas those with the opposite characteristics will not.[1] He finds that the combination of these factors does distinguish the alliances followed by war in five years both in the nineteenth and twentieth centuries (Gibler, 2000: 160–62), as well as for the longer 1495–1980 time span (see Gibler, 1997b; see also Gibler and Vasquez, 1998). In the bivariate analysis he finds that success in the previous war and dissatisfaction (albeit using two different measures)[2] are predictive of war. Alliances consisting of major states are significantly related to war only in the twentieth century.[3]

A different sort of test is to see whether any politically relevant alliance that could be used by a contending party to provide support for its position would increase the likelihood that a MID will escalate to war. In an explicit test of the steps-to-war explanation, Senese and Vasquez (2004, 2005, 2008) look at whether having an outside ally while contending over a territorial MID increases the likelihood of war. They find for the entire period 1816–2001 that this is the case (see also Vasquez, 2004). They also find that having an outside alliance while contending on policy or regime disputes increases the probability of war, although not as high as for territorial disputes. These findings hold for both the dyadic-dispute sample and the dyad-history sample (see Senese and Vasquez, 2008: chs. 5 and 6; Vasquez, 2004).

An examination of the specific probabilities of war illustrates the effect of alliances. For the 1816–1945 period, where the effect is greatest, if one compares the same pair of states over their history to see if they ever have had a war (dyad-history sample), the probability of having a war when

---

[1] Those with mixed characteristics, that is, between the two ideal types, will have a probability of being followed by war within five years.

[2] For the nineteenth century, dissatisfaction as measured by Tau B scores of alliance portfolios is associated with subsequent war, but the outcome of the previous MID is not. For the twentieth century, the reverse is the case (see Gibler, 2000: 156, 158–59).

[3] Gibler (1996) also finds, as discussed in Chapter 10 on territory and peace, that a certain type of alliance that does not threaten security, but actually settles territorial disputes, is hardly ever followed by a war in five years.

relations between the two contending states are dominated by territorial disputes, but they do not have outside alliances, is .368. If the dominant alliance pattern in their history (1816–1945) is one where both sides have outside allies, then the probability of having at least one war significantly increases to .532 (Senese and Vasquez, 2008: Table 5.2, 149). The same relationships hold when using a dyadic dispute sample (Senese and Vasquez, 2008: Table 6.3, 197).

The findings also show, however, that during certain historical periods the effect of alliances can change. For most of history (and for the entire 1816–2001 period) the effect of alliance is bellicose, but during the Cold War (1946–89) this changes. The impact is now negative for certain types of alliance patterns, specifically when both sides have outside allies to aid them. The latter is the condition of the main rivalry of the period – between the USA and USSR. Both sides have plenty of outside allies, yet there is no war between them. This case is the most "disputatious" (Wayman, 2000: 229) and a number of other East–West dyads follow its pattern. Again, an examination of the specific probability of war illustrates the effect. In the 1946–89 period, the probability of war between a pair of states (dyadic-dispute sample) when neither has an outside ally is .178, but when both sides have an outside ally, the probability of war significantly *decreases* to .045.

Even though this finding goes against the expectations of the steps-to-war explanation, it confirms what we know about the Cold War; namely, that the US–USSR blocs never went to war against each other.[4] This research on the steps to war suggests that one of the main factors bringing about the long peace (Gaddis, 1986) is not just nuclear weapons, but the singular thirty-five–forty-year polarized alliance structure (Senese and Vasquez, 2008: ch. 7; Vasquez and Senese, 2007). This alliance structure, no doubt in conjunction with nuclear weapons raising the provocation threshold for war (Lebow, 1981: 277), not only makes each superpower more risk averse, but presumably makes them more tightly control their allies so that what would have made a crisis escalate to war in the previous era no longer does so.

While the alliance portion of the steps to war is not borne out in the Cold War, the research on the explanation has helped elucidate some of the processes by which the long peace worked. In addition to

---

[4] The only East–West dyad involving major states on each side that goes to war is US–China in the Korean War, and some regard this as an inadvertent war (see Whiting, 1991: 122).

highlighting the important role of the polarized alliance structure (i.e. both sides having outside alliances), the research has delineated the role of interaction effects between alliances and rivalry and between alliances and territorial disputes. The precise nature of these relationships had not previously been understood. Senese and Vasquez (2008: ch. 8) find that both sides having alliances interacts negatively with rivalry to greatly reduce the probability of war. Again, since the main rivalries of the Cold War are East–West, this is consistent with what is historically known, but the underlying interaction effect had not been previously detected. Even less expected is the finding that there is a negative interaction between both sides having outside alliances and the presence of territorial MIDs. What this means is that even in the presence of a highly war-prone issue (like territory), the polarized alliance structure reduces the probability of war.

Not all alliance patterns during the Cold War reduce the likelihood of war, however. Dyads where one side has an outside ally increase the likelihood of war, as expected by the steps-to-war explanation, under two conditions. When one side has an outside ally and the dyad is contesting a territorial dispute, there is a positive interaction. There is also a positive interaction when the dyad is engaged in a rivalry. In each of these instances, the presence of this alliance pattern greatly enhances the likelihood of war erupting. These two patterns are the major instances in which the steps-to-war proposition on alliances holds during the Cold War.[5]

These last two findings underline the importance of the polarized alliance structure during the Cold War for managing relations and preventing war. In the absence of the polarized alliance structure, which is what one side having an outside alliance reflects, alliances return to their bellicose effect. Why does this polarized structure have this irenic effect in the Cold War, when both sides having outside alliances has the opposite effect in the pre-1945 era? Part of the answer may be that the tight polarized structure – where the two superpowers had preponderant control – was not present for any extended time previously in history. A more complete answer is that the presence of nuclear weapons made both superpowers highly risk averse. Thus in previous eras, alliance leaders either were unable to exert such tight control and/or they did not have such a high aversion toward war. Both of these claims seem plausible from what we know historically.

---

[5] See Senese and Vasquez (2008: 234–35) for further discussion of the varying impact of alliances in the Cold War and its theoretical implications.

Nonetheless, the anomaly of both sides having alliances reducing the likelihood of war during the nuclear Cold War era raises the question of just how generalizable the steps-to-war proposition on alliances is. Has the nuclear era introduced a new long-term trend with regard to alliances or is this irenic effect unique to Soviet–American competition? Senese and Vasquez (2008: chs. 5–7) probe the short-term post-Cold War period (1990–2001) to address this question. Keeping in mind that this sample consists only of a few years, they find – using an alliance index ranging from no alliances to having any sort of outside alliance – that the probability of a dyad having at least one war when they have no outside ally is .011, but when they do, the probability of a war significantly increases to .097 (dyad-history sample, Senese and Vasquez, 2008: Table 5.7, 167). Probes using the dyadic-dispute sample produce similar results. They conclude that the post-Cold War period is more like the classic 1816–1945 period and that the irenic effect of alliances has disappeared. One of the major conclusions of their analysis is that the Cold War may be fairly unique and that scholars should be cautious in generalizing from it to the future and to previous historical eras. This means that for the bulk of modern history (130 years of the 1816–1945 period and the decade plus of the post-Cold War era), having outside allies increases the likelihood of war. The Cold War is the major exception to this and that exception seems to have come to an end.[6]

Is there other recent scholarship that would indicate a contrary conclusion? Here the work of Smith and of Leeds (including some of her collaborators) is relevant. Smith (1995) argues that sometimes alliances are followed by war and other times they are not. He offers a formal model to explain the difference, arguing that when potential interveners believe that the allies of a target are reliable, they will be "deterred" from attacking, but if they believe that the allies of a target are unreliable, they will be more likely to attack (i.e. intervene). The major problem with Smith's analysis is that he assumes that deterrence (both conventional and nuclear) will work. This can hardly be assumed, but must be systematically tested.[7]

---

[6] A remaining research question is whether the irenic effect of both sides having alliances is confined to the East–West bloc members. It may be the case that the steps-to-war explanation still holds for dyads outside the East–West blocs.

[7] The logic of these two types of deterrence – conventional and nuclear – is also quite different. While nuclear deterrence is more plausible in that there is no clear winner, conventional deterrence is not, in that the probability of someone winning is always considerably greater than zero. On the limits of even nuclear deterrence working, see Kugler and Zagare (1990), Zagare and Kilgour (2000), and Vasquez (1991). Smith (1996) does attempt

In addition, he assumes, based on Sabrosky (1980), that many allies are unreliable and that this can account for a number of cases where wars follow alliances; but Leeds, Long, and Mitchell (2000), using more precise alliance data, show that allies are generally reliable and do live up to their commitments formally expressed in treaties. Thus, even if what Smith says were true, it would apply to only a few cases.

The major empirical research on whether "alliances deter" is Leeds (2003). This study, however, looks at whether alliances that formally target another state reduce MIDs between a pair of states and not whether they deter war *per se*.[8] She does find what might be called a "muting" effect, i.e. a significant diminution of MIDs. This, however, is not deterrence in the classic sense of preventing the outbreak of all MIDs, and it says little about whether any of these MIDs eventually produce war, as she readily points out (Leeds, 2003: 437). Interestingly, when Leeds (2005) does look at war as the dependent variable, she finds no statistically significant relationship between defensive alliances and the outbreak of war, which means they do not "deter" war. In fact, once defensive alliances fail to prevent a MID, there is some evidence to show that the MID will expand, and she finds that multiparty MIDs are more likely to go to war.

Lastly, the tests by Senese and Vasquez (2008: chs. 5 and 6) show that outside alliances are a step to war that is generally independent and separate from the other steps to war. By controlling for the other steps to war they show that the presence of territorial disputes, rivalry, and arms races does not eliminate the effect of outside allies on war, whether it be positive as in most cases, or negative, as in the Cold War.

These tests provide support for proposition 15 (see Appendix I, herein) on alliances, especially for the 1816–1945 period. With the exception of the Cold War period, having outside alliances increases the likelihood of a MID escalating to war within five years. Even during the Cold War, certain alliance patterns, namely having one side with an outside alliance while having territorial disputes or engaging in a rivalry, increase the probability of war. Whatever irenic impact existed during the Cold War seems to be disappearing in the post-Cold War period, where alliances once again

to test some of his claims; however, his research design limits the empirical inferences that can be made.

[8] The main difference between the Leeds (Alliance Treaty Obligations and Provisions [ATOP]) data and the Correlates of War alliance data updated by Gibler and Sarkees (2004) is that the latter do not have explicit targets. Gibler and Senese and Vasquez assume that, even in the absence of an explicit mention of a target, potential targets read the formation of an alliance as a threatening "signal."

seem to be returning to their bellicose impact. The key to distinguishing these impacts may lie with the extent to which alliances increase threat perception. Those made up of states successful in their last war, states that are dissatisfied with the status quo, and major states pose the greatest threats and are most likely to be followed by war within five years.

Rivalry and War

Little empirical research had been conducted on interstate rivalry and war prior to the publication of *The War Puzzle*. Since then there has been a wealth of studies supporting proposition 34 herein. There have been three basic measures of rivalry. The most standard is that of Goertz and Diehl (1992), who classify rivals as: isolated, proto-rivalry, and enduring rivalry. The latter are those that have had at least six MIDs within twenty years. One problem with this measure is that it does not permit MIDs to be used as a dependent variable since it is part of the definition. A good concept of rivalry should be able to predict that the pair of states will have many MIDs (Thompson, 1995; Vasquez, 1996b: 532). Thompson (1995; 2001: 564) tries to overcome this problem by searching histories to pinpoint when decision makers in a given pair of states see each other as threatening, an enemy, and a main competitor. He calls these strategic rivalries. These two different operational definitions produce different lists of rivals (see Thompson, 2001), with the main difference being the inclusion of strategic rivals that do not have MIDs. The Thompson measure has the advantage of being in a position to predict MIDs. It main disadvantage is that it is based on historical judgment (Thompson, 2001: 567) and is not as obviously reliable and transparent a measure as that of Goertz and Diehl (1992). In the review below, the term "rival" is used to indicate the highest level of rivalry whether it be enduring rivalry or strategic rivalry.

Senese and Vasquez (2008: ch. 6) supplement these two measures with an integer variable that looks simply at the number of MIDs between two states. They examine two propositions: the more MIDs the more likely war, and a curvilinear (inverted U) proposition. The integer measure does not assume that six MIDs is a critical threshold and does not employ the Goertz and Diehl (1992) ten-year gap to end a rivalry.[9] Senese and

---

[9] One of the little-known problems in using the ten-year rule is that many of the dyads in World War II, like UK–Germany, are not in an enduring rivalry phase in 1939. This makes the number of war participations starting in the enduring rivalry phase lower than one would expect historically.

Vasquez (2008) use both the categorical Goertz and Diehl measure and the integer measure, with the former being used primarily in the dyad-history sample and the latter in the dyadic-dispute sample.

The most persistent finding in rivalry research is that enduring rivals are likely to go war. This is first uncovered by Goertz and Diehl (1992; Diehl and Goertz, 2000: ch. 3). They find that the probability of enduring rivals having at least one war is .59 (Diehl and Goertz, 2000: 62–63, 200). In addition, enduring rivals account for 49.4 percent of wars and proto-rivals for another 32.9 percent (Diehl and Goertz, 2000: 199). Similarly, in Thompson's historical data, strategic rivalries account for about three-quarters of the wars since 1816 (Colaresi, Rasler, and Thompson, 2007: 88–89). Using ICB data from 1918 to 1995, Colaresi, Rasler, and Thompson (2007: 121–23) also find that strategic rivalries have a greater probability of being involved in crises that escalate to war than non-rivals, even when controlling for a number of other variables. These patterns make it clear that interstate conflict and war are clustered among a comparatively small set of dyads in the post-Napoleonic era (Diehl and Goertz, Diehl, 2000: 199–200; Colaresi, Rasler, and Thompson, 2007: 130). The steps-to-war explanation suggests that it is the underlying relationship between the states in each pair that accounts for this clustering.

Brecher and Wilkenfeld (1997: 832–33), using ICB data, also find that pairs of states engaged in repeated crises (what they call protracted conflict) are more likely to go to war than those that do not.[10] Those with protracted, as opposed to non-protracted, conflict are also generally more violent, more apt to employ violence as their central management technique during a crisis, and have an increased "gravity of threat" (see Brecher et al. 2000; Brecher and Wilkenfeld, 1997: 832–33).[11]

Colaresi, Rasler, and Thompson (2007: 121–30) find, similarly to Brecher and Wilkenfeld, that strategic rivals are more likely to go to war when violent triggers are used, high salience issues are at stake, and there are multiple actors involved. Petersen, Vasquez, and Wang (2004) also find that multiparty disputes, especially multiparty territorial disputes, have a higher probability of going to war than two-party disputes. In an unusual analysis, Colaresi, Rasler, and Thompson find that the rivalry context affects the impact of some well-known variables. For instance, parity

---

[10] See Hewitt (2005) for an analysis that uses repeated crises in the ICB to identify rivals. He finds that crisis-identified rivals have higher levels of hostility than the MID-identified enduring rivals of Diehl and Goertz (2000).

[11] Some of these findings may be inflated because crises occurring within a war (like the battle of Stalingrad) are included in the sample.

is a predictor only outside of rivalry contexts; within strategic rivalries escalation also occurs without parity (Colaresi, Rasler, and Thompson, 2007: 123–24). This is similar to Huth's (1996b: 87–88) finding that weak states contest boundaries even with powerful neighbors. In other words, the hostility engendered by rivalry overcomes "rational constraints" posed by asymmetric capability, which of course makes perfect sense from a rivalry perspective.

The findings based on both MIDs and crises (in the ICB data) make it clear that war typically arises after more than one dispute, although some rivals, like India and Pakistan or Israel and the Arabs, are "born feuding" (see Wayman, 2000).[12] Normally, however, it is believed that rivals require several disputes or crises before they escalate to war. This suggests that Leng's (1983) claim that states escalate their actions as they go from one crisis to the next is an important factor in bringing about war.

Bremer (2000: 25) maintains in his review of the quantitative literature that one of the four main findings of the field is that states that have a history of fighting (in terms of MIDs) will fight again. He offers two explanations, which are not mutually exclusive, of this pattern. The first is that the underlying issue has not been settled and will continue to engender militarized conflict (including war) until it is (see proposition 24, herein). The second is that the process by which the issue is handled generates hostility, which encourages the outbreak of war. Both of these hypotheses are consistent with the steps-to-war explanation, although the latter adds a domestic component that looks at the impact of repeated crises on the number and influence of hard-liners.

There has not been extensive research on "process" since Leng's (1983) original work, but there are two main pieces of research. Maoz and Mor (2002) argue, like Leng, that pairs of states "learn" to become rivals through their interaction.[13] They see rivalries as evolving and use a game theoretic model to analyze that evolution. In an extensive work, they find support for Brams's (1993) theory of moves to explain the process.

---

[12] These rivals tend to be associated with the birth of new states. Maoz (1989), as reported (herein: 157–58, proposition 10) , argues that new states that enter the system through a non-evolutionary process are more apt to have MIDs and wars. Wayman (2000: 230–31) finds that one-third of his enduring rivalries are born feuding and provides an in-depth discussion of each case, arguing that territorial conflict plays a prominent role in the birth of such rivalries. Colaresi, Rasler, and Thompson (2007: 83–84) find that a large number of strategic rivalries (about 56 percent) begin at independence. This suggests that unstable borders may be a problem early on.

[13] On the uses and potential pitfalls of the concept of learning within international relations see Levy (1994).

The second major piece of research is Valeriano (2003). He classifies Diehl and Goertz's (2000) proto- and enduring rivalries into those that exhibit an escalating trend across their MIDs ("escalating rivalries") as distinguished from those that do not have this trend. He finds, in harmony with Leng (1983) and the steps-to-war explanation, that such rivalries are more apt to go to war. Consistent with the finding on escalating rivalries is the finding of Bercovitch and Diehl (1997) that the use of conflict resolution techniques does not have much positive impact in managing rivalries to terminate them or avoid war.

Valeriano (2003) also provides evidence that the use of power politics helps fuel rivalries. In a model he calls the "steps to rivalry," he finds that states that make alliances against each other and that engage in arms racing are apt to become enduring rivals (in the Goertz and Diehl sense). All of this is consistent with the steps-to-war explanation, but goes beyond it by delineating the factors that bring about a sense of rivalry in the first place. Valeriano's work gives us a more precise understanding of the process by which rivalries end up in war and what distinguishes rivalries that go to war from those that do not. More research, however, is needed in this area, especially work that would include some domestic component.[14]

Process, then, as Bremer anticipated, is a key, but so too is the underlying issue. As discussed in Chapter 10, territorial disputes play a critical role. Territorial disputes recur (Hensel, 1998) and most rivalries arise out of territorial MIDs (Vasquez and Leskiw, 2001). Also consistent with research on "process," most enduring rivalries associated with territorial MIDs have more severe MIDs (Tir and Diehl, 2002). Territorial disputes, then, appear to be a peculiar kind of issue that is extremely difficult to settle, that will fester, and increasingly encourage a resort to more coercive tactics. It should come as no surprise that territorial-based rivalries (enduring or proto-rivalries) are more apt to have a war than other types of rivalries (Vasquez and Leskiw, 2001: 308–09; see also Colaresi, Rasler, and Thompson, 2007: 203–13).[15]

---

[14] Hagan (2003) is in the process of collecting systematic data on domestic opposition within the "great powers" from 1815, based on a four-fold typology that would provide some assessment of the role of "hard-liners" versus "accommodationalists". Using "soft" data, Valeriano and Marin (2008) have provided an initial probe of the relationship between hard-liners and the various steps to war (see also Roy, 1997).

[15] It should be noted that this finding is driven by minor–minor states and does not account for many major–major rivals that go to war, because not many of them are dominated by territorial disputes, although five of eleven have more than 25 percent of their MIDs on territory (Vasquez and Leskiw, 2001: 311–12).

Senese and Vasquez (2005, 2008) examine rivalry in light of the other steps to war to assess its relative impact. An interesting finding is that territorial disputes and rivalry have separate and independent effects on escalation to war.[16] Rivalry is also independent from alliance patterns and arms racing for all periods. All this means that rivalry is a key component of the process of war onset and not just a function of other steps to war.

When testing for interaction effects, Senese and Vasquez (2008: ch. 7) also find a positive interaction between territorial disputes and the number of prior disputes (for 1816–1945), which means that in the presence of territorial disputes, rivals have an enhanced likelihood of going to war.[17] Similarly, Colaresi, Rasler, and Thompson (2007: 256) find an interaction among contiguity, contested territory, and strategic rivalry (see also Rasler and Thompson, 2006). They show that this three-fold combination has a high impact on the probability of war. These interactions demonstrate that the rivalry process greatly enhances the likelihood of war in the presence of other variables, especially territorial disputes.

How much of the rivalry process is connected to territorial disputes recurring? Senese and Vasquez (2008) and Vasquez (2004) examine this question by comparing dyads that have four or more recurring territorial disputes with dyads that are labeled rivals by Goertz and Diehl (1992). Using a dyad-history sample, they find that rivalry and recurring territorial disputes have a separate and independent effect for 1816–1945 (but not during the Cold War).[18] This suggests that while the processes can be intertwined, they are separate, which means that rivalries not fueled by territorial disputes are still war-prone.

Wayman (1996) also finds a rivalry interaction process important. In one of the earliest empirical studies of rivalry, he finds that power transitions (and related processes like a rapid approach to parity) work together with rivalry to enhance the likelihood of war among major states. Major states are highly war-prone, so it is sometimes difficult to separate the

---

[16] This holds both for Diehl and Goertz's (2000) categorical measure and for an integer measure (number of prior MIDs) (using a dyad-history sample for the former and a dyadic-dispute sample for the latter). The relationship holds for all three of the major historical eras that they examine, including the Cold War.

[17] When the interaction term is introduced, the (lower order) territorial variable loses significance, but the rivalry measure remains significant, which means that rivals without territorial disputes still have a significant likelihood of going to war; whereas it appears that most territorial disputes that escalate to war are probably doing so in the context of a rivalry.

[18] During the Cold War, recurring territorial disputes are significant only when enduring rivalry is not included in the model.

variables that distinguish the major states that go to war from those that do not. Wayman finds that major states that are rivals and undergoing a power transition are particularly prone to go to war.

These two general patterns – the process of increasing escalation across disputes and the tendency of territorial disputes to recur and fester – raise the question of whether rivals can ever manage their disputes. Mansbach and Vasquez (1981) suggest that states that frequently interact may become accustomed to high levels of hostility and begin to ritualize their behavior and learn to manage their disputes so as to avoid war. They argue that such a process operates during the Cold War and is abetted by explicit rules like detente and crisis prevention techniques (George, 1983).

These claims suggest that there may be a curvilinear relationship between the number of MIDs and the likelihood of war. Senese and Vasquez (2005: 628–29; 2008: 201–2) test this hypothesis and find that there is an inverted U curve operating during the Cold War era, so that war is least likely when dyads have few or many disputes.[19] The upper end of this relationship conforms to the US–Soviet and other East–West rivalries. These dyads have the most MIDs and rarely go to war. It is also important to remember that the US–Soviet rivalry had few territorial disputes, which helps depress the probability of war. The few East–West bloc dyads that had territorial disputes tended to involve a superpower with an ally of the other superpower and not a direct territorial dispute between the superpowers.[20] The general finding on lack of war when both sides have outside allies and territorial disputes are under contention most likely is a result of the risk averseness of the superpowers in such situations and their unwillingness to be drawn into a war with the other superpower by one of its allies. It can be concluded that while rivalry generally increases the probability of war in all historical periods, it may in special circumstances, like those outlined above, be possible to manage rivalry to avoid war. The two key factors seem to be the absence of very highly salient issues, like territory, between the main contenders and a polarized alliance structure that enables the main contenders to control their allies when such issues arise.

---

[19] This relationship holds only for the sample of cases where arms race data are available, but it is also in the right direction for the full sample.

[20] The territorial disputes between the East and West are: USA–USSR (1954); GDR–USA (1958); GDR–FRG (1961); USSR–FRG (1962); USSR–TUR (1957); USSR–UK (1958); USSR–FR (1958); USSR–TAIWAN (1958); USSR–JAPAN (1982) (Senese and Vasquez, 2008: ch. 7: fn. 17).

While the major rivalry of the Cold War did not go to war, there are also other rivalries that have avoided war, a prominent one being the Anglo-American rivalry from 1815 on. Vasquez (1996b) argues that one of the main factors that distinguish those rivalries that go to war from those that do not is the presence of disputes over contiguous territory. A rivalry like the Anglo-American rivalry, or even the Soviet–American rivalry, that is not centered on contiguous territorial disputes is much less likely to go to war than rivalries that are (like the rivalries between India and Pakistan and between Israel and its neighbors). He argues that this territorial path to war is a typical path to war among neighbors and concomitantly that such territorial conflict makes neighbors rivals. States that are not contiguous are less likely to dispute territory and hence less likely to be rivals. If they do become rivals, as many non-contiguous major states do, the source is less likely to be territorial. Nevertheless, many of these non-contiguous and non-territorial rivals will go to war through what Vasquez (1996b) calls a second path to war.

The second path to war is one where states that are rivals become involved in a war with each other by intervening in an ongoing war. In other words, they become involved in a war through a *joining* process (Bremer, 1995), which is best explained by diffusion models and contagion (herein: Chapter 6; see also Valeriano and Vasquez, 2010). Specifically, Vasquez (1996b) posits that the kind of war these rivals are apt to join is a war involving a territorial dispute between a minor state and a major state that is a rival of the state that might intervene. Typically the minor state that is aided is an ally of the intervening major state. Both World War I and World War II (see Vasquez, 1996a and Vasquez and Gibler, 2001 on the latter) are exemplars of the second path to war.

To test the two paths to war idea, Vasquez examines all rivalries and classifies them into contiguous and non-contiguous states (contiguity was used as a proxy for territorial disputes, because there were no direct territorial data at the time of writing). He maintains that if the non-contiguous rivals become involved in a war with each other, it will not be a direct dyadic war between them, but a multilateral war where one of the rivals in the war is a joiner. He finds support for his claims, getting a Yule's Q of -.75 using the Goertz and Diehl measure of enduring rivalry (Vasquez, 1996b: 552–54).

Rasler and Thompson (2000) also pursue the question of contiguity and rivalry. Examining only the major state subsystem consisting of rivals, they find, consistent with Vasquez's (1996b) two paths to war, that: major state rivals tend to be non-contiguous, they rarely fight dyadic wars with each other, and war joining is typical among them. Contiguous dyads tend to be concerned primarily with spatial (i.e. territorial) issues, while non-contiguous dyads tend to be more concerned with positional issues, although they also often have spatial issues mixed in as well. The latter finding is consistent with their own theoretical perspective that positional issues are important, and it adds to our knowledge by showing that the non-contiguous rivalries that join war may be brought to the war by positional concerns. Vasquez and Leskiw (2001: 310–12) also find that major–major rivals tend to be dominated by non-territorial disputes (i.e. policy disputes), but leave open the question of whether these are the issues that bring them into multiparty wars.

Arms Races and War

The final step to war that has been extensively tested is arms races. *The War Puzzle* examined the debate on arms races in 1993 and sided essentially with the position that arms races are an important step to war (see propositions 30, 33). The research since then has amply borne out that position. The major breakthrough came with Sample (1996, 1997).

Sample (1997) was able to resolve the debate between Wallace (1979, 1990) and Diehl (1983) by looking at the deviant cases – arms races that did not go to war. She found that these were of two sorts – those in the 1930s that would eventually go to war by 1939 and those in the nuclear era. She was able to resolve the debate by introducing a five-year window and separating out the post-World War II era. Once she did this, she found that the presence of an ongoing arms race increases the likelihood of a MID escalating to war within five years for the 1816–1945 era. This supports the steps-to-war explanation. For the post-1945 period, arms races were not significant. The data sample was confined to major states, as with Diehl and Wallace, and employed a dyadic-dispute sample, which had become less controversial since Wallace's (1979) use of it.

In subsequent studies, Sample (1998b, 2000) introduced several control variables, in particular high defense burden, capability ratios, and power transition (including variations like rapid approach). Even with these control variables, the arms race variable remained significant. Interestingly, when she combined some of these effects, she found a concomitant increase in the probability of war. In the presence of a mutual military buildup, the probability of a MID escalating to war is .21; if there is also a high defense burden, the probability increases to .40; and if the dyad also has a territorial MID, the probability of war is .59. Adding parity, power transition, and rapid approach raises the probability of war to .69. These probabilities are for the entire 1816–1993 period. To see if nuclear weapons are the key factor making the arms race relationship statistically insignificant for the Cold War, Sample introduces a nuclear weapons variable. She finds that in the presence of a mutual military buildup and nuclear weapons, the probability of war goes down to .05 (Sample, 2000: Table 8.8, 177).

Sample (2002) then collects arms race data on minor states, something not done before. She finds that the arms race relationship also holds for minor–minor states for the 1816–1945 period, but not during the Cold War.[21] Her studies show that arms racing is dangerous, but that danger is muted by the presence of nuclear weapons. This conforms to what we know historically. Unlike other studies, such as those on alliances, Sample (2000) is able to pinpoint the nuclear effect (see also the recent study by Asal and Beardsley, 2007).

What Sample does not examine systematically is the relationship between arms racing and the other steps to war. Senese and Vasquez (2005, 2008; see also Vasquez, 2004) do this. They find that other power politics practices, like alliance making and rivalry, do not eliminate the arms race relationship. In fact, in the presence of the other steps to war, arms races make the probability of war (in the 1816–1945 period) reach its highest levels, in the .90 range for territorial disputes and the .85 to .78 range for policy and regime disputes (Senese and Vasquez, 2008: Table 6.3).[22] Arms races in the pre-nuclear era make war almost inevitable once a militarized dispute emerges.

Like Sample (1997, 2002), they find this arms race effect limited to the pre-nuclear era. However, when they employ the dyad-history sample, they find a significant bivariate relationship between MID escalation to war and there having been an arms race during the 1946–89 period. This relationship persists in the presence of territorial disputes and outside alliances, but when controlling for an enduring rivalry, it disappears. In other words, arms races can still be dangerous during the Cold War period, but their statistical effect is wiped out by enduring rivalry.[23]

---

[21] Nor does it hold for major–minor dyads, which makes sense theoretically.

[22] For the dyad-history sample (1816–1945), the probability of a dyad having at least one war if they ever had an arms race in the presence of the other steps reaches the .90 range for all three issues (Senese and Vasquez, 2008: Table 5.2, 149).

[23] It will be recalled that during the Cold War, rivalry has a curvilinear effect, which means that the dyads with the highest number of MIDs (of which many are East–West dyads) do not have as high a likelihood of going to war as those with a more moderate number

Although arms races can be extremely dangerous, only a few dyads have them. As result, only a few wars are preceded by arms races. Diehl (1983) pointed this out early on, and more recent research by Vasquez and Valeriano (2008) confirms that only a few wars have arms races combined with the other steps to war. Nevertheless, as predicted by the steps-to-war explanation (herein: p. 198, proposition 71), wars preceded by arms races are quite severe and include both World War I and World War II.

One of the criticisms of arms race research is that it might be prone to a selection effect since much of the research looks at arms races in the context of an ongoing MID (see Diehl and Crescenzi's 1998 criticism of Sample and her [1998a] response). In an attempt to address this issue, Gibler, Rider, and Hutchison (2005) collect arms race data based on the presence of a strategic rivalry (Thompson, 1995, 2001). Besides dealing with selection bias, these data – by using strategic rivals as a basis for identifying arms races – eliminate some of the few dyads that may technically have a mathematical arms race, but not the underlying competitive relationship one normally associates with arms racing. Their analyses show that strategic rivals have a significantly greater likelihood of both having a MID and of going to war in the presence of an arms race than in its absence. This provides confirmation of Sample's and Senese and Vasquez's finding using different arms race data.[24] Their analyses also suggest that what makes arms races associated with war is that during arms races the number of MIDs more than doubles – making the chances of war much higher simply because there are more MIDs (Gibler, Rider, and Hutchison, 2005: 144). If sustained (cf. Colaresi, Rasler, and Thompson, 2007: 235, 265), this is an important new finding on the dynamics that bring about war.

Although some of the above studies have looked at arms races in conjunction with other steps to war, there has not been much empirical testing of whether one step leads to another or on the sequence of the steps. This remains a topic for future research. Nonetheless, two studies have begun to look at these questions. Valeriano (2003) examines the Diehl and Goertz (2000) rivals to see if arms racing follows alliance

---

of MIDs. This implies that arms races between nuclear and perhaps even nuclear-allied states are probably not as dangerous as those between non-nuclear (or non-nuclear allied) states. The latter assessment, however, is based more on inference than on a direct test.

[24] One could still claim that a strategic rivalry sample might be subject to selection effects, but if so it is of a different sort. So while the study is not definitive, it does add another piece of evidence consistent with previous results. Gibler et al. (2005) cover the 1816–1993 time span and do not control for the Cold War period.

making or vice versa, and he finds that, generally, arms racing comes in the later stages of rivalry, supporting proposition 27, herein (cf. proposition 19). Rider (forthcoming) looks at Thompson's (2001) strategic rivals and asks what factors make them engage in arms races in the first place. He finds that rivals that have had a territorial MID in the last five years are more likely to have arms races than those that have had a policy or regime MID. Such research opens the question of the impact of combining steps to war.

Combining the Steps

Looking at combinations of steps involves two questions. The first, mentioned above, is whether the steps follow a certain sequence, and the second is whether combining steps has an increasing impact on the probability of war. Although the sequencing of steps is an important topic, for now what matters for testing the steps-to-war explanation is not so much the order of the steps, but that they are mutually reinforcing (Senese and Vasquez, 2008: 23). In other words, an important test of the steps-to-war explanation is to see if the more steps to war present, the more likely a dispute will escalate to war.

The tests of Senese and Vasquez (2005, 2008), using various samples, have found this to be the case. As noted previously, adding each step increases the probability of war in the 1816–1945 period. The highest probabilities of war are always produced when all four steps to war – territorial disputes, alliance making, rivalry, and arms racing – are present. Even in the Cold War period, when both sides having outside alliances reduces the probability of war, adding territorial disputes, rivalry, and arms races increases the probability of war (albeit not always significantly, especially for arms races). Except for complications during the Cold War, each step does produce the kind of step-wise progression predicted by the explanation.

Further evidence on the steps to war is provided by Colaresi and Thompson (2005). Using ICB data from 1918 to 1995 as well as their own data on spatial (territorial) and positional strategic rivalries, they test several steps-to-war propositions using a hazard model. Employing different territorial and conflict data and a different modeling technique provides a robust test for the steps-to-war explanation. They find that spatial and positional rivalries increase the likelihood of war, with spatial rivalry having a much higher probability of going to war than positional, although the latter has a substantial impact. They also find that having two or more crises[25] and an arms race increases the probability of war. These are very similar to the findings of Senese and Vasquez (2005) and Vasquez (2004). What is new in their test of interactions is that they find a positive interaction between: (a) two crises and having an external ally and (b) two crises and having an arms race.[26] External alliances are only significant in the presence of multiple crises. All of this is generally supportive of the steps-to-war logic, as they conclude (see Colaresi, Rasler and Thompson, 2007: 238).

One finding on alliances is close to an anomaly, however. Although they find that when *one* side has an outside politically relevant alliance this increases the likelihood of war, they also find (in contradiction) that when *both* sides have outside alliances in the presence of two or more crises this decreases the probability of war. They conclude that this finding "gives some *prima facie* validity to a deterrence understanding of international politics" (Colaresi, Rasler, and Thompson, 2008: 236). However, it is likely that this finding is solely a function of the nuclear Cold War period, as Senese and Vasquez (2005, 2008) find (see above). Since the ICB data only go from 1918 to 1995, the Cold War will loom large. While both sides having outside alliances has this impact during the nuclear Cold War, it does not prior to 1946, according to Senese and Vasquez (2005, 2008).[27] A splitting of ICB data at 1946 would probably make the findings more consistent with Senese and Vasquez (2008).[28] Nonetheless, this independent test with different data adds confidence that the steps-to-war explanation will continue to survive future rigorous testing.

Additional tests using different data for territory (contested territory derived from Huth and Allee [2002] data) are also generally supportive of the steps-to-war explanation (Colaresi, Rasler, and Thompson, 2007: ch. 9). Colaresi, Rasler, and Thompson again find that contested territory, strategic

[25] Interestingly, they find that two crises is the critical threshold and that three or more crises make no difference. Note, however, that crises reflect a more intense threshold than MIDs; see Hewitt (2003).
[26] Indeed, the lower-order arms race variable is not significant once they control for the presence of two crises.
[27] Senese and Vasquez also note that just because both sides having outside alliances may not result in war does not always mean that "deterrence" works. During the 1938 Munich crisis both sides had outside allies and war was avoided, but this was really a case of "deterrence failure," not success (see Senese and Vasquez, 2008: ch. 7, note 9: 225). Of course, this is only one case and a systematic examination will be needed before any general conclusions can be made.
[28] Colaresi, Rasler, and Thompson 2007: ch. 9, Appendix) do this for contiguity, contested territory, and rivalry, but not for external alliances and arms races.

rivalry, external alliances, and mutual military buildups are significant. However, they now find the triad of contiguity, contested territory, and rivalry particularly potent and considerably so compared to external alliances and mutual military buildups. In fact, in this test, they no longer find the interaction with two or more crises and external alliances and mutual military buildups significant, as they did previously.[29]

The few in-depth case studies that have been conducted to see how the steps to war work together have also been supportive of the explanation. Vasquez (1996a), looking at the period leading up to World War II in Europe and its expansion (1933–41), finds that the steps to war correspond to the way Chapters 5 and 7 herein posit, both in terms of war onset and war expansion. He finds that the war starts because Hitler pursues the broader territorial goals of *Lebensraum* that cannot be accommodated by the nationalist norm for transferring territory (as happened with the Sudetenland). This new goal in the presence of alliances, rivalry (including repeated crises), arms races, and the increasingly hard-line tactics of the Nazis, makes it highly likely that eventually a crisis will come along that escalates to war, which it did in the 1939 crisis over Danzig and Poland. Alliance ties, contiguity, and rivalry make this dyadic war expand, and the breakdown of the political order, other bandwagon effects, and economic dependence on certain non-belligerents makes the war expand further, eventually linking up the war in Europe with the war in Asia.

Vasquez and Gibler (2001), looking at the years before and during World War II in Asia (1931–1945), find that the war has its origin in the Japanese attempts to expand its territory. These cause disputes with China, the Soviet Union, and ultimately the UK and the USA as both of the latter come to the aid of Chiang Kai-shek. All of this supports the territorial explanation of war and Vasquez's (1996b) notion that major state rivals become drawn into ongoing wars (in this case the Sino-Japanese War of 1937). The case also shows that when major states adopt the practices of power politics – making alliances, repeatedly resorting to militarized confrontations, and building up their militaries – the probability

---

[29] They suggest two reasons for this discrepancy (Colaresi, Rasler, and Thompson, 2007: 266–67): One, that alliances and arms races just may not be present as frequently as contiguity, contested territory, and rivalry. Two, that contested territory between rivals "absorbs most of the available variance" in that these kinds of dyads are also the ones most likely to seek outside allies and engage in arms races. The first reason may be more plausible. It may, in fact, be the case that having multiple steps, such as both outside alliances and arms races, is fairly rare because war occurs before an arms race is fully in place. Valeriano and Vasquez (2008) show that sequences with all four steps are fairly rare among the seventy-nine interstate wars.

of war increases. The repeated crises, in this case going back to the 1931 Manchurian crisis, evince a pattern of overall escalating hostility across crises, although this is not precisely measured in the case study. Recurring crises make for the increased influence of hard-liners, especially in Japan, where over time the liberal internationalist coalition is pushed out of power in favor of the nationalist-militarist coalition.

In both this war and World War II in Europe, these steps work in conjunction with the three systemic necessary conditions for world war specified in Chapter 7 to bring about the diffusion of a dyadic war into a world war. The steps-to-war explanation is able in both case studies to provide a plausible historical explanation of two well-known cases, while at the same time highlighting how the logic of combining the steps operates in specific instances of great historical and policy importance.

A third major case study is on the India–Pakistan rivalry. This differs from the other two case studies discussed above in that it is not a study of a specific war, but of a rivalry relationship that has a series of limited wars. Vasquez (2005) draws three major conclusions from this study. First, the source of the rivalry is territorial and results from the inability to reach a mutually acceptable agreement on boundaries before independence. This makes both sides "born feuding" (Wayman, 2000). Starting at independence, both sides are unable to reach a compromise because hard-liners on each side, as well as non-state actors, keep the issue on the agenda and veto any compromise (see also Roy, 1997). Second, with the exception of the first war in 1948, all of the steps to war appear during the rivalry and roughly in the sequence expected. The territorial issue comes first and drives the sense of rivalry. It is also a rivalry between contiguous states contesting territory, which typically results in dyadic wars. An alliance by one leads to a counter-alliance by the other. The same dynamic follows the mutual military buildups leading to arms racing.[30] Domestic hardline reciprocity is also present in the rivalry in that hostile actions by one side reinforce hard-liners on the other side.

The sequence of the steps occurs in the predicted order roughly before each war, except for the first (see Vasquez, 2005: Figure 3.1, 64). The first war (1948) is only preceded by a territorial dispute. The second Kashmir war (1965) is also preceded by one side having an outside alliance and an arms race (but no counter-alliance). The third war (the 1971 Bangladesh

---

[30] A possible exception is that while arms racing comes after the making of the first alliance, it comes before India can make a counter-alliance (see Vasquez, 2005: Figure 3.1, 64). This, in part, is due to the fact that there is no acceptable ally for India at that time. Later (1971) India will sign a non-aggression pact with the Soviet Union.

War) is preceded by both sides having outside allies and an arms race in addition to the underlying territorial dispute. Thus, the last two wars have all four steps, which also seems to be the case with the 1999 Kargil War, although the data in the case study, especially on arms races, do not go past 1992. The case study also supports the finding of Colaresi, Rasler, and Thompson (2007: 123–24) and of Huth (1996b: 87–88) that weaker states, in this case Pakistan, will not refrain from pursuing territorial disputes because of a disparity of power. This tendency is abetted in this case by outside parties and/or allies diplomatically intervening to prevent a military settlement (Vasquez, 2005: 78).

Third, a comparison with the US–Soviet rivalry shows that the sources and dynamics of the two rivalries are different, most likely because of the absence of a serious territorial dispute between the USA and the USSR. In retrospect, it can be seen that nuclear deterrence worked in the Cold War under a set of favorable conditions that are not present in the territorial rivalries between neighbors, like India and Pakistan.

Although the India–Pakistan case study looks at the sequence of the steps to war, most case studies do not. Likewise, there has not been much quantitative investigation of sequencing. Senese and Vasquez (2008: 23–24) maintain that several different sequences are possible (and likely). The typical sequence they suggest, *ceteris paribus,* is that territorial disputes give rise to recurrent crises and a sense of rivalry, which leads to alliance formation and arms racing (see also Colaresi, Rasler, and Thompson, 2007: 241). However, as they point out, war may break out before all four of these steps, especially the last, are taken. Vasquez (2004: 20–23) has done some probing of the sequences of the steps in the context of endogeneity questions and of making inferences from a dyad-history sample. Senese and Vasquez (2008: ch. 5) provide another probe. Valeriano and Vasquez (2010) look at how many of the steps are present before all the complex interstate wars from 1816 to 1997, but not their precise sequence. Nevertheless, their analysis shows that war often occurs with just a few steps, and only a handful of wars have all four steps.

Rasler and Thompson (2006) (see also Colaresi, Rasler, and Thompson, 2007: ch. 9) have the most extensive exploration of possible sequencing, although their study is preliminary due to the nature of the data available. Nevertheless, they are concerned with whether a perception of rivalry precedes or follows contesting territory and militarized disputes. To get at this, they employ Thompson's (2001) perceptual data on strategic rivalries, Huth and Allee's (2002) territorial claims to measure contested territory, and the MID data. Of the 108 cases from 1919 to 1992, they find that fifty-six have a sequence of contested territory leading to militarized disputes (without a strategic rivalry being present). This is followed by forty-nine cases with contested territory occurring in the presence of a strategic rivalry and then being followed by militarized disputes. The remaining six sequences all have fewer than five cases each (Colaresi, Rasler, and Thompson, 2007: 251-52).

The first sequence, for most scholars, is unexpected, because theoretically, rivalry should not be independent of repeated MIDs (in fact Diehl and Goertz define rivalry as repeated MIDs). Nonetheless, Colaresi, Rasler, and Thompson (2007: 251) point out that the sequence that combines contested territory and strategic rivalry has more frequent MIDs than the sequence without rivalry (an average 5.3. MIDs per dyad versus 1.79 per dyad). This last finding supports the notion that the perception of rivalry intensifies hostility and conflict. The presence of multiple paths also supports the claim that war is multicausal and that even within the steps-to-war analysis there can be different paths to war (see Senese and Vasquez, 2008: ch. 1). At the same time, the predominance of two paths shows that the process may not be as complicated as the logical possibilities imply.

The tests on power politics and war have generally failed to falsify the steps-to-war explanation. At the same time they show that its natural domain is the classic 1816-1945 international politics era. For the Cold War only aspects of the explanation – territorial disputes and rivalry – work as anticipated. Both sides having outside alliances works the opposite of what was expected, but this is due primarily to the effect of nuclear weapons. Likewise, arms races during the Cold War, except in a few circumstances, are non-significant.

One would expect, given the logic of the explanation and the above findings, that the absence of power politics would be associated with peaceful eras, regions, and dyads, as was the case when examining the absence of territorial disputes (in the previous chapter). Not much research of this sort has been conducted to date. One of the few studies on this topic (Vasquez, 2001) finds that arms races are considerably less prevalent during peaceful eras. It uses Wallensteen's (1984) classification of historical eras as either particularist or universalist (with the former lacking rules of the game among major states and the latter having them) to test the hypothesis, since Wallensteen finds that during universalist periods there are no wars among major states. Vasquez (2001) therefore predicts that universalist periods should have fewer resorts to the practices of power politics. He has data only on arms races, so the test is confined to that particular practice.

Using the Horn (1987) measure of arms races among major states, he finds that there are no arms races in the peaceful universalist periods and thirty in the war-prone particularist periods.[31] These findings, while far from definitive, do indicate that peaceful periods are not associated with "peace through strength" (Wallace, 1982), but with the avoidance of arms racing. It remains to be seen if other power politics practices, like alliance making and rivalry, are less prevalent in peaceful eras.

Likewise, one would also expect, given the steps-to-war explanation, that peaceful regions and peaceful dyads would have fewer instances of power politics than the more war-prone regions and dyads. There is hardly any research on this topic, but a few aspects of the literature are relevant. Colaresi, Rasler, and Thompson (2007: 92–96) do find that regions differ in the frequency with which strategic rivals appear and that sometimes the same region can have many rivals in one period and few in another. Presumably if the steps-to-war explanation is correct, then this variance should coincide with the presence of peace; i.e. regions with few rivalries should be more peaceful.

Colaresi, Rasler, and Thompson do not test this proposition, but they do provide some pieces of evidence that show the claim is on the right track. We know that prior to 1946 Western Europe was very war-torn and afterward it was not. Colaresi, Rasler, and Thompson (2007: 93) find that prior to 1946, Western Europe had six strategic rivalries, but afterward it had none. Likewise, before 1946 and the founding of Israel, the Mashriq region of the Middle East had four strategic rivalries, and afterward it had twelve; so too with South Asia: prior to 1946 and the founding of India and Pakistan, this region had no strategic rivalries and afterward it had two. These illustrations suggest that a systematic test is worth conducting.

Lastly, the democratic peace literature suggests, as noted several times in passing, that democratic dyads tend not to resort to the use of force to resolve their territorial disagreements, but prefer legal procedures or negotiations (Huth and Allee, 2002; Hensel, 2001; Dixon, 1993, 1994; Raymond, 1994). One would expect from the steps-to-war perspective that a whole host of power politics practices would be absent in joint democratic dyad relations. Analyses of the relationship between the absence of power politics and the presence of peace provide a fruitful area for future research. Likewise, one would expect power politics to be rare within Maoz's (2004) pacifist dyads. All of these ideas await systematic testing.

---

[31] Using the Diehl (1983) measure of arms races, he finds five arms races in the universalist periods and thirty-four in the particularist.

Conclusion

The findings on power politics generally reveal that using the practices of power politics increases the likelihood of war, especially for territorial disputes. The fact that power politics also increases the likelihood of war for non-territorial disputes indicates that it is a separate path to war than the territorial path to war. Three practices – alliance making, rivalry (including repeated militarized confrontations), and arms races – have been examined. Each will be reviewed separately since the findings sometimes differ.

In general, alliances that combine major states, those that have been successful in their last war, and those that are dissatisfied with the status quo, are dangerous and typically are followed by war in five years or less (Gibler, 2000). This holds for both the nineteenth century, when alliances are often more peaceful, and for the twentieth, when they are more war-prone. The major distinguishing factor is whether the alliance increases threat perception. The more characteristics an alliance has that pose a threat to a potential target, the greater the likelihood it will be followed by war.

Examining the likelihood of an MID escalating to war, it has also been found that alliances have a bellicose effect. Having a politically relevant outside ally to provide support increases the probability that a MID will escalate to war, especially if the MID is over territory. The most war-prone alliance pattern is where both sides have outside alliances. These relationships hold for the bulk of the post-1815 era, with the exception of the Cold War, when both sides having outside alliances actually reduces the probability of war (Senese and Vasquez, 2005; 2008: chs. 5 and 6). In the absence of the polarized alliance structure (i.e. when only one side has an outside alliance) the likelihood of war increases when territorial disputes or rivalry are also present (i.e. these two conditions make for a positive interaction with the alliance pattern; Senese and Vasquez, 2008: ch. 7). In the post-Cold War period, the bellicose impact of alliances is once again prevalent.

The impact of outside alliances is not simply a function of the other steps to war. Controlling for rivalry, arms races, and territorial disputes does not eliminate their effect. In fact, territorial disputes that are contested in the presence of outside alliances, with the exception of both sides having outside alliances in the Cold War, have an increased probability of going to war than territorial disputes contested in the absence of alliances. Likewise, policy and regime disputes are more likely to go to war in the presence of outside alliances than in their absence (again with the exception of the Cold War).

The research on rivalry shows that rivalries have a high probability of going to war, and account for half or more of the wars fought since 1815 (Diehl and Goertz, 2000; Colaresi, Rasler, and Thompson, 2007: ch. 3). Typically, war arises after more than one dispute, the major exception being rivals that are born feuding and these are usually fighting over their boundaries (Wayman, 2000). States that have recurring territorial disputes (four or more) also have an increased likelihood of war. This is a separate and independent effect from rivalry (Senese and Vasquez, 2008: ch. 5). At the same time, however, territory-based rivalries account for a number of the rivalries that go to war (Vasquez and Leskiw, 2001). Strategic rivalries that are contiguous and contest territory are particularly war-prone (Rasler and Thompson, 2006; Colaresi, Rasler, and Thompson, 2007: ch. 9).

War seems to come about either because an issue, typically territorial, cannot be resolved and/or the interactions between the contenders engender hostility. In terms of the first pattern, territorial disputes recur and most rivalries arise out of contention over territory (Vasquez and Leskiw, 2001). Rivalries arising out of territorial disputes tend to have MIDs that are more severe (Tir and Diehl, 2002). In addition, conventional conflict resolution techniques do not have much impact on rivalries once they are locked in (Bercovitch and Diehl, 1997).

In terms of the second pattern, we do know that a major process by which states become rivals is by contending parties resorting to power politics practices, i.e. by making alliances against each other and engaging in arms races (Valeriano, 2003). When they engage in such behavior they tend to become rivals.[32] Rivals also tend to escalate their behavior from dispute to dispute. Rivalries that exhibit this escalating pattern are more likely to go to war than those that do not (Valeriano, 2003). Similarly, major states that are rivals that are also engaged in a power transition (or related shifts in capability) have an accelerated probability of going to war (Wayman, 1996). These various processes, all of which are associated with realist practices, seem to increase threat perception and hostility and thereby the likelihood of war. Likewise, rivals that go to war are more likely to use violence as a central management technique, have an increased gravity of threat present, and have high salience issues at stake (Brecher and Wilkenfeld, 1997; Colaresi, Rasler, and Thompson, 2007: ch. 4). Multiple parties in a dispute, especially

---

[32] So power politics not only help bring about war directly, but perhaps also indirectly by making states rivals in the first place.

a territorial dispute, make it more likely that it will escalate to war (Petersen, Vasquez, and Wang, 2004).

Nonetheless, sometimes states with many MIDs become accustomed to them and begin to ritualize their interactions. In doing so, they reduce the probability of war. Such a pattern is found during the Cold War (Senese and Vasquez, 2008: ch. 6). This period also finds a negative interaction between rivalry and both sides having alliances, which means that there is a reduction in the likelihood of war when both rivals have outside allies, as happened with dyads in the East–West blocs.

Rivals come to war basically through two paths. The first and most common path to war is a war between neighbors fighting over territory. The second path to war is a war in which one or more of the rivals join an ongoing war (Vasquez, 1996b). Diffusion plays an important role in bringing non-contiguous major states to war when they do not have ongoing territorial MIDs. They come to war typically by intervening in a war between their rival and a minor state over a territorial question. Often this minor state will also be an ally of the intervening major state. Generally, dyadic wars among non-contiguous rivals are rare and non-contiguous rivals are most apt to go to war by joining an ongoing war (Rasler and Thompson, 2000; see also Colaresi, Rasler, and Thompson, 2007: ch. 6).

In the pre-nuclear era, arms racing is also a factor increasing the likelihood that a MID will escalate to war within five years (Sample, 1997). The findings for arms races hold for both major and minor states and indicate that "peace through strength" is not an empirically accurate hypothesis (Sample, 2002). In the presence of nuclear weapons, this relationship disappears (Sample, 2000), but there is some evidence that arms races are related to war in the Cold War, presumably among non-nuclear dyads. However, the relationship between arms races and escalation to war is no longer statistically significant when controlling for rivalry (Senese and Vasquez, 2008: ch. 5).

The effect of arms races persists for non-nuclear states even in the presence of other variables, such as capability, a high defense burden, and power transitions. In combination with these factors, the effect of arms racing on the probability of war increases (Sample, 1998b, 2000). The same is true when controlling for other steps to war, like outside alliances, rivalry, and territorial disputes. In the 1816–1945 period, these additional steps to war do not wipe out the effect of arms races. Indeed, the presence of arms races with these other factors increases the probability of war to the .90 range (Vasquez, 2004; Senese and Vasquez, 2005; 2008: chs. 5 and 6). As a step to war, arms races tend to follow alliance making rather than precede it (Valeriano, 2003). Strategic rivals that contend over territory are more likely to engage in arms racing than those that do not (Rider, forthcoming), and strategic rivals that have arms races are more likely to go to war than those that do not (Gibler, Rider, and Hutchison, 2005).

As the different steps to war are combined, they should result in a step-wise increase in the probability of war and this is usually found to be the case (Vasquez, 2004; Colaresi and Thompson, 2005). The relationship is strongest for the 1816–1945 period (Senese and Vasquez, 2005, 2008), but even in the Cold War the probabilities are in the correct direction, if not always significant. For the Cold War, territorial disputes and rivalry increase the probability of war, but both sides having outside alliances decreases it. One state having an outside alliance, however, interacts with territorial disputes and with rivalry to enhance the likelihood of war. For the bulk of the post-Napoleonic era, however, the more steps, the greater probability of war. The highest probabilities of war are always reached when all four steps are present. This is true even in the Cold War if one side having an outside alliance is used in the model (and both sides having an outside alliance is not) (Senese and Vasquez, 2008: ch. 6).

Little research has been done on the sequence of the steps to war. Senese and Vasquez (2008: 23) maintain that what matters at this stage of research is not the specific order of the steps but that they are mutually reinforcing. More than one sequence is probable, but disputes preceded by multiple steps are more likely to result in war. Colaresi, Rasler, and Thompson, (2007: ch. 9) show that at least two different sequences are predominant. One sequence is contested territory leading to militarized disputes (without the perception of a strategic rivalry), and the second is contested territory in the context of perceived strategic rivalry followed by militarized disputes. The latter gives rise to more frequent MIDs.

These findings confirm much of what the steps-to-war analysis, going back to Vasquez (1987b), said about power politics. In particular, the various tests are consistent with the claims that power politics bring about a security dilemma that increases the likelihood of war and does not usually prevent war and result in "peace through strength." Outside the nuclear arena, power politics are still very dangerous, as the limited evidence on alliances shows for the post-Cold War era. Although much remains to be done, our empirical knowledge of the impact of outside alliances, rivalry, and arms races is much more complete than it was when *The War Puzzle* was first published.

What is even more important from a philosophy of science point of view is that this knowledge is often the product of deductive testing that could have falsified the explanation but did not do so. Likewise, one of the contributions of the steps-to-war explanation of war is that we now have a body of findings that actually tell us something about the dynamics of territorial conflict and power politics, and their respective roles in bringing about war. As the steps-to-war research program goes forward, more pieces of the puzzle of war will be put together. As they are, we need to shift our attention to the puzzle of peace.

Appendix I:

A Propositional Summary

The propositions listed below provide a detailed summary of the explanation of war provided in the book. Citations following each entry indicate where in the text the proposition is derived and what existing evidence is consistent with the proposition.

The propositions will make it possible to conduct tests of the theoretical model. If the thrust of these propositions can be confirmed and the details refined and elaborated by further research, then it will be possible to move toward a theory of the onset and expansion of war. This is the goal that the analysis has meant to serve.

The cumulation of knowledge involves more than just testing, however; it also involves more exploratory research in light of new theoretical insights. Since this analysis has sought to broaden research on war, several queries that cannot yet be answered are also listed. Answering them will help specify the model. These will be best investigated by further inductive research, especially comparative case studies. It is hoped that these propositions and queries will guide research on war along more theoretically productive lines than has been the case in the past.

A Research Agenda on Causes of War: Propositions and Queries

1. War is a social invention for the use of force; therefore, the goals of war, the ways in which it is fought, and the situations that are handled by war will vary according to the cultural traditions of the global (or regional) system (Chapter 1; Chapter 8: 304–05).

2. The interactions between political actors and the domestic political dynamics preceding war will vary according to the type of war, but specific causal paths to war can be delineated (Chapter 2; Chapter 6: 238).

3. Realist norms and the practices of power politics are more associated with war than with peace (Chapter 3; Chapter 5: 175–77).

4. Major states (i.e. stronger states) are more apt to adopt realist norms and practices; therefore, they are more prone to war (Chapter 5: 177; Bremer, 1980; Singer and Small, 1966).

4a. The longer a major state is a member of the system, the more apt it is to be socialized to its norms and practices. Therefore, the longer a major state is a member of the system, the more alliances and the more wars it can be expected to have (Chapter 5: 175–76; Singer and Small, 1966; Gochman, 1980).

Territorial contiguity

5. Some issues are more apt to lead to war than others. In the modern global system, the single issue that is most likely to result in interstate war (regardless of type) is one that embodies a dispute over contiguous territory (Chapter 4: 137–40, 143, 146–49; Wallensteen, 1981; Diehl, 1985b; Bremer, 1992; Gochman and Leng, 1983).

6. *Ceteris paribus*, two states bordering on each other will early on in their history use aggressive displays to establish a border in an area where they both have frequent contact (Chapter 4: 154–55).

6a. If this is the case, it would be expected that states would divide up the Earth into territorial units and would often claim and hold territory through the use or threat of violence (Chapter 4: 155). Likewise, rationalization for military forces would be in some way related to the need to defend (or gain) territory (Chapter 4: 155).

6b. *Ergo*, the more states in the system, the more militarized disputes and the more wars in the system (Chapter 4: 157, 159; Maoz, 1989; Gochman and Maoz, 1984; Diehl and Goertz, 1988; Small and Singer, 1982).

7. More interstate wars will occur between contiguous states than non-contiguous states. This is especially true for neighbors that are relatively equal (Chapter 4: 144–49; Singer, 1990; Bremer, 1992).

7a. *Ergo*, the more borders a state has, the more wars it will experience (Chapter 4: 156, 159; Richardson, 1960b; Rummel, 1972a; Starr and Most, 1976, 1978).

8. Border areas that are less likely to provoke wars are those where: (a) borders are established by natural frontiers (like high mountains, large bodies of water, or deserts); (b) the area is not inhabited or is seen as having little value; and (c) the people living in the area are not

ethnolinguistically related to people in the neighboring states (Chapter 4: 156; Roy, 1991).

9. How borders are established will have a long-lasting effect on the relationship between neighbors. Borders, especially between equals, established through armed force are much more likely to give rise to recurrent crises and wars than borders established through negotiation, mutual accommodation or agreement (Chapter 4: 161).

9a. There is a curvilinear relationship between how borders are established and the recurrence of disputes. Imposing borders through an overwhelming military victory and the establishment of a border other than through the use of war tends to be associated with relative peace. War that does not result in an overwhelming victory tends to be associated with recurrent disputes and war (Chapter 4: 161).

10. Any new state that emerges poses a threat to existing territorial division and if fears arise that accommodation is not feasible, then war, at some point, is likely. Similarly, any violent revolutionary change in a regime poses a fear that previous territorial accommodations might no longer be accepted, if this turns out to be the case, then war is likely. *Ergo*, as more new states and regimes enter the system, the number of wars in the system will increase (Chapter 4: 157–58; Maoz, 1989).

Rivalry

11. Enduring rivalries (and protracted conflict between unequals) have their origins in attempts to control space. *Ceteris paribus*, enduring rivalries and protracted conflicts between unequals are more characteristic of neighbors than of non-neighboring states (Chapter 4: 147; Wayman and Jones, 1991; Gochman, 1990).

12. The main difference between rivalries that end in a major war and rivalries that end non-violently is the parties' ability to avoid crises involving territorial contiguity. Rival states that are not contiguous tend not to fight a major war with each other unless they are dragged in by third parties (Chapter 5: 211).

12a. Rivals are more concerned with hurting the other side than maximizing their own value satisfaction. For this reason they will tend to oppose the position taken by a rival on any issue. Rivals tend to link all issues on the agenda into one grand overarching issue (Chapter 2: 9–81, 85).

12b. Linking of issues tends to make disagreement persist. Persistent disagreement produces an overreliance on negative acts. These in turn increase negative affect (hostility) (Chapter 2: 79–86).

12c. Interstate interactions (words and deeds) are intended to change issue positions; instead they have a direct impact on psychological affect (friendship–hostility) (Chapter 2: 84).

13. The more disputes and crises that arise between relative equals, the greater the likelihood of their viewing each other as rivals and of adopting an actor dimension (Chapter 2: 85–86).

14. The more disputes and crises that arise between relative equals, the greater the likelihood of their trying to form alliances against each other (Chapter 5: 172–73, 188).

Alliances

15. *Ceteris paribus*, alliances are more frequently followed by war than by peace (Chapter 5: 174–81; Chapter 8: 297, 302; Levy, 1981; Singer and Small, 1966; see also Faber and Weaver, 1984).

15a. However, the bellicose effects of alliances can be reduced depending on the purpose for which they are made and the structural context in which they occur. It follows that certain types of alliances are more war-prone than others (Chapter 5: 177–80, 186).

15b. When the global institutional context limits unilateral acts through the establishment of rules of the game, alliances tend not to be followed by war (Chapter 5: 177, 179; Levy, 1981).

15c. Alliances that control the unilateral acts of states, especially minor states, or that seek to manage rivalry are less war-prone than other types of alliances (Chapter 5: 178–79, 184). *Pacta de contrahendo* (pacts of restraint) are associated with peace between major states, but war between major and minor states (Chapter 5: 178–79; Moul, 1988b; Schroeder, 1976).

15d. Alliances involving major states are more war-prone than alliances without major states (Chapter 5: 178; Levy, 1981).

15e. Younger alliances (up to 5 years)[1] are more war-prone than middle-aged alliances (5–11 years), which tend to be negatively associated

---

[1] Whether the cutoff between younger and middle-aged should be three years, which is what Ostrom and Hoole (1978) employ, or five years, which is Levy's (1981) test period, needs to be ascertained by further research.

with war. Mature alliances (12 years or more) are unrelated to war or peace (Chapter 5: 181; Ostrom and Hoole, 1978).

16. Alliances are not a necessary condition of war, but wars between major states are more likely to have a preceding alliance than wars between unequals (Chapter 5: 180–81; Levy, 1981; Chapter 7: 269).

17. Alliances formed during an ongoing rivalry are much more likely to eventually result in war than alliances formed in other situations (Chapter 5: 179–80, 182–83).

17a. The formation of an alliance increases insecurity, uncertainty, and hostility in the target. In a rivalry, the formation of an alliance by one side leads to the formation of a counter-alliance by the other side and/or a military buildup (Chapter 5: 182–83).

17b. The formation of an alliance by one side and a counter-alliance by the other during an ongoing rivalry leads to a scramble for allies which tends to polarize the system, depending on the extent to which the rivals are the most powerful members of the system (Chapter 5: 182–83).

17c. Polarization of the system (the creation of two blocs) increases hostility, reduces cross-cutting, and encourages persistent disagreement. All of these factors increase the probability of crises erupting (Chapter 5: 182–83).

18. Polarization of the system during a rivalry increases the probability of an arms race in some form (Chapter 5: 186–89; Wallace, 1972, 1985).

19. Alliances followed by military buildups are much more likely to lead to a war between equals than alliances that are not followed by military buildups (Chapter 5: 187–88, 192).

20. The formation of an alliance by a rival crystallizes the hostile and threatening image leaders and the public of the other side have of the rival (Chapter 5: 185, 189–90).

21. Polarization of the system or participation in a severe crisis leads both sides to define situations involving their rival in terms of a threat requiring a firm and hard-line response. Eventually the domestic policy influencers and the public are also biased in this manner (Chapter 5: 189–91; Chapter 6: 230–31, 244).

22. Crises, alliance making, and military buildups form a dynamic in which they interact and reinforce each other to produce increased hostility which in turn institutionalizes and rigidifies images and definitions

of the situation. By producing such cognitive rigidities, rising hostility increases the probability of additional crises erupting (Chapter 5: 191).

23. The presence of hostility produces a step-level effect in subsequent behavior, making actors more sensitive to negative acts and leading them to discount positive ones (Chapter 5: 192–93; Wayman, 1984b; see also Mansbach and Vasquez, 1981: ch. 7).

24. Crises repeat if the parties fail to resolve the major issues at hand. This in turn is a function of the kinds of issues they raise and the way they frame those issues (Chapter 5: 192).

25. Linkage of issues (which is produced by rivalry and polarization) makes it harder to negotiate and resolve issues (Chapter 5: 209–10; Vasquez, 1983b).

Arms races and military buildups

26. Arms races presuppose rivalry and intensify that rivalry (in terms of the actor dimension, disagreement, negative acts, and hostility) once they are under way (Chapter 5: 193). Arms races also increase insecurity (Chapter 5: 193, 200).

27. Because leaders are unlikely to get domestic support for a rapid military buildup without some concrete manifestation of the external threat, arms races usually follow a crisis and/or alliance formation rather than precede them (Chapter 5: 193–94).

28. Since crises make threats clear, the greater the number of crises, the greater the probability of an arms race or mutual military buildup of some sort (Chapter 5: 194).

29. In order to gain domestic political support for power politics practices, leaders exaggerate the threat posed by the other side and frame the issues in transcendent terms (Chapter 2: 81; Chapter 5: 189–94; Chapter 6: 231–32). This increases fear in the other side and creates constituencies more susceptible to hard-line stances, which makes it difficult for leaders to subsequently reduce the salience of the issue or to become more accommodative (Chapter 5: 212; Chapter 6: 231). This dynamic helps produce an arms race spiral (Chapter 5: 193–94).

29a. The presence of this psychological atmosphere and domestic political situation makes it more likely that crises or militarized disputes that arise during an ongoing arms race will escalate to war than crises or disputes occurring in the absence of an arms race (Chapter 5: 194–96, 201; Wallace, 1979; 1982; Morrow, 1989).

Query: Is it the mere presence of arms races that encourages crises to escalate to war or is it the case that arms races change relations so as to produce the *kinds* of crises that are apt to escalate to war (Chapter 5: 200–01)? The latter seems more plausible and suggests that there is a discernible difference in the characteristics of crises before and after arms races (or military buildups) occur (Chapter 5: 206).

30. Militarized disputes that occur in the absence of arms races or military buildups rarely escalate to war (Chapter 5: 194–95; Wallace 1982, 1990; Diehl, 1985a). This implies that among equals inadequate defense preparations tend not to be associated with crisis escalation (Chapter 5: 196; Diehl, 1985a).

Query: Some militarized disputes arise during an arms race that do not escalate to war; what do these have in common? Some common factors might have to do with the disputes themselves, such as being the first or second dispute between equals, being a dispute not involving contiguous rivals, or being a dispute in which nuclear weapons are involved (Chapter 5: 197–98). Other factors might deal with the nature or dynamic of the arms race itself (Smith, 1980; Morrow, 1989; see also Singer, 1970b).

31. Adequate defense preparations prior to a militarized dispute between equals make a party less restrained in its crisis bargaining (Chapter 5: 196, 201; Diehl, 1985a). Likewise, if there is no domestic mobilization (raising an army, taxes, etc.), leaders will not be able to fight and win a war, and therefore will be hesitant to initiate or enter one (Chapter 6: 217).

32. Arms races and military buildups increase the number and influence of hard-liners in each side; they in turn push for a military buildup (Chapter 6: 217).

33. Arms races (and/or military buildups of some sort) increase the probability of war between relative equals by increasing hostility, encouraging the outbreak of the kinds of crises most apt to escalate to war, providing adequate military preparation so that bargaining within a crisis need not be restrained, and helping generate a hard-line domestic political context (Chapter 5: 196–200).

Query: In wars of rivalry, do states follow each of the delineated steps to war, and do they follow them in a particular order? What effects do crises have on moving actors from one step to the next? (Chapter 5: 193, 206, 214).

Crisis escalation to war

34. Rivals usually go to war after a series of crises (typically three or two) with the behavior and outcome of one crisis having an escalatory effect on the subsequent one (Chapter 5: 201; Wallensteen, 1981; Leng, 1983, Diehl, 1985a). Hence most crises do not end in war (Chapter 5: 201–02; Gochman and Maoz, 1984; Cusack and Eberwein, 1982).

Query: An examination of a few cases (see Leng, 1983) shows that war between minor states does not seem to require a series of crises. Is this finding sustained when a larger number of cases are examined? What accounts for this difference between wars between major states and wars between minor states? (Chapter 5: 203, n. 17).

35. Crises and militarized disputes that escalate to war have characteristics that are clearly discernible from crises that do not escalate to war (Chapter 5: 201–02; Leng, 1983; Gochman and Leng, 1983; Diehl, 1985a; Barringer, 1972; James and Wilkenfeld, 1984; Brecher and Wilkenfeld, 1989: ch. 9, 12, 14).

35a. Among equals, a bullying bargaining strategy is usually associated with a dispute escalating to war, while a reciprocating strategy is associated with non-escalation (Chapter 5: 202; Leng and Wheeler, 1979).

35b. In a militarized dispute between equals, the use of threats that are highly credible usually produces a defiant response; between unequals, it more frequently produces compliance (Chapter 5: 202–03; Leng, 1980).

36. Between equals, each side tends to escalate the level of coercion in successive crises. This pattern holds regardless of the success or failure of escalation or decreases in capability (Chapter 5: 203–04; Leng, 1983). The reason for this is that when actions fail to produce a desired outcome, costlier and riskier actions consistent with the overall policy are tried (Chapter 6: 218).

36a. Thus, as the underlying issue fails to be resolved by force, bargaining techniques between equals become more coercive and hence more likely to escalate to war (Chapter 5: 203–04; Leng, 1983).

37. In successive crises between equals, leaders rely on the realist emphasis on power and firmness, but have difficulty in heeding realist advice on prudence (Chapter 5: 203; Leng, 1983, 1986). Coercion produces

hostility which gives leaders a motivated bias to escalate regardless of their immediate prospects of success (Chapter 5: 203). In addition, successive crises and escalation increase the willingness to take risks (Chapter 6: 222, 232–33). Even if a particular decision maker is unaffected by these variables, he or she is biased in favor of escalation by the hard-line domestic political context created by hostility and escalation (Chapter 5: 203; Chapter 6: 231–34).

38. Escalation from one crisis to the next increases the likelihood of a hostile spiral where the actions of one side lead the other to reciprocate in a more hostile manner until the end result is war (Chapter 5: 212; Holsti, Brody, and North, 1968; Maoz, 1983).

38a. In the presence of hostility, one expresses hostility (Zinnes, Zinnes, and McClure, 1972). Perceptions of hostility lead to violence (Holsti, North, and Brody, 1968). Both sides tend to exaggerate threats and both sides think the other side is being more hostile than it is, while misperceiving their own actions as less hostile than they actually are (Holsti *et al*. 1968; Chapter 6: 237).

39. A crisis is most likely to escalate to war when it begins with the use of physical violence on a territorial question (Chapter 5: 204; Gochman and Leng, 1983; James and Winkenfeld, 1984; Maoz, 1984), it is the third in a series of crises, positions harden, bargaining techniques are escalating giving rise to a hostile spiral, and at least one side is prepared for war and is dominated by hard-liners (Chapter 5: 169, 204–05, 211–12; Chapter 6: 217).

40. Crises that involve issues that parties believe are no longer susceptible to negotiation and in which leaders have made a vital public commitment and mobilized the domestic populace are much more likely to escalate to war than crises lacking these characteristics (Chapter 5: 207–08; Barringer, 1972: 1045).

40a. Third party support by a major state encourages escalation to war by discouraging a losing side from negotiating (Chapter 5: 208; Barringer, 1972: 114–15).

40b. Only when issues appear irresolvable through accommodation and reasonable alternatives having been foreclosed is military force likely (Chapter 5: 208; Barringer, 1972: 105).

40c. Persistent confrontations make rivals (leaders and their followers) feel that force is the only way to resolve the issue at hand (Chapter 5: 203).

41. *Ceteris paribus*, multiparty disputes involving at least one major state are more likely to escalate to war than dyadic disputes or disputes involving only minor states (Chapter 5: 209; Cusack and Eberwein, 1982; Gochman and Maoz, 1984; Barringer, 1972: 112, 114).

41a. Multiparty disputes involving a major state are more likely to escalate to war because they tend to be longer and produce less satisfactory outcomes (Chapter 5: 209; James and Wilkenfeld, 1984).

42. Territorial stakes that are linked with intangible issues usually involve multiple parties, are highly intractable, and are prone to successive crises (Chapter 5: 209–10).

43. The side that will initiate the war is the side that has the greater expected utility for the war (as operationalized by Bueno de Mesquita, 1981b and Bueno de Mesquita and Lalman, 1986; Chapter 6: 240).

Domestic politics

44. Prior to war, international interactions and domestic reactions to those interactions produce self-aggravating propensities that encourage leaders to take escalatory actions and make it difficult to initiate conciliatory moves or respond favorably to them (Chapter 5: 212; Chapter 6: 231–33, 236).

44a. The introduction of each new power politics practice – alliance formation, military buildup, and crisis diplomacy – increases the influence of hard-liners and support for more escalatory actions while simultaneously leading to an increase in hostility and greater insecurity (Chapter 6: 244).

44b. This process drives out accommodationist influences in each rival, increases the number and influence of hard-liners, and stiffens the leadership's determination not to give in to the opponent. This increases the probability of war (Chapter 6: 231–32, 244).

44c. From the pattern of interstate interactions, the domestic populace of each side comes to believe that leaders are correct when they say they are facing a situation that can only be handled by going to war (Chapter 6: 230, 244).

Query: Are hard-liners more prone to the most dangerous and least prudent aspect of the realist folklore, and if so, what personal traits push them toward violence (Chapter 6: 222)? What limited research exists on personal predispositions to violence suggests that those prone to advocating war are nationalistic, hold a militaristic view of the world, are distrustful of the other side, feel unable to control events, and tend to have a simple cognitive map of the world (Chapter 6: 223; Crow and Noel, 1965; M. Hermann, 1974; Etheredge, 1978; M. Haas, 1974; Driver, 1977; Brody, 1963; Guetzkow and Valadez, 1981a; Suedfeld and Tetlock, 1977; Suedfeld, Tetlock, and Ramirez, 1977). In crises, they are risk-acceptant, and in personal relations they are prone to dominance (Chapter 6: 222, 225; M. Haas, 1974; Crow and Noel, 1977; Guetzkow and Valadez, 1981b; Etheredge, 1978; Shephard, 1988).

45. Cognitive complexity of information processing and communication are lower in crises that end in unpremeditated war than they are in crises that are peacefully settled (Chapter 6: 223, 237; Suedfeld and Tetlock, 1977; Suedfeld, Tetlock and Ramirez, 1977; Wallace and Suedfeld, 1988). However, when war is initiated in a premeditated fashion cognitive complexity is high (Chapter 6: 222; Levi and Tetlock, 1980).

45a. Since Midlarsky (1988) distinguishes structural wars from mobilization wars on the basis of premeditation, it follows that integrative complexity would be low for structural wars and high (for the initiator) in mobilization wars (Chapter 6: 237).

46. After a war, hard-liners and accommodationists battle over the lessons of the war. Whether hard-liners or accommodationists are favored in a domestic political context depends on whether hard-line policies are judged to have succeeded or failed during the last major war. If the last war was won and adduced to have been worth the costs, then hard-line policies will be seen as having succeeded. If the last war was lost and adduced not to have been worth the costs, then hard-line policies will be seen as having failed. Other combinations produce an unstable and dissonant situation with costs more determinative than outcome. (Chapter 6: 226–29).

46a. Controlling for the type of war (limited vs. total) the higher the casualties in a war, the more likely it will be adduced as not worth the costs, regardless of the outcome (Chapter 6: 227; Mueller, 1971).[2]

47. Over the long term, the images and attitudes of the public toward other political actors are a function of dramatic events and tend to

---

[2] *Ceteris paribus*, the public will be more tolerant of high casualties in a total war than in a limited war, i.e. the same number of casualties in a limited war as a total war will produce different evaluations as to whether a war is worth the costs. This is a reflection of the fact that the issues at stake in a total war are of different salience from those in a limited war.

change in a direction that is consistent with the behavior of their own state (Chapter 5: 193–94; Chapter 6: 230; Wayman, 1984b; Deutsch and Merritt, 1965; Abravanel and Hughes, 1975).

48. A domestic context dominated by hard-liners will constantly push the leadership to take actions that are riskier and more hard-line than they would normally take (Chapter 6: 232).

48a. During a rivalry, in order to keep domestic support, leaders try to placate hard-liners, but in the absence of success this is difficult, since there are always some policy influencers who will advocate riskier actions than the leaders adopt (Chapter 6: 232).

48b. Leaders of states that have been successful in previous wars are more prone to taking risks than leaders of states that have been unsuccessful in previous wars (Chapter 6: 232; see also Singer, 1982).

48c. Leaders and their followers are more willing to take risks to avoid a certain loss than they are to achieve a gain (Chapter 6: 233; Kahneman and Tversky, 1979).

49. The prevalence of hard-liners in the domestic political environment sets up partisan and bureaucratic incentives for taking harder and riskier policies (Chapter 6: 234).

49a. The presence of a set of war plans and the commitment it entails (military buildups and coordination with allies) biases the leadership in favor of actions that increase the risk of war, engender misperception, and increase the sense of threat and insecurity within one's opponent (Chapter 6: 234; see also Snyder, 1984; Van Evera, 1984).

50. As nations get ready for war, each side (leadership and followers) develops mirror images (Chapter 6: 236; White, 1966).

Query: To what extent can White's (1966) findings that each side has a diabolical image of the enemy, a virile self-image, a moral self-image, and decision makers prone to selective inattention, an absence of empathy, and military overconfidence be generalized to other cases of wars of rivalry? To what extent do they hold for wars of inequality? (Chapter 6: 236).

Query: Are crises that have White's (1966) six factors more prone to war than crises in which some of the factors are absent (Chapter 6: 236)?

51. *Ceteris paribus*, hard-liners will prefer power politics practices over all other options, but will first adopt the least costly and those accepted as legitimate by the system (Chapter 6: 231).

51a. The probability that an actor will employ power politics practices and hence increase the prospect of war must be discounted by whether the global institutional context provides effective procedures for resolving issues (Chapter 6: 241–42; Wallensteen, 1984; Kegley and Raymond, 1986).

51b. When accommodationists prevail after a war, their main concern is to establish a post-war order that will prevent the use of force and war. If they are successful, new norms and rules have a legitimacy that requires that they must be tried before any unilateral action be initiated (Chapter 6: 241).

51c. A state dominated by accommodationists is not very threatening because it will have a reduced military, low military expenditures, and a public that is difficult to mobilize. The willingness of the leadership to take accommodative actions also reduces the influence of hard-liners in the other side (Chapter 6: 243).

52. Once power politics tactics are adopted by one side, it is difficult for the target not to eventually respond in kind (Chapter 6: 231, 243).

53. Expected utility calculations affect not so much whether a war occurs, but the timing of the war, once the factors promoting war, both external and domestic, are in place (Chapter 6: 240).

The Global Institutional Context

54. The frequency of war varies in different periods and systems as does the proclivity of states to engage in power politics (Chapter 8: 291; Levy, 1983; Luard, 1986; Holsti, 1991).

55. The global institutional context forms a structure that either encourages or discourages steps to war. War is less likely in an ordered structure (one in which actors are constrained from unilaterally imposing their issue preferences on others, they feel it necessary to follow certain rules of the game, and institutions exist for the resolution of issues) and more likely in a structure where there are no practices permitting interdependent decision making and the few ways of making authoritative decisions rely on unilateral acts (Chapter 8: 286–88, 291, 300–01, 303–04; Wallensteen, 1984; Väyrynen, 1983).

56. Periods in which major states have tried to reduce or eliminate unilateral acts while establishing binding norms and rule-guided means of conducting diplomacy will be more peaceful (reduction in wars and

military confrontations between major states) than other periods (Chapter 8: 291, 299; Wallensteen, 1984; Kegley and Raymond, 1984, 1986, 1990).

57. Peaceful periods and relations are associated with the conscious attempt to geographically separate major states that have a dispute over contiguous territory (Chapter 8: 293–94; Wallensteen, 1984). When major states are able to develop practices and a system for dealing with territorial issues, particularly those involving the contiguity of major states, peace is more likely (Chapter 8: 295, 302–04; Faber and Weaver, 1984).

58. Periods of war are associated with practices of power politics, while periods of peace are associated with an emphasis on other practices (like buffer states, compensation, and concerts of power) that bring major states together to form a network of institutions that provide governance for the system and that can handle certain kinds of issues (territorial, ideological, or life and death) or keep them off the agenda (Chapter 8: 301; Wallensteen, 1984).

59. The greater the number of inter-governmental organizations in the system and the more frequent their use by major states the less likely military buildups and arms races (Chapter 8: 302; Wallace, 1972; Faber and Weaver, 1984). Conversely, prior to the outbreak of war, there is a decline in shared memberships in intergovernmental organizations (Chapter 8: 301; Skjelsbaek, 1971).

60. After major wars, peace settlements attempt to establish a system for resolving future disputes and conducting relations between states (Chapter 8: 288, 301–02; Singer and Wallace, 1970; Faber and Weaver, 1984; see also Doran, 1971; Rummel, 1979; Doran, 1991; Gilpin, 1981).

Query: Doran (1971) finds that some types of peace are more successful in avoiding a repeat of war than others. What characteristics and contextual factors distinguish the successful peaces from the more war-prone (Chapter 8: 289)? How and why do structures of peace break down and give rise to a reliance on unilateral acts (Chapter 8: 305)?

61. *Ceteris paribus*, an actor will select that decision game which will give it the highest probability of winning with the least costs. However, this tendency is overridden by the rules and norms of the system which determine how decision games are selected when there is more than one game. Even when such rules are not formal, the costs associated with certain games order the sequence in which they will be played (Chapter 8: 306–09).

61a. Between equals, especially major states, war breaks out only after actors have failed to resolve their issues by following the nonviolent practices and decision games which the rules have presented as the most legitimate. In the modern global system, as these channels fail to resolve the issue, actors entertain the unilateral solutions of power politics. As each power politics practice fails to resolve the issue, actors shift from one to another, learning that war is the only way to settle the issue and effectively handle the situation they face (Chapter 8: 310–12).

62. If war between major states has been very painful and not very successful in resolving issues, it will not be favored by states. Accommodationists will prevail and attempts will be made to create new ways of resolving issues. The search for new games occurs through the examination of precedents (Chapter 8: 307–10, 313; Mueller, 1989).

A Research Agenda on the Expansion of War: Propositions and Queries:

63. Non-belligerents who have an alliance with a belligerent are more apt to be drawn into an ongoing war than other non-belligerents (Chapter 7: 254–55; Siverson and Starr, 1990, 1991; Siverson and King, 1979).

63a. Alliances that are most likely to act as a contagion mechanism are those between major and minor states, those that are defense pacts, and those that are fairly new (Chapter 7: 255–56; Siverson and King, 1980).

63b. Alliances make wars deadlier (increased battle deaths) and longer (increased months at war) by better preparing each side for war and by expanding war in a manner that makes each side relatively equal (Chapter 5: 183–84, Table 5.1; Singer and Small, 1966; Bueno de Mesquita, 1978; Wallace, 1973).

63c. Prior to world wars, alliances build up in the system (Chapter 5: 257; Chapter 7: 188–89; Midlarsky, 1983, 1986a; McGowan and Rood, 1975).

64. Non-belligerents that share a border with a belligerent are more apt to be drawn into an ongoing war than other non-belligerents, with the exception of those non-belligerents that have an alliance with one of the warring parties (Chapter 7: 257–59; Siverson and Starr, 1990, 1991; Most and Starr, 1980).

64a. Non-contiguous rivals that fight each other in a world war do so by linking the intangible issues in their rivalry with an ally's dispute over territorial contiguity (Chapter 5: 210).

65. An interstate or civil war that occurs within the context of an ongoing rivalry is more apt to expand than a war that occurs in the absence of rivalry (Chapter 7: 261).

66. Intervention by major states into an ongoing war increases the likelihood that other major states will intervene in the war. Conversely, non-intervention by major states increases the likelihood that other major states will not intervene (Chapter 7: 263–64; Yamamoto and Bremer, 1980).

67. Wars involving major and minor states are more prone to expansion than wars involving only minor states (Chapter 7: 250–52; Sabrosky, 1985; Midlarsky, 1988). Major states are more apt to intervene in an ongoing war than minor states (Chapter 7: 251, 259–60; Siverson and Starr, 1990, 1991; Siverson and King, 1979, 1980; Yamamoto and Bremer, 1980).

68. Prior to world wars, disputes of major states are combined with disputes of minor states, making the issues more intractable and prone to a buildup of disputes in the system (Chapter 7: 251–53; Midlarsky, 1988; Leng, 1983).

69. The breakdown of a regional or global political order due to an ongoing war encourages further expansion of the war (Chapter 7: 265–67).

70. The expansion of war is associated with alliances, territorial contiguity, rivalry, intervention by major states, the breakdown of political order, and economic dependence (Siverson and King, 1979; Most and Starr, 1980; Siverson and Starr, 1990, 1991; Yamamoto and Bremer, 1980). Each of these factors has a separate and cumulative effect, with the first three basic factors provoking the initial intervention and the last three promoting further expansion. (Chapter 7: 254, 268–69)

71. The escalation of militarized disputes in the presence of arms races is more associated with complex wars, especially world wars, than with other types of war (Chapter 5: 198; Weede, 1980; Diehl, 1983; Houweling and Siccama, 1981).

Query: Is the association between arms races and complex war a correlate or a cause? Do arms races actually cause wars to expand, and if so how (Chapter 5: 198)?

71a. If there are several arms races ongoing before a war, the war, once it comes, is likely to be deadlier (battle deaths) and longer (months) than wars that are not preceded by several ongoing arms races (Chapter 5: 198).

72. The use of coercion is contagious; the initiation of one serious dispute increases the likelihood that another serious dispute will emerge, involving other parties in the system as well as increasing the probability of a second dispute between the same parties (Chapter 7: 264–65; Bremer, 1982).

72a. As coercion spreads, it weakens prohibitions and norms against the use of violence and unilateral behavior, which in turn increases the likelihood and frequency of coercion and violence (Chapter 7: 265; see also Gurr, 1970: 170).

73. The probability of a civil war becoming internationalized or a revolution provoking intervention goes up if domestic opponents have foreign allies (Chapter 5: 208; Chapter 7: 266; Maoz, 1989; Barringer, 1972).

74. A state that is weakened by revolution or civil war and had previously settled a territorial question to its advantage by the use of force can now expect that issue to be raised again by the losing party (Chapter 4: 158; Maoz, 1989).

75. World war occurs only in the presence of three necessary conditions: (1) a multipolar distribution of capability in the system; (2) an alliance system that reduces this multipolarity to two hostile blocs; and (3) the creation of two blocs in which one side does not have a clear preponderance of capability over the other (Chapter 7: 268).

75a. A multipolar distribution of capability that has been polarized into two blocs accounts for the scope of the war (Wayman, 1984b; Levy, 1985a; Bueno de Mesquita, 1978), the lack of preponderance and relative equality of capability for the severity (Singer et al., 1972); and the alliance commitments for the length of the war (Chapter 7: 272; Bueno de Mesquita, 1978; Kennedy, 1984).

76. When the core territory of a state is at issue, a war becomes a total war. World wars become total wars because the core territory of a major state becomes an issue of contention. Complex wars which do not have the core territory of a major state at issue (e.g. the Crimean War) remain limited (Chapter 2: 69; Chapter 7: 278; Kugler, 1990: 202–3).

Query: Are there other factors that keep a limited complex war (like the Crimean War) from becoming a total war among major states (Chapter 2: 69)?

Query: Sometimes concurrent wars involving major states are linked into one grand war (e.g. the European war and the Sino-Japanese war in World War II) and at other times they are kept separate (e.g. War of Spanish Succession and the Great Northern War in the early eighteenth century). Are alliances the main factor associated with the linking of wars? What conditions promote or prevent alliance making in one situation and not the other? What role, if any, does rivalry play? (Chapter 7: 254).

Appendix II

Major Findings on the Steps to War

Territory

Conflict (dispute onset, rivalry)

1. The presence of a territorial claim (disagreements that have not yet resorted to the threat or use of force) between two states increases the probability of a militarized interstate dispute (MID) (Senese and Vasquez, 2003; see also Colaresi, Rasler, and Thompson, 2007: 253).

2. Dyads that are neighbors (i.e. contiguous) are more apt to have a MID than non-contiguous dyads (Senese, 2005).

3. Intangible territorial claims are more apt to have a MID than tangible territorial claims (Hensel and Mitchell, 2005).

4. Not all territorial issues are equally likely to escalate to the threat or use of force (as in a MID). Territorial issues (claims) involving ethnic questions are the most conflict-prone (Huth, 1996b; Hensel and Mitchell, 2005; Hensel *et al.*, 2008), strategic territory the next, and territorial claims involving economic resources the least conflict-prone (Huth, 1996b; Huth and Allee, 2002: ch. 9).

4a. Salient territorial issues (i.e. those involving homeland territory, ethnicity, or a long history of sovereign rule) are more apt to have a MID (Hensel *et al.*, 2008).

5. Territorial disputes are more apt to be reciprocated (Hensel and Diehl, 1994; Hensel, 1996a) and tend to recur (Hensel, 1994, 1996a, 1998) (see also finding 14 below).

6. A sense of rivalry and contesting territory produce militarized disputes (Rasler and Thompson, 2006; Colaresi, Rasler, and Thompson, 2007: ch. 9).

7. Territorial disputes are the source of most interstate rivalries (Vasquez and Leskiw, 2001; Tir and Diehl, 2002), particularly among minor–minor dyads and neighbors (Vasquez and Leskiw, 2001).

8. States that have territorial disputes with each other are more apt to have fatal MIDs (Senese, 1996; Hensel, 2000).

9. Enduring rivals that are territory-based have more severe MIDs (Tir and Diehl, 2002).

War onset

10. Territorial disputes have a higher probability of going to war than other types of disputes (Hensel, 1996a; Vasquez and Henehan, 2001; Vasquez, 2001, 2004; Senese and Vasquez, 2005, 2008). This holds for major–major, major–minor, and minor–minor dyads (with few exceptions) and for the 1816–1945, 1946–89, and 1990–2001 periods.

10a. Controlling for the effect of territorial claims at the MID onset stage does not eliminate the effect of territorial disputes (MIDs) at the escalation to war stage, i.e. territorial MIDs increase the probability of war, even while controlling for the effect of territorial claims on dispute onset (Senese and Vasquez, 2003).

10b. Controlling for the effect of contiguity at the MID onset stage does not eliminate the effect of territory at the escalation to war stage (Senese, 2005).

10c. Territorial claims and contiguity increase the likelihood of a MID, but the presence of a territorial dispute is the primary determinant of whether a MID is likely to escalate to war (Senese and Vasquez, 2003; Senese, 2005).

11. States with policy disputes are more apt to avoid war compared to states with territorial disputes or even regime disputes (Vasquez and Henehan, 2001; Vasquez, 2004).

12. Not all territorial issues are equally likely to go to war. Those that are the most intrinsically salient, namely those involving homeland territory, ethnic questions, and previous possession, are the most war-prone (Hensel and Mitchell, 2005; cf. finding 4 above).

13. Intangible territorial issues (claims) are more likely to go to war than tangible territorial issues (Hensel and Mitchell, 2005).

14. Dyads that have recurring territorial MIDs (four or more) have an increased probability of having a war (Senese and Vasquez, 2008: ch. 5). This is a separate and independent effect from rivalry (see finding 26 below).

14a. Dyads that have a history of territorial MIDs will go to war sooner than dyads that have a history of non-territorial MIDs (Petersen, 2008).

15. Dyads that have territorial disputes are more likely to have a war whether or not they are contiguous. Controlling for the presence of territorial disputes wipes out the significance between contiguity and war onset (Vasquez, 2001; Senese, 2005). The same is true of fatal MIDs (Hensel, 2000). These findings indicate that the territorial explanation of war is superior to the contiguity explanation of war.

16. Territorial disputes that are handled through the use of power politics are more apt to go to war than those that are not. Dyads that have outside alliances, a pattern of rivalry (recurring disputes), and an ongoing arms race are subject to a step-wise increase in the probability that the territorial MID will escalate to war. This pattern holds for the entire post-Napoleonic period for rivalry, for 1816–1945 and 1990–2000 for alliances, and for 1816–1945 for arms races.

16a. The use of power politics to handle policy and regime disputes also increases the likelihood that they will escalate to war (following the same pattern as in finding 16). This indicates that power politics have a separate and independent effect from territory.

Peace

17. Dyads that have legally accepted their borders are considerably less likely to go to war (Kocs, 1995) or raise a territorial claim (see Huth, 1996b: 182). Likewise, dyads that have stable borders are unlikely to have MIDs (Gibler, 2007).

18. Alliances that settle territorial disputes are less likely to be followed by war than other alliances (Gibler, 1996).

19. Once states settle their territorial claims, the probability of having any future MID goes way down (Hensel, 2006).

19a. Enduring rivals that settle their territorial disputes experience a significant reduction in future MIDs (Gibler, 1997a).

20. Leaders will resort to legal settlement procedures to deal with territorial disputes rather than make concessions during negotiations, if they face political opposition or anticipate adverse domestic costs (Allee and Huth, 2006a, 2006b; Simmons, 1999).

21. Peaceful historical eras have few territorial disputes on the agenda (Henehan and Vasquez, 2006).

22. Joint democratic dyads tend not to have many territorial disputes (Mitchell and Prins, 1999). Even when they have territorial claims against each other, they rarely threaten or use force over these claims (Huth and Allee, 2002: 267).

23. States with stable borders are more apt to become democracies (Gibler, 2007). The absence of external territorial MIDs is related to a higher level of domestic political tolerance (Hutchison and Gibler, 2007).

Power Politics and War

24. The probability of war increases if states possess politically relevant outside alliances prior to the onset of a MID (holds for the 1816–1945 and 1990–2001 periods) (Senese and Vasquez, 2004, 2005, 2008).

25. Alliances composed entirely of major states, those that have been successful in their last war, and/or dissatisfied states tend to have a greater likelihood of being followed by a war within five years than those without these characteristics (Gibler, 1997b, 2000).

26. Rivals have a higher probability of going to war than non-rivals. A majority of wars fought since 1815 are associated with rivals (Goertz and Diehl, 1992; Colaresi, Rasler, and Thompson, 2007: ch. 3).

26a. As the number of prior disputes between states goes up, the likelihood of war also goes up (Senese and Vasquez, 2005; 2008: ch. 6).

26b. However, some rivals can learn to manage their disputes. There is an inverted U-shaped relationship between the number of prior disputes and the probability of war for the Cold War (1946–89) period (Senese and Vasquez, 2005, 2008: ch. 6).

27. Major states that are rivals and engaged in a power transition (or related power shifts) are more apt to go to war (Wayman, 1996).

28. Rivals that use violence as a central management technique in crises have an increased gravity of threat present, and highly salient issues at stake are more apt to go to war (Brecher and Wilkenfeld, 1997: 832–33; Colaresi, Rasler, and Thompson, 2007: ch. 4).

29. Multiparty disputes are more apt to escalate to war than dyadic disputes; this is especially true of multiparty territorial MIDs (Petersen, Vasquez, and Wang, 2004; see also Colaresi, Rasler, and Thompson, 2007: ch. 4).

30. There are two paths to war; one involves contiguous states contesting territory, and a second non-contiguous states often contesting policy issues (or positional issues). Non-contiguous rivals come to war primarily by joining ongoing wars rather than fighting each other directly in a dyadic war (Vasquez, 1996b; Rasler and Thompson, 2000; Colaresi, Rasler and Thompson, 2007: ch. 6).

31. Strategic rivalries that are contiguous and contest territory are highly war-prone (Rasler and Thompson, 2006; Colaresi, Rasler, and Thompson, 2007: ch. 9).

32. Dyads that resort to the practices of power politics (alliance making and arms races) are more likely to become rivals (proto- and enduring) (Valeriano, 2003).

33. Rivals tend to escalate their interactions from one dispute to the next. Rivals that have this escalating pattern are more likely to have a war (Valeriano, 2003).

34. In the pre-nuclear era, militarized disputes between states engaged in an arms race are more likely to eventuate in war compared to those between states not engaged in an arms race (Sample, 1997, 2000, 2002; Senese and Vasquez, 2005; 2008: chs. 5, 6).

35. Among rivals, alliance making tends to precede arms racing (Valeriano, 2003).

36. Strategic rivals that contend over territory are more apt to engage in arms racing (Rider, forthcoming), and strategic rivals that have arms races are more likely to go to war than those that do not (Gibler, Rider, and Hutchison, 2005).

37. For the 1816–1945 period, a dyad has a higher probability of war if it has a territorial dispute and simultaneously has outside allies, has been engaged in an enduring rivalry, and has had an arms race. A dyad experiences ever-increasing probabilities of going to war as each of these factors is present. Although this pattern is most prominent in the presence of territorial disputes, any dispute (e.g. regime or policy disputes) will have an increased proclivity to going to war if handled in the above manner, although the probability of war is lower than that for territorial disputes (Senese and Vasquez, 2005; 2008: chs. 5, 6).

37a. The steps to war are mutually reinforcing; the more steps each side takes, the greater the probability of war. For the 1816 to 1945 period, the most dangerous condition (i.e., producing the highest probability of war) identified in research is when two states (1) engage in territorial MIDs; (2) have politically relevant outside alliances; (3) engage in repeated disputes; and (4) are involved in arms races. During the 1946 to 1989 span, only the first and third factors are strong indicators of a high probability of war (Senese and Vasquez, 2005; 2008: chs. 5, 6; see also Colaresi and Thompson, 2005).

37b. Each of these "steps to war" has an impact even while controlling for the other steps (Senese and Vasquez, 2005; 2008: chs. 5, 6; see also Colaresi and Thompson, 2005).

38. During the Cold War both sides having outside alliances reduces the likelihood of war, but having one side with an outside alliance still increases it under certain conditions.

39. The larger the war the more likely that key dyads will have engaged in power politics prior to the outbreak of the war. This implies that the resort to power politics helps wars expand (Valeriano and Vasquez, 2010).

40. Peaceful historical eras are associated with the absence of arms races among major states (Vasquez, 2001).

Interactions

(Except as noted, the source of all of the following is Senese and Vasquez, 2008: ch. 7)

41. Multiplicative processes are not the typical means by which escalation to war occurs. Interaction does occur where it would be expected theoretically: mostly with territorial disputes, occasionally with rivalry, and hardly ever with arms races.

For the 1816–1945 period:

42. Territorial disputes have an enhanced likelihood of escalating to war as disputes repeat (i.e., when states are in a rivalry). As the number of prior disputes increase in the presence of territorial disputes, there is a higher likelihood of war than with the simple addition of the individual effects of each.

43. Territorial disputes have an enhanced likelihood of escalating to war when states have outside alliances (specifically [a] one side having an outside alliance, and [b] being allied to each other but also having an outside alliance). For this period there is no positive interaction

between having a territorial MID in the presence of both sides having an outside alliance.

43a. There are no significant interaction effects between territorial MIDs and arms races.

44. Rivalries (those with an increasingly greater number of MIDs) have an enhanced likelihood of escalating to war when both sides have outside alliances. Other forms of outside alliances do not exhibit this tendency.

44a. There is also no positive interaction between rivalry and arms racing.

44b. Arms races have no positive interactions with any of the other steps to war.

For the 1946–89 Cold War period:

45. The long peace in the Cold War is associated with considerably fewer positive interactions involving the steps to war (compared to the 1816–1945 and 1990–2001 periods). The Cold War has only two positive interactions, whereas the other two periods have five and four, respectively.

46. During the Cold War there are negative interactions between both sides having outside alliances, in the case of rivalry and in the case of territorial disputes. This means that the polarized alliance structure of the Cold War greatly reduces the likelihood of war when states are rivals or have ongoing territorial disputes. However, when only one side has an outside ally in these same two conditions (rivalry and territory), the probability of war is enhanced.

For the 1919–95 period (Colaresi and Thompson, 2005; see also Colaresi, Rasler, and Thompson 2007: 264–65):

47. After two crises, having an external alliance greatly enhances the hazard of war.

48. After two crises, having a mutual military buildup greatly enhances the hazard of war.

~

References

Abel, Theodore (1941) "The Element of Decision in the Pattern of War," *American Sociological Review* 6: 853–59.

Abravanel, Martin, and Barry Hughes (1975) "Public Attitudes and Foreign Policy Behavior in Western Democracies" in W. Chittick (ed.), *The Analysis of Foreign Policy Outputs*, Columbus: Charles E. Merrill, pp. 46–73.

Alcock, John (1989) *Animal Behavior: An Evolutionary Approach*, 4th ed., Sunderland, Mass.: Sinaver Associates, Inc.

Alexander, Richard (1987) *The Biology of Moral Systems*, Hawthorne, New York: Aldine de Gruyfer.

Alker, Hayward R. (1996a) "The Presumption of Anarchy in World Politics" in H. Alker, *Rediscoveries and Reformulations*, Cambridge: Cambridge University Press, pp. 355–93.

(1996b) *Rediscoveries and Reformulations*, Cambridge: Cambridge University Press.

Alker, Hayward R., Jr., and P. G. Bock (1972) "Propositions about International Relations: Contributions from the International Encyclopedia of the Social Sciences" in J. Robinson (ed.), *Political Science Annual*, vol. III, Indianapolis: Bobbs-Merrill, pp. 385–495.

Allan, Pierre (1983) *Crisis Bargaining and the Arms Race: A Theoretical Model*, Cambridge, Mass.: Ballinger.

Allee, Todd L., and Paul Huth (2006a) "Legitimizing Dispute Settlement: International Adjudication as Domestic Political Cover," *American Political Science Review* 100 (May): 219–23.

(2006b) "The Pursuit of Legal Settlements in Territorial Disputes," *Conflict Management and Peace Science* 23 (Winter): 285–307.

Altfeld, Michael (1983) "Arms Races? – and Escalation? A Comment on Wallace," *International Studies Quarterly* 27 (June): 225–31.

Ardrey, Robert (1966) *The Territorial Imperative*, New York: Atheneum.

Asal, Victor, and Kyle Beardsley (2007) "Proliferation and International Crisis Behavior," *Journal of Peace Research* 44 (20): 139–55.

Ashley, Richard K. (1981) "Political Realism and Human Interests," *International Studies Quarterly* 25 (June): 204–36.

(1984) "The Poverty of Neorealism," *International Organization* 38 (Spring): 225–86.

(1987) "The Geopolitics of Geopolitical Space: Toward a Critical Social Theory of International Politics," *Alternatives* 12 (October): 403–34.

(1988) "Untying the Sovereign State: A Double Reading of the Anarchy Problematique," *Millennium* 17 (2): 227–62.

Bachrach, Peter, and Morton Baratz (1962) "The Two Faces of Power," *American Political Science Review* 56 (December): 947–52.

Bailey, Thomas A. (1948) *The Man in the Street*, New York: Macmillan.

Banks, Michael (1985) "The Inter-Paradigm Debate" in M. Light and A. J. R. Groom (eds.), *International Relations: A Handbook of Current Theory*, Boulder: Lynne Rienner, pp. 7–26.

Barringer, Richard (1972) *War: Patterns of Conflict*, Cambridge, Mass; MIT Press.

Bateson, Patrick (1989) "Is Aggression Instinctive?" in J. Groebel and R. Hinde (eds.), *Aggression and War*, Cambridge: Cambridge University Press, pp. 35–47.

Ben-Yehuda, Hemda (1997) "Territoriality, Crisis and War: An Examination of Theory and 20th Century Evidence," Paper presented at the annual meeting of the International Studies Association, Toronto, March 19.

(2004) "Territoriality and War in International Crises: Theory and Findings, 1918–2001," *International Studies Review* 5 (December): 85–105.

Bennett, D. Scott, and Alan Stam (2004) *The Behavioral Origins of War*, Ann Arbor: University of Michigan Press.

Bercovitch, Jacob, and Paul F. Diehl (1997) "Conflict Management of Enduring Rivalries: The Frequency, Timing, and Short-Term Impact of Mediation," *International Interactions* 22 (July–September): 299–320.

Bercovitch, Jacob, and Jeffrey Langley (1993) "The Nature of Dispute and the Effectiveness of International Mediation," *Journal of Conflict Resolution* 37 (December): 670–91.

Berger, Peter L., and Thomas Luckmann (1966) *The Social Construction of Reality*, New York: Doubleday.

Bismarck, Otto von (1862) Speech before the Prussian Diet, September 30 (quoted in *Bartlett's Familiar Quotations* [Boston: Little, Brown, 1955]: 696a, note 1).

Bobrow, Davis, and Neal Cutler (1967) "Time-Oriented Explanations of National Security Beliefs: Cohort, Life-Stage and Situation," *Peace Research Society (International) Papers* 8: 31–57.

Boswell, Terry, and Mike Sweat (1991) "Hegemony, Long Waves, and Major Wars: A Time Series Analysis of Systemic Dynamics, 1496–1967," *International Studies Quarterly* 35 (June): 123–49.

Boulding, Kenneth (1962) *Conflict and Defense: A General Theory*, New York: Harper and Row.

Braithwaite, Alex, and Glenn Palmer (2003) "The Escalation and Geography of Militarized Interstate Disputes, 1993–2001," Paper presented at the annual meeting of the Peace Science Society, Ann Arbor, November.

Brams, Steven J. (1993) *Theory of Moves*, Cambridge: Cambridge University Press.

Braudel, Fernand (1966) *The Mediterranean and the Mediterranean World in the Age of Philip II*, English translation, 1973, New York: Harper and Row.

Brecher, Michael, and Patrick James (1988) "Patterns of Crisis Management," *Journal of Conflict Resolution* 32 (September): 426–56.

Brecher, Michael, Patrick James, and Jonathan Wilkenfeld (2000) "Escalation and War in the Twentieth Century: Findings from the International Crisis Behavior Project" in J. Vasquez (ed.), *What Do We Know about War?* Lanham, Md.: Rowman & Littlefield, pp. 37–53.

Brecher, Michael, and Jonathan Wilkenfeld (1989) *Crisis, Conflict and Instability*, Oxford: Pergamon Press.

——— (1997) *A Study of Crisis*, Ann Arbor: University of Michigan Press.

Bremer, Stuart A. (1980) "National Capabilities and War Proneness" in J. D. Singer (ed.), *The Correlates of War*, vol. II, New York: Free Press, pp. 57–82.

——— (1982), "The Contagiousness of Coercion: The Spread of Serious International Disputes, 1900–1976," *International Interactions* 9 (1): 29–55.

——— (1990) "Dangerous Dyads: Conditions Affecting the Likelihood of Interstate War," Paper presented at the annual meeting of the Peace Science Society (International), New Brunswick, N.J., November 12.

——— (1992) "Dangerous Dyads: Conditions Affecting the Likelihood of Interstate War, 1816–1965," *Journal of Conflict Resolution* 36 (June): 309–41.

——— (1995) "Advancing the Scientific Study of War" in S. A. Bremer and T. R. Cusack (eds.), *The Process of War: Advancing the Scientific Study of War*, Amsterdam: Gordon and Breach, pp. 1–34.

——— (2000) "Who Fights Whom, When, Where, and Why?" in J. Vasquez (ed.), *What Do We Know about War?* Lanham, Md.: Rowman & Littlefield, pp. 23–36.

Bremer, Stuart, Cynthia Cannizzo, Charles W. Kegley, and James Ray (1975) *The Scientific Study of War*. New York: Learning Resources in International Studies; reprinted in J. Vasquez and M. Henehan (eds.), *The Scientific Study of Peace and War*, New York: Lexington Books, 1992, pp. 373–437.

Brody, Richard A. (1963) "Some Systemic Effects of the Spread of Nuclear-Weapons Technology," *Journal of Conflict Resolution* 7 (December): 663–753.

Bronfenbrenner, Urie (1961) "The Mirror Image in Soviet–American Relations: A Social Psychologist's Report," *Journal of Social Issues* 17 (3): 45–56.

Brown, Robert (1963) *Explanation in Social Science*, Chicago: Aldine.

Bueno de Mesquita, Bruce (1978) "Systemic Polarization and the Occurrence and Duration of War," *Journal of Conflict Resolution* 22 (June): 241–67.

(1981a) "Risk, Power Distributions, and the Likelihood of War," *International Studies Quarterly* 25 (December): 541–68.

(1981b) *The War Trap*, New Haven: Yale University Press.

(1985) "The War Trap Revisited: A Revised Expected Utility Model," *American Political Science Review* 79 (March): 157–76.

Bueno de Mesquita, Bruce, and David Lalman (1986) "Reason and War," *American Political Science Review* 80 (December): 1113–29.

(1988) "Empirical Support for Systemic and Dyadic Explanations of International Conflict," *World Politics* 41 (October): 1–20.

Bull, Hedley (1977) *The Anarchical Society*, New York: Columbia University Press.

Burton, John W. (1982) *Dear Survivors*, London: Frances Pinter.

(1984) *Global Conflict: The Domestic Sources of International Crisis*, Brighton: Wheatsheaf.

Burton, J. W., A. J. R. Groom, C. R. Mitchell, and A. V. S. de Reuck (1974) *The Study of World Society: A London Perspective*, Occasional Paper No. 1, International Studies Association.

Campbell, David (1989) "Security and Identity in United States Foreign Policy: A Reading of the Carter Administration," Ph.D. dissertation, Australian National University.

Carr, E. H. (1939) *The Twenty Years' Crisis* (1964 ed.), New York: Harper and Row.

Chan, Steve (1984) "Mirror, Mirror on the Wall ...: Are the Freer Countries More Pacific?" *Journal of Conflict Resolution* 28 (December): 617–48.

Chay, John, and Thomas E. Ross (1986) (eds.) *Buffer States in World Politics*, Boulder, Colo.: Westview.

Chernoff, Fred (2004) "The Study of Democratic Peace and Progress in International Relations," *International Studies Review* 6 (March): 49–78.

Chi, H. (1968) "The Chinese Warlord System as an International System" in M. Kaplan (ed.), *New Approaches to International Relations*, New York: St. Martin's Press, pp. 403–25.

Choucri, Nazli, and Robert C. North (1975) *Nations in Conflict*, San Francisco: W. H. Freeman.

Choucri, Nazli, Robert C. North, and Susumu Yamakage (1992) *The Challenge of Japan Before World War II and After: A Study of National Growth and Expansion*, London: Routledge.

Claude, Inis L., Jr. (1962) *Power and International Relations*, New York: Random House.

Clausewitz, Carl von (1832) *On War*, J. J. Graham translation, 1874 (1966 ed.), London: Routledge and Kegan Paul.

Colaresi, Michael P., Karen Rasler, and William R. Thompson (2007) *Strategic Rivalries in World Politics: Position, Space, and Conflict Escalation*, Cambridge: Cambridge University Press.

Colaresi, Michael P., and William R. Thompson (2005) "Alliances, Arms Buildups and Recurrent Conflict: Testing a Steps-to-War Model," *Journal of Politics* 67 (May): 345–64.

Coplin, William D., Stephen L. Mills, and Michael K. O'Leary (1973) "The PRINCE Concepts and the Study of Foreign Policy" in P. J. McGowan (ed.), *Sage International Yearbook of Foreign Policy Studies*, vol. I, pp. 73–103.

Coplin, William D., and Michael K. O'Leary (1971) "A Simulation Model for the Analysis and Explanation of International Interactions," Paper presented at the annual meeting of the International Studies Association, San Juan, Puerto Rico.

Craig, Gordon A., and Alexander L. George (1983) *Force and Statecraft*, New York: Oxford University Press.

Crow, Wayman J., and Robert C. Noel (1965) "The Valid Use of Simulation Results," La Jolla, Calif: Western Behavioral Sciences Institute.

   (1977) "An Experiment in Simulated Historical Decision-Making" in M. Hermann with T. Milburn (eds.), *A Psychological Examination of Political Leaders*, New York: Macmillan, pp. 385–405.

Cumings, Bruce (1981) *The Origins of the Korean War, vol. I: Liberation and the Emergence of Separate Regimes*, Princeton: Princeton University Press.

   (1990) *The Origins of the Korean War, vol. II: The Roaring of the Cataract*, Princeton: Princeton University Press.

Cusack, Thomas R., and Wolf–Dieter Eberwein (1982) "Prelude to War: Incidence, Escalation and Intervention in International Disputes, 1900–1976," *International Interactions* 9 (1): 9–28.

Cutler, Neal E. (1970) "Generational Succession as a Source of Foreign Policy Attitudes: A Cohort Analysis of American Opinion, 1946–66," *Journal of Peace Research* 7 (1): 33–48.

Dahl, Robert A. (1950) *Congress and Foreign Policy*, New York: Harcourt, Brace.

Dean, Dale P., Jr., and John A. Vasquez (1976) "From Power Politics to Issue Politics: Bipolarity and Multipolarity in Light of a New Paradigm," *Western Political Quarterly* 29 (March 1976): 7–28.

Dehio, Ludwig (1962) *The Precarious Balance*, New York: Vintage.

Denton, Frank H., and Warren Phillips (1968) "Some Patterns in the History of Violence," *Journal of Conflict Resolution* 12 (June): 182–95.

Der Derian, James, and Michael J. Shapiro (1989) (eds.) *International/Intertextual Relations: Postmodern Readings of World Politics*, Lexington, Mass.: Lexington Books.

Dessler, David (1991) "Beyond Correlations: Toward a Causal Theory of War," *International Studies Quarterly* 35 (September): 337–55.

Deutsch, Karl W., and Richard L. Merritt (1965) "Effects of Events on National and International Images" in H. Kelman (ed.), *International Behavior*, New York: Holt, Rinehart, and Winston, pp. 132–87.

Diehl, Paul (1983) "Arms Races and Escalation: A Closer Look," *Journal of Peace Research* 20 (5): 205–12.

(1985a) "Arms Races to War: Testing Some Empirical Linkages," *Sociological Quarterly* 26 (3): 331–49.

(1985b) "Contiguity and Military Escalation in Major Power Rivalries, 1816–1980," *Journal of Politics* 47 (4): 1203–11.

(1991) "Geography and War: A Review and Assessment of the Empirical Literature," *International Interactions* 17 (1): 11–27.

Diehl, Paul F., and Mark Crescenzi (1998) "Reconfiguring the Arms Race–War Debate," *Journal of Peace Research* 35 (January): 111–18.

Diehl, Paul F., and Gary Goertz (1985) "Trends in Military Allocation since 1816: What Goes Up Does Not Always Come Down," *Armed Forces and Society* 12 (1): 134–44.

(1988) "Territorial Changes and Militarized Conflict," *Journal of Conflict Resolution* 32 (March): 103–22.

(1991) "Enduring Rivalries: Theoretical Constructs and Empirical Patterns," Paper presented at the annual meeting of the International Studies Association, Vancouver, British Columbia, March 20–23.

(2000) *War and Peace in International Rivalry*, Ann Arbor: University of Michigan Press.

Dixon, William J. (1993) "Democracy and the Management of International Conflict," *Journal of Conflict Resolution* 37 (March): 42–68.

(1994) "Democracy and the Peaceful Settlement of International Conflict," *American Political Science Review* 88 (March): 14–32.

Doran, Charles F. (1971) *The Politics of Assimilation: Hegemony and Its Aftermath*, Baltimore: Johns Hopkins University Press.

(1989) "Systemic Disequilibrium, Foreign Policy Role, and the Power Cycle," *Journal of Conflict Resolution* 33 (September): 371–401.

(1991) *Systems in Crisis: New Imperatives of High Politics at Century's End*, Cambridge: Cambridge University Press.

Doran, Charles F., and Wes Parsons (1980) "War and the Cycle of Relative Power," *American Political Science Review* 74 (December): 947–65.

Doyle, Michael W. (1986) "Liberalism and World Politics," *American Political Science Review* 80 (December): 1151–69.

Driver, M. J. (1977) "Individual Differences as Determinants of Aggression in the Inter-Nation Simulation" in M. Hermann with T. Milburn (eds.), *A Psychological Examination of Political Leaders*, New York: Free Press, pp. 337–53.

Duvall, Raymond (1976) "An Appraisal of the Methodological and Statistical Procedures of the Correlates of War Project" in F. Hoole and D. Zinnes (eds.), *Quantitative International Politics: An Appraisal*, New York: Praeger, pp. 67–98.

Easton, David (1965) *A Framework for Political Analysis*, Englewood Cliffs, N.J.: Prentice-Hall.

Eberwein, Wolf-Dieter (1982) 'The Seduction of Power: Serious International Disputes and the Power Status of Nations, 1900–1976," *International Interactions* 9 (1): 57–74.

Etheredge, Lloyd S. (1978) *A World of Men: The Private Sources of American Foreign Policy*, Cambridge, Mass.: MIT Press.

Faber, Jan, and R. Weaver (1984) "Participation in Conferences, Treaties, and Warfare in the European System, 1816–1915," *Journal of Conflict Resolution* 28 (September): 522–34.

Fanon, Frantz (1968) *The Wretched of the Earth*, New York: Grove Press.

Farrar, L. L. (1977) "Cycles of War: Historical Speculations on Future International Violence," *International Interactions* 3(1): 161–79.

Fearon, James D., and David D. Laitin (1996) "Explaining Interethnic Cooperation," *American Political Science Review* 90 (December): 715–35.

(2003) "Ethnicity, Insurgency, and Civil War," *American Political Science Review* 97(1): 75–90.

Ferguson, R. Brian (1984) "Introduction: Studying War" in R. B. Ferguson (ed.), *Warfare, Culture, and Environment*, New York: Academic Press, pp. 1–81.

(1987) "War in Egalitarian Societies: An Amazonian Perspective," Paper presented at the annual meeting of the American Anthropological Association, Chicago, November 20.

Fischer, Fritz (1967) *Germany's Aims in the First World War*, New York: W. W. Norton.

Flint, Colin, Jurgen Scheffran, Paul F. Diehl, John Vasquez, and Sang-hyun Chi (2008) "The Spread of World War I in Conflict Space." typescript in progress.

Foucault, Michel (1972) *The Archaeology of Knowledge*, New York: Pantheon.

(1980) "Truth and Power" in M. Foucault, *Power/Knowledge*, edited by C. Gordon, New York: Pantheon.

Franke, W. (1968) "The Italian City-State System as an International System" in M. Kaplan (ed.), *New Approaches to International Relations*, New York: St. Martin's Press, pp. 426–58.

Freud, Sigmund (1930) *Civilization and Its Discontents*, London: The Hogarth Press.

(1933) *Why War?* (Letter to Einstein) in J. Strachey (ed.), *The Standard Edition of the Complete Psychological Works of Sigmund Freud*, vol. XX, London: The Hogarth Press, 1964, pp. 203–15.

Fried, Morton (1967) *The Evolution of Political Society: An Essay in Political Anthropology*, New York: Random House.

Frohock, Fred (1974) *Normative Political Theory*, Englewood Cliffs, N.J.: Prentice-Hall.

Fukui, Katsuyoshi and David Turton (1979) (eds.) *Warfare among East African Herders*, Osaka: National Museum of Ethnology.

Gaddis, John Lewis (1986) "The Long Peace: Elements of Stability in the Postwar International System," *International Security* 10 (Spring): 99–142.

Galtung, Johan and T. Hoivik (1971) "Structural and Direct Violence," *Journal of Peace Research* 8: 73–76.

Gamson, William A., and Andre Modigliani (1971) *Untangling the Cold War*, Boston: Little, Brown.

Gantzel, Klaus Jurgen (1981) "Another Approach to a Theory on the Causes of International War," *Journal of Peace Research* 18 (3): 39–55.

Garnham, David (1976) "Power Parity and Lethal International Violence," *Journal of Conflict Resolution* 20: 379–94.

Geiss, Imanuel (1976) *German Foreign Policy, 1871–1924*, London: Routledge and Kegan Paul.

Geller, Daniel S. (1992) "Capability Concentration, Power Transition, and War," *International Interactions* 17 (3): 269–84.

George, Alexander (1983) (ed.) *Managing U.S.–Soviet Rivalry: Problems of Crisis Prevention*, Boulder, Colo.: Westview.

Ghosn, Faten, Glenn Palmer, and Stuart A. Bremer (2004) "The MID3 Data Set, 1993–2001: Procedures, Coding Rules, and Description," *Conflict Management and Peace Science* 21 (Summer): 133–54.

Gibler, Douglas M. (1996) "Alliances that Never Balance: The Territorial Settlement Treaty," *Conflict Management and Peace Science* 15 (Spring): 75–97.

(1997a) "Control the Issues, Control the Conflict: The Effects of Alliances that Settle Territorial Issues on Interstate Rivalries," *International Interactions* 22 (April): 341–68.

(1997b) "Reconceptualizing the Alliance Variable: An Empirical Typology of Alliances," Ph.D. dissertation, Vanderbilt University.

(2000) "Alliances: Why Some Cause War and Why Others Cause Peace" in J. Vasquez (ed.), *What Do We Know about War?* Lanham, Md.: Rowman & Littlefield, pp. 145–64.

(2007) "Bordering on Peace: Democracy, Territorial Issues and Conflict," *International Studies Quarterly* 51 (September): 509–32.

Gibler, Douglas M., Toby Rider, and Marc Hutchison (2005) "Taking Arms against a Sea of Troubles: Interdependent Racing and the Likelihood of Conflict in Rival States," *Journal of Peace Research* 42 (March): 131–47.

Gibler, Douglas M., and Meredith Sarkees (2004) "Measuring Alliances: The Correlates of War Formal Interstate Alliance Dataset, 1816–2000," *Journal of Peace Research* 41 (March): 211–22.

Gibler, Douglas M., and John A. Vasquez (1998). "Uncovering the Dangerous Alliances, 1495–1980," *International Studies Quarterly* 42 (December): 785–807.

Gibler, Douglas M., and Scott Wolford (2006) "Alliances, Then Democracy: An Examination of the Relationship between Regime Type and Alliance Formation," *Journal of Conflict Resolution* 50 (February): 1–25.

Gilpin, Robert (1981) *War and Change in World Politics*, Cambridge: Cambridge University Press.

(1987) *The Political Economy of International Relations*, Princeton: Princeton University Press.

(1989) "The Theory of Hegemonic War" in R. Rotberg and T. Rabb (eds.), *The Origin and Prevention of Major Wars*, Cambridge: Cambridge University Press, pp. 15–37.

Gleditsch, Kristian S. (2002) *All International Politics is Local: The Diffusion of Conflict, Integration, and Democratization*, Ann Arbor: University of Michigan Press.

Gleditsch, Nils Petter, and J. David Singer (1975) "Distance and International War, 1816–1965," *Proceedings of the International Peace Research Association (IPRA)*, Fifth General Conference, Oslo, Norway, pp. 481–506.

Gochman, Charles S. (1980) "Status, Capabilities, and Major Power Conflict" in J. D. Singer (ed.), *The Correlates of War*, vol. II, New York: Free Press, pp. 83–123.

(1990) "The Geography of Conflict: Militarized Interstate Disputes since 1816," Paper presented at the annual meeting of the International Studies Association, Washington, D.C., April 10–14.

(1991) "Interstate Metrics: Conceptualizing, Operationalizing, and Measuring The Geographical Proximity of States since The Congress of Vienna," *International Interactions* 17 (1): 93–112.

Gochman, Charles S., and Russell J. Leng (1983) "Realpolitik and the Road to War," *International Studies Quarterly* 27 (March): 97–120.

Gochman, Charles S., and Zeev Maoz (1984) "Militarized Interstate Disputes, 1816–1976: Procedures, Patterns, and Insights," *Journal of Conflict Resolution* 28 (December): 585–616.

Goddard, Stacie E. (2006) "Uncommon Ground: Territorial Conflict and the Politics of Legitimacy," *International Organization* 60 (Winter): 35–68.

Goertz, Gary, and Paul F. Diehl (1988) "A Territorial History of the International System," *International Interactions* 15 (1): 81–93.

(1992) *Territorial Changes and International Conflict*, London: Routledge.

Goldmann, Kjell (1982) "Change and Stability in Foreign Policy: Detente as a Problem of Stabilization," *World Politics* 34 (January): 230–66.

Goldstein, Joshua S. (1987) "The Emperor's New Genes: Sociobiology and War," *International Studies Quarterly* 31 (March): 33–43.

Gourevitch, Peter (1978) "The Second Image Reversed: The International Sources of Domestic Politics," *International Organization* 32 (Autumn): 881–912.

Grotius, Hugo (1625) *The Law of War and Peace*, translated by Francis W. Kelsey (1925), Carnegie Endowment for International Peace.

Guetzkow, Harold (1950) "Long Range Research in International Relations," *The American Perspective* 4 (Fall): 421–40; reprinted in J. Vasquez (ed.), *Classics of International Relations*, Englewood Cliffs, N.J.: Prentice-Hall, 1986, 81–89.

Guetzkow, Harold, and Joseph J. Valadez (1981a) "International Relations Theory: Contributions of Simulated International Processes" in Guetzkow and Valadez (1981b), pp. 197–251.

(1981b) (eds.) *Simulated International Processes: Theories and Research in Global Modeling*, Beverly Hills: Sage.

(1981c) "Simulation and 'Reality': Validity Research" in H. Guetzkow and J. J. Valadez, *Simulated International Processes*, Beverly Hills: Sage, pp. 253–330.

Gurr, Ted R. (1970) *Why Men Rebel*, Princeton: Princeton University Press.

Haas, Ernst B. (1953) "The Balance of Power: Prescription, Concept, or Propaganda?" *World Politics* 5 (April): 442–77.

Haas, Michael (1970) "International Subsystems: Stability and Polarity," *American Political Science Review* 64 (March): 98–123.

(1974) *International Conflict*, Indianapolis: Bobbs-Merrill.

Hagan, Joe D. (2003) "Oppositions, Ruling Strategies, and the Domestic Road to War: Political Explanations of Foreign Policy and the Great Powers since 1815," Paper presented at the CEEISA/ISA International Convention, Budapest, June 26–28.

Halvard, Buhang, and Nils Petter Gleditsch (2006) "The Death of Distance? The Globalization of Armed Cinflict" in M. Kahler and B. Walter (eds.), *Territoriality and Conflict in an Era of Globalization*, Cambridge: Cambridge University Press, pp. 187–216.

Hanson, Norwood (1965) *Patterns of Discovery*, Cambridge: Cambridge University Press.

Hassner, Ron E. (2006/2007) "The Path to Intractability: Time and the Entrenchment of Territorial Disputes," *International Security* 31 (Winter): 107–38.

Hassner, Ron E., and Ann Hironaka (2002) "Can Time Heal All Wounds?" Paper presented at the annual meeting of the International Studies Association, New Orleans, March 24–27.

Hempel, Carl G. (1952) *Fundamentals of Concept Formation in Empirical Science*, Chicago: University of Chicago Press.

(1966) *Philosophy of Natural Science*, Englewood Cliffs, N.J.: Prentice-Hall.

Henderson, Errol A. (2002) *Democracy and War: The End of an Illusion?* Boulder, Colo.: Lynne Rienner Publishers.

Henehan, Marie T. (1981) "A Data-based Evaluation of Issue Typologies in the Comparative Study of Foreign Policy," Paper presented at the annual meeting of the International Studies Association, Philadelphia, March.

(1989) "Congressional Behavior on Foreign Policy Issues: A Longitudinal Analysis," Ph.D. dissertation, Rutgers University.

(2000) *Foreign Policy and Congress: An International Relations Perspective*, Ann Arbor: University of Michigan Press.

Henehan, Marie T., and John A. Vasquez (2006) "The Changing Probability of Interstate War, 1816–1992" in R. Väyrynen (ed.), *The Waning of Major War: Theories and Debates*, London: Routledge, pp. 289–99.

Hensel, Paul R. (1994) "One Thing Leads to Another: Recurrent Militarized Disputes in Latin America, 1816–1986," *Journal of Peace Research* 31 (August): 281–98.

(1996a) "Charting a Course to Conflict: Territorial Issues and Interstate Conflict, 1816–1992," *Conflict Management and Peace Science* 15 (Spring): 43–73.

(1996b) "The Evolution of Interstate Rivalry," Ph.D. dissertation, University of Illinois at Urbana-Champaign.

(1998) "Interstate Rivalry and the Study of Militarized Conflict" in F. P. Harvey and B. D. Mor (eds.), *Conflict in World Politics: Advances in the Study of Crisis, War and Peace*, London: Macmillan, pp. 162–204.

(2000) "Territory: Theory and Evidence on Geography and Conflict" in J. Vasquez (ed.), *What Do We Know about War?* Lanham, Md.: Rowman & Littlefield, pp. 57–84.

(2001) "Contentious Issues and World Politics: The Management of Territorial Claims in the Americas, 1816–1992," *International Studies Quarterly* 45 (March): 81–109.

(2006) "Territorial Claims and Armed Conflict between Neighbors," Paper presented at the Lineae Terrarum International Borders Conference, University of Texas – El Paso, New Mexico State University, Colegio de la Frontera Norte, and Universidad Autonoma de Ciudad Juarez, March.

Hensel, Paul R., and Paul F. Diehl (1994) "It Takes Two to Tango: Non-Militarized Response in Interstate Disputes," *Journal of Conflict Resolution* 38 (September): 479–506.

Hensel, Paul R., and Sara McLaughlin Mitchell (2005) "Issue Indivisibility and Territorial Claims," *Geojournal* 64 (December): 275–85.

Hensel, Paul R., Sara McLaughlin Mitchell, Thomas E. Sowers II, and Clayton L. Thyne (2008) "Bones of Contention: Comparing Territorial, Maritime, and River Issues," *Journal of Conflict Resolution* 52 (February): 117–43.

Hermann, Charles F., and Robert E. Mason (1980) "Identifying Behavioral Attributes of Events That Trigger International Crises" in O. Holsti, R. Siverson, and A. George (eds.), *Change in the International System*, Boulder, Colo.: Westview, pp. 189–210.

Hermann, Margaret G. (1974) "Leader Personality and Foreign Policy Behavior" in J. Rosenau (ed.), *Comparing Foreign Policies*, New York: Halsted, pp. 201–34.

(1978) "Effects of Personal Characteristics of Political Leaders on Foreign Policy" in M. East, S. Salmore, and C. Hermann (eds.), *Why Nations Act*, Beverly Hills: Sage, pp. 49–68.

(1980) "Explaining Foreign Policy Behavior Using the Personal Characteristics of Political Leaders," *International Studies Quarterly* 24 (March): 7–46.

Hewitt, J. Joseph (2003) "Dyadic Processes and International Crises," *Journal of Conflict Resolution* 47 (October): 669–92.

(2005) "A Crisis-Density Formulation for Identifying Rivalries," *Journal of Peace Research* 42 (March): 183–200.

Hintze, Otto (1902) "The Formation of States and Constitutional Development: A Study in History and Politics" in F. Gilbert (ed.), *The Historical Essays of Otto Hintze*, New York: Oxford University Press, pp. 156–77.

(1906) "Military Organization and the Organization of the State" in F. Gilbert (ed.), *The Historical Essays of Otto Hintze*, New York: Oxford University Press, pp. 178–215.

Hobbes, Thomas (1651) *Leviathan* (1950 ed.), New York: E.P. Dutton.

Hoffmann, Frederick (1970) "Arms Debates – A 'Positional Interpretation'," *Journal of Peace Research* 7 (3): 219–28.

Hollis, Martin, and Steve Smith (1991) *Explaining and Understanding International Relations*, Oxford: Clarendon Press.

Holsti, Kalevi J. (1991) *Peace and War: Armed Conflicts and International Order 1648–1989*, Cambridge: Cambridge University Press.

Holsti, Ole R. (1972) *Crisis, Escalation, War*, Montreal: McGill-Queen's University Press.

Holsti, Ole, Robert North, and Richard Brody (1968) "Perception and Action in the 1914 Crisis" in J. D. Singer (ed.), *Quantitative International Politics*, New York: Free Press, pp. 123–58.

Holsti, Ole R., and James N. Rosenau (1984) *American Leadership in World Affairs: Vietnam and the Breakdown of Consensus*, Boston: Allen and Unwin.

Horn, Michael Dean (1987) *Arms Races and the International System*. Ph.D. dissertation, University of Rochester.

Houweling, Henk W., and Jan G. Siccama (1981) "The Arms Race–War Relationship: Why Serious Disputes Matter," *Arms Control* 2 (September): 157–97.

(1985) "The Epidemiology of War, 1816–1980," *Journal of Conflict Resolution* 29 (December): 641–63.

(1988a) "Power Transition as a Cause of War," *Journal of Conflict Resolution* 32 (March): 87–102.

(1988b) *Studies of War*, Dordrecht: Martinus Nijhoff.

Howard, Michael (1976) *War in European History*, New York: Oxford University Press.

Hughes, H. Stuart (1961) *Contemporary Europe: A History*, Englewood Cliffs, N.J.: Prentice-Hall.

Hunter, John E., Frank L. Schmidt, and Gregg B. Jackson (1982) *Meta-analysis: Cumulating Research Findings across Studies*, Beverly Hills: Sage.

Huntingford, Felicity Ann (1989) "Animals Fight, but Do Not Make War" in J. Groebel and R. Hinde (eds.), *Aggression and War*, Cambridge: Cambridge University Press, pp. 25–34.

Huntington, Samuel P. (1968) *Political Order in Changing Societies*, New Haven: Yale University Press.

Hutchison, Marc, and Douglas M. Gibler (2007) "Political Tolerance and Territorial Threat: A Cross-national Study," *Journal of Politics* 69 (February): 128–42.

Huth, Paul K. (1996a) "Enduring Rivalries and Territorial Disputes, 1950–1990," *Conflict Management and Peace Science* 15 (Spring): 7–41.

    (1996b) *Standing your Ground: Territorial Disputes and International Conflict*, Ann Arbor: University of Michigan Press.

Huth, Paul K., and Todd L. Allee (2002) *The Democratic Peace and Territorial Conflict in the Twentieth Century*, New York: Cambridge University Press.

Huth, Paul, and Bruce Russett (1991) "General Deterrence Between Enduring Rivals: Testing Three Competing Models," Paper presented at the annual meeting of the International Studies Association, Vancouver, British Columbia, March 20–23.

Intrilligator, Michael D., and Dagobert L. Brito (1984) "Can Arms Races Lead to the Outbreak of War?" *Journal of Conflict Resolution* 28 (March): 63–84.

James, Patrick, Johann Park, and Whan Choi (2006) "Democracy and Conflict Management: Territorial Claims in the Western Hemisphere Revisited," *International Studies Quarterly* 50 (December): 803–18.

James, Patrick, and Jonathan Wilkenfeld (1984) "Structural Factors and International Crisis Behavior," *Conflict Management and Peace Science* 7 (Spring): 33–53.

Jervis, Robert (1976) *Perception and Misperception in International Politics*, Princeton: Princeton University Press.

    (1980) "The Impact of the Korean War on the Cold War," *Journal of Conflict Resolution* 24 (December): 563–92.

Johnson, James Turner (1975) *Ideology, Reason, and the Limitation of War*, Princeton: Princeton University Press.

    (1981) *Just War Tradition and the Restraint of War*, Princeton: Princeton University Press.

Johnston, Alastair Iain (1996) "Cultural Realism and Strategy in Maoist China" in P. J. Katzenstein (ed.), *The Culture of National Security: Norms and Identity in World Politics*, New York: Columbia University Press, pp. 216–68.

Jones, Daniel, Stuart A. Bremer, and J. David Singer (1996) "Militarized Interstate Disputes, 1816–1992: Rationale, Coding Rules, and Empirical Patterns," *Conflict Management and Peace Science* 15 (Fall): 163–213.

Jones, Joseph M. (1955) *The Fifteen Weeks*, New York: Harcourt, Brace, and World.

Kahneman, Daniel, and Amos Tversky (1979) "Prospect Theory: An Analysis of Decision under Risk," *Econometrica* 47: 263–91.

Kegley, Charles W., Jr., and Gregory A. Raymond (1982) "Alliance Norms and War: A New Piece in an Old Puzzle," *International Studies Quarterly* 26 (December): 572–95.

(1984) "Alliance Norms and the Management of Interstate Disputes" in J. D. Singer and Richard J. Stoll (eds.), *Quantitative Indicators in World Politics: Timely Assurance and Early Warning*, New York: Praeger, pp. 199–220.

(1986) "Normative Constraints on the Use of Force Short of War," *Journal of Peace Research* 23 (September): 213–27.

(1990) *When Trust Breaks Down: Alliance Norms and World Politics*, Columbia: University of South Carolina Press.

(1991) "Alliances and the Preservation of the Postwar Peace: Weighing the Contribution" in C. Kegley Jr. (ed.), *The Long Postwar Peace*, New York: HarperCollins, pp. 270–89.

Kegley, Charles W., Jr., and Richard J. Skinner (1976) "The Case-for-Analysis Problem" in J. Rosenau (ed.), *In Search of Global Patterns*, New York: Free Press, pp. 303–18.

Kehr, Eckart (1977) *Economic Interest, Militarism, and Foreign Policy: Essays on German History*, translated by G. Heinz, Berkeley: University of California Press.

Kelman, Herbert (1965) (ed.) *International Behavior*, New York: Holt, Rinehart and Winston.

Kende, Istvan (1971) "Twenty-Five Years of Local War," *Journal of Peace Research* 8 (1): 5–22.

(1978) "Wars of Ten Years," *Journal of Peace Research* 15 (3): 227–42.

Kennan, George F. (1951) *American Diplomacy, 1900–1950*, Chicago: University of Chicago Press.

Kennedy, Paul (1984) "The First World War and the International Power System," *International Security* 9 (Summer): 7–40.

(1987) *The Rise and Fall of the Great Powers*, New York: Random House.

Keohane, Robert O. (1984) *After Hegemony*, Princeton: Princeton University Press.

Kissinger, Henry (1957) *Nuclear Weapons and Foreign Policy*. New York: Harper.

Kitcher, Philip (1987) "On the Crest of 'La Nouvelle Vague'," *International Studies Quarterly* 31 (March): 45–52.

Kocs, Stephen (1995) "Territorial Disputes and Interstate War, 1945–1987," *Journal of Politics* 57 (February): 159–75.

Kratochwil, Friedrich (1986) "Of Systems, Boundaries, and Territoriality: An Inquiry into the Formation of the State System," *World Politics* (October): 27–52.

(1989) *Rules, Norms, and Decisions*, Cambridge: Cambridge University Press.

Kugler, Jacek (1990) "The War Phenomenon: A Working Distinction," *International Interactions* 16 (3): 201–13.

Kugler, Jacek, and A. F. K. Organski (1989) "The Power Transition: A Retrospective and Prospective Evaluation" in M. Midlarsky (ed.), *Handbook of War Studies*, Boston: Unwin Hyman, pp. 171–94.

Kugler, Jacek, and Frank C. Zagare (1990) "The Long-Term Stability of Deterrence," *International Interactions* 15 (3–4): 255–78.

Kuhn, Thomas S. (1970) *The Structure of Scientific Revolutions*, 2nd ed. enlarged, Chicago: University of Chicago Press.

Lakatos, Imre (1970) "Falsification and the Methodology of Scientific Research Programmes" in I. Lakatos and A. Musgrave (eds.), *Criticism and the Growth of Knowledge*, Cambridge: Cambridge University Press.

Lapid, Yosef (1989) "The Third Debate: On the Prospects of International Theory in a Post-Positivist Era," *International Studies Quarterly* 33 (September): 235–54.

Lauren, Paul Gordon (1983) "Crisis Prevention in Nineteenth-Century Diplomacy" in A. L. George (ed.), *Managing U.S.–Soviet Rivalry*, Boulder, Colo.: Westview, pp. 31–64.

Lebow, Richard Ned (1981) *Between Peace and War: The Nature of International Crisis*, Baltimore: Johns Hopkins University Press.

Leeds, Brett Ashley (2003) "Do Alliances Deter Aggression? The Influence of Military Alliances on the Initiation of Militarized Interstate Disputes," *American Journal of Political Science* 47 (July): 427–39.

(2005) "Alliances and the Expansion and Escalation of Militarized Interstate Disputes" in Alex Mintz and Bruce Russell (eds.), Lanham, Md.: Lexington Books, pp. 117–34.

Leeds, Brett Ashley, Andrew G. Long, and Sara McLaughlin Mitchell (2000) "Reevaluating Alliance Reliability: Specific Threats, Specific Promises," *Journal of Conflict Resolution* 44 (5): 686–99.

Leng, Russell J. (1980) "Influence Strategies and Interstate Conflict" in J. D. Singer (ed.), *The Correlates of War*, vol. II, New York: Free Press, pp. 124–57.

(1983) "When Will They Ever Learn? Coercive Bargaining in Recurrent Crises," *Journal of Conflict Resolution* 27 (September): 379–419.

(1986) "Realism and Crisis Bargaining: A Report on Five Empirical Studies" in J. Vasquez (ed.), *Evaluating U.S. Foreign Policy*, New York: Praeger, pp. 39–57.

(1993) *Interstate Crisis Behavior, 1816–1980: Realism vs. Reciprocity*, Cambridge: Cambridge University Press.

Leng, Russell J., and J. David Singer (1988) "Militarized Interstate Crises: The BCOW Typology and Its Applications," *International Studies Quarterly* 32 (June): 155–73.

Leng, Russell, J., and Hugh Wheeler (1979) "Influence Strategies, Success and War," *Journal of Conflict Resolution* 23 (December): 655–84.

Lenin, V. I. (1916) *Imperialism: The Highest Stage of Capitalism* in Lenin, *Selected Works*, vol. I (1967 ed.), New York: International Publishers.

Levi, Ariel, and Philip E. Tetlock (1980) "A Cognitive Analysis of Japan's Decision for War," *Journal of Conflict Resolution* 24 (June): 195–211.

Levy, Jack S. (1981) "Alliance Formation and War Behavior: An Analysis of the Great Powers, 1495–1975," *Journal of Conflict Resolution* 25 (December): 581–613.

——— (1983) *War in the Modern Great Power System, 1495–1975*, Lexington, Ky.: University Press of Kentucky.

——— (1985a) "The Polarity of the System and International Stability: An Empirical Analysis" in A. Sabrosky (ed.), *Polarity and War*, Boulder, Colo.: Westview, pp. 41–66.

——— (1985b) "Theories of General War," *World Politics* 37 (April): 344–74.

——— (1989) "The Causes of War: A Review of Theories and Evidence" in Philip E. Tetlock *et al.* (eds.), *Behavior, Society, and Nuclear War*, vol. I, New York: Oxford University Press, pp. 209–333.

——— (1990) "Big Wars, Little Wars, and Theory Construction," *International Interactions* 16 (3): 215–24.

——— (1991) "Long Cycles, Hegemonic Transitions, and the Long Peace" in C. Kegley, Jr. (ed.), *The Long Postwar Peace*, New York: HarperCollins, pp. 147–76.

——— (1994) "Learning and Foreign Policy: Sweeping a Conceptual Minefield," *International Organization* 48 (Spring): 279–312.

Levy, Jack S., and T. Clifton Morgan (1984) "The Frequency and Seriousness of War: An Inverse Relationship?" *Journal of Conflict Resolution* 28 (December): 731–49.

Lider, Julian (1977) *On the Nature of War*, Farnborough, England: Saxon House.

Lorenz, Konrad (1966) *On Aggression*, New York: Harcourt, Brace, and World.

Lowi, Theodore J. (1964) "American Business, Public Policy, Case Studies and Political Theory," *World Politics* 16 (July): 677–715.

——— (1967) "Making Democracy Safe for the World: National Politics and Foreign Policy" in J. Rosenau (ed.), *Domestic Sources of Foreign Policy*, New York: Free Press, pp. 295–331.

Luard, Evan (1986) *War in International Society*, New Haven: Yale University Press.

McClelland, Charles (1972) "The Beginning, Duration, and Abatement of International Crises: Comparisons in Two Conflict Arenas" in C. Hermann (ed.), *International Crises: Insights from Behavioral Research*, New York: Free Press, pp. 83–105.

McDougal, William (1915) "The Instinct of Pugnacity" in L. Branson and G. Goethals (eds.), *War: Studies from Psychology, Sociology, Anthropology*, New York: Basic Books, 1964: 39–43.

McGowan, Patrick J., and Robert M. Rood (1975) "Alliance Behavior in Balance of Power Systems: Applying a Poisson Model to Nineteenth-Century Europe," *American Political Science Review* 69 (September): 859–70.

McGuinness, Diane (1987) (ed.) *Dominance, Aggression, and War*, New York: Paragon House.

Malinowski, Bronislaw (1968) "An Anthropological Analysis of War" in Leon Bramson and George W. Goethals (eds.), *War*, rev. ed., New York: Basic Books, pp. 245–68.

Mannheim, Karl (1952) "The Problem of Generations" in K. Mannheim, *Essays on the Sociology of Knowledge*, P. Kecskemeti (ed.), London: Routledge and Kegan Paul, pp. 276–320.

Mansbach, Richard W., Yale H. Ferguson, and Donald E. Lampert (1976) *The Web of World Politics*, Englewood Cliffs, N.J.: Prentice-Hall.

Mansbach, Richard W., and John A. Vasquez (1981) *In Search of Theory: A New Paradigm for Global Politics*, New York: Columbia University Press.

Mansfield, Sue (1982) *The Gestalts of War*, New York: Dial Press.

Maoz, Zeev (1982) *Paths to Conflict: International Dispute Initiation, 1816–1976*, Boulder, Colo.: Westview.

(1983) "Resolve, Capabilities, and the Outcomes of Interstate Disputes, 1816–1976," *Journal of Conflict Resolution* 27 (June): 195–229.

(1984) "A Behavioral Model of Dispute Escalation: The Major Powers, 1816–1976," *International Interactions* 10 (3–4): 373–99.

(1989) "Joining the Club of Nations: Political Development and International Conflict, 1816–1976," *International Studies Quarterly* 33 (June): 199–231.

(1996) *Domestic Sources of Global Change*, Ann Arbor: University of Michigan Press.

(2004) "Pacifism, and Fightaholism in International Politics: A Structural History of National and Dyadic Conflict History, 1816–1992," *International Studies Review* 6 (December): 107–33.

Maoz, Zeev, and Nasrin Abdolali (1989) "Regime Types and International Conflict, 1816–1976," *Journal of Conflict Resolution* 33 (March): 3–35.

Maoz, Zeev, and Ben D. Mor (2002) *Bound by Struggle: The Strategic Evolution of Enduring International Rivalries*, Ann Arbor: University of Michigan Press.

Maoz, Zeev, and Bruce Russett (1993) "Normative and Structural Causes of Democratic Peace, 1946–1986," *American Political Science Review* 87 (September): 624–38.

Masters, Roger D. (1989) *The Nature of Politics*, New Haven: Yale University Press.

May, Ernest R. (1973) *"Lessons" of the Past: The Use and Misuse of History in American Foreign Policy*, New York: Oxford University Press.

(1984) "The Cold War" in J. Nye, Jr. (ed.), *The Making of America's Soviet Policy*, New Haven: Yale University Press, pp. 209–30.

Mayer, Arno, J. (1981) *The Persistence of the Old Regime: Europe to the Great War*, New York: Pantheon.

Mead, Margaret (1940) "Warfare is Only an Invention – Not a Biological Necessity," *Asia* 40/8: 402–5.

Mearsheimer, John J. (1990) "Back to the Future: Instability in Europe after the Cold War," *International Security* 15 (Summer): 5–56.

(2001) *The Tragedy of Great Power Politics*, New York: W. W. Norton.

Midlarsky, Manus I. (1978) "Analyzing Diffusion and Contagion Effects: The Urban Disorders of the 1960s," *American Political Science Review* 72 (September): 996–1008.

(1983) "Alliance Behavior and the Approach of World War I: The Use of Bivariate Negative Binomial Distributions" in D. Zinnes (ed.), *Conflict Processes and the Breakdown of International Systems*, University of Denver Monograph Series in World Affairs, vol. 20, pp. 61–80.

(1984) "Preventing Systemic War," *Journal of Conflict Resolution* 28 (December): 563–84.

(1986a) *The Disintegration of Political Systems: War and Revolution in Comparative Perspective*, Columbia: University of South Carolina Press.

(1986b) "A Hierarchical Equilibrium Theory of Systemic War," *International Studies Quarterly* 30 (March): 77–105.

(1988) *The Onset of World War*, Boston: Allen and Unwin.

(1990) (ed.) *Big Wars, Little Wars – A Single Theory?* Special Issue of International Interactions 16 (3): 157–224.

Miller, Benjamin (2007) *States, Nations, and the Great Powers: The Sources of Regional War and Peace*, Cambridge: Cambridge University Press.

Milstein, Jeffrey S. (1972) "American and Soviet Influence, Balance of Power, and Arab–Israeli Violence" in B. Russett (ed.), *Peace, War, and Numbers*, Beverly Hills: Sage, pp. 139–66.

Mintz, Alex (1985) "The Military-Industrial Complex: American Concepts and Israeli Realities," *Journal of Conflict Resolution* 29 (December): 623–39.

Mitchell, Sara McLaughlin (2002) "A Kantian System? Democracy and Third Party Conflict Resolution," *American Journal of Political Science* 46 (October): 749–59.

Mitchell, Sara McLaughlin, and Paul. R. Hensel (2007) "International Institutions and Compliance with Agreements," *American Journal of Political Science* 51 (October): 721–37.

Mitchell, Sara McLaughlin, and Brandon D. Prins (1999) "Beyond Territorial Contiguity: Issues at Stake in Democratic Militarized Interstate Disputes," *International Studies Quarterly* 43 (March): 169–83.

Modelski, George (1978) "The Long Cycle of Global Politics and the Nation-State," *Comparative Studies in Society and History* 20 (April): 214–35.

(1990) "Is World Politics Evolutionary Learning?" *International Organization* 44 (Winter): 1–24.

Modelski, George, and William R. Thompson (1989) "Long Cycles, and Global War" in M. Midlarsky (ed.) *Handbook of War Studies*, Boston: Unwin Hyman, pp. 23–54.

Morgenthau, Hans J. (1951) *In Defense of the National Interest*, New York: Knopf.
(1960) *Politics Among Nations: The Struggle for Power and Peace*, 3rd ed. New York: Knopf.
(1970) "The Origins of the Cold War" in J. Huthmacher and W. Susman (eds.), *The Origins of the Cold War*, Waltham, Mass.: Ginn, pp. 79–102.

Morrow, James D. (1989) "A Twist of Truth: A Reexamination of the Effects of Arms Races on the Occurrence of War," *Journal of Conflict Resolution* 33 (September): 500–29.

Most, Benjamin A., Philip A. Schrodt, Randolph Siverson, and Harvey Starr (1987) "Border and Alliance Effects in the Diffusion of Major Power Conflict, 1815–1965," Paper presented at the annual meeting of the International Studies Association, Washington, D.C., April.

Most, Benjamin A., and Randolph Siverson (1987) "Substituting Arms and Alliances, 1870–1914: An Exploration in Comparative Foreign Policy" in C. Hermann C. Kegley, Jr., and J. Rosenau (eds.), *New Directions in the Study of Foreign Policy*, Boston: Allen and Unwin, pp. 131–57.

Most, Benjamin A., and Harvey Starr (1980) "Diffusion, Reinforcement, Geopolitics, and the Spread of War," *American Political Science Review* 74 (December): 932–46.
(1984) "International Relations Theory, Foreign Policy Substitutability, and 'Nice' Laws," *World Politics* 36 (April): 383–406.
(1989) *Inquiry, Logic, and International Politics*, Columbia: University of South Carolina Press.

Moul, William B. (1988a) "Balances of Power and the Escalation to War of Serious Disputes among the European Great Powers, 1815–1939: Some Evidence," *American Journal of Political Science* 32 (May): 241–75.
(1988b) "Great Power Nondefense Alliances and the Escalation to War of Conflicts Between Unequals, 1815–1939," *International Interactions* 15 (1): 25–43.

Mousseau, Michael (2000) "Market Prosperity, Democratic Consolidation, and Democratic Peace," *Journal of Conflict Resolution* 44 (August): 472–507.

Mueller, John E. (1971) "Trends in Popular Support for the Wars in Korea and Vietnam," *American Political Science Review* 65 (June): 358–75.
(1989) *Retreat from Doomsday: The Obsolescence of Major War*, New York: Basic Books.

Nagel, Ernest (1961) *The Structure of Science*, New York: Harcourt, Brace, and World.

Newman, David (2006) "The Resilience of Territorial Conflict in an Era of Globalization" in M. Kahler and B. F. Walter (eds.), *Territoriality and Conflict in an Era of Globalization*, Cambridge: Cambridge University Press, pp. 85–110.

Nicholson, Michael (1983) *The Scientific Analysis of Social Behavior: A Defense of Empiricism in Social Science*, London: Frances Pinter.

(1985) "The Methodology of International Relations" in S. Smith (ed.), *International Relations: British and American Perspectives*, Oxford: Basil Blackwell, pp. 56–70.

(1987) "The Conceptual Bases of The War Trap," *Journal of Conflict Resolution* 31 (June): 346–69.

Niebuhr, Reinhold (1946) "The Myth of World Government," *The Nation* 162: 312–14.

NSC-68. National Security Council memorandum 68. Declassified in 1975 and published in *Naval War College Review* 27 (May–June, 1975): 51–108.

Oglesby, Carl (1967) *Containment and Change*, New York: Macmillan.

O'Loughlin, John, and Luc Anselin (1992) "Geography of International Conflict and Cooperation: Theory and Methods" in M. Ward (ed.), *The New Geopolitics*, New York: Gordon and Breach, pp. 11–38.

Organski, A. F. K. (1958) *World Politics*, New York: Knopf.

Organski, A. F. K., and Jacek Kugler (1980) *The War Ledger*, Chicago: University of Chicago Press.

Osgood, Robert (1957) *Limited War: The Challenge to American Strategy*, Chicago: University of Chicago Press.

Osgood, Robert, and Robert W. Tucker (1967) *Force, Order, and Justice*, Baltimore: Johns Hopkins University Press.

Ostrom, Charles W., Jr., and Francis W. Hoole (1978) "Alliances and War Revisited: A Research Note," *International Studies Quarterly* 22 (June): 215–36.

Palmer, R. R. (1961) *Historical Atlas of the World*, Chicago: Rand McNally.

Peffley, Mark, and Robert Rohrschneider (2003) "Democratization and Political Tolerance in Seventeen Countries: A Multilevel Model of Democratic Learning," *Political Research Quarterly* 56 (3): 243–57.

Petersen, Karen (2008) "History Matters: An Analysis of the Effect of Territorial Disputes on Dyadic Interstate Relations, 1816–2001." Draft typescript.

Petersen, Karen, John Vasquez, and Yijia Wang (2004) "Multiparty Disputes and the Probability of War, 1816–1992," *Conflict Management and Peace Science* 21 (Summer): 1–16.

Phillips, Nancy Edelman (1973) "Militarism and Grass Roots Involvement in the Military Industrial Complex," *Journal of Conflict Resolution* 17 (December): 625–56.

Phillips, Warren R. (1973) "The Conflict Environment of Nations: A Study of Conflict Inputs to Nations in 1963" in J. Wilkenfeld (ed.), *Conflict Behavior and Linkage Politics*, New York: David McKay, pp. 124–47.

Phillips, Warren R., and Robert C. Crain (1974) "Dynamic Foreign Policy Interactions: Reciprocity and Uncertainty in Foreign Policy" in P. McGowan (ed.), *Sage International Yearbook of Foreign Policy Studies*, vol. II, pp. 227–66.

Popper, Karl (1959) *The Logic of Scientific Discovery*, London: Hutchinson.

(1963) *Conjectures and Refutations*, London: Routledge.

Putnam, Robert D. (1988) "Diplomacy and Domestic Politics: The Logic of Two-Level Games," *International Organization* 42 (Summer): 427–60.

Randle, Robert F. (1987) *Issues in the History of International Relations*, New York: Praeger.

Rapoport, Anatol, and A. M. Chammah (1965) *Prisoner's Dilemma*, Ann Arbor: University of Michigan Press.

Rasler, Karen (1986) "War, Accommodation, and Violence in the United States, 1890–1970," *American Political Science Review* 80 (September): 921–45.

Rasler, Karen, and William R. Thompson (1983) "Global Wars, Public Debt and the Long Cycle," *World Politics* 35 (July): 489–516.

(1985a) "War and the Economic Growth of Major Powers," *American Journal of Political Science* 29 (August): 513–38.

(1985b) "War Making and State Making: Governmental Expenditures, Tax Revenues, and Global Wars," *American Political Science Review* 79 (June): 491–507.

(1989) *War and State Making: The Shaping of the Global Powers*, Boston: Unwin Hyman.

(1992) "Concentration, Polarity and Transitional Warfare," Paper presented at the annual meeting of the International Studies Association, Atlanta, Georgia, April 1–4.

(2000) "Explaining Rivalry Escalation to War: Space, Position, and Contiguity in the Major Power System," *International Studies Quarterly* 44 (September): 503–30.

(2006) "Contested Territory, Strategic Rivalries, and Conflict Escalation," *International Studies Quarterly* 50 (March): 145–67.

Ray, James Lee (1995) *Democracy and International Conflict*, Columbia: University of South Carolina Press.

(2003a) "Explaining Interstate Conflict and War: What Should be Controlled For?" *Conflict Management and Peace Science* 20 (Fall): 1–31.

(2003b) "A Lakatosian View of the Democratic Peace Research Program: Does it Falsify Realism (or Neorealism)?" in M. Fendius Elman and C. Elman (eds.), *Progress in International Relations Theory: Metrics and Methods of Scientific Change*, Boston: MIT Press, pp. 205–44.

Raymond, Gregory A. (1994) "Democracies, Disputes, and Third-party Intermediaries," *Journal of Conflict Resolution* 38 (March): 24–42.

Raymond, Gregory A., and Charles W. Kegley, Jr. (1985) "Third Party Mediation and International Norms: A Test of Two Models," *Conflict Management and Peace Science* 9 (Fall): 33–51.

Reed, William (2000) "A Unified Statistical Model of Conflict Onset and Escalation," *American Journal of Political Science* 44 (January): 84–93.

Richardson, Lewis F. (1960a) *Arms and Insecurity*, Pacific Grove, Calif.: Boxwood Press.

(1960b) *Statistics of Deadly Quarrels*, Pacific Grove, Calif.: Boxwood Press.

Rider, Toby (forthcoming) "Understanding Arms Race Onset: Rivalry, Theory, and Territorial Competition," *Journal of Politics* 71 (2).

Robinson, Ronald, and John Gallagher (1961) *Africa and the Victorians*, London: Macmillan.

Rock, Stephen R. (1989) *Why Peace Breaks Out: Great Power Rapprochement in Historical Perspective*, Chapel Hill: The University of North Carolina Press.

Rosecrance, Richard (1966) "Biopolarity, Multipolarity and the Future," *Journal of Conflict Resolution* 10 (September): 314–27.

(1973) *International Relations: Peace or War?* New York: McGraw-Hill.

Rosen, Steven (1972) "War Power and the Willingness to Suffer" in B. Russett (ed.), *Peace, War, and Numbers*, Beverly Hills: Sage, pp. 167–84.

(2005) *War and Human Nature*, Princeton: Princeton University Press.

Rosenau, James N. (1966) "Pre-Theories and Theories of Foreign Policy" in R. Farrell (ed.), *Approaches to Comparative and International Politics*, Evanston: Northwestern University Press, pp. 27–93; reprinted with revisions in J. Rosenau (1971) *The Scientific Study of Foreign Policy*, New York: Free Press.

Roy, A. Bikash (1991) "False Prophecies of Doom: The Territorial Relations of the United States with Canada and Mexico in the Nineteenth Century," Paper presented at the annual meeting of the Northeast International Studies Association, Philadelphia, November 14–16.

(1997) "Intervention across Bisecting Borders," *Journal of Peace Research* 34 (August): 303–14.

Rubin, Jeffrey Z., and Bert R. Brown (1975) *The Social Psychology of Bargaining and Negotiation*, New York: Academic Press.

Rummel, Rudolph J. (1972a) *The Dimensions of Nations*, Beverly Hills: Sage.

(1972b) "U.S. Foreign Relations: Conflict Cooperation, and Attribute Distances" in B. Russett (ed.), *Peace, War, and Numbers*, Beverly Hills: Sage, pp. 71–113.

(1979) *War, Power, Peace (Understanding Conflict and War)*, vol. IV, Beverly Hills: Sage.

(1983) "Libertarianism and International Violence," *Journal of Conflict Resolution* 27 (March): 27–51.

Russett, Bruce, M. (1970) *What Price Vigilance?* New Haven: Yale University Press.

(1975) "The Americans Retreat from World Power," *Political Science Quarterly* 90 (Spring): 1–21.

(1993) *Grasping the Democratic Peace*, Princeton: Princeton University Press.

Russett, Bruce, and John R. Oneal (2001) *Triangulating Peace: Democracy, Interdependence and International Organizations*, New York: W. W. Norton.

Sabrosky, Alan Ned (1975) "From Bosnia to Sarajevo: A Comparative Discussion of Interstate Crises," *Journal of Conflict Resolution* 19 (March): 3–24.

(1980) "Interstate Alliances: Their Reliability and the Expansion of War" in J. D. Singer (ed.), *The Correlates of War*, vol. II, New York: Free Press, pp. 161–98.

(1985) "Alliance Aggregation, Capability Distribution, and the Expansion of Interstate War" in A. N. Sabrosky (ed.), *Polarity and War*, Boulder, Colo.: Westview, pp. 145–89.

Salmore, Stephen A., and Don Munton (1974) "An Empirically Based Typology of Foreign Policy Behaviors" in J. Rosenau (ed.), *Comparing Foreign Policies: Theories, Findings, and Methods*, New York: Halsted, pp. 329–52.

Sambanis, Nicholas (2000) "Partition as a Solution to Ethnic War: An Empirical Critique of the Theoretical Literature," *World Politics* 52 (4): 437–83.

Sample, Susan G. (1996) "Arms Races and the Escalation of Disputes to War," Ph.D. dissertation, Vanderbilt University.

(1997) "Arms Races and Dispute Escalation: Resolving the Debate," *Journal of Peace Research* 34 (February): 7–22.

(1998a) "Furthering the Investigation into the Effects of Arms Buildups," *Journal of Peace Research* 35 (January): 122–26.

(1998b) "Military Buildups, War, and Realpolitik: A Multivariate Model," *Journal of Conflict Resolution* 42 (April): 156–75.

(2000) "Military Buildups: Arming and War" in J. Vasquez (ed.), *What Do We Know about War?* Lanham, Md.: Rowman & Littlefield, pp. 165–95.

(2002) "The Outcomes of Military Buildups: Minor States vs. Major Powers," *Journal of Peace Research* 39 (November): 669–92.

Scheffler Israel (1967), *Science and Subjectivity*, Indianapolis: Bobbs-Merrill.

Schroeder, Paul W. (1976) "Alliances, 1815–1945: Weapons of Power and Tools of Management" in K. Knorr (ed.), *Historical Dimensions of National Security Problems*, Lawrence: University Press of Kansas, pp. 227–62.

Schuman, Frederick L. (1933) *International Politics* (1958 ed.), New York: McGraw-Hill.

Schumpeter, Joseph (1919) "The Sociology of Imperialisms" in J. Schumpeter, *Imperialism and Social Classes*, New York: A.M. Kelley, 1951, pp. 3–130.

Searle, John (1969) "How to Derive an 'Ought' from an 'Is'" in W. D. Hudson (ed.), *The Is/Ought Controversy*, New York: Macmillan.

Senese, Paul D. (1996) "Geographic Proximity and Issue Salience: Their Effects on the Escalation of Militarized Interstate Conflict," *Conflict Management and Peace Science* 15 (Fall): 133–61.

(2005) "Territory, Contiguity, and International Conflict: Assessing a New Joint Explanation," *American Journal of Political Science* 49 (October): 769–79.

Senese, Paul D., and John A. Vasquez (2003) "A Unified Explanation of Territorial Conflict: Testing the Impact of Sampling Bias, 1919–1992," *International Studies Quarterly* 47 (June): 275–98.

(2004) "Alliances, Territorial Disputes and the Probability of War: Testing for Interactions" in P. F. Diehl (ed.), *The Scourge of War: New Extensions on an Old Problem*, Ann Arbor: University of Michigan Press, pp. 189–221.

(2005) "Assessing the Steps to War," *British Journal of Political Science* 35 (October): 607–33.

(2008) *The Steps to War: An Empirical Study*, Princeton: Princeton University Press.

Shapiro, Michael J. (1966) "Cognitive Rigidity and Moral Judgments in an Inter-Nation Simulation," Evanston, Ill.: Northwestern University.

(1981) *Language and Political Understanding: The Politics of Discursive Practices*, New Haven: Yale University Press.

Shaw, R. Paul, and Yuwa Wong (1987a) "Ethnic Mobilization and the Seeds of Warfare: An Evolutionary Perspective," *International Studies Quarterly* 31 (March): 5–31.

(1987b) "Inclusive Fitness and Central Tendencies in Warfare Propensities," *International Studies Quarterly* 31 (March): 53–63.

(1989) *Genetic Seeds of Warfare: Evolution, Nationalism, and Patriotism*, Boston: Unwin Hyman.

Shepard, Graham (1988) "Personality Effects on American Foreign Policy, 1969–84: A Second Test of Interpersonal Generalization Theory," *International Studies Quarterly* 32 (March): 91–123.

Simmons, Beth A. (1999) "See You in 'Court'? The Appeal to Quasi-Judicial Legal Processes in the Settlement of Territorial Disputes" in P. F. Diehl (ed.), *A Road Map to War: Territorial Dimensions of International Conflict*, Nashville, Tenn.: Vanderbilt University Press, pp. 205–37.

Singer, J. David (1958) "Threat-Perception and the Armament-Tension Dilemma," *Journal of Conflict Resolution* 2 (March): 90–105; reprinted in Singer (1979), pp. 27–47.

(1970a) "Escalation and Control in International Conflict: A Simple Feedback Model," *General Systems Yearbook* 15: 163–75; reprinted in Singer (1979), pp. 68–88.

(1970b) "The Outcome of Arms Races: A Policy Problem and a Research Approach," *Proceedings of the International Peace Research Association* 2: 137–46; reprinted in Singer (1979), pp. 145–54.

(1979) (ed.) *The Correlates of War, vol. I: Research Origins and Rationale*, New York: Free Press.

(1981) "Accounting for International War: The State of the Discipline," *Journal of Peace Research* 18 (1): 1–18.

(1982) "Confrontational Behavior and Escalation to War 1816–1980: A Research Plan," *Journal of Peace Research* 19 (1): 37–48.

(1984) "Getting at Decision Rules in Major Power Conflict," Paper presented at the ECPR workshops on decision making, Salzburg, Austria.

(1990) "Accounting for International War in the Twentieth Century," Olin Lecture Series, US Air Force Academy, December 7.

Singer, J. David, and Sandra Bouxsein (1975) "Structural Clarity and International War: Some Tentative Findings" in T. Murray (ed.), *Interdisciplinary Aspects of General Systems Theory*, Washington, D.C.: Society for General Systems Research, pp. 126–35.

Singer, J. David, Stuart Bremer, and John Stuckey (1972) "Capability Distribution, Uncertainty, and Major Power War, 1820–1965" in B. Russett (ed.), *Peace, War, and Numbers*, Beverly Hills: Sage, pp. 19–48.

Singer, J. David, and Thomas Cusack (1981) "Periodicity, Inexorability, and Steersmanship in International War" in R. Merritt and B. Russett (eds.), *From National Development to Global Community*, London: George Allen and Unwin, pp. 404–22.

Singer, J. David, and Melvin Small (1966) "National Alliance Commitments and War Involvement, 1815–1945," *Peace Research Society (International) Papers* 5: 109–40.

(1968) "Alliance Aggregation and the Onset of War, 1815–1945" in J. D. Singer (ed.), *Quantitative International Politics: Insights and Evidence*, New York: Free Press, pp. 247–86.

(1972) *The Wages of War, 1816–1965*, New York: John Wiley.

(1974) "Foreign Policy Indicators: Predictors of War in History and in the State of the World Message," *Policy Sciences* 5 (September): 271–96; reprinted in Singer, 1979: 298–329.

Singer, J. David, and Michael D. Wallace (1970) "Inter-Governmental Organization and the Preservation of Peace, 1816–1964: Some Bivariate Relationships," *International Organization* 24 (Summer): 520–47.

Singer, Marshall R. (1972) *Weak States in a World of Power*, New York: Free Press.

Siverson, Randolph M., and Paul F. Diehl (1989) "Arms Races, the Conflict Spiral, and the Onset of War" in M. Midlarsky (ed.) *Handbook of War Studies*, Boston: Unwin Hyman, pp. 195–218.

Siverson, Randolph M., and Joel King (1979) "Alliances and the Expansion of War" in J. D. Singer and M. Wallace (eds.), *To Augur Well*, Beverly Hills: Sage, pp. 37–39.

(1980) "Attributes of National Alliance Membership and War Participation, 1815–1965," *American Journal of Political Science* 24 (February): 1–15.

Siverson, Randolph M., and Harvey Starr (1990) "Opportunity, Willingness, and the Diffusion of War," *American Political Science Review* 84 (March): 47–67.

(1991) *The Diffusion of War: A Study of Opportunity and Willingness*, Ann Arbor: The University of Michigan Press.

Siverson, Randolph M., and Michael P. Sullivan (1983) "The Distribution of Power and the Onset of War," *Journal of Conflict Resolution* 27 (September): 473–94.

Siverson, Randolph M., and Michael R. Tennefoss (1982) "Interstate Conflicts: 1815–1965," *International Interactions* 9 (2): 147–78.

Skjelsbaek, Kjell (1971) "Shared Memberships in Intergovernmental Organizations and Dyadic War, 1865–1964" in E. Fedder (ed.), *The United Nations: Problems and Prospects*, St. Louis: Center for International Studies, University of Missouri at St. Louis, pp. 31–61.

Skocpol, Theda (1979) *States and Social Revolutions: A Comparative Analysis of France, Russia, and China*, Cambridge: Cambridge University Press.

Small, Melvin (1980) *Was War Necessary?* Beverly Hills: Sage.

Small, Melvin, and J. David Singer (1976) "The War Proneness of Democratic Regimes," *Jerusalem Journal of International Relations* 1 (Summer): 49–69.

(1982) *Resort to Arms: International and Civil Wars, 1816–1980*, Beverly Hills: Sage.

Smith, Alastair (1995) "Alliance Formation and War," *International Studies Quarterly* 39 (December): 405–25.

(1996) "To Intervene or Not to Intervene: A Biased Decision," *Journal of Conflict Resolution* 40 (March): 16–40.

Smith, Steve (1987) "Paradigm Dominance in International Relations: The Development of International Relations as a Social Science," *Millennium* 16 (2): 189–206.

Smith, Theresa C. (1980) "Arms Race Instability and War," *Journal of Conflict Resolution* 24 (June): 253–84.

Smoke, Richard (1977) *War: Controlling Escalation*, Cambridge, Mass.: Harvard University Press.

Snyder, Glenn H., and Paul Diesing (1977) *Conflict among Nations: Bargaining, Decision Making, and System Structure in International Crises*, Princeton: Princeton University Press.

Snyder, Jack (1984) *The Ideology of the Offensive: Military Decision Making and the Disasters of 1914*, Ithaca: Cornell University Press.

Somit, Albert (1990) "Humans, Chimps, and Bonobos: The Biological Bases of Aggression, War, and Peacemaking," *Journal of Conflict Resolution* 34 (September): 553–82.

Spanier, John (1973) *American Foreign Policy since World War II*, New York: Praeger.

Spiezio, K. Edward (1990) "British Hegemony and Major Power War, 1815–1935: An Empirical Test of Gilpin's Model of Hegemonic Governance," *International Studies Quarterly* 34 (June): 165–81.

Starr, Harvey (1991) "Joining Political and Geographic Perspectives: Geopolitics and International Relations," *International Interactions* 17 (1): 1–9.

Starr, Harvey, and Benjamin A. Most (1976) "The Substance and Study of Borders in International Relations Research," *International Studies Quarterly* 20 (December): 581–620.

(1978) "A Return Journey: Richardson, 'Frontiers,' and Wars in the 1946–1965 Era," *Journal of Conflict Resolution* 22 (September): 441–67.

Stedman, Stephen John (1990) "Bayonets in Search of Ideas: War Aims and War Endings in Total Wars," mimeo.

Stoll, Richard J. (1980) "Two Models of Escalation of Serious Disputes to War, 1816–1976," Paper presented at the annual meeting of the International Studies Association, Los Angeles, March 18–22.

Suedfeld, Peter, and Philip Tetlock (1977) "Integrative Complexity of Communications in International Crises," *Journal of Conflict Resolution* 21 (March): 169–84.

Suedfeld, Peter, Philip Tetlock, and Carmenza Ramirez (1977) "War, Peace and Integrative Complexity: U.N. Speeches on the Middle East Problem, 1947–76," *Journal of Conflict Resolution* 21 (September): 427–42.

Suganami, Hidemi (1989) *The Domestic Analogy and World Order Proposals*, Cambridge: Cambridge University Press.

Sullivan, Michael P. (1979) "Foreign Policy Articulations and U.S. Conflict Behavior" in J. D. Singer and M. Wallace (eds.), *To Augur Well*, Beverly Hills: Sage, pp. 215–35.

Thompson, William R. (1983a) "Cycles, Capabilities, and War: An Ecumenical View" in W. Thompson (ed.), *Contending Approaches to World Systems Analysis*, Beverly Hills: Sage, pp. 141–62.

(1983b) "Succession Crises in the Global Political System: A Test of the Transition Model" in A. Bergesen (ed.), *Crises in the World-System*, Beverly Hills: Sage, pp. 93–116.

(1983c) "The World-Economy, the Long Cycle, and the Question of World-System Time" in P. McGowan and C. Kegley, Jr. (eds.), *Foreign Policy and the Modern World System*, Beverly Hills: Sage, pp. 35–62.

(1985) "Cycles of General, Hegemonic, and Global War" in U. Luterbacher and M. Ward (eds.), *Dynamic Models of International Conflict*, Boulder, Colo.: Lynne Rienner, pp. 462–88.

(1988) *On Global War: Historical–Structural Approaches to World Politics*, Columbia: University of South Carolina Press.

(1990) "The Size of War, Structural and Geopolitical Contexts, and Theory Building/Testing," *International Interactions* 16 (3): 183–99.

(1992) "Dehio, Long Cycles and the Geohistorical Context of Structural Transition," *World Politics* 45 (October): 127–52.

(1995) "Principal Rivalries," *Journal of Conflict Resolution* 39 (June): 195–223.

(2001) "Identifying Rivalries in World Politics," *International Studies Quarterly* 45 (December): 557–86.

Thompson, William R., and Karen Rasler, (1988) "War and Systemic Capability Reconcentration," *Journal of Conflict Resolution* 32 (June): 335–66.

Thorndike, Edward L. (1898) "Animal Intelligence: An Experimental Study of Associative Processes in Animals," *Psychological Review*, Monographical Supplement 2.

Tilly, Charles (1975a) *The Formation of National States in Western Europe*, Princeton: Princeton University Press.

(1975b) "Reflections on the History of European State-Making" in Tilly (1975a), pp. 3–83.

(1990) *Coercion, Capital, and European States, AD 990–1990*, Cambridge, Mass.: Basil Blackwell.

Tir, Jaroslav, and Paul F. Diehl (2002) "Geographic Dimensions of Enduring Rivalries," *Political Geography* 21 (February): 263–86.

Tir, Jaroslav, and Douglas M. Gibler (forthcoming) "Settled Borders and Regime Type: Democratic Transitions as Consequences of Peaceful Territorial Transfers."

Toft, Monica (2003) *The Geography of Ethnic Violence: Identity, Interests, and the Indivisibility of Territory*, Princeton: Princeton University Press.

Tolman, Edward C. (1932) *Purposive Behavior in Animals and Men*, New York: Appleton-Century-Crofts.

Toynbee, Arnold, J. (1954) *A Study of History*, vol. IX, London: Oxford University Press.

Truman, Harry S. (1956) *Years of Trial and Hope, Memoirs*, vol. II, Garden City, N.Y.: Doubleday.

Valeriano, Brandon (2003) "The Steps to Rivalry: Power Politics and Rivalry Formation," Ph.D. dissertation, Vanderbilt University.

Valeriano, Brandon, and Victor Marin (2008) "The Steps to War: Causal Processes of Interstate War," Paper presented at annual meeting of the International Studies Association, San Francisco, March.

Valeriano, Brandon, and John A. Vasquez (2010) "Identifying and Classifying Complex Interstate Wars," *International Studies Quarterly*, forthcoming.

Valzelli, Luigi (1981) *Psychobiology of Aggression and Violence*, New York: Raven Press.

Van Evera, Stephen (1984) "The Cult of the Offensive and the Origins of the First World War," *International Security* 9 (Summer): 58–107.

(1994) "Hypotheses on Nationalism and War," *International Security* 18 (Spring): 5–39.

Vasquez, John A. (1976) "A Learning Theory of the American Anti-Vietnam War Movement," *Journal of Peace Research* 13 (4): 299–314.

(1983a) *The Power of Power Politics: A Critique*, New Brunswick, N.J.: Rutgers University Press.

(1983b) "The Tangibility of Issues and Global Conflict: A Test of Rosenau's Issue Area Typology," *Journal of Peace Research* 20 (2): 179–92.

(1985) "Domestic Contention on Critical Foreign Policy Issues: The Case of the United States," *International Organization* 37 (Fall): 643–66.

(1986) "Explaining and Evaluating Foreign Policy: A New Agenda for Comparative Foreign Policy" in J. Vasquez (ed.), *Evaluating U.S. Foreign Policy*, New York: Praeger, pp. 205–29.

(1987a) "Foreign Policy, Learning, and War" in C. Hermann, C. Kegley, Jr. and J. Rosenau (eds.) *New Directions in the Study of Foreign Policy*, Boston: Allen and Unwin, pp. 366–83.

(1987b) "The Steps to War: Toward a Scientific Explanation of Correlates of War Findings," *World Politics* 40 (October): 108–45.

(1991) "The Deterrence Myth: Nuclear Weapons and the Prevention of Nuclear War" in C. Kegley, Jr. (ed.), *The Long Postwar Peace*, New York: Harper Collins, pp. 205–23.

(1992) "World Politics Theory" in M. Hawkesworth and M. Kogan (eds.), *Encyclopedia of Government and Politics*, London: Routledge, pp. 839–61.

(1993) *The War Puzzle*, Cambridge: Cambridge University Press.

(1995) "Why Do Neighbors Fight? Proximity, Interaction, or Territoriality," *Journal of Peace Research* 32 (August): 277–93.

(1996a) "The Causes of the Second World War in Europe: A New Scientific Explanation," *International Political Science Review* 17 (April): 161–78.

(1996b) "Distinguishing Rivals That Go to War from Those That Do Not," *International Studies Quarterly* 40 (December): 531–58.

(1996c) "Territorial Issues and the Probability of War: A Data-based Analysis," Paper presented at the annual meeting of the Peace Science Society (International), Rice University, Houston, Texas, October 26.

(1998) *The Power of Power Politics: From Classical Realism to Neotraditionalism.* Cambridge: Cambridge University Press.

(2000) "Re-examining the Steps to War: New Evidence and Theoretical Insights" in M. Midlarsky (ed.) *Handbook of War Studies II*, Ann Arbor: University of Michigan Press, pp. 371–406.

(2001) "Mapping the Probability of War and Analyzing the Possibility of Peace: The Role of Territorial Disputes," Presidential Address to the Peace Science Society (International), *Conflict Management and Peace Science* 18 (Fall): 145–74.

(2002) "Realism and the Study of Peace and War" in M. Brecher and F. Harvey (eds.), *Millennium Reflections on International Studies*, Ann Arbor: University of Michigan Press, pp. 79–94.

(2004) "The Probability of War, 1816–1992," *International Studies Quarterly* 48 (March): 1–28.

(2005) "The India–Pakistan Conflict in Light of General Theories of War, Rivalry, and Deterrence" in T. V. Paul (ed.), *The India–Pakistan Conflict: An Enduring Rivalry*, Cambridge: Cambridge University Press, pp. 54–79.

Vasquez, John A., and Douglas M. Gibler (2001) "The Steps to War in Asia, 1931–1941," *Security Studies* 10 (Spring 2001): 1–45.

Vasquez, John A., and Marie T. Henehan (2001) "Territorial Disputes and the Probability of War, 1816–1992," *Journal of Peace Research* 38 (March): 123–38.

Vasquez, John A., and Christopher S. Leskiw (2001) "The Origins and War Proneness of Interstate Rivalries," *Annual Review of Political Science* 4: 295–316.

Vasquez, John A., and Richard W. Mansbach (1984) "The Role of Issues in Global Cooperation and Conflict," *British Journal of Political Science* 14 (September): 411–33.

Vasquez, John A., and Paul D. Senese (2007) "How, and Why the Cold War Became a Long Peace: Some Statistical Insights." Paper presented to the annual meeting of the Midwest Political Science Association, Chicago, April 14.

Vasquez, John A., and Brandon Valeriano (2008) "A Classification of Interstate War." Draft typescript.

Väyrynen, Raimo (1983) "Economic Cycles, Power Transitions, Political Management and Wars Between Major Powers," *International Studies Quarterly* 27 (December): 389–418.

de Waal, Frans (1989) *Peacemaking among Primates*, Cambridge, Mass.: Harvard University Press.

Wallace, Michael D. (1972) "Status, Formal Organization, and Arms Levels as Factors Leading to the Onset of War, 1820–1964" in B. M. Russett (ed.), *Peace, War, and Numbers*, Beverly Hills: Sage, pp. 49–69.

(1973) "Alliance Polarization, Cross-cutting, and International War, 1815–1964," *Journal of Conflict Resolution* 17 (December): 575–604.

(1979) "Arms Races and Escalation: Some New Evidence," *Journal of Conflict Resolution* 23 (March): 3–16.

(1982) "Armaments and Escalation: Two Competing Hypotheses," *International Studies Quarterly* 26 (March): 37–51.

(1985) "Polarization: Towards a Scientific Conception" in A. Sabrosky (ed.), *Polarity and War*, Boulder, Colo.: Westview, pp. 95–113.

(1990) "Racing Redux: The Arms Race-Escalation Debate Revisited" in C. Gochman and A. Sabrosky (eds.), *Prisoners of War*, Lexington, Mass.: Lexington Books, pp. 115–22.

Wallace, Michael D., and Peter Suedfeld (1988) "Leadership Performance in Crisis: The Longevity–Complexity Link," *International Studies Quarterly* 32 (December): 439–51.

Wallensteen, Peter (1981) "Incompatibility, Confrontation, and War: Four Models and Three Historical Systems, 1816–1976," *Journal of Peace Research* 18 (1): 57–90.

(1984) "Universalism vs. Particularism: On the Limits of Major Power Order," *Journal of Peace Research* 21 (3): 243–57.

Wallerstein, Immanuel (1974) *The Modern World-System: Capitalist Agriculture and the Origins of the European World Economy in the Sixteenth Century*, New York: Academic Press.

(1980) *The Modern World-System II: Mercantilism and the Consolidation of the European World-Economy, 1600–1750*, New York: Academic Press.

(1983) "An Agenda for World-Systems Analysis" in W. Thompson (ed.), *Contending Approaches to World System Analysis*, Beverly Hills: Sage, pp. 299–308.

Walt, Stephen M. (1987) *The Origins of Alliances*, Ithaca: Cornell University Press.

Walter, Barbara (2002) *Committing to Peace*, Princeton: Princeton University Press.

(2003) "Explaining the Intractability of Territorial Conflict," *International Studies Review* 5 (December): 137–53.

Waltz, Kenneth N. (1959) *Man, the State, and War*, New York: Columbia University Press.

(1967) *Foreign Policy and Democratic Politics*, Boston: Little, Brown.

(1979) *Theory of International Politics*, Reading, Mass.: Addison-Wesley.

(1989) "The Origins of War in Neorealist Theory" in R. Rotberg and T. Rabb (eds.), *The Origin and Prevention of Major Wars*, Cambridge: Cambridge University Press, pp. 39–52.

Ward, Michael D. (1982) "Cooperation and Conflict in Foreign Policy Behavior: Reaction and Memory," *International Studies Quarterly* 26 (March): 87–126.

(1992) (ed.) *The New Geopolitics*, New York: Gordon and Breach Science Publishers.

Waterman, Harvey (1981) "Reasons and Reason: Collective Political Activity in Comparative and Historical Perspective," *World Politics* 33 (July): 554–89.

Wayman, Frank Whelon (1983) "Power Transitions, Rivalries, and War, 1816–1970" (January). University of Michigan-Dearborn, mimeo.

(1984a) "Bipolarity and War: The Role of Capability Concentration and Alliance Patterns among Major Powers, 1816–1965," *Journal of Peace Research* 21 (1): 61–78.

(1984b) "Voices Prophesying War: Events and Perceptions as Indicators of Conflict Potential in the Middle East" in J. D. Singer and Richard J. Stoll (eds.), *Quantitative Indicators in World Politics: Timely Assurance and Early Warning*, New York: Praeger, pp. 153–85.

(1985) "Bipolarity, Multipolarity, and the Threat of War" in A. N. Sabrosky (ed.), *Polarity and War*, Boulder, Colo.: Westview, pp. 115–44.

(1990) "Alliances and War: A Time-Series Analysis" in C. Gochman and A. Sabrosky (eds.), *Prisoners of War*, Lexington, Mass.: Lexington Books, pp. 93–113.

(1996) "Power Shifts and the Onset of War" in J. Kugler and D. Lemke (eds.), *Parity and War*, Ann Arbor: University of Michigan Press, pp. 145–62.

(2000) "Rivalries: Recurrent Disputes and Explaining War" in J. Vasquez (ed.), *What Do We Know about War?* Lanham, Md.: Rowman & Littlefield, pp. 219–34.

Wayman, Frank Whelon, and Daniel M. Jones (1991) "Evolution of Conflict in Enduring Rivalries," Paper presented at the annual meeting of the International Studies Association, Vancouver, British Columbia, March 20–23.

Wayman, Frank Whelon, J. David Singer, and Gary Goertz (1983) "Capabilities, Allocations, and Success in Militarized Disputes and Wars, 1816–1976," *International Studies Quarterly* 27 (December): 497–515.

Weede, Erich (1976) "Overwhelming Preponderance as a Pacifying Condition among Contiguous Asian Dyads, 1950–1969," *Journal of Conflict Resolution* 20: 395–411.

(1980) "Arms Races and Escalation: Some Persisting Doubts," *Journal of Conflict Resolution* 24 (June): 285–87.

White, Ralph K. (1966) "Misperception and the Vietnam War," *Journal of Social Issues* 22 (July): 1–164.

(1970) *Nobody Wanted War*, Garden City, N.Y.: Doubleday.

Whiting, Alan S. (1991) "The U.S.–China War in Korea" in A. L. George (ed.), *Avoiding War: Problems of Crisis Management*, Boulder, Colo.: Westview Press, pp. 103–125.

Wilkenfeld, Jonathan, Michael Brecher, and Stephen R. Hill (1989) "Threat and Violence in State Behavior" in Michael Brecher and Jonathan Wilkenfeld (eds.), *Crisis, Conflict and Instability*, Oxford: Pergamon Press, pp. 177–93.

Wilkenfeld, Jonathan, Gerald Hopple, Paul Rossa, and Stephen Andriole (1980) *Foreign Policy Behavior: The Interstate Behavior Analysis Model*, Beverly Hills: Sage.

Wilson, Edward O. (1975) *Sociobiology: The New Synthesis*, Cambridge, Mass.: Harvard University Press.

Winch, Peter (1958) *The Idea of a Social Science*, New York: Humanities Press.

Wish, Naomi Bailin (1980) "Foreign Policy Makers and Their National Role Conceptions," *International Studies Quarterly* 14 (December): 532–54.

Wittkopf, Eugene R. (1987) "Elites and Masses: Another Look at Attitudes toward America's World Role," *International Studies Quarterly* 31 (June): 131–59.

Wittkopf, Eugene R., and Maggiotto, Michael A. (1983) "Elites and Masses: A Comparative Analysis of Attitudes Towards America's Role," *Journal of Politics* 45 (May): 303–34.

Wright, Quincy (1942, 1965) *A Study of War*, 1st and 2nd eds., Chicago: University of Chicago Press.

Yamamoto, Yoshinobu, and Stuart A. Bremer (1980) "Wider Wars and Restless Nights: Major Power Intervention in Ongoing War" in J. D. Singer (ed.), *The Correlates of War*, vol. II, New York: Free Press, pp. 199–229.

Young, Oran R. (1978) "Anarchy and Social Choice: Reflections on the International Polity," *World Politics* 30 (January): 241–63.

Zagare, Frank C., and D. Marc Kilgour (2000) *Perfect Deterrence*, Cambridge: Cambridge University Press.

Zinnes, Dina A. (1968) "The Expression and Perception of Hostility in Prewar Crisis: 1914" in J. D. Singer (ed.), *Quantitative International Politics*, New York: Free Press, pp. 85–119.

(1975) "Research Frontiers in the Study of International Politics" in F. Greenstein and N. Polsby (eds.), *Handbook of Political Science*, vol. VIII, Reading, Mass.: Addison-Wesley, pp. 87–198.

Zinnes, Dina A., and Robert G. Muncaster (1984) "The Dynamics of Hostile Activity and the Prediction of War," *Journal of Conflict Resolution* 28 (June): 187–229.

Zinnes, Dina A., Robert C. North, and H. E. Koch (1961) "Capability, Threat, and the Outbreak of War" in J. Rosenau (ed.), *International Politics and Foreign Policy*, New York: Free Press, pp. 469–82.

Zinnes, Dina A., Joseph L. Zinnes, and Robert D. McClure (1972) "Hostility in Diplomatic Communication: A Study of the 1914 Crisis" in C. Hermann (ed.), *International Crises: Insights from Behavioral Research*, New York: Free Press, pp. 139–62.

Zolberg, Aristide R. (1983) "'World' and 'System': A Misalliance" in W. Thompson (ed.), *Contending Approaches to World System Analysis*, Beverly Hills: Sage, pp. 269–90.

Zur, Ofer (1987) "The Psychohistory of Warfare: The Co-Evolution of Culture, Psyche and Enemy," *Journal of Peace Research* 24 (June): 125–34.

INDEX

4

Wayman, Frank, 78, 86, 147, 148, 170,
181, 187, 189, 192, 194, 235,
269–70, 271–72, 275–77, 281,
283, 379, 385, 387–88, 396, 401,
407, 415–16, 421, 426
Weaver, R., 303–04, 408, 418
Weede, Erich, 161, 194, 197, 279, 420
WEIS, 192
Wheeler, Hugh, 202, 204, 412
White, Ralph K., 212, 236, 416
Whiting, Alan, 379
Wilhelm II, Kaiser, 56, 187, 232
Wilkenfeld, Jonathan, 83, 204, 209,
384, 412, 414
Wilson, Edward O., 33–34, 78
Wilson, Woodrow T., 221, 313
League of Nations, 228
Winch, Peter, 91
Wittgenstein, Ludwig, 95
Wittkopf, Eugene R., 219, 222, 226
Wolford, Scott, 364
Wong, Yuwa, 34, 153, 333, 384, 401–02,
426
world order, 241, 306
world war, 168, 419
defined, 65, 247–48, 254
duration of, 183, 214, 248–50, 270,
280–83
factors related to, 114, 246, 250–54,
283–84, 417

necessary conditions of, 246, 254,
269–80, 421
as a type of war, 245–49, 254, 279,
327
World War I, 52, 60, 62, 71, 74, 100, 101,
109, 112, 117, 120, 183, 188–89,
197, 198, 211, 228, 237, 238,
241–42, 246, 247, 250, 251, 260,
261, 271, 274, 275–77, 300, 312,
368, 389, 392
World War II, 22, 60, 62, 69, 71–72, 74,
75, 109, 110, 117, 195, 198, 211,
228, 229, 238, 246, 250, 251,
260–61, 271, 274, 276–77, 319,
341, 365, 383, 389, 392, 395–96
Wright, Quincy, 3, 18, 26–30, 30–31,
33, 36, 38, 64, 73

Yamamoto, Yoshinobu, 263, 420
Young, Oran, R., 49
Yugoslavia, 356

Zagare, Frank, 381–82
zero sum games, 82, 85, 164, 165, 311,
355, 356
Zinnes, Dina A., 36, 42, 73–74, 212,
237, 238, 413
Zinnes, Joseph L., 237, 413
Zolberg, Aristide R., 88
Zur, Ofer, 36

CAMBRIDGE STUDIES IN INTERNATIONAL RELATIONS